ART, ARTISTS
AND GAUGUIN

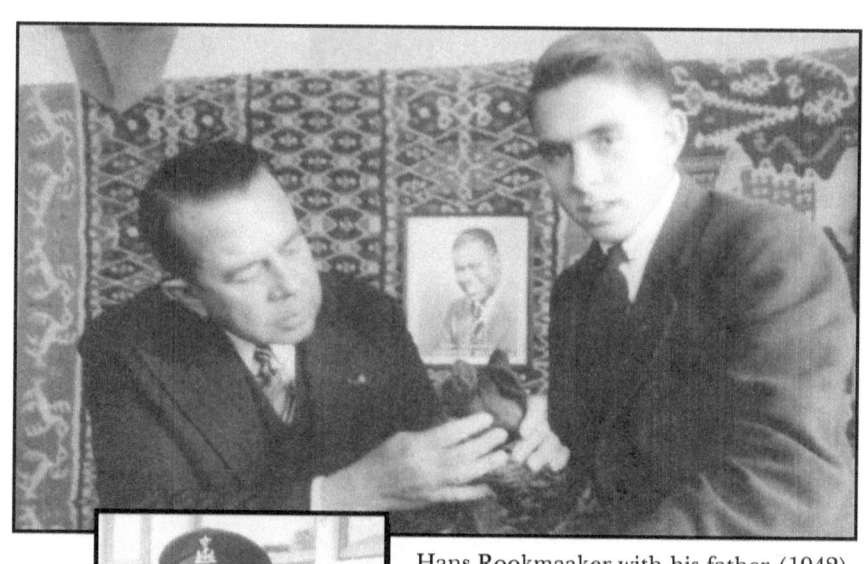

Hans Rookmaaker with his father (1942).

As a marine cadet in 1939.

ART, ARTISTS AND GAUGUIN

The Complete Works of Hans R. Rookmaaker

Volume I

Edited by
Marleen Hengelaar-Rookmaaker

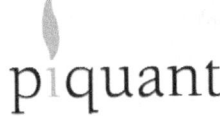

Copyright © 2002 by Marleen Hengelaar-Rookmaaker

This edition copyright © 2021 by Piquant Editions in the UK

Piquant Editions
Website: www.piquanteditions.com

First edition 2002
Paperback edition 2021

ISBN for this volume: 978-1-909281-80-6

The right of Marleen Hengelaar-Rookmaaker to be identified as author of this work has been asserted by her in accordance with the Copyright, Designs and Patents Act, 1988.

All Rights Reserved. No part of this publication may be reproduced, stored in a retrieval system or transmitted, in any form or by any means, electronic, mechanical, photocopying, recording or otherwise, without the prior written permission of the publisher or the Copyright Licensing Agency.

Synthetist Art Theories, copyright ©1959 by H.R. Rookmaaker
(Amsterdam: Swets & Zeitlinger, 1959); copyright © 2000
by Marleen Hengelaar-Rookmaaker
Gauguin and 19th Century Art Theory, copyright © 1972 by
H.R. Rookmaaker (Amsterdam: Swets & Zeitlinger, 1972);
copyright © 2000 by Marleen Hengelaar-Rookmaaker
Art review articles from *Trouw*, 1949–1956,
copyright © by H.R. Rookmaaker; copyright © 2000 by
Marleen Hengelaar-Rookmaaker (translated into English for
this edition by Evelyn Kuntz Hielema)

British Library Cataloguing-in-Publication Data
A catalogue record of this book is available in the UK from the British Library.

ISBN 978-1-909281-80-6

Cover art: Marc de Klijn, detail from
Monuments in the (pre)history of modern art (2000)
Cover design: Jonathan Kearney

Piquant Editions actively supports theological dialogue and an author's right to publish but does not necessarily endorse the individual views and opinions set forth here or in works referenced within this publication, nor guarantee technical and grammatical correctness. The publishers do not accept any responsibility or liability to persons or property as a consequence of the reading, use or interpretation of its published content.

Overview Contents for the Six Volumes of the Complete Works of Hans Rookmaaker

The contents of volumes 1 to 6 have been organized partly chronologically and partly thematically. Most of the writings compiled in volumes 1 and 2 date from before 1960, while most of the materials brought together in volumes 3 to 6 were written after 1960. Each of the volumes contains one or more books as well as articles. Two books, previously published in Dutch only, appear in English for the first time: *Jazz, Blues and Spirituals* (1960) and *Art and Entertainment* (1962). In addition, roughly a thousand pages of Dutch articles have been translated into English: exhibition and music reviews; many short articles on art, music, and Christianity and culture written for Christian periodicals; articles that are scholarly and art-historical; and articles that are long and philosophical like the ones for *Philosophia Reformata*. Also included are the lectures given at l'Abri and Westminster Seminary. The two series of lectures, on 'God's Hand in History' and 'Revelation', have been integrated by Colin Duriez into one unit entitled 'God's Hand in History'.

Volume 1: ART, ARTISTS AND GAUGUIN

- Foreword by Jeremy Begbie
- Scholarly introduction by Graham Birtwistle
- Gauguin and Nineteenth-Century Art Theory (*Synthetist Art Theories*)
- Rookmaaker as art critic (1949–1956): exhibition reviews

Volume 2: NEW ORLEANS JAZZ, MAHALIA JACKSON AND THE PHILOSOPHY OF ART

- Philosophy and aesthetics: articles on style, world view, philosophy of art and education
- *Jazz, Blues and Spirituals*
- Music articles: African-American music, blues, spirituals and gospel, jazz, rock, and classical music

Volume 3: THE CREATIVE GIFT, DÜRER, DADA AND DESOLATION ROW

- *Art and Entertainment*
- *The Creative Gift*
- Articles on history, faith and culture, faith and lifestyle, and faith and scholarship

Volume 4: WESTERN ART AND THE MEANDERINGS OF A CULTURE

- Articles on Western art from the Middle Ages until the nineteenth century: themes and motifs, general reflections on art, plus an unfinished manuscript
- *Art Needs No Justification*
- Art and the Christian: articles, letters, and the Westminster discussion sessions 'Comments on Art and Culture'
- Miscellaneous articles and exhibition reviews

Volume 5: MODERN ART AND THE DEATH OF A CULTURE

- *Modern Art and the Death of a Culture*
- *Art and the Public Today*
- Articles on twentieth-century artists and streams, modern art, and the question: Do we need to be modern in order to be contemporary?
- Reviews of books on modern art and reviews of expositions of twentieth-century sculpture

Volume 6: OUR CALLING AND GOD'S HAND IN HISTORY

- Biography of Hans Rookmaaker by Laurel Gasque
- Interviews
- 'God's Hand in History' and the l'Abri lectures
- Indexes to all six volumes of the *Complete Works*

Contents of Volume I

Acknowledgments   xi
Foreword by Jeremy Begbie   xiii
H.R. Rookmaaker: The Shaping of his Thought, an introduction
by Graham Birtwistle   xv

Part I: Gauguin and Nineteenth-Century Art Theory

Preface by Hans Rookmaaker to the Second Edition   3
1. Introduction   5
   The art of the Salons (6)
2. The Precursors of the Synthetists   11
   David, Ingres, Gros, Géricault (11); Constable, Turner (12); Goya (13); Delacroix (15); Baudelaire (19); Swedenborg (25); Baudelaire (continued) (27); Edgar Allen Poe (31); Schopenhauer (33); Carlyle (35); Art in the Realist tradition (38); French landscape (41); Impressionism (43); Japanese art (44)
3. The Genesis and the Character of Symbolism   46
   William Blake (46); John Ruskin (48); Pre-Raphaelite movement (50); Rose†Croix (57); Symbolism and Synthetism (60); Symbolist art (61); Negative attitude to reality (62); Symbolist art (continued) (68)
4. Kindred Spirits   73
   Impressionism (73); Seurat (76); Puvis de Chavannes (80); Cézanne (81); Van Gogh (84); Rive Droite (89)
5. The Artistic Ideals of the Synthetists   91
   Anti-naturalism (91); Subjectivism (92); Individualism (93); Synthesis (93); Freedom (94); Realism (95); Art and nature (97)
6. The Origin and Development of the Synthetist Theory of
   Art 1885–1890   99
   Gauguin's early development (100); The early development of Bernard (103); The events of the summer of 1888 (107); Gauguin with van Gogh in Arles (110); Sérusier (112); Gauguin in Paris in 1889 (113); Gauguin and his friends at Le Pouldu (114); Gauguin in 1890 (116)
7. The Definitive Formulations   119
   Morice (119); Gauguin (124); Mallarmé (125); Gauguin's escape from France (126); Aurier (128); Maurice Denis (133); Sérusier (137); The theory of correspondences (138); Sérusier (continued) (139); Bernard (143)

8. Some Terms and Concepts	147

Synthèse (147); Imagination (156); Rêve (157); Symbol (160); Art as revelation (162); Symbol (continued) (166); The iconic – the real achievement of Synthetist art theory (169); Musicality (175); Mystère (183)

9. Gauguin's Last Years	187

Gauguin's Realism (188); Manau Tupapau (189; D'où venons-nous? Que sommes-nous? Où allons-nous? (191); Later writings (197); Freedom (199); Gauguin's legacy (200)

Bibliography	202

On art, art theory and aesthetics before the nineteenth century (203); Philosophy and aesthetics in the nineteenth century (204); Literature and culture in the nineteenth century (up to 1885) (205); General works on nineteenth-century art (207); Precursors of the Synthetists (208); Art and art theory in the naturalistic-realistic tradition (209); Art and literature outside the circle of the Synthetists (211); Kindred spirits of the Synthetists, writers and painters (215); Writings by or about the Synthetists (1885–1900) (218); Writings by Gauguin (219); Writings concerning Gauguin (219); Memoirs and writings after 1900 of eye-witnesses (222); Later literature on Synthetism and the Synthetists (222); Writings concerning Gauguin after 1959 (223)

Theses Accompanying the Dissertation	225

Part II: Rookmaaker as Art Critic (1949–1956)

Middle Ages and Renaissance	231

Art treasures of the Lower Rhineland: grand culture from around AD 1000 (231); From the treasuries of the Middle Ages (233); Painting in the late Middle Ages (235); From Gothic to Renaissance (236); Alsation art in Delft I (237); Alsation art in Delft II (239); Rhineland's art in Arnhem (240); Beauty from the Middle Ages in the Rijksmuseum (242); Religious art in Tournai (244); Burgundian splendour by Flemish masters (245); The portrait in the Old Netherlands (246); Jan van Scorel: universal artist (248); Leonardo da Vinci: brilliant and universal (250); Italian drawings: breaking with the Renaissance (251)

Seventeenth and Eighteenth Centuries	253

Caravaggio's influence on the school of Utrecht (253); Painters of architecture (254); Dutch still lifes (256); The Rembrandt House in Amsterdam (257); Fame and value of a great artist: Rembrandt exposition in Amsterdam (259); Rembrandt as graphic artist (262);

Rembrandt and the Bible (264); The Gospel of Rembrandt (265); Rembrandt's pupils (266); 120 Famous paintings in the Rijksmuseum (268); The story of the portrait in the Rijksmuseum (269); Three centuries of portraits in the Rijksmuseum (270); Rubens and Antwerp (272); The Venetian art of painting (274); The French landscape (276); Swiss graphic art in the Print Gallery of the Rijksmuseum (277); Drawings from two centuries in the Rijksmuseum (278); Gainsborough in Bath (280); Goya's accusations (281)

Nineteenth Century 283

Romantic painting: entitled to more recognition and a little fame (283); The Romantic painting (284); Romantic works from the nineteenth century (285); Nuyen: a gifted Romantic (287); Beautiful Nuyen discovered (288); The Hague school of art (289); Verster in Lakenhal (290); Pier Pander – an overdue classicist (290); Constantin Guys (292); A hundred years of Norwegian painting (293); The British school of the hunting scene (295); Early works by van Gogh (296); Van Gogh: visual phenomenon (297); James Ensor: a great graphic artist (297); Bresdin: etcher and lithographer (298); Van Gogh's contemporaries (299); Monet: a mirror of Impressionism (301)

Twentieth Century 303

E. Munch: forerunner of modern art (303); Europe 1907, an important year for art (304); What is Expressionism? (305); Beckmann: violent Expressionism (308); Macke: pure talent (309); Paula Modersohn-Becker (309); Female compassion in painting: Käthe Kollwitz, Charley Toorop, and the Joffers (311); Modern Italians in the Stedelijk Museum of Modern Art in Amsterdam (312); The Picasso of Eindhoven (313); Picasso's Guernica in Amsterdam (315); De Stijl in the Stedelijk Museum of Modern Art (318); Bart van der Leck (319); Guggenheim collection in the Gemeentemuseum (320); Unbelief as emptiness (322); Collection Urvater in Museum Kröller-Müller (324); Willink, envisioner of existential angst (325); W.Schumacher: magical and Romantic (327); German art after 1945 (328); Joseph Zaritsky: chaotic work without clear substance (329); Belgian art (330); Three friends who gave expressions to a Flemish view of life (331); G. Rouault: modern Christian art (333); Healthy French art (334); Works by André Petroff (335); Humour in drawing: mirror of modern life (336); Saul Steinberg's mockery: nihilistic games (337); Modern American graphic art (338); Comparative exposition of modern art (339); The Experimental in (or out of) the Stedelijk Museum of Modern Art (341); Domela Nieuwenhuis (342); Modern art as national property (343); Meritorious work of Paul Citroen (345); Charley Toorop: mature talent in full bloom (347); Berserik: one of the best (347); Escher's graphic art: puzzling cleverness (348); Graphic work of Henk Krijger (350); Poorly organized exposition (350); Christian art in Amstelveen (352); Van Meegeren: genius forger and decadent artist (352); Contact between art and the public (355); Monumental arts (356); Emergence of a style (358); Poster art, a living art (360)

Notes to Volume 1   363

Acknowledgments

How do most Complete Works come about? Is it usually enthusiastic kindred spirits who decide that the writings of their peer or preceptor should be collected, presented to this generation, and preserved for the next? Or is it perhaps more often the family that takes the initiative? In the case of this collected Complete Works, it was Pieter Kwant, first as Managing Director of Paternoster Publishing and subsequently as the owner of the publishing partnership Piquant, who had the vision, the courage and the know-how to make this project happen. For each of these three invaluable gifts, sine qua non, I am deeply grateful to him. Thanks are also due to his wife Elria, who collated these volumes with great skill and precision.

When I am writing this it is almost 24 years ago that my father was very unexpectedly taken away from us. It is cause for great gratitude to see that his work has not been forgotten and his memory is still alive. One can even speak of a renewed interest in his legacy. *Modern Art and the Death of a Culture,* his most well-known book, was not only republished in English in 1994 but over the past seven years has also been translated into Korean, Czech, Romanian, Russian and Spanish. The book may even be published in Dutch during 2002! Isn't it interesting that in the last few years most copies of this book were sold in Korea? Also *Art Needs No Justification* recently appeared in such diverse languages as Spanish, Polish, Russian and Greek.

I would like to acknowledge the patient labour of two people, Wendy Morrison Sereda and Roger Henderson, who started collecting my father's materials and worked on a bibliography at a time when it was not at all clear that anything would ever come of their efforts. Thanks for Frans Klaasse's contribution to the bibliography in its early stages as well. An early interest in my father's work was furthermore shown by Wheaton College, where, especially due to the dedication of Mary Dorsett, Paul Snezek and Larry Thompson, all relevant materials are now kept in the Special Collections section of the Buswell Memorial Library.

I am very grateful to G. Bromiley, Evelyn Kuntz Hielema, Herbert Donald Morton, Edith M. Reitsema, Alida L. Sewell, and Marion Vorage, the translators. They kindly offered their time and translation skills to altogether render around 1500 pages of Dutch text into English. Without their help these Complete Works would not have been possible. A word of thanks is due also to William Clarke, Paulien Daudeij, Marga van Gent-Petter, Robb Ludwick, Joël Valk and Ruth Slater who so generously gave of their time to transcribe lectures. I moreover want to acknowledge the committed enthusiasm of Colin Duriez. Even before the possibility of a Complete Works was considered he started on a new book based on my father's lectures on 'God's Hand in History' and 'Revelation'. The results of his editing expertise can be found in Volume 6, along with the other l'Abri lectures.

Books on art ask for artful covers. Marc de Klijn and Jonathan Kearney designed the splendid series of covers to complement this work. I would like to thank Tricia Porter and Sylvester Jacobs, who kindly gave permission to include some of their photographs.

As to Volume 1, I would like to offer a big word of thanks to Roger Henderson who looked through eight years' worth of *Trouw* issues, i.e. 8 x 52 x 6 copies of this daily Dutch newspaper, to find and photocopy all the exhibition reviews written by my father. These reviews were translated by Evelyn Kuntz Hielema. I thank Graham Birtwistle for reading the proofs of 'Gauguin and Nineteenth-Century Art Theory', and Joëlle Eykerman and Liesbeth Razzano for checking the French quotes in the endnotes.

Last, but not least, I would like to express the immense debt I owe to my husband, Albert, for his sound advice and steady support. Thanks also to Gerbert, Marieke and Dieke, for the many hours they allowed me on the family computer to handle a never-ending stream of e-mails. It is to them, the son-in-law and grandchildren my father never knew, that these volumes are dedicated.

Marleen Hengelaar-Rookmaaker
Ommen, The Netherlands

Foreword by Jeremy Begbie

Years ago, a friend put Hans Rookmaaker's *Modern Art and the Death of a Culture* into my hands. I was immediately struck by the directness and courage of this extraordinary book. Its grounding of art in an objective order, its rehabilitation of the notion of beauty, its pungent critique of many streams of artistic modernism – all this was highly foreign to the fashionable art schools of the 1970s, to say the least.

Rookmaaker's piercing prose both disturbed and enthralled me. It may well be that the world of painting has changed in important ways since then, it may well be that some of the judgments in that seminal paperback have been contested sharply. But, in the last few decades, what other single piece of writing has had more influence on Christian artists? What other book has done more to persuade Christians, not only those from the Reformed tradition, to take visual depiction seriously? What other book has done more to provide a specifically Christian intellectual environment for the practice and understanding of art? And what other book has done more to convince Christian artists that theirs is a true and worthy calling?

That relatively short masterpiece was, of course, only one item in a huge output of writing, extending over an enormous field of topics, and we are indebted to Rookmaaker's daughter, Marleen, for carefully gathering together and arranging for its editing and translation.

Why is the publication of these writings so important? What does Rookmaaker's legacy have to offer us in the new millennium?
First, his books and essays stand as a monument to the importance of rigorous Christian art-historical scholarship. For many years Professor of Art History at the Free University of Amsterdam, Rookmaaker was a fastidious scholar. Today, when a postmodern fascination with all things 'aesthetic' and 'spiritual' can easily engender scholarly carelessness and an ignorance of specific artworks, Roomaaker reminds us that Christian commitment must never be used to avoid the kind of precise, intellectual engagement which is so evident in his written words, a painstaking attentiveness to the details of particular pieces of art, and to the particularities of society and culture in which they are embedded. Second, we are reminded of the importance of breadth as well as depth. Rookmaaker's interests ranged far beyond the visual arts. He had a fascinated interest, for instance, in music (especially the spirituals and jazz), and in broader cultural concerns (youth culture, scientific discovery, and much more). In an age of increasing specialization and blinkered vision, Rookmaaker shows us that it is quite possible to be a specialist and to be alert to the links between these specialisms and much wider issues. Third, Rookmaaker sets the arts in the midst of a rich and full-blooded Christian world view. For him it was not good enough to claim that the arts are important for the Christian, and then justify

this with a few verses carelessly plucked from Scripture. We need to demonstrate carefully what place the arts have in the grand and sweeping purposes of God for history, and it was to Rookmaaker's immense credit that for thousands he made this breathtakingly clear. In a climate when the contribution of a distinctively Christian perspective on the arts is so often ruthlessly marginalized, often to the point of extinction, Rookmaaker's voice is one we sorely need to hear. Fourth, nourished by the Dutch Neo-Calvinist philosophy of Dooyeweerd and his followers, Rookmaaker provides a vision of the arts that does justice both to their irreducible integrity and to their interrelatedness with other aspects of God's world. Western post modernity relishes in the 'aestheticization' of culture, sometimes to the point that the aesthetic threatens to swallow up everything else in a wash of images. In his own day Rookmaaker saw that a proper refusal to isolate or downplay the arts must not be countered by a Neo-Romantic exaltation of the aesthetic. He knew there was another much more fruitful option, implicit in the Christian faith. We need to find it and celebrate it more than ever today.

It is a wonderful thought that this man's rare wisdom, which so radically changed the lives of those who knew him, can now find its way to a wider audience in the pages that follow. Rookmaaker's is a timely wisdom, and it will inspire thousands for decades to come.

Dr Jeremy Begbie is the Director of Theology Through the Arts (Cambridge and St Andrews), Associate Principal of Ridley Hall (Cambridge), Affiliated Lecturer in the Faculty of Divinity, University of Cambridge, and a Reader at the University of St Andrews in the newly-established Institute of Theology, Imagination and the Arts.

H.R. Rookmaaker: The Shaping of his Thought
an introduction by Graham Birtwistle

The texts to be republished in these volumes date from as long as thirty, forty or even fifty years ago. In fact, since Hans Rookmaaker typed his last sentence in 1977 a whole generation has been born, raised and come to adulthood. Quite likely, therefore, a good many people who will now be turning these pages were either very young or not yet born when the texts were first written. Such readers may be tempted to ignore the original dates and take Rookmaaker's articles and books as though they are freshly written and addressed to issues we are facing today. Readers using that approach would certainly not come away empty-handed, and I would be the first to acknowledge that there is a sense in which these writings by an eminent Christian thinker contain a clear and abiding message. But there is also a sense in which Rookmaaker was a man of his time addressing problems of his time. With the passing of the years, the historical and personal context in which Rookmaaker's writings took shape has inevitably become less easily accessible to new generations, so that not all his original intentions and concerns will simply spring out from the pages to the present-day reader. In writing this introduction to his work I have seen it as my main task to tell something about the context in which Rookmaaker wrote, the limitations imposed on him as well as the possibilities afforded him in his day, and about the challenges he took up.

Rookmaaker in context

How, then, do we begin to define the historical context in which Rookmaaker developed his characteristic ideas? In the broadest terms, it can be described as that of the postwar period in Europe. But the term 'postwar' is more than merely a convenient chronological label for the years that followed on 1945. For Rookmaaker, as for many other people of his generation in Europe, living and working in the postwar period meant that personal experiences of the devastating realities of the Second World War and Nazi occupation of his country remained long in the memory and provided a powerful stimulus to establish a saner society. More specifically, we can see his response to the postwar context as that of a Dutchman, a Christian, and a scholar. However, none of these three aspects of his identity turns out to be as uncomplicated as it might seem at first sight.

Rookmaaker was indeed Dutch, and shared traits in common with many other Dutch people: a certain social bluntness, for example, as well as the kind of linguistic agility and flexibility towards other cultures that undoubtedly have to do with belonging to a small nation in close proximity to much larger ones. But among his fellow countrymen he belonged to a special category. He was the child of parents in the higher echelons of the colonial service in what used to be called the Dutch East Indies – the country of many islands that gained its independence in the later 1940s to become The Republic of Indonesia. Rookmaaker grew up in the last phase of Dutch colonialism in the East, alternately spending time in the tropics and being schooled in Holland. In his teens it had already become plain to him that his future would have to lie in returning to the more cramped environment of the Netherlands. But the exotic circumstances of his childhood – he loved to tell about them in later life – marked his personality and his imagination and lent complexity to his Dutch identity. It was perhaps in no small way the mixed culture of his own Dutch-Indonesian background that gave Rookmaaker a continuing urge to travel and made him so fervent an advocate of another richly mixed culture: that of African-Americans.

There was complexity, too, in his identity as a Christian. Most Dutch believers of his generation, and particularly those who became Christian leaders, were firmly rooted in carefully demarcated denominational traditions that embraced just about all aspects of life. Being raised in one or other branch of the Dutch Reformed churches, for example, stamped one's education, politics, and cultural attitudes with a strong sense of identity and loyalty, and the situation was very similar for Roman Catholics. Rookmaaker, however, was brought up outside any church affiliation. His Christian faith came through conversion when, imprisoned by the Nazis during the war, he spent a good deal of time studying the Bible and became convinced of its truth. Though he subsequently became an active member of the Reformed Churches in the Netherlands (Liberated) he was also shaped by Christian influences from outside Holland, brought by a deep and lasting friendship with the American minister Francis Schaeffer who founded the study centre l'Abri Fellowship in the Swiss Alps. The Rookmaaker family went on to share the l'Abri work with the Schaeffer family and also shared a good deal of the Schaeffers' Evangelical-Presbyterian approach to the life of faith, which was considerably more outgoing than that of most Dutch Reformed men and women. A close colleague of Rookmaaker, himself born and bred Reformed, once commented to me that he felt Rookmaaker always remained a kind of outsider in Reformed life; despite participating in it enthusiastically he lacked the rootedness in its strong traditions that an insider had. Other people have made similar remarks about him, and I think we have a good clue here to the special nature of Rookmaaker's contribution to Dutch and international Christianity. Since conformity to Reformed tradition was not bred into him, Rookmaaker was able to enrich the faith and cultural life of Dutch Christians in ways that were not 'typically Reformed': for example by his American-influenced approach to personal faith, and not least by opening eyes to the significance of modern art and attuning ears to the sounds of jazz, blues and spirituals. And, by the same token, through his lectures and writings he was able to introduce an international audience to those aspects of the Dutch Reformed tradition which he had learned to value deeply.

When we come to look at Rookmaaker the scholar, we have to reckon again with a certain complexity. Though his reputation is firmly linked to his work as an art historian, he initially embarked on an entirely different career. He chose for a schooling that was technical rather than arts-oriented and trained as a cadet officer in the Dutch Navy, studying engineering at the Technical College of Delft. Something of the engineer's mentality always remained with him, I feel: a no-nonsense grasp of reality coupled with a low tolerance for whatever struck him as vaguely mystical or sentimental. Then the War effectively put an end to his first career and laid the foundations for another. Not only did he become a Christian while interned by the Nazis but as more books became available to the prisoners of war he developed a taste for reading in the arts and humanities. And crucially, in prison camp he was coached by an older officer, J.P.A. Mekkes, in contemporary Calvinist philosophical theory. The Calvinist philosophy movement, with its regular forum of discussion centred on the theories of Herman Dooyeweerd and D.H.Th. Vollenhoven, was to provide Rookmaaker with an academic milieu that was both Christian and intellectually rigorous. After the War ended in 1945, however, it was not in philosophy but in art history that he decided to make his new career. In fact, it was not unusual for Calvinist philosophers to develop their thinking in relation to specific fields and disciplines (Dooyeweerd's own 'home' discipline was law) and Rookmaaker saw in art a field of study relatively untouched by other Calvinist thinkers. But it was a close thing, he once told me, whether he had opted for musicology instead of art history. At that time he had a more intimate knowledge of music than of the visual arts. As a teenager he was already an irrepressible jazz enthusiast, and in the post-war years he rapidly became one of the leading Dutch experts on jazz, blues and spirituals and built up a fine collection of African-American records. Rookmaaker's interest in the arts was undoubtedly first awoken by music, and music was to remain both an important feature in his lecturing and writing and a primary source of enjoyment for him.

Art history, on the other hand, offered him the kind of fertile academic ground in which his ideas on art and culture could grow. Studying art history for many years (1946–1953) at the University of Amsterdam also provided Rookmaaker with the challenge of training in a secular environment and testing his qualities against those of other leading lights in the discipline. He was appointed assistant to Professor Van Regteren Altena in 1949, and in the 1950s he was a contemporary of Hans Jaffé (then curator at the Stedelijk Museum of Modern Art in Amsterdam) when both men were preparing their doctor's theses at the university.

The two Hanses maintained their differences and disagreements in friendly rivalry – Jaffé the humanist and modernist, Rookmaaker the Reformed Christian – and by the mid-sixties both had themselves become professors in the history of art: Jaffé at the University of Amsterdam, where the tradition was humanist, and Rookmaaker at the Free University of Amsterdam, which had been founded by Calvinists.

It is now time to draw some preliminary conclusions. Rookmaaker patently did not fit into any regular slot in the context of his day. Among his colleagues in art history and art criticism he was unconventional in being a forthright Christian. But among fellow Christians he was also unconventional, partly because of the foreign influences he brought to Dutch churchmanship and partly because in the Christian community his commitment to studying and teaching about such matters as art history, jazz and popular music marked him out as different. It is as though Rookmaaker re-drew the boundaries of the various circles in which he participated so that in his own person and work they overlapped in new and surprising ways. It helps us to understand his work better, I think, when we bear in mind that he was combining worlds of thought that usually did not have much to do with one another. Sometimes tensions between these different worlds are apparent in Rookmaaker's writings. Sometimes, as in his well-known book *Modern Art and the Death of a Culture*, we can marvel at the unforced way Rookmaaker combined the diverse resources of Christian witness, Calvinist philosophy, art-historical expertise, and musical connoisseurship to create a seamless and challenging account of modern cultural history. To no small degree, then, Rookmaaker's work represented the meeting of different cultural circles, different worlds of thought, or – in the jargon of late twentieth-century theorists – different discourses.

Different discourses

The term 'discourse' has been overworked by postmodernist theorists, but it is useful for my purposes here because it refers to the way people of a particular group or persuasion communicate to like-minded people, as well as what they communicate. Generally speaking, ideas and communicatory habits within a group will tend to have both an inclusive and an exclusive side; they will be distinctive enough to make some people feel at home with their peer group and others feel outsiders to the debate in question. Clearly, to engage in differing but distinctive discourses will take a conscious effort, and attempts to 'translate' from one discourse to another may provoke irritations or misunderstandings along the way. So which discourses are apparent in Rookmaaker's writings, and how did he cope with their differences?

With Rookmaaker's first major publication we have a good example of a text that bears all the hallmarks of belonging to one very distinctive discourse. His 'Sketch for an Aesthetic Theory based on the Philosophy of the Cosmonomic Idea', a longish article published in two parts in 1946 and 1947 in the Calvinist philosophical journal *Philosophia Reformata*, fell so totally within the ambit of Dooyeweerd's philosophical thought and terminology that it could only be fully appreciated by fellow members of the movement. In fact, this article was basically conceived and written during the War, under the tutelage of Captain (later Professor) Mekkes, and it is probably best seen as a kind of supervised exercise in which Rookmaaker demonstrated his ability to work with Dooyeweerdian concepts (such as 'modalities', 'anticipations' and 'retrocipations') and apply them to his own chosen field of art and aesthetic theory. This article did not so much set the course for Rookmaaker's future writings as mark the close of a relatively brief and condensed learning phase. After this first major publication he did not go on to pursue the systematic philosophical analysis of aesthetics any further. Moreover, he appears to have taken a conscious decision not to allow his own writing to be so dominated by Dooyeweerd's rather exclusive terminology as he had done in that first article. Rookmaaker always remained deeply indebted to Dooyeweerd's systematic philosophy and analyses of the history of Western thought, but the conviction seems to have come to him quite early that these ideas were best translated into 'ordinary' language. In that respect, Rookmaaker became one of the most effective channels whereby Dooyeweerd's basic insights reached a new international audience, though perhaps he paid a price for this since at least some of Dooyeweerd's more conventional followers never really recognized Rookmaaker as a fully-fledged Calvinist philosopher.

Rookmaaker certainly preferred to write in an easily accessible mode rather than to flaunt specialist terminology, and many of his readers will be grateful to him for that. But his use of ordinary language reflected more than just a personal preference or a concession to his readers; it was intimately linked to one of his deepest teachings. Throughout his writings runs the insistent theme that reality is God's creation and as such is neither strange nor incomprehensible to man. Rookmaaker taught that to know and experience reality as God intends us to do it is not necessary to approach it as a puzzle that can only be solved theoretically or scientifically, or as a secret that is hermetically locked from the common gaze. In his own theories he used this firm grasp of a created and reliable reality as his guideline for norms and values, and his fiercest polemics were usually directed against those who he felt were trying to alienate us from reality or distort our image of it. The use of plain language rather than specialist jargon suited him well in working out this theme in his writings and lectures, and he also liked to return apparently tortuous theoretical problems back to their earthy roots by telling anecdotes or even jokes. For example, he related a funny story about a horse who came into a bar in Amsterdam and ordered a cocktail that normally had a fig on top, but it told the barman not to add the fig. It drank the cocktail and when people gathered around in astonishment, the horse said to them: 'What's the matter, do you find it so odd that I don't like figs?' This story can be found in Rookmaaker's article 'Science, Aesthetics and Art', published in 1949 in the *Journal of the South African Academy* (*Complete Works 2*, p.94). He used it to show that we can get into all kinds of theoretical contortions if we try to define what is real and unreal about the horse and his cocktail, but then we miss the joke itself. That the joke has its own very firm and significant place in Creation was something Rookmaaker certainly believed – and practised, as those of us who knew him remember. He may have told the joke about the horse to make a serious point about a Christian understanding of reality, but he also told the story at much greater length than I have done here, building up the suspense and using the timing and authentic discourse of the joke-teller. One hopes that his learned South African readers could appreciate his humour as well as the point he was making.

Calvinist philosophy was not the only specialist discourse he translated into a more popular idiom; there was also, of course, the field of art and the academic discipline of art history. In the immediate postwar years he already began teaching and writing about art for church groups and other interested parties while at the same time studying art history at the university. In fact, Rookmaaker was educating others while he was still being educated himself. This two-way educational process was particularly apparent when he began writing art criticism for the daily newspaper *Trouw* in 1949, the year in which he passed his candidate's examination (equivalent to BA-level) and also became an assistant at the university. For the next seven or so years he visited national, and occasionally international, art exhibitions on a regular basis and wrote (usually once or twice a week) reviews of them for the generally Calvinist readership of *Trouw*. While some of his reviews discussed relatively 'safe' subjects, such as the works of Rembrandt, a good many of them dealt with the difficult phenomenon of modern and contemporary art. It has to be remembered that around 1950 not only the Calvinist public but also the public in general – prompted by what the Dutch art-critical establishment wrote in the newspapers – was extremely wary of most modern art. Especially art that was abstract, or close to abstraction, could usually expect an antagonistic reaction. The standpoint of modernist artists was in those days shared by just a few supporters in positions of authority, such as curator Hans Jaffé and director Willem Sandberg at the Stedelijk Museum of Modern Art in Amsterdam. Moreover, the discipline of art history at the universities was still dominated by erudite studies of the art of earlier centuries so that a study of modern art history was not then, as it is now, generally acknowledged as a task for a real scholar. Rookmaaker and Jaffé were in fact among the first Dutch art historians to write their doctoral theses on modern art: Jaffé on the movement De Stijl of around 1920 and Rookmaaker on the art theory of Gauguin and his circle in the late nineteenth century. During the long years of research and preparation for his study on Gauguin, Rookmaaker was obviously using his regular art criticism to train himself in looking closely at modern art and in accounting for what he saw. Allowing his art-historical research to interact with his popular art-critical writing, and his experience of modernist art to interact with his orthodox Christian faith and values, meant that in Rookmaaker's earlier career these different discourses were continually cross-pollinating one another. This, I feel, amounted to an apprenticeship that shaped his character as a writer for the rest of his career.

Rookmaaker on modern art: reviews and researches

The reviews signed 'H.R.R.' that were written for Trouw between 1949 and 1956 constitute a substantial part of Rookmaaker's total output. Yet because they were published half a century ago, in Dutch, and in the most ephemeral category of publications, they have tended to be eclipsed by his better known texts. To my mind the English translations of these reviews can provide a rich hunting ground for the reader who wants to understand the development of Rookmaaker's ideas better. Most importantly, the reviews can help to correct a misapprehension about Rookmaaker that has arisen in some circles, namely that he was an implacable opponent of all modern art.

In fact, the prevailing impression one gets from his reviews is of Rookmaaker's curiosity and eagerness to examine the works of modern artists. Time and time again we can note his insistence that his readers take the works seriously and do not dismiss or scorn what at first sight might seem strange to them. Rookmaaker would often begin a review by showing that he could identify with the reader's presumed bewilderment and latent suspicion about modern art, before going on to explain what particular works were about and coming to an evaluation of them. His judgments were often nuanced, so that comments such as 'talented', 'good composition', or 'technically good' could be applied to artists or works which he then went on to criticize on other grounds, such as content or spiritual direction. This distinction between technical artistic matters and the world view of the artist meant that relatively few of his reviews of modern art amounted to outright condemnations. On one rare occasion (an exhibition by Joseph Zaritzky in October 1955 in the Stedelijk Museum of Modern Art) Rookmaaker's exasperation gained the upper hand and he confessed to having no contact whatsoever with the 'chaotic work' and no desire to delve into it. Usually, however, he offered his readers a reasoned critique. A more or less consistent pattern can be seen, in which his most severe judgments tended to deal with two extremes in contemporary art. On the one hand, he obviously came to dread his annual visits to the mass exhibitions of the St Luke Association of Painters. Several years running he panned their exhibitions as put together indiscriminately and their art as mostly old-fashioned and mediocre, in December 1953 using the headline 'Boring Exhibition' and in November 1954 that of 'Poorly Organized Exposition'. On the other hand, he deeply disliked the more irrationalistic and primitivistic tendencies in modern art that he saw represented by the work of the Surrealists, Miró, and the Experimental artists of the Cobra movement. In November 1949 the major Experimental/Cobra exhibition at the Stedelijk Museum of Modern Art in Amsterdam elicited the following passages from Rookmaaker in *Trouw*:

> Experimentalism is the most consistent kind of nihilism: people don't believe in anything any more, not even in the world created by the revolution itself. The result is a constantly prolonged and renewed revolution. Civilization, conventions, norms, morality, beauty, these are obsolete concepts to be rid of. [...] Therefore, let us not mock all this, or call it charlantry; let us not cry 'woe and alas' but let us take note of this sign of the times. For it is here, right here in these extreme expressions in painting and poetry, that the spirits make themselves manifest (*Complete Works* 1, pp.341/2).

I read these passages with more than a casual interest because I have written a good deal about Cobra myself and I cannot agree that it was a nihilistic movement without norms and values. However, I have to remember that Rookmaaker was not alone in seeing Cobra as a threat to cherished values in 1949; critics in all the major Dutch newspapers condemned the Cobra exhibition under such headlines as 'Barbarians in the museum' and 'World-changing artists show their lack of skill'. What distinguished Rookmaaker's review from the others was the Christian dimension in his critique. Not only did he urge his readers to test the spirits and 'signs of the times' but in placing Experimental/Cobra art and poetry in a line of descent from the French Revolution of the eighteenth century he took up a familiar Calvinist anti-revolutionary theme (the main Dutch Calvinist political party in 1949 was still called the Anti-Revolutionary Party). In establishing that link between Cobra and ongoing revolution Rookmaaker was certainly not mistaken, though at the time he failed to notice that these young artists with their Marxian inclinations were really looking for authenticity and were criticizing bourgeois culture for its false facade, much as Rookmaaker himself was to do (though from his own Christian perspective) in his later book *Modern Art and the Death of a Culture*. Of course, it is one thing to write about Cobra at a safe distance of several decades and quite another to have faced these developments when they were new and provocative.

If Rookmaaker's wrath was directed at the two extremes of old-fashioned mediocrity and revolutionary Experimental spontaneity, his warmest appreciation was reserved for certain artists who, in his eyes, employed modern techniques not to assault traditional human values but to maintain and develop them. When he used the accolade 'sympathetic work' it meant that Rookmaaker felt at home with an artist's view of humankind and the world. Among contemporary Dutch artists he particularly liked the figurative sculpture of John Rädecker, for example, and also the quirky Realism of the (then) young painter Herman Berserik. As far as the well-known names of international modern art were concerned, his warmest words of praise were for artists such as Paula Modersohn-Becker and August Macke, two painters who shared the aims and methods of German Expressionist art without pushing it to the primitivistic extremes of a Nolde or the abstract extremes of a Kandinsky. In fact, Rookmaaker's own taste as a man of the twentieth century quite obviously inclined towards a moderate or mainstream Expressionism. He liked art to be figurative rather than abstract but he could applaud the use of highly simplified shapes or non-naturalistic colours when they served to elicit a richness of feeling. Nevertheless, in the work of an Expressionist such as Max Beckmann he found the images of a broken humanity too violent and disturbing.

Like many other critics of his day, Rookmaaker obviously struggled with the problems posed by abstract art. It is interesting to note that in his reviews he did not show the degree of aversion toward the abstraction of De Stijl artists such as Piet Mondrian or Bart van der Leck that he showed toward Surrealism and its associated artists such as Miró and the Experimentals. This was mainly, I suspect, because he saw Surrealists and their line as revolutionaries intent on dislocating our rational grasp of reality, while Mondrian's abstraction was at least understandable on a rational level as a step-by-step development of a new and rigorous means of pictorial composition. Several times in his reviews Rookmaaker suggested that abstract works of art could be valued for their 'decorative' qualities. This may sound like faint praise indeed, if we take it that he was asking his readers to look at abstract paintings as though they were pieces of mass-produced patterned wallpaper. But we have to be careful here since for Rookmaaker the term 'decorative' denoted something other than a second-rate or superficial kind of art. It had become important to him to refute the kind of hierarchical thinking that elevated works of Art (with a capital A) to a much higher plane than works of design or decoration. There was a Christian dimension to this critique, since he saw a danger that High Art could all too easily rise above its station to become the object of idolatry. But Rookmaaker was also drawing on his researcher's knowledge of Gauguin's art theory to lend a deeper significance to the term 'decorative'. For Gauguin and his circle, the decorative did not imply superficiality but carried positive connotations derived, among other things, from their admiration for the symbolic and expressive character of non-Western art. When he finally published his dissertation *Synthetist Art Theories* in 1959,

Rookmaaker openly admired the 'decorative principle' in Gauguin's art, 'according to which a far greater emphasis was laid on aesthetic arrangement, the rhythmic and harmonious play of lines and colours, than had been done in the art of the preceding period' (*Complete Works* 1, p.201). In that respect, Rookmaaker saw Gauguin's 're-discovery of the iconic element' as a positive contribution to modern art. Iconic values were to be found in the way Gauguin re-affirmed the flat picture plane and the significance of composition as the primary elements in painting, and though Gauguin turned away from naturalistic depiction he maintained an 'adherence to reality' and a 'humanity' that satisfied Rookmaaker. But the legacy of Gauguin's synthesis, his balance between pictorial renewal and maintaining a grasp of reality, was to be squandered by later twentieth-century artists: 'Gradually freedom is more and more stressed, reality loses more and more of its meaning until, at last, non-figurative art made its appearance – in particular that branch of it which may be called irrational.'

In this evaluation of Gauguin and his legacy, the contours of Rookmaaker's characteristic assessment of modern art were clearly drawn and were to remain more or less unchanged through the rest of his career. He thoroughly appreciated modern artists' search for a new pictorial language, but the more these developments seemed to alienate art from reality the more Rookmaaker's critique was aroused. Once again, therefore, we see that a rational grasp of God-given reality was pivotal in Rookmaaker's thinking. It was on that issue, not on any rejection of non-naturalistic pictorial methods, that his main objection to certain modern artists turned.

As a corollary to this, he warned against those instances in which artists had pushed beyond a rediscovery of the iconic element to elevate works to the status of icons of a modern spirituality, thereby encouraging a kind of idolatry. In the theses accompanying Synthetist Art Theories he applied such a critique to Mondrian's abstraction, first establishing in his Thesis IX that the Second Commandment in the Bible does not forbid the making of works of art but 'forbids the use of them for cultic purposes, i.e. to worship or adore them', and then going on in Thesis X to assert: 'Jaffé's thesis that the non-figurative art of Mondrian can be explained by his Calvinist past – in connection with the Second Commandment – is a misapprehension. Rather, Mondrian contravened this Commandment.'

Here Rookmaaker was following the usual practice of enlivening his doctoral defence by trading punches with a fellow scholar (his reference was to Hans Jaffé's own dissertation on De Stijl defended three years earlier). But Rookmaaker was also making serious points about the nature of a Calvinist – and in a broader sense, Christian – understanding of art in relation to the Second Commandment, and about the danger he saw in giving abstract art such as that of Mondrian a cultic significance.

Synthetist Art Theories established Rookmaaker's international reputation as a scholar and as a substantial contributor to research in the history of modern art. The fact that another dissertation on a similar subject was published in Stockholm in the same year – Sven Lövgren's *The Genesis of Modernism* – came as something of a surprise to Rookmaaker, but in no way did this detract from the success of his own book. By selecting, analysing and translating into English a great many key passages from late nineteenth-century French art theory, Rookmaaker had performed a service for international scholarship that was to be appreciated for decades. It was not just that a few key specialists in his field got to know of his study. When in 1968 the American art historian Herschel B. Chipp made prominent use of Rookmaaker's research and translations in editing *Theories of Modern Art* – for the last thirty years the most widely used general source-book on the subject – Rookmaaker's name and contribution became known to just about every art history department in the Western world.

Modern art and the death of a culture

While *Synthetist Art Theories* was warmly appreciated by academic art historians, the same could not be said of *Modern Art and the Death of a Culture* when it came out in 1970. This new book was based on lectures Rookmaaker had been giving on modern art and popular music and culture to an international audience in the sixties, and its worldwide success – particularly among Christians studying or working in the arts – saw it rapidly translated into several European languages and even into Japanese. For Christians and for those investigating the claims of Christianity it was a timely and strategic book that provided the kind of authoritative support and rationale for their involvement in the arts that was not always forthcoming from the churches. And its influence extended beyond a specifically Christian debate, for example when the prominent British journalist Malcolm Muggeridge, who had made no secret of his own pilgrimage towards Christian faith, championed *Modern Art and the Death of a Culture* on various occasions in the public media, proclaiming it a 'book of the year' in a major newspaper and even discussing it in a review for the distinctly urbane periodical *Esquire* in March 1971. But this most widely read of all his books also opened up a rift between Rookmaaker and the Dutch art-historical establishment. Among his fellow scholars *Modern Art and the Death of a Culture* quickly gained a negative reputation as too frankly Christian, too free-ranging in its references to popular culture and – worst of all – too critical of modern art.

It is important to note that by 1970 it had become de rigueur among reputable Dutch art historians to write about modern art from an implicitly modernist standpoint. Their aim as scholars was to write accurate and factual accounts of modern art history, but it had become a matter of consensus that the history to be written was that of modernism and its succession of avant-garde movements. In that Dutch intellectual climate of the sixties and early seventies, to question the canon and values of modernism in any kind of fundamental way was to challenge the symbols of a hard-won postwar freedom and cultural progress, and therefore to risk being lumped together with ultra-conservatives and cranks. In that respect, Rookmaaker's book was something of an embarrassment in the eyes of many of his colleagues in university and museum circles. Though one can wonder how many of them really read the book, most of them knew about it and the message was spread around that Rookmaaker had written something other than a factual account and that his approach was therefore unscholarly. Among the academic gossip that reached me at the time were even assertions that Rookmaaker was a 'charlatan'. Hans Jaffé would not have stooped to using such language, and in any case his estimation of Rookmaaker as a scholar was high. Nevertheless, Jaffé was to pass on this consensus view in his own gentle and circuitous fashion when he wrote in his obituary on Rookmaaker in 1978 that the latter's contribution to the study of art was 'not at all "unbiased"'.

Nowadays, of course, it is evident to all and sundry that those who (like Jaffé) wrote their histories from a modernist standpoint were themselves biased. But this revised opinion about modernist assumptions only became widespread after Rookmaaker had died and when postmodernist theory got into its stride in the 1980s. Since then, a new scholarly consensus has emerged in which it has become the norm to offer a critique of modernism and to expose its ideological roots and power bases in the art world and in scholarship. Not uncommonly, postmodern accounts have come to portray modernism as a kind of surrogate religion, a faith in the redeeming power for mankind of a new art and architecture. The conclusion is irresistible, therefore, that in the postmodern era historians and critics have finally found their way to issues that Rookmaaker was dealing with back in 1970 (and indeed much earlier). It is not simply that Rookmaaker's Christian critique prefigured postmodern accounts by exposing modernism's religious or ideological commitments, but Rookmaaker showed postmodernists the way on other counts too. He challenged the exclusive claims of modernist orthodoxy by emphasizing the plurality of streams in modern art, among which he saw plenty of opportunity for freedom of choice; today, historians of modern art have also turned to presenting a pluralistic picture and it has now become the accepted thing to pay attention to artists whom the modernist accounts preferred to ignore. And in 1970 Rookmaaker daringly interwove his discussion of modern art with themes and issues drawn from popular music and culture; today, a narrow emphasis on the history of fine art is generally frowned upon and university courses are now widely teaching about the interaction of 'High and Low' cultural histories.

That is not to say, however, that we can simply regard *Modern Art and the Death of a Culture* as a postmodern book in the same sense as publications that were to be given that label some fifteen or twenty years later. Not only should we avoid treating the book anachronistically but it is important not to gloss over some fundamental differences between Rookmaaker and the later postmodernists. For example, if Rookmaaker pointed to a plurality in modern art developments there was certainly no room in his thinking for the relativism and pragmatism that have tended to mark postmodernist conceptions of plurality. And some of the favourite themes of postmodernist theory – for example the notion of the simulacrum and the general fascination with disconnecting appearances and signifiers from firm realities and meanings – have broken in new and extreme ways with the belief in a created and reliable reality that Rookmaaker so prized. In some respects, then, postmodernism has given rise to ideas even more alien to Rookmaaker's mentality than modernism ever did. But on the other hand, theorists in the postmodern era have indeed brought indictments against modernism similar to those Rookmaaker was making and even drawn some conclusions that are reminiscent of his. So it remains fascinating to note that by the mid-1980s postmodernists were widely proclaiming 'the end' – the end of the modernist era, the end of a Western tradition, the end of history, the end of art, and the end of a great many other things as well – after Rookmaaker had already charted 'the death of a culture' in 1970.

Rookmaaker and histories of cultural decline

However, to see Rookmaaker's theme of 'the death of a culture' as a kind of forerunner of postmodernist critique is to approach it only from one angle and to link it only with a discourse that emerged after 1970. Should we not also view it from another angle, and ask if it was linked with traditions of thought that already existed before 1970? This is an important question since it returns us to the context in which Rookmaaker's ideas were shaped. Some critics of his work have had no hesitation in locating *Modern Art and the Death of a Culture* within a well-established genre in academic and popular-academic writing, a genre which is usually typified by Oswald Spengler's famous book *The Decline of the West*, which was first published in German as early as 1918. Indeed, Spengler and a good many other historians and theorists in the twentieth century have portrayed modern history and culture in terms of decline, decadence, death, and loss. Extremist variants, sometimes claiming a quasi-scientific basis, have included such abominations as the Nazi theories and policies that gave rise to the persecution of all that was deemed 'decadent' in art, culture and race. If *Modern Art and the Death of a Culture* was more or less ostracized by the Dutch art-historical establishment of its day this was perhaps in part because its title and theme reminded some people of that most unhappy period in history. Rookmaaker himself, of course, had no truck whatsoever with such extremist notions of decadence; nor, I want to suggest, is there any reason to link Rookmaaker with the secular ideas and cultural pessimism of Spengler.

If we want to link Rookmaaker's work with other accounts of some kind of decline in modern culture we can better look to traditions that were specifically Christian. One such tradition was to be found in the circle of Calvinist philosophers in which Rookmaaker moved since his conversion during the war. Rookmaaker was grafted into a theoretical movement that, from its inception in the nineteenth-century writings of the Dutch Christian statesmen Groen van Prinsterer and Abraham Kuyper, had specialized in a critique of those Enlightenment and Revolutionary principles that had denied God and attempted to establish an autonomy and freedom for mankind. Calvinist thinkers saw in the eighteenth-century Enlightenment a fundamentally flawed project that nevertheless gained a grip on many minds, leading to an increasing breakdown in values and finally to a crisis in twentieth-century Western thought and culture. It was this story of worsening problems as a consequence of unbelief that was dealt with by Dooyeweerd from a philosophical perspective in his book In the *Twilight of Western Thought* (1960) and then taken up by Rookmaaker from an art-historical perspective in *Modern Art and the Death of a Culture* some ten years later. There is an obvious similarity between their titles as well as a sharing of their underlying themes, and Dooyeweerd's title may even have been meant to recall Spengler's *The Decline of the West*. Dooyeweerd had no compunction in speaking of 'the fundamental crisis of contemporary, secularized Western thought', but he also made it clear that there was an important difference between Spengler's cultural pessimism and his own Christian analysis, which was concerned with diagnosing ills in order to treat them. Dooyeweerd saw Spengler as a radical historicist who thought Western culture was doomed because it had run its fatal course in history:

> Radical Historicism, as it manifested itself in all its consequences in Spengler's Decline of the West, deprived the history of mankind of any hope for the future and made it meaningless. [...] There would be no hope for mankind and for the whole process of man's cultural development if Jesus Christ had not become the spiritual centre and his kingdom the ultimate end of world history. (pp. 111–112)

Much the same Christian outlook pervaded Rookmaaker's discussion of the death of a culture; we find the crumbling of a culture and expressions of hopelessness portrayed on many of its pages, but the major theme of Rookmaaker's book, leading to its emphatic conclusion, was an affirmation of Christian hope and a call for a reformation of values. To view *Modern Art and the Death of a Culture* from the angle of its close relationship to Dutch Calvinist philosophical studies, as I do here, is in no way to detract from the originality of Rookmaaker's book. Rather, it is to affirm that there was a well-defined spiritual and intellectual tradition that stimulated and supported Rookmaaker's ideas – a tradition of thought that was itself highly critical of the Spenglerian prophets of cultural doom.

Rookmaaker and Sedlmayr

But we need to take another Christian approach to modern history into account, and in this second context questions have indeed been raised about the originality of Rookmaaker's book. It has been suggested by some critics that Rookmaaker's *Modern Art and the Death of a Culture* owes much to earlier publications by the Austrian art historian Hans Sedlmayr, in particular his *Verlust der Mitte* (literally 'Loss of the Centre', though the English edition was entitled Art in Crisis) of 1948 and his *Die Revolution der modernen Kunst* ('The Revolution of Modern Art') of 1955. Sedlmayr was one of the leading names in his discipline, the author of books on Renaissance and Baroque art and architecture and on art-historical method, and also a Roman Catholic. His faith was strongly in evidence when he published *Verlust der Mitte* in 1948, a book that accounted for the rise of modern art from the eighteenth to the twentieth century in overwhelmingly negative terms. 'People's relationship to God became disturbed', wrote Sedlmayr, and as a consequence man's relationship to himself, man's image of man, became more and more disturbed, the symptoms of which Sedlmayr traced in art history. Sedlmayr saw a dehumanization in art as polarized into two extremes, both of which showed a 'loss of the centre': at one extreme there was a search for a higher 'inhuman' purity in abstraction and machine-like forms, while at the other extreme there was a falling back into a 'subhuman' underworld to present the dark and irrational side of man, and a world of monsters and chaos. Not only was the image of man deformed but art lost its original character, too. Since the end of the eighteenth century the various arts (such as painting, sculpture, architecture) diverged and each sought to become autonomous and pure. Sedlmayr wrote in this context of the 'death' of artistic forms and principles: the death of the total work of art (*Gesamtkunstwerk*), the death of iconology, the death of ornament. The only remedy, wrote Sedlmayr at the conclusion of his book, is to recover 'the eternal image of man', but this can only come through faith and the realization that man is created in the image of God to live in an ordered world. His book achieved considerable fame and success, and also notoriety in the field of art scholarship, where its polemic against modern art worked as an irritant for many years. Since Rookmaaker acquired *Verlust der Mitte* in 1952 and underlined and annotated passages, and then went on to write a review of Sedlmayr's later book *Die Revolution der modernen Kunst* in 1959, there can be no doubt that he absorbed their contents during a formative phase in his own career. To what extent, then, could Rookmaaker's thinking have been shaped by his reading of Sedlmayr? And more particularly, to what extent was *Modern Art and the Death of a Culture* modelled on Sedlmayr's books about the 'loss' and 'death' of values in modern art?

The spiritual themes and conclusions of Sedlmayr's books must have struck Rookmaaker as broadly familiar and akin to those of his own Calvinist circle, and indeed similar to those he was already applying to art in his reviews for *Trouw*. In that respect, he did not need Sedlmayr to set him on the course he was already following. But I think that Rookmaaker must have been impressed to see such arguments being applied so systematically to his own field of the history of art – and by a much older and highly reputed member of his discipline. In other words, Rookmaaker could well have been inspired by Sedlmayr's example to think of writing such a book himself, from his own standpoint. In some respects his *Modern Art and the Death of a Culture* did follow a pattern established by Sedlmayr's books. For example, both authors used the rhetorical device of picking out and numbering phases or categories in modern art: Rookmaaker picked out and exemplified the 'three steps to modern art', while in *Verlust der Mitte* Sedlmayr had identified 'the three revolutions in art of the eighteenth century' that set the course towards modern art, and in *Die Revolution der modernen Kunst* he had gone on to discuss four main categories. But if there is similarity at the level of the broad spiritual themes and the rhetorical patterns of their books, there are not many points at which the more detailed contents of Rookmaaker's and Sedlmayr's accounts coincide. One or two artists (Goya, for example) took on similar significance in their arguments, but the artists and cultural issues chosen for discussion by Rookmaaker grew from his own special interests in years of lecturing and writing, and suggest to my mind no particular debt to Sedlmayr. Moreover, whoever reads their books with an eye to comparison will find some fundamental differences that have to do with the fact that Sedlmayr was a Roman Catholic while Rookmaaker was a Protestant. Sedlmayr saw the Reformation as a contributing factor in the rise of individualism and a consequent disintegration in culture, and made it clear that he valued the medieval cathedral as a 'total work of art' and a high point in Western art. Rookmaaker, on the other hand, argued as man of the Reformation and found in Reformational influences on seventeenth-century Dutch art many of the values he most admired. That he found much to agree with in Sedlmayr's view of modern art is quite clear from the review Rookmaaker wrote for *Opbouw* in 1959. It is especially illuminating, however, to note a substantial point of disagreement in Rookmaaker's closing words in that review:

> We can warmly recommend Sedlmayr's little book. Although there is a 'but' involved. It is our belief namely that this study does not sufficiently teach us to look, does not tell us enough about the origins and the grammar of that new language that is also in some respects modern art. The study is

somewhat too one-sided in its focus on spiritual problems, and while everything that the author mentions is certainly real, it is also good to look a little further and inspect the other side of this coin. Sedlmayr is so fascinated by the countenance of the god Hai-Hai [i.e. modern art seen as worthless blah-blah – GB] that he forgets to notice the people involved in it, neglects to hear their song, neglects to listen in to their everyday conversations. It is surely an unmistakable fact that art is art, and not philosophy or life and world view, however much art may have to do with these as well.

So if Sedlmayr's books were an inspiration to him, and I think that almost certainly was the case, then Rookmaaker decided quite early on what it was in Sedlmayr's approach that needed correction. We can safely establish that when he went on to write his *Modern Art and the Death of a Culture* it was not only about principles but emphatically about real people and their hopes and fears; one of the striking things about Rookmaaker's book is that he so evidently listened with compassion to their songs and to the conversations to be heard on the streets. Rookmaaker's book is also explicitly not only about negative aspects of modern art, but about positive ones as well. But in writing *Modern Art and the Death of a Culture* did Rookmaaker successfully avoid the one-sided focus on spiritual problems that he had formerly criticized in Sedlmayr's books? Was his own book sufficiently about art as art, and about the new pictorial language that was also modern art?

Calvin Seerveld, for one, did not think so when he included a chapter pointedly entitled 'Modern art and the birth of a Christian culture' in his book *Rainbows for the Fallen World* (1980). Seerveld, an American colleague of Rookmaaker in the circle of Calvinist philosophers, had no compunction in asserting:

> Contemporary christian critics have sometimes slipped into the lazy opinion that 'Cubism' or 'abstract' modern art is fragmented and defective, therefore a sure sign if not abetting cause of the breakdown of Western civilization. But that sweeping judgment about modern art is simply wrong. Braque, and Picasso too, among certain other gifted artists, raised the painting consciousness of people by showing the painterly strength of allusive, styleful colour compositions that carried perspective, insightful meaning without using devices of mimetic illusions. (pp.175–176)

In his note to this passage Seerveld made it clear that he had Sedlmayr's *Art in Crisis* and Rookmaaker's *Modern Art and the Death of a Culture* in mind. In bracketing Sedlmayr and Rookmaaker together as targets for his critique, Seerveld was obviously more interested in profiling his own theory than in elaborating on differences between the two other authors. In fact, in Rookmaaker's book, but not so easily in Sedlmayr's, Seerveld could certainly have found passages to cite that would have supported his own argument concerning the value of the new pictorial language developed by modern artists – though not, it is true, about the

Cubism of Picasso, which Rookmaaker described in terms of spiritual loss. So perhaps Seerveld was a little unfair. Nevertheless, he found a tender spot since *Modern Art and the Death of a Culture* is indeed much more about the spiritual problems of the age than about the artistic perspectives opened by the new styles. In that respect, it is rather more like Sedlmayr's books than one might have expected from Rookmaaker's critique of Sedlmayr in 1959.

Conclusion

I suggested earlier that the contours of Rookmaaker's attitude to modern art were already drawn by the late 1950s. I still hold to that, but I now have to conclude that within those contours Rookmaaker shifted his emphasis somewhat in the 1960s. *Modern Art and the Death of a Culture* still contained passages affirming the value of modern art's new languages and styles but, as the last chapter made clear, Rookmaaker was now more than ever convinced that the most important thing to share with his public about modern art concerned its content and meaning, not its aesthetic and technical aspects. This conviction can have had little to do with his reading of Sedlmayr, which had come so much earlier in his career. Rather, I am sure it grew during the sixties, through the direct contact Rookmaaker had with an increasingly interested public on his many lecture tours, to become a calling. The sense of calling and the passion with which he wrote the book can be felt by the reader. At the same time, the discerning reader must know that in order to write such a book some things had to be left out that the art historian Professor H.R. Rookmaaker might otherwise have wanted to explain about modern art. Rookmaaker knew that himself. In conversations we had after *Modern Art and the Death of a Culture* was already a widely acclaimed book, he confessed that in an ideal world it would have been better to complement the book with another one, a more technical study of modern art that even the Dutch art historians could not ignore. But we live in a real world, not an ideal one, and we may be thankful for the combination of strengths and limitations that was the real Rookmaaker.

What would have come if Rookmaaker had lived longer? Such speculations verge on forbidden terrain, but one cannot help entertaining them. In this respect I feel it worth sharing something that in all honesty I had forgotten until I reopened some boxes marked 'Rookmaaker' for the purpose of preparing this introduction. There I rediscovered several letters dated 1977, written shortly after Rookmaaker's death to the Free University and to the Schaeffer family, by Joseph Masheck, editor of the journal *Artforum* in New York. Masheck expressed a 'serious interest in the work of this man who contributed so much to the scholarship of modern art' and told that he had contacted Rookmaaker just before his death with the intention of publishing material on contemporary Photo-Realism from lectures that Rookmaaker had given at Grace Church in New York. At the moment Rookmaaker died, *Artforum* – the most prestigious modern art journal of the seventies – was wanting him.

Dr Graham Birtwistle is a former student and colleague of Hans Rookmaaker. At present he is Associate Professor of Art History at the Free University of Amsterdam.

Part I

GAUGUIN AND NINETEENTH-CENTURY ART THEORY

Preface by Hans Rookmaaker to the Second Edition[1]

In the introduction to the first edition of this book, more than ten years ago, I suggested that the artists at the end of the nineteenth century were aware of what they were aiming at, and what was involved in their search for a new style. These artists were not mysterious beings who created new things out of unconscious urges, but their artistic innovations were in many ways connected with cultural and philosophical trends. The most important innovation of Gauguin and the group around him, in trying to overcome the restrictions of the prevailing naturalism, was their understanding of the visual arts as using a pictorial language, which I called iconic.

I still feel that this study of the art-theoretical notions of the Post-Impressionists offers a key to the understanding of some of the most important aspects of the arts in the twentieth century. The arts of the twentieth century cannot simply be equated with the modern movement characterized in its different streams by Cubism, Dada, Surrealism, Abstract Expressionism, Pop, Op and Neo-Dada. This modern movement is not a style, but more an attitude, a spiritual insight, a feeling for the predicament of humankind. Modern art is defined by its content, not its style. It uses different styles: naturalism, a certain kind of mannerism, and cubistic or expressionistic iconic types of visual communication. But these different pictorial languages are also used in contemporary visual arts that are not 'modern' even if they are contemporary. And I feel that the iconic type of visual communication is one of the most important and lasting characteristics of the arts of our century.

This second edition is almost completely unchanged – some printing errors and some mistakes in the translation are corrected. Ten years have passed and the world has changed greatly during the revolutionary sixties, but I don't feel that the argument of this book is obsolete. If I were to touch this book again I should have to rewrite it – but I doubt that it would really be improved. Since the first edition was published I have devoted most of my time to the study of modern art and its background, in relation to the problems of our own age, which has resulted in my *Modern Art and the Death of a Culture* (London: IVP, 1970).

I have only to add one new and final proof of my argument concerning Gauguin's 'Whence? What? Whither?' in Boston.

In my discussion on page 193 I put forward some reasons for the likelihood that Gauguin knew Carlyle's *Sartor Resartus*. That he certainly did read it, has now become evident as the *Mercure de France* of 1895 to 1897 (Vol. XVI-XXI), to which Gauguin was a subscriber, published a translation of Carlyle's book by E. Barthelemy in instalments. In the issue of January – March 1897 on page 64 we read the translation of

'But whence? – O, Heaven, whither? for *Mais d'où venons-nous? – O Cieux, où allons-nous?* I should like to thank the person who called my attention to this evidence – but unfortunately this correspondence has zaccidentally been lost.

Further, I have added a few titles to the list of books and articles directly concerning Gauguin that were published since my book first came out, although I haven't aimed at providing a complete bibliography.

I wish to thank Dr J. Q. van Regteren Altena, Professor of History of Art at the Amsterdam University, for his careful reading of my manuscript and for his many clarifying remarks. Many other scholars have helped me in some way or another with my study of the subject treated in this book. I want to mention specifically: the late Prof. Dr H. J. Pos, Prof. Dr J. M. Romein, the late Dr J. Suys, Prof. Dr H.M.J. Oldewelt, Prof. Dr A. H. van der Weel, all of the Amsterdam University; Prof. Dr H. Dooyeweerd, Prof. Dr D. H. Th. Vollenhoven, of the Free University, Amsterdam; Prof. Dr J. P. A. Mekkes, Prof. Dr H. van de Waal, of the University of Leiden; Prof. Dr C. G. Seerveld, Trinity College, Palo Heights,Ill.; Prof. D. E. H. Gombrich, of the Warburg Institute, London. Beside these who have advised me as only scholars of profound learning can do, there were those who helped me by lending or giving me books and other material. It would be impossible to name them all, but I wish to stress that without their generous aid this study would not have been possible. I may not pass over in silence the amiable help of the publisher of this book, Mr R. J. Swets, and of Mr H. van Krimpen, who looked after the lay-out and typography. Thanks are also due to my wife, who has spent much of her energy in order to make this study ready for publication, as she has done all the typewriting and correcting.

H. R. Rookmaaker, 1972

I
Introduction

After having proclaimed the omnipotence of scientific observation and deduction for eighty years with childlike enthusiasm, and after asserting that for its lenses and scalpels there did not exist a single mystery, the nineteenth century at last seems to perceive that its efforts have been in vain and its boasts puerile. Man is still walking about in the midst of the same enigmas, in the same formidable unknown, which has become even more obscure and disconcerting since its habitual neglect. A great many scientists and scholars today have come to a halt, discouraged. They realize that this experimental science, of which they were so proud, is a thousand times less certain than the most bizarre theogony, the maddest metaphysical reverie, the least acceptable poet's dream, and they have a presentiment that this haughty science which they proudly used to call 'positive' may perhaps be only a science of what is relative, of appearances, of 'shadows' as Plato said, and that they themselves have nothing to put on old Olympus, from which they have removed the deities and unhinged the constellations.[2]

This is how Aurier characterizes the position around 1890, functioning as the spokesman for many of his generation. No wonder that they tried to strike out new paths and wanted to free themselves out of the quandary into which especially art had been brought by the exclusive positivistic focusing on visible things.

What was the state of affairs in the plastic arts? Was there any justification for fulminating against naturalism since academism reigned supreme and, to quote Toynbee, had changed from a creative minority into a ruling majority? Or are we to hold such pronouncements applicable only to the domain of literary art? True, there also prevailed a naturalism founded in the positivistic mentality and, no doubt, Aurier stems from an environment of writers and poets. But our quotation is the initial part of an article on contemporary painting that enters more thoroughly into the subject of naturalistic pictorial art, which was nothing but 'the short-sighted copy of social anecdotes, the imbecile imitation of the warts of nature, the flat observation, the trompe l'oeil, the glory of being as faithfully and vulgarly exact as a daguerréotype'.[3]

It should not be supposed that in the period around 1890 there existed a criticism like this with respect to the Impressionists, and that Aurier's strictures were levelled at them. For the Impressionists were only just beginning to find a certain amount of recognition in these years, and were fighting their own battle against the prevailing taste. For the latter reason the newcomers felt some affinity with them and admired them. Only now did they get acquainted with this kind of art, although it had flourished since the seventies. For it should be borne in mind that the generation of artists of 1890 was very young – apart from a pioneer like Gauguin, who notwithstanding his passing through Impressionism did not yet sharply oppose it. It was, however, impossible for them to see in the Impressionism of Monet, Renoir, Sisley and Pissarro the realization of their ideals. They were of too different a mind for this – for in their art they wanted to dig deeper than was compatible with a faithful representation of light and atmosphere, however brilliant it might be. Very soon they were to formulate their objections but, quite different from their attitude towards the naturalists, this criticism would not exclude their appreciation and admiration.

The art of the Salons

This disqualified naturalism was, properly speaking, the art of the Salons displayed at the great annual exhibitions in Paris. What were the aims of that large group who proudly called themselves 'academicians', a name that in the mouths of their adversaries was almost synonymous with the words 'bad, meaningless'. They prided themselves on continuing the great tradition of French pictorial art and on faithfully preserving the ancient principles, that is to say, those artistic principles that had been formulated by Raphael in the sixteenth century and renewed as well as adapted to the French mind in the seventeenth century by Poussin, Vouet and Lebrun. Subsequently they had been undermined by the Rococo with its pastorals and courtly love-scenes and 'rendezvous', to be renewed in the cool, manly classicism of the late eighteenth century.

This lofty tradition, this 'grand manner' did not only mean a particular way of painting, but mainly particular kinds of themes. The artist was expected to observe the required 'decorum'. As long as this decorum was not violated, widely different techniques were permitted, provided the deviations from what was hallmarked were not too obvious. So, for instance, in the case of the debate around Courbet's work the academicians seem to have taken offence almost exclusively at his realistic themes, his attention for what they considered to be too trivial a kind of reality. This appears, among others, from Couture's caricature of a Realist, a man who chooses a pig's head as his model, painted in a technique that, after all, differs only very little from Courbet's.[4] The exalted myths of a remote past, especially that of the Greeks and the Romans, the great heroic events of history, the ideal person, beautiful in body and mind, such were the subjects worthy of art,[5] while as to beauty as such, its highest norm could be what the Greeks had bequeathed to us, for it was they who had formulated the ideals in such a pure and almost inimitable way. On the other hand, if we examine the works made at this time by the painters who ruled the Salons, we discover that these ideals were only rarely a concrete guiding principle. In reality academism was merely the acceptance of one single dogma, namely that there are fixed rules for art, particular technical precepts that ought to be observed – especially as regards the method of drawing – and that these can be learned.[6]

Consequently there is more than a little truth in Gauguin's statement:

> At the beginning of the nineteenth century art is no longer a language as it used to be formerly, in every country, with the memory of beautiful traditions. It is in a way a kind of Volapük formed with the aid of recipes. A unique language taught by certified teachers, giving the assurance of perfection and of an immense mediocrity. This Volapük is still spoken.[7]

This certainly holds for the classicistic painters in the narrower sense, for those who stuck most faithfully to the academic tradition proper, artists like Gleyre, Gerôme, and the proverbial Bouguereau. But on examining their work, we see that both in technique and in their themes they had not been left untouched by what was the spirit of the age, and that they, too, were much more realistic than the classicists of the past. For one thing, they were no longer able to follow the anachronisms of the earlier painters, who represented the lofty events of the past in the contemporary style of clothing – now they 'knew better'.[8] They regretted the fact, but they acquiesced to it. And, for a second thing, they followed nature much more closely, especially when painting nudes, in which case they based themselves less on the classical norms of ideal bodily beauty than on a well-chosen model.[9] Thus this art had degenerated into genre painting, reporting, as it were, everyday incidents of a distant past or giving us a glimpse of a quasi-ideal world in which nymphs and satyrs, gods and goddesses walk or fly about naked.

Looking, for example, at Bouguereau's *Satyr and nymphs*[10] we get the impression of seeing a snapshot taken in a nudist camp. The figures are represented in such naturalistic detail, so palpable are the beautiful people performing a round dance with their bodies bare, that it is difficult for us to take the title seriously. The same holds for *Venus bathing* painted by Baudry in 1859 (and bought by the Museum of Bordeaux): this Venus is certainly a beautiful woman, but a real one, of flesh and blood, standing bare in a (very naturalistically painted) wood. There is nothing left of the sculpturally idealizing and abstract-timeless quality of the genuinely classicistic nudes of the time of David.

There is no longer any belief in the classical themes, the allegorical figures or the ideal human figures that are painted. These subjects, which had a profound meaning for an artist like Rubens, because they were directly connected with his vision of life, are now no more than pretexts. Themes such as Venus, Magdalene, and others in which beautiful naked women could be the artist's subjects without loss of decorum, or without shocking the public, were very much in favour. But it was precisely the naturalistic way of painting that often rendered them unpalatable and vulgar, rather bare than naked, more sensual than aesthetic. In this connection Gauguin even speaks of 'an obligatory brothel'.[11] How great the deviation from the classical ideal might be can be experienced in the *Madeleine* by Falguière, a sculpture which was on view at the 'Exposition Centenale de l'Art' [12] offering us nothing but the full-length portrait of a bare female dancer, whose body had been considerable deformed by the corsets of those days. The title has to save the situation, and in that way the 'decorum' has been observed. But the examples are as common as grass.

And finally, if contemporary themes were chosen, the unreal embellishing gave rise to namby-pamby sentimentalism. This is the case with *Brother and sister* by Bouguereau in the catalogue cited above,[13] which depicts some too sweet children in too beautiful clothes with too neatly combed long hair, but with nothing of the aristocratic air and the natural ease based on a grand style of living that made such a theme convincing and truly beautiful in the hands of a painter like Reynolds.

However, also other tendencies could be discovered in the Salons, sometimes in straight contradiction to the classicistic tradition. But there was hardly question of a conflict, and a writer like Castagnary, an advocate of naturalism, asserted that he could comprise by this term 'the whole of the younger idealistic and realistic generation'.[14] The artists referred to in this context, Bastien-Lepage, Lhermitte, Roll and the like, were influenced in more than one respect by Realists like Courbet, Manet, and even by the Impressionists. But they mitigated this Realism to such a degree that buyers at the Salons should not be deterred. They continued the tradition of the painters of history who already in a previous period had come very near to photographic accuracy – recall Boissard de Boisdenier's *La retraite de Moscou* of 1835, now in the Rouen Museum,[15] and similar works by Meisonnier, Neuville and Detaille, reconstructing the events very exactly in retrospect as an elaborate photographic record. Although the art of these Realists within the Salons was very naturalistic, it was rarely personal, and always adapted to the taste of the indispensable clients. This was one of the reasons why they were never attacked, however much their subjects must have violated the academic 'decorum'. In this connection one might think of Gervex' scenes in hospitals, preferably representing operations, in a cold and would-be scientifically objective way, but not without a melodramatic accent.

In addition to the inoffensively smooth surface of their paintings, the firm position of these painters in the Salons was due also to the fact that with their themes they remained within the prevailing social class, or, when 'lower-class people' were represented, they viewed them with the eyes of the bourgeoisie. We might mention Dantan's studio-pieces: they satisfied the curiosity of those who wanted to know how things were done at the studios of the naturalistic sculptors, where images of living models were cast for the making of clay figures (and perhaps also for the production of works of art). Never was there any revolutionary sentiment in this art, and very rarely was there a hint at the contrast between the social classes in a socialistic spirit. Even if this should ever have happened, it would have been done in such a way that nobody's feelings could be hurt.

Perhaps there may have been a few genuinely good artists among these 'academicians' who, as we have seen, were in reality naturalists. It is possible that they will be re-discovered when the artistic tide turns and an art that is directed to the visual aspect of things has a stronger appeal than at present.[16] However, it is still difficult for us to look at works of this kind with an open and unprejudiced mind, free from the excessive criticism made by the artists outside of the world of the Salons and their adherents, the more so as in many cases they rightly poured out the vials of their wrath. But some of the works of Bastien-Lepage and of Lhermitte certainly testify to their originality and their daring. They are free of the empty display of technique intended to curry favour with a public that had lost taste and a genuine love of art. The above-mentioned artists, for instance, were highly praised by van Gogh, [17] who became thoroughly acquainted with them when he was working for an art dealer. But he, too, has his criticism to offer, the gist of which is directed against the academic technique. This technique turns painting into applying a certain number of rules. 'Without your being aware of it, that academy is a mistress preventing a more ardent, more serious, more fruitful love from awakening in you – leave that mistress alone, and fall head over heels in love with your real beloved lady nature or reality . . . She renews, she gives fresh vigour and courage, she gives life!'[18]

The very sharp condemnation of the arts of the Salons by artists and critics not belonging to that circle is not to be explained, however, only by a different attitude. There is something else, which perhaps plays the decisive part. Aurier summarizes this in a masterly way in his discussion of the Salons of 1891: 'floods of articles of a purely commercial nature . . . there would be no question at all of art, of artists, but simply of a luxury industry'.[19]

This criticism was not a novelty. In the course of the nineteenth century there had been repeated complaints about the low artistic level of the Salons. Of course they came from those circles who wanted to go in another direction, or from those who had been seized by revolutionary ideas and opposed the leading social groups. No wonder that most of the criticism came from the socialists, or that Baudelaire wrote with reference to the Salons that 'mediocrity . . . prevails more than ever'.[20]

Yet there is a great difference between the older kind of criticism and that made at the end of the century. For a man like Baudelaire did not at all shun the task of subjecting the Salon artists to an elaborate discussion. And in his comment on a picture by Tassaert he devotes many words of praise to it.[21] Yet this work, a very naturalistic representation of a market of female slaves, might certainly have been used by us as an example of an academism of a dubious kind. It would no doubt also have occasioned sharp criticism on the part of the generation of 1890. For it is true they had inherited Baudelaire's negative attitude with regard to the art of the Salons as a whole, but were not merely content with stating its bad quality. They tried to dig deeper and to lay bare the cause of this artistic decadence. Thus they came upon positivism, upon the fact that French culture was overgrown with the natural scientific mentality, and were induced to make a pronouncement like that of Aurier.

It is impossible for us to give an account of the artistic situation around 1890 without considering the art of the Salons. For this art dominated the situation, and the newcomers in the artistic field had to stand up against it. They linked up with an entirely different tradition which, alongside that of the painters of the Salons, had determined the artistic climate of the nineteenth century. In many respects this tradition held on to the French artistic achievements of the past in a deeper, more essential way. It did not degenerate into the insipid banality of a photographic art without a trace of the artistic or even of good taste, although in the course of the century these figures, though marginal in the official world of art, came also to manifest a growing tendency towards Realism in their choice of themes.

In this study we propose to institute a thoroughgoing investigation of the theories advanced by the generation of 1890, which has created an art that has become decisive in every way for the twentieth century – witness the Fauves in particular, who would have been unthinkable but for the men of 1890. The development of art in the circles outside of the Salons became of such eminent historical importance that very often, even apart from the far superior artistic quality of their creations, it represents for us the nineteenth century proper. The art of the Salons is, therefore, no more than a *repoussoir* enabling us to get a better insight into the development which is our chief interest.

It should not be supposed, however, that outside of the Salons there is only one single line of development to be discovered in the history of the art of the nineteenth century. For here, too, the state of affairs is very involved, and there are tendencies to be discovered which at times deviate strongly from each other. A closer study of the genesis and the character especially of the art theories of Gauguin and his circle will necessitate a sharp analysis if we are not to lose our way in the thick tangle of trends and movements around 1890 that are more or less related to one another and sought to strike out new paths. It is especially imperative for us to distinguish their art and their ideas clearly from those of the Symbolists, with whom they are too often classed together.

2
The Precursors of the Synthetists

David, Ingres, Gros, Géricault

The nineteenth century opened with the supremacy of classicism under the undisputed leadership of David. More than ever before the classicistic dogma of following the Greeks found adherence. As a reaction to the art of the Rococo, which had concentrated on the erotic and the feminine elements, the artists now laid emphasis on the masculine. Their favourite subjects were taken from Roman history and were concerned with examples of heroism, patriotism, generosity and loyalty. They strove after a formal clarity and balance. Again they adopted the principles of the seventeenth-century classicism as Poussin had defined them. Even more than David it was to be Ingres who embodied this old ideal as far as the nineteenth century is concerned, no doubt also because he worked on far into the century, raising high the classicistic torch. This is why the discussions about classicism were concentrated on his art. In his words and works he continues to acknowledge the drawing, *le dessin* – always a characteristic of the academic tradition – as the foundation of the painter's work, although at times he could be very fascinating as a colourist.

Gros and Géricault, too, considered the *grande histoire* as the highest aim of painting. Only, they were more inclined to follow the Baroque. The former, it is true, made desperate attempts to be a classicist in the line of David, but often maintained a greater measure of freedom in composition, a greater mobility in his figures and groups. That which in his heart of hearts Gros would have liked to do, was realized by Géricault, who followed him in the beginning and always continued to admire him. He is through and through a Romantic artist in the French understanding of the term, but more clearly related to the Baroque than anybody else. This does not only appear from the masters he admired and studied, Rubens and Michelangelo, but also from his strongly mobile compositions built on the diagonal. We are introduced into a heroic world in which powerful figures and noble animals move about. Following new tendencies in historical painting, which had already asserted themselves in the eighteenth century,[22] he also selected an event of contemporary history for his principal work. But notwithstanding his scrupulous accuracy of detail he did not fall into the error of a kind of photographic naturalism. After the manner of the Baroque, he strove after an ennobled summary of the meaning of an event. The history of this work *Le radeau de la Méduse*, from the year 1819, is extremely instructive in this respect. After first researching the facts, also by means of conversations with the survivors of the wreck of the French warship – a scandal that had made a great stir – he experimented in his preliminary studies until the composition achieved maximum artistic effect.[23]

Constable, Turner

It is Constable who became very important for the further course of events. In many respects he continued the tradition of such seventeenth-century Dutch landscape painters as Ruysdael and Hobbema. But he aimed at something new insofar as he tried to represent the changing aspects of nature – recall his studies of clouds – as exactly as possible, which betrays an almost scientific attitude[24] that, as such, had been alien to our great [Dutch] landscapists. For the purpose of noting the rapidly changing effects of the weather he developed a very direct and quick manner of painting, adding to the quasi-scientific tendency in his observation a marked subjective element that was also foreign to his predecessors. It is remarkable that the nineteenth century was to be a constant witness of this new and peculiar manner. In the very method of painting it made the tension palpable, as it were, between nature and freedom which has always dominated humanism:[25] on the one hand there is a concentrated study of nature in its visible outward appearance; on the other, we find a strictly subjective manner of representing what has been observed.

This complex mentality later on found its most explicit realization in Impressionism. Zola's well-known pronouncement that the artist should represent 'a corner of nature seen through the medium of a temperament'[26] concisely formulated this.

We do not believe that one is justified in depreciating Constable's more elaborate finished works in favour of his rapidly painted sketches, which most clearly manifest what has just been said. Constable is certainly not likely to have belied his own nature when finishing the symphonic pictures, and to explain this peculiarity one need not say that he yielded to the prevailing taste and to tradition.[27] But, as so often happens, the new tendency comes to the fore in its most unpurified form in a study and in a sketch. Also in the completed works the new elements were not lacking. Was it not the *Haywain* in its elaborated version that opened the eyes of Delacroix at the Salon of 1824 to a new method of working in which the colours were put on the canvas unmixed, a procedure that made them give the impression of freshness and naturalness?

The influence of Constable – and artists of kindred spirits like Bonington – on French painting, indirectly via Delacroix, and above all directly on the landscapists of the school of Fontainebleau, can hardly be overestimated. It is exactly the direct inspiration derived from nature, without any Romantic admixtures, which has again and again been a guiding principle. Turner's influence was to remain much more restricted, due also to his much more pronounced subjectivity with respect to natural scenery. This is the consequence of his sense of composition, an academistic trait derived from Claude. His too great freedom in the realization of his effects, together with his always noticeable idealizing tendency after the manner of Claude Lorrain, caused his work to be less in line with the tendencies of the French painters. There is no doubt that he took a great interest in light and colour, but they remained a means for him to express feeling, to make the dream acceptable.[28] There was always something in Turner's work that was not naturalistic. This striving to give more than nature as such we also find clearly formulated in Ruskin's work *Modern Painters*, devoted to Turner's art. Here, for instance, we read that Turner not only knew and studied the clouds, but 'to him . . . the stormclouds seemed messengers of fate. He feared them, while he reverenced; nor does he ever introduce them without some hidden purpose, bearing upon the expression of the scene he is painting.'[29]

Goya

We should not altogether leave Goya out of the picture, although we must not overestimate his direct influence. The problems of the artists around 1890, to be investigated in more detail later, are concerned with the relation between a work of art and reality. They have rejected naturalism but are by no means prepared to indulge in a fantastic art that has become detached from reality. It is precisely at this point that they might have made an appeal to Goya, although they never did, as far as we know. For Goya's art was not easily accessible. Some of them will no doubt have known about him because of what Baudelaire wrote about him, and possibly, via Delacroix in particular, there must have been some indirect influence. In this connection we refer to his famous print in the series of the *Caprichos*,[30] with the striking title *El sueño de la razón produce monstruos*. It represents a man asleep, with his head on a table – behind him there are all kinds of monsters resembling bats, owls, and a cat. The title should not be translated as 'the sleep of reason produces monsters', as is done in Levitine's note – which, by the way, is a particularly important one[31] – but as 'the dream of reason produces monsters', which is the rendering given by Gombrich in his no less important article.[32] This term 'dream' (*rêve*) was in very frequent use among the generation of 1890. But in this case we find it for the first time applied to great art in the sense of the artist's mind being a creative spirit that invents a whole world of images and symbols. This world is not the realm of fantasy but bears the closest relation to the world in which the artist lives. This dream is not at all a means to escape from reality into the freedom of fantasy. On the contrary, the attempt is made to come to close grips with reality by means of an image.[33]

Gombrich shows that this method had already been applied by the English graphic artists and caricaturists of the latter half of the eighteenth century, men like Gillray. The dream, fantastic figures, ghosts, and more, are used to represent, in an image, that which cannot be rendered in a naturalistic way.[34] In this way an attempt is made to avoid the incongruity that has existed in the visual arts since the Renaissance, because on the one hand the artists tried to represent everything in accordance with what the eye perceives, and on the other they stuck to the allegorical-symbolical method of the Middle Ages.[35] For in this way the spectator was shown things in the picture that had the appearance of being real, but that never occur together in such a context in actual reality. A simple example of such incongruity is the picture of an angel represented as a human being with wings. To interpret such an image naturalistically is mere folly. However, now that the world represented in the picture is called a dream, a fiction, the artist has become free to depart from the outward appearance of everyday reality. And exactly in this way the artist is able to satirize the events of the day all the more sharply, or to elucidate them critically in an image.

Also Goya's *Caprichos*, although they are the *monstruos* of his *sueño*, are not really dream castles but works which in many cases bear the character of genre pieces, if we study their titles and descriptions. They are glimpses of daily life in the Spain of Goya's time. It is true that, already at an earlier period, namely in the work of Tiepolo, we find *capricci* – he sometimes also calls them *scherzi di fantasia*[36] – but we think that Gombrich is right in discovering some connection between Goya's work and that of the English caricaturists, because the technique used in both is new and certainly different from that of Tiepolo. For Tiepolo gives either a world of fantasy or simply a genre piece. He does not know this element of the 'dream', namely the creative daydream, in which there is always a vision of what is found in the immediate surroundings, however slight the naturalism of the representation might be.

Certainly new were the peculiar character and the contents of this vision which, by way of a pun, we had better call a 'daymare' than a daydream, and which Baudelaire characterized with the words 'Le monstrueux vraisemblable'. In fact, 'these contortions, these bestial faces, these diabolical grimaces are imbued with humanity.'[37] For in Goya's case even the strangest representations rarely create the impression that the artist is giving free reins to his imagination. Even in the case of that remarkable print entitled *Quien lo creyera* – a significant inscription – representing two fighting naked old hags, it seems that Baudelaire's interpretation, a summary of 'all the vices the human mind can conceive of'[38] is the only right one. In this connection the very clearly non-naturalistic first print in the series *Desastros de la guerra* is also characteristic.[39]

Here the horror of war is summarized in a birdlike monster. It resembles a bird because there is no possibility of human contact with this kind of creature, for we do not know and cannot predict its reactions. It is a symbol that we meet again in our own time in many ways – as in drawings by Zadkine made during the last world war.

Delacroix

Delacroix's influence reached the generation of 1890 in three different ways. In the first place, of course, there were his works, which, comparatively speaking, were within the reach of every painter. But alongside these grand works he also left a number of no less fascinating writings, while Baudelaire's articles containing a brilliant analysis as well as an enthusiastic glorification of his art will certainly have been of great importance.[40] In many respects Baudelaire was the teacher of the generation of 1885-1890. But he would not have occupied that influential position among the artists if he had never written about Delacroix's art. This is why Delacroix and Baudelaire belong together, and the influence of the one is not conceivable without that of the other.

When studying Delacroix's work the first thing that strikes us is the way in which colour is handled. It is so different, so much more lively and fascinating than in the works of his contemporaries. Also Ingres who, to be sure, had some qualities as a colourist, at times used bright and telling colours. But there is always this distinction: the works of Delacroix are, so to say, vibrant. This is the result of a very easy manner of painting, a striking technical quality of Delacroix's work that has always fascinated artists. He did not discover this new technique without an effort. The examples of Rubens and Constable pointed the way, but his own studies and thought were also necessary for him to attain perfect mastery. Many passages in his *Journal* and in his other writings dealing with this subject bear witness to it. And they have not remained unknown to the artists. Van Gogh writes about them in his Nuenen period,[41] while Signac's book is one elaborate homage to the colourist Delacroix.[42]

Yet Delacroix never aimed at colour for the sake of colour, just as an art for art's sake was foreign to him. The colouristic realization of his work was subservient to the effect he wanted to achieve, namely directness and fluency, in opposition to the painful accuracy with which Ingres as well as the Salon artists worked. In the rare cases of a certain ease and fluency of execution in the works of the latter we can nearly always trace it back to Delacroix's influence – we are referring to Decamps, Couture, and similar artists. Delacroix did not strive after Romantic fire, the direct and unrestrained expression of the self but, according to his own formula, 'One should make sketch-like pictures that have the freedom and the frankness of rough drafts.'[43] A few days before he wrote this he had noted down in his diary a criticism of painters whom he calls *des prosateurs* ['the prose writers'] – the classicists – in which he makes the remark that, 'It looks as if the tones have been assembled by luck and the lines of the composition have been arranged by chance. The poetic or expressive idea does not strike one at the first glance.'[44] So he is in search of a kind of ease and freedom of execution that does not imply casualness. And the sentence last quoted approaches much more closely that which he considers to be essential in this respect, namely that the colour and the composition, built up in a colouristic way, should bear and underline the emotional expressiveness of the subject. He gave a pregnant expression to this idea which frequently occurs later on with his admirers:[45] 'There is an impression evoked by a certain arrangement of colours, lights and shadows etc. . . . This is what one would call the music of the picture.'[46]

The vivid impression of reality that his paintings call up, and which immediately strikes the spectator as genuine and natural, has been achieved by means of a technique and a manner of execution which are not in the least naturalistic in the sense of the Salon painters. 'For', Delacroix says, 'the artist's imagination not only represents to himself such and such objects, but combines them for the purpose he wants to realize; it produces pictures, images he composes as he pleases.'[47] His view of art embodies a strong urge for freedom, in perfect agreement with the impression we get from his work. This freedom, however, is not licence but aims at the poetic expression, the representation of reality. For, according to him, it is indeed right to compose a fine arrangement of lines and colours,

> but if, to a composition already interesting by the choice of subject, you add a disposition of lines which increases the impression, a chiariscuro which catches the imagination, a colour adapted to the character, you have resolved a more difficult problem and once more, you are superior: it is harmony and its combinations adapted to make a song that is unique.[48]

So in Delacroix's art we witness two requirements that might contradict each other if they had not been brought to a synthesis in such a convincing way, namely the inclination to develop harmonies of colour in full freedom and the demand to render reality in a pure and telling manner. That which Delacroix tries to define is something that in former centuries artists had done intuitively without raising so many problems. The artistic act representing reality, without the inclusion of so many details of what was to be seen somewhere at a certain moment, now required more precise justification. For humankind's relation to nature had become problematic in all manner of ways: either a freedom was sought that was detached from nature (in Romanticism), or only the depiction of what the eye can perceive was thought to be meaningful (in a naturalistic conception). We might almost say that here Delacroix upholds an old painter's tradition, which before him had found its most beautiful formulation in the works of Rubens and Rembrandt. He does so at a time when this tradition was no longer understood and thus hands it down to the next generation. As we hope to show, it is precisely at this point that we must look for the most positive value of the art and the theories of the Synthetists, at the end of the nineteenth century.

So to Delacroix the great problem was that of the relation between work of art and reality, because his observation and his manner were different from those of his contemporaries. 'Our moderns,' he says, 'no longer paint the feelings, they describe the exterior, they analyse everything.'[49] Yet he does not condemn a thorough study of nature; on the contrary, as may appear from his landscapes, his *coins d'atelier* ['corners of the studio'], and his studies of the model. But we shall never find him using a study such as the one of *Mademoiselle Rose* of 1821, in the Louvre, in the great compositions that cannot be considered as studies. On the contrary, more than once he speaks of his experience, that work done directly from nature is not really good, and that he only comes nearer to his ideal when he works out what he has found by directly studying nature, because 'my intentions are more pronounced and useless particulars have been removed'.[50] For he abides by his opinion that human interpretation, human feelings with respect to the facts of nature, to what the eye perceives in the strict sense of the word, are essential, both to human experience and to art. He may say as sharply as he can – and here he follows the motif of freedom in humanistic Romanticism – that 'The most careful execution of details will not give the unity that results from I-do-not-know-what creative power, of which the origin is indefinable.'[51] He certainly does not strive after the unrestrained expression of absolute freedom in the modern sense. He has certainly reflected on the relation between the sensorily given facts and that which is in the artist's mind as an ideal first, that which he creates according to his 'imagination'.[52] It can hardly cause any surprise that his answer is in line with eighteenth-century philosophy,[53] which has struggled with this problem from its strictly subjectivistic, sensualistic standpoint.[54]

> The fact counts for nothing because it will pass. Nothing is left but the idea; in reality the fact even exists only in the idea, since the latter lends its colour to it ... [This is] what happens when the creative faculty seizes the idea in order to animate the real world given in the transitory facts and to derive from them pictures of the imagination. It composes, that is, it idealizes and selects.[55]

Thus Delacroix almost inevitably arrives at the thought which was to be at the centre of the meditations on the theory of art at the end of the century, namely that the figures and the things represented in a work of art are mere signs, symbols. This is why Delacroix writes about painting: 'These figures, these objects, which seem to be the things themselves to a certain part of your intelligent being, seem to be a solid bridge on which the imagination leans in order to penetrate to the mysterious and profound sensations of which the forms are somehow the hieroglyph.'[56] In direct contact with Delacroix, Baudelaire was to express and elaborate this thought.

It now remains to make a few observations on Delacroix's subjects. Although by the end of the century his admirers had never criticized him in this, they rarely followed his example. Delacroix represents reality very vividly and directly, but embodies it in images that only rarely have been derived from the reality around him. He remains entirely in line with the generation of great artists of pre-Revolutionary times when engaged with historical and allegorical subjects or deriving his inspiration from such authors as Walter Scott. In this respect, certainly, he is not so much in opposition to the art of his own time as he is in his execution. Consequently he has never been criticized on this point by his contemporaries, nor by his opponents. He belongs to his time in his striving after historical exactitude in dress and environment just like his contemporaries. He can no longer follow the older generations of painters in their way of depicting historical scenes, with subjects dressed in outfits that bore no resemblance to the way people dressed at the time of the event.[57] But his paintings never impress one in their depiction of costumes or manners as an exact reconstruction of the past.

In this lies the essential difference between Delacroix and his contemporaries: the handling of historical data. Delacroix is fully aware of the fact that a photographical reconstruction of the events has serious deficiencies, 'In the first place, because a picture has to bring to light the historical meaning of the event recorded, to interpret the latter and to express it through line and colour.'[58] His treatise on this matter, as recorded in his diary on 4 October 1854, is well worth reading. But in addition, Delacroix wants above all to be modern; he wants to reflect the spirit of his own time. As a result the subject itself thus becomes a kind of metaphor of the view that his own time has of human being and of human history. He therefore states that there is no point in producing a Greek Achilles. Not even Homer himself has done so, for as Delacroix rightly observes, 'Homer's Achilles and the hero who lived on in the imagination of the poet's contemporaries a long time after the death of the real Achilles with his whole generation and all their ideals . . . And perhaps in reality he had not at all been such a superhero.'[59]

This view for a great part explains the secret of Delacroix's paintings. Even now they do not strike us at all as cold or too photographically exact and soulless, like those of Delaroche. It is true that a picture of the Revolution of 1830 makes an impression that is hardly different from that of a work representing the capture of Constantinople or the battle of Taillebourg. For in all these paintings we have to deal with the same living human beings, animated by a similar spirit, which renders the depictions hardly historically exact but not for that reason less meaningful. Their meaning is to be sought in the fact that they reflect the contemporary spirit in various ways. No doubt it was this circumstance to which Delacoix referred in his diary when he made a note saying that in his dictionary – which remained a project only – he should devote a long article to philosophy: 'Without this philosophy as I understand it there will be no duration for a book or a painting, or rather no existence.'[60] In short, a work of art must be based on a view of human being and human actions, otherwise one will never achieve anything better than a photograph or a reporter's reconstruction after the event. This very important thought at the same time implied the severest criticism of the art of the Salons of his time.

In Delacroix's work the whole of the great artistic tradition of Western culture was as it were formulated anew and integrated into the contemporary pattern. The heritage of Constable, Goya, Géricault, who had done the same thing in their own way, with all their personal contributions and additions, was epitomized in a grand way and animated and seeded for the future. But only Baudelaire's words were able to make the true import of all this clear to later generations.

Baudelaire

The great difference between the ideals of Baudelaire and those of his contemporaries, not only of the Salon artists but also of those of the still highly esteemed school of Fontainebleau is clear when we read his elaborate criticism of them in the *Salon* of 1859. Especially its conclusion in which he once more states his own wishes explicitly: 'I wish to be taken to the dioramas whose bold and enormous magic can force their useful illusion on me . . . These things are infinitely nearer to truth because they are false; whereas the majority of our landscapists are liars for the very reason that they have forgotten to lie.'[61] These desires appear to have been satisfied by Victor Hugo's drawings, in which Baudelaire discovered a 'a magnificent imagination',[62] drawings which can in no way be called naturalistic but, rather, Romantic.

Yet Baudelaire did not strive after an excessive kind of imagination, disorderly, uncontrolled and unconnected with reality. It was not absolute free play he wanted but truth, the full human truth, which he could not find in the naturalistic art of his time because there was too little truly human interest in it, too little vision. But also Grandville's art, a kind of pre-Surrealism, did not give him the truth he wanted. Grandville at times succeeded in making beautiful and good things, but too often he changed reality for the apocalyptic and turned the world upside down.[63]

Baudelaire's attitude can be best understood by taking into account that he was ultimately rooted in Romanticism and at the same time aware of the influences of positivism. In his own person he felt the consequences of the former and he was keenly aware of its faults, 'the disorder and the shameless displays'.64 But he certainly did not like the other tendency, to be found in the works of the landscapists and of Courbet and his followers, whose art derived from an attitude towards nature that was similar to that of positivistic philosophy. To him, the child of Romanticism, this positivism left too much to be desired. That is why he tried to avoid the shortcomings of the one influence as much as those of the other. In some way or other he attempted to satisfy the two fundamental requirements of human freedom and subjectivity, on the one hand, and an interest in reality outside of human being, on the other.

Baudelaire was perfectly aware of this situation. That Romanticism was the cause of many of his difficulties and of his inner depression he explicitly stated, in the words of the autobiographical main character in his *Fanfarlo*:

> Pity me, or rather, pity us, for I have many fellows of my kind; it is the hatred of all and of ourselves that has induced us to tell lies like these. It is through the despair of ever attaining to nobility and beauty by natural means that we have painted our faces so strangely. We have so much set ourselves to sophisticate our hearts, we have so much abused the microscope to study the hideous excrescences and the disgraceful warts that cover our hearts and which we have a pleasure in enlarging, that it is impossible for us to speak the language of other people ... We have altered the accent of nature, one by one pulled out the decencies of virginity that covered the honesty of our inner man. We have psychologized like fools who add to their folly by trying to understand it ... Woe, three times woe to our fathers who made us rachitic and undersized.65

More than lengthy theories, this pronouncement by the young Baudelaire makes it clear that the situation in which he and his fellows of the same generation found themselves was the fruit of the development of the eighteenth and the early part of the nineteenth century. To begin with, the value of the revelation in Holy Scripture and that of the traditional – Roman Catholic – faith with its certainties were denied and considered to be without any real importance. And then the attempt was made to regain an insight into reality through psychologistic epistemologies. Later on came Romanticism, which laid even more emphasis on human subjectivity and cultivated its expressions in all directions.

So this trend of events evidences the revival of the old humanism,66 which had been thwarted in its development by the Reformation and the Counter-Reformation. By the end of the seventeenth century it had again begun to reflect upon its own starting point and consequences. At first the effort was made to subject reality to human supremacy in a practicalistic way, with the aid of the insight and the knowledge gained by means of science and philosophy. As the scientific ideal concretized more and more human freedom was endangered, for this science aimed at the formulation of universally valid laws. In the name of freedom a sharp reaction started, especially in Germany and England and, under its influence, a little later also in France.[67]

The results were manifest in the situation in which we find Baudelaire. Although he certainly showed the influence of Christian (Roman Catholic) thinkers – for instance Xavier de Maistre[68] – he did not turn his back on the humanistic past. On the contrary, his starting point remained the opposition between human freedom and nature. And this was also the reason why to him this reality – which he still viewed through the eyes of the eighteenth-century French philosophers – was a strange and incomprehensible power, a world that fitted into his conception only with difficulty and that put up a strong resistance to that thirst after freedom which was the central, nodal point in his view of life.[69] In this way an estrangement from reality arose, a feeling of 'the hostility of the atmosphere',[70] a dread that Baudelaire expressed as 'the complaint about the emptiness and nothingness of existence of a soul that had withered early in the storms of life'.[71] Perhaps it was more applicable to his own work than to that of Delacroix when he wrote that 'All this work . . . is like a terrible hymn composed in honour of fatality and irremediable sorrow.'[72] And most clearly, perhaps, he laid bare his heart in the final lines of *Les Fleurs du Mal*:

> 0 death!
> Pour out your poison that it may comfort us!
> This fire burns our brain so much that we wish
> To plunge into the depths of the abyss, into hell or into heaven,
>   it does not matter!
> Into the depth of the unknown to find something new.[73]

For the very fact that this contact with reality had become problematical and this reality seemed to be a strange, mysterious power outside of human being, his most personal basic experience of reality was one of looking into the abyss, into the abyss of death. As this reality of doom – for thus eighteenth-century scientists had represented it – oppressed him he had to look for new impulses and values 'at the bottom of the unknown' of this reality itself.[74]

Yet he rejected the consistent expression of freedom, as we have already stated. On the contrary, retaining a strongly pronounced subjectivism and laying great stress on human freedom in opposition to nature, he wanted to give nothing in his art but this very same reality. Baudelaire did not wish to be a dreamer, building beautiful daydreams alongside an outside reality, erecting a paradisaic dream palace to take refuge in. He wanted to look full in the eye of those oppressing and horrible depths that constituted reality.[75] He wanted to live fully in the world of his own times and to reflect it in his art. The demand for contemporaneousness, the reflection of the spirit motivating a person, the expression of the heart as it really is, had always been the guiding principle in all his critical and theoretical views of art. Or, as he put it himself: 'What is pure art according to the modern conception? It is the creation of some suggestive magic comprising at once the object and the subject, the outer world and the artist himself.'[76]

It is this effort which is new, this search for a synthesis between the free experience of the strictly personal and the adherence to what reality has to offer. This synthesis is one of the fundamental characteristics of the theory of art advanced by the Synthetists, as we hope to show later on. For it may be true that he wrote: 'Romanticism is not to be pinpointed in the choice of subjects, or in the exact truth, but in the manner of feeling.' But he supplemented this sentence immediately with the following: 'Above all, one must know the aspects of nature and the situations of man, which the artists of the past disparaged or which they did not know.'[77]

How did Baudelaire set about to effect such a synthesis? By means of the idea of the 'imagination' to which he devoted the best pages in his *Salon* of 1859. This imagination, 'the queen of the faculties' (*la reine des facultés*), comprises analysis and synthesis,[78] and contains *la sensibilité* but is more than that. It is the human creative power:

> It is the imagination that has taught man the moral sense of colour, outline, sound and smell. At the beginning of the world it created analogy and metaphor; it breaks up the whole of the creation and with the materials collected and arranged according to rules the origin of which can only be found in the depths of the soul, it produces the sensation of the new. Since it has created the world – one may put it like this, I believe, even in a religious sense – it is only right for it to rule.[79]

If we study this passage, which was written in an almost religious rapture, philosophically, we are close to Kant's conception, according to which in his *reine Vernunft* man is supposed to create order in his chaotic sensory impressions. Or, perhaps, because we are dealing with a Frenchman, we may refer to Maine de Biran,[80] whose voluntaristic theories are related to those of Baudelaire in many respects. To the best of my knowledge Baudelaire was unacquainted with de Biran's work or, at least, he was not influenced by it to any noticeable degree.[81] It is doubtful whether Baudelaire carried his reflection so far, or lent to his thoughts on the 'imagination' such a far-reaching import. We are here much rather confronted with an art theory as such, which (and this is typical of those days, as has already been observed in the case of Delacroix) is engaged in a penetrating study, in a way that is closely akin to the philosophical problem of epistemology, of how humans relate to reality.

However, we shall revert to Baudelaire's 'imagination' and read this passage: 'The imagination is the queen of truth, and the possible is one of the provinces of the truth.'[82] We must not take this pronouncement in a strictly literal sense, to imply that there are consequently more worlds 'possible' that can be created by the imagination in total freedom. By this 'possible' he much rather meant reality as understood by the *doctrinaires* in question, with whom he was carrying on a debate, the people who demanded that an artist copy nature. The meaning of this passage in the theory of art must be conceived in the light of the statement made a little further on to the effect that 'The chief formula ... of true aesthetics [will be that] the whole of the visible creation is only a storehouse of images and signs to which the imagination assigns a place and a relative value; it is a kind of food that the imagination has to digest and transform.'[83] In this idea that reality is nothing but a 'dictionary' in which the true artists look for the elements that can be adapted to their conception Baudelaire not only very nearly approached Delacroix, who had advanced the same thought more than once,[84] but he had undoubtedly been influenced by the latter's thought, a fact that he admitted himself.[85]

The criterion for the selection of the suitable facts from that 'dictionary' is that 'Everything must serve to illuminate the generative idea and still bear its own original colour, its livery, so to say.'[86] And this 'generative idea' is undoubtedly the work of the imagination, or, as he indiscriminately called this faculty of the true artist, the work of *le rêve*, explicitly defined as a creative daydream: 'The dream is a vision produced by intense meditation.'[87]

Here Baudelaire is one of the first writers who penetrated to the admission that artists worthy of the name will attempt to make their work into something meaningful because it is related to their fundamental view of reality, to their view of life and the world. This relatedness to that which a person has very much at heart finds expression both in his or her choice of subject, and in the way in which the chosen subject is realized – in the approach, the composition and the execution. The one as well as the other must be relevant to a person, it must bear on his or her outlook and fundamental attitude towards reality. In this way we shall perhaps be better able to understand such a pronouncement as the following: 'A picture must above all reproduce the intimate thought of the artist which dominates the model as the creator does the creation.'[88] It is quite understandable that especially Baudelaire – and the kindred spirit Delacroix – were the first to see this, and that they took it as the starting point of their theory of art. For to them the relation between reality and a work of art had become problematic, partly due to the fact that reality itself was no longer a matter of fact for them, and partly because their starting point was placed in the experience and the expression of what was peculiar to their own personality, in which humanistically conceived freedom assumed a particular subjective form.

This explains why Baudelaire was always greatly and profoundly interested not only in the way in which a work had been realized, as to technique and composition, but also in its theme. To him 'l'art pour l'art' did not at all mean that art ought to be abstract and purely aesthetical, as this phrase is often taken to mean nowadays.[89] In his final discussions of the landscapists in the *Salon* of 1859 he himself laid full emphasis on this thought, as we have seen. He even went so far as, for a moment, to wish back the Romantic landscape, in which was found 'all that would have to be invented if it did not exist'.[90] But this passage was an exception; much stronger was his call for subjects that have the heroism of his own times as their starting point. As has been said, his conception was determined by a yearning for reality, genuine and living reality, and for a desire to know it, to penetrate it, to experience it passionately.[91]

How was such relevancy to be brought about, how was the artist to choose from that 'dictionary' which comprised the whole of reality? For an answer Baudelaire called in the help of very ancient theories. They were to ensure a firm basis for the 'imagination' and to guarantee its relatedness to reality without losing the freedom inherent in it. This duality between reality or nature and freedom is typical and determinative. Baudelaire was perhaps as sharply opposed to the older Romantics – with whom he had, notwithstanding, so much in common and whose starting point he wanted to modernize (recall the quote from his *Fanfarlo* that we mentioned above) – as he was to naturalism. For he did not simply mean to realize the artist's subjectivity, the strictly personal.[92] He wanted more; in addition to the subjective, he wanted also to attain to something that had universal validity, revealing a fixed and permanent truth and reality. As the Christian religion – in its true sense, as the belief in God's revelation – had lost its hold on the culturally formative minds, it became necessary for them to know and understand the meaning of reality in some other way. This was also the mission of the positivists, who tried to find it in their own way. But Baudelaire wanted something more; he wanted to get a deeper insight and a more comprehensive view than was afforded by the social and psycho-physical 'exterior' of things only. It is not sufficient for art, he says, to be merely a cultivation of form, for 'The absence of what is just and true is equal to the absence of art', because 'The entire man has vanished.'[93] That is why, he says, art should go hand in hand with science and philosophy, for otherwise it would mean suicide to art itself.[94]

So Baudelaire wanted to furnish the imagination with a firm basis in its creative activity, enabling it to function as a means to reveal the essence of reality – this was no less than absolutizing the personal outlook to become the deepest truth itself.[95] He clearly indicated the way in which this was done when he wrote: 'The imagination is the most scientific of the faculties, for it is the only one that understands the universal analogy, or that which a mystical religion calls the "correspondence".'[96] And in these words he referred to the ancient theories that have already been hinted at.

That very old tradition had come down to him especially via Swedenborg, whose work he had come to know mainly in an indirect way through Balzac and others. For Swedenborg had made a deep impression on the Romantics by means of his strange theories, which deviated so far from the tendencies in philosophy during the eighteenth century. The Romantics had been in very close contact with mysticistic movements[97] that drew their inspiration from similar sources as Swedenborg did, whose views, however, succeeded in fascinating people the most. At least, the resultant non-rationalistic, non-sensualistic tradition was linked with his name. This conception gave a different answer to the question of how we can attain to the knowledge of the principles determining reality.

Swedenborg

Swedenborg came from the family of a Lutheran clergyman. He devoted the first part of his life to research in the natural sciences.[98] However, he soon began to long for a summarizing philosophical insight into the whole of the cosmos, so that we need not expect from him an elaborate and patient investigation of some particular phenomenon.[99] This brought him into close contact with the new insights that occupied the contemporary minds, especially with regard to epistemology. Locke became the determining influence and, like him, Swedenhorg denied any innate knowledge and was also an empiricist.[100] But no more than Locke did he find a firm basis in this. On the contrary, Swedenborg as well as Locke inferred from it that our knowledge shows a deficiency because it is entirely dependent on our (sensory) experience. This was the starting point for all of his further development, which is, as it were, an attempt to restore along a different route the lost certainty of human insight into the totality of cosmic relations; an attempt to defend the Christian truth against the relativistic consequences of the rationalistic natural sciences, which undermined certainty. These sciences reasoned God away and denied revelation any firm content of truth. For his defensive purpose Swedenborg did not take recourse to the testimony of Holy Scripture itself but sought for an equally rationalistic theory as Locke's to achieve insight into the 'supernatural' and foundational truths. With a view to this he consulted mystical and Neoplatonic traditions.[101] Especially his allegorical way of interpreting the Bible made him closely approach the already very old attempts to synthesize the Platonic or Neoplatonic and the Christian heritage.[102]

According to Swedenborg it is an effect of the fall into sin that humankind has to rely on sensory experience in order to acquire knowledge. Things were originally different when humans had a direct insight into the deeper relationships by means of a kind of radiation of the divine Light.[103] To an increasing degree Swedenborg also tried to acquire knowledge by means of the anima – about which he theorized in a way that is strongly suggestive of Plotinus[104] – and he more and more wanted to give up the unreliable knowledge gained by means of the senses.

In this way he drew up his theory of the *Entsprechungen* or correspondences based on the agreement between things in different spheres: 'For all divine things are examples; intellectual, moral and civil things are types but the images of nature as such and things physical are merely likenesses.'[105] This was in itself the consequence of a Platonic, or rather a Plotinian thought, saying that all things in the different spheres are reflections, depictions of the ideas in the intelligible world.[106] Also Plotinus' conception of the meaning of the soul is found to surface again in Swedenborg: 'The soul adds the form of the world to the four elements and provides them with it; but it is the intelligence which furnishes germinal reasons.'[107] This might be a summary of Swedenborg's view although it really reflects Plotinus' thought. Swedenborg uses this theory for the conclusion that 'consequently' the lower things agree with the higher ones, and 'so' what is lower can be used in order to arrive at the knowledge of what is higher.[108] Swedenborg's very close agreement with Plotinus is further indicated by the fact that he then started to refer to Egyptian hieroglyphs, which are supposed to be no mere representations of natural things but to express the inner essence of things because they indicate the correspondences themselves. Plotinus had come to literally the same 'conclusion'.[109] Remarkably enough, though, Swedenborg continues to formulate a theory to explain the idolatry of the heathens but does not speak of art in general.

The inference might, therefore, be that the Renaissance had taken over the old theories that had from the outset been directly related to art – we think of Gombrich's article on the *Icones Symbolae*, which demonstrates the spread of these ideas especially in the seventeenth century[110] – and that Swedenborg transmitted them to the nineteenth century without, however, applying them to art theory. Balzac was to draw the same old conclusions again in his *Louis Lambert*,[111] and they were worked out in full detail by Baudelaire, who made these theoretical ideas of art fruitful for the remainder of the nineteenth century. But maybe this reconstruction of the course of events is too bold and we should consider the possibility that Baudelaire had some personal acquaintance with the work of Plotinus and that of other Neoplatonists, like Porphyry, or that of the mystics.[112]

On the other hand it should be borne in mind that Swedenborg was much more accessible to the nineteenth-century minds than the old philosophers and mystics. For not only had his work been published in a French translation around 1820 by Moët and Hindmarsch but

Swedenborg also struggled with, and applied the old theories to, the same problems as they had encountered. He wanted to compose an epistemology which far transcended any natural-scientific limitation but was in actual fact equally rationalistic. The old theories were re-formulated anew, as it were, within the framework of the problems of the eighteenth century and detached from their scholastic or humanistic environment,[113] which was perfectly alien to men like Baudelaire. It enabled them to solve the tension between nature and freedom or, to put it in another way, between the ideals of individual personality and of science[114] within the problems of their time. In such a way, at least, the two elements could be given their due in a kind of equilibrium – even though it was only a labile kind of equilibrium – and artists were able to choose their own way of expressing their personality, in freedom, while keeping up the appearance of being founded in reality.

Thus we can agree with Evans who, in his study on Balzac's *Louis Lambert*, writes: 'The eternal dialectic of idea and facts that has always tormented him is at last resolved by Balzac in favour of the idea, but the facts remain in his work as the images of the idea.'[115] We need not occupy ourselves here with a penetrating investigation of the depth of Swedenborg's actual influence, nor with the question whether 'Van der Elst is right in his assertion that Balzac really developed his theories independently and only cited Swedenborg as an authority to lend his own conception the required importance.'[116] For it is clear that actuated by the impulse issuing from Swedenborg – and possibly also from other mystics – Balzac arrived at a theory which at least differed from theirs in that he had given up any reminiscences of a synthesis with (biblical) Christianity. If he did borrow directly he also removed very carefully from Swedenborg's philosophy every element relating to God, the Bible, heaven and hell, angels and devils.

Baudelaire (continued)

It is, of course, simply conceivable that Baudelaire got acquainted with such theories via Balzac, after their purification of Christian and 'supernatural' admixtures. For it is well known that Balzac had a great influence on Baudelaire, especially in the latter's early years. The very search for a synthesis testifies to their spiritual affinity. This also explains why later on, at the end of the century, people again turned to Balzac, the Balzac of *Seraphita* and of *Louis Lambert*.[117]

However, Baudelaire had elaborated these ideas in a theory of art and made them accessible to posterity. One of the reasons for this accessibility was the fact that he divested his thoughts of their abstract philosophical character. In his *Salon* of 1859, when discussing the imagination, he hardly mentioned this theory and straightway applied it in his examination of the artist's method. But his exposition was charged with the driving power of his view of life, which imparts its force and influence to these passages. He also summarized them in a poem entitled 'Correspondences'[118] for literary artists to derive inspiration from. In this poem, by the way, Baudelaire elaborated an image taken from Balzac's *Les Lys dans La Vallée*.[119]

Baudelaire's ideas have had an enormous influence on the generation of 1890. First of all he considered the theory of correspondences to be the foundation of the artistic possibility of suggesting one thing by means of another, a sound by a colour, a colour by a melody, and so on, or an idea by one of the means just mentioned. He thought this so essential and natural that it would be astonishing 'if sound could not suggest colour, or colours could not give the idea of a melody, and if sound and colour were unfit for the translation of ideas; things have always been expressed by reciprocal analogy (another word for 'correspondence') since the day God produced the world as a complex and indivisible totality'.[120] But Baudelaire wanted to dig even deeper. As Swedenborg has already taught us – so he says – that everything, both in the spiritual realm and in the realm of nature, has a signifying function, is 'correspondent', so that

> we cannot but arrive at this truth that everything is hieroglyphic, and we know that symbols are only relatively obscure, i.e., according to the degree of purity, benevolence or innate clear-sightedness of the souls. Well, what is a poet – I take the word in its widest sense – if not a translator, a decipherer? With all good poets there is no question of metaphors, comparisons, or epithets which are not mathematically exact adaptations in the actual circumstances, because these comparisons, metaphors and epithets have been drawn from the inexhaustible source of universal analogy and they cannot be drawn from anywhere else.[121]

Just as in the seventeenth century, as Gombrich demonstrated, the aid of Neoplatonic theories was called in[122] to give every image, or every comparison, every metaphor, an ontological value far above mere playing or arbitrariness. But even more, in this way art became a means enabling us to get an insight into the deepest meaning of reality, into that which determines reality. Thus art became revelation. Baudelaire rarely says so *expressis verbis*, but it is very instructive to compare that part of his essay on Théophile Gautier with a paragraph of Poe's *The Poetic Principle*, which he follows more or less closely. Thus Baudelaire writes: 'It is this admirable, immortal instinct of the beautiful that makes us consider the earth and its spectacles as a summary, a correspondence of Heaven.'[123] Poe says that man's sense of beauty 'administers to his delight in the manifold forms, and sounds, and odours, and sentiments amid which he exists'. And Baudelaire continues: 'The unquenchable thirst for all that is beyond and is revealed by life is the most striking proof of our immortality',[124] while in this part of his essay Poe apparently does not at all feel the need for any proof of his immortality but states that this joy in the beauty of things is not enough for a person, because he or she thirsts for something more important:

> This thirst belongs to the immortality of Man. It is at once a consequence and an indication of his perennial existence ... It is no mere appreciation of the Beauty before us, but a wild effort to reach the Beauty above. Inspired by an ecstatic prescience of the glories beyond the grave, we struggle by multiform combinations among the things and thoughts of Time to attain a portion of that Loveliness whose very elements perhaps appertain to eternity alone.

Of the latter we can 'attain to but brief and indeterminate glimpses . . . through the poem, through the music'. These thoughts are summarized in Baudelaire's translation as follows: 'It is at once by and through poetry, by and through music that the soul gets a glimpse of the splendours beyond the grave.'[125] This is something more because here, a little nearer to Christian thought, there is a reference to a fullness of reality revealed by art. That is why in Poe fine art evokes tears, because we are aware that it does not yet attain to that fullness of 'Loveliness' that he has mentioned above. This may be called a purely Platonic thought. In Baudelaire, on the other hand, 'Those tears are evidence of sensitive melancholy . . . of a nature exiled in what is imperfect, and which would immediately seize upon a revealed Paradise on this very earth.'[126] The difference in the use of words in theses quotations – 'glimpses' (Poe) and 'revealed' (Baudelaire) – speaks volumes.[127]

To summarize Baudelaire's view of art we might take as our point of departure his statement that the artist after his own heart, says: 'I wish to illuminate things with my mind and project their reflection on other minds.'[128] Here the starting point is strictly subjective. The artist must not be ruled by a universally valid ideal outside himself or formulated by his predecessors.[129] On the contrary, 'The ideal is the individual restored by the individual.'[130] But this does not mean that Baudelaire wishes artists to set to work in perfect freedom, to give free reins to their ima-gination. He wants the work to be well thought out and under perfect control. This thought is already to be found in his *Salon* of 1846,[131] but later on he became no doubt more convinced of this by his contact with Poe's work, especially with the latter's treatise on the poem 'The Raven'.[132] For Baudelaire is not interested in the artist's own subjectivity as such, by which the artist would fixate in his work what is strictly personal and peculiar. Rather, his concern is with the artist's personal *vision of reality*. He can give such a vision by means of the 'correspondences', and the relevant and appropriate images and comparisons will occur to him through his 'imagination'. For this purpose he makes use of the images that his mind has collected, images supplied to him by reality as if by a dictionary, and which he now produces from his remembrance. This remembrance, *ce souvenir*,[133] is therefore the direct link between the artist and reality that, as such, must never be merely copied. For then the artist would kill his or her thinking and feeling inner person.[134]

Something new is the amply elaborated concept of the 'imagination'. In it Baudelaire combines ideas that flow to him from different sources such as, for instance, Swedenborg's philosophy. The knowledge of this philosophy he may have owed to Balzac, or to somebody else, and he combines it with the existing idea of *le rêve* as a creative daydream, an idea that is also found in Balzac,[135] and especially in Goya. Baudelaire would certainly have agreed with the latter's pronouncement with reference to his *Capricho 43* – the well-known work discussed at the beginning of this chapter: 'Imagination, deserted by reason, begets impossible monsters. United with reason, she is the mother of all arts, and the source of their wonders.'[136] In this there is also the equalization of dream and imagination. Further, Delacroix is sure to have influenced the formation of Baudelaire's 'philosophy of the imagination' – thus we might almost call his theory – for Delacroix generally uses this term and rarely uses the word rêve. Lastly, we should not forget the great influence of Poe in those days. There is a striking agreement when one compares, for instance, Baudelaire's ideas found in his *Salon* of 1859 with Poe's statement: 'That the imagination has not been unjustly ranked as supreme among the mental faculties appears from the intense consciousness, on the part of the imaginative man, that the faculty brings his soul often to a glimpse of things supernal and eternal.'[137]

It is remarkable that Baudelaire nowhere gives a theory of beauty in the narrow sense of the word. He did have a keen eye for the importance of colour and composition, even for the *dessin* ('drawing') in Ingres' sense, and there are few art critics before his time who realized as strongly as he did that a work of art is worthless if it is below the mark in this respect – one should read his treatise on colour in the *Salon* of 1846[138] – but as soon as he goes on to speak about art, such terms as 'intimacy, spirituality, aspiration towards the universe'[139] flow from his pen. He himself is aware of this and even explicitly mentions it. He says that he has devised as many systems as he has rejected. So, 'I have contented myself with feeling . . . I prefer to speak on behalf of feeling, of morals, and of pleasure.'[140]

As soon as he discusses art that is important in his eyes, for instance that of Delacroix, his thoughts try to penetrate deeply and to grasp the sense and meaning of this art, not exclusively in its artistic vehicles but in that which this art has to say. And the deeper such art penetrates, the more it satisfies the requirements that he, Baudelaire, posits with his own version of Romanticism, the more he speaks of exactitude and truth. And then he even tries to fathom the depths of religion, which he considers as the fundamental relation between humankind and reality –

the Creator and Normgiver has practically already been excluded from his view, and consequently also redemption and joy. That is why this religion is not a joyful one. To the contrary. For the present we shall conclude our discussions of Baudelaire's views of art – it was not necessary to go into his literary work, or into his personality – by quoting his words on Delacroix:

> But to explain ... that only Delacroix knows how to make religion, I will point out to the observer that, if his most interesting pictures are nearly always those of which he has chosen the subjects, that is those of the imagination, nevertheless the serious sadness of his talent is perfectly in harmony with our religion, a religion of universal sorrow, which on account of its very catholicity[141] leaves the individual entirely free and requires nothing better than to be celebrated in each man's own language – if he knows sorrow and if he is a painter.[142]

Edgar Allen Poe

We have already mentioned Edgar Allen Poe's role as a co-determinant of the climate in which the artists worked around 1890. They were well acquainted with his work, since it had been made accessible to them in excellent translations by Baudelaire. Indirectly this interest in Poe favoured Baudelaire's own influence, as the latter prefaced many of his editions of Poe's works with an introduction. Of course we shall not enter into Poe's theories, nor into his development,[143] but into that which may have struck his French readers, into that strictly individual quality of Poe's that fascinated them again and again.

It goes without saying that they will have been struck by the eccentric nature of Poe's stories, on the one hand gruesome, strange, exceptional, weird, and on the other hand never so fantastic that they could not have taken place in reality. Even the very sharp analysis of the events, which were in themselves no more than natural, contributed to the total effect of something grisly and fantastic. It must have made a deep impression on those who sided with Baudelaire or were influenced by him.[144] For this work was properly speaking Romantic, yet never lost sight of reality. And also, these stories were written in such a purely objective manner, sometimes almost in a cool and matter-of-fact way, like a report for a court of justice[145] (a style that Poe deliberately allowed to influence him).[146] Without a trace of sentiment or of a personal emotional statement, they must have made a special appeal to those who wanted to retain the fundamental characteristic of Romanticism, namely to live out of human freedom, but who rejected the Romantic method.

Gautier concisely summarized this personal quality of Poe's style in the formula *mathematiquement fantastique*.[147] Remarkably prophetic were the words that the Goncourts wrote in their diary, expressing a similar sentiment:

> Poe, a new literature, the literature of the twentieth century, the scientifically miraculous, fiction by A + B ... imagination by means of analysis, Zadig judge of instruction, Cyrano de Bergerac a pupil of Arago's ... finally, the novel of the future whose call it is rather to relate things that happen in the brain of man than things that happen in his heart.[148]

This typically non-Romantic trait in presentation and form, by the absence of any very personal expression of feeling, is very important. Mauclair – and here we quote an author and critic belonging to the generation of 1890 – therefore writes about Poe:

> The tales of mystery treat of subjects without the aid of allegory, presented with all the relief belonging to the facts of real life; and the strangest of them always end with a plausible explanation. The artist in Poe shrinks from all gratuitous and illogical suppositions; he detests the melodramatic, just as he does over-charged style and fortuitous inspiration. Far from drawing his fantastic element from an arbitrary distortion of life, he makes it, on the contrary, grow out of a more careful study of what seems to the generality of people natural and commonplace.[149]

What is said here is exactly what these artists sought themselves. Poe pointed them the way, or at least, he showed that the synthesis they strove for was possible. True, Poe had something new to offer – something that had a strong appeal to those who sought so passionately for what was new, unheard of and unprecedented – but these qualities were after all new aspects of the reality in which we all live. That is why he is honoured, for 'The profound sense he has of that aspect of nature and man that has not yet been observed ... the grotesque and the horrible ... the sense of the exceptional, the spiritual sense of beauty in intensity, and lastly, the lyrical sense of science – these are the three glorious claims Poe has to eternal admiration.'[150] So wrote Morice in 1889.

All this Poe attained by letting the imagination, rooted in human freedom, dominate over natural facts and events – something that ought to have struck Gauguin too, who after all sought for the same thing. According to Morice he often quoted Poe's statement: 'Matter is the artist's slave, it belongs to him.'[151]

Also Carlyle and Schopenhauer influenced the formation of the art theory of the Synthetists. At the time with which we are now mainly concerned, around the middle of the nineteenth century, both of them had finished their work but were mostly still unknown in France. Their influence, therefore, was felt later, but then in a very direct way without any intermediaries and without being associated with any artistic or pictorial trend or leading figure, while to a certain extent there were such connections in the cases of those we have discussed above: Balzac – and through his *Louis Lambert* and *Seraphita*[152] also

Swedenborg – Poe and Baudelaire. Directly or indirectly they had something to do with the great French tradition that manifested itself in such a magnificent way in Delacroix.

Schopenhauer

The philosophy of Schopenhauer became increasingly better known in France in the course of the nineteenth century. The work of Ribot and other writers on philosophy, and that of translators, bore fruit. In a large measure Schopenhauer's work attracted so much attention and, consequently, influenced the circle of artists – most of them authors – mainly because his idealistic philosophy was really a theory of art, whereas his other treatises, his observations and remarks seemed to be less *Deutsch-gründlich* than those of the other great German philosophers. Whoever dips into an edition of translated fragments of 1880 – *Pensées, Maximes et Fragments*,[153] a second edition – will understand that a writer presented in such a way was bound to appeal to the French. This holds especially for authors who were accustomed to deal with more or less theoretical works, it is true, but to whom the genuinely German and technical philosophical literature with its typical jargon and problems was too exacting a test of their patience – apart from the question whether they knew enough German or whether there were translations of these works available. As a result, Schopenhauer became the connecting link between the German idealistic philosophy and this late nineteenth-century literature. It seems that Moréas was the first to point their attention to Schopenhauer,[154] but whether this statement is correct or not, they were certainly willing to listen to Schopenhauer's thoughts. These artists desired to assign a very high place to art with the help of a philosophical justification and Schopenhauer provided it, whereas through Baudelaire, Poe, Balzac and Swedenborg they had become familiar with a world of thought ruled by Platonic ideas as well as by a strong subjectivism. This combination is also the most characteristic feature in Schopenhauer.

A look into his principal work *Die Welt als Wille und Vorstellung* cannot but give the art historian the impression that Schopenhauer tried to modernize and bring up to date the classicistic theories of Winckelmann and his followers – which were connected with the Enlightenment.[155] The following introductory sentences of this book strongly remind us of the Kantian world of thought: 'The world is my conception . . .'[156] We shall not follow the elaboration of this philosophical theme any further here. For our purpose the most important part is his third chapter in which he combines the Kantian doctrine of the Categories with Platonism by positing that the will – which he identifies with Kant's *Ding an sich* – objectifies itself in different stages, in which we can recognize Plato's ideas, while in time and space we can find the *principium individuationis*.157 As, however, all knowledge is dependent on the *Satz vom Grunde*, the concept of causality, to which the ideas are not subjected, the great problem becomes this: How can we know these ideas in order to get an insight into the true and profound meaning of reality? The answer is:

> As has been said, the possible transition – though it is to be considered as an exception – from the common knowledge of individual things to the knowledge of the Idea is something sudden, if knowledge detaches itself from the service of the will, so that the subject ceases to be something merely individual and is now a pure unvolitional subject of knowledge, which no longer investigates relations according to the category of sufficient ground, but rests and is merged into the fixed contemplation of the given object apart from the latter's coherence with any others ... In such contemplation the individual thing at one blow becomes the Idea of its class, and the contemplating subject becomes the pure subject of cognition.158

These two statements of Schopenhauer contain a summary of his epistemology, a development of his thought, so full of leaps. But the important thing is that this stage, which is necessary for the knowledge of true reality detached from the *principium individuationis*, is attained in and through art, 'the work of a genius'.159 Of art, whether pictorial art or literature, it may be said that 'Its [i.e. of art] sole origin is the knowledge of the Ideas, its sole purpose is the communication of the Ideas, . . . the essence of genius is the predominant capacity for such contemplation'.160 When these thoughts are worked out in more detail we come upon an artistic ideal with a strongly classicistic stamp, for which Schopenhauer had great enthusiasm, especially through the work of Goethe and that of Fernow. We need not concern ourselves any further with this, as it did not have a strong appeal to the later generation who had entirely outgrown the old classicism.

They will, however, have been struck by the fact that Schopenhauer declared art to be an eminent means to reveal deeper ideas of reality. It could penetrate deeper than the exact sciences without losing any of its certainty, and without losing sight of reality. And as the artist was considered a genius, human freedom was preserved, and the artist was not forced into a straitjacket of fixed norms and laws – that was, as long as Schopenhauer's clearly delineated artistic ideals were not taken too seriously.

What made the authors and poets around 1890 so willing to listen to Schopenhauer as a kindred spirit will no doubt have been his pessimism, his contempt for all 'ordinary' reality. 'The world is hell, and men are divided into tortured souls and torturing devils.'161 They could read and sympathize with these words in his above-mentioned anthology. And pronouncements like those that will follow now, which from Schopenhauer's own theory are perhaps not so easy to defend, will have been highly appreciated by them, taught as they had been by Baudelaire and the others we have already mentioned: 'A novel is of an order which is all the more noble and elevated as it penetrates deeper into the inner life, and has fewer adventures . . . The novelist's task is not that of telling about great events, but that of making small things more interesting' or, to conclude: 'Style is the physiognomy of the spirit.'[162] Such pronouncements explain why these men turned to Schopenhauer. For without his pessimism and without such less intrinsically philosophical opinions on art they would probably never have penetrated to Schopenhauer, even though he provided them with ever such a beautiful armature for the defence of their own views. For in the last analysis Schopenhauer's criticism of the German way of writing, with its long paragraphs, was also applicable to his own style, which was no less cumbersome and obscure.[163]

For the same reason the influence of Eduard von Hartmann with his biologistic philosophy will not have been of much importance. In addition, we should not forget that he had no theory of art and no playful observations to offer alongside his principal work. It will therefore have been rather a matter of fashion to speak about von Hartmann, although he was nearer to them insofar as he really tried to work the exact data of natural science into his metaphysics. His tone and the totality of his conception, however, are by no means positivistic. He formulated his purpose as a search to gain 'speculative results obtained by the inductive method of natural science'[164] in an effort to bring about a synthesis between the results of idealistic philosophy and those that positivism had yielded. We cannot help getting the impression that in this procedure there is something laboured; there is something strained in his passion for systematizing, as in his earlier totality conceptions. However this may be, there is scarcely a trace of any real influence to be found, and it would be hardly conceivable. For, notwithstanding the mutual affinity of their strivings, there was too great a difference in their environments, intentions and direct aims for the artists to study von Hartmann's abstruse principal work.

Carlyle

It is not surprising that Carlyle as a thinker influenced the circle of the authors and artists of the last quarter of the nineteenth century. Anyone who studies his works enters into a world of thought that is in many respects related to that of Baudelaire and Schopenhauer. The agreement with the latter's work is striking, especially so when viewed as the above-mentioned artists will have considered them – for both were not interested in strictly technical philosophical questions and no more will have cared about problems relating to the history of philosophy. But what will certainly have rendered Carlyle more palatable than Schopenhauer is the form in which he had presented his ideas. His *Sartor Resartus* is in itself almost a work of art, fascinating and written in a richly imaginative style, playful, not in the least dry and yet strictly matter-of-fact in its logical argumentation. No doubt there is some scholarly pedantry, but it changes into playful wit owing to the somewhat bantering way in which Carlyle advances his thoughts. The very fact of his jotting down his views, as if he hardly understands them himself and does not in the least take them seriously, renders his work so attractive. We can, therefore, hardly be surprised that Gauguin occupied himself with this book – Gauguin, too, liked to make fun of what others took so seriously and what was really also near to his own heart. Witness, for instance, the dish in which he wrote 'Vive la sintaize'[165] and to which we will return later. That Gauguin really knew Carlyle's *Sartor Resartus* may appear from his portrait of Meyer de Haan,[166] in which it lies on the table by the side of Milton's *Le Paradis Perdu*('Paradise Lost').

The interest in Carlyle was especially roused by the work of Taine, the positivistic philosopher who busied himself so much with art, particularly in his *Histoire de la Littérature Anglaise* of 1864, and *L'idéalisme anglais, étude sur Carlyle* of the same year. It would be inconceivable for the Symbolists and the Synthetists not to have immediately tried to find out more about this author on reading the following quotation from the former work: 'The facts seized upon by this vehement imagination melt away as in a flame . . . The ideas, changed into hallucinations, lose their solidity; beings resemble dreams . . . Mysticism makes its appearance like smoke within the over-heated room of the intellect which bursts.'[167] What Symbolist or Synthetist would not have liked his own work to have been described in this way?

In his *Sartor Resartus* Carlyle writes about a German philosopher, Professor Teufelsdröck – who personified German idealistic philosophy, inclusive of Schopenhauer – who lives at Weissnichtwo in the Wahngasse. Carlyle happened to find out about the Professor's remarkable philosophy of dress and lavishly quotes from his confused notes and books. For, although he may be muddleheaded, Teufelsdröck's chief thoughts are perhaps not unimportant. And in this disguise Carlyle explains his ideas in the most fantastic way. We learn that he gets into a great crisis when he has been seized by the 'Spirit of Inquiry': 'Thus must the bewildered Wanderer stand, as so many have done, shouting question after question into the Sibyl-Cave of Destiny, and receive no answer but an Echo. It is all a grim Desert.'[168] 'From Suicide only a certain afterglow (*Nachschein*) of Christianity held me.'[169] But when this mood has been on him, he shakes himself loose and becomes aware of being a 'Child of Freedom'.[170] As such he does not turn his back upon reality but, on the contrary, claims:

> Yes here, in this poor miserable, hampered, despicable Actual, wherein thou even now standest, here or nowhere is thy Ideal: work it out therefrom; and working, believe, live, be free. Fool! The Ideal is in thyself, the Impediment too is in thyself: thy Condition is but the stuff thou art to shape that same Ideal out of: what matters whether such stuff be of this sort or that, so the Form thou give it be heroic, be poetic?[171]

Will not such a train of thought – expressing essentially the same as Baudelaire had said, but in an entirely different way – have been exactly the answer to the questions that occupied the French artists so strongly in the late nineteenth century?

When we read on we see that Carlyle uses also the same combination of 'imagination' and symbol that is found in Baudelaire; and in a similar way personal freedom is upheld while, at the same time, individual work is given a deep, deep significance as the unveiling of truth. 'Fantasy' is seen as 'the organ of the godlike' and 'Man thereby, though based, to all appearance on the small, visible, does nevertheless extend down into the infinite deeps of the Invisible[172]... And this happens because he creates symbols in which there is concealment and yet revelation'. He continues:

> For it is here that Fantasy with her mystic wonderland plays into the small prose domain of Sense, and becomes incorporated therewith. In the Symbol proper, what we call a Symbol, there is ever, more or less distinctly and directly, some embodiment and revelation of the Infinite; the Infinite is made to blend itself with the Finite, to stand visible, and as it were attainable there ... He everywhere finds himself encompassed with Symbols ... the Universe is but one vast Symbol of God; nay, if thou wilt have it, what is man himself but a symbol of God; is not all that he does symbolical; a revelation to Sense of the mystic god-given Force that is in him; a 'Gospel of Freedom', which he, the 'Messiah of Nature', preaches, as he can, by act and word?[173]

The relation between nature, as investigated by science, and the imagination is like this: 'The understanding is indeed thy window, too clear thou canst not make it; but Fantasy is thy eye, with its colour-giving retina, healthy or diseased.'[174] For Carlyle, too, these thoughts are directly connected with the meaning of a work of art, in accordance with a very old tradition that started with Plotinus: 'Let but the Godlike manifest itself to Sense; let but Eternity look, more or less visibly, through the Time-Figure (*Zeitbild*)!' For this is found in a true work of art: 'In them wilt thou discern Eternity, looking through Time; the Godlike rendered visible.'[175] With Carlyle we close the series of literati and theorists who influenced the world of thought of the generation of 1885 to 1890. These figures showed the artists how to form their ideas on art. With each of these writers we see old traditions re-appearing in a new guise, old ideas re-thought in the light of the new spiritual climate in an attempt to overcome scientialistic thought, which over-estimated the value of the natural-scientific method, in order to make room for human freedom.

Art in the Realist tradition

Turning to pictorial art again, we will first follow the line of Realism. It had its roots as early as the eighteenth century, as we have seen, but it became something typically nineteenth-century in the hands of Gros and Géricault. In their works we find pictures of important events of their own time which are exact representations but not without some rhetoric in a Baroque sense. The principal work of Géricault, *Le Radeau de la Méduse*, is the grand and new formulation of this conception. The interest in reality itself is great, also, or perhaps especially in its deviations, in its vehement appearance as distinct from the commonplace. We are referring to the portraits of lunatics that Géricault did on behalf of the scientific study of his friend Dr Georget.[176] It is especially the latter element that is new, and more than the style it is precisely the subjects that constitute the great and striking difference between this kind of art and the Baroque paintings of the seventeenth and the eighteenth centuries.

The next important artist in this tradition is Daumier. In principle, and as a starting point, his art is occupied with everyday occurrences, politics, customs and social abuses. He is a Realist, but if anywhere it is here in this work that the term comes to denote something quite different in France from what it meant in seventeenth-century Holland. For here the artist does not in the least try to contemplate lovingly the ordinary and the familiar about him, to sing a song about the beautiful things presenting themselves to his eyes; on the contrary, according to Baudelaire, we see here 'marching past before your eyes in its fantastic and harrowing reality all the living monstrosities a great city may contain'.[177] Daumier expressed his view of the politics of his time with such conviction that many people can look at the events of his time only through his eyes. He was a typical republican revolutionary. He not only exposed the personal frailties and faults (which he may have very shrewdly detected) of the various bearers of authority, but he did so in a manner that struck a blow at their office as such. For this office, this authority, Daumier had no respect. More than once one feels that he was concerned with their authority rather than with the individual personalities as such. He also mercilessly castigated what was bourgeois, all that did not wish or was unable to conform to the revolutionary style of living. And though more than once he hit the nail on the head, one asks oneself whether he did not pull down rather than build up, drag through the mire rather than show the relative nature of things in a truly humoristic vein.

The most important work for our subject is probably his series *L'histoire ancienne*. In this series he disposes of every kind of classicism in such a radical way that it will no longer have been possible for an artist in all seriousness to paint a classical Narcissus of rare beauty and dignity after having seen, for example, Daumier's *Narcissus*. After all,

Daumier achieved his results by thoroughly re-thinking these stories from antiquity in a sober and realistic way and then having them enacted by ordinary people whom he represented in a way that was the exact opposite of the idealizing method. This is one of the reasons why later on the classicistic subjects are no longer found, not even when it is possible to speak of a 'renaissance of classicism' in the sense of R. Rey's book.[178] What would the art of someone like Seurat, for example, have been like if this strong realistic anti-classicist trend, in which his series of lithographs represents an important phase, had not caused every classical subject as such henceforth to appear as meaningless and untruthful, lifeless and unreal? There is no point in analysing this series in great detail here, but it is difficult to overestimate the importance of this work (be it in a negative sense) especially for the iconography of the art of the latter half of the century.

In Constantin Guys we find a man who as an illustrator and draughtsman directed all his energy to the easy, direct notation of the commonplace, the typical life, manners and customs of people. With him every drawing was a summary of what he had seen, observed and retained in his mind. He did not play an important role in the history of art, despite the long and extremely laudatory article that Baudelaire devoted to his work.[179] Together with Guys we might mention many other illustrators and draughtsmen like Gavarni, Monnier and others.

The work of Courbet raised a great deal of discussion in the middle of the century. Yet we may wonder what made it so remarkable. For, as has already been observed in our introduction, his method did not really differ so very much from that of the Salon artists.[180] His reform was chiefly concerned with the subjects treated. In his art there is no question of idealization, or of the interpretation of a subject from a particular idealizing or romanticizing point of view.[181] It represents reality as it is seen, or at least experienced, by the ordinary person – which Courbet himself was, after all. This is the opinion of, for examle, Delacroix who, when he first met Courbet's work, wrote in his diary: 'I have been astonished at the vigour and dash of his principal painting; but what a painting! What a subject! The vulgarity of the forms would not matter, it is the vulgarity and uselessness of the idea that are abominable; even if this idea as such was clear.'[182] We need not in more detail discuss Delacroix's criticism, which partly follows from his own specific considerations – namely that a landscape should be in agreement with its figures so that the latter are truly standing in it – for its tenor is clear and shows at the same time that the name of 'Realist' was well chosen indeed. As a matter of fact, Courbet himself expressed his views in the same spirit: 'Painting is an essentially concrete art and can only consist in the representation of things that really exist. An abstract object, invisible, does not belong to the domain of painting. The imagination in art consists in finding the most complete expression of an existing thing.'[183] These few words clearly reveal a view of art which is entirely different from that of Baudelaire, notwithstanding the fact that the latter might have subscribed to the following pronouncement: 'Beauty, like truth, is something relative to the time in which we live and to the individual able to conceive it.'[184] Courbet's special importance for our investigations is that he approached art more intent on reality and that he was more radical in killing any interest in allegories and in historical, mythological or literary subjects.

Thus he also pointed out the way for young painters, who furthermore ignored the social implications found in Courbet's art in connection with his socialistic interest. Manet's *Olympia* of 1864 is a good example of the way in which reality can be made the subject of a picture without any literary, social or other connotation. On the contrary, the new generation of painters, the naturalists, whose defender and literary equivalent was Zola, might be said to have purposely chosen subjects that had never before been deemed worthy of artistic interest. There is a marked preference for what is ugly, un-beautiful, vulgar – which in the eyes of the painter's contemporaries was certainly true in the case of the *Olympia*.[185] Every kind of 'artistry' in the age-old sense of an idealization, heroizing or rhetoric was dropped. It was exactly this feature that made this art increasingly difficult to understand; this constituted its novelty. For even Manet's technical reforms, with his insistence on brushwork, on paint, we would almost say, was after all not so very new. It was already done by Delacroix or, in connection with Manet, we had better mention the great Spanish art of the seventeenth century.

The theoretical considerations bearing on this art are especially found in Castagnary, who calls it naturalism to distinguish it from Courbet's Realism. 'The naturalist school declares that art is the expression of life under all phases and all levels, and that its sole aim is to reproduce nature by carrying it to its maximum power and intensity; it is truth balanced with science. The naturalist school re-establishes the broken relation between man and nature.' Ultimately also this view is one that concentrated chiefly on the subjects. The following pronouncement clearly represents the way in which every view was rejected that followed from a conception of society that deviated from the basic ideas of the great French Revolution. These ideas had been formulated by the socialism and positivism of that time. 'This naturalistic art,' Castagnary wrote, 'springs from our politics, which, by posing as a principle the equality of individuals and as a desideratum the equalizing of conditions, has caused false hierarchies and deceptive differentiations to disappear from the mind.'[186] Thus the artist was tightly bound to reality. But, showing the typical humanistic character of this movement, it was emphatically asserted that this conception would not and should not destroy the artist's freedom. 'It says to the artist: Be free!'[187] and get rid of traditional forms and ideas with respect to that which is, or is not, in accordance with the 'decorum' of art. It is precisely this 'decorum' that used to play an important part in classicistic and Baroque art,[188] but which now disappeared entirely.

The younger generation, who at this very time began to find their feet, basing themselves on the work of Courbet and especially on that of Manet, still had quite different considerations originating in the art of the landscapist. They will now claim our attention.

French landscape

The French painters who in the early part of the nineteenth century concentrated on landscapes had to struggle free from something akin to a fossilized tradition. It is true that, not long before, artists such as Fragonard and Moreau l'Aîné had set them an example, but they had to re-discover, as it were, the possibilities this genre offered the painter. For the period preceding them was ruled by classicism, which was not particularly beneficial to this artistic genre and attached importance to landscapes only if they were painted after the style of Claude Lorrain or, better still, Poussin. It is quite natural that alongside Bonington also Constable became very important.[189] His magisterial *Haywain*, for example, exhibited at the Salon in Paris in 1824, proved that it was possible to practise the art of the landscapist in a fresh and direct way while reflecting the contemporary mind. More convincing than many words such a painting refuted the prevailing view which, also in 1824, was formulated as follows:

> What would become of the landscapist's art if, through overtimidity, he feared to burst into the domain of history? What poetry, what high inspiration, could fire him, and sustain him in his labours? Continually trees and shrubs, and air and space and surface – what do I care for all these things if the artist does not throw upon these objects some sentiment of living animated nature, if he does not invest them alternately with sadness or serenity, violence or calm.[190]

No, to the young generation of painters visible nature was sufficient to quicken their inspiration, for it was precisely nature that fascinated them without all those side-reflections and rhetoric. They tried to express what lived in their hearts in accordance with the spirit of the times, which, after the manner of the French positivistic tradition,[191] or in a Romantic vein, looked upon nature in itself as something significant that needed no justification.

Thus arose the new art of the landscapists such as Corot and others, mostly collectively designated by the term 'the school of Fontainebleau'. As painters they were absorbed in the study of natural scenery in order to record nature in all its changing aspects. Their efforts were not concerned with the structure of the scenery as a whole in a particular part of the country, and that is why we can very well understand Baudelaire's criticism of Rousseau, for example, 'And then he falls into the notorious modern error originating in a blind love of nature, of nothing but nature; he takes a simple study for a composition.'[192] And further: 'I understand that a mind applying itself to taking notes cannot indulge in the stupendous daydreams contained in the scenes of present nature.'[193]

To note down the visible effects of nature directly and quickly a new technique was necessary. Corot mentions it when he says that his academic teachers had not taught him how to draw. For he could not even represent what fascinated him because people – and we may add, the effects of nature – would vanish before he had barely started to draw them. 'For the first time I essayed drawing in the mass, rapid drawing – the only drawing possible. I set myself to take in a group at a glance; if it stayed for a short time only, at least I had got its character, its general unconscious attitude; if it remained long I could add the details.'[194]

And thus it may be said that these painters removed the veil cast over nature by Poussin and Lorrain, rendered opaque by the methods of the faux classiques, and that they represented nature in its own beauty and value.[195] It has often been asserted, also in their own time,[196] that in the nineteenth century landscape painting became an important, if not the most important, genre of pictorial art because of the desire to escape from the social and other problems connected with growing industrialization. Perhaps we should look for a likelier and more positive reason in the new view of life that sought to express itself in an entirely different manner, a view already manifest in Courbet and Castagnary. We shall not try to decide this point; possibly both factors cooperated in the same direction.

The new attitude towards landscape painting only gradually gained ground and its consequences were only slowly realized. Thus this first generation of the great French landscapists rarely worked in the open, *sur le motif*, and there remained a great deal of arrangement and composition in their art. Especially Corot often introduced such figures as Homer, Orpheus, women making music, and others, into his landscapes. A more striking feature is that these figures are really standing in the landscape and that they move in it in the same way as 'ordinary' people do in nature, whereas on the whole his women were painted in a much more naturalistic manner than was possible in the classical tradition after the manner of Poussin and Lorrain. They were real people of flesh and blood, notwithstanding their occasional classical garments – Orpheus, for example – or the fact that they sometimes acted in a way which in a strictly realistic sense could not be defended – such as a half-naked woman who has her hair dressed in the middle of a wood.[197]

Impressionism

The painters who are known by the name of Impressionists started from these two traditions, namely the Realism of Courbet and Manet, and the influence of the painters of the school of Fontainebleau. For them it became of prime importance to record the changing aspects of a scenery, painted immediately on the spot while, when they incorporated persons in their art, they represented them as they were in their daily occupations – for instance, boating or lounging at La Grenouillère. Degas, the figure-painter who associated himself with the Impressionists, made it his main object to portray them, as it were, unaware of the fact that they were being painted. Degas, and also Manet, distinguished themselves from the earlier realistic art by the directness of their vision, a building up of the composition in such a way that we seem to be confronted with a more or less accidental snapshot. In this they availed themselves of new principles of composition which they had found in Japanese art (to which we shall devote a special section below).

It is possible that the landscapists had less difficulty in their quest than figure-painters like Manet and Degas, for the very reason that landscapes were considered to be of minor importance by the painters and critics of the world of the Salons, where the traditional formulation for landscapes was as a consequence far less defined and settled. As a matter of fact, the school of Fontainebleau had already paved the way to a certain extent. For the figure-painters, however, there was a very firmly rooted tradition to combat, a view of art and its task which was still generally accepted in spite of the work of their predecessors and from which they could only struggle free with difficulty. For Degas too had done work in the classicistic spirit during his early years. That is why they talked and wrote much more often about their subject, and formulated their ideas in a much more articulate way. They embodied their view of human being in their work, unhampered by the 'decorum' as it was understood by the ruling groups of their day. A landscape did not require any justification and this is why its devotees could concentrate on technical questions, also in their meditations and conversations. On this point, therefore, they were attacked.[198] But very soon they attracted followers, even in the circle of the Salon painters. We are referring to a man like Bastien-Lepage.

Reverting to the figure-painters, especially to Degas, we find them very aware of the new things they introduced into the domain of their subjects. This is directly reflected by Duranty's pamphlet of 1876 which summarized the new ideals of art as follows:

> And the purpose of the drawing according to the ideals of these moderns is exactly to investigate nature so accurately, to embrace it so strongly, that the drawing is irreproachable with respect to the coherence of the forms, that it captures the inexhaustible diversity of the characters. Farewell to the human

body treated as a jar from the viewpoint of the decorative vase; farewell to the uniform monotony of the frame, to the anatomy of the limbs showing under the nude; what we want is the special note of a modern individual in his clothes, in the midst of his social habits, at home or in the street. The job becomes particularly tricky now, it is like fitting a torch into its shaft with a pencil, it is the study of habits reflected in the faces and the dress, the observation of the intimacy of man with his apartment, of the special trait imprinted on him by his profession, the gestures it entails, the aspects by which he manifests and assert himself best.[199]

Indeed, this art was practised in a positivistic spirit so that Duranty was able to call even Diderot a witness to the fact that this art was undoubtedly founded in a French tradition.[200] It had been a tradition, however, which up till then had always been obliged to remain in the shadow of what had been officially recognized as valuable. The once creative minority had after all become a ruling majority, to speak with Toynbee, and was not likely to cede its place to this new trend straightway, a trend which carried on the ideals that had once fed the French Revolution. With respect to politics, these ideals lived on in revolutionary republican and socialistic ideas. That is why it is not surprising that in political and social matters most of these artists were in agreement with such worlds of thought. But these are problems that need not concern us at this particular moment.

Japanese art

It would perhaps not be out of place to say a few words about the unquestionably great influence exercised by Japanese art. Especially in the circles of Realists like Manet and Degas and among the Impressionists the interest in Japanese prints – we are not concerned now with pottery, clothes and small sculptures – was very great already soon after they had been discovered.[201] It would be possible that the analogous position occupied by the Japanese Okiyoye art in its own country and that of the Frenchmen mentioned in theirs had some influence. For in both cases we are confronted with art that has to maintain itself alongside the art that is officially recognized and considered to be important. But although such an observation has sometimes been made,[202] we think it more likely that this interest was aroused because these artists strove after a similar purpose: 'a new aesthetics, an aesthetics allowing greater freedom, a drawing at first sight, an exuberant fantasy and at the same time a servility of the right kind to follow nature in its most rapid transformations,'[203] as Renan put it in 1888. Especially the latter fascinated them.[204]

A far stronger appeal was made by this art to the generation that came to the fore in the 1880s. For these artists sought something absolutely new. It is true, they did not work in a naturalistic way, but nevertheless they kept the bond with reality intact. The Japanese woodcuts are inspired by ordinary reality but altogether lack the characteristics of European naturalistic art, the sculptural quality of the figures, the representation of depth by means of perspective, the absorption in visible nature with its shadows, delicate shades of colour and such like things. Japanese art has the courage to simplify, to omit shadows as inessential, to represent depth in a quite different way so that the picture plane as such is not broken. This art is able to render the typical nature of things and living beings in their movements without surrendering to the very accidental aspects caused by the fall of the light and by the position with regard to surrounding objects. And yet it is an art that manages to present very unexpected views. These are due not to the natural objects but to the artist, who succeeds in arranging these natural objects on the surface of the paper in a completely new way.

And all this fitted in beautifully with the considerations and wishes of the artists of the 1880s and the 1890s. This is why we find the same terms used when they discussed Hokusai as when they formulated their own theoretical ideas on art: 'It is evident that there are two sides to the author of the Mangua: the naturalist and the idealist. The latter term need not astonish anybody. Hokusai is not only in love with visible nature; he is also a dreamer, an imaginative painter.'[205] And thus we need not be surprised that Ary Renan, whom we have quoted here, immediately points out an analogy with those artists whose conception of art we have already discussed, and who were so very important with respect to the formation of the new theory of art. After mentioning the names of Poe and Baudelaire, Renan continues: 'Is it not something remarkable to find the plastic realization of these dreams of "the beyond" in an artist from the Far East, nostalgic dreams that the most advanced literary art in Britain and France believed themselves to have had an exclusive glimpse of.'[206] The fact that he does not yet mention the painters is understandable, as there was then (ca. 1888) hardly any question of a school of artists equivalent to the literary men referred to, or at least they had not yet clearly given public evidence of their existence.

3
The Genesis and the Character of Symbolism

If we wish to occupy ourselves especially with the theories of those artists working at the end of the nineteenth century whom we will identify by the name of Synthetists, it will be necessary to distinguish them sharply from another group, working at the same time but with entirely different ideals. The latter group we will call the Symbolists. In various respects they are related to the Synthetists, but the differences between them are very marked and so fundamental that the two movements can certainly not be classed together. Symbolism also flourished in another environment, in closer contact with the poets, less removed from artistic life in its more public manifestations. It will be necessary to examine it more closely in order to show more fully our view of the Synthetists against this background.

William Blake

The first artist of any importance found outside of the 'academic' tradition in nineteenth-century England was William Blake. In contrast with Turner and Constable and their followers Blake was not interested in nature as such. 'I assert for myself, that I do not behold the outward creation, and that to me it is hindrance and not action.'[207] His attitude towards reality is closely related to that of gnosticism, as he held also that the creation as such is evil, enclosing the infinite within the finite.[208] 'What is called corporeal nobody knows of; its dwellingplace is a fallacy, and its existence an imposture.'[209] He sharply opposes rationalism or scientialism, which had dominated the age of the Enlightenment and had certainly not lost its hold on the minds of the people yet. He considers all this as evil because it shuts a person off from life ruled by the 'imagination'.

It is remarkable that we are again confronted with Swedenborg's influence. For not only does Blake take over the latter's theory of the correspondences but also the idea that man has lost the insight into them owing to his inordinate interest in what is material. For originally humans were very well able to know the correspondences, namely in paradise – but we should not think of the historical Paradise, described in the Scriptures, but of a state or condition of being thus indicated in a mythologizing way (in accordance with the method used by Swedenborg to explain Genesis). Thus Blake writes: 'One day the world was a Paradise and Imagination was its principal Goddess. If the doors of perception were cleaned, everything would appear to men as it is: infinite. For man has closed himself up until he sees all things through the narrow chinks in his cavern.'[210]

We need not dwell on the Platonic image he uses, but would point out that both Swedenborg and Blake try to gain an insight into those things of which the senses cannot give us a clear and true idea, into the deeper reality which alone is true and genuine. According to Swedenborg this is achieved by a very direct contact with the world of the angels; for Blake it is the art based on the 'imagination' that will point the way. Thus Blake says that his great task is 'to open the eternal worlds, to open the eternal eyes of Man inwards, into the worlds of Thought, into eternity, ever expanding in the bosom of God, the human Imagination'. Thus love and imaginative art are perceived to be the powers that redeem humanity.[211]

Art will have to start from the 'imagination' in order to grasp what is eternal and true. Or, perhaps, we must put it even more sharply – for here we find the same identification of the subjective view of man with truth and meaningful reality itself as in Baudelaire and Schopenhauer – by saying that the 'imagination' itself embodies the eternal truth. Thus Blake says that 'In Paradise they are not talking of what is good and what is evil, or what is right or wrong, and puzzling themselves in Satan's labyrinth; but are conversing with eternal realities, as they exist in the human imagination.'[212] And therefore art will have to represent that true reality, not the material world in its 'vegetative' appearance. 'I question not my corporeal or vegetative Eye any more than I would question a Window concerning a sight. I look through it and not with it.'[213] And so he is able to say that in his imaginative art reality itself is represented, that it is a revelation of reality: 'Vision or Imagination, is a representation of what actually exists, really and unchangeable.'[214] His art may be said to be allegorical only if it is borne in mind that to him this allegory represents reality itself and does not depict it indirectly: 'Allegory addressed to the intellectual powers while it is altogether hidden from the corporeal understanding [naturalistic scientialism, we might say], is my definition of the most sublime poetry.'[215]

A closer study of his art (either of his pictures or of his poetry) shows that in a mythologizing way he describes the deeper forces and spirits determining society and the world around him.[216] These spiritual realities are personified and their mutual relations and struggles explained by having the personifications speak or act with each other. It appears that Blake's thought is contradictory,[217] because according to him the world comes into being by the interplay of opposing forces, by a 'Marriage of Heaven and Hell'. His mythologizing method is, for instance, very clearly manifested in the following passage describing what we now call the Industrial Revolution. This revolution is a negative force, especially because 'the horses of instruction' (i.e., the science ideal) are let loose, whose work consists of 'petrifying all the Human Imagination into rock and sand.'[218] In another passage industry is portrayed as follows:

> 0 Satan, my youngest born, art thou not Prince of the starry Hosts.
> And of the wheels of Heaven, to turn the Mills day and night?
> Get to thy Labours at the Mills and Leave me to my wrath
> Thy work is eternal Death with Mills and Ovens and Cauldrons.[219]

This is the way in which Blake's art is 'Imagination, vision, a revealing of the eternal, the Word made flesh, the Marriage of Heaven and Hell.'[220]

In a stylistic sense Blake's pictorial art might best be characterised as mannerism. True, there are different kinds of mannerism, and this term is not always used in a accurately defined sense. But there is certainly a question of mannerism when an artist plays with forms that belong to a way of representation which is no longer employed in its original meaning. Blake's figures are plastic whereas his drawings often have a markedly graphic character. In many respects they remind us of the artistic method used subsequent to the Renaissance. But they sometimes display a remarkable slimness and an excessive degree of stretch, moving often in a supple manner that is by no means ordinary to give rise to flowing and slightly rounded contours. Thus Blake – whose style was certainly influenced by Fuseli – tries to make clear that he wants to express something spiritual, that his figures express more than mere reality on the corporeal and visible plane. This is also clear in his interpretation of biblical scenes,[221] in which he succeeds more than once to make it clear that those stories have a meaning for him that is quite different from historical events. They are the embodiment of a deeper, timeless truth. His intention is even clearer when he depicts persons who do not exist in visible reality, like God, angels, or mythological visionary figures of his own conception, such as Enitharmon and others.

So Blake operates with forms borrowed from the naturalistic (or classicistic) tradition, but he uses them for his frankly non-realistic purposes. Thus there arises a certain tension between the artistic means derived from naturalism and his decidedly anti-naturalistic[222] conception of art in connection with his non-realistic subjects. This remarkable state of affairs is always to be found with the Symbolists discussed in this chapter: they use artistic means in the construction of their figures, the rendering of space and so on, that are connected with a view of life from which they have actually detached themselves.

John Ruskin

John Ruskin became famous for his *Modern Painters*, a work designed to defend Turner's landscape art which developed into perhaps one of the most comprehensive theories of art ever written. He does not build up a system but supplies a truly admirable number of observations and reflections. He emphasizes the art of the landscapist, no doubt, and one might ask whether this is due to his purpose of defending a landscapist, or whether he really felt that the heart of contemporary art was in it. As a matter of fact he gives a classification of art reminiscent of the old theories,[223] in which the subject is decisive and according to which that art is thought to be the highest which depicts what is noblest. Later on, however, he occupies himself with 'the novelty of landscape' and tries to find out what can have caused the emphasis on this genre in the nineteenth century.[224] Finally he defines the peculiar character of this modern art of the landscapists,[225] so that by this light he can examine the sublime reforms introduced by Turner, in particular,[226] whom he describes as 'the first poet who has, in all their range, understood the grounds of noble emotion which exist in landscape'.[227]

What is the essential element in art according to Ruskin?

> I say that the art is greatest which conveys to the mind of the spectator, by any means whatsoever, the greatest number of the greatest ideas; and I call an idea great in proportion as it is received by a higher faculty of the mind, and as it more fully occupies, and in occupying, exercises and exalts, the faculty by which it is received.[228]

Ruskin's way to achieve this is by a very close study of nature in all its details. But the important thing in this procedure is not the rendering of a particular subject in its smallest details – he fulminates again and again against the Dutch painters who are supposed to have done that[229] – rather, the important matter is the specific character of this natural datum, its structure and meaning, especially in connection with the greater whole of the work of art.[230] Nothing in the work of art will be left to the 'imagination', except for the arrangement and the coherence of things – in which 'All so-called invention in landscape is nothing more than appropriate recollection'[231] – until the work of art has been completed in all its parts. For when this has been done, the artist may 'dash as much as he likes: throw, if he will, mist around it, darkness and confused light, whatever in fact, impetuous feeling or vigorous imagination may dictate or desire'. For thus 'The imagination, strengthened by discipline and fed with truth, will achieve the utmost of creation that is possible to finite mind.'[232]

To Ruskin also the imagination is of supreme importance, notwithstanding his elaborate naturalism set forth with such great emphasis. 'The imaginative artist . . . owns no laws. He defies all restraints, and cuts down all hedges. There is nothing within the limits of natural possibility that he dares not do, or that he allows the necessity of doing. The laws of nature he knows; these are to him no restraint. They are his own nature.'[233] In view of this there is doubtless some relationship with

Delacroix and Baudelaire in their idea of nature as a 'dictionary'. But there are also great differences. Ruskin much more strongly emphasizes the study of the structures of natural objects, of nature which has nothing problematic to him, perhaps also on account of his Protestant roots. Baudelaire and Delacroix, on the other hand, lay the stress on what is strictly personal and subjective, and assign to nature a less important role in a work of art. This is the reason why the passage just quoted sets out a direction for the construction of a work of art that is the exact opposite of what Delacroix had sought, whose pronouncement Ruskin could never have subscribed to:

> Man has in his soul inborn feelings that will never be satisfied with real things, and to these feelings the imagination of the painter or the poet is able to give a form and life ... The most accurate execution in details will never give this unity that results from I know not what creative power of which the source is indefinable.234

Such pronounced individualism, and such freedom with regard to the natural object, would have deterred him.

There is no doubt that these things are also determined by the differences between English and French art as such. Ruskin and Baudelaire had something different in mind when they wrote or thought about art. For, despite the mutual influences exercised between French and English art over the course of centuries, they were of distinctly different characters, as diverse as a French person is from an English one.235

Pre-Raphaelite movement

What kind of art are we to examine in connection with Ruskin's views? We shall not discuss Turner again, nor the other landscapists such as Constable, but turn to the younger generation of painters making their debut around the middle of the century, namely the Pre-Raphaelites. Among the three leading personalities it was undoubtedly Holman Hunt who followed Ruskin the closest.236

Holman Hunt was an avowed naturalist who was only satisfied when he had painted an exact copy of his subject, in its smallest details, on the spot. For this purpose he made journeys even to Palestine and he was one of the first artists in Europe who painted out-of-doors.237 Reading his autobiography – *Pre-Raphaelitism and the Pre-Raphaelite Brotherhood* – one cannot help getting the impression of something forced in his method, a stubbornness which is not quite justified by its results. He might be compared with Courbet, and certainly so when one studies a work like the *The hireling shepherd* of 1861,238 a realistic representation of a shepherd with his girl. But in connection with Courbet we had sooner think of Ford Madox Brown, who was a little older and very much akin to Hunt. His *Work* (1852-1865)[239] gives a direct image of people working on the public road. If we compare it with Courbet's *Stonebreakers* (1849, Dresden Museum), the difference is also conspicuous. Madox Brown and Holman Hunt depict reality very accurately indeed, but in accordance with the requirements formulated by Ruskin their aim is to express a deeper thought.[240] A typically English trait is to colour the realistic vision with a moralistic tendency. This shows up also a much stronger bond with the Christian (Puritan) tradition than displayed by the French artists who, after all, were sons of the French Revolution. A work such as Hunt's *The awakening conscience*[241] is in every respect almost the opposite of Manet's *Lunch on the grass*.[242] The former picture represents a man and a fully dressed woman, who is conscience-stricken; in the latter there are two dressed men and a naked woman, who appears to consider the situation as quite normal.

Holman's art clearly reveals one of the aspects of Pre-Raphaelitism: the representation of universally human feelings and thoughts with a certain moralistic tendency by means of realistic subjects and a very elaborate naturalistic technique. The fact that Hunt's art did not develop into something truly great was probably due to his lack of 'imagination' – which, after all, Ruskin too required from an artist after his own heart.

We shall not pay special attention here to Millais, who was originally closely related to Hunt but rather soon chose the paths of the Salon artists, who were to be found in England just as well as in France. It is much more necessary to examine Dante Gabriel Rossetti more closely. For his influence was very great and when the Pre-Raphaelites are mentioned his name, and those of his imitators, is called to mind, sooner than the names of Hunt and his followers, who perhaps initially had taken the lead. Therefore Hunt may be right in saying that Rossetti had drifted from the original Pre-Raphaelitism. But we must bear in mind that the latter had as a matter of fact worked in a spirit akin to that of Hunt only for a short time – properly speaking only in his *Found* of 1853.[243]

Rossetti's ideas of art at the time when he was without doubt a faithful member of the Pre-Raphaelite Brotherhood are found in his essay, written at the end of 1849 for *The Germ*. This essay shows clearly that already at this stage his art aimed at something quite different from what Holman Hunt was trying to achieve. It is a kind of art-historical study about an artist of the Trecento who existed only in Rossetti's mind. He traced the development of this artist. At first 'Chiaro' tried to serve God by means of beauty, but very soon he discovered that he worshipped beauty rather than God himself. So he turned away from beauty and determined in future to produce only those works that aim at 'The presentment of some moral greatness that should impress the beholder: and in doing so he did not choose for his medium the action and passion of human life, but cold symbolism and abstract impersonation'.[244] So, we might say, he did not do what the Pre-Raphaelites tried to do, namely to represent 'moral greatness by means of real human actions and passions'. Thus every allegorical art is rejected, although Rossetti's own works warrant the conclusion that he did not strive after the naturalism of such men as Hunt. For he rarely represented contemporary reality and visible nature as far as it can be painted. Chiaro, the trecentist painter created by Rossetti, however, was not very successful in his work, especially because the people did not like it very much. Some incidents revealed to him that this was not the right way, because he could not by this means get in touch with people. Then his own soul paid him a visit in a vision – which along with Dante also reminds us of Blake, whose work Rossetti was well-acquainted with, as we shall see presently – and tells him to give up those cold abstractions. 'How is it that thou, a man, wouldst say coldly to the mind what God hath said to the heart warmly?' If he wished to serve his fellows, he was instructed, he should 'Work from thine own heart, simply; for his heart is as thine, when thine is wise and humble; and he shall have understanding of thee . . . Set thine hand and thy soul to serve man with God.'[245] And then Chiaro sets about, like Blake, to paint his vision. In short Rossetti's view boils down to this, that artists must express their heart in their work and not only their intellect. Their art should be warm and true to life, and spring from the depths of their soul and give expression to its movements.

In the spring of 1847 Rossetti got acquainted with the art of Blake after he had come upon a bundle of papers of the latter that have since been known as *The Rossetti Manuscript*. It contained also 'A Vision of the Last Judgment', which was the treatise on art from which we have quoted when discussing Blake. There is no doubt that Rossetti was strongly influenced by Blake. The latter's idea about not working from nature and producing one's images from one's own mind was bound to appeal strongly to Rossetti.[246] For, with his mind formed by the study of Dante and the medieval poets he preferred giving expression to the soul by working with 'hand and soul' adapting himself with difficulty to reality as understood by the naturalists. He lacked the interest in it that his contemporaries had – it is characteristic of him that he did not take an interest in the inventions and discoveries made by natural science. He also had little interest in theories, as may appear from his judgment of the 'middle period' of Chiaro. But there is no doubt that he was struck by Blake's idea of the different states a person had to go through, and by his doctrine of the correspondences.[247] As is so often the case, it is hardly possible to decide whether the ideas shaped the man or the man selected the ideas that connected with his natural disposition. For although Rossetti's mind, as we have observed already, had been prepared to appreciate such ideas as Blake's, it is certainly also true that his acquaintance with the latter carried him ever further away from that which others, like Hunt, were striving after.

He does not formulate his own typical art before he has detached himself from the ideas of Hunt and the latter's followers. Remarkable enough, he then all at once masters the technique which had given him a great deal of trouble before that time. His most important works of this period are his portraits of women, rarely if ever exact representations of the subjects but always stylized in accordance with the ideal type he had in mind. He is in his true element only in his symbolical portraits of women, which were no cold intellectual products but warm-blooded expressions of his soul. He imparted to them a general meaning by embodying in them a 'state' and its corresponding emotions in a sensuous and spiritual sense. The lower part of the face then represents the lower element, directed to the senses, whereas the upper part with the eyes is related to the higher element, the eternal.[248]

It is possible that Blake's influence, which Rossetti assimilated in such a characteristic way, asserted itself most definitely only after 1861, the year of the death of Gilchrist, who had been working on a biography of Blake. At that time Rossetti was intensely occupied with Blake's ideas and art because he contributed significantly to the preparation for publication of Gilchrist's manuscript.[249] Although after 1861 his style is not materially different, and he had already worked before that time in the same spirit as that of his later work in his treatment of subjects like *Paolo and Francesca*,[250] the first of his symbolical women's portraits appeared after that date, especially the *Beata Beatrix* of 1863.[251]

It is remarkable, or at least striking, that in his essay on Blake in Gilchrist's work he gave some critical notes with reference to Blake's use of colour. Obviously he had not understood its symbolical or expressive meaning, which cannot be measured by naturalistic criteria.[252] As a matter of fact such arbitrary use of colour is rarely if ever applied by Rossetti, but this does not detract from the fact that his art is really less naturalistic, at least further removed from the classicistic style, than Blake's. It is certainly less graphic in character, although perhaps his book illustrations also show traces of the influence of Blake's style on their forms. In any case, he sticks to the method of representation determined by European tradition, which since the fifteenth century had started from the representation of actual reality. Thus his art no doubt has its mannerisms, although less than Blake's. In comparison with the work of his contemporaries it could not but appear to be very wilful, mysterious and manneristic.

Rossetti's influence was very great. In the first place he directly influenced a number of pupils, among whom Burne-Jones and William Morris rank first, and also indirectly, or via the last named artists, a group of younger men who worked in a Pre-Raphaelite style during the last ten or fifteen years of the century. The term Pre-Raphaelite must then be interpreted in the spirit of Rossetti; for all this has little to do with Hunt and his circle. We are especially referring to Ricketts, Sturge Moore, and

Reginald Savage, who published graphic works in 1893 in *The Dial*. But the style was much more generally accepted, especially by illustrators. For the influence of the Pre-Raphaelites was particularly strong in this division of art. For their original contributions to typography and to the illustrator's art, which up till then had been mostly neglected, started with the publication of Tennyson's work, illustrated by Hunt, Millais and Rossetti in 1857 – the Moxon edition. In this department especially Morris, more than once in cooperation with Burne-Jones, created something quite original in his own editions of books which were of a very high standard.[253] In this connection we must also mention the work of Walter Crane who was closely related to those we have mentioned. Especially his children's books published around 1880 have been very important for the spread of this new style, not only in England but also on the continent of Europe, where there was a great interest in this new way of presenting children's books.[254] It is possible that even Gauguin made use of some reminiscences of this (illustrator's) art in the formation of his own style. But such influence will not have been very deep, and, if it existed at all, it concerned the method rather than the particular stylistic characteristics.[255]

The art of the Pre-Raphaelites had social implications, for a great deal of their work contained an implicit criticism or even rejection of the attitudes of their contemporaries.[256] In this respect also Ruskin no doubt showed the way, struck as he was by the avalanche of ugly products which resulted from the Industrial Revolution. A symptom of his interest in these things is the fact that he had part of his *Stones of Venice* printed separately under the title of 'The Nature of Gothic' to be distributed among the labourers. In it he praises earlier working methods, which he perhaps idealized a little, in opposition to working with machines, which was death to the spirit and to beauty.[257] Characteristic of the attitude of the Pre-Raphaelites in this respect is also their joint cooperation in the Working Men's College of F. D. Maurice, where it was attempted to teach labourers taste and artistic insight.[258] Thus we see that they have a growing interest in social questions, and an increasingly clearer awareness that in human society itself something ought to be changed if art and beauty were to flourish again as in former times, especially the Middle Ages, according to their view.[259] That is why Ruskin occupied himself for years at a stretch with more or less utopian projects in the economic field. But the most practical activity, perhaps, was the work of the firm of Morris, in which many of the artists cooperated who were associated with the Pre-Raphaelites. It was based on the principle of the self-activity of all the labourers, without treating them simply as extensions of the machines. This is not the place to examine the further development of these things,[260] but the important consequence was that the style of Rossetti, Morris, Burne-Jones and Crane was transplanted into the field of the decorative arts.[261]

So originated the style that under the name of Art Nouveau also conquered France around the year 1890. It was a decorative style with very strong linear qualities, supple curves and no doubt often very imaginative ones, assimilating naturalistic elements. Especially the herbaceous dominated it.[262] In addition to Blake[263] – who had a considerable influence on the graphic artists, chiefly via the publication of Gilchrist – also the products of Japanese 'industrial art' had a stimulating effect. As far as France is concerned, the publication of *Le Japon Artistique* (in 1888) was symptomatic of this. According to Bing's introduction this influence was explicitly intended.

In England all this created around 1890 an atmosphere among the younger artists that was not only revolutionary and socialistic but undoubtedly aestheticistic.[264] For the whole of Pre-Raphaelitism, insofar as it was concerned with social problems, had an aesthetic drive, in the sense that the artistic element was the starting point and the aim of the entire movement. The art of Rossetti, Burne-Jones and their comrades and followers aimed to evoke a beautiful world. There was no Realism to be found among them. They created a dreamworld, a beautiful daydream, which sometimes assumed decadent traits because beauty was sought also in what is ugly and bad.

This movement was characterized by its opposition to what was generally accepted and bourgeois, of which the art of the Salon was considered to be typical; it was opposed also to the naturalistic character of the latter and its lack of imagination. It was a kind of revival of Romanticism. 'At base it was a revolt of the spirit against formal subservience to mere reason.'[265] Naturally the movement in England differed from that in France, where positivism and naturalism had been much more influential in art and literature. It is, for instance, characteristic that in the nineties there was still a group of young English artists who could turn to Impressionism and whose subjectivistic unconventionality was highly esteemed,[266] whereas in France this Impressionism was considered as a dated view by the same generation.

With regard to ideas there was a strong French influence, that of Baudelaire[267] and of writers like Huysmans. But it should not be forgotten that these theories were already known, in their direct application, through the work of Rossetti. Not only in his pictures but also in his poetry he adopted the ideas of Blake, who was in many respects related to those Frenchmen just mentioned. After all, the French theories could not have sounded too strange to those who were used to Carlyle?

The Pre-Raphaelite art of the nineties aimed especially at the poetic. Its subjects were, therefore, often derived from literature. There was a special predilection for what is strange, mysterious, horrible: *Oedipus and the Sphinx* by Ricketts,[268] scenes from Coleridge's 'Rime of the Ancient Mariner' by Sturge Moore, sentences from Poe's poems, such as 'But evil things in robes of sorrow assailed the monarch's high estate' or 'The night's Plutonian shore' by W. Heath Robinson. There were also subjects of their own invention: Reginald Savage's *Behemoth* in which a monster inspired by Dürer's rhinoceros is seen to fly from a burning palace – on its walls there is a Cassandra wandering about, and a two-headed Phoenix dives into the fire; or the majestic mountains in human shapes by Sturge Moore. But what is lovely was not wholly absent, for example in *Daphnis and Chloe* by Ricketts, pleasant scenes of country life by Lucien Pissarro or *Centaurs*, an experiment in line by Reginald Savage. Elsewhere we find a kind of sublime mythical world with beautiful girls: Burne-Jones' *The golden stairs* and *The mirror of Venus*, in which we see them admiring themselves in the water of a pond.[269] The atmosphere of the fairytale was not lacking – Crane's flower figures – and are not Burne-Jones' versions of biblical stories really fairytales? The erotic element was present although it played a subordinate part; it was indirect rather than direct – the girlish female figures were rarely represented in a sensual way, and the art of Beardsley, who was extreme in this respect, was an exception.[270]

Personifications, allegorical figures, symbolic forms, animals and things, were frequently part of this tranquil pictorial poetry with its fanciful, flowing play of lines and its evocative rather than clear, descriptive compositions. We call this art tranquil because its figures rarely move passionately, they are never active and there is little happening – this is primarily mood art and narrative ranks second, if it is present at all. The images are called up gently and, as it were, in a whisper.

This art can certainly not be called realistic and in a stylistic respect it displays strongly manneristic traits, as in the excessive elongation and the linear elegance of the figures, whereas the play of lines on the surface possesses strongly decorative qualities. But its means, its images, are not new. In this respect it is based on the forms of the European art of the Renaissance. A considerable influence may be traced to Venetian book illustrations of the late fifteenth century and to painters from the same period, such as Perugino and Botticelli. This is why we sometimes find surprisingly naturalistic details.

The world of these artists, which Holbrook Jackson describes in such a masterly way in his *The Eighteen Nineties*, was certainly not a world of artworks and abstract discussions only. This view of life was put into practice and determined the attitude of those who had been grasped by this spirit of the times – no wonder that dandy-ism was revived.[271] That is inevitable, for art is not something apart from reality and man cannot be divided into an artistic and a non-artistic part. For the very reason that this was a question of aestheticism, the influence of art (and of the theory of art) must have been stronger than ever: 'In our time we are agreed that we "make our souls" out of one of the great poets of ancient times, or out of Shelley, or Wordsworth, or Goethe or Balzac, or Flaubert or Count Tolstoy . . . or out of Mr Whistler's[272] pictures.'[273] So writes

Yeats, a typical exponent of this period. Well, the typical young man of this time, the young Symbolist, is caricaturized in a masterly way in the following lines from Gilbert and Sullivan's 1890 opera *Patience:*

> If you're anxious to shine in the high aesthetic line, as a man of culture rare,
> you must get up all the germs of the transcendental terms and plant them everywhere.
> You must lie on beds of daisies and discant us novel phrases of your complicated state of mind.
> The reason doesn't matter if the subject only chatter of a transcendental kind.
> And everyone will say, as you walk your mystic way,
> If this young man can understand these things that are far too hard for me,
> Why, what a very cultivated, clever young man, this clever young man must be.

And elsewhere:

> Then a sentimental passion of a vegetable fashion must exite your languid spleen.
> An attachment à la Plato, to a blashful young potato or a not too French French bean.
> Though the Philistines may jostle you will rank as an apostle in the high aesthetic band,
> If you walk down Piccadilly with a poppy or a lily in your mediaeval hand.[274]

Rose†Croix

This English art, especially that of Rossetti and Burne-Jones, had a great influence in France. There was a similar artistic climate there, evoked by the symbolistic poets and by the Art Nouveau movement. There are many witnesses to this influence who may be quoted, for instance Mauclair later on, when giving a survey of this movement, writes that there are artists who are indicated by the terms Symbolists or Idealists, 'who up to a certain point have accomplished in France a work analogous to that of the English Pre-Raphaelites, or at least to that of some of them, notably Rossetti, Watts[275], and Burne-Jones. This has been a protest against the academy and against Realism, and in this respect it is an interesting subject for study.'[276] Criticism of the English artists that we are discussing was far from always favourable, thus G. Geffroy who, on the occasion when three works by Burne-Jones were exhibited in the Salon, speaks of 'still-born images'[277] and also includes Aman-Jean in his criticism.[278]

This Aman-Jean exhibited at the Rose†Croix exhibition of 1892. In this group, assembled by the remarkable Sar Péladan, a typical representative of this period, we find the painters that we would call Symbolists to distinguish them from the Synthetists we shall discuss later on as our principal subject. How very correct Mauclair's characterization was, may appear from what Péladan himself wrote in the introduction to the catalogue: 'We should simply have been permitted to witness the concentration of the idealistic forces, the renewal of mysticism finally victorious over science, materialism, the Revolution, modern times.'[279] This pronouncement at once points out the absence of a trait that had been very characteristic in Baudelaire and his adherents, namely the starting point in contemporary reality in their art. On the contrary, it may be said here that 'Art is neither a torso, nor a head, or a body, it is the soul, faith, passion, sorrow . . . All art is ideographic'[280] – in which the last term should not suggest to us what Baudelaire or Delacroix would have meant by it, but what we have quoted above from Péladan.[281]

At the exhibition of the Rose†Croix of 1892 there were works on view by Séon, C. Schwabe, Aman-Jean, Henry Martin, Pozieux, Dampft, artists who according to Germain truly worked in accordance with these ideals. Of course, there were also those among them who for some (perhaps more opportunistic) reason had joined them, but whose tendencies were different – we shall not investigate here whether or not Hodler, who also exhibited here, belonged to those we have mentioned. It is rather striking that several of these painters are said to be under English influence. It is even asserted that the Rose†Croix movement was characterized by it.[282]

However, this movement was not so very strongly represented in France. The reason was perhaps that here naturalism had created a brilliant art, also outside the world of the Salon, in that of the Impressionists. The important painters worked in an entirely different climate. There were, therefore, no artists of a high order among these exhibitors. The movement was much stronger abroad where it had its centre in the XX in Belgium. For although there also the Synthetists, and congenial painters, such as Seurat and his followers, often exhibited their works, the attention was above all directed to such figures as Khnopff. The attention to the English was very marked here. It was said of Khnopff that he was losing influence in proportion to the degree in which the works by Burne-Jones, Rossetti and also Gustave Moreau became better known.[283] But also elsewhere – in the Netherlands, where the Symbolists had very important representatives, such as Toorop;[284] in Norway in the works of Munch; in Germany and Austria in the works by the painters of the different Sezessionen – there are many works in this spirit to be found. Nearly always the English influence is very strong,[285] although it often worked indirectly via the circle at Paris.[286]

This art was often the pictorial equivalent of a literary movement in the given country, which is very clear in the case of, say, Munch in Norway – in him, perhaps, the English influence is the least marked.

That this art is entirely different from that of the artists we will call the Synthetists, such as Gauguin and his followers, is at once obvious when we have a look in Dr Bettine Polak's study devoted to the Symbolist subjects.[287] Here the subjects mentioned as characteristic of the movement are the femme fatale, the sphinx, the snake, the chimera, the centaur, the bride, the lily and so on, subjects that are hardly if at all met in the works by the Synthetists just mentioned. Symbolistic art often presented such subjects, borrowed from literature, in an allegorical way by means of metaphors and above all by means of personifications. They avoided almost scrupulously the use of the old generally accepted allegorical figures, for most important was the objectification of strictly individual emotions and ideas in subjects which were often perfectly new to pictorial art. This art flourished for too short a time to develop a fixed system that was to a certain extent universally understandable. This is why their art is often obscure and their imagination sometimes far-fetched and bizarre in the eyes of the uninitiated. Entirely apart from their work, their theory sometimes suggests that of the Synthetists, but the 'application' was so very different that we can hardly speak of a direct relationship. When for instance we read about Thorn Prikker that he does not want to represent 'the outward appearance of things, but the beautiful remembrance that has remained', then this is a thought that we also find in Gauguin. But when he goes on to say that pondering on a flower he comes to view it quite differently from what it is, 'for example as a sharply outlined piece of white colour . . . with little stars round it, lines which move quietly and say how beautiful she was, how delicate her whole existence, that she was so perfect',[288] then we can imagine that a man like Gauguin, on reading this, would have burst into scornful laughter at this 'Symbolist whim, another kind of sentimentalism'.[289]

As to style we may for the most part repeat what we wrote about the English style of this period. Its forms are still derived from those of the naturalistic style that had already existed for centuries, although they are now applied in a typically manneristic way and provided with graphic additions, formal exaggerations – for example, the hairs of Toorop's female figures of this period.[290] This is characteristically expressed in Séon's method: 'So, measure figure and form, fit one's composition into a framework of decorative arabesques, choose luminosity and tints in accordance with the subject to be dealt with . . . enclose one's fiction in the verisimilitude.'[291]

Although this art was entirely new and foreign to the ideals of the painters of the Salon, they excercised more influence on it than Gauguin and his supporters did. And this is plausible, for they do not break with the representational forms of the past, however manneristic they may be, and their subject matter stays as far removed from daily life. Thus mysticism could become a fashion.[292] But, of course, with regard to style they kept within the limits of what was generally accepted and shunned anything that might look too strange. Perhaps we may even recognize a faint echo of it in a Marguerite – Goethe's 'Gretchen' – by Dagnan Bouveret at the Salon of 1912,[293] a very realistic painting of a half-nude figure with some vague phantom-like shapes in the background.

Symbolism and Synthetism

We have already indicated that the painters we group under the term Synthetists do not think much of this Symbolism. Did not Signac speak of 'the miserable deformations of the Symbolists'[294] and did not Denis say emphatically that they were anything but 'painters of the soul' themselves.[295] In fact, the same Denis had said in his famous definition of the art of painting, just like Péladan, that the essence of art did not lie in a head, or a torso, or whatever subject of reality, but whereas Péladan spoke of passions, sorrow and so on, Denis asserted that, more than anything else, a picture was a flat surface covered with colours and lines. As a matter of fact Denis emphatically stated that it was wrong 'to confound mystic and allegoric tendencies, such as the search for the expression by means of the subject, with the Symbolist tendencies to seek for the expression by means of the work of art'[296] – in which he called our Synthetists, Symbolists.

Indeed, the latter characteristic marks the most striking difference. We find a remarkable comparison mentioned by Bettina Polak, when she compares Toorop's *De anarchist* with that of Vallotton. The former is full of allegorical personifications, streaks of hair rising high up, whereas the latter represents an anarchist who is collared by policemen in the street.[297] An analysis of the stylistic elements would show that Vallotton makes a much less direct use of the old representational system than Toorop, whose figures, although a little stylized, are after all more or less academic in their anatomy and plastic structure. Vallotton simplifies a great deal more and builds up his composition in very distinct black and white contrasts (without shadows) that cooperate in elucidating the subjects.

That the Symbolist artists were above all concerned with non-realistic subjects – and not so much with a new way of representation – is also implied in the criticism that Diepenbrock once made of this entire movement. We believe that its correctness may also appear from the fact that after all this movement did not develop into a truly general one. Their pretentions had too little foundation in reality and were not sufficiently proved by the works themselves. In 1893 Diepenbrock wrote about symbolic art as follows:

Well, I can see nothing in the symbolic art of painting but the most extreme individualism, which is possessed by the delusion of expressing universal metaphysical things, so the opposite of individual things, and has arrived at this delusion by the element of reflection, and the handling of anti-naturalistic motifs.298 But what is anti-naturalistic is not therefore supra-naturalistic, still less metaphysical and approaching the absolute.299

Symbolist art

We have seen that around 1890 we can discover two sharply distinguishable groups side by side. They are two entirely different spheres notwithstanding their mutual points of contact. We should like to distinguish a third tendency, if it did not seem a little strange to speak of a tendency in this case, as properly speaking we are referring to one or two artists only, namely Bresdin and Odilon Redon.

These three different movements are also found in literature. They run parallel to each other. For Michaud distinguishes three movements, rightly so in our opinion,300 which all of them more or less clearly start from Baudelaire and are the continuation of tendencies that had already been found in Romanticism.301 One movement, that of the *poésie affective* had Verlaine for its grandmaster, and may be called the movement of the *décadents*. The third is that of the *poésie fantastique* and it centres on the figure of Rimbaud, whereas the second main stream is that of symbolisme, the *poésie intellectuelle*, with Mallarmé as its epoch-making exponent.

In the years 1885 and 1886 the formation of their own art theory is supposed to have started in the group mentioned last, no doubt also under the influence of Mallarmé's ideas. At that time Sarrazin drew attention to the Pre-Raphaelites,302 but their influence was slight in this circle. Much greater was the influence of Russian novels, on which Vogué published a book in 1885. It was precisely the interest in reality itself, including the spiritual forces at work in it, that struck them in these novels. Ghil is one of the first who gives a more detailed theory, entirely in the footsteps of Mallarmé, in which he clearly rejects 'the sad verses', 'the egotist reveries', in a word 'decadent poetry'.303 At the same time also Moréas published his well-known manifesto of Symbolism. These Symbolists were, doubtlessly, important for the formation of the theory of art on the part of the painters, and this is why we shall discuss the individuals who are most important for our subject later on when dealing with Synthetist art theory. The development of this literary movement need not be discussed here, as it has been elaborately treated in Michaud's work. In fact, the theories of the poets have always been given a great deal of attention, so that they have been studied in much more depth.

No more shall we enter into the movement of the decadents. They shared the demand for freedom and the anti-naturalistic attitudes of the Symbolists.[304] From Michaud we shall borrow the following brief characterization of their strongly marked subjectivistic attitude:

> This is the content of decadent poetry: the inner world but reduced to its lowest levels, to its undefinable emotions, its most exasperated sensations, to dreams ruled by repressed desires and by the demands of the flesh ... a new expression: ... a subjective correspondence between the music of the words and the music of the soul caught in its mobile and fugitive course.[305]

Indeed we find here what Kahn expressed in the following words:

> The essential aim of our art is to objectify the subjective (the externalization of the Idea) instead of subjectifying the objective (nature seen through the eyes of a temperament). Thus we carry the analysis of the Self to the extreme, we let the multiplicity and intertwining of rhythm harmonize with the measure of the Idea, we create literary enchantment by annulling the pattern of a forced and spiritual modernism.[306]

The last few words show where they deviate from Baudelaire's ideals, in contradistinction to the movement of Mallarmé and the Synthetist painters, whereas in the use of the term Idea we may see them makea bow in the direction of Schopenhauer who had a great influence in this environment.

Negative attitude to reality

This movement – and not only these decadents, but also the Symbolists and, in a certain sense, the Synthetists – is characterized by a very explicit aversion to reality. This is one of the reasons, if not the deepest cause, of their flight into what is subjective and detached from the outer world, modern or not. To understand the art of this period, at least some important aspects of it, it is almost indispensable to have an insight into the nature and the origin of this negative attitude towards reality.

This feeling of depression was characteristic for the Romantics. Thus Sénancour wrote in his *Obermann*:

> Thus seeing relations in things that are hardly there and seeking for what I shall never obtain, a stranger in the real world[307], ridiculous among men, I shall have only vain affectations and whether I live in accordance with my own taste, or in accordance with the way of other men, I shall not have anything but the eternal torment of a permanently suppressed and miserable life – in the oppression from outside or in my own limitation.[308]

This author has probed his mind very deeply, and he knows also that his estrangement from reality, his depression as such, is the consequence of the fact that he wants something more than this reality, more than is humanly possible in the creation.[309] It is the attempt to control everything, the wish to be limitless, lawless, which again and again causes him to come into conflict with that reality itself, because it cannot offer him this freedom. 'I seek elsewhere, for some unknown good the urge for which pursues me. Is it my fault if I find boundaries everywhere, if all that is finite has not any value to me?'[310]

The urge for freedom found here is of a religious[311] character,[312] and implies humankind's wish to be self-determining, not subject to laws or norms they have not made or created themselves. It is the old humanistic freedom motif that is again fervently and consciously avowed as the starting point of all human (cultural) activity. Morice, in his influential book *La littérature de tout à l'heure* written in 1889, in which he enters into these things very elaborately, also sees this sharply when, writing on Byron as a typical Romanticist, he says: 'In order to find and to combine the evolutions and sudden changes of his poem and his drama he had only to carry to their extreme consequences his feelings, imaginary but sincere, the feelings that upset his soul when exalted by the very fumes of his genius and by the electricity of the stormy air: If I were omnipotent, what should I do to my enemies, what to the world?'[313]

And although it is important to know that around 1890 this profoundly spiritual urge was understood like this, it may plead in Morice's favour that in Carlyle there is a direct pronouncement to be found which confirms Morice's view of Romanticism in this respect. It is even possible that what will follow was also in Morice's mind. Carlyle wonders how even a simple man like a shoeblack might be made happy. Nobody can do so, for 'the shoeblack also has a soul quite other than his stomach; and would require, if you consider it, for his permanent satisfaction and saturation, simply this allotment, no more, and no less: God's infinite Universe altogether to himself, therein to enjoy infinitely, and fill every wish as fast as it rose.'[314] Essentially, therefore, humans demand no more, and no less, than being God's equal, the old wishful dream, ever renewed, which Satan held out to humankind in Paradise.

Also in this respect it was Baudelaire who formulated the spirit of Romanticism anew and thus carried it over to the generation working at the end of the century. In his *Salon* of 1855 he elaborately discusses the cultural situation in connection with the position of the artist. From the latter he demands that he shall be 'his king, his priest, and his god',[315] in short, a man who in the true sense of the word is driven on by the religious 'dynamis'[316] of the personality ideal.[317] All this had been threatened with grave dangers by positivism, which supposed it could bring freedom and the control of nature by means of the natural sciences but risked this foundational freedom by its very starting point. For this positivism wished to formulate laws for everything according to natural science, and there was no certainty at all that it would stop at human freedom. On the contrary, the ideal of the domination of reality by the application of economic laws would drive humankind onto a road that would ultimately lead to the very annihilation of this human freedom. Baudelaire saw this sharply when he asked himself:

> If, in a delicate way, proportionate to the new enjoyments brought by it [the ideal of science] the indefinite progress would not be man's most ingenious and most cruel torture; if, preceding with the obstinate negation of himself, it would not be a method of incessantly renewed suicide, and if, enclosed within the fiery circle of divine logic, he did not resemble a scorpion that pierces its own body with its terrible tail, this eternal yearning which causes his eternal despair?[318]

This revival of the Romantic attitutude at the end of the century made the conflict with reality still sharper. For the nature with which they came into conflict was no longer nature in its self-evident existence, but a reality viewed through the glasses of the positivists and, as such, loaded with a power that ran counter to the freedom intended in the personality ideal. Reality in this sense consisted of a complex mix of fixed law-conformities without any subjective freedom under this law. Thus writing about de Goncourt, Morice says: 'In the uniform mask that science casts on nature wherever it is in direct relation to man, he has seen mankind lose its hold on things, and in a menacing silence things resuming their own individual lives, alien to humanity, thus vanquished by its victory and unable to reconquer its ruins which return to nature.'[319] Viewed as a complex mix of fixed law-conformities, this reality turns into 'the robe of Nessos from which nothing can deliver us'.[320] There would be an escape in the knowledge that everything is merely a dream, 'Only he who dreams us would do well to hasten the hatching of his opium.'[321]

It was exactly this spiritual situation that was felt by the generation of 1885 to 1890 to have caused their trouble in trying to achieve an art which was truly beautiful, in accordance with their ideals. For, as Morice says, 'As our life is such a terrible thing that art has not had the means for a perfect realization of our dreams of happiness, it was really necessary to maintain ourselves mourning for the joys that life denies to us and which could only be realized in dreams.'[322] Indeed they were even denied the beautiful dream of life which art ought to offer. Thus Valin writes in 1892 that it was 'the impotence from which especially the artists suffered, incapable of fully realizing their dream, i.e., clothing an eternal idea in a truly real form'.[323] The question is whether it was really the ugliness of reality which incapacitated them to produce a good and sound art, just as we may ask ourselves whether their feeling of discomfort was not rather caused by their own attitude to life than by that reality as such. In truth, positivism was a danger to human freedom, but this did not make it necessary by way of reaction to put every norm and every tradition out of action in the name of freedom, in the sense of Romanticism. That is why we may speak of the *perversité* with which they turned away *volontairement de la norme*. They followed 'the advice of perversity, which wants all things to be dislodged from their proper niche and deprived of their natural balance'.[324]

They wanted to escape from the world as positivism had explained and disclosed it, the reality of the statistically observed facts and futilities.[325] They wanted to get free from the everyday world, with its multitudes of things and events, this world, which oppressed a free man and forced the artist to live as commonplace and superficial a life as 'everybody'. Positivism had dethroned every value and equallized everything by its natural-scientific method. For if only individual, visible, palpable and measurable events are meaningful the insight into the difference between what from a human standpoint is meaningful and what is not will be lost. That is why there is a certain amount of truth in Radiot's assertion that 'The spirit has become incapable of hierarchy.'[326] It is characteristic of Western civilization, so very profoundly influenced by Greek thought, to seek the contrast again between soul and matter, or, at this time, coming after the eighteenth-century sensualism, between the soul and the senses. 'It is no longer the soul as commander-in-chief which speaks but each of the mutinous soldiers, the so-called senses'[327] And so Aurier writes: 'The present only hurts and is ugly only on account of its being material.' And what is the remedy? 'While believing that we are inventing the most fabulous chimeras we do nothing but call up the visions we remember unconsciously of the times when our souls relaxed in the marvellous garden of the Eden of the pure Ideas.'[328] The human mind is mortal, 'because it indulges in the sweet ephemera of contingency; immortal because it can lift itself to the Paradise of the absolute'.[329]

Here we hear that the solution is sought in the spirit of Plato, as we have seen already more than once, also in the previous chapter. What may have induced them to take up these ancient thoughts again? Perhaps the same cause that had so often made people advance them in former centuries, namely in order to supply a firm basis for non-naturalistic art. They provide a justification that does not only exempt the artists from the necessity 'to copy' the reality given by the senses but even elevates them to the status of 'visionaries' who are better able than anyone else to render visible the Ideas behind reality that determine its meaning. Of course, Plato himself could not be appealed to directly, as he had declared art to be an inferior kind of activity, the imitation of natural objects.[330] But they turned to Plotinus who, simply stating that it was pre-eminently art which 'imitated' the Ideas, elevated art to one of the highest of human activities.[331] From this thought the aestheticists of the fifteenth century had started, and this had been the core of the theory of Mannerism.[332] Later on, around 1800, these thoughts had been revived when a theory of art was wanted which would enable the artist to indulge in his or her own fantasy without lapsing into wild fancies without any sense or content. For it was an issue of that time also to secure a high view of art.[333] These thoughts really pronounce the artist free, and that which Aurier posited above – after all, just give your own imagination the reins, then we shall walk about in the Eden of the Ideas – is entirely in accordance with tradition.[334]

It is quite possible that Shestov is right in saying that Plotinus conceived these ideas because ultimately he thought the world too beautiful, preferred to enjoy it, and was not in the least minded to withdraw from it into asceticism. But it would have been consistent if he had arrived at conclusions similar to those of the gnostics who also affirmed that the creation, man's living-space as such, was evil and worthless.[335] The artists of this generation agreed with Plotinus that reality itself is something inferior. 'The starting point of the speculative thought of Plotinus . . . is a feeling of uneasy discomfort, the feeling that in its actual form human life is a checked sort of life diminished by obstacles caused by bodies and passions.'[336]

The generation of 1890 was not at all unacquainted with these old traditions. Not only did they always come across them when reading the works of their predecessors, mentioned in the previous chapter, but at least those who were actively engaged in forming the new theory of art studied the old works of the Plotinian tradition.[337]

So Plotinism was a very useful way out of the difficulty of escaping from actual reality and of depreciating it as such while retaining all the joy that art can give us. This view was an answer to his 'need to escape from the horrible reality of existence, to cross the borders of thought, to grope for some certainty without ever arriving at it, in the mist of the beyond of art',[338] as it is put by des Esseintes, the main character in *A Rebours* by Huysmans, published in 1884.

But having thus found a way of escape, they kept feeling that the kind of art they longed for was not to be achieved in the world of their time. We have already seen that Morice, while wishing to create an art that was to realize their beautiful dream, at the same time posits that such fulfilment is impossible in view of the miserable reality in which they find themselves. For there is no real freedom, only 'the natural order, so that if all that lives lives as a slave, there is nothing in accordance with the laws of nature, as each life is chained by another life, or by a vice, or by artificial obligations outlined by society as it is'.[339] And the consequences of the latter state of affairs were obvious. There was not only a crisis within art, but also a crisis of art, to use Redeker's distinction,[340] so that according to them it was necessary to change society itself in order to arrive at a truly good kind of art. And although a few idealists of Péladan's type will no doubt have fancied this change to be possible by means of art itself, it was nevertheless obvious that art *qua talis* is too weak or wholly unfit for such a task.[341] Thus it is not surprising that in such an artistic sphere the revolutionary sentiment ran high – in this respect they were the continuation of their naturalistic predecessors[342] and they even preached anarchism, generally in words rather than in actions. But we shall not study this aspect of their activity any further.[343]

On the whole the ideas just mentioned did not have any considerable influence on their view of art as such. On the contrary, in the years immediately before and after 1890 there was plenty of optimism so that Morice was able to say that the wish 'anywhere out of the world'[344] even implied something positive with respect to art, for 'This complaint is something of our time, and it is a great deal more than a complaint: it is the supreme law of supreme art.'[345] Yet their negative sense of reality was very important for the nature of their art. For a person will seek after truth in his or her art, after that which seems to be meaningful and valuable. And as this was not 'ordinary' reality, the latter was something inferior also for art. Thus it was possible to say about a decadent person that 'he withdrew more and more from reality, and above all from the contemporary world which he considered with increasing horror; this hatred had strongly influenced his literary and artistic tastes, and he turned away most from pictures and books whose limited subjects were inspired by modern life.'[346]

But this person will also somehow look upon one or other depiction of a glorious paradise as a lie. This was perhaps the real reason why at this time it seemed to be impossible to realize truly 'beautiful' art. Already in Baudelaire this is clear from the direct connection between the view of reality and the character of the works of art that were preferred: 'Nature is ugly, and I prefer the monsters of my fantasy to the trivial positive.'[347] And even more explicitly:

> I have found the definition of what is beautiful, of what I call beautiful. It is something passionate and sad, something a little vague ... I can hardly conceive a type of beauty (would my brain be an enchanted mirror) in which there is no despair. Supported – others say obsessed – by these ideas I think that it would be difficult for me not to arrive at the conclusion that the most perfect type of manly beauty is Satan – after the manner of Milton.[348]

Therefore the choice of subjects on the part of the Symbolist painters is not so very surprising.[349] They were almost always *fleurs du mal*, beauty sought in what is ugly, in all that violates the norms and the tender relations. It is quite understandable that Salome should become one of the most important subjects of this period. Salome, who danced very beautifully in order to commit a horrible crime in a truly satanic mingling of over-refined beauty, sensuality, deeply rooted cruelty and purposeful cunning. She was the classical personification of decadence in whom almost all the motifs were united that were dear to this mentality: aestheticism, the freedom of the individual (in a past which was far superior to the banality of the present), although not without the fatal subjection to the power of the passions, life on a different plane from the vulgarly commonplace, full of irrationality and mysteriousness in which, after all, sin committed in a charming way is given its beautiful form.

Symbolistic art (continued)

This decadent sense of life had been given its first brilliant form in Huysmans' *A Rebours* written with the explicit purpose of getting out of the impasse of naturalism.[350] The book made quite a stir and had an immense influence both in France and abroad.[351] It portrays the decadent person, and thus is able to show what is relevant to his or her character. Through this work a number of painters were brought to the notice of a much wider audience of people, in the first place those belonging to the decadent authors and poets themselves. Huysmans was better acquainted with what was going on in the sphere of pictorial art than most of his colleagues as he had been an art critic for many years.[352] We first wish to pass in review these painters because their work runs parallel to that of the decadent literary artists. Their art is entirely different from that of the Synthetists, such as Gauguin, and consequently had hardly any influence on the latter. It is, however, conceivable that through the contact with this work, especially with that of Redon, these artists were encouraged to strike out on their own. The only possible influence by these painters on Synthetism was to function as catalysts.

Gustave Moreau perfectly fitted the definition Baudelaire once gave of an artist after his own heart:

> And as a painter proud of my genius
> I should enjoy in my picture
> the intoxicating monotony
> of metal, marble and water
> ... and heavy cataracts
> hanging down like crystal curtains
> dazzling from crystal walls.[353]

The agreement with a particular aspect of Baudelaire, the Baudelaire of the *fleurs du mal*, was also sharply recognized by Huysmans when he wrote about Moreau as follows: 'In his erudite works full of despair there was a singular enchantment, a kind of incantation that stirs you to the bottom of your soul like certain poems by Baudelaire.'[354]

That Huysmans' words on Moreau were not merely the reading of the former's dreams or wishes into Moreau's work, but the latter's actual ideal and meaning, will appear when we consult the explanation or accompanying text that the painter wrote for some of his paintings himself. The following description may serve as a brief summary of what we have written above – the subject is the painting entitled *Les Chimères*:

A satanic Decameron. This island of fantastic dreams encloses all forms of passion, fantasy, and caprice in the woman, woman in her primary essence, the unconscious being fond of the unknown, the mysterious, in love with evil in the form of a perverse and diabolic seduction. The dreams of children, of the senses, monstrous dreams, melancholy dreams, dreams that carry the spirit and the soul into the unknown of the spaces, into the mystery of gloom, everything must experience the influence of the seven deadly sins, everything is found in these satanic precincts, in this circle of the vices and the guilty ardours, from the as yet innocent germ to the monstrous and fatal flowers of the abyss ... In the distance, the dead town with the dormant passions. And this town is real life, true life, that which is hidden, enclosed within the sombre walls, under flat roofs. But the mountainous roads ... rise and some figures ... are climbing while always clinging to the sharp points of that barren and hard rock ... Perhaps they will arrive at that redemptory cross that rises humbly in the ether, the last stage of life, the last evidence of what is creative and beneficent, the last refuge of a being that has been able to avoid or to vanquish the visionary dream after the cruel afflictions, the terrible dream of ruin, of sorrow and death.[355]

It may be called characteristic of this milieu that the cross is hardly visible in the picture itself, and is certainly not victorious. It can only be reached after a long and dangerous journey, perhaps. The terrible though beautiful daydream of reality itself is predominant.

Moreau's views were characterized by a strong gnostic strain, as we can read in his note on his *Jupiter et Sémélé*, in which the earth, personified as Pan, 'bends its head sadly full of regret that it is enslaved and in exile, while at his feet are assembling the gloomy phalanx of the monsters of Erebus and the Night . . . [while there is] an ascension to the higher spheres, to the Divine, [by which] the great mystery is accomplished'.[356]

There is a striking affinity with Blake, not in the subjects as such but in their treatment. Here, too, mythological personifications are used, the scenes are represented by means borrowed from the naturalistic tradition, which often gives rise to some marked mannerism. Indeed there are more than once direct borrowings from sixteenth-century art reminding us of Bronzino or of the school of Fontainebleau.[357]

Moreau's influence, inextricably connected with that of Huysmans' *A Rebours*, was especially great on the men of letters. Fontainas says about it: 'The *Salome* by Gustave Moreau haunted us'[358] and then he quotes Huysmans, a brilliant description which does not fail to impress, perhaps even more than the picture itself. The interest in this kind of art was not at all restricted to France. Jan Veth devotes an article to it in *De Nieuwe Gids* of 1890,[359] and in England Moreau was discussed in *The Dial* of 1893,[360] and in *The Pageant* of 1897.[361] Also at the first exhibition of the Grosvenor Gallery in London (which specialized in the Pre-Raphaelites) there was a work by Moreau on view.[362] These articles may prove that painters too were interested in him as all three had been written by fellow artists. In fact, two painters of the group of the Rose†Croix, namely Ary Renan and F. Aman-Jean had been his pupils. Those pupils who did not come to the fore until 1900, such as Rouault, we shall leave out of account here. But we must observe that the interest in Moreau was restricted to the group of those we have called the 'decadents' when discussing literature, or Symbolists when painters were concerned. Moreau finally played an important role in spreading the knowledge of the Pre-Raphaelites in France.363

The pictoral artists that may be considered as parallel to the third group of authors distinguished by Michaud – Rimbaud and others – on the whole do not try to represent gnostic Platonic truth with the aid of some mythological allegory after the manner of Moreau. Rather, they try to give direct expression to a negative sense of reality, a feeling of estrangement from reality that is experienced as a hostile incomprehensible power. This was done either by a direct depiction of the products of an irrational phantasy, as Redon did, or by trying to represent reality in a way that laid special emphasis on that which seemed to them to be relevant in it.

> The lawless concrete – all that remains to man after the departure of the gods – the civilized supra-nature, irrational, and psychic, creates phantoms which people call the Black Novel. The phantom does not express the myths of nature or the infinity of what is real like a Greek god or like a fairy. It is a particular event that is transformed into a psychism, a part of reality transposed to the interior of man and which is reincarnated – in irreality. These immaterial creations express the terror of men threatened by the exterior evil which has become a psychism.364

This is how some adherents characterized this art.

Meryon was one of the first to take this road, but Bresdin became better known. In his work he represents his view of reality, often rendering the latter in its smallest details. The concentration upon those details brings home to us the strangeness, the irrational, killing, mysterious, hostile, sinister character of reality – what the Germans call *unheimisch*, where we do not feel at 'home' (*Heim*). Only rarely – especially in his earlier work – he specifies his view by 'peopling' his reality with gnomes, skeletons proclaiming their triumph, for instance in his *Comédie de la mort* of 1854.365 In most cases he suffices by representing some conceivable reality to express this horror and this estrangement. Thus the congenial Redon, who, although younger, had known Bresdin well, writes about him as follows: 'What is found everywhere in his work, from one end to the other, is man in love with solitude, flying from the world, flying desperate and homeless under the sky, into the terrors of an exile without hope and without end.'366 This work is like self-torture, an absorption in the minutest details of reality to discover in it the horror, the estrangement, that which is hostile to him as a human being without any contact with this reality. It stands to reason that he could not copy reality and gave free reign to his imagination, but it is characteristic of his vision to remain a conceivable reality, or rather, it is reality itself viewed in one of its aspects.

The latter statement also applies to Redon to a certain extent,[367] although in his case the products of the imagination are a great deal more spectral, irreal. But Redon, who is no doubt the most important artist of this group and – just as Moreau had been brought to the fore by Huysmans in *A Rebours* – was also highly esteemed by the Symbolist writers,[368] himself always laid stress on the representation of his dream 'by this semblance of truth'.[369] because he puts 'the logic of the visible at the service of the invisible as much as possible'.[370] Whereas Bresdin concentrates on landscape, transposed to give expression to the artist's sense of life, Redon focuses on the figure as central, whether a human or some imaginary being.

Redon's art, too, is a direct concretizing of his 'pain of life',[371] in relevant images, the evocation of an atmosphere described by Aurier as 'a shiver of fear in the endless night'.[372] It is not necessary to argue this point elaborately as practically all the authors who wrote about Redon interpret his art in this sense,[373] while he himself more than once spoke about it in this way in his diary.[374]

The spiritual ancestors who inspired Redon and led him on his way are Goya and Poe – he devotes an album containing lithographs to both of them. More often than they did, he created phantastic beings that do not exist in reality, but apart from this there are parallels enough in their approaches to the subject. The subject is detected by a close scrutiny of reality – it expresses all that is terrible, horrific, hideous, in a word, all that is relevant to their negative sense of reality. There remain differences between them: Redon is more subjective, more hallucinatory in his dreams, less exact than Poe, less directed to contemporary events than Goya.

Already in 1883 Huysmans mentioned Baudelaire in addition to Poe as one of the 'teachers' of Redon.[375] It is something remarkable that nearly all the trends existing at the end of the century, however much they differed, were not only able to appeal to Baudelaire but were also influenced by him and could have started from his work. As a matter of fact, Michaud had shown this already in his scheme of classification.[376] Also Redon could appeal to Baudelaire. Witness the latter's pronouncement in *Curiosités Esthétiques:* 'Nature is ugly, and I prefer the monsters of my fantasy to the trivial positive.'[377] In Baudelaire's work he could find subjects that suited him – in 1890 he made lithographs illustrating *Les Fleurs du Mal.*

It is striking that Baudelaire's own critical work started from entirely different premises, apart from an isolated sentence like the one just quoted. On the other hand the agreement is very clear when we consider Baudelaire's literary work. Perhaps we may put it like this: in his own (literary) art Baudelaire pointed the way to those whom we have discussed in the present chapter. But in his theory of art his attitude towards reality is different, a much more important place being assigned to it in the synthesis. This fact can only be explained by taking into account the great admiration for and the great influence of the art and the ideas of Delacroix. This enabled him to point the way to the Synthetist artists round Gauguin. The latter owed an immense debt to Baudelaire, but exactly on account of those elements in which he agreed with Delacroix.

None of the Symbolist artists dealt with in this chapter broke with the old familiar method of representing their subjects. Their art is new with respect to its content, often oriented to literature. They did not shrink from deformation or from fantastic beings, but in their forms they always followed the naturalistic way of representation, using perspective, shade and plastic quality. As we have more than once indicated, the result was that their art often fell into mannerism. This Symbolism was the last flowering of the art which had been born in Flanders and Italy during the fifteenth century.

The artists we wish to discuss next are on the whole very different from these. 'But I think these melancholies of Meryon's utterly horrible.'[378] So van Gogh once wrote, and thus became the spokesman for them all. In spite of the contacts and the points of agreement in their theory of art there was an immense difference in their approach to the artistic problems.

4
Kindred Spirits

That which unites all the painters to be dealt with in this section, in contradistinction to those of the previous chapter, is the fact that they build on what the Impressionists had achieved. They share the admiration of the Symbolist[379] painters for a few artists like Redon, but they consider Delacroix, the painters of Fontainebleau and Manet as the pioneers and their great predecessors. They have a more or less pronounced aversion to the Pre-Raphaelites: 'Beware of the Pre-Raphaelites.'[380] They also have in common their Realism as regards their subjects. This shows in the clearest way perhaps, however sharply they may have expressed their critical views of Impressionism that, after all, they took their origin from the realistic-impressionistic tradition. Denis very clearly defines the difference between these artists and the Symbolists when he says that we must sharply distinguish between 'the mystic and the allegorical tendencies, i.e. the search for the expression by means of the subject, and the Symbolist[381] tendencies, i.e. the search for the expression by means of the work of art'.[382]

Impressionism

Impressionism had been realistic as far as the subjects were concerned. It clearly showed a disposition that was born by a positivistic view of reality. 'Faith is by sight,' the artists of the Renaissance already claimed. This is why they had sought to give expression in their art to truth as they understood it by trying to design a picture that showed some agreement with what the eye could see and observe. Only in the eighteenth century had the epistemological consequences been drawn from this viewpoint and had sensualism taught that the outer world can primarily be known by the 'sensations'[383] – recall for example Condillac's *Treatise on Sensations*.[384] And it is precisely this conception of how we know reality and truth that found expression not only in the subjects of the Impressionists but also in their method of painting. 'Nature . . . was the direct source of pure sensations, and these sensations could best be reproduced by the technique of small dots and strokes which . . . retained the general impression in all its richness of colour and life'[385] – which at the same time may prove that 'sensations' and 'impressions' were pretty well synonymous (in fact they had been synonyms already in eighteenth-century sensualistic philosophy).[386]

It cannot be surprising that the Impressionists took such a great interest in the problems of light and colour. For it was precisely in the years during which they were forming a style of their own that not only the physical science but also the theoretical problems surrounding the nature of light were in the centre of general interest. The results of the scientific investigations were followed by the public at large with great interest.[387] Physical science was of course also based for the greater part on the eighteenth-century philosophical conceptions, which were formulated and elaborated anew by positivism. The 'experimenting with effects of light and colour'[388] was related to the attempt to record sensations directly without any emotional interpretation. This view of reality had penetrated French thought in the nineteenth century so deeply that they did not even suspect that in reality they were following a theory. 'I have always had a horror of theories . . . I have only the merit of having painted directly from nature, trying to convey my impressions in the presence of the most fugitive effects.'[389] This late pronouncement by Monet simply clarifies that the artist equalizes the representation of nature with the (unproblematic) notation of impressions or 'sensations'.

These things became clearer to the next generation who reacted strongly against the positivistic view of life. They began to understand that reality is more than the sum total of impressions but kept looking upon nature through the eyes of the positivists. As a result they blamed the Impressionists for having merely represented nature while forgetting what was truly human, such as emotions, thoughts, ideas. Mauclair said with reference to them: 'The eye and the hand! superb, and it was enough: but nothing else.'[390] All the same, the decadent authors, although they were akin to the Symbolist painters whose art was a far cry from Impressionism, defended this style. 'At bottom they had nothing in common, it was their common reaction against the ill will of the press which united them', Mauclair explained.[391] This situation was due to the fact that Impressionism (really the work of a very small group of artists), had been entirely hidden from the eyes of the official world of art. The prevailing tendency, that of the Salons, would have nothing to do with them and deliberately closed its eyes to what was new and important in their achievements. Though Impressionism flourished especially between 1870 and 1880,[392] the Impressionists came to the fore later only, and simultaneously with the Symbolists – taking this latter term in a very wide sense. When they aroused the public interest it was at first no doubt a spirit of rejection and condemnation.

As a matter of fact, the original Impressionism in the most literal sense of the word was already a thing of the past by 1890. Nearly all the artists that might be called Impressionists had started searching for new ways after 1880, in order to get out of the deadlock into which their too exclusive interest in the 'sensations' of light and colour had brought them. For this very reason it is important to inquire how it is that in, for instance, all kinds of textbooks on the history of music we again and again find the opinion defended that Debussy was pre-eminently an

Impressionist in music, a statement based on *La cathédrale engloutie* and similar compositions.[393] So this is considered to be the musical parallel to Impressionism. But, even apart from the real character of his art, it is well known that Debussy moved especially in a Symbolist environment[394] – taking this term again in as wide a sense as possible. Did he not compose music to Maeterlinck's *Pelléas et Mélisande* and did he not write a tonal poem inspired by Mallarmé's *L'aprés midi d'un faun* – in which, by the way, he hit off the atmosphere and the mood of this far-from- realistic work in a masterly way?

In its atmosphere, its conception or its starting point there was hardly any connection between genuine Impressionism and the 'Symbolist' music of Debussy. Yet there is some truth in the current opinion, but only if we consider the later development of Monet who very consistently followed the lead of sensualism. He had started as a Realist and worked in the spirit of the painters of Fontainebleau, as can be seen in an early work from 1865, *A small street in Normandy*.[395] One notes here the way the structures of the houses were made clear in it. Afterwards he had come to emphasize the pure and exclusive representation of the sensations of colour and light, thus intensifying the subjective element at the same time. After 1875, as his courage increased, he drew more and more far-reaching conclusions from his viewpoint. In this way his art became exclusively a fixation of the effects of light and colour based on close observation in all kinds of weather – recall his well-known series of the cathedral of Rouen in the early 1890s – with the result that all matter seemed to have vanished so that his reality consisted only of a rarefied, vague totality composed of vibrations of colour and light. For the very reason that the matter and structure of things no longer seemed to exist in his eyes, his art became something ethereal and nebulous. For the spectator the work of art thereby loses its immediacy and the impression that a very particular moment has been fixed, as we sometimes experience with Constable. But this indefinite vagueness is also characteristic of the literary art of the decadents and the Symbolists.

This affinity might be more accurately described by paying attention to the meaning of the word *rêverie*, a term rarely used at the end of the nineteenth century. It probably evoked too many associations with the past. But it was perhaps avoided even more on account of the fact that the word *rêverie* implied a more passive attitude to nature. As we shall see, the Symbolists and the Synthetists strove much more after the *rêve* (the dream), the active and creative daydream. The word *rêverie* in the sense intended here was connected with an attitude of life, a very particular attitude towards reality that was first embodied in a concrete artistic form by Jean Jacques Rousseau in his *Rêveries d'un Promeneur Solitaire*.[396] In it nature inspires people to indulge in a stream of thoughts and feelings that as such is entirely subjective and not immediately connected with the peculiar character, structure and nature of a particular natural phenomenon. Although neither this term, nor this thought as such, were of frequent occurrence among the generation of 1890, the character of their work was nevertheless more than once determined by this attitude towards reality. Both Verlaine and Mallarmé sometimes suggest a *rêverie* rather than a *rêve*, at least, the line of demarcation between these two, theoretically speaking, clearly distinct conceptions of the relation between the artist and reality cannot be sharply indicated.[397]

Indeed, several of Monet's works of the series mentioned above, and his Nymphéas even more, might suggest a *rêverie*, just as some of Debussy's works like *La cathédrale engloutie'* or *L'aprés midi d'un faun*. Viewed in this light the later lyrical Monet had remained an 'Impressionist' and had many points of contact with the art of the 1890's and with Debussy. For then he was also strongly subjective and dreamy, evoking a mood rather than giving an exact description. How very much Monet thus kept pace with the times may also appear from a comparison of these later pictures with the great decorative works by Vuillard, produced during the years 1894 to 1900, who had after all come from the Synthetist milieu.

Yet not only was Monet very far apart from the Synthetists proper but also from the Symbolist literary men – much further than he was from the decadents of the school of Verlaine. This becomes clear when Aurier makes the critical remark that

> It is permissible . . . to take exception to this constant sacrifice of significant forms and this deliberate plunging of beings into those atmospheres which have been so splendidly conceived that those beings seem to be vaporized in them; it is, no doubt, just as well legitimate to wish for an art that is less immediately, less directly sensational, an art of a more distant dream and of the idea.[398]

This is a criticism of the *rêverie* from the standpoint of the *rêve*.

Seurat

A painter who will probably have satisfied the wish implied in the words just quoted is Seurat, although Aurier is not likely to have had him in mind. Seurat and his friend and kindred spirit Signac aimed at 'reflection' and 'permanence' in contradistinction to the method 'of instinct and instantaneousness'.[399] He had been subject to various influences, among which we must not underestimate that of Delacroix, whose work he had closely studied already at the time when he was forming his own conceptions,[400] whereas Signac repeatedly cited Delacroix when elaborately discussing Neo-Impressionism (as their art was soon called). He especially quoted Delacroix's pronouncement that nature is nothing but a dictionary for the artist in which to look up the words required to frame his own sentences.[401]

Their own pronouncements and the treatises written by their supporters (such as Fénéon) who had known them personally make it clear indeed that instead of what is just momentary and transient, *le fugace*, they sought for what is permanent and durable in order 'to confer authenticity on nature tired at last of its precarious reality', [402] as Signac expressed it. This meant that they attempted to capture the permanent character of things, the meaning and structure of their subject, in opposition to the momentary impression which is perhaps not representative at all: 'To synthetize a landscape in a definitive aspect that perpetuates the sensation it gives,'[403] wrote Fénéon.

In their works we find Baudelaire's aim again to create an art in which chance does not play a part, and in their way of realization everything is under control to the minutest details. They differ from Baudelaire only in that he demands at the same time that the method be easy and fluent, without constraint, direct, and looking spontaneous, which is made possible by the previous thoroughly considered conception. The latter requirement is maintained by Neo-Impressionists but their technique, which by necessity consists of planning even the smallest details, is the opposite of spontaneous and direct.

They want to render their vision of the subject in its permanent character and meaning by different means of expression which are purely aesthetic and can certainly not be understood in a naturalistic way. This is at once clear when we study their conception of colour. For at first sight the pointillist's technique, founded in the theories of light propounded by Chevreuil and others, has all the appearance of being purely Impressionist, but only according to a method that has been thought out in a more scientific way. Their method had arisen indeed under the influence of the Impressionists, but the colours were chosen with a view to their aesthetic effect on the eye, their mutual contrast, optical mingling and such, owing to which they can become the bearers of the expression[404] and of artistic meaning. The very first lines of Seurat's own summary of his aesthetics clearly show this: 'Art is harmony. Harmony is the analogy between contrasts, the analogy of similarities of tone, colour, line, viewed against the dominant element and under the influence of a particular light, in gay, calm or sad combinations.'[405] In this theory we do not find a statement to the effect that thus the natural effects of light are rendered in a better way but, on the contrary, that by this method the work of art can be realized in a much better way aesthetically.

Also with regard to tonal values and to the lines on the surface of the canvas these artists searched for aesthetical laws. For example, the direction of the lines was said to represent different emotions. Their aim was by no means the detection of psychological laws but rather aesthetical regularities, fixed rules to be observed for a composition to be truly harmonious. They supposed that it was possible to formulate these laws in the same way as was done in the natural sciences.[406] The (mathematical-natural) science ideal dominated their thought and their action. At the same time, however, they rightly presupposed the existence of a close mutual coherence of purely aesthetical values – harmony – and iconic meaning[407] – *calme, triste* and such like.

The primacy of the science ideal in Seurat's artistic attitude is also evident from the fact that he consulted all kinds of scientific treatises on light – those by Chevreuil, Helmholtz[408] and others – and consequently in this respect he was much more consistently positivistic than the Impressionists proper. But at this point the great difference between them is revealed, for he did not at all strive after the fixation of 'sensations' in their direct momentariness but tried to render what is more general and permanent. His art was summarizing and human in its interpretation.

At first sight this statement might suggest an anti-positivistic attitude, because human freedom seems to be given greater emphasis. This element is there – it has never been absent in Western humanism – but it remains of subordinate importance. We find it in Signac's pronouncement that 'Subordinating colours and lines to the emotion that he has felt and wants to render, the painter will do the work of a poet, of a creator.'[409] But for a correct understanding of what he meant by this it will he useful to read the following words of Sutter's:

> Rules do not hinder the spontaneity of the inventive power or that of the execution in spite of their absolute character ... Science delivers us of all uncertainties and permits us to move in perfect freedom and within a very vast circle. As all rules have been derived from the laws of nature themselves, there is nothing so easy to know in principle, nor so indispensable. In the arts everything must be planned.[410]

So the wish to give human freedom free scope is there, but it is entirely bound to following the laws of nature. The motif of freedom was very weak indeed in the idea that 'We must see nature with the eyes of the mind and not exclusively with the bodily eyes like a creature destitute of reason.'[411] For although this writer argues against naturalism, which wished to render only that which the eye could see, this seeing, *avec les yeux de l'esprit* means nothing but the application of the aesthetic laws conceived of as laws of nature.

The above quotations are from David Sutter, who had explained his ideas in a series of articles in 1880 entitled 'Les phénomènes de la vision', which are concluded with his positing 167 rules for art. Consequently this constituted an aesthetics in the scientific sense of the word, akin to the somewhat later work by Henry regarding composition and method. The titles of some articles of Henry's are telling enough: 'A scientific Aesthetics'[412], 'The Aesthetics of Forms'[413] and the article which was so important to Seurat and his followers 'The Chromatic Circle and the Sensation of Colour'.[414] They were in direct contact with Henry, and Seurat made a very thorough study of Sutter's article. This is one of the very rare cases in the nineteenth century where aesthetics in the proper sense directly influenced artists – as long as we keep the academic art of the Salons out of the picture.

The idea of art being bound to fixed rules as to its purpose and execution is closely related to classicism. This relationship is very profound, so that R. Rey could rightly speak of *La renaissance du sentiment classique* (1921) in the title of his book, also with a view to Seurat and his adherents. Later artists, too, have been occupied with the search for artistic rules, although their art could by no means be called classical of expression. But if we look at Seurat's *Baignade* in the National Gallery in London, done in 1884 before he had arrived at pointillism through his contact with Signac, then the total impression is really classicistic or, if you will, classical: a quiet surveyable composition, a harmonious reality in which the figures suggest perfect calmness and ease of movement, without any vehement emotions in a clearly defined space. These are qualities that are also found in Raphael.

As a matter of fact, the first words in Seurat's 'manifest' quoted above were: 'l'art c'est l'harmonie'. In view of his 'origin',[415] as a pupil of Lehmann, who himself was an adept of Ingres, so much admired by Seurat, we need not find this strange. It is rather much more remarkable that he was never a classicist with respect to his subjects, but immediately took the side of the Realism of his time. Already his first important work, the *Baignade* just mentioned, is about a contemporary subject far from sublime. Not only in his subjects, but also in the forms he chooses, Seurat keeps entirely clear of any reminiscence of the art of antiquity or of that of classicist tradition. This once more clearly proves that classicism (in a traditional sense) had lost its hold on this generation. It had been owned too much by the academic works of the painters of the Salons like Bouguereau. Daumier's criticisms, contained in his lithographs which ridiculed classical subjects, had been deadly.

Seurat seems to have thought this so much a matter of course that he hardly mentions it. Fénéon accounts for it, though, when writing on the Neo-Impressionists in 1887. Then he said that, in contradistinction to the Impressionists who wished to fixate very evanescent effects, they strove to 'synthesize landscapes in a definite aspect which will preserve the sensation implicit in them . . . Objective reality is to them a simple theme for the creation of a higher and sublimated reality.'[416] Also Verhaeren was occupied with this facet when writing about Seurat's work at the exhibition of the XX: 'What the masters did to express their time, he attempts for his, and with equal care for exactness, concentration and sincerity . . . The gestures of the promenaders [in Seurat's *Grand Jatte*], the groups they form, their goings and comings, are essential.'[417] These pronouncements even more clearly illustrated the classicist tendency in Seurat's work. Thus a classicist of the academic tradition was likely to have spoken about his subjects and the relation to reality, although Seurat's classicist contemporaries (and their nineteenth-century predecessors) only wished to restrict themselves to so-called sublime subjects.

The great difference between Seurat and the Realists of his own time was especially to be found in his giving up naturalism, and his regaining the insight that a work of art represents reality in an iconic way. Goldwater has rightly pointed out that in building up his compositions Seurat sometimes worked from different visual points[418] and thus succeeded in rendering reality distinctly and clearly – even though in this way he came into conflict with the naturalistic laws of perspective. Seurat might also have been influenced indirectly, via the work of his contemporaries, by Japanese woodcuts. We are thinking, for example, of the dark figure at the bottom of the *Chahut*. So Seurat's art was determined by two directly related elements: the strong, rigorously balanced composition, entirely directed to the creation of aesthetic harmony, and the lucid and surveyable rendering of the permanent, essential meaning of the subject, in a configuration of representational forms that could only be understood iconically and not in a naturalistic way.

Finally, when Denis writes of Seurat, saying: 'He had the merit of attempting to regulate Impressionism ... this first effort against freedom,'[419] we understand at the same time why Seurat was not held in such high esteem by the Synthetists. For they wanted to maintain their freedom, however much their art and their art theory were akin to Seurat's.

Puvis de Chavannes

Puvis de Chavannes was held in high esteem by the artists who are the subject of our investigation.[420] If we pay exclusive attention to composition he was very much related to Seurat. But apart from technique, the greatest difference is to be sought in the subjects dealt with. For Puvis de Chavannes was certainly no Realist. All the same, he is not an academician either, no more in his subjects, as he generally avoided traditional allegories and tried to bring home to the spectator a particular idea or atmosphere, to express the latter, as it were, poetically in his pictorial compositions of figures elevated beyond time. In themselves these figures appear to be very naturalistic in that the nudes are free from the classicistic idealizing stylization. In this respect his work sometimes bore a strong resemblance to Corot's figure paintings. But at the same time there is a strong tendency to simplification: he omitted all that was superfluous, all (photographic) details. He made efforts to compose genuine mural paintings which filled larger areas decoratively and were clear and surveyable, without giving the impression of enlarged easel-pictures.

His compositions were very carefully done. By means of the play of line and colour, in the rhythmical arrangement of the groups and figures, he wanted to elucidate and to underline the poetic idea.[421] It is exactly at this point that the younger generation must have felt a kinship to him and must have been prepared to be taught by him. The structure of reality as we see it remains intact – as has been observed already, there was a distinctly naturalistic strain in his work in spite of his subjects and his simplifications. Did not Fontainas rightly observe with reference to his figures: 'They have not been disembodied by some vain caprice, but figured strictly in accordance with the essential necessities of matter.'[422]

That which Puvis really had in common with the Synthetists – and in this respect he may be called a predecessor – was the fact that he did not at all elaborate his poetic ideas as if they were (photographic) illustrations of a poem. And as far as historical pictures are concerned, as in his series in the Pantheon devoted to St Geneviève, they were not, as it were, a photographic reconstruction of the events. But he represented his subjects in a purely pictorial manner, elucidating the meaning and contents in a telling way by means of the structure of the composition and the arrangement of the colours. That he was thoroughly conscious of this procedure may appear from his pronouncement that 'For all clear ideas there exists a plastic thought that translates it.'[423] This idea must be made clear in an iconic way; 'I seek a scene that translates the idea exactly.'[424] And then he added that this kind of art might be called 'symbolism'.

Cézanne

The brilliant artist Cézanne played an important part in the formation of Synthetism, not personally so – for he had not only retired to Aix, but in addition he had broken off every contact with Gauguin – but by means of the works of his that were on view at Tanguy's[425] or were in the possession of Gauguin. We must, however, also take into account that Gauguin (together with Pissarro) had cooperated with him for some time[426] and that Cézanne's ideas may certainly have influenced Gauguin already in 1881. The question that must be asked, therefore, is what were Cézanne's theories in those days?

Looking through Cézanne's correspondence, it appears that hardly any theories of art occur in his earlier letters. In 1866 he wrote about the use of working in the open air,[427] and in 1878 he said something about the art of painting as a 'a means to express sensation'.[428] This observation made at the time when Cézanne was an Impressionist in the full sense of the word is only remarkable on account of the use of the term 'expression' instead of 'notation'. Perhaps we might detect here the first symptoms of a growing consciousness of what he expected from art. But then we have to wait till the end of the century before there is again any distinct utterance on the nature of his art and his views. He himself placed his work before anything, and in this respect he wished to be put in the right only 'on nature'[429] though he also felt the need to give his art a more or less theoretical foundation.[430]

Our impression is that there is a great deal of truth in Mauclair's statement, written down in 1922: 'All the theories on Cézanne's pictorial genius, all the praise of his synthetic art have been made afterwards, I saw their birth.'[431] In the Synthetist milieu the first efforts may have been made under the lead of Gauguin and Bernard to formulate the peculiar character of Cézanne's art also theoretically. And thus, together with the growing interest in his art, also a considerable dose of their own interpretation may have become common property for the Symbolists and Synthetists after 1890. Later on Cézanne repeatedly came into contact with younger artists who plied him with their questions about his art. In answer to their sympathetic questions he started formulating his ideas more adequately, the result of which we find in his letters written since 1900 or thereabouts, and also in other books that recorded contacts with the by then old Cézanne.[432]

Owing to the negative reactions to their compositions and the scantiness of the interest in their work the Impressionists faced a crisis around 1880[433] – which is why in the years that followed they all started to reflect thoroughly on their art and their method.[434] It is quite possible that precisely in these years Cézanne began to strive deliberately to 'Make of Impressionism something solid and durable like art in museums.'[435] And by the reflections and discussions that took place in this sense Gauguin as an artist who had only started around 1881 may have been deeply impressed. This might appear from a letter he wrote to Pissarro: 'Has M. Cézanne found the exact formula for a work acceptable to everyone? If he discovers the prescription for compressing the intense expression of all his sensations into a single and unique procedure, try to make him talk in his sleep.'[436] We may possibly find a precipitation of what was then discussed in a letter written by Gauguin in 1885 to Schuffenecker, in which he enters into details about the meaning of colours and lines as means of expression for what inspired the artist. And then he immediately goes on to say: 'Look at Cézanne, who was not understood, who had the essentially mystical nature of the East . . . in the form he loves a mystery and the heavy tranquility of a man lying down to dream, his colours are grave like the character of orientals', and he continues by saying that 'The further I go the more I come to work in the way of translating thoughts by entirely different means from those of literature.'[437]

Even if we should have to assume that, in his view of the symbolic meaning of lines and colours, and in his wish thus to give more than is perceived by the eye, he was inspired by the ideas advanced at that period by literary men or possibly even by Seurat, the fact remains that he cites Cézanne as evidence. It may be that via Cézanne, Gauguin had got into touch with the first start of the new ideas that were taking shape in authors such as Huysmans – for Cézanne followed their work closely.[438] For the rest, both Cézanne and Gauguin had been acquainted with the writings of Baudelaire and Balzac and, of course, with the art of Delacroix (perhaps also with the latter artist's writings published shortly after his death). Although, therefore, the part that Cézanne played with respect to the formation of the new theories of art is by no means clear, it is certain that Gauguin considered his own art with an eye to this. And that he thought he was working in accordance with Cézanne's ideas may appear from the fact that later on, around 1890, when preparing to make a picture he often used to say: 'Let's make a Cézanne.'[439] And yet Gauguin's work had hardly anything in common with Cézanne's as far as style is concerned – which all the more proves that this was in the first place a matter of conception and approach.

Considering Cézanne's art-theoretical contemplations as he formulated them later on when Synthetism had fully developed, we may say that he wished to combine two elements in his art. He wanted to produce an art which should be an interpretation of nature, giving a human vision of what is permanent and meaningful, but at the same time the result of direct observation after the manner of the Impressionists. This is expressed most clearly and concisely in the demand: 'What is needed is to renew Poussin looking at nature.'[440] What he meant by it will become clear when we read: 'In a painter there are two things: his eyes and his brains, which should help each other; we must try to further their mutual development but as a painter: the eye, by looking directly at nature; the brains, by means of the logic of the organized sensations which supply the means of expression.'[441] That in this we are confronted with the striving to retain that which Impressionism had brought and at the same time to give human freedom its due, thus bringing about a synthesis of nature and freedom, may appear from the following: 'One is neither too scrupulous, nor too sincere, nor too much submissive to nature; but one is more or less master of one's model, and above all of one's means of expression. Penetrate what one has in front of one and persevere expressing oneself as logically as possible.'[442]

Cézanne did not in the first place seek to render what is transitory and momentaneous in the impressions of nature but much rather to elucidate nature in its structure and meaning for the thinking and feeling person: 'Nature is always the same but nothing of it remains of what appears to us. Our art should give us a shiver of its duration with the elements, the appearances of all the changes.'[443] We get the impression that Cézanne in his work as well as in his ideas found great difficulty in accomplishing something that previous generations, for instance Jan van Goyen, considered as a matter of course. Just as in the case of Delacroix we are aware of the consequences of the increasing influence of the epistemological theories that had occupied the minds of people since the eighteenth century. Did he not say that 'The painter concretizes his sensations and his perceptions by means of the design and the colours.'[444]

It stands to reason that in this attempt Cézanne was obliged to occupy himself thoroughly with the pictorial means as such. This is clear from the previous quotations, and it is especially obvious in his frequently occurring pronouncement that intensive observation was at least as indispensable as 'the knowledge of the means of expressing emotion'.[445] And while working and thinking in this direction, he again came upon the insight that a work of art can never catch hold of reality as such, that which is given by our observation; but that such reality must be represented in a different, that is to say, in an iconic way. 'I have wanted to copy nature – I have not been successful. I was satisfied about myself when I discovered that, e.g., the sun [the objects in the sunshine] could not he reproduced, but that it was necessary to represent it by something else than by what I saw – by colours.'[446]

No doubt Cézanne's toilsome striving testifies to a high degree of originality. With respect to his art this is incontestable. But it is possible indeed to hesitate with respect to his art-theoretical ideas. For to what extent had he been influenced by what was going on in Symbolist-Synthetist circles? Even if he rarely came into contact with them, he is sure to have read about them, and to have made acquaintance with their (literary) work in whatever measure this may have been. And, besides, in what sense were the younger artists who came to him around the turn of the century contributors to his ideas? For already by the questions they asked they influenced his thoughts. Although we cannot ignore the influence of Synthetism without more ado, Cézanne's formulations are certainly his own and original. They were bound to be so, for his own art, which had by no means arisen 'spontaneously' but owed its existence to careful consideration, was totally different in style and partly also in its subjects from that of the Synthetists.

In summary, and in an attempt to define Cézanne's position in relation to Gauguin and his followers, we might submit the following quotation, which probably contains more truth than would be supposed at first sight: 'The reconstruction of Art started by Cézanne with the means of Impressionism has been continued by Gauguin with less sensibility and scope, but with greater theoretical rigour. He has rendered Cézanne's thought more explicit.'[447]

Van Gogh

Although van Gogh was a Dutchman, his art can scarcely be said to have its origin exclusively in the Dutch artistic traditions or to be directly connected with what was produced in the Netherlands at the time.

He may have studied with Mauve for a short time and may have had a good look at the work of his contemporaries, but already from the beginning he was very well acquainted with what was achieved in the art of painting abroad, especially in England and in France. He learnt about art as an employee in an art business and therefore especially about the more or less 'current' art. Only during his stay in Paris after 1885 did he come into direct contact with the Impressionists and with others who worked outside the official art world.

Both from his choice of authors – Michelet, for instance[448] – and from his predilection for particular artists – Lhermitte, Millet and others[449] – it is clear that from the moment he began to devote himself to the art of painting he was a whole-hearted adherent to Realism. And so he remained all his life. This becomes clear from his controversy with Bernard concerning the treatment of biblical subjects:

> It is undoubtedly wise and just to be moved by the Bible, but the realities of today have so taken hold of us that, even when attempting abstractly to reconstruct ancient times in our thoughts, our meditations are broken into by minor events of our daily life and we are brought back forcibly by our own experiences into the world of personal sensations – joy, boredom, suffering, anger and laughter.[450]

This preference for Realism was, doubtless, very deeply rooted, namely in a view of life and the world in which the humanistic motif of nature was given main emphasis. Did not his brother Theo – who knew him through and through – write that Vincent considered living beings as tightly bound to nature?[451] That is why he objected to working from a dream – the creative daydream as the Synthetists understood it. He much rather started from a thought which is more closely bound to natural reality.[452] This shows that he nevertheless did not want to fixate the fugitive impressions of nature as the Impressionists tried to do but wished to express the human view of it, inclusive of the subjective feelings aroused by the subject. With a view to this he is sure to be much more arbitrary in his use of colours,[453] which also shows his urge for freedom.

Van Gogh's mind may also be understood when we study the names of the artists he appeared to admire most once he had made a thorough acquaintance with French art in its different facets, also outside the Salons. They are Daumier, Ziem, Millet, Théodore Rousseau,[454] Monticelli and, of course, Delacroix.[455] He strongly disliked Ingres, Raphael and Degas.[456] It is quite possible that his being a Dutchman played some part in his reaction to the latter artists. For in the Northern Dutch mentality the Calvinistic Protestant tradition is a strong co-determinant, for which ultimately the world of beautiful harmonious forms created by the classicist masters with refined aestheticism implies a lie. The more Roman Catholic humanistic dream of the harmonious human being is foreign to it, while in building up the ideal reality in the pictorial image too little account is taken of the fact of our living on a cursed earth. All this was certainly true in van Gogh's case as he came from a church minister's family, however modernist they were and however estranged he was from them. For the formative influence of a view of life that has been dominant for many centuries cannot be turned into an entirely different direction at a moment's notice, and certainly not in these deeper strata of a person's being where judgments are more or less 'instinctive'[457] and taste and commitment to a position are more or less unreasoned.

On the other hand his predilection proves that he understood the Realists, as well as those who manifested a profoundly Romantic sympathy with nature. Surely he wished to keep within the limits of what is possible: 'Personally I love things that are real, that are possible.'[458] The atmosphere Baudelaire or Meryon evoked in their works was uncongenial to him, not only on account of their estrangement from reality, which he certainly felt to be present in them – did he not speak about 'the melancholy after the manner of Meryon'[459] – but also because of their search for what was irrational, strange, and unreal – did he not oppose 'the Baudelaire aspect of Paris' and prefer the 'the possible, the logical, the real'?[460]

Although later on he became mentally deranged, it appears that – apart from the periods in which he had an attack which made every kind of orderly thinking or working impossible – he was not at all open to a 'morbid' mental attitude that was capable of being entirely wrapped up in the *fleurs du mal*. It is perhaps possible to explain his extreme sensitivity, his inconceivably fast and fiercely concentrated way of working during his Arles period, like one possessed, as signifying the approach of a fit of mental derangement. But the opposite interpretation is also possible! We consider it to be rather risky to explain his artistic ideas as the effects of a diseased mind. When, for instance, Jaspers supposes that van Gogh's striving after the symbolic use of colours is connected with this derangement[461] it would amount to declaring that the whole of this group of artists, inclusive of Delacroix and Baudelaire, were mentally diseased!

But the fact that he was such a pronounced Realist does not at all imply that he was a naturalist. On the contrary! Already at the time when he was at Antwerp he rejected the academic naturalistic method. 'That academy is a mistress preventing a more serious, more ardent, more fruitful love from awakening in you – leave that mistress alone and fall head over heels in love with your proper beloved lady nature or reality.'[462] He seeks for a method that will be better suitable to do justice to reality than the naturalistic manner: 'Well, one loses that general harmony of tones in nature by painfully exact imitation; one keeps it by recreating in a parallel colour scale which may be not exactly, or even far from exactly, like the model,'[463] he wrote when still living in Brabant.

His thoughts developed in this direction later on, especially in response to the stimulating influence of people like Gauguin and the influence of Japanese art. And this is why he was not only very proud – with a pride born of modesty – when in 1890 at St Remy he read Aurier's article about him, but he also thought that the latter had written how he ought to paint.[464] For Aurier wrote:

> He is no doubt very conscious of pigment, of its importance and beauty, but also, and most frequently, he considers his enchanting pigment only as a kind of marvelous language destined to express the Idea. Almost always he is a Symbolist . . . feeling the constant urge to clothe his ideas in precise, ponderable, tangible forms, in intensely corporeal and material envelopes.[465]

As a matter of fact he himself more than once wrote in the same spirit. A very frank instance is the following: 'I am always in the hope of making a discovery there, to express the love of two lovers by a marriage of two complementaries, their mingling and their opposition, the mysterious vibrations of kindred tones. To express the thought of a brow by the radiance of light tones against a somber background.'[466] That he expressed himself rather modestly and metaphorically when speaking of his hope to discover something, may appear when we read what he wrote about the painting representing his bedroom. He explained how he expressed quiet and peace precisely in the colours and the manner in which he had treated the subject.[467]

In such a way he tried to find the synthesis, that is, the expression of the human vision of a very realistically conceived subject as such. Thus a thought will be expressed by means of an image which does not violate reality. In connection with his controversy with Bernard about the latter's *Christ in the Olive Garden* he wrote to Theo that Bernard was wrong in omitting to try and make a clear image of the reality of things and that 'This is not the way to synthesize.'[468] But in order to make the representation of (visual) reality into an expression of a thought it is of course necessary to lay some particular emphasis on colour and line which deviate from what is perceived with the eye. He then called such use of colour 'arbitrary'.[469] This shows that naturalism had had such a profound influence on the minds of people that a deviation from strict naturalism was felt to be something arbitrary, even by him who practised it with full conviction. It was, therefore, possible only for a person with a strong disposition to enable his or her own personality and own subjectivity to express themselves. In this particular sense of synthesis there is the search for more than a new method only, for there was also a striving after a kind of equilibrium that would allow both the motif of nature and that of freedom to be given their due.

As a direct consequence of this striving van Gogh made the re-discovery of the iconic, that is, he became conscious of the fact that artistic painting is intended to express a human vision by means of pictorial art, without copying reality in a naturalistic-photographic way. He appeared to be thoroughly aware of this state of affairs: 'I cannot work without a model. I don't say that I do not frankly turn my back upon nature in order to transform a study into a picture by arranging the colours, by enlargement and simplification.'[470] He also saw sharply the difference between this method and that of earlier artists who had expressed their thoughts primarily by means of their subjects, while their way of painting itself had remained naturalistic.[471] This is why he said: 'It is not a return to Romanticism or to religious ideas, no. However, by passing by Delacroix even more than it appears, by colours and by the drawing which are much more arbitrary than deceptive exactness, one would express a country scene.'[472] That this quotation is really concerned with the subjects (so not with Romanticism or Christianity in the sense of a view of life) may very clearly appear from what he wrote to Bernard half a year later 'to remind you that to create an impression of agony one may try to perform this without straightway aiming at a Garden of Olives in historical Gethsemane, in order to give a sweet and consoling motif it is not necessary to represent the characters of the Sermon on the Mount'.[473]

Van Gogh no doubt arrived at these conceptions on his own account – the fact that he had to teach a lesson on these views to Bernard who later on asserted to have been the inventor of Synthetism, is very remarkable – although we should not exclude the influence of such contemporaries as Gauguin, Seurat and possibly a few others. But Delacroix was certainly very important for van Gogh, and this pretty well without the former's literary writings or the explanations of Baudelaire. It appears from this brief summary by van Gogh himself: 'I rather come back to what I sought before coming to Paris, and I do not know if anyone before me spoke about suggestive colour, but Delacroix and Monticelli produced it without having talked about it.'[474] So he seemed to have forgotten that at one time he had sent Theo cuttings from a paper on Delacroix's use of colour, in which there occurred various quotations from the latter's literary work. For the rest, it is quite conceivable that also Carlyle's Sartor Resartus had exercised some influence on the formation of these ideas during the days at Nuenen.[475]

But, though it appears that at the time when the theories of the Synthetists were elaborated van Gogh is not likely to have had a direct influence on them – for he was in the south of France and far removed from them at that time – it is possible that he may have inspired the thoughts of these Frenchmen on two occasions: the first being when, having just arrived in Paris from the North, he came into contact with Gauguin and Bernard. On the whole, however, we think that he was then rather receptive than suggestive, and sure to have abandoned this theory (recall the above quotation) rather than to have passed it on to others. The second opportunity was when Gauguin stayed with van Gogh at Arles during 1888.[476] Although the importance of a few letters should not be entirely passed over in silence, we do not believe that they were of decisive significance in this respect. If we were to give a short summary of the role of van Gogh with regard to the Synthetists, we might say that he was a parallel figure who exercised some influence on them.

Rive Droite

In addition to the view of life and the world and the conceptions of art founded in it, the formation of the individual character of a particular art is also influenced by the style of living, the social environment that is sought, and the way one behaves in it. If anywhere, this is especially clear in the case of the artists of the *Rive Droite*. As soon as we make a closer investigation of their work, we hear about clubs, cabarets and so on, and we are obliged to get acquainted with the motley nightlife of Montmartre as it was spent at the end of the century at the *Chat-Noir* of Rodolphe Salis[477] and among such ephemeral groups as that of the Hydropathes, Hirsutes, Zutistes and Jemenfoutistes, whose very names can already enlighten us about the *blague* and *esprit* cultivated there.

One of the first typical artists in this milieu was Félicien Rops, originally a Realist who was in close contact with what was going on in this field in Belgium in the 1860s. Later on, however, he was entirely taken up with the production of prints, drawings and illustrations which were not quite free from pornography. 'Rops has nothing mystical or neurotic. He is a sane mind in a sound body disdainful of all weak bashfulness, happy in exalting his virility,'[478] wrote one of his admirers. 'I simply and stupidly try to render what I feel with my nerves and what I see with my eyes: this is the whole of my theory of art,'[479] he wrote himself. But, of course, then the question is what he felt and saw. And this is very concisely described by the words: 'Up till now nobody has so profoundly handled the catholic notion of lewdness, the demoniac pleasure of perversity, that which lies beyond evil.'[480] He had wanted to be a great painter, and might have become one under the influence of Baudelaire, whom he knew very well, but ultimately he occupied himself exclusively with illustrating the works of such writers as the Goncourts, Huysmans, Verlaine and others, and between 1880 and 1890 was most sought after as an illustrator.[481]

After 1890 or thereabouts Rops' role was at an end, but the painters of Montmartre like Villette, Léandre, Forain and Steinlen (whose work strongly influenced by socialistic ideas we shall leave out of account at present), continued working in the spirit of Rops. Their work may perhaps best be characterized by the 'Programme' that Forain inserted in his paper *Le Fifre*:

> Telling about the life of every day, showing the ridiculousness of certain sorrows, the sadness of a great many joys, and stating roughly sometimes in what a hypocritical manner vice is inclined to manifest itself in us: this is my

project. I am an imaginative seeker, I will go everywhere endeavouring to render distinctly and immediately, and as sincerely as possible, the impressions and emotions that I feel.[482]

It is exactly this term *fantaisiste* ('imaginative') which denotes their wide difference from the Synthetists proper, with whom they had a great deal in common, but from whom they were separated by the wide and deep Seine. For the Synthetists lived and worked on the *Rive Gauche*: 'The symbolists looked down upon the *Chat-Noir* and on the artists of Montmartre: they were of the 'Rive Gauche' (the left bank of the Seine), stand-offish, rather lofty, and though they allowed humour, they would have thought laughter at a joke unworthy of themselves.'[483] This was written by Mauclair, a faithful follower of Mallarmé and a reliable witness who lived at the time.

At the moment it is not necessary to discuss Toulouse-Lautrec, the greatest artist in this milieu, who obtained a lighter tone and strove after a kind of 'Degas-Realism' in an easy style that appreciated the strictly subjective 'handwriting'. His art was in the first place graphic and he was influenced by Japanese art – via Gauguin, Art Nouveau, and also directly. All this did not make him that different from his contemporaries, however. He differed from them rather by his sharper observation, his more telling characterization, his faultless composition and his controlled delicate style of drawing.

Trying to define the greatest common denominator of the artists dealt with in this chapter and that which united them, we may point out that they all started from Realism or Impressionism, with the exception of Puvis de Chavannes who had, after all, greater affinity with Ingres. They were contemporaries of the Symbolist painters such as Moreau, but there was hardly any relationship. No more did they play a part in, or belonged to the Art Nouveau movement. Although they wished to conquer the world of the Salon, they remained faithful to Realism with respect to their subjects. And at least two of them, Cézanne and van Gogh, gained insight into the characteristic element peculiar to the art of painting, namely the iconic element, of which van Gogh once said: 'It is not the deceptive appearance of Realism,[484] but is it not something really existing?'[485] Indeed, in art the issue is always this: What is expressed? And, what does reality ultimately mean to the artist?

5
The Artistic Ideals of the Synthetists

Anti-naturalism

The generation that came to the fore in the 1890s was not only mature enough but also anxious to adopt new ideas, to help build up a new art. Thus Denis wrote that a number of younger men working in the studios of Cormon and Julian were favourably disposed to all that was new and attacked the old: 'We went to those who had done away not only with academic teaching but also and above all with naturalism, either of the Romantic or the photographic kind, at that time universally acknowledged as the sole theory that was worthy of a scientific and democratic epoch.'[486] They felt the artistic and the cultural situation connected with it to be very unsatisfactory; especially the fact that the art with which they came into contact in no way presented an elevated aspect will have induced them to search for something else. Another factor doubtlessly was the presence of a strong movement among the young men of letters who wanted to strike out on new paths to find an art that would be different from the prevailing naturalism according to Zola's sense. They discussed it a great deal.[487] The climate of their thoughts will be found reflected in Aurier's works of a somewhat later date which better formulated all this:

> The natural sciences, or the inexact sciences, in opposition to rational or exact sciences which are by definition insusceptible of absolute solutions, have the fatal tendency to lead to scepticism and to the fear of thought. We must, therefore, accuse them of having made for us this society without faith, so common-place, incapable of those thousand intellectual or sentimental manifestations that might be comprised under the name of devotion. They are, consequently, responsible ... for the poverty of our art to which they have assigned imitation as its unique domain, the only aim that can be verified by experimental methods.

Thus we have arrived at 'pure animality', and that is why a reaction was needed: 'We must again cultivate the higher qualities of the soul.'[488] But not only the literary groups of their time with their numerous periodicals will have caused them to react against the prevailing mentality with its faith in the sciences. Also Delacroix and Baudelaire had already pointed out how much art was impoverished by the predominance of positivistic naturalism. The latter wrote: 'With us the painter of nature ... is almost a monster. The exclusive preference for truth[489] suppresses and suffocates the sense of what is beautiful ... He [the artist] feels or rather judges in succession, analytically.'[490]

Baudelaire's *Curiosités Esthétiques* from which we quoted was published at this time, in 1884. Also Delacroix had more than once expressed himself in the same spirit,[491] and they may have been acquainted with it by means of G. Dargenty's book: *E. Delacroix par lui-même*, published in 1885. No doubt Delacroix's own work was also important in this respect.

Gauguin too frequently fulminated against every naturalism: 'We have lapsed into the abominable error of naturalism.'[492] This pronouncement leaves nothing to be desired as regards clarity. He, too, seeks the cause of the error in the science ideal: 'They sought what was visible round about them and not what was in the mysterious centre of thought, and thus they fell into scientific reasonings.'[493] And even at the end of his life he deems it necessary to explain to Morice that the past period was so much influenced by physics, chemistry and the study of nature that the artists had lost 'the force to create'.[494]

This is how matters looked in the milieu to which we are directing our attention at the moment, one in which 'The short-sighted copy of social anecdotes, the imbecile imitation of the warts of nature, the flat observation, the trompe l'oeil, the glory of being as faithfully and vulgarly exact as a daguerréotype, no longer satisfies any painter worthy of the name.'[495] But we shall have to resist the temptation to give more quotations that illustrate what Denis summarized in one short sentence: 'They have propagated the hatred of naturalism.'[496]

It is clear that these artists could not develop or approve of a view of art with a scientific tinge. This is no doubt the basis of their rejection of Seurat's theories – Seurat's style was quite new and original, and in some respects he showed affinity with these artists, but his theory was too much determined by this hateful physics. With reference to the creation of his own work, Gauguin therefore says explicitly: 'Where does the execution of a picture begin and where does it end? At the moment when the extreme sentiments are being fused in the deepest of being, when they explode and all thought is thrown out like lava from a volcano, is not there a breaking forth of the work which is suddenly created? The cold calculations of reason have not preceded this explosion.'[497]

Subjectivism

We cannot be surprised to find the demand for an art that was subjective, in which consequently the maker's personality expressed itself. 'Instead of working round about the eye we looked for the mysterious centre of thought,' as Gauguin put it. The imagination again became the queen of the faculties, as Baudelaire had demanded. 'Thus we liberated our sensibility, and instead being the copy of nature art became the subjective deformation of nature,' wrote Denis.[498]

It is, of course, true that also Impressionism, and even the positivistic philosophy and aesthetics – say, of Taine – were already subjectivistic. This has been pointed out by Aurier in his article on the *peintres symbolistes*, in which he said that also naturalism represented reality 'seen through the medium of a temperament'. But he is not satisfied with that which Zola (who is not mentioned here) meant. For the work of art as such must be 'a visible sign of this temperament' or, better still, a symbol of this personality, 'the symbol of the ideational and sensitive totality of the worker'.[499]

Individualism

Without a doubt there is a strongly individualistic trait in all this. 'We strove after the joy of self-expression as the young authors demanded at that period,'[500] Denis wrote. But then he immediately goes on to say that the theory of the equivalents provides him with the means to accomplish this so that, as we shall see, the bond with reality is retained. We should not think this individualism to be of the extreme philosophical kind approaching solipsism, but rather to be the artist's freedom to express in a strictly personal way what he or she considers to be meaningful in reality – which, therefore, has a claim to being truthful.[501]

Synthesis

One of the remarkable things in the world of thought at that time was a striving to clarify in the work of art the artist's personal vision, that which impresses him or her in a strictly individual sense, but at the same time to represent and elucidate reality itself in its deepest essence. The fundamental idea of the *synthèse* has been developed precisely to solve this contradiction. Thus Aurier says: 'What is a poem? A synthesis of all the general ideas perceived by a given self.'[502] Which satisfies Baudelaire's demand made upon 'pure art according to the modern conception; the creation of a suggestive kind of magic containing the object simultaneously with the subject, the outer world and the artist himself'.[503] Baudelaire, however, also wrote: 'The artist does not reveal but himself ... He has been his own king, his own priest and his own god.'[504] This proves that the contradiction had existed already earlier on.

We might summarize the actual state of affairs best as follows: these artists wanted to claim freedom for human beings again, also as individual persons. For this purpose a person had to be freed from the grasp of nature as it had become predominant by positivistic science. But they themselves were tied down very tightly by this reality as well, so that a complete realization of their freedom in the work of art was not yet possible to them.

What they sought was in fact to get free from the making of a photographical record of reality as seen in a positivistic view, hence the freedom from naturalism. There was as yet no question of getting loose from nature in its concrete real structure. They did not yet think of abstract (non-figurative) art, such as was to arise some twenty years later. At any rate they never wrote about it. And the individualistic realization of their own freedom apart from any reality outside of human being, as is found among experimentalists, tachists and similar groups, was still entirely beyond their horizon. But the urge for such absolute freedom was alive in their hearts and drove them on in their search for a new art not bound by nature.

Freedom

In what has so far been said we have already come upon the motif of freedom which assumed the form of the personality ideal,[505] the wish to express oneself, to note down and objectify one's own internal vision and motives. This freedom motif[506] also manifested itself in the wish to dominate nature. The difference between the primacy of the motif of nature in the science ideal and in artistic naturalism and his own attitude is very clearly indicated by Gauguin's words:

> Primitive art proceeds from the spirit and uses nature. So-called refined art proceeds from the senses and serves nature. Nature is the housemaid of the former and the mistress of the latter, but the housemaid cannot forget her origin and degrades the spirit by allowing him to adore her. This now is how we have fallen into the abominable error of naturalism.[507]

Thus they aimed at an art in which one could use nature at will to express one's own ideas. Hence their frequent demand not to paint from the model, but from memory. Their ideals of that time found splendid expression in Denis' (later) summary of the development of their art in those years:

> In Paris, every year, with the Independents ... he[508] sees what work is going on, apparently towards more freedom, in reality towards more reason and order, a new order, paradoxical, an order derived from the Symbolist arduous toil and whose success indicated the triumph of the spirit of synthesis over that of analysis, of the imagination over sensation, of man over nature.[509]

As has been observed above, the extreme profession of freedom in its ultimate consequences was not yet found at the time around 1890. Also the letters of that period that have come down to us are silent about it. It was especially Gauguin whose thought turned in this direction consistently in later years, and who posited that by realizing the artist's freedom over against nature his work made absolute freedom possible for later generations. This is also the reason why he posits that the artists rather than the public will have to be grateful to him.510 This new conception of freedom that urged them on implicitly in all their efforts to create a new style in the years between 1885 and 1890 had not yet become explicitly conscious. It became so in Gauguin's words in 1902:

> While taking into account the efforts and the investigations, even those of science, it was, necessary to think of a complete liberation, to break the windowpanes at the risk of cutting one's finger, to leave it to the next generation, henceforth independent, free from any shackles, to solve the problem completely. I do not say definitively, for it exactly means an art without strict boundaries, rich in all kinds of technique, fit to translate all the emotions of nature and man. For this purpose it was necessary to risk body and soul in the struggle, a struggle against all the schools, all of them without any distinction, not by disparaging them, but by something else, by offending not only the officials but also the Impressionists, the Neo-Impressionists, the older and the newer kind of public ... And as to the work, a method of contradiction, if you like, venturing into the strongest abstractions,511 doing all that was forbidden, and reconstructing more or less happily, without any fear of exaggeration, even with exaggeration. Learning anew, and then, once having learnt, learn again. Conquer any timidity however much ridicule it may occasion. In front of his easel the painter is no slave, either of the past or of the present, either of nature or of his neighbour. He is himself, again himself, always himself. This effort of which I am speaking was made twenty years ago in silence in a state of ignorance, and then it began to assert itself.512

Rarely has an artistic ideal been formulated so lucidly and exactly – Gauguin himself has hardly realized this program. That was to be the work of the twentieth century.

Realism

Summarizing the requirements made by the Synthetists, we can say that they aimed at a subjective kind of art trying to clarify what is strictly personal, also in the reaction to the outer world, in a way that was not naturalistic. It would be possible to say the same thing about Delacroix's work, so that it is not surprising that they admired it very much. But they were not trying to revive Romanticism. They attempted to express this mental attitude in an entirely new way.

In 1892 somebody wrote: 'Their ideal is no doubt different from that of Romanticism; they take no pleasure in the vehement expression of the passions nor of the feelings of the heart . . . they clothe an abstract truth in the garb of dazzling realities.'513 Indeed, in their opinion Romanticism did not penetrate deep enough and remained too superficial. For what was Romanticism? According to Morice: 'It is not the deepest essence of the passions, it is their exterior gesticulation, their active manifestation.'[514] In other words, it remained too much only human passion as such, and did not give an insight into full reality. For, above all, they wanted to grasp this full reality in their art. In connection with this we should never forget that all these artists originated from the school of the Realists – in Courbet's sense – and from the Impressionists,[515] and that in this respect they were separated by a large gulf from the painters we have called Symbolists and who are characterized by Denis as 'painters of the soul'.[516] They were very keenly aware of the shortcomings of the positivistic ideal of art but wanted to keep hold of nature in their art. Their objection is exactly the fact that naturalism does not do sufficient justice to some part of reality,[517] whereas we have seen that Romanticism took too little account of nature and rendered the external appearance of passions only. They might be said to have aimed at correcting both Romanticism and positivism by not only uniting them but by digging deeper than was possible for either by virtue of its starting point. Thus Denis writes about his fellows: 'They were minds with a passion for truth, living in communion with nature . . . If they were induced to deform, to compose – things that had not been done by their immediate precursors – it was also in order to achieve greater sincerity in the rendering of their sensations.'[518] Their predecessors had failed somewhere in the realization of their own starting point, according to Denis. The literary artist who was closely related to them, Morice, expressed all this in a little more obscure and poetical language, but it boiled down to the same thing. He spoke of 'that intense contemporaneous desire of the human mind to combine the mystic and the scientific stream into one large and living river of Beauty united with Truth in joy'.[519] Then there would be 'Integral Art'.[520]

They did not give up Realism in their subjects. For there was another valid reason why in giving up naturalism they did not resort again to expressing their vision allegorically, as for instance the Symbolists had done. This reason was expressed tersely and concisely by Delacroix in a note dating as far back as the year 1820. How much more it must have been applicable to the situation at the end of the century when academism had become increasingly more superficial. Delacroix observed the following in his note: 'I contend that anyone who plunges into allegory will be compelled to find such strong, novel and sublime ideas that without the resource of Pallas, Minerve, the Graces, Amor, Discord, etc., turned a hundred different ways, he will be cold, obscure, flat, common.'[521] And however paradoxical it may seem to be, the avoidance of such vulgarity and obscurity was the very reason (for these were also their grievances against the art of their time) why they stuck to Realism in their subjects. In rendering 'ordinary reality' they tried to express its meaning rather than what was seen with the eye. For this, too, they could appeal to Baudelaire, and from this point of view it is easily understood why they admired such works as Balzac's *Séraphita*[522] – seemingly so naturalistic (in Zola's sense) but in reality presenting so much more.

In art they tried to grant the artist freedom to express him or herself, even to rule, it is true, but in such a way as to embrace everything that escaped the positivistic analysis of reality, and to incorporate all this into the whole that they designed. Again Gauguin and Morice[523] gave clear expression to these things in the following words – which should be understood as an artistic ideal rather than as an instance of overestimation of themselves:

> [The artist] is master of truth, of life. He brings you living nature. The invention that you reproach him for, which you mistrust, is precisely the soul of his work, the breath that makes it alive, the warmth and the water that flowers cut off from their stem lack, causing them to wither too soon – Invention is the life of the works, the invention that circulates like blood through the elements borrowed from Nature by imitation.

For the highest thing will be if,

> a great artist has crowned one of the innumerable beautiful figures of Nature with his genius when the artist, himself a child of Nature,[524] nourished by her, living on her, rises to express the beauty of his mother: when Nature by one of the changing aspects of her mysterious countenance eternalize the word of her enigma in the work of art. [525]

Art and nature

Denis expressed this ideal less poetically when he wrote:

> Perhaps one day they will attain to Nature: that is, their conception of things will possibly become complete and profound enough for the work of art realized by them to preserve all the logical relations that form the essential character of living Nature, and thus there will be a greater analogy between the object and the subject, between the creation[526] and the image that they will have reconstructed.'[527]

What this meant to him appears from what he says about Gauguin's *Calvaire* and kindred works: 'From the canvas itself, a flat surface covered with colours, springs the bitter or the soothing emotion, "literary" as the painters put it, without any need to interpose the memory of another old sensation (like that of the motif of nature utilized).' The latter statement constitutes their great difference from the Symbolist painters we have discussed in our third chapter. 'In one the form is expressive, in another nature wants to be so.'[528]

Indeed they aimed at elucidating the meaning of nature, and at expressing their idea of it with the aid of purely artistic means, without expressing this idea in an explicitly figurative way by means of allegory and the like. And for this purpose they sought for the expressive power implied in particular lines and colours. 'Look about you in the immense creation of nature and you will see if there are no laws to create all human sentiments with altogether different means and yet similar in their effect,'[529] Gauguin wrote in 1885 in a letter we shall revert to later.

'Instead of evoking our mental states by means of the subject represented, it was the work itself which was to transmit the initial sensation and perpetuate the emotion.'[530] They strove after this and the idea was to have a great influence later on, especially in Expressionism. This was the new element separating them from the Symbolist painters. But this was not their sole aim. The arrangement of colours and lines had to be beautiful too.

Much more than the Symbolist milieu these artists were always occupied with purely painterly questions. From a reaction against academic art they again clearly realized that after all a picture is a two-dimensional area. This idea was given a very extreme form of expression in Denis' now famous utterance – too famous, because it denoted a facet of their striving, it is true, but not the essence of their art: 'to remember that a picture – before being a warhorse, a nude woman or whatever sort of anecdote – is essentially a flat surface covered with colours arranged in a particular order'.[531]

6
The Origin and Development of the Synthetist Theory of Art 1885–1890

Gauguin and the artists of his circle were no doubt revolutionaries striving after a complete break with the existing state of affairs. But they did not look down on the achievements of the past. On the contrary, they often felt they were merely winning back what had been lost over the course of time – especially during the previous hundred years. Gauguin often explicitly confessed his admiration for Raphael and Ingres [532] and Denis calls this movement of 1890 'neo-traditionalism'. They also admired Delacroix and Cézanne, whom they considered earlier masters and precursors.

Reflection and contemplation always accompanied their artistic work proper. This is almost a matter of course. If an artist does not just paint according to the 'fashion' of the times, the 'current' method, but fiercely reacts against contemporary and current things, it is necessary for him or her to have a clear realization and not merely to adopt a negative attitude. What former generations had considered as only a matter of course had to be recovered by reflection and ratiocination. The Synthetists sometimes felt their own non-naturalistic method to be something 'arbitrary'.[533] This proves that they were so much imbued with the naturalistic way of thought that any deviation from it seemed to them to be a deviation from the norm. This is the reason why the revolutionary character of their work is less obvious to us now than it was then. We look back on this development and we witness the realization of the freedom of the twentieth century. They were still very close to naturalism and Impressionism, and when they simply gave their figures an outline or slightly stylized them, this process was experienced as an extreme conquest of their own freedom.

In view of this situation it is to be understood that these first works made the spectators ask 'why?' and 'wherefore?' – just as is the case at present with abstract art or other kinds of modernistic work – so that the artists were compelled to give an account of their own activities and aims. For, as Aurier says, 'It was necessary to justify (ideist art)[534] by abstract and complicated reasonings, so much did it seem to be paradoxical to our decadent civilizations that had forgotten all about initial revelation.'[535] Besides, the introductory word was also important to convince fellow artists of the rightness of their starting point. For this purpose it was necessary to show that the impasse into which art had landed could be overcome. It is, therefore, not surprising to hear Denis say: 'Besides, Sérusier proved to us by means of Hegel, and the difficult articles by Albert Aurier insisted on the fact that, logically and philosophically speaking, Gauguin was right.'[536] Very often, no doubt, the words and thoughts of the predecessors rather than their works as such will have induced young painters to prefer the new movement.

It should not be supposed that the theories were made afterwards only to justify the works of the artists. On the contrary, when examining the development in this circle we shall more often find that theory and reflection preceded its realization or concretizing in a work of art. As a matter of fact, with them action and thought, painting and talking, always accompanied each other and were indissolubly interwoven in the totality of their evolution. For their art was not an 'applied theory' however much reflection influenced their method. This is why in our expositions of the development of their theories we shall often have to refer to the pictures themselves to illustrate the stylistic evolution.

Gauguin's early development

We have already seen Cézanne's probable influence that led to the first formation of a trend of thought in Gauguin that deviated from strict Impressionism. But this cannot possibly explain the ideas that Gauguin expounded in his famous letter from Copenhagen to Schuffenecker in the year 1885. We must, doubtless, remember that Gauguin was acquainted with what was going on in Paris.[537] Although Gauguin was not actively or thoroughly preoccupied with the literary developments during those years, the main points will not have escaped him, even if only through what he had probably read in the *Figaro*.[538] He will no doubt have read Baudelaire's *Curiosités Esthétiques* published in 1884 – even if only on account of his great interest in Delacroix, whom he held in high esteem all his life and some of whose work he had seen at Arosa's already at an early age. It is possible that in those years he also read one of the editions of Delacroix's writings that were in existence.

What particular ideas may have influenced Gauguin in those years? We need not be under the illusion that Gauguin should have studied the works of Baudelaire and Delacroix, as we tried to point out earlier in our second chapter. On the other hand, however, it is not necessary to suppose that he was content to be influenced by a few slogans without grasping the basic ideas. Not only was he close to them in time and place but he also knew Delacroix's paintings very well. Therefore Baudelaire's expositions and Delacroix's observations that reached him[539] could be immediately related to things seen and experienced, so that they were far removed from being a drab theory only.

In addition to Baudelaire's introductions to translations of Poe, Gauguin will have acquainted himself with Baudelaire's *Curiosités Esthétiques*. The primacy of the personality ideal found in that work, the vindication of the artist's freedom without any violence done to reality, are motifs that will no doubt have influenced Gauguin in realizing his own attitude with respect to such problems. We shall insert a few quotations that may have had a strong appeal to Gauguin. Although in the literal sense of the word they are not actually found in Gauguin's writings, the thoughts embodied in them are unmistakably there. 'It is a happy thing to dream, and it would be glorious to express what one dreamt.'540 Then there is the idea of the musicality of painting, also found in Delacroix's writings, to which we shall revert later on, and on the same page: 'There are bright and playful tones, playful and sad ones, rich and bright ones, rich and sad ones, common and original ones.'541

As for Delacroix we will suffice with a quotation from a work published in 1885. It is not a quotation from the great artist himself, it is true, but the thought will no doubt have had a strong appeal to Gauguin in connection with the artistic ideal formulated in it:

> The work of Eugène Delacroix contains feeling, constant emotion, sharp emotion leading the spectator instantly through all the phases of the excited intellectual activity. The fixed idea of the master, if I am not mistaken, has been to render the struggles going on in the secret chambers of the soul and to make them, so to say, palpable, visible by means of colours and forms.542

Gauguin speaks in a similar way in his letter to Schuffenecker from Copenhagen on the 24th of May 1885. He asks for a photo of the *Barque de Don Juan*543 and then he says: 'In the same way with Delacroix arms and shoulders are always turned round in a manner that is foolish and impossible to reason, but nevertheless express the real passion.' And further on he speaks of 'nothing but the painting, no *trompe l'oeil*', and then 'The line with him (is) a means to accentuate an idea.'544

But already before this, on the 14th of January, he had written the famous and often quoted letter to the same gentleman. In it he starts with thoughts that are closely akin to those quoted above with respect to Delacroix:

> To me the great artist is the model of the greatest intelligence, to him occur the most delicate and, therefore, the most invisible feelings and translations of the brain. Look about you in the immensity of the creation of nature and see if there are no laws to create all the human feelings with means that are totally different and yet similar in their effect.545

In this couple of short sentences we have the quintessence of the whole programme of Gauguin's later art. We especially point to his search for a different kind of representation which should tell us more of the subject than was possible to the naturalistic artist, but maintains the latter's reality. 'From this I draw the conclusion that there are noble lines, mendacious ones, and so on.'546 This is his not quite logical or convincing conclusion from a short exposition to the effect that a particular object, such as a spider, arouses a multitude of feelings in us which contain more than only the visible aspect as such. The idea of lines that express something in an iconic way is found in hardly any of the precursors or contemporaries[547] discussed by us. But we do find the idea that colours may express something, as appears from the above quotation from Baudelaire. Gauguin has assimilated the latter thought entirely, so that he had no need to use the same examples as Baudelaire. He writes: 'Colours are even more explanatory although less manifold than lines owing to their power over the eye. There are noble tones, others are common, tranquil harmonies, soothing ones, others that exite you by their audacity.'[548] And what follows suggests that which we have already quoted concerning Delacroix: 'Would not lines and colours also give an impression of the more or less grandiose character of the artist?'[549] But instead of continuing with Delacroix, he speaks of Cézanne. It remains possible that Cézanne had spoken of these things – although he hardly makes use of it himself or refers to it later on. But Gauguin does not say here that Cézanne himself searched in this direction. He rather quotes him in evidence of his thesis quoted here. And then he formulates the thought that actually contains the whole theory of Synthetist art in a nutshell: 'The further I get the more I feel the necessity[550] to render thought by something quite different from literature.'[551] Finally he summarizes his ideal clearly in the words: 'Work in freedom and like mad . . . a great feeling can be rendered immediately, dream about it, and find its simplest form.'[552] Here the term *rêver* is used in exactly the same way as Baudelaire used it in the quotation above.

It is true that his work of this period and of the following years hardly does justice to these words. Theory is many years ahead of its realization. Yet in his work he seems to have been occupied with it. Did not he often speak in 1886 about the 'synthesis' he is aiming at?[553] The sole use of the term shows that he is entirely ahead of, or at least abreast with, his time.

Yet also his work of the time immediately after this makes it clear that his art was gradually changing, that he was searching for a method, a new approach, to give a more summarizing vision. We find no genuine break with the past,[554] but we do find strong influences of Cézanne and Degas.

We are referring particularly to some landscapes from Martinique.[555] In this we see how the choice of a high visual point (suggesting Degas' Japanizing manner) enables the whole painted surface to play a part in the realization of the subject and how this breaks through naturalism in landscape painting, also because the interplay of the lines of the composition assumes a more independent meaning. This is further underlined by the network of the treetrunks on the surface in a manner reminiscent of Cézanne,[556] although we cannot say for certain that Gauguin knew the latter's works of the eighties – he may have seen them at Tanguy's. Another new aspect of those landscapes is the absence of any perspective in the sky. This feature had been suggested by Cézanne's work from around 1880.[557] But in contradistinction to Cézanne and Degas, Gauguin used these means to impart to colour and line an artistically expressive value of their own.

These statements make it clear that in his letter of 1885 Gauguin was not concerned with a kind of Symbolism, but with that which Baudelaire called 'musicality', which we have discussed before,[558] namely that the atmosphere of a picture as a composition, by the artistic interplay of lines and colours, is the bearer of the expression of the subject. Already at this time Gauguin broke with Impressionism in that the conception of his composition includes the human evaluation of the meaning of things. This appears from the role he assigned to human figures in his pictures. It is true, the manner of painting itself was still impressionistic, with little strokes side by side; and the manner in which he described the forms in their plastic quality and in their own colours was in principle similar to what he had learnt from Pissarro. But the vision embodied in the picture was by no means derived from what is visible only – and this is, in fact, what was new in it. So Gauguin very carefully tried to extend the possibilities of the art of painting. His development was certainly not rectilinear. In 1886 he painted the portrait of Laval, a work which anticipated the future in many respects,[559] but two years later, after his return from Martinique, he still made an almost purely Impressionist view of Pont Aven.[560] Yet in his *Three dancing Breton girls*[561] from the same year he very nearly approached a more academic kind of art after the manner of Cottet.

Living at such a long distance from these events we have a difficulty in evaluating the true magnitude of the changes, because later artists broke with the past in a much more violent, more consistent and more extreme way. It is clear, however, that in his art Gauguin tried to find ways to represent more than what is strictly visual. We do not think it correct to say that he strove in his art after that which he knew how to express in comparatively clear language, so that he may be said to have remained an ordinary Impressionist. Indeed, also his own words about the work he made, contradict this supposition. From Martinique he wrote: 'I have never had such a clear and lucid painting (a great deal of fantasy for instance).'[562] Especially the words 'lucid' and 'fantasy' point in the direction of his new conception of art.

The early development of Bernard

In many respects it is difficult to form a clear idea of what Bernard thought about art in those years before 1888. We do not possess direct pronouncements made by him, but we have all the more at our disposal of what he noted down himself later on, or of what others wrote down of his utterances. But in view of the controversy with reference to these later considerations, we should not attach too much value to them in our opinion. And certainly not if accurate definitions are required.

There is no doubt that before 1888 Bernard had achieved a few things that might be called new. His art is an effort to strike out new paths. In this he was strongly influenced by Cézanne – he saw the latter's work at Tanguy's[563] – although the influence is not easy[564] to point out in his own style. It seems to us that the Japanese influence was more important, which does not only appear from the choice of a high viewpoint in the landscape[565] but especially from the composition. He aims at a well-considered 'decorative'[566] composition, built up of large areas of colour. The forms are sometimes as surprising as in Japanese art: although on the whole they are fascinating and striking blots of colour, their exact meaning is not immediately clear at first sight. Later on we discover that a particular form certainly has an iconic meaning.[567] The interplay of forms thus has a twofold function: on the one hand it has a fascinating decorative function and, on the other, it has a very accurately defined iconic sense.

As mentioned, it is difficult to say what conceptions of art Bernard had in those years. It is, of course, clear that he rejected naturalism, and also classicism was not particularly congenial to him. This latter fact was perhaps chiefly due to the influence of his milieu, for later on he comes into his own when he changes over to a kind of classicism. In 1886 he often came into contact with Vincent van Gogh; but it is not easy to say if the latter had any influence on his thoughts on art. In view of the fact that van Gogh often discussed art with him, we think it probable that Bernard learnt a few things from him. It is striking that in 1885 Bernard started making biblical pictures, but from 1886, with one exception, he devoted himself entirely to painting landscapes, farmer's wives from Bretagne, and a portrait.[568] Later on, in 1889, when van Gogh's direct influence had increased, he again reverts to biblical subjects. To this van Gogh reacts with slashing criticism.[569] Van Gogh may have explained to him that art should represent the peculiar individual character of persons and things. These thoughts had already been expressed by him earlier with reference to the *Potato-eaters*. However, he did not mean it in a naturalistic sense, but in a realistic sense not excluding deformations, if necessary. Thus van Gogh's views might be characterized.[570]

Already at the beginning of his career Bernard had come into contact with Impressionism and had sympathized with it in some measure. But very soon he tried to overcome this Impressionism. His contacts with men like van Gogh, Gauguin (his contact with Gauguin was slight, but all the same it was sufficient for him to know what Gauguin was doing), Signac Cézanne[571] and, perhaps more important, his knowledge of what was going on in literary circles, opened his eyes to the deficiencies of Impressionism. After a very short impressionistic period he is immediately in the centre of the movement of 1885. He even wrote poems in the symbolistic spirit.[572]

In 1888 his views would have been something like the following:[573]

> Since the idea is the form of things acquired by the imagination, one should not paint in front of things but by calling them back into the imagination that had acquired them, which preserved them in the idea; thus the idea of a thing gives the suitable form to the subject of the picture, or rather to its ideal (the sum total of the ideas) it gives the simplification purporting to be the essential in things perceived, and consequently details are rejected.[574]

These thoughts are closely related to those advanced by the literary artists around 1885. And instead of referring vaguely to the generation of 1885 we can be more precise and, like Michaud, speak of the Symbolists who are clearly distinguished by him from the decadents and the people of the 'fantastical poetry'.[575] If we consider the opinion expressed by Ghill in 1885, who was a member of Mallarmé's school and also strongly opposed to the decadents,[576] his relationship is very clear. This is why it is no accident that in spite of his admiration for Redon, Bernard himself never dared to make such works of (pictorial) art as we have called Symbolist. As a matter of fact, the entire social milieu in which he moved was averse to it.

To circumscribe the influence exercised by the men of letters on Bernard's thought we may quote Moréas' famous manifesto, which Bernard will no doubt have known: 'Symbolic poetry endeavors to clothe the Idea in a sensitive form which, nevertheless, could not be an end in itself, but would be subordinate to the Idea while serving to express it . . . art can derive from objectivity only a simple and extremely succinct point of departure.'[577]

But, no doubt, other influences too determined his ideas of pictorial art. The use of the word 'imagination' immediately calls up reminiscences of Baudelaire's *Curiosités Esthétiques*, a work that Bernard is sure to have known. Besides there are many points of resemblance between the way in which in the above quotation he defines the relation between the idea and the reality perceived and what Delacroix had written in his diary.[578] It is true, this diary had not yet been published, but the passage referred to by us occurs as a quotation in Dargenty's book on Delacroix published in 1885, and there Bernard may have found it.[579]

For our examination of Bernard's view of art in the years before he met Gauguin in Pont Aven in the summer of 1888, van Gogh's letters to Bernard are very valuable. In these we read that Bernard is busy studying old Italian and German art in order to discover 'the symbolic meaning that the abstract and mystic drawing may contain' and a little further on he again mentions 'your investigations with regard to the properties of lines with opposite movements'.[580] So van Gogh here points out certain ideas in Bernard concerning the manner of composition, and the meaning the latter attaches to the language of lines and colours in a composition. This is a purely Synthetist thought that we have already come upon in Gauguin, and which we shall find again in a more elaborate form later on. And the fact that van Gogh cautiously warns him against the danger of *stériles méditations métaphysiques* at any rate suggests that at that time Bernard was occupied by art-theoretical problems – problems in which van Gogh took little interest when they were thus posited and thought out.

Finally we wish to mention another possible source of influence on Bernard's thought. We are referring to the Art Nouveau movement which precisely in those years began to assume more distinct features. With the rise of this kind of art in France there were two decisive factors at work, namely the example of the English – the work of William Morris and his followers, such as Crane with his illustrations of children's books – and Japanese art. Art Nouveau was in the first place a revival of decorative art. And it is remarkable in this connection that Bernard himself so strongly emphasizes the decorative element. Thus, later on, he wrote that in those days he had asserted: 'Painting, being decorative, should above all please the eye and the mind: and for this there were but two means; colour on one hand, invention of the picture on the other.'[581] When in an essay by Gonse published in March 1888 we read about this Art Nouveau milieu, we are struck by his emphatic statement that it seems necessary to some people for a work of art also to contain 'a body of psychological and quasi literary ideas' and that the Japanese may perhaps lack this element, but that on the other hand they have something else, namely 'the absolute predominance of the decorative principle in all the branches of art'. And this is why he wishes to honour them as the greatest ornamental painters of the world. The Japanese, he says, possesses 'a natural talent for synthesis', 'a marvellous instinct for the resources of colour', 'a profound knowledge of their harmony', and 'infinite delicacy in varying their use'.[582]

The English influence is even harder to establish from the source material; this is certainly so with respect to art theories. Yet the artists in question are sure to have known English art, both from the pictures they saw at Bing's in Paris and from books. Gauguin appears to have possessed a book of illustrations by Caldecott and praises it highly.[583] But it is really almost unthinkable that Bernard should have been ignorant of English art in the spirit of Morris and so on,[584] not only because he took such a great interest in everything that presented itself as something new, but especially because the carved wooden cabinet doors he made at Pont Aven in 1888[585] would else be almost inexplicable in their style and construction. The same thing applies to his stained-glass windows of this period.[586]

The events of the summer of 1888

We have arrived now at the events of the summer of 1888 which has always attracted a lot of attention.[587] For then Gauguin and Bernard entertained a close contact with each other at Pont Aven for a somewhat longer period of time. The younger man is supposed to have induced the older one to produce an entirely new kind of art. There is no doubt that Bernard was ahead of Gauguin as to style, and that the latter will have borrowed the former's use of flat colours, *cloisonné*,[588] at least temporarily. Prior to meeting Bernard, Gauguin still stuck to a loose and shaded way of painting in small strokes, even in those works of which he explicitly mentions that he was working in the spirit of the Japanese artists.[589] When, however, we examine the compositions concerned, it is clear to us that Gauguin had developed a new art and was by no means any longer a mere Impressionist. In fact he realized this himself, for in the letter in question he explicitly adds these words 'it is not at all like Degas'.[590]

But the most important thing for us is what was thought and said in the field of the theory of art. Here it is quite plausible that Bernard had a great deal to say to Gauguin, for the former knew what was going on at Paris. Gauguin was, indeed, not entirely ignorant of these things, but Bernard's mental disposition and his greater literary interest naturally enabled him to be better informed of art-theoretical matters than Gauguin.

It is not unlikely for Bernard to have rendered the same service to Gauguin that he did to Cézanne later on. He compelled Gauguin to realize and to define his own ideas more precisely, for Bernard asked him questions and was very much intent upon theoretical clarity. He wanted to realize discursively what a painter really does when he is painting. At the same time Bernard may have brought Gauguin's terminology up to date. So we do not believe that Gauguin was now, as it were, confronted by an entirely new trend of thought, but we think that their conversations carried both Gauguin and Bernard further. If it were the case that Gauguin took over everything from Bernard after the true manner of a pupil, it is not quite understandable why exactly at this time Bernard conceived such a great admiration for him.[591] As a matter of fact, although these two men now came into closer contact with each other for the first time, they had had an indirect contact through Theo and Vincent van Gogh and many mutual friends and acquaintances among the Parisian vanguard. The almost immediate agreement that arose between these men at Pont Aven in the summer of 1888, exactly with respect to their conceptions of pictorial art, is therefore in no way a miracle.

Indeed, it remains to be seen whether Bernard really wanted to say that he had shown Gauguin the way to a new art theory. For it is true that Bernard says that 'Gauguin truly saw in my work and learnt from the exposition of my ideas all that could be derived from Cézanne,'[592] but this does not mean that he transferred entirely new ideas of art to Gauguin. It is possible that this concerned only some theories on colours and their effects, of which Gauguin admitted their correctness. Perhaps Bernard's contribution was connected with purely technical matters, such as the fact that colours which have been applied unmixed and flat have a much greater effect, which may be intensified by means of black-blue contours.[593] Bernard's influence, on account of which he considered himself to be the real 'father' of Synthetism, is therefore less a matter of theories than one of a new style, based on Bernard's manner of composition described above.

Nevertheless we really think that in the summer of 1888 an important step was taken in the direction of a new art theory, that of Synthetism. And although we do not seem to be warranted to say that Gauguin only now started to think things through and break with the presuppositions of the older Impressionism, it is not possible to entirely rule out the stimulating influence exercised by Bernard in this respect.[594] This also appears in a later letter of Gauguin's from Arles, in which Bernard and Laval asked him what part is played by the shade in a picture. If Bernard had formed the new ideas on art on his own such a question would have been foolish and Gauguin would rather have asked Bernard about it. But in our opinion Bernard's contribution to the new development consists exactly in his asking such questions. For without this Gauguin would probably never have found such a definite answer to this problem, which was certainly not unimportant with respect to the representation of reality.[595]

We have ignored one important remark, namely Bernard's assertion that his expositions had induced Gauguin to derive his inspiration from Cézanne more intensely than he had done up till then. This assertion is rather remarkable, for a comparison of Gauguin's work before this time and that after it will have to arrive at the conclusion that Gauguin had moved further away from Cézanne rather than nearer to him. What did Bernard consider to be essential to Cézanne's work? In one of the pictures he had taken along with him from St Briac to Pont Aven that is given much praise by Gauguin,[596] Cézanne's influence is very clear.[597] In this landscape, a somewhat accidented terrain without trees, the depth has been built up after the manner of Cézanne, so without the use of aerial perspective. Owing to this method the surface of the picture retained its brightness of colour and the light aspect was not disturbed. Just as in the case of Cézanne, the structure of the subject of this work was made clear by a lucid composition. But it is precisely this painting that shows little resemblance to Synthetism which was to arise shortly afterwards. Properly speaking the much older *Railway bridge at Asnières* (1885)[598] is much more closely related to it. The problem is, therefore, far from easy to solve. Perhaps Bernard saw that in Cézanne's work Impressionism had been broken through exactly at the point where a transparent composition was concerned in which the whole surface is of a bright colour. But in Synthetist works in the proper sense of the term – such as *Breton women in a meadow* and *Vision after the sermon* –

this thought has been realized entirely apart from Cézanne's stylistic characteristics.[599] For now that art arose of which Cézanne said that it proved that Gauguin had never understood anything of him and that such Chinese art seemed to him to be a mockery.[600]

But to revert to the art-theoretical considerations proper: what kind of thoughts were formulated in the summer of 1888? In the first place, then, that the artist is free with respect to nature as given in its visual appearance. The issue is about what is essential and meaningful to a person in what has been observed and spiritually experienced. And this can be best painted from the memory which acts like a sieve, selecting and retaining from the object only that which the artist as a human person thinks important. He or she chooses the essential thing from a multitude of visual impressions.[601] Similar ideas – how very much they are akin to Baudelaire's – are found in Gauguin as well as in Bernard, although the latter wrote them down from memory only later on.[602] According to Morice, Gauguin is reported to have said:[603] 'It is better to paint from memory, in that way your work will be yours; your sensation, your intelligence and your soul will then survive for the eye of the amateur . . . Seek harmony.'[604] And also in a letter to Schuffenecker, shortly after Bernard's arrival, he wrote: 'A piece of advice, do not paint too much from nature. Art is an abstraction;[605] borrow it from nature by dreaming in front of it and think more of the creation that will result.'[606]

What could be meant by the word 'abstraction' mentioned here? We think that it clearly expresses the idea that a work of art has a structure of its own which may be widely different from nature perceived naturalistically, although there is an invariable intention to represent the subject according to its structure and meaning. This is clear from the advice about the shadows referred to above. In it he says that the Japanese, it is true, do not make use of shadows, and yet 'Only using colour as a combination of tones, as different harmonies, they still give the impression of warmth, etc.'[607] Thus the artist may use shadow when he wants it for his composition, but he may also leave it out: 'In a way the shadow is at your service.'[608] A similar thought must be read in the letter he wrote a short time before in which he gave a brief summary of his own work as 'a synthesis of form and colour while only considering the dominant'.[609]

We may also refer in this connection to a letter to Schuffenecker at this time with the remarkable pronouncement: 'Why do you talk to me about my terrible mysticism. Be an Impressionist to the end and fear nothing.'[610] In the first place it shows that Gauguin had communicated a few things about his ideas,[611] and that in this Schuffenecker had recognized such a great deal of similarity to the thoughts of the decadents or to the (pictorial) Symbolists that Schuffenecker thought he should warn him. 'No,' Gauguin said, 'soyez impressionniste', in spite of the fact that he rejected Impressionism. Just like van Gogh,[612] Gauguin sticks to this term, because it clearly denoted the distance from the academic art of the Salons, whereas he did not think it necessary at this time to lay too much emphasis on the difference from the Impressionists proper. Exactly in this context it is all the more clear that this term also means something else, a non-academic art which is realistic – for he distinguishes Impressionism from a mystic kind of Symbolism (after the manner of Moreau, for instance).

The most important works of this period are Bernard's *Breton women in the meadow* and Gauguin's *Vision after the sermon*. Both lay strong stress on composition, the artistic form. Yet in both the subject remains important, although to a lesser degree in Bernard's case. His work is more like a decoration and is much nearer to what may be called Art Nouveau than Gauguin's work, of which the content is much more telling and important, and this is not something accidental for this content is fully borne by the artistic configuration. This was Gauguin's deliberate aim.[613] This work is really the explicit and very clear pictorial expression of the thoughts found in the famous letter of 1885. But we must emphatically state that this does not mean that it happened for the first time. Only – and this was the part played by Bernard – this ideal again presented itself very clearly to his mind and he began to see better how to realize it. Bernard's method connected with Japanese art and with the Art Nouveau suggested the means to him.[614] Gauguin would never allow the work of art to merge into mere decoration; he always wanted to go further and dig deeper. This is not only the difference between Gauguin's art and that of Bernard, but also between their theories.

Gauguin with van Gogh in Arles

Shortly afterwards Gauguin went to Vincent van Gogh at Arles. Their discussions there no doubt made Gauguin even more conscious of his own ideas and induced him to put them into words even more clearly. From the debate about the different artists it appears that Gauguin considered a finely balanced composition as an essential requirement, not only life caught in an image: 'I think I have to mix Puvis with the Japanese manner.'[615] Even before Gauguin's arrival van Gogh had stated that he wanted to express something of the object by means of colours.[616] He was thinking of a direct iconization and not of aesthetic effects for their own sake – the poetry was to be in the subject of the painting, in the artistic expression of it.[617] Gauguin, however, laid the accent on the aesthetic aspect, on the beautiful composition of the work which was to be poetic in itself, apart from the subject.[618] This composition, however, was to be related to the subject. Thus an aesthetic configuration should be created, which, although meaningful itself, was an accompaniment to the subject of the work and underlined that subject while accompanying it.

It was characteristic of Gauguin that at Arles he found 'a source of fine modern style'.[619] He indeed made some pictures here which were stylistically strongly akin to the Japanese and English elements in Art Nouveau.[620] These pictures exhibited that element more clearly than all the other works by Gauguin. Van Gogh followed his example,[621] in a composition which (obviously after Gauguin's manner) was explicitly made from motifs of remembrance – a remembrance of their garden at Etten.[622] The idea of painting from memory and not directly from nature here found an extreme application. Owing to this we can be sure, at any rate, that Gauguin advanced this conception at the time. This *Garden at Etten*[623] is pretty well the only picture van Gogh did in this manner.

When very early in 1889, shortly after Gauguin had left, he set about doing the famous *Berceuse* in the Synthetist spirit, he certainly painted from the model and did not perform a stroke of the brush, not even when making a replica, without having her, Madame Roulin, before him. He tried to arrange the colours in this work in such a telling way that it was a significant work even for that alone. 'I leave it to the critics to say whether or not I have sung a lullaby with the colours.'[624] 'Perhaps in *Berceuse* ("the one who rocks the cradle") there is an effort to compose some colour-music about her.'[625] It is remarkable that in these two pronouncements the iconic sense of the harmony of colours was related to something different. Later on this method, the method of 'abstraction', was considered as a blind alley by van Gogh, at least as far as he himself was concerned.[626] But precisely owing to this course of events the characteristic element in the Synthetism of Gauguin (and Bernard) has become clear to us. But for these sources we should perhaps have been unable to reconstruct their theory in the way we did, namely that the effect of the colours and the play of the lines in themselves should in the first place make for harmony, and in addition relate to the subject. The above statements made by van Gogh even suggest that as early as 1888 the term *musicalité* (following Baudelaire) was used in this connection. It is true, already before Gauguin's sojourn at Arles, van Gogh had also repeatedly spoken of an iconic, non-naturalistic use of colours,[627] but then the question was how to render the typical trait of the object which, as it were, was thus pictorially described in a direct way. It was not meant to be an aesthetic whole working in parallel to the subject, without coalescing with it *qua talis*. The contrast pointed out by Gauguin between van Gogh and himself, 'painting in the manner of Daumier', or 'in the manner of a colourful Puvis mixed with Japanese elements', is clear enough in this respect.

Sérusier

Finally we wish to call special attention to another event which may be conducive to getting an insight into the ideas that were formed in the circle of Gauguin in 1888, namely the meeting with Sérusier. This young artist was the enthusiastic leader of a small group of pupils of the Académie Julian. Under his influence their interest was much more comprehensive than was mostly the case in such company. It was especially he who called their attention to all that was new and occupied the minds of their contemporaries – from Wagner to the decadent literature[628] – while Sérusier, in connection with the anti-positivism that was in the air, also displayed a great interest in Plotinus.[629]

In the summer of 1888 Sérusier stayed at Pont Aven for some time, where he established a hesitant contact with the people around Gauguin – Bernard, Filiger, and others. Shortly before his definite departure he at last ventured to approach Gauguin himself. In connection with the controversy about the question who was the 'initiator' of the new movement it is a remarkable and instructive fact that Bernard referred Sérusier to Gauguin for further information.[630] Although we do not possess direct contemporary reports of al this, we may trust Denis' later writings to provide the information, especially in connection with their general agreement with each other. The more so as later on Sérusier never repudiated or corrected Denis' opinions, not even in his private correspondence. Denis relates how after returning from Pont Aven to the Académie Julian, Sérusier showed the lid of a cigar box on which he had made a painting under Gauguin's guidance, 'a formless landscape, by dint of being formulated synthetically, in violet, vermilion, veronese green and other pure colours as they come out of the tube almost without any mixture with white'. ' "How do you see that tree?" Gauguin asked in front of a nook in the Bois d'Amour, "Is it green? Put on green then, the most beautiful green of your palette; and that shade, rather blue? Be not afraid to paint it as blue as possible".'[631]

It is striking that here Gauguin did not tell Sérusier to work from memory, but exactly with his eyes on nature, although the pupil was advised to maintain a great measure of freedom with respect to it. Again we are aware of the idea that in its aesthetic composition as such the work should be beautiful and telling – for 'take the finest green of your palette' means on the pictorial surface there must be a beautiful patch of green, and it does not matter whether this green is exactly in agreement with the green of the tree in question.

It is difficult to decide whether the passage given below means that in his exposition of Gauguin's ideas, Sérusier said all this, or that we are here dealing with the result of later contemplation embodying the fruits of more prolonged discussions on this new view. But even if this is so, the essential part of the new ideas on art transmitted by Sérusier has been preserved.

By the way, in this case we would point out the generative influence of the spoken word and art theory, together with the direct example of the painting. Denis continues: 'Thus, in a paradoxical, unforgettable form, we were for the first time presented with the fertile concept of the "surface covered with colours arranged in a certain order".'[632] (We shall revert to the last sentence when discussing Denis' manifesto of 1890.) The final conclusion drawn from this confrontation with a new method is at once that here reality was not rendered naturalistically, but that in an iconic sense 'Every work of art was a transportation, a caricature, the passionate equivalent of a sensation received.'[633]

It is a remarkable fact that at the very outset the young artists were engaged in the formation of the new art although they hardly knew Impressionism as yet. They will indeed have felt that here was something that (in its anti-naturalism) was akin to the new movement in literature of which they knew something. The Synthetists of Pont Aven had apparently initiated Sérusier also into the recent events in French art and had shown him the way to find out about it. For, as Denis tells us, since that day they frequented the gallery of Theo van Gogh and Tanguy's shop to get acquainted with the work of Vincent, Monet, Degas, and Cézanne.[634]

The fact that here Gauguin handled the matter quite differently from his method when he was with van Gogh some time later shows that he was by no means a dogmatist with regard to his manner of working. He was especially concerned with an art that should leave the artist a larger measure of freedom than naturalism and Impressionism did, so that the work of art might give something that was peculiar to the artist. This ideal inspired Gauguin and directed his development and consequently also the guidance he gave to the younger men. This is also made clear by Denis' observation: 'Gauguin was no teacher . . . On the contrary, he was an intuitive person. In his conversation as in his stories there were happy aphorisms, profound insights, finally assertions of a logic that was stupefying to us.'[635]

Gauguin in Paris in 1889

In the early part of 1889, after the tragical events at Arles, Gauguin was again at Paris. He does not seem to have met Sérusier there,[636] but to have cooperated with Bernard. At this time he will also have made acquaintance with Meyer de Haan, and will have met some other pupils, such as Filiger. His old friend Schuffenecker again entertained him. All this, however, is of minor importance for the history of art theory, as we do not know what was discussed at that time. Also the fact that Gauguin exhibited with the XX at Brussels may be important for the history of the appreciation of Gauguin, but does not take us a step further.

Sérusier and some others of his group of the Académie Julian no doubt met Gauguin a little later in the year, namely in the latter part of the summer, when after a short stay in Brittany (where Sérusier visited him)[637] he was again at Paris in connection with the exhibition at Volpini's.[638]

It remains questionable whether or not he had already met the 'avant-garde' of the literary men that year – the source material almost exclusively speaks of the year 1890 in this connection. But if perhaps he did not make any contacts in the winter of that year, he certainly made them in the summer at – or in connection with – the exhibition organized by him and his followers, because various young critics of the Symbolist circle wrote about the show.[639] It is almost certain that he then met Aurier, who knew Bernard to whose paper *Le Moderniste* Gauguin shortly after contributed some articles.[640] However this may be, it is pretty well inconceivable for him not to have got acquainted with the work of the avant-garde of authors and poets and of their ideas, in view of Bernard's and Sérusier's interest in these things. We think we can reconstruct his reaction. For in this year he made a number of works in conception akin to the Symbolist poetry. They are the exception among Gauguin's works, but for this reason they are all the more important, as indicators of a new and alien influence. We are especially referring to his large wooden relief: *Soyez amoureuse, vous serez heureuse*.[641] Stylistically this work again testifies strongly to a Japanese influence assimilated more or less after the manner of Art Nouveau, but with a stronger literary element in the painting: 'the fox, an Indian symbol of perversity'.[642] This introduced a new element into Gauguin's art. The composition itself with its peculiar configuration was new and different from the old naturalism. This new manner had already been found in his *Vision after the sermon*. But in addition to it the composition as such could only be understood symbolistically, that is, the different figures were a rendering of a poetic thought in their iconic relation, and any bond with a visual entity had vanished. But in the details there are enough realistic elements – in the female nude – showing that Gauguin did not at all renounce his Realist Impressionist past and was absolutely disinclined to adopt the idealizing method characteristic of the Symbolist art after the manner of Moreau.

Gauguin and his friends at Le Pouldu

It would be conceivable that Gauguin had arrived at such a method without any personal contact with the avant-garde of the men of letters or with their work, but directly under the influence of Baudelaire's *Les Fleurs du Mal*. It is certain that in this relief we may also recognize a reflection of what occupied him and his circle in *Le Pouldu*. Notwithstanding the almost total absence of exact information, we may be sure that there was no end of discussions on art theory, in which Sérusier's and de Haan's real knowledge of philosophy is sure to have contributed a deepening influence. From the portrait of de Haan made by Gauguin, with both Carlyle's *Sartor Resartus* and Milton's *Paradise Lost* [643] on a table, we know a little about what kind of works appealed to them. Carlyle, in addition to Baudelaire, may have imprinted the idea of 'musicality' deeper into their minds. Baudelaire's work was no doubt also read and discussed, and together with Milton's poem it will have inspired Gauguin to make his 'satanic' self-portrait.[644]

It is difficult to say exactly what theories were elaborated there or in what way. Apart from the source material mentioned there are few documents to inform us of these things. In any case, Gauguin still appears to be searching for the synthesis. This cannot only be gathered from the title of the exhibition held in the summer of 1889, 'Groupe impressionniste et synthétiste', or from the drawing representing Bernard, Schuffenecker, and Gauguin against a background inscribed with the word *Synthétisme*,[645] or from the cry 'Vive la sintaise' proving that Gauguin is capable of ridiculing that which he takes very much to heart,[646] but above all from an exposition given by him in a letter to Bernard. In it he says he can appreciate work done from observation – *la sensation* – as well as work constructed according to strict rules of composition. And he continues to say that this is why 'we have to work in both directions'.[647] It is clear that we should not read any eclecticism in these words, but that this shows the way to supply the deficiency that Gauguin felt in the works of 'sensation', namely a 'lack of the beyond'.[648]

There is another source of information on this period in Le Pouldu in 1890 which deserves our attention, namely two letters written from there by Sérusier to Denis. He started writing the first when he had just arrived – Gauguin had disappointed him. In this letter written *Jour de Vénus*[649] he immediately started with a problem which occupied him and for which he had apparently not yet received a solution from Gauguin, namely 'What has especially embarrassed me is this: what should be the part of nature in the work? Where should one stop? and finally, from the material point of view, the execution, should we work from nature or only look and remember?'[650] It seems possible that he hit upon this specific question, which was not without some importance with regard to the working method, on account of a contradiction in Gauguin which he could not explain. For in the year before, Gauguin had taught him to work with his eye on nature and to seek for the synthesis from there, and now he had probably been told to work from memory. It was the same contradiction in Gauguin's views that we have referred to above and then ascribed to the fact that this point was of minor importance to Gauguin.

A few days later Sérusier wrote a second letter which he opens with the remark: 'I am sorry for what I have said about Gauguin, he has nothing of the humbug, at least with regard to those whom he knows can understand him.'[651] This quotation supports our opinion that Sérusier had at first thought that Gauguin had been poking fun at him and had only assumed an air of having a conception of his own. The rest of the letter will claim our attention in a later context.

Although all the source material proves that Gauguin and his friends were occupied with art-theoretical problems, we should not think that they tried to build up an abstract kind of aesthetics. On the contrary, aesthetics as a branch of philosophy that is concerned with beauty as a given phenomenon did not interest them. Their discussions about art, although touching the very foundations, were certainly not abstract but immediately directed to their own work, to their manner of approach and to their working method. And connected with these things there were all kinds of strictly technical problems, from the use of special brushes and colours to questions of composition and the harmony of colours. This is why it is not contrary to what has been said when in a letter written later in the year Sérusier says: 'Of all my theories[652] that have been tried this winter only this simple law is left: avoid bringing together two tones that are too wide apart unless there is at least a kinship between them.'[653]

Gauguin in 1890

In 1890 Gauguin often came into contact with authors and poets of the new movement. Morice tells us how he started propounding the new art in the midst of those literary men (with an air he had at times also adopted before his pupils). This manner did not seem to meet with such a very favourable reception at the time,[654] but it proves that after all Gauguin had definite ideas on art – on this and on other occasions he will have realized that where theories were concerned he still had a lot to learn.

The quintessence of his exposition on that evening in the *Café La Côte d'Or* has been summarized by Morice as follows:

> Primitive art proceeds from the spirit and uses nature. So-called refined art proceeds from the senses and serves nature. Nature is the housemaid of the former and the mistress of the latter, but the housemaid cannot forget her origin and degrades the spirit by allowing him to adore her. This now is how we have fallen into the abominable error of naturalism.[655]

It is as clear as daylight that he rejects naturalism. But this is not saying that he considered the kind of (literary) Symbolism, which we have indicated above as 'decadent', as parallel to what he sought himself. It is not at all certain that he made a sharp distinction between the different tendencies after the manner of Michaud; but we think it very likely that he had his likes and dislikes with regard to the one or the other. This might appear from the people with whom he had a closer contact, Morice and Aurier, and less intensively, also with Moréas – who changed over to a kind of neoclassicism at that time – while we should not underestimate the importance of his contact with Mallarmé – in the sense that Mallarmé, with his erudition, now admitted Gauguin to his Tuesday-evenings, although the artist would probably not have understood much of what was said.

At first sight we should, therefore, be inclined to consider as a foolish tale, unworthy of any belief, the myth that Gauguin with Sérusier had heard the theory from a set of men of letters and had not understood much of it – especially because Sérusier was present who was himself an erudite theorist to the core. But the circumstances indicated above make us suspect that there might be some foundation for this story,[656] namely that Gauguin will have responded to the ideas and ideals of the decadents in a strongly negative and disapproving way. In this light we shall, therefore, have to read a (later) pronouncement – in a letter from Sérusier to Verkade in 1893: 'Gauguin is coming back, I have received his tidings. He tells me he has studied without looking for symbolism. Oh! all the better. He has risen above people, who make me detest even this word',[657] whereas later on Gauguin himself said that he had liberated art from the 'the shackles of symbolism'.[658] That such pronouncement cannot have been meant to deny his earlier art and to imply that he had started developing new ideas is clear from his own development as an artist, and from his letters which every now and again explain his work.

There is, indeed, another indication that we may interpret Gauguin's attitude thus, namely his attack on Huysmans, the decadent. He rejected the latter's interpretation of Redon's work[659] and found in it something far more profound and essential than a mere decadent play with the lugubrious and monstrous, an exaltation of what is abnormal and morbid. It appears that Gauguin no doubt understood this art and highly appreciated it. It was a kind of proto-Surrealism parallel to the poetical movement characterized by the writings of Rimbaud, the movement of the poètes maudits in the narrow sense of the word.[660] Gauguin himself, however, did not take this road but stayed clear of any influence exercised by it. The fact that in the portrait of Moréas[661] he quite clearly worked in Redon's manner is an isolated case implying nothing, for Gauguin made more or less a caricature here.

But his attack on Huysmans' preference for Gustave Moreau is sharper and stronger. At the same time it becomes clear why he was never guilty of this pictorial kind of Symbolism: he looked upon it as an art which did not really render 'literary' ideas in a pictorial way, but was much rather content with illustrating old stories (which, therefore, roused the opposition of the Realist in Gauguin) in the naturalistic manner. He also sharply rejected the typically decadent preference for all kinds of jewelry: 'His impulsive moment is very far from the heart and he loves the richness of material wealth.' In short, what he found lacking in Huysmans and Moreau was 'simplicity, nobility'.[662]

All this may show that Gauguin's power of judgment was no doubt sharp enough at times. Nor should we think that Gauguin was an illiterate man who did not know about anything. On the contrary, he was a great reader. Rotonchamps relates an anecdote showing that as early as 1880 Gauguin had read Poe,[663] while at the time we are discussing he had certainly read a great deal. From a later letter to Morice it plainly follows that he knew the latter's *Littérature de tout à l'heure* quite well, and was also acquainted with Renan's work.[664] And further, we have Morice's witness in his Gauguin biography of a much later date, which we can trust on this point, namely that Balzac and Poe were his favourite authors, and of their works he preferred especially Balzac's *Études philosophiques* like *Séraphita*.[665]

Finally, the fact that he was in close contact not only with the men of letters personally but also with their works is proved by Gauguin's own writings. There was a clear change in style in those years, not so much when factual information or questions were concerned, nor in his perennial complaints about money and such, but in the description of his own works. In these descriptions he sometimes appeared to have developed a style that is truly literary and of a peculiar kind of beauty. Its abruptness, its telegraphic character sometimes suggests Mallarmé. He himself pointed to Mauclair.[666]

Also at this time Gauguin rarely took the path of (pictorial) Symbolism in his paintings and notwithstanding many renewals his work remained realistic. Only in a few cases did he make something that revealed a stronger influence of literature in a Symbolist spirit. The most striking example of this kind was no doubt his *Perte du Pucelage*.[667] The choice of the subject as well as the way in which the symbols are used are not realistic. With regard to the composition, the way in which the subject is treated, we might point to influences exercised by Puvis de Chavannes, however much the colours deviated from the latter's art. It is a debatable question as to whether or not this work has the 'nobility' of which he spoke at this time himself, but the 'simplicity' that he failed to find in Moreau is there. Although in this Gauguin comes nearest to a conception akin to Moreau, the real distance between them remains immense, especially owing to the fundamental difference in their use of pictorial means. For Moreau derived them from naturalism, while Gauguin developed new means.

7
The Definitive Formulations

Morice

In 1890 and later Gauguin had a rather intensive contact with Morice, whose ideas will certainly not have failed to influence him. Although it is difficult to decide exactly what are formulations and ideas advanced by Morice himself and what represent the words of Gauguin as summed up by Morice in his Gauguin-book of 1919, these summaries no doubt represent the gist of the artist's views as expressed in their conversations. Morice tells us that Gauguin was in his own way interested in philosophy:

> He 'philosophizes' when he demonstrates his way of understanding general ideas ... [saying] 'Philosophy is difficult if it is not in me by instinct. It is sweet in our sleep with the dream that adorns it – it is not science ... it is not a logical conclusion as grave persons would like to teach us, but it is a weapon that we make for ourselves as savages. It does not present itself as a reality but as an image: like a picture, admirable if the picture is a masterpiece.[668]

The style of this quotation strongly suggests Morice himself, but the thoughts and images employed are likely to be Gauguin's – they nowhere contradict later pronouncements in the latter's writings. These quotations show at any rate that Gauguin will have been very much interested in Morice's theoretical explanations (whose book, as already noted, he had read thoroughly) if only to convince younger men of the correctness of his own views.

In this respect Morice was the right man to turn to. For Morice was one of the prominent men of letters of the younger generation who are grouped together under the name of 'Symbolists'. He owed this position to his book: *La littérature de tout à l'heure* [669] published in 1889, a work in which he once for all gave Symbolism its fixed form by his closed and well-considered exposition – we are using the term 'Symbolism' in the narrower sense of the word for the literary group related to pictorial Synthetism. In lucid language and without any wavering or doubt, Gauguin explained his own conceptions of the function of art in the human world, of the meaning and the purpose of every artistic activity, of the high respect that was due to it and of the corrupt state in which it was found to exist in many respects. If anywhere, it is in this book that the fundamental meaning of synthesis was elaborated and proclaimed as an essential part of any art that understands its time and its task.

Indeed the search for synthesis was not something new – we have already met with it rather often. But let us not forget that men like Baudelaire, Poe, and others with whom we have found it before, indeed presented it as something new. They tried to retain Romanticism and to connect it with contemporary scientialistic positivism or, considered from the other point of view, it was an effort to compensate for the one-sidedness and the shortcomings of positivism with its sociological and naturalistic tendencies by clinging to the passion for freedom of the Romantic personality ideal. The seekers for this synthesis – among whom Baudelaire took the lead and became one of the determining influences that framed the future of France owing to his enormous influence – had been isolated figures, to such an extent that more than twenty years after Baudelaire's death the viewpoint of synthesis was still something new in French cultural life. We should not forget that Baudelaire wrote his articles, which were to bring him such fame later on, only a short time after Comte had finished his most important work – in 1842 the last volume of his *Cours de philosophie positive* appeared – whereas only two years before the death of Baudelaire, Taine published his *Philosophie de l'art* (1865), a work in which the positivist way of thought was also elaborated for art history and art theory.

It is true, in 1889 Morice was justified in saying that Baudelaire and Poe 'elevate to dogmas that will have no heretics among true poets'[670] the fundamental conceptions of the viewpoint of synthesis. But he also appeared to think it necessary to open his book with an attack on the science ideal, 'the popularization of the sciences'[671] resulting in 'Mediocrity. The fatal product of the diffusion of light – the enormous joke, that monstrous modern ecstasy',[672] by which the battle-axe which had been lifted by Baudelaire was taken up and handled in an almost similar way. Morice is still able to state that 'They want nothing but formulae, 2 and 2 is 4, there is only this at the back of everything.'[673]

But however this may be, he said, even though the poets no longer have an audience, they must write all the same. This is their fate. And then he continued with a theory of art based on an ontology that follows Plotinus very closely.[674] 'Emanations of God, sparks escaped from the fire of the All-Light, they – the poets – return into it.'[675] This is 'the universal law of life, of the souls'. And, 'These souls are the exterior manifestations of God who emits them with the mission to cooperate, each in their own way, to the luminous harmony of the world.'[676] And it is art that can best bring this about. For, Morice said,

> A book, a work of art, a musical phrase, pure thought itself ... are eternalizations of the I. From this we make as many means to disengage our I-ness from contingencies, and it is in this way also that the human I comes back as soon as it escapes from contingencies to the seat of the absolute, to the metaphysical place of the Ideas, to God.[677]

So it appears that for Morice the activity of artists in their creative work consisted of liberating themselves into freedom (in the humanistic sense of the word), which at the same time directed them to the intellectual, mystical merging with the Plotinian god.

According to Morice, a true work of art is directed to the totality of a person, not only to the mind nor only to the senses. It will be perfect in form precisely to please the senses, for 'the form in the work that is thus perfect and ideal is only the bait offered to seduce the senses to let themselves be appeased; they have fallen asleep in a delicious drunkenness and leave the spirit free, the senses are enchanted to recognize the lines and the primitive sounds, the forms that have not yet been betrayed by an artifice and which a genius finds in his communion with Nature.'[678] Thus a genuine work of art will have a strong and living bond with natural reality exactly because then the meaning of the work of art will have its import. For in this case 'the vague and charming apparition of a divine entity of the Infinite'[679] will be left to the liberated spirit. And this is decisive for the high value of art, for, 'Understood thus, art is only the revelator of the Infinite, it is the very means to penetrate into it. It goes much deeper than any philosophy, it prolongs and reverberates the revelation of a Gospel.'[680]

And then he emerges with his creative principle as with a triumphant manifesto: 'Here is the great, the most important, the first sign of a new Literature, here, in this ardour to unite Truth and Beauty, in this desirable unity of Faith and Joy, Science and Art.'[681] How does this connection between art and (philosophical or religious) truth arise? By means of the idea of the symbol: 'We seek the truth in the harmonic laws of Beauty, deducting from the latter all metaphysics – because the harmony of the nuances and the sounds symbolizes the harmony of the souls and worlds – and all morals.'[682] He then enlarges upon the history of nineteenth-century art with its Romanticism and its naturalism, to point out that there were predecessors who strove after an *idéal esthétique plus complet*, mentioning the names of Chateaubriand and Goethe.[683] They and Stendhal, de Vigny, Sénancour, Gérard de Nerval wrote for the generations that were to read them, around 1890, announcing the desire 'to let the mystic and scientific movement join in a single grand and living river of Beauty united with the Truth in Joy'[684] – a synthesis, therefore, of the personality ideal and that of science, of (human) freedom and nature, as we have characterized these basic motifs of humanism above. But we should remember, of course, that in the humanism of these people coming from a (however much secularized) Roman-Catholic milieu there are strong influences of Plotinus and of Christianity at work, of motifs that had become manifest in the first few centuries of our era in the attempt to combine Greek philosophy and Christian doctrine.[685] Morice identifies Balzac and Wagner as the great forerunners and builders of this art, and Baudelaire and Poe as the dogmatic theorists.[686]

But, although Morice enthusiastically proclaims that he wants a synthesis in which science is given a place and is taken full account of in the work of art as well as mysticism and human freedom, there remains an important restriction with respect to science. First we read the accusation that art asked the advice of science, but that the latter took advantage of it in order to dominate over art. He is no doubt referring to naturalism in literature. And it is still more clear that by this science he certainly does not merely mean positivistic science when we read: 'While waiting for the moment when science has decidedly turned to mysticism, the intuitions of the dream forestall science and celebrate such an as yet future and already definitive alliance of the religious with the scientific sense in an aesthetic fête where the very human desire for a reunion of all the human powers is glorified by a return to original simplicity.'[687]

We have already found the word 'simplicity' used in this way in Gauguin – in his letters in which he speaks of Redon, Huysmans, and Moreau[688] – and we have no doubt that this may be interpreted as evidence of Morice's influence on Gauguin's thought (and the way of formulating his thought).[689]

A little further on in his book he comes back to the subject of synthesis, and thus clearly shows that in his opinion – as in that of Gauguin and his followers – nature does play a certain part in art and that they do not at all seek for a 'non-figurative' art which in its exaltation of the freedom motif cuts through any bond with (observable) reality. The real issue was how to find an art that would realize the demand 'to suggest the whole of man by the whole of art'.[690] All the elements that were essential for the creation of a work of art in Romanticism and naturalism will have to cooperate together. For, 'The synthesis cannot be localized in a pure psychology of the passions, nor in a dramatization of the sentiments, nor in the pure observation of the world as we see it immediately round us, for then it would run the risk of ceasing to be a synthesis and become analysis again.'[691] A little further on he even more clearly states the real issue – leaving out all Plotinian philosophizing he had used to give his art theory a firm ontological basis, 'The work of art is a transaction between the temperament of the artist and nature.'[692]

This Plotinian thought is evidence of the working of old motifs in the christian world.[693] We need certainly not suspect Morice of pulling our leg in a somewhat erudite way, but we should thoroughly realize that at base this synthesis is a matter that should be understood from the dialectic of humanism,[694] in which the religious dynamic of the freedom motif is the determining impulse. This is very clear when we read the first point of his programme, drawn up to arrive at the realization of the new art: 'In art the soul regains its own depth in order that (!) the soul may free itself from all fetters for the joy and the understanding of the world and itself.'[695] And then he starts with an exposition[696] which shows that the freedom he is after is something characteristically humanistic, and of an entirely different nature from the biblical freedom. 'Every life is chained to another life', he says to prove that the freedom he desires does not yet exist in this world, so that there is 'the disorder of the world'.[697] But already the Second great Commandment given by

Christ Jesus shows that our human task and our glory is to be sought in this very bond with other human persons – 'Thou shalt love thy neighbour as thyself', for Christian freedom implies the love of all men (2 Peter 1:7) in a very concrete sense, and not all the loneliness that is the result, according to Morice, of the attainment of or even the search for freedom – 'This recovery of the self through freedom.'[698] And the thesis that this freedom gives a person 'a feeling of unlimited power'[699] throws an even clearer light on the radical difference between this humanistic striving of a person to be a god – compare what we have quoted from Carlyle in an earlier chapter[700] – and the biblical Christian striving after being a good and faithful servant who expects everything from his Lord, whose kingdom is sure to come.

This humanistic ideal of freedom is always connected dialectically with the nature motif, as absolute freedom is necessarily unrealizable and humankind will always have to capitulate to reality itself if the latter is felt to be the non-I and is identified with nature. Thus Morice may land in an antinomy, although he is no apostate from humanistic tradition, when after the quotations given above he continues, saying:

> Man's glory in the world is that instead of the dubious honour of being elected for kingship (what a chimera!) – this is an obvious allusion to the biblical Christian view – he is really reduced to being merely the servant of Nature (with a capital letter) and its confidant. Here, natural science intervenes to make a pact for a fertile alliance with metaphysics.[701]

But we shall no longer follow his trend of thought closely. We have only entered into this matter to show that what we have said above about the synthesis that was sought at this time is not some construction of ours. On the contrary, in the history of humanism this synthesis is an element in which the attempt was made to connect the two basic motifs of nature and freedom; and the more profound thinkers in this artistic milieu were aware of the fact and understood it in this sense.

The second point of Morice's programme, *Synthèse dans l'idée: Fiction*, again shows clearly that this group of artists did not at all shun contemporary reality as a subject to start from in the work of art. According to them a poet is concerned with *de symboliser sa pensée*, but for this purpose he may very well start with 'the contemporary moment'. Then 'The Dream that escapes himself may reach the appearance of everyday reality.'[702]

The third and last point of Morice's programme is *Synthèse dans l'expression: Suggestion.* Of this he says: 'Suggestion can do what expression cannot. Suggestion is the language of the "correspondences" and of the affinities of the soul and nature.' This makes it possible, for 'Suggestion alone can render in a few lines the perpetual crossing and recrossing and the mingling of details to which expression would devote whole pages,' a thought that is further elucidated by what follows: 'It has ascended to the very source of all language, to the laws of the adaption of the sounds, and the colours, of the words to the ideas.'[703] Here Morice falls back on a well-known pronouncement made by Baudelaire in the opening passage of his article on Wagner, namely that colour and sound may mutually suggest each other and that each of them may 'translate' the ideas in their own way, a thought he found in the theory of the correspondences. Both Baudelaire and Delacroix expressed similar views, also elsewhere when referring to the 'musicality' of a picture.

Gauguin

Because of the strongly personal way in which Gauguin assimilated the influences exercised on him with regard to theories and ideas, and because there was a great deal that was important for him in addition to the ideas of Morice, it is not easy to point out the latter's direct influence. To our mind it is most obvious in the remarkable 'Paragone' that Gauguin wrote. It is not easy to determine the exact date of this article that was published posthumously. But considering the style in which it is written, it is almost inconceivable that he wrote it before his Parisian time of 1890. In this article we read: 'A poet is the necessary intermediary not only between humanity and nature, but also between man and thought. The arts form a hierarchy according to the more or less numerous means with which they furnish the poet for the accomplishment of his function as an intermediary.'[704] This thought shows a strong resemblance to the idea developed in the first few pages of Morice's book.

For the rest Gauguin's ideas with respect to the question as to which of the arts is best are interesting enough, and are certainly his own. Not any man of letters would have dreamed of assigning the highest place to painting. It is typical of Gauguin's world of thought that the element of remembrance plays such an important part in it – the meaning of the 'imagination' is strongly suggestive of Baudelaire, but has been worked out in a very personal way. About pictorial art he writes:

> Painting is the most beautiful of all the arts, all the sensations are summarized in it, looking at it everybody can create a novel, as his imagination prompts him, at one glance he can have his soul overwhelmed by profound remembrances; with no efforts of the memory everything is summarized in one single instant. A complete art, comprising all the others and completing them.[705]

And indeed, here again nature – *toutes les sensations* – as well as freedom – in the 'imagination' – play an important part and the synthesis has been realized in a way that is entirely his own, although these two motifs have not really been united but remain opposites. For Gauguin may say that 'the art of the colourist' is a rich means 'to enter into an intimate relation with nature',[706] but just a moment earlier he detached the viewers from nature as persons able to project the image they wanted in their own freedom and in connection with their own remembrances. This constituted one of the most important gains of pictorial art – 'You can freely dream while you listen to music just as when you look at a picture,'[707] whereas when reading a book one would be a slave of the thoughts of the author.

Mallarmé

Through Morice, Gauguin also came into contact in 1890-1891 with Stéphane Mallarmé, the poet and theorist who was in very high esteem with the poets and writers of the generation of 1885 and was even considered to be their leader and predecessor. Gauguin attended some of his famous Tuesday-evenings and etched a portrait of Mallarmé, showing that they must have made more than just a fleeting acquaintance.

Mallarmé had a philosophical view which was peculiarly his own[708] and which was by no means shared by the group of younger men referred to a moment ago, although their thinking moved in a similar direction. The influences of Plotinus, and more directly those of English philosophers such as Berkeley – whose views of language and word will no doubt have interested him[709] – certainly played an important part, and his reaction to the positivistic-naturalistic method[710] was very sharp and vehement. This also appears clearly from the following quotation which is very characteristic of Mallarmé and, as it were, embodies a summary of his art theory. It clearly reveals his strong urge for freedom, although he asserts reality as based in our experience – 'the divine transposition for whose accomplishment man exists goes from the fact to the ideal'[711] – so that he certainly does not propose art to be exclusively occupied with the creation of a world of the imagination, nor calls up phantoms in the spirit of Redon, notwithstanding a close relation to and appreciation of the latter. He wrote:

> Abolished is the pretention – aesthetically speaking an error, although it dominates masterpieces – that it would be possible to put on the thin paper of a volume anything else but, e.g., the horror of the wood or the threat of thunder silently waiting in the foliage: not the wood as a whole in the d ensity of its trees ... Monuments, the sea, the human face, in their inherent fullness, retain a force so much more lovable that a description would only veil them, which ought to be said by evocation, allusion, I know, suggestion. This terminology that is a little random testifies to the tendency, perhaps a very decisive one, to which literary art has been subjected, and by which it has been determined as well as freed. Magic it has if it only liberates, loose from a handful of dust or reality, without binding it in the book, even as a text, the volatile dispersion that is the spirit, who is only concerned with the musicality of the whole.[712]

We may wonder what Gauguin could have learnt from Mallarmé. The latter's view of art, though showing differences from Gauguin's, was internally related to Gauguin's aims in the sense that there was a striving after freedom and, moving away from naturalistic description, both made the attempt to represent the object in its fullness. It is not impossible that Mallarmé's strong emphasis on the freedom of the artist, loose from the material (in a literal sense) made a deep impression on Gauguin. As we shall see further on, he spoke much more clearly about artistic freedom in his later years than earlier on. To him this freedom was essential to the new art of painting, of which he considered himself to be one of the leaders and builders; it was what distuinguished the new art from what had gone before. But we think we can find evidence of a direct influence exercised by Mallarmé in the sense of the quotation given just before, in the letter in which he comments upon his *D'où venons-nous? Que sommes-nous? Où allons-nous.* In this letter Gauguin made reply to a critic who had posited the thesis that 'Nothing would reveal the meaning of the allegory to us.'[713] The artist answered, 'My dream is not tangible, it does not contain any allegory; like a musical poem, it can do without a libretto' (quoted from Mallarmé). Consequently the essential thing in a work (of art) is immaterial and superior and consists exactly of 'that which has not been expressed: it results from the lines, without the colours or the words, it has not been constituted in a material sense'.[714]

To say nothing of the reference to Mallarmé, his influence is discernible even in the style of Gauguin's writing. And there is certainly a very strong agreement with Mallarmé[715] in Gauguin's use of the idea of the 'musicality' of a work of art. In addition, they agreed on the idea that the artist should use suggestion rather than description, a thought that is not found as such anywhere else in Gauguin's writings.[716]

Mallarmé did not give an art theory adapted to pictorial art, although he was a lover of this art, as can be witnessed by his own collection.[717] This is why he could not lead painters like Gauguin any further. He restricted himself to the transmission of some general thoughts and new ideals. But this was important enough.

Gauguin's escape from France

It is not easy to say to what extent Mallarmé contributed anything of decisive importance to Gauguin's ideas and plans to go to the tropics and to escape from France.[718] Morice once showed him a poem by Mallarmé which made a deep impression on him:

> Fly! Yonder! Fly! I feel that the birds are intoxicated
> Because they are in the foam of the unknown waves and
>   in the heavens ...

> I will go! Steamer with thy dancing masts
> Weigh anchor to depart for an exotic nature![719]

This expresses the spirit in which Gauguin will have felt these things. And it is certainly not impossible that on one of the Tuesday-evenings at Mallarmé's such a subject was discussed. However this may be – and there is nothing to prove it – if Mallarmé should have influenced Gauguin in this respect, he really did nothing but intensify an existing tendency. He merely urged Gauguin to realize plans and ideas that the latter had already been entertaining for some time. As was so often the case, his influence was only to intensify existing inclinations.

For there is no proof needed that Gauguin had been entertaining such plans for a long time. Had he not carried out a similar plan many years earlier, when he set out for Martinique? And had he not more than once expressed such desires himself?[720] But only in 1890 did these ideas assume a more definite form, as appears from his correspondence with Bernard.[721] He will no doubt have wished to escape from his constant financial worries and from the continuous struggle and obloquy – the result of misconception or jealousy – while he will also have been attracted by the prospect of not needing to exercise any restraint in sexual matters. 'Free at last, without any financial worries, and I shall be able to love, sing and die.'[722]

But this was certainly not the only reason. There was a deeper motive, namely his wish to have an opportunity to renew his art by tearing loose from the influence of his Western environment: 'The Western world is corrupt and whoever is a Hercules can obtain new strength by touching the soil over there, like Antaeus.'[723] Also in a letter to his wife he lays emphasis on his wish to find his own way, and he points out to her that it is a gain rather than a loss to be far away from the artistic life: 'My artistic centre is in my brain and nowhere else, and I am strong because I am never led astray by the others and because I make what is in me.'[724] And then he continues to refer on the one hand to the deaf Beethoven and on the other to Pissarro, who always followed the trends of the times.[725]

Baudelaire may have suggested to him already at an early date that a journey to a distant country might be conducive to the renewal of his art. For Baudelaire wrote: 'If . . . I take . . . an intelligent (person) and transport him into a remote country I am sure . . . this will create a new world of ideas in him . . . all this unknown vitality will be added to his own vitality; some thousands of ideas and sensations will enrich the dictionary of his mortal being.'[726] And indeed, this was what Gauguin tried to achieve; he wanted to receive new impressions in order to enrich and to deepen his art. At this time, while he still hesitated whether he would go to Madagascar or to Tahiti, he wrote: 'Besides, Madagascar offers more resources with respect to types, religion, mysticism, symbolism.'[727]

Aurier

The literary writer and critic who contributed most to the elaboration of the Synthetist art theory was no doubt Aurier. He was of course most intimately connected with the literary movement and knew all about what was being written. He had studied philosophy and had been in direct contact with Bernard – who had met him in Brittany for the first time in 1888[728]– and with Gauguin.[729] And what was most important of all, he was thoroughly acquainted with the work of these young painters.[730] Unlike Morice's theories (which no doubt had a great influence on Aurier) Aurier's reflections on painting were written with a clear idea of the kind of art he was actually talking about.

There are two articles written by him that are worth considering a little more closely, namely one from the year 1891 on Synthetist art and Gauguin,[731] and one from 1892 explaining the theory of this art again, a little more elaborately this time, with a survey of the young artists who worked in this direction.

The latter article opens with the quotation with which we started this book, a splendid piece of rhetoric with a profound background. In it nineteenth-century positivism is accused of having chased poetry away in its naïve optimism of being able to solve all mysteries, whereas actually man walks about more than ever in 'this formidable unknown'.[732] But this state of affairs can be changed if the poets (here he uses this term in the broad sense of artists in general) are called back into the world of those who shape culture, for they are the 'guardians of eternal knowledge'.[733]

Materialistic art, 'experimental and immediate' will have to go – that naturalist art starting from this, 'the antinomy of all art: concrete truth, illusionism, trompe l'oeil',[734] an art that leaves no room for any further suggestion and thus kills the insight into the idea, the true reality. This art can no longer satisfy anybody, this art with 'the short-sighted copy of social anecdotes, the imbecile imitation of the warts of nature, vulgar observation'.[735] He is clearly referring to the naturalistic art of the Salon. But just as clearly he rejects the thought that the academic art, the older 'idealistic' art of classicism, might be a solution. For, he says, the latter may produce objets beaux, but here too the artist is a 'poor, stupid prisoner of Plato's allegorical cave'.[736]

> Everywhere they are vindicating the right to the dream, the right to pasture in the azure heavens,[737] the right to wing their way towards the stars to which the absolute truth has been denied.[738]

This new 'Symbolist' art was not called into existence out of nothing by the new generation, for it already existed with men like Puvis de Chavannes, Moreau, Henner, Carriére, Rodin, and the Pre-Raphaelites, although not yet as a lucid doctrine of art.[739] What did these artists search for that was also striven after by the new generation? 'They have made efforts to understand the mysterious meaning of lines, the effects of light, and shadows, in order to use these elements, like the letters of an alphabet, to write the beautiful poem of their dreams and of their ideas.'[740] This thought is exactly like the one that Gauguin had already advanced in 1885. Here he immediately points out the peculiar characteristic of the new art, namely that the object in nature is not rendered in a merely naturalistic way. Neither is its essential character to be sought in the subject as such but in the way in which the artist's thought concerning the object, the idea of the thing, is represented. It is remarkable that he connects this theory – heard perhaps from either Gauguin or Bernard – with the thought advanced by Baudelaire (and Delacroix), namely that reality is a 'dictionary' for the artist. But the emphasis has been shifted: for Aurier does not compare the natural object as seen by the artist to a word in a dictionary – such a word is given its meaning only by its position in the context of other words – but here the artist exclusively uses the aesthetic elements of line and colour, of whose expressive value he is aware, for the writing of his 'poem'. In comparison with Delacroix and Baudelaire this means a further remove from the objects of nature and a stronger emphasis on the elements by means of which the work of art is composed iconically. This shift is also made clear in the metaphor as such: Aurier no longer speaks of words but of letters. The artist is entitled to exaggerate, to weaken, to deform 'these directly signifying characters (forms, lines, colours, etc.)'[741] that he derives from reality, not only in connection with his individual vision but also in order to give a clearer expression to the idea. For in two ways a work of art will show deviations from the strict imitation of nature given by a daguerréotype,[742] namely on account of *un tempérament* – here he implicitly refers to Zola's well-known definition – and secondly because a work of art should represent the idea of a natural object.

And then he tries to give the latter thesis a philisophical foundation and elaboration, although, just like Baudelaire in his article on Wagner, he first posits a priori that it is impossible to imagine that 'art, the supreme way of expression, could not express the universality of the souls'.[743] After this he sets forth a clearly Plotinian theory saying that every *objet* – this word is best rendered by 'being' or 'entity' in view of the fact that he also refers to a person as an object – has self-consciousness (*conscience de son être*), it is *la Pensée* – which will become clear if we look upon the word *pensée* as a translation of the Greek Plotinian word *Nous*[744] – and a form which is also the *objet* itself. This form must, therefore, be in direct relation to that *pensée* by which assertion the theory of the equivalences is there: 'The form . . . the body of every object is . . . the tangible modality of its being, i.e., the visible signification of a *pensée.*'[745] Thus he arrives 'through all this repulsive jargon and through all this hoary scholasticism'[746] at this definition: 'In nature everything is ultimately only a signified Idea,'[747] in which he again identifies *pensée* with 'Idea'[748] without giving any further account of this fact. Thus, according to Aurier, the possibility is here given of a more profound symbolism than what the naturalists accepted implicitly – for they said that a work of art reflects something of its maker's temperament.[749]

But the average man does not know the *réalité idéique* – only 'the superior minds of our poor blind humanity', the true artists, should know it.[750] The artist is 'the expressor of the absolute Beings', because 'as a superior man he is the tamer of the monster illusion;' he knows how to 'walk as a master in this temple of fantasy',

> where living columns
> sometimes utter confused words ...

whereas 'the imbecile human herd, duped by appearances that make them deny the essential ideas', will in eternal blindness

> pass through the forests of symbols
> that watch them with familiar glances. [751]

This quotation proves that he has combined these Plotinian thoughts with metaphors borrowed directly from Baudelaire.

Then he reverts to the idea that 'The various combinations of lines, plans, shades, colours, constitute the vocabulary of a mysterious language which is miraculously expressive.'[752] which every true artist ought to know. This thought is not clearly connected with the symbol theory or founded in the latter with the concept of equivalence associated with it. For to say that the form of a thing is the symbol of the idea of a thing – which is a purely philosophical theory – is something different from saying that in a work of art, lines and colours and so on can express something about a thing – which is an art-theoretical assertion, or rather, an experience gained from looking at works of art.

The elaboration of this theory of expression is something new, namely that 'This language, like all languages, has its alphabet, its orthography, its grammar, syntax, even its rhetoric which is: the style.'[753] Later on Gauguin made an observation on style which suggests to us that he had taken over this thought. He writes: 'Many persons say I cannot draw, because I make special forms. When will they understand that the execution, the drawing, and the colour (the Style) must be in accordance with the poem?'[754] This is especially clear if we consider this pronouncement in the light of Gauguin's explanation of his manner of working:

> In a way I work like the Bible, in which the doctrine ... announces itself in a symbolic form presenting a double aspect, a form which first materializes the pure Idea in order to make it better understandable ... this is the literal, superficial, figurative, mysterious meaning of a parable; and then the second aspect which gives the Spirit of the former sense. This is the sense that is not figurative anymore, but the formed, explicit one of this parable.[755]

This exposition shows that Gauguin had a similar art theory – derived from Balzac, Baudelaire, and especially Morice – so that he did not meet with any difficulties in taking over Aurier's theory on style.

According to Aurier, therefore, a work of art symbolizes a spiritual datum in the first place by reflecting the artist's mind – this is unavoidable and secondly because the artist has expressed in it the Idea of things. Thus the art object is 'At best a fragment of the spirituality of the artist, and at worst the whole spirituality of the artist plus the essential spirituality of the various objective beings.'[756] Then the object of art is a new being with a life of its own owing to a soul 'which is the synthesis of two souls, the soul of the artist and that of Nature'.[757] In proportion to the depth of this soul of the work of art it is able to convey to the spectator emotions, ideas and feelings. 'It is this influx, this sympathetic radiation felt at the sight of a masterpiece which is called the feeling of beauty, the aesthetic emotion.'[758]

There are two remarks to be made here. In the first place, that this art theory is perfectly subjectivistic: for beauty is considered to be only a particular state of mind evoked by the work of art in the spectator. And further, this theory makes the beauty of a work of art dependent on the degree to which it expresses spiritual truths, and not on the presence or absence of its agreement with particular aesthetical norms, nor on its having certain qualities inherent in the structure of the work of art as such. The correctness and the force with which a work of art expresses something about the artist and the object in nature with which it is concerned are decisive for its beauty. Consequently it must be judged according to some criterion of truth (however subjective this may be) rather than according to abstract-aesthetical norms. This remarkable trait in the theory of art is found in exactly the same way in Plotinus: 'The aesthetics of Plotinus is really impregnated with this idea, that beauty is not added to things as an exterior, accidental quality but constitutes their true essence (*Ennéades* I, 2) . . . beauty must, therefore, be the reflex of an Idea that makes this being what it is. Aesthetic value and intellectual value coalesce.'[759]

This aesthetic feeling arising from the contact between the work of art as an (active) agent and the spectator as a (passive) receptor is very much analogous to Love – a purer love than human love which is always impaired by 'some muddy sexuality', thus Aurier continues. This is a very important point to him. For according to him, on account of positivism we have landed in 'pure and simple animality', and 'We must again learn what is love, the source of any comprehension.'[760] However, owing to sensualism we cannot discover anything in a woman but flesh to gratify material desires; and through scepticism God himself has become a mere nominalistic abstraction so that this love of him has also become impossible.[761] 'Only one love has still been permitted to us, that of works of art. Let us throw ourselves on that last plank of salvation.'[762]

These kinds of ideas, founded in Plotinian Swedenborgian theories about the 'correspondences', making art to take the place of the divine revelation and thus elevating it to religion, were of rather frequent occurrence in the circles with which we are now concerned. Already Baudelaire expressed himself in this spirit,[763] and – even more explicitly – Morice, whose *Littérature de tout à l'heure* Aurier will, of course, have known thoroughly, and whose art-theoretical views must have had a great influence on him. For Morice wrote: 'Understood thus, art is merely the revealer of the Infinite ... So by nature, and in essence, art is religious.'[764]

Continuing his discourse, Aurier says that this art is the true and absolute art – and it is only because our positivistic society has obliterated any fundamental revelation that such a complicated theoretical argumentation has become necessary. It is true and absolute because it is legitimate, theoretically, but also because 'It is found to be at roots identical with primitive art, art as it was discovered by the instinctive geniuses of the earliest times of humanity.'[765] This is a thought he may have derived from Gauguin – recall the latter's discourse when he met men of letters at Paris for the first time[766] – or he may have read it in Denis' expositions, or he owed it to both sources. Denis even called the new art *neo-traditionaliste* in his article of 1890 which we shall consider in more detail below.

All this is brilliantly summarized in Aurier's rhetorical passage on Gauguin, the artist and leader and most important exponent of the art that Aurier was referring to as follows: 'It is the plastic interpretation of Platonism done by a savage genius.'[767] The latter additional observation was certainly not superfluous. Aurier was too well informed of the art of his time not to know that the mere adherence to some correct theory does not yet produce masterpieces – as a matter of fact we have already pointed out that he looked upon great artists as exceptions, as men who can see and are thus able to reveal what others cannot understand. But, at least in his first article, he also points to the necessity of *le don d'émotivité* which, if translated into a more sober idiom than Aurier's terminology, only means the artist's talent.[768]

Finally we wish to consider what Aurier really meant by the slogan-like rhetoric in the summary of his artistic ideals at the end of his article on Gauguin when he claims that the new art is to be:[769]

1. Ideational, for its unique ideal will be the expression of the Idea.[770] [This may be clear after what we have discussed so far.]

2. Symbolistic, for it expresses this Idea by means of forms.[771] [With this he refers to his expressivistic theories.]

3. Synthetistic, for it will write these forms, these signs, according to a method which is generally understandable.[772] [This is far from clear. Aurier rarely mentions synthesis – we have come upon the term only once,

namely in the second article, in which he uses this term in the same sense as Morice. [773] Here, in this important passage, this notion is put in the foreground for the first time. It is as if Aurier suddenly realizes that he has not yet used this term which was so often employed by Gauguin and his fellow artists in particular, and therefore Aurier apparently just jots it down here. His short digression probably means that this art speaks clearly and is not esoterically strange and only intelligible to the initiated.]

4. Subjective, for the object will never be considered as an object but as the sign of an idea perceived by the subject.[774] [This thought, too, was not plainly expressed in his expositions although it was given eo ipso in the view that only a genius can 'read' the signs of the Idea that are represented by the objects.[775]]

5. Decorative, for decorative art in its proper sense, as the Egyptians, very probably the Greeks and the Primitives understood it, is nothing but a manifestation of art at once subjective, synthetic, symbolic and ideational.[776] [Again he introduces a new thought into his 'summary'. He possibly wants somehow to do justice to an idea of Bernard's. If we take this digression seriously, this decorative character is the centre of this entire theory of art, for the decorative quality implies all the positive qualities he has ascribed to the new art. His reference to the Egyptians might be considered to be reminiscent of ideas that Gauguin took very much to heart,[777] or perhaps this passage is only a free rendering of a passage in Maurice Denis' article of 1890, of point XXIV of that 'manifesto'.]

Indeed in surveying these articles we cannot but grant to Denis that he was right when he observed that Gauguin must have been astonished when, on his arrival in Paris in 1890, he saw what proportions the new art theory had assumed that had started from his up till then only fragmentary thoughts about the new art.[778] All this was very important to Denis, for 'Sérusier proved to us by means of Hegel – and the abstruse articles by Albert Aurier insisted on the fact – that logically, philosophically, Gauguin was right.'[779]

Maurice Denis

We shall now have to consider the theories developed in this circle to which we referred a moment ago, the group of Denis and Sérusier, young artists that knew each other intimately from the time they had spent together at the Académie Julian. Denis does not leave us in doubt of the fact that Sérusier was the motivating power; this appears from the quotation given above.[780] Yet Denis was the first to publish an article, all the more important as it was the result of discussions and conversations carried on among the artists themselves, unlike the articles dealt with above which were all by literary men – although Aurier had been in close contact with the painters. But Denis' article shows us what the painters themselves around the year 1890 thought of these things.

The article opens with a thesis which has later on been quoted again and again and which became a kind of slogan at the time of the rise of non-figurative art: 'Remember that a picture – before being a warhorse, a nude woman or whatever sort of anecdote – is essentially a surface covered with colours arranged in a certain order.'[781] It may be doubted whether the appeal made to this pronouncement later on was justified. Denis in the first place turns on the art of the Salon of his time. This polemical element cannot be ignored. It also appears from the theses immediately following this pronouncement, which relate to Bouguereau, Meisonnier and Dagnan-Bouveret. For this Salon art was naturalistic in the extreme and sought to represent the natural object in the picture as exactly (as much as a photograph) as possible. This method overlooked the view that a work of art is an iconic representation, an artistic achievement that is not identical with what is given in reality. And it is the renewed insight, that a work of art is an artistic object representing reality iconically, which was posited in this first thesis of Denis. It is true, a year later Denis said: 'I think that above everything else a painting should be an ornament. The choice of subjects or scenes means nothing. It is through its coloured surface, through the value of tones, through the harmony of lines that I attempt to reach the mind, arouse the emotion.'[782] But from his memoirs of a slightly later date it appears that this thesis was certainly not intended in an abstract-expressionistic sense. In his memoirs of the time spent at the Académie Julian he tells how from Brittany Sérusier brought the 'talisman' that embodied the result of an afternoon lesson given by Gauguin. His comment is as follows: 'Thus for the first time the future concept of the "surface covered with colours arranged in a certain order" was given to us in a paradoxical, unforgettable form.'[783] On reading further we see more clearly that this concerns what we have called 'the iconic aspect': 'Thus we came to know that every work of art is a transposition, a caricature, the passionate equivalent of a sensation perceived.'[784]

After quoting Gauguin in his thesis XV, 'There is art when the figures are given with plastic modelling',[785] exposing again the defects of the entire art of the Salons with its *trompe l'oeil, modelé en ronde bosse,* in short its quasi classicistic hyper-naturalism, he continues in thesis XX with a discussion of Gauguin's *Calvaire Breton*: 'From the canvas itself, a surface area coated with colours, springs the bitter or the consoling emotion, "literary" as the painters say, without there being any need to interpose the memory of another earlier sensation (like that of the given natural object used).'[786] We notice how much Denis is struggling with the difficulty of putting these new thoughts into words. For his use of the term *littéraire* is, properly speaking, incorrect – in the quotation that will presently be given below this word is used in a different and more correct way. If, however, we should not yet be convinced of the fact that Denis is not engaged in drawing up a theory of non-figurative art – which in itself would be an anachronism, as a tendency in this direction was out of the question in 1890, at least certainly not in such a deliberate and conscious form – the clarifying passage immediately after this one is no doubt convincing enough: 'A Byzantine Christ is a symbol; the Jesus of modern painters, even if rendered most accurately, is merely literary. In the first it is the form that is expressive; in the second, nature (being imitated) wants to be as such.'[787] Here the term 'literary' is used in its proper sense[788] of 'descriptive, rendering something elaborately and literally'.

Once more we wish to emphasize the fact that Denis was no Symbolist. Thus in 1892 he wrote:

> We are astonished that informed critics ... take pleasure in confusing mystical and allegorical tendencies, i.e., the attempt to express oneself by means of the subject and the symbolistic[789] tendencies, i.e., the search for an expression by means of the work of art.[790]

Later on he explains that the precursor of Synthetism is not to be found in academic art, nor in the art of Pre-Raphaelitism or in art that was entirely determined by Symbolist poetry but much rather in the Realism of the previous period: 'The inaugurators of Synthetist art were landscapists, still-life painters, not at all "painters of the soul".'[791]

When studying the history of art there are always three elements to be distinguished. Each of them must be examined separately if we are to gain an insight into the nature and character of a particular movement. First there is the class of subjects that are treated – they will always be relevant or related to the artists' view of life and the world, and be connected with the function a work of art is to have; second there is the style or the way in which the different motifs (figures or things) are rendered, *peinture* and (idealizing or not) 'deformation';[792] finally there is the purely aesthetic quality, the composition, the interplay of lines and colours on the painted surface. Of course, these three elements will have to be adapted to each other as, properly speaking, they presuppose each other, in order that they may together elucidate the content of the work of art.[793] In a true work of art of high standing they will, therefore, form a unified coherence in such a way that it will not be possible to speak of one of them without saying something about the other at the same time, and vice versa. This insight was not consciously realized in this way by Maurice Denis or by any of the other art theorists, although it is remarkable that Denis showed these elements in their close mutual relation. As an artist he starts from this interrelatedness, as it were, as a matter of course. This fact was already clear to us when we discussed the first of his theses in his article of 1890, of which thesis XXIV is also important in this respect.

In thesis XXIV he wrote:

> Art is the sanctification of nature, of the nature of everybody who is content to live. What is the great art that is called decorative, the art of the Hindus, the Assyrians, the Egyptians, the Greeks, the art of the Middle Ages and the Renaissance [all art that has ever been important] and the decidedly superior modern artworks [he may be referring to Cézanne and Gauguin]? What else is it but disguising common sensations – of natural objects – as sacred icons, lofty,[794] impressive.[795]

He reveals a realistic attitude with regard to his subjects, or at least with regard to his motifs,[796] which are derived from everyday reality and experience. But they are treated in such a way that a picture elucidates those objects, as it were, in their permanent sense; we could almost say the picture reveals their permanent meaning. Thus arises beauty – our third element, already referred to by the term *decoratif*. 'The universal triumph of the imagination of the aesthetes over the stupid efforts at imitation; the triumph of the feeling of beauty over the naturalist lie.'[797] The coherence of the elements mentioned by us is even clearer expressed by the following quotation derived from an article of a somewhat later date: 'They [the first generation of the new art] were willing to submit to the laws of harmony governing the relations between the colours, the arrangement of lines [the researches of Seurat, Bernard, C. Pissarro]; but it also served to bring more sincerity in the rendering of their impressions.' After this he gives in one single sentence the following brief summary containing what is essential in the Synthetist theory of art: 'There was, therefore, a close correspondence between forms and sensations.'[798]

The latter, namely the correspondence, is the prerequisite for the artistic unity in the work of art. It enables the artist's activity to make also the (purely aesthetic) composition into something of an expression that at the least runs parallel to the object represented. We purposely use the word 'parallel', for neither Denis, nor Gauguin, Aurier and so on, succeeded in arriving at a conception that really explained the unity in the work of art of the aesthetic qualities and the expressive rendering of the object. Again and again in their views we find the demand, on the one hand to deform the given object in order to elucidate it in accordance with the artist's vision; on the other hand to realize the 'decorative' beauty in the work of art. It is as if, notwithstanding their expositions, there is to them something static or abstract in this beauty, an obedience to universal laws apart from any expressiveness. This appears clearly from Denis' distinction (in a later article) of objective and subjective deformation. The former is related to the universal laws of beauty, the latter to the artist's subjective vision of his object:

> From an objective standpoint, the decorative, aesthetic, and rational composition ... became the counter part, the necessary corrective of the

theory of the equivalents. This theory justified all possible transpositions with regard to the expression, even those that had the character of caricatures, excessive renderings of character; the objective deformation in its turn compelled the artist to turn everything into Beauty. To summarize: the expressive synthesis, the symbol of a sensation or a feeling, had to be an eloquent transcription and, at the same time, an object composed to please the eyes.[799]

This emphasis on the purely aesthetic element is hardly found in the authors we have discussed above. However much they tried to explain the peculiar character of pictorial art – to give an account of its relation to nature, on the one hand, and to the creative artist, on the other – their art theory was defective. It was rather a kind of epistemology than a formulation giving an answer to the question of what constituted the beauty of a work of art. We may be glad that they laid such a great emphasis on the demand for truth and concentration on what is meaningful. Yet their views were often hardly an answer to the question what after all is essential in a picture as a work of art, and how together with the *idéique* it also embodies beauty proper. It is possible that Denis being a painter himself was conducive to laying a stronger emphasis on the purely aesthetic elements. But perhaps Sérusier's influence was more important in this connection. Denis repeatedly referred to him at that time (c. 1890) as the man whose influence and guidance were so decisive precisely with respect to his views of art.

An overview of all of Denis' conceptions of art shows them to be largely free of any philosophizing. What Denis wrote about the movement of 1890 much later is hardly applicable to his own article on that period: 'We made a singular mixture of Plotinus, Edgar Poe, Baudelaire and Schopenhauer.'[800]

Sérusier

No doubt Sérusier was very important with respect to the more exact formulation of the Synthetist art theory. Denis claimed that Sérusier had been his teacher in this matter.[801] Therefore we may suppose that Denis' article of 1890 contained a great deal of Sérusier's thought; at the same time we must not overlook the possibility that, as early as 1889, Serusier influenced Gauguin and his circle at Le Pouldu. He was certainly co-responsible for the further formulation and extension of the theory. It is not possible to say in how far he influenced Aurier directly. However this may be, Aurier is sure to have learnt a great deal from Morice's book from the year 1889; but as Morice's theories and those of Sérusier – also on account of the fact that they drew their inspiration from the same sources – were very much akin, they could be easily combined. Sérusier too was influenced by Plotinus; he also admired Balzac's *Seraphita* and

Louis Lambert[802] and had had direct contact with old mystic traditions via Schuré's book, *Les grands Initiés*.[803] We have already pointed out that Aurier may have learnt some things from Denis' article.

The theory of correspondences

Before examining the way in which Sérusier practically gave the Synthetist art theory its definitive formulation and final content we wish to see how the theory of the correspondences (or equivalences) had developed.

Its first clear exposition in connection with contemporary art is found in Baudelaire who, as a matter of fact, had derived it from all kinds of older sources.[804] Baudelaire actually points out how colours may have a particular meaning and effect,[805] and in connection with Delacroix he shows that the latter's colours are in perfect harmony with the subject of the picture.[806] He does not explicitly base this thought in his *Salons* on the theory of the correspondences, perhaps to avoid diminishing the intelligibility of these articles, although the discussion *in extenso* in the *Salon* of 1859 is really based on this theory. In it he focuses on the 'imagination', which does not work in an arbitrary way but is based on 'a collection of rules required by the organization of the spiritual being'.[807] Only in his article on Wagner he gives a very concise and dogmatic exposition of his view – colours and sounds can express ideas on account of the analogies or correspondences.[808]

Yet we can hardly maintain that Baudelaire bases his theory on the thought that colours (and lines) can represent ideas – rather, among others, these are means for the artist to arrive at a grand conception. Delacroix achieved his impressive results, according to Baudelaire, 'by the whole, by the profound, complete harmony between his colour, his subject, his drawing, and by the dramatic gestures of his figures'.[809] And although he did not say so literally, we may suspect that when Baudelaire spoke of reality as a dictionary to the artist,[810] he did not exclusively, or even in the first place, refer to colours (and lines) but to figures, human beings, things observed in reality. In fact, on reading carefully what Delacroix observed in this connection,[811] we shall see that also to him colour and composition play an important part in the work of art as co-determinant elements, but he certainly did not mean to say that it is not necessary to select real data from reality for the artist to realize his conception. Finally, however much Baudelaire's views were concerned with the art of painting, things literary played a great part in it; and recalling his poem 'Correspondances' we shall have to think of some symbolical language, some kind of metaphor, to understand it correctly, rather than of abstract-aesthetical means like colour, rhythm and so on, which, as a matter of fact, he himself said clearly elsewhere.[812]

Directing our attention to Morice, we see that the state of affairs has really remained what it was. Morice mentions 'suggestion' as one of the main points of his programme. In explanation he appears to mean that line, colour and sound can elucidate a particular situation better than a possibly much more elaborate description. This thought is based on the theory of correspondences; however, it remains only one of the building blocks of the work of art, and the whole theory of art as such is not restricted to it.[813]

Aurier goes a step further. The elements with which the pictorial artists write their *poème de leurs rêves* are, indeed, the purely pictorial means of lines, colours and so on. But, strictly speaking, the art theory that he bases on Plotinus is not the foundation of this thought. For he does not say how it is that lines and colours can represent an idea, though his meaning is clear, namely that lines, colours and so on are the means by which the forms can be made to speak, to reveal the idea.

It is as if in Aurier we come upon two theories, derived from two different sources: the literary Plotinian source of the correspondences; and the expressive force of lines and colours, which he had taken over from the Synthetist painters. But he does not succeed in composing a (theoretical) tightly reasoned whole out of these.

In the articles developing his ideas Denis speaks typically as a painter. For he says: 'There was, consequently, a close correspondence between forms and sensations',[814] but he does not enter any further into the theoretical implications of the theory of the correspondences. The impression is made that he has borrowed the term from usage current in his circle, it is true, but that he uses it as it were naïvely, as founded in an experience of the iconic aspect by looking at art. And, characteristically, he does not mention ideas that must be represented but 'sensations' (visual experiences). The laws determining the coherence of lines and colours are properly speaking always related by him to a purely aesthetic harmony, side by side (by no means identical) with the expressive deformation artists apply to elucidate their vision. Summing up Denis' various articles we cannot avoid having the impression that in his first article, perhaps directly influenced by Sérusier, the immediate connection between the iconic representation and the purely aesthetic composition of the work (called the 'decorative element') is posited clearest of all, but that later on these two elements are considered more and more separate from each other, while the philosophical foundation is omitted.

Sérusier (continued)

And thus we come to Sérusier himself, who immediately continues the work of the great forerunners Delacroix, Gauguin and Baudelaire in building up an expressivistic theory as well as tries to explain what constitutes the pure beauty of a work of art in this connection. For this purpose he connects the theory of the correspondences with the ideas obtained in the circle of Seurat, and later on also with the closely related ideas of the Beuroner school. In this way what used to be merely one of the means at the disposal of the artist became the basis of a total theory of art. For the theory of the correspondences was almost invariably a main part of the art theory of the authors we have reviewed so far, though in most cases it provided the foundation for a kind of metaphor rather than explicitly concerned itself with pictorial means as such.

We have more or less reconstructed Sérusier's thought of the 1890s from the scanty data at our disposal in letters and other sources. Thus in a letter of 1892, addressed to his pupil Verkade, we read:

> I want a firm, simple and finished drawing. By this I do not mean that it should contain all the details, but that each line should be planned and have its own function, its expressive and decorative role in the whole; I wish every line to be necessary. But if this end is to be attained one should know one's subject thoroughly.[815]

This latter observation clearly shows that we need not expect to find him striving after non-figurative art. His formulation is a very concise and brilliant summary of the world of thought of Gauguin and his circle. Here the synthesis so eagerly sought for at that time has been found in an almost irreproachable form. Human freedom is implied, no doubt, in the concept *expressif* – although this is not entirely separated from nature or from the world in which we live, for it explicates the meaning of the object (as it is understood by the artist) – while nature plays a role in the work of art in an entirely different way, namely in the 'natural laws' of aesthetic harmony. This was perhaps implicitly intended in Gauguin's views though he never clearly expressed it. Also the idea of the decorative element – still to be considered as a more or less secondary matter for Bernard and Gauguin, a motif derived from art that was essentially foreign to them, namely Art Nouveau – has here become an intrinsic element of art theory.

If it should be thought that we are inferring far too much from this short quotation, we could refer to other data we have from 1896. In a small book, Mellerio briefly summarized the ideas of different artists of the new generation, among whom also Sérusier. According to Mellerio, Sérusier thought the following about the origin of a picture:

> The direct spectacle of nature exciting the feelings – the memory which calls them back to the mind – the imagination that creates them by means of combinations – bring us into an involuntary mental state. Then the Idea is formed in our mind. It is superior to our lower nature on account of its logic, and its harmony appearing to the artist, he exerts himself to express it in its integral intensity, a result that he can all the better achieve if he ignores

details and only retains the characteristics. Then the artist puts the spectator in the same frame of mind that he was in – which is the purpose of art.[816]

This shows clearly that Sérusier closely followed what Gauguin had taught him. We wish to point out how strong the voice of the freedom motif is: both in apprehending what is given and in representing it, a person is free to transcend reality, which is meaningless in itself and functions as a stimulant only. Alongside this, in a letter in the same year from Verkade to Sérusier, we see how much the latter was constantly submitting the pictorial means themselves to closer examination and how he concentrated the expressivistic theory on this: 'We have followed the right ways, seeking the Idea expressed by decorative forms and explained by simple colours.'[817] We know that Sérusier was also busy with a *cercle chromatique* and with other investigations in the field of the laws of pure aesthetics, in a way that no doubt shows the influence of Henri (and Seurat).[818] We may also note that, alongside the expressivistic idea based on the theory of the correspondences applied by Sérusier in the purest and most consistent way, the scientific element is not lacking in this synthesis.

So we are confronted here with an almost seamless texture of two interwoven motifs, namely that of the primacy of human personality (in its freedom) and that of the primacy of science (in its search for laws of nature). We have found the former in the first quotation from 1896 – which as such did not posit absolute freedom but allowed nature to play a role, albeit a subordinate one. The second motif was implied in the second quotation, although alongside pure law-conformity human freedom of choice was not lacking (in the conception of the Idea, as explained in the first quotation, though subordinated to the aesthetic norms conceived of as laws of nature).

Only in this light can it become clear how it was that in the following years Sérusier gave up the splendid unity of his theory. We hear him promulgate very contradictory opinions – which alternately lay the main stress now on the one motif, then on the other. After all, the synthesis is not really possible and the two motifs remain mutually contradictory in their ultimate consequences.[819] In a letter written in 1905 to Willibrord Verkade we read:

> I believe that our age is rather less advanced as far as Christian art is concerned, than the earliest times of Christianity. So I believe that we can apply to our age what he (P. Didier) says about these times: that the search for beauty would prevent the direct and natural expression of the ideas; let us express ourselves anyhow and above all let us be sincere with ourselves: this constituted the spirit of the primitives; the correction will come little by little, it cannot precede the ideas without barring them the way. For the rest, there is no agreement among us about the meaning of the word. Beauty . . . I think you take this word in an objective sense, whereas I take it in a subjective

meaning. This difference separates the schools of this century, which have ended in Cabanel and Bouguereau, from those to which I have belonged.[820]

The latter statement clearly shows that he rejected any academic art, whereas his own ideals pointed in the direction of intuitive and free expression. A year afterwards however, his words were very emphatically in favour of the opposite tendency – here he demanded what he had condemned a year earlier as putting obstacles in the way of the artist's self-expression:

> I now believe that the only thing that can make an artist is the establishing of a harmony in forms and colours. Harmony is the only means, like prayer, to bring us into communion with God. All the rest in art is only illustration, personal sentiment, individualism, human poetry. As to copying natural objects, especially models that are not even natural, I think it horrible.[821]

In this case this one element in his view of art had ousted nearly all the others, to such an extent even that he drew conclusions in a direction that very nearly approached a theory of abstract art. At that time he was indeed the life and soul of a group of young artists of whom Delaunay was to be the first to realize literally the thought expressed in this quotation.[822]

Sérusier's activity was completed with his booklet *A.B.C. de la peinture* in 1921, a summary of all that he had thought out and sought in former years. The work opens with a sharp rejection of any naturalism and any idea of imitation and then it continues with a discourse about the way our knowledge and understanding of things is determined by experience, remembrance, the relative situation with respect to other facts, and our own situation and condition at the moment when we observe all these things.[823] As the given facts, apprehended thus, are translated by us in the work of art by means of pictorial signs (with iconic means, we should say) and, as we can do so only in a personal way – because absolute beauty is impossible for us to reach on account of our human limitations – this gives rise to style.[824]

But, he says, in and behind this style, which is peculiar to a personality, a period or a nation, there is 'A superior quality, a language that is common to every human intelligence. Without some trace of this universal language there does not exist any work of art . . . These elements are inherent in our constitution, therefore inborn.'[825] Owing to the present low standard of education and culture, however, we are compelled to rediscover these elements *par l'abstraction et la généralisation*. And then he goes on to give a treatise on these general laws of art based on the numerical laws and especially on geometry, where he refers to the golden section, and so on.[826] But this aesthetic is only a means, the alphabet[827] with the aid of which artists express themselves – here we notice that in this well thought-out treatise he reverts to the well-balanced synthesis of the 1890s: 'Thoughts and moral qualities can only be represented by formal equivalents. It is the faculty of perceiving these correspondences that makes the artist.'[828] This may be achieved if the artist studies 'the exterior world in its laws and not in its accidents'.[829]

This shows clearly that Sérusier is aware of the fact that art is an iconic representation clothed in the idiom of a pictorial language of what is given in human experience, an expression of what a person has grasped and understood of some given reality. It is striking that although he appeals to the theory of the correspondences he did not think it necessary to elaborate it or to give it a philosophical basis. This is all the more striking as, apart from what others have said about him, he himself relates that in the period around 1890, when all this had been formulated, they were absorbed in the study of Plato, Aristotle and the Neoplatonics.[830] It is as if that philosophical background is taken for granted. Men like Morice and Aurier, not to mention Balzac and Baudelaire, had already laid the foundation. He was now concerned with the elaboration of a theory of art that was genuinely directed to art itself and to artistic methods, one that did not lose itself in philosophical speculation. This constitutes Sérusier's great merit, and the transparency of his views makes him the strongest exponent of the Synthetist art theory.

Nevertheless, it must be admitted that there is also some rigidity in his theory, for it systematized Gauguin's conceptions in too rigorous a framework,[831] so that the fullness and liveliness, the richness of ideas found in Gauguin, was crumpled up and lost in more than one respect. We might draw a direct parallel with a comparison of the art of the two men. Sérusier's art is inferior in terms of warmth, richness and variation when compared with Gauguin's – so much so that when Sérusier happened to use a motif from Gauguin it was deprived of its staggering impact, the surprise it gives the spectator, even today still, long after it has lost its revolutionary meaning and has become a tradition of the past.[832]

Bernard

Now there is only one more figure to be considered, namely Bernard in his later development. We shall not go into the controversy – or should we say the quarrel and breach – between Gauguin and Bernard. Let us only examine in what sense he himself elaborated the theories advanced before 1890. Entering more deeply again into these views of art, we discover a remarkable complication in the typically Roman Catholic personality of Bernard. We might have pointed it out elsewhere and in an earlier context, but nowhere does it come out so clearly as here. For we have already found more than once that the ideas (as well as the concrete activities) of these shapers of culture and artists we have dealt with were determined by the basic motif of humanism, with its internal duality of nature and freedom. In order to solve this tension, or at least to reduce it to a kind of balance, they had recourse already very early on (in Baudelaire, for instance) to theories of which the origin was to be sought in an entirely different world view from that of humanism, in this case in late antique Neoplatonism. But the latter itself was dependent on a completely different basic motif, namely that of form and matter.[833] This form-matter motif always raises the question of the interrelation between a permanent, self-supporting 'eternal' form and an always 'flowing', changing matter that composes and decomposes itself perpetually, and in which that form manifests itself in some way or another.[834] We might say that in the synthesis between Greek and humanistic thought the 'nature' of humanism is as such conceived after the manner of the Greek form-matter duality – in which the latter is deprived of its intrinsically religious sense.[835] There is a further complication in the case of Bernard, who was a very well-informed Roman Catholic believer and whose thought was determined in all kinds of ways by the motif of nature and grace which had been given its more elaborate formulation and determination during the Middle Ages – a motif which in itself was also the result of a synthesis between Christian-biblical and classical thought, starting with the form-matter polarity.[836]

Let us now consider how these things were concretely formulated by Bernard in his views of art. In an article written in 1895 we read: 'For if visible things are the figure of things invisible – this is a Greek way of thinking, or to be more exact it is Neoplatonic – man's essence partaking of the divine and endowed with harmony, coordinates and transforms nature according to its own supremacy in order to make it express his real supranatural origin.'[837] The latter part of this quotation is clearly the expression of the primacy of the personality embodying the freedom motif. It is hardly christianized by its references to the 'divine'. Especially the expression 'supremacy' is significant. The same state of affairs is found a little further on and expressed in the following way: 'So through God there is a latent creation in man which is superior to the visible world.'[838]

Next he dwells on the symbol, appealing (with elaborate quotations) to Pseudo-Dionysius Areopagite,[839] to present us with a pure Neoplatonism only slightly christianized.[840] Finally he fits all this into a framework which is strongly suggestive of the scholastic doctrine of the *donum super additum*, for he writes of 'the beautiful which is the result of a special illumination and which is the gift of the Holy Ghost'.[841] Meanwhile it appears that in all this Bernard also implicitly understood that a work of art has an iconic nature – this was the real discovery of his generation. And a great part of their philosophizing was intended to justify and to prove it, for they felt this to be something perfectly new. Thus he can give an elaborate and no doubt adequate defence of the meaning and the composition of the (Greek Catholic) icons leading to the thesis: 'The lines are arranged in a coherence which is more or less significant, colours are characters (alphabetical symbols), their combinations are phrases . . . Young and old formulas are, therefore, a kind of script that we should always understand, always know and not deny.'[842]

That the significance of the theories developed by the Synthetists really far transcended the style of their own group – whom they wanted to defend with it against naturalism and all its implications – may appear from the fact that even after Bernard had turned his back upon Synthetism as such, he continued to defend this theory and to adhere to it. He did so, for example, in a short exposition in 1926 (his polemical afterthought, to defend his own authorship, is left out of the account here), in which he wrote as follows: 'In nature there is no form that is not a sign for the spirit [this is the Greek *nous* concept, or Aurier's notion of *pensée*]; all nature is, therefore, a symbol as such.'[843] This purely Plotinian thought is elaborated in an exposition of the method by which an artist can achieve the desired result, working from memory, because thus the image will be 'purified' (which idea we have come upon more than once before), with his conclusion: 'There is an internal work done unconsciously; all that cannot be united with my temperament is effaced from me; what is left is in accordance with myself.'[844] It is remarkable how this theory then results in a purely humanistic, and even purely individualistic, view of art, with its ideal of giving expression to the strictly personal.

Speaking about Gauguin, Bernard continues with a striking thought about 'the great directions of the lines, the simplification of colours which become more significant for the subject than representative of light and tone'.[845] Here we see him trying to attain to a direct result of the insight into the iconic character of a work of art, that of the *Indifferenzlicht*, the true meaning of which had no longer been recognized owing to the *natürliches Naturlicht* of nineteenth-century art.[846] It is a really striking thing that in the work of Gauguin and his circle the *Beleuchtungslicht* had vanished. This *Beleuchtungslicht* belonged to post-Renaissance art, which always assumed the observer to be standing in the same spot. It was replaced by the iconic representation of persons and things in a painting by means of the *Indifferenzlicht*. As a matter of fact, Gauguin had been aware of this to a certain extent when, in answer to a question asked by Bernard and Laval about shadows, he said that the latter as such are by no means indispensable.[847]

To come back to the remarkably complicated synthesis, which is so obviously manifest in Bernard, we would in summary quote his pronouncement that in his art he sought 'to unite the visible truth of the outer world and the divine of the inner life'.[848] The former agrees with the symbol theory founded in the Greek basic motif and is used here to give 'nature' (in the sense of the humanistic polarity) its due, whereas the latter clearly expresses the personality ideal. We see on closer examination that the synthesis that was aimed for in those days was even more complicated than it appeared to be at first sight. Remarkably enough, the Roman Catholic basic motif did not have any profound influence on art-theoretical thought in general, although it was noticeable in men like Bernard.

8
Some Terms and Concepts

In the Synthetist movement at the end of the nineteenth century a definitive reaction against positivism forces its way through, against naturalism, against the primacy of the ideal of natural science. The exact opposite is sought of what at one time Darwin wrote in the preface to his *The Botanic Garden* (1789): 'The general design of the following sheets is to enlist the Imagination under the banner of Science.'[849] Gauguin formulates the contrast sharply in his exposition (quoted by Morice): 'So-called refined art proceeds from the senses and serves nature;' whereas the art to come was quite different, art that 'proceeds from the spirit and employs nature'.[850]

Synthèse

In this connection the term *synthèse* was often used in those days, so often that it occurs almost on every written or printed page. For this reason it is impossible and meaningless to enumerate all the passages where it is found. But it is important to examine how the term was used.

It is certainly unnecessary to enter into all kinds of cases where the word is used carelessly or only more or less rhetorically, so that it is difficult to discover any real sense in it. Such usage, however, evidences the popularity of the term. Its meaning in these instances will no doubt be remotely related to the one that we are trying to discover in this section. To give an example of what we mean we will quote Maurice Denis: 'Thus by choice and synthesis there is a certain habit formed by the modern artist, an eclectic and exclusive habit of interpreting optical sensation.'[851] Here he discusses the Salon artists with their naturalism and in the term 'synthesis' we cannot detect anything more than the assertion that the artists worked from a particular artistic point of view.

More than once we can translate *synthèse* by artistic unity, harmonious composition, internal unity of conception, the understanding and the coherence of forms and colours. Thus Aurier says in a review of the Salons of 1891 about the art exhibited there: 'It is . . . above all the complete neglect of style, of a true style which at base is nothing but the comprehension of the intellectuality of the forms, and which has become impossible, in the first place on account of the neglect of any synthesis in art.'[852] The same Aurier wrote about Sérusier that 'His last canvases, of a poetic kind of symbolism, a beautiful and skilful synthesis of lines and colours, hold out a promise of an artist of the first class.'[853] The term 'synthesis' is really used here in a way that does justice to Sérusier's own conception. For he himself writes: 'The synthesis consists in embodying all forms in the small number of forms in which we can think, straight lines, some angles, circular arcs and ellipses; if we depart from there we get lost in an ocean of varieties.'[854] And perhaps we find the term used most correctly in this sense by Denis. When speaking of the classics and the classicists he says: 'What dominates is the idea of synthesis. There is not a classic who is not sparing of his means, who does not subordinate all the graces of detail to the beauty of the whole, who does not attain to greatness by conciseness.'[855]

But (apart from the last quotation) it is difficult to abide by the translation given. In this term we feel a connotation which has a wider meaning than merely 'a consciously balanced composition' – it also denotes something of the relation between a work of art and reality.[856] This becomes clearer when, referring to the new art, we read of 'the triumph of the spirit of synthesis over that of analysis, of the imagination over sensation, of man over nature'.[857] At the same time this shows the origin of the term.

For originally 'synthesis' is a scientific term meaning 'combination', considering things in their interrelation. As such it is mostly used in opposition to 'analysis', a setting apart that makes a sharp distinction between the parts viewed separately and by themselves. In French *synthétique* often means something that we could translate by 'inductive'.[858] Also in Baudelaire we come across this original meaning when, for example, he writes about the (naturalistic-academic) artists of his day: 'He feels, or rather, he judges successively, in an analytic way', as opposed to others who 'feel immediately, everything simultaneously in a synthetic way'.[859]

Already here Baudelaire uses the term in connection with artistic questions, and we can understand that it thus gradually gained ground in the world of the artists. Thus in a dictionary we find *sub voce* 'the synthetic language' defined as that 'which expresses complex relations in one single word, and which groups accessory ideas round the principal idea in rounded sentences'.[860] And although we have never found in any dictionary that the men of letters indicated in this way a particular technique or attitude with respect to the artistic use of language,[861] we may assume that it certainly existed. How else can one explain the sudden rise and popularity of the term after 1885? Also the painters no doubt used the term in a similar way, which we will examine in a later context.[862]

The artists of this generation opposed naturalism blaming it for its (positivistic) analytical attitude. They themselves strove after a new art which was to represent reality in a new synthetic way. It is, therefore, understandable that the term was very suitable to express their ideal, especially on account of its scientific connotations, and also in connection with the linguistic (and art-technical)[863] sense given to it in their own circle. And as these artists were so occupied with all kinds of theories to give their own view its foundation and to defend it, quite naturally the term was burdened still more, in a very specific sense connected with their art-theoretical considerations, which in turn were connected with their starting point based on their view of life. Even more so, in philosophy proper the term had been used in this sense since a much earlier time, as we shall see in what follows.

We have already explained more than once that in those years they were sharply aware of their own position with respect to their view of life: they wanted to wrench themselves free from the primacy of the science ideal and to vindicate personal freedom again without giving up what the nineteenth century had yielded in terms of the domination of nature. They sought to find a way of doing equal justice to the two basic tendencies in the humanistic motifs of nature and freedom.

'At the base of their thought there is the longing for ALL. Aesthetic synthesis that is what they are after.'[864] Thus Morice briefly summarized their main thought. The attempt was made to recapture human freedom – after the period of slavery in the service of nature – without, however, giving up nature. Thus it was hoped they could grasp the fullness of being, while there was a deep-seated feeling that only in art such a synthesis could be fully realized. Morice even more amply formulates this 'artistic synthesis' in his sensational book of 1889, *La Litérature de tout à l'heure*. 'It is there, in this ardent wish to unite Beauty with Truth, in this desirable unity of Faith and Joy, Science and Art',[865] in which we clearly see truth and natural-scientific insight and even faith placed on the same level and opposed to beauty, joy and art. And if this pronouncement is to be taken seriously, it entails remarkable consequences. For, if the new art aims at a synthesis of the elements mentioned, but nevertheless truth and beauty, science and art remain clearly opposed to each other, how can art ever reach a synthesis? For art is only one of the elements to be synthetized and, as such, a different kind to the element of truth found in natural science.

In fact, we are confronted with an internal contradiction here: on the one hand they stuck to the view of reality based on the primacy of the ideal of science; on the other, they wanted to oppose it and at the same time connect with it art and beauty – which in the sense intended by them (cf. chapter 5) are connected with the personality ideal.[866] It is understandable that not long after this, at the turn of the century, both elements contained in the synthesis tear themselves loose from each other. Painting then becomes the direct expression of human freedom and is not to be related to truth in any way in the sense of conformation with reality as such, whereas there is also a tendency toward a kind of supernaturalism with a multi-dimensional colour-film as its ideal (evoking an image that does not in any way deviate from the natural visual objects).

Also in Aurier we meet with the term and the concept 'synthesis' in a very elaborate form. Especially in his plan for his *Oeuvre*, as a totality made up of poems:

> What is a poem? The synthesis of all the general ideas perceived by a given self. The synthesis of the sensations constitutes the sciences. The synthesis of the sciences constitutes the philosophies. The synthesis of the philosophies constitutes the dogmas. The synthesis of dogmas constitutes a poem. A poem is, therefore, pre-eminently an intellectual conclusion; a poem is the essential synthesis of the self.[867]

In part he understands by 'synthesis' what is generally understood by it in science – summary, total view – but on examining the final conclusion we notice that thus in art a synthesis is achieved (and now the term is used as in the passage from Morice mentioned above, as the combination of the two polar tendencies within the humanistic view of life and the world) between the given (natural) reality and human personality. Somewhere else Aurier expresses himself more clearly and more simply when he says of the work of art that it is 'a new being ... since it has to animate a soul which is the synthesis of two souls, the soul of the artist and the soul of nature'.[868]

The demand for such a synthesis gives rise to a special problem for art, a problem which was not new, as a matter of fact, but which had been anticipated by men like Baudelaire. It had even presented itself before, namely in the first attempts of the Romantics to assign a place to nature, before they abandoned themselves entirely to positivism. At that time the artists sought the new art in what was natural but would not relinquish the peculiar character of Romanticism. This was the very opposite to what was seen at the end of the century. Van Tieghem has very sharply formulated the problem:

> The purpose ... of introducing contemporary life into literature constituted one of the newest tendencies, one of the boldest ... of the Romantic movement; also the most difficult one to realize if one insisted on maintaining and developing the rights of the imagination, sensibility, the ideal, on keeping the divine mantle of poetry free from any dirt in its contact with prosaic reality, on avoiding the prosaic form and the vulgar content.[869]

How it was thought possible to solve such a problem has been explained by Paul Adam, writing in 1886 as follows:

> Modern life does not remain forbidden to us ... But it will be permitted to transfigure it in a synthesis[870] different from that hitherto given by the impressionism of the novel. We shall not paint it as it subjectivizes itself in the brain of a stableboy or of a signboard painter, but as our individual retina makes it to us, our much more comprehensive vision. We shall put in the phantoms of our dream, our hallucination, our remembrance, the imaginary evocations, for all this is found in life and constitutes it.[871]

But we now know that this effort failed: the movement defended here ultimately lead to art that we have called 'decadent' in an earlier context. In this art the natural and contemporary datum had practically disappeared to make room for a kind of traditionalistic or allegorical-symbolistic subject matter – such as is found in pictorial art with the Rose†Croix group, which even had the following formulation in their rules: 'Here are the rejected subjects . . . Any representation of contemporary private or public life,' and recommended as subject-matter, for example, 'the interpretation of oriental theogonies except those of the yellow races' and prescribed that 'An allegory should be expressive like "modesty and vanity", or decorative like the work of Puvis de Chavannes.'[872]

The best solution to the artistic problem posited was affected by those who broke with naturalism not only as a starting point but also as a style. For thus it was possible to maintain Realism in the subjects fairly well without any proviso – without introducing queer phantoms and hallucinatory subjects – and yet to avoid 'the prosaic form and the vulgar content'.[873] This is what we find in the group we have called the Synthetists. But here, too, the synthesis has proved to be of a transitory character, for the anti-naturalistic element had overgrown everything to such an extent that in the end the naturalness was lost, notwithstanding the ostensibly realistic subject matter (e.g. in Picasso's still lifes from around 1910 or in the work of the Fauves).

In the above we again and again came back to the tension between abiding by Realism, which at the time implied the risk of relapsing into naturalism and copying nature as in photography, and promoting the artist's personality in a realization of his or her vision in personal freedom. The tension between the science ideal and the personality ideal, with its striving for freedom, may manifest itself also in another way. We have already discussed this point in the preceding chapter when dealing with Sérusier. Denis again sharply formulates the antinomy we have in mind when writing down his reminiscences of the 'great' time of 1890:

> Instead of being the copy of nature, art became the subjective deformation of nature. From an objective viewpoint, the decorative, aesthetic, and rational composition, of which the Impressionists had not thought because it ran counter to their preference for improvisation, became the counterpart, the necessary corrective of the theory of the equivalences. This theory justified all possible transpositions with regard to the expression, even those that had the character of caricatures, excessive renderings of character; the objective transformation[874] in its turn compelled the artist to turn everything into Beauty. To summarize: the expressive synthesis, the symbol of a sensation or a feeling, was to be an eloquent transcription and, at the same time, an object composed to please the eyes.[875]

By 'objective deformation' Denis no doubt means working in accordance with fixed laws such as Sérusier had formulated (in line with

Henry and others), namely the rational, mathematically exact laws alleged to determine the aesthetical. And of course these laws are in sharp contrast with the freedom sought and found in the expression of the strictly personal vision – *la déformation subjective* legalized by means of the theory of the equivalences.[876]

The antinomy has certainly been posited more correctly here. For here we are concerned with a conflict within the artistic creation itself, a question of artistic means and the way to use them. Before that time the real antinomy was found in the artist's attitude towards reality, while the question of artistic realization was not raised or, if raised at all, was not formulated in such a sharp way. The latter case was especially found in the Symbolist circle such as, leaving literature aside, the Rose†Croix movement. We have already seen how it was realized there, whereas the antinomy formulated by Denis can only be found in circles that have radically broken with the academic-naturalistic method.

It stands to reason that also the attempt to effect a synthesis in the sense so correctly formulated by Denis could not last. When consistently thought out in one direction this effort leads to work created in the spirit of Delaunay after 1914. The aim was to evoke a kind of pure beauty by affirming the aesthetic laws, using circles and contrasting colours, while any meaning or any expression had disappeared. The other direction led to the Expressionists and the Fauves, to the art, made for instance by Kandinsky in his *Blaue Reiter* period, lacking any 'rational' composition.

'Among all the others, painting is the art that will pave the way to resolve the antinomy of the sensible and the intellectual world,'[877] claimed Delaroche in an article on Gauguin, quoted with approval by the latter. The general opinion of those days was indeed that the synthesis sought for could be realized especially in and through art.

This thought was certainly not new. We find it already strongly represented in Romanticism. At that time too a synthesis was sought, similar to that at the end of the century. The most striking example is found in Krug, whose philosophy is called 'transcendental Synthetism' in which the fundamental idea is that 'Real and ideal are posited in our mind as equally original and related to each other.'[878] Art was in a position to concretize this synthesis. Thus Kant wrote: 'In the field of human rational activity the desired synthesis of freedom and nature, of teleology and necessity, of the practical and the theoretical function is represented by Genius which produces the works of the fine arts in a teleology without utility.'[879] These thoughts were carried through in the circle of the Jena idealists in the aesthetic idealism,[880] in which we must especially refer to Schiller[881] and Schelling.[882]

No doubt the German idealistic philosophy influenced thought in France at the end of the nineteenth century,[883] but generally speaking we shall not have to think of the two men just mentioned; rather of

Schopenhauer (and Eduard von Hartmann). We have already spoken about this in the second chapter, where we have also pointed out that above all Carlyle must be looked upon as an important link between the German philosophy of the early part of the nineteenth century and French thought – especially in artistic circles. For the painters in whom we are in the first place interested Carlyle was no doubt very important. The influence of German idealistic philosophy was only indirect as may appear for instance from Morice's book, repeatedly quoted by us (and the talks we know he had with Gauguin and possibly also with others). Whatever may have been the state of affairs among the literary artists and the painters, we must always consider that there was only question of a purely philosophical interest on their part in so far as it enabled them to elucidate or to promote their own new ideals. And in any case we should guard against the thought that the new tendency arose under the influence of the idealistic philosophy from Kant up to and including Schelling and Hegel. Neither need we suppose that there was any contact or any acquaintance with German Neo-Kantianism, which came very markedly to the fore in those very same years.

Here we are concerned with the use of the term 'synthesis'. This term was indeed current in the German thought referred to in a sense similar to what we found with the French in the latter part of the nineteenth century. But it was less frequent than might have been expected. Even in Kant's *Kritik der Urteilskraft* it occurs rarely, and never explicitly in the sense obtaining among the French.[884] At any rate, in the specific sense in which the latter used it so often (at that time and in that context), the term occurs too seldom in the German philosophers for us to seek the origin of its popularity in these thinkers – also considering their rather indirect and far from important influence.

In 1915 Sérusier wrote: 'The movement to which we belong preceded the German influences. In philosophy we spoke about Plato, Aristotle, the Neoplatonics and never about Kant.'[885] This shows that at least with regard to the painters any question of a direct and conscious influence on the part of the German idealistic philosophy is precluded – a conclusion we dare to risk because especially Sérusier was the most philosophically minded and philosophically grounded figure among them.

It seems to be meaningful in connection with our present inquiry, to try and find out what Neoplatonism may have contributed both as regards the ideas and as regards the term used. The short summary of some of its principal thoughts given by Windelband will immediately make things clear:

> In it the Mind appears as the synthetic function which creates plurality out of its own higher unity. From this general point of view the Neoplatonics worked out the psychology of knowledge under the principle of the activity of consciousness. For according to this view the 'higher soul' can no longer

be considered as passive, but in accordance with its essence only as active also in all its functions. All of its insight rests on the synthesis of various moments; even where knowledge is related to the sensible datum the body only is passive, whereas the soul is active in becoming conscious of it; and exactly the same thing holds for sensory feelings and affects.[886]

Calling to mind the theories advanced by Gauguin and his followers around 1890 we are at once aware of being in a kindred climate. The question of whether this is due to the fact that such ideas appealed to the artists of that period as a more exact foundation for their artistic aims or, that such ideas became common property via Swedenborg, Balzac, Baudelaire and others in such a way that this kinship was only a matter of time, cannot be answered directly. And yet it is striking that these ideas were not found in other movements of this period or of the time immediately prior to it. Perhaps the situation can be best explained as follows: once the search had been made for ways of realizing the primacy of the human mind over nature, the Neoplatonism contained in their tradition directed thought, as it were, automatically and determined the formulations.

Finally however, and we shall not extensively elaborate this theme, also in the Plotinian world of thought art was the ideal way in which humanity could free itself from materiality and concretize its view of the Ideas. Perhaps Plotinus himself casually referred to something that we should call art when, in this connection, he spoke of hieroglyphs.[887] At any rate, he advanced these thoughts in principle. But they were elaborated by the later Neoplatonists, for example by Ficino, a typical Renaissance man in his emphasis on the freedom of the human will who considered the freedom of the human mind to be humankind's supremacy. This may also explain the great similarity to the Synthetist art theories when Ficino posits that 'Art does not copy nature: it has its own laws. The supremacy of human art is rooted in man's power of self-determination. Thus Zeuxis' bunch of grapes, Appelles' horses and dogs, Praxiteles' Venus are superior to what nature could do: for they are evidence of the triumph of the human mind over matter.'[888] But although it is clear that this Neoplatonism might be a source of the idea of the synthesis or at least might have further determined it in its concrete formation, and although the term 'synthesis' actually occurs in this movement, as we have seen, it does not seem plausible that we have found its origin here. For this philosophy and the literature in which it was discussed lay too far outside the interests of these artists and literary men. Yet we must not ignore Neoplatonism as a co-determinant of the popularity of the term.

Barre thus summarizes Moréas' ideas: 'The synthetic relation between the Idea and its appearances can only be fixed by an archetypal and complex style.'[889] This is a good example showing how the word is directly borrowed from the Plotinian sphere of thought and applied as an art-theoretical term indicating one of the principal elements of the new art.

Especially in the circle of the painters the term 'synthesis' seems to have been very popular. This may appear from the fact that one day Gauguin, supreme scoffer as he is, makes a pot on which he writes 'Vive la sintaize',[890] and still more undeniably from the fact that the first exhibition at which the group of artists round Gauguin made their collective début in 1889 during the World Exposition was entitled 'Groupe impressionniste et synthétiste'.[891]

Would it be possible to trace how the painters used this term in actual practice, what it implied for them with respect to their manner of working? In 1888 Gauguin wrote about his own work that it contained 'synthesis of a form and a colour without considering one to be the dominant'.[892] This clearly means the composition, the combining organization, a meaning that nearly approaches the one we quoted in connection with language.[893] It is, however, evident that summarizing and subordinating to one facet is immediately connected with the question of what and how the artist is to select – and certainly at a time when they were so sensitive to the problems concerning the relation between nature and art. In this term, therefore, the art-theoretical and the philosophical opinions as well as their view of life were always implicitly comprehended. Perhaps we might explain these things best with the aid of the following short survey of Gauguin's theories, given by Dom Eduard Verkade in 1926:

> The impression of nature must be wedded to the aesthetic sentiment which chooses, arranges, simplifies and synthesizes. The painter ought not to rest until he has given birth to the child of his imagination ... begotten by the union of his mind with reality ... Gauguin insisted on a logical construction of composition, on a harmonious apportionment of light and dark colours, the simplification of forms and proportions, so as to endow the outlines of forms with a powerful and eloquent expression.[894]

On quietly reading the first sentence we realize that there, and in all other cases in the world of artists, the terms 'choose', 'arrange', and 'simplify' are more or less synonymous with 'synthesize'. In this use the primacy of (artistic) humanity over nature given in the impression is concretized. This thought is further qualified by the successive sentences of the quotation. The synthesis implied, therefore, meant concretely what we read in the last sentence: great attention paid to the individual, peculiar character of the artistic realization, so that it may forcefully express what reality meant to the artist. When we have become aware of this state of affairs with regard to 'synthesis' we also see how it is possible for the term to have so many apparently diverging acceptations, and how it is that the same writer uses it now in this, now in that sense, for at one time the same fundamental thought or leitmotiv is viewed according to its philosophical aspect, then again according to its practical-artistic meaning, or considered in a more close relation with the artist's view of life, or according to the artistic form in which it has been concretized.

Imagination

In the quotation we have just been studying we left one sentence out of account, namely that a work of art is supposed to be 'a child of [the artist's] imagination'. It is clear that in this way one of the elements in the synthesis is emphasized, the element of the freely creating human personality, that is to say, one of the two poles of the basic motif (which is to be brought into a relation of equilibrium or, at least, into some coherence with one another).

We can hardly be surprised to find this term frequently used during this period. As we have already seen, it plays an important role also with those whom we have called precursors, especially with Baudelaire. It was not only in current use among the artists outside of the Salon, but even in the latter circle. Thus a certain Ph. Gauckler devotes a whole section to it in his book *Le Beau et son histoire*.[895] This author is perhaps best characterized by his definition of *le beau*: 'the true manifestation of the unity of being by finite phenomena'.[896] After an elaborate explanation of all kinds of concepts like *le sublime*, *le joli*, and *le goat*, remaining within the world of thought of the academicians although not without some originality, he discusses *l'imagination*. He starts from the statement that even if in our work we have followed all the correct precepts and methods – which he had treated elaborately before – it is still possible that the result may be dead and meaningless. This is due to the lack of the imagination: 'Dragged through the mire by the moderns,[897] who did not understand it and thought it beneath them to understand it, it was highly appreciated by the Ancients who under the name of inspiration assigned to it a divine origin.'[898]

The Synthetists and their nearest adherents nearly always use the term in direct opposition to the servile copying method of naturalism, to the soulless art of the Salon. In this, too, their precursors had shown them the way. Thus Baudelaire writes, more or less repeating Delacroix's own words, that 'nature is nothing but a dictionary', and says, 'Those who have no imagination copy the dictionary. The result is a great vice, the vice of banality.'[899] For Delacroix had said 'The true art of painting is that in which the imagination speaks above all',[900] and more exactly he observed elsewhere: 'With the artist the imagination does not only represent such and such objects, but it combines them for the purpose he wants to reach, it makes pictures, images that he composes at will.'[901]

It needs no further argument that the latter statement was bound to appeal to the generation of 1890. Thus Denis calls to mind his reminiscences of that period and says: 'Instead of working on the basis of the the eye, we searched "in the mysterious centre of thought", as Gauguin had said. Thus the imagination again becomes the queen of the faculties according to the wish of Baudelaire.'[902]

'Imagination', therefore, besides inspiration, means above all creative artistic power – using the given object as material for arriving at a very personal, free expression in the work of art.

Rêve

As we have seen, these precursors at that time also rendered the concept 'imagination' by the term *rêve*, 'dream'. It is certainly true that more than once the term loses its sharply defined meaning through its frequent use and becomes a slogan, with little meaning – more an indication of an atmosphere, always with the connotation 'non-naturalistic'.[903] For the term was extremely frequent in oral and written use among this young generation. This may be proved from *Les Deliquescences d'Adoré Floupette, poèmes décadents*, a booklet published in 1885 containing a mocking caricature of the circle of literary artists. It is here we find the sentence that is so significant in the present context: 'The dream, the dream! friends, let us embark for the dream.'[904]

The original 'dream' – but we should not think of a dream in the sense of what happens to us when we sleep – still plays a role, namely the *rêve*, the daydream, the ideal, something we aspire after, something we hope will happen or that we wish to attain to. This is the meaning of the word in a sentence like the following: 'His dream of art began to take shape.'[905] For also this dream is something made by a person, a projection. As soon as this projection into the future is directed to the work of art that one intends to produce, thus concentrating it on a very particular piece of work, one very nearly approaches the meaning attached to the word, especially by the artists of the nineteenth century whom we are discussing. Extending this meaning a little, we arrive at the acceptance of style, artistic ideal, vision or conception. In view of the use of the term by artists like Baudelaire and the attitude that was so strongly opposed to naturalism, it is not surprising that *rêve* also came to mean 'the free self-projected vision of the artist'. Besides, the term was naturally adaptable to such use: is not a dream the opposite of commonplace everyday reality? It explains a pronouncement made by Bernard (even without attaching the art-theoretical connotations proper to the term, as we shall see): 'What deceives the eye is identity. What delights and elevates the mind – for a picture is first of all a dream written down and from a certain viewpoint a kind of illusory springboard for the mind itself – is harmony, that which has been felt.'[906]

Le rêve consequently refers to the daydream, and for our understanding of their ideas of art it is very instructive to recall Gauguin's pronouncement: 'A waking dream, almost the same thing as a dream in sleep. The dream in sleep is often bolder, sometimes a little more logical.'[907] Thus the *rêve* is less concerned with the style, the artistic realization, than with the subject matter, this being a difference of nuance we should always bear in mind when we come upon the term. This will be clear when we read what Gauguin wrote about his picture *Te Rerioa (Le rêve)* of 1897: 'Everything is a dream[908] in this picture; whether it is the child, the mother, the horseman on the path, or the painter's dream! All this is beside the painting, they will say. Who knows? Perhaps not.'[909]

In the theory of art of the circle of Poe, Baudelaire, Mallarmé, Morice, the men of letters who precisely as thinkers had such a great influence on the painters round Gauguin, the word *rêve* had an even wider implication. Baudelaire, directly influenced by Poe, writes about the 'dream' as follows: 'But the dream is also a means to acquire knowledge, a mode of perceiving what is real or, rather, some super-reality of which our stable universe is only a simplification and, so to say, a caricature.'[910]

But it was Mallarmé's view that had been thought out sharpest and most consistently. Wyzewa summarizes his view concisely in the following words: 'He admits the reality of the world, but he admits it as the reality of fiction. Nature with its shimmering fairy scenes, the rapid and coloured spectacle of clouds, and the startling human societies are dreams of the soul; real: but are not all dreams real?'[911] Mallarmé's application of these thoughts to literature in his *Poème en prose, un spectacle interrompu* is very characteristic. He describes his ideal of a paper 'that notes the events in the light that is proper to a dream'. For, he continues, 'Reality is an artifice suitable to orientate an average intellect among the mirages of a fact; but owing to this it rests on some universal agreement: let us therefore see if in the ideal there is not a necessary, evident, simple aspect serving as a type.'[912]

In what might be called a typically artistic-aristocratic attitude, this is a view of reality and of our knowledge about it that is strongly reminiscent of Berkeley. The latter denies the existence of any matter and says that all reality consists in 'ideas' that persons possess. He distinguishes 'ideas of sense' from 'ideas of imagination' - the latter are the product of our activity, the former are created in us by God – by means of which Berkeley tries to escape the scepticistic consequences of his conception. The unity of our experience of reality – which to Berkeley can only consist in the combination of 'ideas', which when considered in themselves are always individual – is not an original datum but is the product of the combination of activities in a person. As such it is arbitrary, although experience always works regularly and constantly in this, an activity of combining. This shows that here an important step is taken in the direction of subjectivizing knowledge, in the sense that the contribution made to knowledge by that which is knowable consists exclusively of its being knowable. Later on, in Kant, both thought about what is given and our experience of it in time and space became a priory categories, qualities of human understanding, thus changing epistemology into 'transcendental logic'. At this stage there is no longer any question of a reality apart from human logic.[913]

When we call to mind what Plotinus had said in this connection (as mentioned above in the discussion on 'synthesis') the agreement with his conception is obvious. Discovering a tradition that leads via Plotinus and Berkeley to Mallarmé, we understand why Mallarmé, who at first sight does not seem to quite fit in with the rest of the circle we are discussing, fits there perfectly. He is just less directly influenced by Plotinus and handles the same conception (philosophically speaking) in a modern way, and therefore the connection between him and the Neoplatonic tradition in art theory is less obvious and less marked.

But the term *rêve* is very heavily burdened for Mallarmé: it denotes Berkeley's 'ideas of imagination' and at the same time it emphasizes his scepsis with regard to the knowledge of reality. Everyday knowledge is based on a *universelle entente*, and as a matter of fact everything is *rêve*, the product of a person's creative imagination – although, as we have seen in the previous chapter, Mallarmé does not entirely cut through the bond with given reality, certainly not in (artistic) practice. This term rêve is consequently something new in comparison with the old tradition. It is the contribution of the nineteenth century that it gives a positive sense to this rêve, which first had a negative content in, for instance, Kant's *Träume eines Geistessehers*. Its origin in the literary sphere seems to be an established fact; it's introduction to the world of the painters happened already earlier, with Goya.[914]

Morice (as well as Aurier) used the term in a similar sense and applied it to art theory in a characteristic way. Thus Morice writes: 'Beauty . . . the dream of the true. But what is this delight of the spiritualized sense if not the radiation of truth in symbols that deprive it of the dryness of abstraction and complete it in the joys of the dream?'[915] Thus it becomes clear for what purpose these thoughts were used, namely to get free from the primacy of analysis as used in natural science.

We may ask whether the painters were aware of all this. They were certainly not aware of the philosophical meaning we have tried to define above. Still less did they realize the historical background – in which they probably took no interest. On reading again the quotations from the painters in this connection, it appears that there was always a certain apprehension about this connotation, some understanding of the deeper meaning expressed by this term and put in words by the men of letters.[916] But even then it is almost identical with 'imagination' – recall that Berkeley did not speak of *rêve* but of 'ideas of imagination'. So *rêve* is generally speaking (and certainly in the case of the painters) distinguished from 'imagination' only by some vague connotations, a certain tone of feeling – the word strongly emphasizes the free, self-creating aspect of the imagination, even more markedly subjective and individual. We might find a further confirmation of this in the way Gauguin uses the term *rêve* in his letter to Fontainas in 1899. There we might translate it by 'imagination', but then we would fail to express a shade of meaning that we might retain if we translated *rêve* by 'artistic daydream', artistic conception of a strictly individualistic, and in any case obviously subjectivistic, view of reality: 'The idol ... embodying my dream ... and all this is sadly singing in my soul and in my scenery, while I am painting and dreaming at the same time ... I close my eyes in order to see without understanding the dream in the infinite space receding before me.'[917]

Symbol

The typically Synthetist standpoint has been sharply expressed by Bernard in a short summary: 'There is only symbolism at this price: a symbol is nothing but the mind presented in a form, the ideal in the sensible.'[918] This shows how the idea of the symbol is used in order to effect the synthesis we are discussing. Less kind but very clear and no doubt with some foundation is Poizat's description – it is true, he speaks of the decadents in this case (their pictorial equivalent we have called the Symbolists), but in this matter the theories of both trends are very alike: [919] 'The decadents had rallied to subjectivism ... they no longer looked at things except through the distorting mirror of their dreamy souls. And as on the other hand they were great reasoners, they very soon came to look upon things, thus thought of and immaterialized, as merely emblems and symbols.'[920]

As a matter of fact, the art-theoretical notion of the symbol is no novelty. We come upon it already in the time of the Romantics. Even such a man as Heine – the connecting link between German Romanticism and French literature – makes use of it and in his exposition even excels in clarity and lucidity:

> Tones, words, colours, and forms, phenomena in general, are merely symbols of the idea, symbols arising in the soul of the artist when he is moved by the holy spirit of the world, his works of art are only symbols by means of which he communicates his own ideas to other souls ... Is the artist so entirely free in the choice and the arrangement of his mysterious flowers?[921] Or does he only choose and combine because he has to do so? I answer this question about a mystical constraint in the affirmative ... In art I am a supernaturalist. I believe that the artist cannot discover all his types in nature, but that the most significant types are, as it were, revealed to his soul as the innate symbolism of inborn ideas.[922]

This thought is also clearly found in Baudelaire:[923] 'With the most excellent poets there is no metaphor, comparison or epithet which is not a mathematically exact adaptation in the actual situation, because these comparisons, metaphors and epithets have been drawn from the inexhaustible fund of the universal analogy and cannot be drawn from anywhere else.'[924] After all that has been said we need not argue any longer that such a pronouncement will certainly have influenced the artists of the generation of 1885-1890. Also Mallarmé's similar theory will have strengthened this thought and made it almost inevitable. Ghil's *Traité du verbe* of 1885, the influential publication that explained and distributed Mallarmé's ideas, will have contributed a great deal too. Among other things he writes in it as follows: '[For the poet to compose] the sole worthy vision: the real and suggestive symbol in which the primary and final Idea, or truth, will rise in its naked integrity palpitating for the dream.'[925]

But if it is so clear where these artists got their ideas from, the question remains where is the origin of this thought. After what we have written especially about Aurier and Morice the answer is not difficult to find. Without doubt we are dealing here with a Neoplatonic tradition. As a matter of fact they were well aware of this state of affairs. Thus Bernard, for instance, has an elaborate quotation from Pseudo-Dionysius Areopagita:[926] 'We, therefore, have some difficulty to believe words relating to divine mysteries which we only contemplate through the veil of sensory symbols . . . the various forms in which a sacred symbolism clothes the divine, for, looked at from outside, are they not full of some inadmissible and imaginary monstrosity?'[927] Is it not as if we hear a direct echo of such thoughts when in Rémy de Gourmont we read: 'One should seek the eternal in the diversity of the momentary forms, the truth that remains in the False that will pass away, perennial logic in the instantaneous illogical?'[928] But we need not look for ideas like these in the works of the literary men who had hardly any contact with the painters we have been examining. Aurier expresses very similar thoughts,[929] and that while appealing to Swedenborg – who himself derived his thoughts from similar Plotinian sources. Aurier concludes: 'Well if this has been admitted, then the possibility and the legitimacy have been granted for the artist to be preoccupied in his work by that ideistic substratum that is found everywhere in the universe and which, according to Plato, is the sole true reality.'[930]

Indeed, when we go more deeply into the literature handled by these artists and men of letters, we again and again come upon the same considerations. We are referring to Carlyle, for instance, who in his turn started from the German idealistic philosophy, Romantic literature and art theory: 'In the symbol proper . . . the Infinite is made to blend itself with the finite, to stand visible, and as it were attainable thereby.'[931] Of this we find as it were a direct, though flowery, translation in Morice, when he speaks of 'the work of art which reveals, and whose perfection of form above all consists in effacing that form in order not to let anything persist to disturb thought but the vague and charming appearance, the charming and dominating, the dominating and fecund appearance of a divine entity of the Infinite'.[932]

It is to be understood that they were so strongly convinced of the truth of these ideas that art was considered to be impossible without them: 'A simple imitation of material things that does not signify anything spiritual is never art, in other words there is not, there is never art without symbolism.'[933]

Art as revelation

If we allow the thoughts concisely summarized in the above to be impressed in our mind, the conclusion is unavoidable that art reveals a higher reality to us, *L'Infini*, the Ideas found behind reality according to the theory of Plato. And in fact the view that art is the pre-eminent instrument of divine revelation is found especially with the literary men, and is repeatedly placed in the foreground.

This thought was already old and was found implicitly at least in Plotinus. But we meet with it explicitly in Ficino, for whom it was connected with the typical religious basic motif of modern times, which assumes such a clear form especially with these men, namely the theme of the freedom and independence of the human mind.[934] Thus he can claim that art has its own laws and does not copy nature, for the exalted character of human art is rooted in the human power of self-determination. 'Thus the grapes of Zeuxis, the horses and dogs of Apelles and Praxiteles' Venus are works that are superior to those of nature, for they testify to the triumph of the human mind over matter.'[935]

Via all kinds of mysticistic and occultistic movements that were strong during Romanticism (and we have to point out again the importance of Swedenborg) this kind of thought penetrated also to the world of the artists. V.E. Michelet makes this clear in the following passage of his writing in 1891:

> What is a poet? He is one of the incarnations in which is manifested the Revealer, the Hero, the man whom Carlyle calls: 'a messenger sent by the impenetrable Infinite with tidings for us'. This conception of the Hero, expressed by a visionary genius is the direct consequence of another conception which is universally admitted by occultists and mystics and was formulated as follows by Novalis: 'Every created being is a revelation.'[936]

In *Noa Noa*, Morice elaborates these ideas in connection with Gauguin in his own poetical way:

> Somewhere outside of the world, in the heaven of joy and beauty it is the day of the supreme epiphany when a great artist has crowned with his genius one of the innumerable beautiful figures of Nature, when the artist, himself the child of Nature, fed by it, living on it, rises to proclaim the beauty of his mother: when Nature allows one of the changing aspects of its mysterious visage to eternalize the word of its enigma in a work of art.[937]

But already some years earlier Morice had preached this gospel of beauty very clearly in his important book: 'Art is nothing but the revealer of the Infinite: for the poet it is even a means to penetrate into it. He penetrates much deeper than any philosophy, he prolongs and re-echoes in it the revelation of a Gospel, he is a light that calls up light.'[938] How is the truth found in a work of art? 'We sought the truth in the harmonic laws of Beauty and deduced all metaphysics from the latter – for the harmony of nuances and of sounds symbolizes the harmony of the souls and the worlds – and all morality.'[939]

Reading the quotations just given, which sometimes border on profanity, and knowing that kindred thoughts did not only remain restricted to the world of the artists but also penetrated the ecclesiastical environment, we cannot but consider it understandable, and even a matter of course, that criticism was inevitable. And thus it is perhaps not so surprising that it was precisely Dr Abraham Kuyper who in 1898 subjected Symbolism to a penetrating criticism. We will study the contents of his paper here.[940]

Kuyper starts with a survey of the symptoms of the new movement as it manifested itself in the churches: a growing interest in liturgy, especially as regards its artistic aspect[941] with much interest in symbolism; a lesser regard for the importance of the preaching of the word, in particular through sermons; the ignoring of the differences between the various ecclesiastical gronps;[942] a depreciation of the values of the confession of faith and of dogmatic clarity. Then he says: 'Childish it would be not to realize at once the inner connection between the general increase of love of the symbolical in literature, in painting, in sculpture, in service of worship outside our own churches,[943] and the clearly distinguishable change of religious appreciation by which no keen observer can keep from being impressed with in our own circles.'[944]

He rightly continues: 'It is not art but symbolism . . . that took hold of the mind . . . a new religion has set in.'[945] We may also speak of

> a predilection for mystical piety ... [but] it is devoid of any personal and definite character ... no demand at all for deliverance from sin; no desire for a conscious personal reunion with the living God ... Their watchword is the merging of the soul in the ocean of the Infinite; the afterthrilling of the soul of the Cosmos in the vibrations of their own heart: the perception of an all-pervading power inspiring them, and the coveting of an unattainable ideal.[946]

How true the latter statement is, may appear from the plan for a novel found among the papers of Aurier and published in his *Oeuvres posthumes*. After all kinds of blasphemous incidents have happened, which have greatly depressed the mistress of the principal character (Aurier's mouthpiece), he observes:

> Poor child! Don't be sad ... There is redemption. Where I would find it? In yourself ... Descend into your soul ... Do I have in myself, without knowing it, such a power? Do I carry a whole universe in my flesh? – A universe, my child, greater and finer than the universe! A universe of which you are the god ... When we believe we invent the most fabulous chimera do we not do anything else but call up visions that we remember unconsciously from the times when our souls relaxed in the marvellous Eden of the pure Ideas?[947]

At this point it is not necessary to point out the clearly Platonic inspiration, nor to enter into the connection with mysticism, which advances such thoughts usually in a christianized way – still less are we in a position here to examine whether such a combination of the Christian tradition with Platonic thoughts can really be attained without cutting through the bond with Holy Scripture as the divine revelation in a more or less explicit way (although we think this question must certainly be answered in the negative).

After discussing the further characteristics of such mysticism, Kuyper draws the conclusion that 'Their constant endeavour is not to fear, to serve and to love the living God . . . but to enjoy fully the mystical titillations of a delightful religious feeling.' What are the sources of the movement, rightly called a purely aristocratic one, according to Kuyper? He mentions three of them: the new German philosophy, the historical school, and the revival of the arts. The first of the three and the second are to be conceived of as a reaction to the disintegration of life and thought brought about by the French Revolution, and the too superficial and reckless severing of all historical ties. The question may be asked if German philosophy itself had been so far removed from the ideas of the French Revolution. After all, the young Hegel, Schelling and many others had danced round the tree of liberty and had sung revolutionary songs.[948] No doubt Kuyper knew Groen van Prinsterer's book on the French Revolution[949] too well to think that the Restoration in Europe had really attacked the basic principles of the French Revolution and had liberated itself from it. For it is probable that for the sake of brevity Kuyper formulates his thought this way, and that he wanted to bring to light that positivism, which in its essence as well as in its tradition of thought was developed by the spirit that had borne the French Revolution and was combated most in Germany in the nineteenth century. However this may be, as we have repeatedly pointed out, there was certainly a connection between German idealism with its Romantic art theory,[950] and the movement of the 1890s in France.

We are more concerned with what Kuyper says about art there. As one of the origins of the symbolic movement he mentions the 'revival of art life, under the all permeating influence of Lessing and Goethe, in its adoration for the classical beauty [951] of the Greek world, [which] must feel scandalized by the ridiculous extolling of uncultured nature, as was to the French evolutionists the real point of depart for their system.'[952] No doubt he is referring to German classicism, while it is not so easy to guess what he is thinking of with respect to French art. Zola's naturalism, or that of the art of the Salons? We shall have to seek in this direction probably. Or are we to go further back and to think of Rousseau?

'About the middle of the century France sank, Germany rose.'[953] It is certainly not easy to say what Kuyper had in view with respect to the pictorial arts. Hildebrand, Böcklin, Feuerbach? Or did he not at all think of painting and sculpture, and was it rather Wagner he had in mind, or was he especially concerned with German literature of the latter half of the nineteenth century? However this may be, there will at present be few people who would repeat Kuyper's words.

Next Kuyper points out Plato's importance and that of Phidias for the forms and ideas of the German movement mentioned above. 'In this abstract form, however, this new leading thought could not radiate from the German to the Anglo-Saxon mind . . . until Darwin gave it its material basis . . . The Idea of the Infinite becoming phenomenal in the finite, by means of a material process, adapted itself to the Anglo-Saxon mind.'[954] A very remarkable utterance, showing at any rate how little Kuyper was familiar with English and American thought – we only mention the names of those who contradict the former hypothesis: Coleridge, Emerson, Carlyle, Poe, Rossetti and his school, although we must admit that also in England the positivistic ideal of natural science dominated the minds of people, whose most spectacular representative was no doubt Charles Darwin.[955]

Kuyper is clearer and less easily refutable when in the following pages, coming to his own sphere of interest, he is occupied with the nature and character of Revelation and of Symbolism.

> Everyone who, moving in the finite, becomes aware of the existence of something Infinite, has to form a conception of the relation that exists between both. Either the Infinite reveals itself to man, and by this revelation unveils the really existing relation, or the Infinite remains mute and silent and man himself has to guess, to conjecture and to represent to himself this relation by means of the imagination; that is, in an artificial way. The first is the Christian one ... Paganism ... wants the symbol and creates it in its idols. Symbol means a fictitious link between the invisible Infinite and the visible finite. Derived from symballein, i.e. bringing two different spheres together, Symbolism is the grasping of something outward and material upon which the imagination may put the stamp of the unseen and unspeakable. The symbol is the middle link, being related from one side to what you can see

and grasp, and from the other side to what you feel, fancy and imagine ... what she [Symbolism] is longing after is a comprehensive impression of the Infinite in its totality, in its all-pervading and all-permeating action ... such an infinite sensation only Symbolism can produce.

This exposition is to the point, sober-minded and transparent, and explains a great deal of what we have been discussing.

The conclusion is obvious: 'Revelation and Symbolism are in principle opposed, one to the other.' In the one case the acceptance of Revelation by faith will be the way to gain fundamental knowledge of the basic principles of reality; in the other, art will be the medium: 'art, by the wonderful power of its imaginative gifts, creating the corresponding symbols'.[956] It is a confirmation of the correctness of his view that here Kuyper uses exactly those terms that we have found in the Symbolist or in the Synthetist theories of art. Recall only what Baudelaire said about the 'imagination'.[957]

Also his next statement can immediately be corroborated by a quotation from Morice. Kuyper said: 'Accomodation to existing religion has always been in leading thought, and this accomodation is achieved at once by taking as poetry what the church confesses as the highest reality.'[958] In Morice we read:

> Modern criticism does not allow us to believe unbelievable things, and yet the modern mind, like the Ancients, remains eager for beautiful mysteries: has Wagner not understood that, since religion cannot live for art unless it veils its element of truth in an ever increasing accumulation of unbelievable things,[959] and since men do not want these beautiful chimeras proposed to their reason, they must exclusively be offered to their imagination?[960]

After this quotation, Kuyper continues, saying that 'all actions of worship' are interpreted as 'mere symbolical utterances', thus humanizing and subjectivizing them. According to Kuyper, who refers back to a thought expressed already in the beginning of his paper, this explains the great interest in Roman Catholicism, which is so much better adaptable to this mentality than Protestantism. And then he points out the many conversions to Roman Catholicism during the Romantic period. No doubt this also holds in many respects for the circle of men who are the subject of the present study: we think of Huysmans, and in the Netherlands of Toorop, while Maurice Denis, Emile Bernard and the entire group of kindred minds were strong representatives of Symbolist thought although they were fervent Roman Catholics – apparently they were unaware of the contradiction between the faith in Revelation and that in Symbolism.

Symbol (continued)

What we have written above about the symbolic was mostly concerned with theory. It remains to be examined what these artists meant by their Symbolism in a concrete and practical sense, what it meant for their view of a work of art in its concrete shape.

Exclusively occupying himself with the men of letters, Lehmann has tried to answer this question by examining carefully how the term 'symbol' was used and what meanings were attached to it. He recapitulates his findings as follows:[961]

> 1. Any isolateable member of the external world or any quality, which bears witness (to the mystic) of the supranatural unity and 'universal analogy' in the world (Baudelaire). [This is the meaning that we, too, have found, and which no doubt may be called the ordinary sense, nearest to the generally accepted meaning attached to this concept.]
>
> 2. Any sensible thing or any word in so far it suggests to the Mallarmean poet the Platonic Idea immanent in it (Mauclair). (Properly speaking this is not a new meaning of the word, but only a particular explanation of the origin and the meaning of the symbol as we have seen in an earlier context. It is only a further definition of what has been said in (1) above, as also Baudelaire and his followers tried to found their theory of the symbol in a similar direction.)
>
> 3. Any representation serving as a sign or a general attitude which either tradition or supernatural decree has invested with powerful emotional resources (Yeats). [This, too, is merely a further determination of what has been given in (1) above. We have not dealt with Yeats in further detail as he was not in any way important for the (French) painters, nor did he write during the first few years of the new movement (his work belongs to the end of the 1890s). On the other hand, his occult-magical symbolism is interesting enough.[962]]
>
> 4. An allegory, provided always that the art possesses, or tended to possess, a high degree of artistic integration. Hense, also, all myth, and by extension, pseudo-myth (Wyzewa, etc.). [Here we are in the climate of Wagner and of the art theory influenced by him, which for the rest is in all kinds of ways closely related to that of the ideas of the group we have called the 'decadents'. And this conception is, therefore, most conspicuous in the typical Symbolist painters (those of the Rose†Croix and people like Toorop) with respect to their choice of subjects and their manner.]
>
> 5. A single representation abstracted from a complex of experience involving many associated representations, which is intended to do duty for its fellows as the most characteristic (Kahn). [Here we are nearer to the practical application of the theory, and so nearer to the answer to the question raised above.]
>
> 6. Any work of art, not being an allegory or myth, whose evident purpose is to express the artist's attitude (Verhaeren). [Here the term is used to denote

the typical subjectivism in its own colour, in its artistic, concrete form. Properly speaking this view is perfectly inherent in the views of, say, Baudelaire, although the latter would perhaps not use the term in this particular application.]

7. A formal construct or poetic image of great force which constantly recurs in the poet's work as his mind circles around a certain predominant attitude (Valéry etc.). [This conception is a near approach to the one mentioned under (7) above; it is, as it were, its practical consequence.]

8. Any work of art at all, considered as a formal unity, or embodying an aspiration to formal unity (Gide). [Here we are not at all far removed from the theories explained in the previous numbers, but this is a particular application. We have, however, found that this thought was expressed particularly by the term 'synthesis'.]

Lehmann now tries to reduce all these meanings to one common denominator and that is the concept language. 'Language . . . embraces everything and anything which an artist appropriates to himself from tradition and uses as a vehicle for expression,'[963] and a little further: '"Symbol" is the form – and of course the content – of a book or other piece of writing. And the formal construction of a work of art is simply the way in which its creator expresses an attitude – is an attitude.'[964]

We cannot agree with Lehmann's words, at least not without some qualifications. For when we pay attention to the way in which he explains his thesis, that this generation was concerned especially with 'language', we see that he is formulating the structure of a work of art. Before giving the summary we have quoted in great detail, he himself says that these artists are urged on by the desire for 'a revival of the claims of art against not-art'.[965] Yet this confusion of language and (literary) art is quite understandable. For the issue in this case was not language as such, nor a theory of language, but the recovery of the insight into the essential character of a work of art precisely also in its use of language.

In this circle the attempt was made to give a new formulation of the peculiar character of a work of art, of its peculiar way of expression and representation of reality. And as this was done in a strong spirit of reaction to naturalism, which for all kinds of reasons had become unacceptable in its view of life, this generation was bound to fall a victim to all manner of mysticistic theories, which as it were, were readily available in a strong tradition. Naturalism had degraded art to a kind of copy of everyday life, owing to which also the artistic use of language had been lost. Metaphors, poetically exact but not therefore scientific ways of expression, an artistic manner of giving expression to what is relevant by means of language, all this and a great deal more was implied in their endeavours, because in the tradition based on the (natural-) science ideal the peculiar character of art, its structure and meaning, had been lost for the greater part.

All this is really much more apparent in pictorial art. Here the naturalistic art of the Salon was all powerful, which as a matter of fact meant a vulgar photographical naturalism, an art which did nothing but copy what the eye saw. It made even the most sublime subject vulgar and (or) theatrical without the least trace of an interpretation of its meaning. Here the peculiar nature of a work of art had been completely lost sight of. The pictorial means had become so much a matter of course, they were so much determined by a tradition that started from the idea that a picture should 'imitate' the reality that we know by means of our senses, that in consequence it was forgotten that every pictorial artistic achievement makes use of iconic means which (in their own way but similar to language) are not identical with the given object represented by them.[966] Indeed, for pictorial art the important thing was to regain an insight into the peculiar character of the pictorial manner of expression by means of an image. This was more obvious and urgent in pictorial art than in literature.[967]

In two ways the artists tried to rehabilitate the artistic and peculiar character of a work of art over against the Salon tradition. The one tendency sought to renew the subject matter, more or less mythologizing in an extensive use of allegorical and metaphorical ways of representation, a method closely akin to that of literature – the way of the Symbolists. The other tendency applied itself rather to the structure of the work of art as such, and kept faith with Realism as it had been formulated in the progression of Fontainebleau – Courbet – Manet – Impressionism. In the former case the way of depiction continued to progress in line with art since the Renaissance, as we have already tried to show in an earlier context. The latter case found an entirely new way of artistic expression, one that shows its relationship with all pictorial art except that of the classical and the modern period. But the latter remark should not blind us to the fact that also Raphael, Rubens and Rembrandt – to mention only a couple of names – were certainly alive to the peculiar character of pictorial 'language'. In this section we will not consider the background of their view of life, but will try to define what was the real discovery made by these artists, by which they recovered something that had been lost in the naturalism of especially the art of the Salons.

The iconic – the real achievement of Synthetist art theory

We are referring to the 'iconic'[968], a term which we have used a few times already, but which we shall have to explain further. By the word 'iconic' we want to express something that might be indicated by the Dutch word *beeldspraak* (literally, 'speaking in images'), if this term were not a little confusing because it means 'metaphor'. For the important fact is that iconically we can express something by means of lines, colours, and three-dimensional forms – in a way similar to what happens in language by means of sounds. Language does not express something by means of sounds alone, because it requires 'organized (i.e. speech) sounds'— an organization that will have to be brought about according to the norms of language. The icon operates in the same way. Both belong to the same modality:[969] the relation between the word 'table' and the concrete thing denoted by this word is in principle identical with the relation between a drawing or painting of a table and a real table. In naturalism there is sometimes — not always — a question of a mimetic relation (*Abbildrelation*) — which is comparable to onomatopoeia in language — but this is by no means necessary for an iconic image. Surveying the great number of ways in which through the course of history the objects of the reality around us — both the realia and the invisible things — have been represented, we see that there are many image-languages possible. But if the typical norm of the iconic is to be observed, namely clarity (as it should also be in language), the structure of things must be represented. Take for example the way in which a child draws a human being. It may be a clumsy expression, an image in which he or she may have rendered only the most elementary state of affairs, and it may not contain any nuance or complication, but we recognize a human being in a children's drawing because iconically that has been clearly indicated by it.

It needs no comment that by means of the iconic quite different things may be expressed or represented from that which can be denoted by language. There are states of affairs that can hardly be made clear in an iconic way — such as a philosophical theory, an adjunct of place or time and so forth — but there are also many cases in which language fails us, whereas the iconic means may be very clear and unambiguous. Think for instance of geographical maps, portraits, topographical drawings and so on. The iconic 'language' — which is generally speaking international but may certainly change with the times to such an extent that to a later generation the iconic representation is not at all clear [970] — has its own norms that again and again require further positivizing, further concrete formulation.

We might call the latter 'style' if there were no objections to be raised against this term. For the iconic element as such is not artistic, just as language as such is not artistic. The example of the geographical map just mentioned — we might also refer to graphical representations of statistics — makes this clear. Yet it is understandable that our thoughts are immediately turned to style. For this positivizing of iconic norms is nearly always done by artists in their works — in which they sometimes look for new iconic means to express particular new visions. Here, too, appears the profound and non-metaphorical but real agreement with language. For it is literary artists particularly who often give language and linguistic usage (a new) form in prose and poetry. In the pictorial arts, as well as in literature, the iconic and the linguistic expression respectively are turned in an artistic direction; they are aesthetically disclosed or expanded. The latter statement will be explained after we have seen how the generation of 1885-1890 had regained a clear insight into this aspect of a work of art (although they had not always found a lucid formulation for it). It is precisely the extreme denial of this state of affairs by the Salon artists that held it under their very noses, so to say, and made them aware of something that had really been a matter of course before their time (that is, before the nineteenth century), something that had implied nothing problematical, at least.

Delacroix is without doubt one of the first to posit the question at stake here in a clear way. Thus we read in his *Journal*: 'There are no contours nor brushstrokes in nature. We must always come back to the conventional means in each art which are the language of art.'[971]

We shall not again investigate the difficult problem of the way in which Delacroix's ideas had found their way to Gauguin and his followers. It is striking, however, that as soon as Gauguin liberated himself from the Impressionists and started seeking for new ways he posited the problem very lucidly: 'The further I get the more I feel the necessity to render thought by something quite different from literature.'[972] And some time later his answer to Bernard's and Laval's question concerning the shadows in his pictures shows that in his entire 'instruction' it was exactly the question of the *iconic* representation that came to the fore again and again. It is characteristic that here he rightly points to the Japanese artists who, indeed, exercised a totally different manner of positivizing the iconic element, a manner which could certainly not be explained on the basis of some representational relation. 'You discuss shadows with Laval and ask me if I don't care about it. As far as the explanation of light is concerned, yes. Look at the Japanese who nevertheless make such excellent drawings and you will see life in the open and in the sun without any shadows. They use colour only as a combination of tones, various harmonies giving the impression of heat, etc.'[973] Much later, in Tahiti, he still appeared to realize this state of affairs thoroughly and clearly, almost more sharply than before. He discusses the Tahitian world and his artistic picture of it: 'All these fabulous colours, this glowing but sifted, silent air. But all this does not exist! [the critic objects, but Gauguin goes on to reply:] Yes, this exists as the equivalent of that grandeur, that depth, of the mystery of Tahiti, when one has to express it on a canvas of a square yard.'[974]

If Lehmann is right, the men of letters in their field were also clearly conscious of this circumstance – although in their case, in view of the character of literature, which makes use of language, of which the proper nature can never be misinterpreted, the direct focus on its artistic use is much more explicit than in the case of the painters. For painters first had to re-conquer the conception of the iconic element as such after a long period in which this element had been ignored. It is understandable that Aurier had a keen insight into this matter, although we should certainly not underestimate the direct influence of Gauguin and his followers on Aurier in this respect. In opposition to the idea of the mimetic relation in a naturalistic sense, he writes: 'The ideistic painter's duty is, therefore, to bring about a reasoned selection from the many elements combined in objectivity, to use in his work only the lines, forms, general distinctive colours serving to describe the ideistic signification of the object clearly.'[975] The latter statement, freed from the Neoplatonic scheme of interpretation, really means that the structure of what has been represented should be rendered in an iconic way.

In another passage Aurier is very explicit and concentrates on what occupies us here: 'This boils down to saying that the objects, i.e., abstractly, the various combinations of lines, planes, shadows, colours, constitute the vocabulary of a mysterious language, but wonderfully expressive, which one must know in order to be an artist. This language, like every language, has its own handwriting, its orthography, grammar, syntax, even rhetoric, which is "the style".'[976] If many present-day art historians and aestheticians can unreservedly agree with Aurier in this case,[977] it is because the fundamental discovery made in this respect has become more and more clear and evident via the Synthetist art theory and the works of art in which this discovery was made use of.

It need not cause any surprise that this insight is also found with Gauguin's pupils, especially Sérusier and Denis.[978] It is remarkable that together with Gauguin himself and his example also Cézanne played an important part for them. Cézanne's opinion (published only later on) is quoted again and again in the short slogan: 'Let us consider this word of Cézanne's: "I have wanted to copy nature. I did not succeed. I have been satisfied about myself since I discovered that the sun, for instance (things lit up by the sun) could not be reproduced, but that one must represent it by something else than what I saw – by colour."'.[979] Elsewhere the phrase *autre chose* is still further explained as *par des équivalents plastiques.*[980]

It is certainly not inconceivable that Gauguin had also learnt something from Cézanne precisely on this point – the latter being indebted to Delacroix and others, although the creative and personal element in this cannot be denied to either Cézanne or Gauguin. This thought urges itself all the more strongly upon our minds as Gauguin used the same word *équivalent* more than once in this connection (whereas this synonym for *correspondant* is rare in the case of the men of letters). We have already come across the term in one of the quotations from Gauguin made a moment ago. But this passage is by no means the only one.[981]

That people were aware of the fact that they had finished with the naturalistic theory of imitation may appear from the following quotation from Denis:

We have replaced the idea of 'nature seen through the medium of a temperament' by the theory of the equivalence or the symbol. We assert that the emotions or states of the soul, evoked by some spectacle, bring about in the artist's imagination signs or plastic equivalents capable of reproducing these emotions or states of the soul without the necessity to furnish the copy of the initial spectacle; that with every condition of our sensibility there must be a corresponding objective harmony, which is capable of translating it.[982]

And Sérusier – from whom we might quote extensively – observes that this method of working is really the ordinary one: 'Well, thoughts and moral qualities can only be represented by formal equivalents.' (It is, of course, not accidental that Sérusier and the others so often talked of the invisible human experiences that must be depicted, for in this respect the extreme form of naturalism was deficient in the clearest and most serious way). 'This faculty of perceiving those correspondences constitutes the artist. Every man possesses this faculty as a possibility already at birth; his personal work can develop it, a bad education may annihilate it.'[983] The last statement certainly refers to the academicians.

It is quite understandable that the art of other periods, especially the non-naturalistic kind, was an aid in making these artists aware of the meaning and the character of the iconic element, especially also in their confrontation with the art of the Salons. We have already mentioned Japanese art in this connection. Bernard writes about the Byzantine artists as follows: 'At last I understood again that in an icon . . . everything must be imprinted with a simple, explicative, exact and symbolic character, that every actor should have a dimension proportionate to the importance of his role.'[984] And Denis says quite rightly and sharply: 'A Byzantine Christ is a symbol; the Jesus [985] of the modern painters, even if rendered most accurately, is merely literary. In the the first it is the form that is expressive; in the second it is nature (being imitated) that wants to be as such.'[986] And, finally, also Gauguin owed a great deal to his study of the art of Giotto,[987] Cambodia (even though this was in reality the Burubudur on Java),[988] the Egyptians and so on.[989]

Naturally, these artists were not concerned with a theory of the iconic element as such, a theory of the image and imaging. No more were the men of letters concerned with language and linguistic theory apart from the works of art, or the painters with the iconic element apart from the artistic aspect. On the contrary, their view of language and of the iconic aspect are always directly connected with the use of these means in a work of art: the issue is the literary language, the artistic icon. The aesthetic aspect is a modality[990] which is of a different nature than the iconic element and qualifies a work of art. And this is why the iconic elements in a work of art will be arranged in such a way that they help to build up a composition[991] that is aesthetically justified. But in the aesthetic modality itself, the iconic (or the linguistic) moment will be reflected as an analogous element,[992] that is, the aesthetic form as such will be adapted to the iconic (linguistic) aspect in a work of art. This state of affairs makes it possible for a work of art to be a unity – as an artistic object its unity consists in the close coherence of the aesthetic and the iconic (linguistic) factors. In poetry, for example, this appears in the 'plastic' quality of a poem. In its 'aesthetic symbolism' we find rhythm, hiatus, assonances and consonances used to underline the meaning of the poetic subject (comparable to madrigalism in music).[993] By way of an example we shall quote a line from Coleridge's 'Rime of the Ancient Mariner': 'Down dropt the breeze, the sails dropt down', where in a typical aesthetic way the first word 'dropt' underlines the sudden falling away of the wind mentioned in the (linguistic) text.[994]

But although the artists of the generation of 1890 were not in the least intent upon the theoretical analysis of such questions, they were certainly aware of them. When they speak of the iconic element, they often do so in immediate connection with the aesthetic organization of the image – the quotations given above have been chosen with some care, so that this aspect would not come to the fore too much in order not to make the discussion too complicated – while they denoted this 'aesthetical symbolism'[995] by the term 'musicality', as we shall try to show in what follows.

So these artists were in the first place aware not only of the iconic character of the image, but especially of the requirement that the work of art as such should represent the meaning of the object, and that a narrative, or, as the case may be, imitative depiction of the given visible thing in itself does not imply anything artistic. That is why Denis wrote: 'Instead of evoking our states of mind by means of the subject represented, the work itself must transmit the initial feeling, perpetuate the emotion.'[996] In this circle the expression by means of the subject was simply called 'literary' – because it ignored the expansion of the iconic by the aesthetic modality qualifying a work of art. This is what Gauguin was referring to when he wrote: 'Suffice it to warn the visitor that Gauguin is a cerebral artist – I won't say, indeed, "a literary man" – that he does not express what he sees but what he thinks by means of an original harmony of lines, by a drawing which is curiously comprised in an arabesque.'[997]

Writing in connection with Gauguin's art, Morice explains this situation very clearly:

> It was natural that the synthesis should lead the artist to the symbol. Sacrifices and an order in the composition intended to make the author's thought intelligible, a liberation from the immediate dependence on direct observation, must inspire the artist with the wish to retain only those aspects of nature in which he read a significant allusion to that thought, and to unite those aspects in some great image, liberated from any verisimilitude [i.e. the naturalistic representation instead of the iconic rendering], as well as profoundly, that is to say vitally and artistically, true.[998]

And then he adds: 'Cette image, c'est le symbole.' This is the meaning of the word 'symbol' given by Lehmann, points 5 and 8 above, which was in every way a sufficient reason to consider the fundamental meaning of the symbol as an aesthetically expanded language.[999]

Musicality

We shall now examine the meaning and the use of the term 'musicality' more closely. No doubt it was Delacroix who was the first to use this term with great emphasis, the first in a tradition that led to Synthetism. He wrote:

> There is a kind of emotion which is very particularly proper to painting. There is an impression which results from such an arrangement of colours, lights, and shadows, etc. ... This is called the music of the picture.[1000] Before knowing what the painting represents you enter a cathedral and you find yourself placed at too great a distance from the picture for you to know what it represents, and often you are caught by this magical harmony: sometimes the mere lines have this power ... Here is the true superiority of painting to any other art, for this emotion is directed to the most intimate part of the soul ... To what would be the spectacle of nature painting adds this element which verifies and selects, the soul of the painter, his particular style.[1001]

Enquiring after the exact meaning of Delacroix's utterance, we are induced to study Baudelaire's elaboration of this thought – which he had almost certainly heard from the artist. Such a study will no doubt explain things:

> A painting by Delacroix, placed at too great a distance for you to judge of the charms of the outlines or the more or less dramatic quality of the subject, penetrates you already with supernatural delight ... And when you come nearer, the analysis of the subject will not deprive you of anything and will not add anything to your primitive pleasure, of which the source is elsewhere and far away from any secret thought. I can invert the example. A well-drawn figure penetrates you with a joy that is entirely alien to the subject. Voluptuous or terrible, this figure only owes its charm to the arabesque it cuts out in space.[1002]

This quotation should be supplemented with the following pronouncement: 'A good way to judge whether a painting is melodious is to look at it from a distance great enough for us not to understand the subject or the lines. If it is melodious it already has a meaning and it has already occupied its place in the repository of the memories.'[1003]

In the quotations given here we see that factually Baudelaire says that colours and lines are already brimful of meaning in themselves, even apart from the motif represented, or rather: their expressiveness is due to a quality that is not identical with their representational function as such. When reading that the metaphorical term 'melody' – of which the meaning is identical with that of the term 'musicality' – is intended to describe this state of affairs, we may perhaps infer from these quotations from Baudelaire when viewed alongside one from Delacroix that the former here refers to the purely aesthetic moment. As, however, these colours (and lines) are also expressive – 'There are bright and playful tones, playful and sad ones, rich and bright tones, rich and sad ones,'[1004] Baudelaire observes two lines further than the last quotation – we must not think of aesthetic meaning entirely apart from the thing represented. The qualities of the colours and the lines that iconically give the motif or subject represented its artistic sense (which thus has such a strong human appeal) will have to be in accordance with the character of the object. This is also clear from the entire discussion of the colourists in the *Salon of 1846*, of which the passage just quoted was a detail. And as we are here concerned with a purely aesthetic quality having a certain expressive value, although it is not iconic as such, we think we are justified in taking the term 'musicality' to refer to the iconic analogy in the aesthetic aspect of the work of art (the 'aesthetic symbolism'), as we have already established above, without giving a more detailed explanation.

The predilection for music, appearing from the use of the term 'musicality', to indicate the aesthetic element was not something new. Already in the eighteenth century there was a shift in terminology noticeable: the earlier invariable comparison of poetry with painting – *ut pictura poesis* – disappears almost entirely from the art-theoretical discussions. Especially the pre-Romantics compared poetry with music, for the very reason that the latter did not contain any imitative element. Music was considered as the art which gave the most direct expression to emotion and to mental qualities. This is stated very explicidy by Wackenroder: 'Music . . . (depicts) human feelings in a superhuman way, because clothed in golden clouds of gay harmonies it depicts all the movements of our emotions in an incorporeal form over our heads.'[1005] A little further on he writes: 'And thus also is the state of affairs with respect to the mysterious stream in the depth of the human heart, language tells and names and describes its changes in an alien material – music makes this stream pass in front of us . . . in the mirror of the tones the human heart learns to know itself, by feeling them it learns to feel.'[1006]

The idea that music may be a direct expression of human feelings is not at all new: it was found as early as in Aristotle's *Poetics* – also with respect to music he calmly speaks of mimesis,[1007] especially referring to human feelings and emotions. Via the classicistic-humanistic art-theoretical literature such ideas had naturally penetrated deeply into Western thought. Although in Romanticism the term 'expression' was preferred to the word 'mimesis', practically speaking they come to the same thing. Adam Smith made a characteristic pronouncement – which may represent the average opinion on this matter in the eighteenth and the early part of the nineteenth centuries: 'The effect of instrumental music upon the mind has been called its expression. Whatever effect it produces is the immediate effect of the melody and harmony, and not of something else which is signified and suggested by them: they in fact signify and suggest nothing.'[1008]

At the same time it was said that music was consequently meaningless and that it was the direct expression of the human mind itself, of the promptings of the human heart. We may observe that this state of affairs is best explained by remembering that, while speaking of the aesthetic element, people referred in particular to 'aesthetic symbolism', as we have already tried to explain above. There is, therefore, a striking agreement between the (German) pre-Romantics and the (French) painters with respect to the direction of their attention.

We are pointing out this state of affairs because it may explain why we come across these ideas so often in the nineteenth century. We need not assume that Delacroix was entirely original as to his views of these things; to the contrary, even though we do not have any inclination to belittle the importance and also the originality of his observations.

A very remarkable utterance is that by Carlyle, who assigned a very high place to this concept of musicality. We quote the following passage from his chapter 'The Hero as a Poet' in *On Heroes, Hero-worship, and the Heroic in History* because we find it translated in Taine's book *L'idéalisme anglais*, a book that introduced Carlyle's ideas into France and one that will no doubt have been well known in the circle of artists we are discussing:

> Poetry being metrical, having music in it, being a song ... If your delineation be authentically musical, musical not in word only, but in heart and substance, in all the thought and utterances of it, in the whole conception of it, then it will be poetical; if not, not. – Musical: how much lies in that! A musical thought is one spoken by a mind that has penetrated into the inmost heart of the thing, detected the inmost mystery of it, the inward harmony or coherence which is its soul, whereby it exists, and has a right to be, here in this world. All inmost things, we may say, are melodious; naturally utter themselves in Song. The meaning of Song goes deep. Who is there that, in logical words, can express the effect music has on us? A kind of inarticulate, unfathomable speech, which leads us to the edge of the Infinite, and lets us for a moment gaze into that ... ! All deep things are Song. It seems somehow the very central essence of us; of us, and of all things ... See deep enough, and you see musically; the heart of Nature being everywhere music, if you can only reach it.[1009]

This passage shows how a thought such as Wackenroder, for instance, had formulated was carried to its extreme; we could almost say, to absurdity. The essence of a poem is its musicality – for in its musical quality the human soul, a person's inner being, will express itself most directly and without any inhibitions, without logical precision, without the need of describing reality in a metaphorical or any other way. But in a characteristically subjectivistic manner, namely by locating the knowable in the (absolutized) subject,[1010] in line with German idealism, this direct expression of the soul is equalized with the revelation of the essential 'inner nature' of reality as such. This is a remarkable utterance on the part of Carlyle, and this was all the more a reason for the generation of around 1890 to lay emphasis on this 'musicality': for it was not only beauty that could thus be achieved, not merely expression, but reality itself could be caught in its essence and embodied artistically in a work of art.

Bearing this development of the idea of the musical element in mind we shall also better understand a passage of Aurier's which might at the first glance have seemed a little too flowery. He writes:

> A work of art is only really a work of art if like a mirror[1011] it reflects the psychological emotion experienced by the artist in the presence of nature or in that of his dream. This emotion can ultimately be only a pure sensation: a sensation of a particular harmony of lines, of a symphony determined by colours.[1012]

So the metaphors in this passage derived from music have a much more profound sense than might appear at first sight. Here, too, music is mentioned in connection with strictly subjective emotions: for this *sensation pure* can only be an emotion apart from observation or experience, a perfectly internalized experience. It is, indeed, evoked by observation, but it does not constitute the observational 'content'.

If thought out, matters are as follows: in the image – Aurier speaks about pictorial art – reality is represented iconically, whereas in the strictly aesthetical 'musicality' the deepest and innermost feelings (in accordance with the given object) are expressed. If we turn again to our quotation from Baudelaire and study it in this light, namely the passage about the picture seen from a distance and so on, the quotation will be even clearer. We think we are justified in assuming that the Synthetists read Baudelaire in this way, whereas he himself will presumably not have been so sharply aware of this state of affairs – or of this supposed state of affairs.[1013]

Especially in his later years Gauguin more than once spoke about 'musicality'. In *Diverses Choses* he closely follows the quotation from Delacroix that we, too, have given,[1014] without, however, mentioning the latter's name. Perhaps when he was back in Paris in the years 1893 to 1895 he had read Delacroix's article again. Possibly we should consider this article as the direct source that motivated Gauguin to assign such great value to this notion in his later writings.

In a letter to Fontainas he wrote: 'Think also of the musical role that will henceforth be played by colour in modern painting. Colour is vibration just like music, and is in the same way able to attain to that which is most general and consequently most vague in nature, namely its interior form.'[1015] The meaning of this statement may become clear when we think of what Carlyle had written in this connection, going only a little further than the immediate leaders of the Synthetists, Delacroix and Baudelaire.

The idea we have characterized by the term 'musicality' occurs again and again with Gauguin's 'pupils'. We quote only one example (from Sérusier): 'Sounds, colours, words have a wonderfully expressive value apart from any representation, apart even from the literal meaning of the words.'[1016] In this passage – and we have seen that there are more such in Sérusier – a thought given implicitly by Gauguin and other leaders is made explicit by means of a very clear and short summary, however devoid of any poetry.

After our elaborate discussion of Denis' views in a previous chapter, especially in connection with the question whether he strove after non-figurative art, we think there is now no need to explain again that none of the painters or men of letters we have quoted directed their efforts to anything like that. But we can certainly indicate factors that might have led them in that direction – we shall revert to this point later on. They had too high an opinion of art to go that way. To put the issue clearly we shall quote Ruskin and Raymond with approval. Both in their own way explained the obvious misconception that might follow from carrying through the idea of musicality and why it should be avoided.

Ruskin has more than once been accused of it that his insistence on truth in art was in reality favouring a kind of supernaturalism and that he did not attach any proper significance to the purely aesthetical element. Yet, though he should never have said anything about it, even a cursory look through his work would show that this is a man who took an intense delight in art. Although he was not without marked prejudice and passion in his rejection and his approval, he was certainly capable of appreciating beauty of colour, line and composition for its true value. Perhaps we should say that the very fact of his wholehearted engagement in positive as well as in negative criticism, in short, that his very prejudices are the conclusive evidence of his love of beauty and his full appreciation of its importance. For only a man who is not really moved by the image before him can talk about it in an 'objective' and unprejudiced way.

But there are indeed pronouncements made by Ruskin – and, remarkably enough, he also avails himself of the metaphor of music:

> These abstract relations and inherent pleasantnesses, whether in space, number or time, and whether of colours or sounds, from what we may properly term the musical or harmonic element in every art; and the study of them is an entirely separate science. It is the branch of art-philosophy to which the word 'aesthetics' should be strictly limited, being the inquiry into the nature of things that in themselves are pleasant to the human senses or instincts, though they represent nothing, and serve for nothing, their only service being their pleasantness.[1017]

And elsewhere, too, as Dougherty has pointed out,[1018] Ruskin spoke of the significance of the purely aesthetic qualities of art with great emphasis. For the very reason that he valued them highly and did not like to be unjust to them, he refrained from talking a great deal about them.

But Ruskin would never have been able to accept non-figurative art. He had too high an opinion of the human significance of art. As a result of the creative activity of a person a work of art will have to appeal to him or her as a totality; it will have to possess a fullness and richness consisting precisely of the close relation between the iconic element representing reality and the aesthetic element constituting the beauty of the work of art. Dougherty rightly says in a brief summary:

> Rodin's famous remark: 'A woman, a mountain, a horse – they are all the same thing; they are made on the same principles' would have brought the retort from Ruskin that a man who thinks so has little knowledge of or love for women, mountains or horses. They are not the same thing, and they are not made on the same principles.[1019]

Marcel Raymond's words are more directly related to the question we have considered, and therefore his observations are of more immediate importance for our discussion. He points out that even the most 'musical' poem in the sense of the Symbolists or Synthetists does not leave a musical emotion as such in us. This is true, for who can remember Verlaine's 'Les sanglots long/Des violons/De l'automne/Blessent mon coeur . . .' apart from the words, purely as a melody? The poem cannot be explained from the relations between the sounds – the writers we have quoted so far have never asserted such a thing; to the contrary. Rather, here we have to do with the associations evoked in us.

> The 'musical' poet must be capable of feeling the affinities existing between the world of sound and the world of thought. Here again, the problem is to bring out mysterious *correspondances,* certain syllables, thanks to an infinitely subtle accord with the meaning of the words which they compose, by virtue of the confused memories evoked by this word even more than by its sonorous charm, actually 'move' the mind, magnetize it in a specific direction. But in no case can the psychological value of the word and its virtual treasury of images and associations be considered independently of its sonorous qualities. Consequently, the 'music' of words can be distinguished only arbitrarily from their meaning – in the broadest sense – and a certain 'inner music' must always be placed above a quasi-material harmony, which is pleasing only to the ear.[1020]

We have quoted Raymond extensively as he has given an excellent analysis of the state of affairs with respect to poetry. In pictorial art matters become even more complicated: words have sounds, but neither colours nor lines possess anything like that in reality. Yet Raymond's exposition is valid for colours and lines as well if only we bear in mind that aesthetic symbolism as such cannot be explained psychologically; it is a purely aesthetical quality having an aesthetic meaning only, although this is a case of an analogon of the iconic aspect. This does not detract from the fact that some specific associations connected with colours and lines can find their basis in purely psychic reactions. But the fact remains that those colours and lines reveal their 'musical' meaning only when viewed in connection with the iconic representation – which, sometimes literally, has been 'coloured' by it in a particular way. Would not the content of one of van Gogh's last paintings, the ravens above the field, be changed entirely if the birds were not black but white or blue, or whatever other colour?

Let us now again consider Sérusier's pronouncement given a moment ago on the expressive meaning of colour and line. It strikes us that – as he so often does – he posits issues as if it is only a matter of purely artistic laws, and that he manages to camouflage the instigation issuing from the artist's view of life that led to a particular formulation. It is quite possible that to him this seemed to be the real state of affairs, and we have to admit that he sometimes discovered how matters truly are. But even then we cannot consider the views of these painters and poets apart from that which prompted them in the depth of their hearts. It is far too obvious for us to prove that in their case we are by no means dealing with scholars intent upon the discovery of factual truths that have little bearing on themselves. As a matter of fact, such scholars too as we are referring to by way of example are rarely mere machines registering laws; they are people of flesh and blood, driven by a particular idea, which is ultimately based in a view of life and the world that expresses a religious choice of position. Even though the latter will not be clearly put in the foreground, let alone be professed consciously by the persons in question, that which they consider relevant – and almost even more important, what they judge to be irrelevant – will reveal this state of affairs on closer analysis.

The generation of artists of 1885 to 1890 is certainly not a set of dry-as-dust aestheticians examining the state of things without any personal inner involvement. On the contrary, the problems we have analysed, of which the origins had to be sought in a remote past, were very near to their hearts. And the new discoveries they made were due to their devoting all their efforts to the realization of a very particular artistic ideal. Their search was concerned with an art (a style) that should satisfy them because it consciously or unconsciously reflected their spiritual attitude.

We once more state this view in order to prevent misconceptions. For we have deliberately eliminated these latter questions when dealing with the iconic element and 'musicality' in order to be able to arrive at a clearer definition of the concepts concerned. But now that we want to say something about Mallarmé, we see that this is made almost impossible for us by the author himself.

For Mallarmé also mentioned 'musicality', in a passage which is characteristic of his style, his way of thought and his attitude:

> Monuments, the sea, the human face, in their inherent fullness, retain a force so much more lovable that a description would only veil them, which ought to be said by evocation, allusion, suggestion. This terminology that is a little random testifies to the tendency, perhaps a very decisive one, to which literary art has been subjected, and by which it has been determined as well as freed. Magic it has if it only liberates, loose from a handful of dust or reality, without binding it in the book, even as a text, the volatile dispersion that is the spirit, which is only concerned with the musicality of the whole.[1021]

To understand an utterance like this we shall have to ask what Mallarmé is really saying with it: in a work of art the spirit should get free of matter, of commonplace reality, and be concerned with what is implied in the facts of reality – the sea, the human face and so on – and can be suggested by them, namely the 'musicality of the whole'. For a correct understanding of this latter phrase it is necessary to examine Mallarmé's world of thought somewhat closer. Things will perhaps be clearer when (in a letter from 1866) we read:

> Yes, I know, we are only vain forms of matter – but very sublime for having invented God and our soul. So sublime, my friend, that I will give to myself this spectacle of matter, having consciousness of being, and yet throwing itself forcibly into this dream, which it knows it is not, singing of the soul and all similar divine impressions that have accumulated in us from the earliest times and proclaiming these glorious lies in the face of the Nothingness which is the truth. Such is the plan of my book, lyrical and such will probably be its title, the Glory of the Lie, or the Glorious Lie. I will sing it as one who is despairing.[1022]

We see that here the real meaning, the basic idea and the essence of reality, the highest truth, is Nothing or Nothingness – a matter he already mentioned in the former of the two quotations above. He is indeed willing to sing (in a Carlylian sense) the praise of this reality, given in matter, because he cannot help it – it is his profoundly felt experience of Heidegger's *Geworfen-sein* ('thrown-ness')[1023] that is expressed in it – but he sings 'as one despairing'. Yet in this way he can also try to show the truth of this Nothingness, this essential fact 'behind every concreteness also in description', this 'musicality'. Thus he will attempt to abstract all the non-essential elements from the objects in the no longer descriptive 'allusion' and 'suggestion' – compare also his famous pronouncement in Hurot's enquiry[1024] – knowing he will never reach the essential element, for this is Nothingness itself. As soon as we make use of the word we have passed from essence to existence, even though this realization is the manifestation of the spirit.[1025] Thus Mallarmé's 'musicality' hovers around the borders between Nothing – it is not nothingness in the full sense of the word, for that absolute stage (*le moi projeté absolu*) would entail the disappearance of the 'I' itself – and material reality, which, however, must be free from every concrete determinateness in order to approach that absolute kernel in it, its essence, as nearly as possible. For this purpose the term 'musicality' is excellently suited as it hits the heart of the matter (recall what Delacroix and Baudelaire said about it) without making it concrete and definite in a visible way.[1026]

In 'musicality', consequently, Mallarmé seeks to find not only the abstract aesthetical element but, in and together with the latter, also what is permanent in the temporal, the Idea in the object. We may ask what it was that drove him – and less explicitly also the other art-theoreticians (and artists) of 1885 to 1890 – in this direction. Why, after all, was that 'materiality', the concrete object, so lustreless, such a 'Lie'?

We hope we shall be able to find an answer to this question in the analysis of the term *mystère* and 'mystic' so often used by all these poet-writers and writing painters.

Mystère

In 1886 the result of an inquiry was published in *Vogue* by a certain L. d'Orfu – in answer to the question what poetry is. Mallarmé's answer (it had already been given in 1884) was: 'Poetry is the expression of the mysterious sense of the aspects of existence by human language restored to its essential rhythm: thus it endows our sojourn with authenticity and constitutes our sole task.'[1027] So Mallarmé wants to represent especially the mystery of reality in art – and this is not in conflict with what we have found above – for to his mind this mystery is the essential thing.

In this opinion he is certainly not alone. Aurier – possibly influenced by him – even goes so far as to say:

> At present we need mysticism, and mysticism alone can save our society from brutalization, from sensualism, and utilitarianism. The noblest faculties of our soul are being atrophied ... on account of positive science we shall have returned to pure and simple animality. We must react. We must again cultivate the superior qualities of the soul. We must again become mystics. We must learn again what is love, the source of all understanding.[1028]

Such a quotation shows clearly that these writers sought after mysticism in their reaction to positivism; they made an effort to free themselves from naturalism and natural science in their approach to reality – and age-old traditions surviving especially in the Roman Catholic world were to help them. Their immediate predecessors in this respect are found in Romanticism, which in its own way had reacted to the positivism of the Encyclopaedists and sensualists of the eighteenth century. What those

Romanticists had preached in their period had become known and passed on to them through the intermediary action of men such as Balzac, Baudelaire and so on, as we have pointed out more than once. Thus it becomes clear that what had once been said about the Romantic mystics is applicable also to them:

> Their definitions are based on the theory of direct inspiration. To release this 'interior self' by imitation, this 'divine spark' that exists in the human personality, to enjoy this 'intuition', this profound insight into things resting on a 'spiritual illumination', those 'relations of an exceptional nature with the denizens of an invisible world', to possess 'the inner vision of the principle of the reality of this world', these are the hopes of the adepts.[1029]

Both at the time of Romanticism and now at the end of the century it was an effort to take hold of certainty behind or beyond of commonplace reality, in a naturalistic sense, whilst retaining a purely individualistic subjectivism. Therefore Viatte is right when he says: 'A great many souls looking down on the beaten paths sought new or neglected roads. Born under the protective shadow of a church or in the absence of any creed, they combine their doubt with religious anxiety.'[1030]

For two reasons their mysticism was eminently suited for their purpose. In the first place mysticism had always been something esoteric in Western civilization, something that was not precisely the privilege of everybody – mysticism dated from very early times, it is true, but to their minds it was by no means a trodden path – while, secondly, mysticism had always pretended (under the strong influence of Neoplatonism or Plotinus) that it opened up a source of knowledge, revealing the deep essence of reality without the intermediary of the senses which acquainted a person with the 'exterior aspect' of things only. For mysticism, just like the life and world view of the generation of 1885 to 1890, was fed by a strongly negative sense of reality.

Mysticism, with its fusion of Neoplatonic thoughts and Christian traditions, had indeed always given form to a particular religious attitude. Mystics like Saint Teresa have always directed their efforts to attain to a *unio mystica* with the divine, although the latter often had very few traits in common with the Lord, the Father in heaven, given in the biblical revelation. In such Christian mysticism there was often a strongly individualistic and subjectivistic tendency, and also in this the revelation of the Scriptures had been depreciated to a lower kind of revelational source at the most.[1031]

But there also existed a mysticism outside the Christian world and detached from the direction to a personal God. And the mysticism of the Synthetists and Symbolists showed a much stronger affinity with the intellectualistic mysticism of a man like Plotinus than with that of a Saint Theresa. For their first concern was a new source of knowledge.

Their mysticism was an effort to gain a new certainty, apart from the dogmas of the Church – although of course dogmas do play a part with some of these artists, the fervent Roman Catholic ones like Denis, Sérusier and Bernard – a source of knowledge which, because it is not concerned with the 'exterior' of things, considered to be contingent and accidental, accessory and superficial, might reveal the absolute to them.

The way of this mysticism is that of art – thus it was hoped that via the purely subjective they might reach something transcending all (human) limitations, something permanent, and therefore something that should make the contingent in the cosmos meaningful. They hoped they would get free from reality in its actual form, which in their opinion had been moulded too much after the positivistic pattern and was consequently an obstacle to the free personality and kept them trapped in too tight a straitjacket.

Thus Morice wrote:

> A book, an art object, a musical phrase, pure thought as such ... are eternalizations of the self. We make as many means of them to disengage our I-ness from the contingences and also in this manner, and as soon as it escapes from these contingences, the self comes back ... to the hearth of the absolute, to the metaphysical place of the Ideas, to God.[1032]

In a similar context Aurier writes that in this way the fetters are shattered and we get away *loin du cruel cachot naif,* which is reality itself.[1033]

This is also the meaning of the search for symbols, which are related to reality only via the correspondences or, to put it in another way, in which reality is deprived of its proper character and remains merely as a metaphor of the authentic absolute 'reality' – where the term 'reality' is meant in a Platonic (Greek) sense.[1034] Michaud truthfully summarizes Mallarmé's ideas as follows: 'Since it concerns the attainment of the absolute, must not poetical language try to find the necessary symbols that escape from any relativity?'[1035]

Behind and in all this they were driven by the strong *dunamis* of their religious attitude, by their urge for freedom in a humanistic sense, freedom from any commandment, any rule, any limitation, to be like a god, to be self-determining and free from all that is non-I, which is considered an irksome counter-instance that forever reminds a person of the fact that he or she is really only a human being, only a creature. Thus in connection with the creation of a work of art we read in Morice:

> And indeed, from these three fundamental virtues liberty, order and solitude there immediately results a feeling of unlimited power, which is the adviser himself of the Infinite; immediately the soul acquires certainty about its own eternity in this exceptional solitude and that there is no death and no birth, and that veritable life is to be one of the conscious centres of the infinite vibration.[1036]

The humanistic personality ideal with its free self-determination was the motivating power also for these artists. And the whole of this esoteric theory, this entire mysticism, was to serve this purpose, as we read in Bernard: 'For, if things visible are the outward form of things invisible, the essence of man near to the divine and endowed with harmony arranges and transforms nature in accordance with his supremacy to make it express his own supernatural origin.'[1037]

In the next chapter we will examine how Gauguin elaborated such thoughts in the last years of his life. He still held to figurative art, like all the other artists of this group. Only later on were these tendencies towards freedom and towards the representation of the absolute, free from the world known to us through the senses, to urge the artists on towards non-figurative art. Then 'musicality' would become the essence of the work of art, which would be *geistig* – we are referring to Kandinski and Mondrian. On paper, at least, such thoughts had been expressed in the 1890s by some figures who started from the development outlined above, namely Bahr and Endell who were Germans, which might be no accident.[1038]

9
Gauguin's Last Years

Gauguin went to Tahiti in 1891. He did so for several reasons which we have tried to analyse in an earlier context. Thus he followed in the path that had already been found by Bougainville and Cook[1039] in the eighteenth century, the path to an earthly paradise. In the eighteenth century, and even as late as the year 1890,[1040] the natives reminded men of Greek gods; they were 'noble savages', as it were, and the living evidence of Rousseau's theories and those of his followers with respect to the glorious state of nature. Kunstler has compared Gauguin to Rousseau,[1041] and not entirely without reason for Gauguin too held a rather idealized view of the Tahitians. 'And they are called savages? They sing, they never steal . . . they do not murder. Two Tahitian words characterize them: *Iorama* (= goodday, good-bye, thank you, etc.) and *Onatu* (=I don't care, it doesn't matter, etc) and are they called savages?'[1042] It is a remarkable fact that, unlike most other Westerners at the time, he immediately joined the natives and proved to be free of any colonial attitudes by which Westerners put themselves above these people, at least as regards social standing. This led to difficulties with government officials later on when he was in the Marquesas islands.

A comparison with La Fargue,[1043] who visited Tahiti only a very short time before Gauguin, is instructive. It appears that the American displayed a typically nineteenth-century attitude, not so much in that he, too, idealized these native people but in his great interest in the ethnological aspect of their folklore and traditions. Gauguin, however, nowhere adopts such a (semi-) scientific attitude, and as a matter of fact his paintings are no dependable sources to learn anything about the life and thought of the Tahitians, however intimate he may have been with the population. For it is true that he seemed to be engrossed in the study of their religion, to which his *Noa Noa* would testify, but in actual fact he was listening to Moerenhout, as Huyghe has established conclusively[1044] and his would-be absorption in their religion was properly speaking merely apparent, for all of this mythology had for a great part disappeared from the world of thought of the Tahitians themselves. At any rate, he learnt and heard little about it from his Tahitian friends. His treatise on it is more of a rêve than a genuine study, more of an interesting fabrication with a local colour than ethnology or the result of investigations in the line of the science of religion.

Ultimately Gauguin's stay in the Pacific islands was determined for a small part only by these idealizing motives. In addition to the economic motive it were no doubt in the first place artistic motives that led him.

He always remained the artist and did not aim to identify himself with the population, to live their life in order thus to turn his back upon Western culture. He had his *centre artistique*[1045] with him, kept pace with what happened in France and finally boasted that he had conquered new possibilities for the rising generation of artists, as we shall see at the end of this chapter. All this may also appear from his observation in a letter of 1892: 'I have a great many worries and if it was not necessary for my art (of this I am sure), I would leave at once.'[1046]

Gauguin's Realism

In his book on Gauguin, Morice writes that this artist had always been occupied with reality, even in the remote parts of the world to which he had retired. He made notes, in the form of drawings and written annotations, and from these documents he started: 'His imagination has its starting point and its references in what is real.'[1047] There are two negative pronouncements by Bernard which prove that this opinion is correct. In a publication of the letters that Gauguin had sent him, Bernard makes the slightly sour remark: 'Paul Gauguin was in reality rather a decorative painter than a symbolistic one; for in none of his pictures there ever appeared any idea.'[1048] We hope to prove that the latter remark is wrong, but this utterance does prove that in the eyes of Bernard, Gauguin stuck too much to reality. On the academic standpoint there is hardly a sharper kind of criticism conceivable of the theory and the work of Gauguin, but this very circumstance makes it all the more clear what Gauguin aimed at. We can understand this remark better when we bear in mind what Bernard wrote later on about Anquetin. After the account of the latter's development till around 1896, when Anquetin still adhered to a kind of art which was related to that of Daumier and Courbet, Bernard saw a fundamental change: 'His imagination, up to now a prisoner of reality, had been awakened and desired to express itself in the images of which the great masters have availed themselves. Suddenly he realized how very vain it was to attach oneself to the transitory aspects of his time.' He now sought something else: 'To the summary knowledge of the palette and the current practices he opposed the great science of art; to the false styles he opposed form; to the anemia of methods he opposed force; to the immediate subjects the great commonplaces of humanity . . . no longer a beautiful Parisian woman bathing but a nymph watched by a satyr.'[1049]

Morice, more positively, stated that Gauguin made use of his observation and experience of reality, of his notes written and drawn in his search for *des équivalents plastiques de la nature*[1050] or, in other words, to represent this reality in an iconic and non-naturalistic way. For Gauguin remained a Realist as to his subjects and he did not break with the tradition that had radically cut ties with the *grands lieux communs* by means of the work of Daumier, Courbet, Manet and the Impressionists and had ended in a strongly pronounced Realism with Degas, Lautrec and van Gogh.

We will try to explain this fact with the aid of two important works of art.

Manau Tupapau

Manao Tupapau is the title of a picture from 1892 which Gauguin calls: 'The most rigid and . . . the one which I want to keep or to sell dear,'[1051] a picture he valued very highly himself and the only one from this period that he dwells upon elaborately. He also tells us on what occasion he had made it – how one day he came home very late and then he saw his mistress lying in bed in great fear[1052] – this experience is a 'documentation' of the kind Morice mentions. But Gauguin is not merely content with painting the situation; in it he summarizes an aspect of the life of the Maori. We will first quote in full his explanation of the picture:

> A young girl of the South Sea Islands is lying on her stomach showing part of her frightened face. She rests on a bed adorned with a blue *paréo* and a bright-chrome yellow sheet. The violet-purple background is strewn with flowers, resembling electric sparks; a slightly strange figure stands by the side of the bed. Attracted by a form, a movement, I paint them without any other preoccupation than to make a study of the nude. As such it is a slightly indecent study of the nude, and yet I want to make a chaste picture of it by giving the Pacific spirit, its character, its tradition. The *paréo*, which is intimately connected with the existence of a Pacific islander, I use as the top of the bed. The sheet, made of a material like the bark of a tree, must be yellow because this colour suggests something unexpected for the spectator; it suggests the light of a lamp, which enables me to avoid the effect of a lamp. I want a slightly terrible background. The violet has been strongly indicated. This is the musical part of the painting fully exhibited.
>
> What can an entirely naked Pacific girl on a bed do in such a position? Prepare herself for love? This is indeed in her character, but it is indecent, and I won't have it. Sleep? That would be the end of the amorous action, which is also indecent. I only see fear. What kind of fear? Certainly not the fear of a Susan surprised by the greybeards. This does not exist in Oceania.
>
> The *Tupapau* (the spirit of the Dead) has been entirely indicated. For the South Sea Islanders this means constant fear. At night they always have a lamp burning. Nobody walks about on the roads unless with a lantern and even then they go, several of them together. Once I found my Tupapau, I entirely attached myself to it and made it into the motif of my painting. The nude is relegated to the second plane.

> What can an apparition be to a woman of the Pacific Islands? She does not know about the theatre, nor does she read any novels, and when she thinks of death she necessarily thinks of somebody she has already seen. My ghost can only be any simple woman. The decorative sense induces me to sprinkle flowers on the background. The flowers are the flowers of the Tupapau, phosphorescences showing that the ghost is occupied with a person. These are Tahitian beliefs.
>
> The title *Manao Tupapau* has two meanings: either she is thinking of the ghost, or the ghost is thinking of her.
>
> To recapitulate. The musical part: horizontal undulating lines, harmonies of orange and blue, connected by yellows and violets, their derivative tints, brightened by greenish sparks; the literary part: the spirit of a living human being connected with the spirit of the Dead. Night and Day. This genesis has been written for those who always want to know the why and the wherefore. If this is not the case it is simply a study of an Oceanian nude.[1053]

We are really grateful to Gauguin for his explanation – for after all we are among those people who always want to know the how and the why, as a matter of fact this is the origin of all science. Gauguin's last utterance should not be taken to mean that he did not consider his expositions to be of any importance. He rather wanted to point out that even without his explanation the contents of his painting were clear even if we did not know in every detail why the painter had done his work thus and what his considerations had been. Had not he once written about similar observations with respect to another picture saying: 'All this is besides painting, one will say. Who knows? Perhaps not.'[1054] These reflections clearly show his manner of working which was really in accordance with what we have found concerning his art-theoretical views. Reality was the starting point but more was expressed about it than was visible to the eye. As a matter of fact, he preferred making an impression by means of purely iconic means to painting an exact imitation of the visual object,[1055] as is seen in the passage where he speaks of avoiding the effect of the lamp whereas he did want to suggest such a fall of light by means of the colour of the sheet.

We also note how in such a painting various experiences and observations are summarized. What he says about the *paréo* on the bed shows that we must never use Gauguin's pictures as a a source of exact information on the customs of the Tahitians. Yet this *paréo* is certainly in its place, it is like an indication of place – in this respect the work is comparable to the nude of Anna the Javanese painted in Paris a few years later, which by the mere presence of the chair makes it clear that we are not in the tropics. His remarks concerning the reason why he represents the figure of death or of the ghost as a somewhat mysterious old woman are very striking. This old woman has been deliberately made entirely different from the traditional figure of a ghost in Western art (and rightly so).

The subject – the 'literary part' – has not only been represented iconically, it has been underlined by the whole aesthetic structure in line and colour – the 'musical part'. It is clear in this case that the harmony of colours and lines, although as such of a purely aesthetic nature and representing nothing, are an accompaniment to the iconic aspect, an intensification made in tune with it and clarifying it. Thus an artistic whole is achieved embracing a great deal more than a mere naturalistic depiction of visual things. In this work Gauguin is realistic, and any symbolism that tries to clarify the atmosphere and the object by means of allegorical figures or metaphorical indications[1056] is alien to him.

Actually more than one layer of reality is embraced by this picture – as was also the case with paintings of former times:[1057] first of all we see only the back of a nude with a woman beside it (a variation of the subject of Manet's *Olympia*). But in and by means of this representation a great deal more is told, namely about the world of thought of the Tahitians with their fears and their belief in ghosts. The realistic trait in all this is the fact that the artist derives his inspiration immediately from ordinary reality so that we cannot at all speak in this case of a *lieu commun de l'humanité*, the expression of a profound thought in the allegorical and personifying way of humanism.[1058] True, it is a nude, but more, one that evokes a whole world of thought.

Gauguin's work proves to be in perfect agreement with the views of art he had advanced when still in Paris. The supposition that he had then been a Symbolist but had turned his back upon this tendency later on is clearly refuted by this work.

D'où venons-nous? Que sommes-nous? Où allons-nous?

At the time when Gauguin painted his principal work *D'où venons-nous? Que sommes-nous? Où allons-nous* (1897–1898) there was hardly any longer question of a Synthetis movement.

Bernard had gone in a different direction, which was much more traditional and academic, even though he continued to adhere to some of the chief tenets of the theory propounded between 1888 and 1890. In his own way Denis had developed what he had then achieved, while more and more deriving his inspiration from the Florentine quattrocento. Theoretically speaking Sérusier was still purely Synthetist, but in his art he had not the courage to deviate very strongly from the traditional style, and the famous *Talisman* – the cigar box painted on according to the suggestions made by Gauguin – was to remain his most advanced work. And many of the artists who had been influenced by Gauguin and his followers only indirectly, such as Bonnard, Vuillard,

Lautrec, Maillol, built on what they had learnt, sometimes more directly and at other times less clearly so, and found their own way.

Yet this great work by Gauguin, which is now in the Boston Museum of Fine Arts,[1059] may be considered as the principal work of the whole movement. For this was after all the mature fruit of Gauguin's development and a summary of the aims and the work of this whole group. In it their artistic ideals were given a very adequate form. And even if it were true that some of Gauguin's smaller works were aesthetically as strong or even stronger, we think that after all Ruskin's definition still holds when he said that 'The art is greatest which conveys to the mind of the spectator, by what means whatsoever, the greatest number of the greatest ideas,' if we bear in mind that also in Ruskin's view the stress is not laid on 'number' but rather on the quality of the 'ideas'.[1060] And there is no doubt that *D'où venons-nous? Que sommes-nous? Où allons-nous?* is a work with a very complex content in which many motifs and thoughts have been embodied.[1061]

In February 1898 he wrote about this work for the first time, to his faithful friend Daniel de Monfreid. He also relates his futile effort at suicide after he had completed his great picture. One gets the impression that he had as it were staged this scene: committing suicide and leaving behind as a testament a striking canvas which is at the same time the summary of all that he had always striven for. A theatrical death, leaving not only a perfect oeuvre ending in a summarizing masterpiece but also a death that finishes his self-determined course of life in setting a future biographer the great task of elaborating a grand theme, which could end on a more triumphant note, a different and more glorious one, than the life of the master of Balzac's *Un chef d'oeuvre inconnu* – a death resembling the suicide of de Nerval.[1062]

In that letter Gauguin continues with an exact description of the canvas measuring 4.5 by 1.7 metres, which he compares to a fresco – probably having in mind Puvis de Chavannes (whose name he mentions in connection with this work later on). He also speaks of a white goat, which is not white in the picture now, and of a squatting figure near an idol, which is absent – it is possible that he made some alterations later on. A little further on he briefly indicates the principal contents, *le poème*, of the work, after which he triumphantly concludes: 'I have finished a philosophical work on this theme comparable to the Gospel . . . I think it is good.'[1063]

The subject of this picture was neither new nor uncommon. Yet we do not believe that he had been inspired by the German publications quoted by Bettina Polak in connection with the Dutch Symbolists, nor by writers belonging to Maeterlink's circle,[1064] people with whom Gauguin had not had any contact and whose writings he almost certainly had not read.

We get a great deal nearer to Gauguin's world when we refer to Balzac's *Séraphita*, a work he no doubt knew and appreciated highly. When Wilfred has fallen into a hypnotic sleep – and will not Gauguin have dreamt that his picture would do the same thing to the spectator as was done by Séraphita's words to Wilfred:

> That my words may clothe the brilliant forms of dreams which they adorn with images, flamboyant and descending on you ... Do you understand the destination of humanity by means of this visible thought? From where it comes and where it goes to ... Do you understand ... such spectacles would take away and tear to pieces your intelligence ... you understand?[1065]

We are for a moment reminded of these words – if the whole work does not already speak of this – when reading the description of his work quoted above where he says: 'A figure . . . lifts up its arms into the air and astonished, looks at these two personages who dare to think of their destination.'[1066]

But there were also other sources of inspiration for Gauguin with respect to this work. We are especially referring to Carlyle's *Sartor Resartus*.[1067] In this book Carlyle penetrates to great depth, also in consequence of the remarkable form in which he clothed his thoughts. He speaks of the spiritual crisis into which Teufelsdröckh gets involved when he had lost his (Christian) faith, and when for this reason he had lost all hope because to him the whole of this world seemed to be one great meaningless process:

> Thus must the bewildered Wanderer stand, as so many have done, shouting question after question into the Sibylcave of Destiny, and receive no answer but an Echo ... no Pillar of Cloud by day, and no Pillar of Fire by night, any longer guides the Pilgrim.[1068] To such length has the spirit of Inquiry carried him.[1069]

These fundamental questions occur again and again in this book: 'Who am I? What is me? A Voice, a Motion, an Appearance; – some embodied, visualized Idea in the Eternal Mind? *Cogito, ergo sum.* Alas, poor Cogitator, this takes us but a little way. Sure enough, I am; and lately was not: but Whence? How? Whereto?'[1070] And this question remained even after Teufelsdröckh had reached a turning-point and had recognized his place and accepted it, 'a revelation to Sense of the mystic god-given Force that is in him; a "Gospel of Freedom", which he, the "Messiah of Nature", preaches, as he can, by act and word'.[1071] For – and this trend of thought is very similar to that of Balzac's *Séraphita*[1072] – we read: 'On the hardest adamant some footprint of us is stamped in; the last Rear of the host will read traces of the earliest Man. But whence? – O, Heaven, whither?'[1073]

It might be asked whether Gauguin had also read all this. There is no certainty about this. Yet, at Le Pouldu we may assume that the *Sartor Resartus* had been discussed – in the portrait of Meyer de Haan from this period there lies a copy of this work on the table,[1074] – and that Gauguin was acquainted with its contents. It is possible that de Haan had read out loud some characteristic parts, such as the one we have quoted. For the possibility that Gauguin had also read it himself depends on the question whether Gauguin could read English, and if so, whether he read it so well as to be able to understand this, by no means simple, kind of English.[1075]

But there is still another way in which Gauguin might have come into contact with Carlyle's work. For Taine wrote a book on this philosopher in which there are all kinds of quotations.[1076] Also the forever recurring question in Carlyle's book: 'Oh Whence – Oh Heaven, Whither?' is found in Taine's French work. He translates these words,[1077] not quite accurately although correctly according to the meaning, as follows: 'Mais d'où venons-nous? O Dieu, où allons-nous?'[1078] In view of the importance of this book for the Symbolist authors – about which we have spoken in our second chapter – it is not at all impossible that Gauguin was acquainted with it, even if only indirectly by means of a talk with Morice, for instance.

Gauguin did not embody these thoughts in his work in an allegorical way, he did not have them 'staged' by metaphorical figures. On the contrary we are confronted with a work that at first sight does not give more than a (realistic) view of daily life in Tahiti – even if it is immediately clear that it gives a particular summary. But if we saturate ourselves with the whole of it, even the spectator who has not read Gauguin's reflections will understand that in and with these figures and these motifs more has been given than the daily life of the Tahitians, that a particular vision has been given, that this painted world is metaphorically related to a deeper reality, the nature of the life of man and woman there, and in this nature, we would almost say, the structure of human life in general. In this the question about the meaning of life has also been posited. The colours and the composition are by no means unimportant in this connection; on the contrary, precisely by their means it becomes clear that we do not have before us some folkloristic-ethnological study of life there, such as was for instance given by La Fargue. The title is an aid to the spectator's meditations, which is not exclusively 'literary', in the sense that here thoughts are presented that are really unconnected with the picture and its own artistic qualities – on the contrary, the work will reveal its meaning, its 'great number of ideas' in various layers of reality when we study the work thoroughly. Thus also the meaning in its most profound sense, in its relatedness to what lies nearest to the painter's heart, his or her view of life and the world, will become poetically visible. For the relevance, the relation between the work and this view, imparts to every colour and every line, to every figure and every stroke with the brush its profound artistic sense – iconically, 'musically', and aesthetically.

Gauguin himself also speaks about these questions when in connection with this work he compares his own manner of working with that of Puvis de Chavannes.

> Puvis explains his idea, yes but he does not paint it. He is Greek [i.e. he joins the classicistic-academic tradition] whereas I myself am a savage. Puvis will entitle a picture 'Purity' and in explanation he will paint a young virgin with a lily in her hand – a well-known symbol, so it is understood. Gauguin will paint a landscape under the same title with limpid waters with not any stain of civilized man, perhaps one personage. Without my entering into details it is clear that there is a whole world of difference between Puvis and me. As a painter Puvis is a lettered man, whereas I am not a lettered man but perhaps a man of letters.[1079]

The latter pronouncement means probably that he is certainly not a naturalist who tells his thoughts merely by the figures represented.

According to the art theory of the Synthetists the work of art was a child of the 'imagination' – a free creation in which the artist embodies and summarizes what he has observed and thought out in an artistically justifiable and meaningful image, representing it not allegorically but metaphorically with iconic means. In this case Gauguin has explained the way in which his 'imagination' worked – although his *rêve* was noted down a long time afterwards, we do not believe that his description is a mere fiction; rather it is a short, poetic analysis of the atmosphere in which the work of art came into existence. He wrote to Fontainas in 1889:

> Here, close to my cottage, in complete silence, I dream violent harmonies in the natural perfumes that intoxicate me. A refined delight of I don't know what holy horror which I presume in the immemorial. The past, the fragrance of joy which I inhale in the present. Animal figures, of a statuesque rigidity: I do not know what ancient, glorious, religious flavour in the rhythm of their gestures, in their rare immobility. In their dreamy eyes the surface is blurred by an unfathomable enigma. And it is night – peace everywhere. My eyes are closed in order to see without understanding the dream in infinite space which recedes in front of me, and I have a feeling of the doleful march of my hopes.[1080]

All this has been really given in the work in the way described by Gauguin himself (immediately below the quotation given just now), *sans aucune allégorie* ('without any allegory'). Although its motifs are realistic, the real meaning of the work is 'that which has not been expressed', that which is not contained in the motifs as such, which 'follows implicitly from the lines without colours or words, it has not been materially constituted'.[1081] So this is the 'musicality' again – he speaks of his *poème musical* – ultimately revealing the meaning of the work, in its composition, in its aesthetic arrangement.

We now have to consider the different figures and motifs as he explains them in his letter to Morice in 1901:

> In this large picture:
> Whither?

> Close to the death of an old woman,
> A strange stupid bird concludes.
> What?
> Daily existence.
> The man of instinct asks himself what all this means.
> Whence
> Source.
> Child.
> Communal life.

The bird concludes the poem by comparing the lower being with the intelligent being in this great whole which is the problem announced by the title.

> Behind a tree two sinister figures, enveloped in clothes of a sad colour near the tree of knowledge, make their note of sadness, caused by this very knowledge in comparison with the simple beings in a virginal nature that might have been a paradise conceived by man, abandoning themselves to the bliss of living.[1082]

If anywhere it is here in this last paragraph that Gauguin comes very close to Jean Jacques Rousseau.

It is very remarkable that in this work he has represented the course his thoughts took by starting at the right and moving to the left.[1083] Should this be viewed as a last effect of the influence of Japanese art which construes its compositions from right to left?[1084]

A last trace of Japanese influence, we said, for in contradistinction to the principal work of the first period in Brittany, *Vision after the sermon* this work is not at all Japanese in its structure. We do not look down on the scene as it were from above, and the figures are never cut at the border of the picture. Its decorative effect is due to something quite different, namely the frieze-like arrangement of the figures in a few planes parallel to the front area. It would be possible to ascribe this feature to the influence of Puvis – and there is certainly such an influence – but, as Dorival has established, we must above all bear in mind that Gauguin possessed some photos of the Burubudur friezes.[1085] They exhibit a similar rhythmical arrangement of the figures side by side, also in at most a few parallel planes. The landscape in the background is a real background, one that evokes little sense of depth. Also in this case Gauguin's composition has been kept rather flat although the figures in the foreground have been given the necessary moving space. For, however satisfying the arrangement on the surface may be called, it is certainly not a 'flat' composition in the exclusively decorative sense.

In this work we are really face to face with the direct application of some of the artistic ideals Gauguin had formulated in his mythical exposition, his story of the painter Mani-Vehli-Zumbul-Zadi who gives his pupils all kinds of precepts, such as 'Look for harmony . . . that with you everything breathes peace . . . Avoid the pose in movement. Each of your personages should be in a static condition. Apply yourself to the silhouette of each object.'[1086] Although this writing had been made at a much earlier period[1087] it certainly suits a painting like this better than his earlier art, though the latter also shows very little movement.

This painting deals with profound and fundamental problems, with the basic questions of human existence itself. As a matter of fact Gauguin has no answer to offer – a Christian answer is impossible to him, as he is of the opinion that 'Putting oneself in the hands of one's Creator is annulling oneself and dying,'[1088] and its vagueness is more than a question of an artistic ideal only; rather, it is the expression of his resignation to the fact that it is insolvable: 'The idol is there . . . forming part of my dream in front of my cottage with the whole of nature, reigning in our primitive soul, the imaginary consolation of our sufferings [note the use of 'imaginary'] in what they imply of vagueness and of the incomprehensible with respect to the mystery of our origin and our future.'[1089]

Later writings

After the work we have just been discussing Gauguin did not make many more paintings. He was hampered by illness, monetary difficulties and adversities. He only devoted himself more intensively to writing what might be called his memoirs, which also embodied his creed. It is as if after the completion of his oeuvre he wished to leave a series of reflections to posterity by way of a testament. Of course we must not expect that Gauguin now became a philosopher in the technical sense of this term – but this is not saying that his thought lacked depth or clarity. He explained his thoughts in a very sharp way, occasionally in Nietschean turns of phrase, partly as a summary of all that in the preceding ten or fifteen years he had striven after and had thought out in connection with it. But there are also new subjects, new thoughts, sharper conclusions with a new emphasis. In the writings of these years he sometimes merely repeats what he had written before, as in his letters, but there is also a great deal that we have not come across before.

Gauguin does not aim at a system: 'And then you know that if the others have gratified me with a system, I myself have none and I will not be condemned to it. To paint as I like, bright today, dark tomorrow, etc. . . . for the rest, an artist should be free or he is not an artist.[1090] This explains clearly what is the issue – not some aesthetics as with Sérusier and his colour circle, nor a system as the one that the Neo-Impressionists tried to formulate and apply, not a fixed manner of working, which would only mean a new kind of academism. All this Gauguin scrupulously avoided. But this does not mean that he was without any definite ideas on art, that he had no artistic ideal, excluding certain kinds of art, or on the other hand that he did not want a work of art to satisfy particular requirements. In this sense he certainly had an art theory, which formulated general principles and defined the relation of a work of art to reality in a more philosophical way than any mere formula of style, or any manner of working could do.

In fact, if anywhere it is clear in the case of Gauguin that reforms in art never arise merely spontaneously, owing to accidental influences and circumstances, from the character and the nature of the reformer as such, without reflection and without any conscious mental attitude and ideals. The artist who as it were automatically draws purely from his talent and discovers what is new is a Romantic conception, which only rarely does justice to reality. Such art is considered to be apart from any conscious reflection – and the artist is really considered as a thoughtless improvisator, which testifies to a low rather than to a high opinion of art.

Such a view must be rejected for, as Gauguin himself puts it, 'If a work of art were something accidental, all these notes would be useless.'[1091] He maintains that his expositions are 'all rays to the vital centre of my art'.[1092]

In a negative way Gauguin always described his art as the opposite of the academicism and naturalism of the Salon artists, while notwithstanding his admiration of the great personalities among the Impressionists he rejected Impressionism. 'The machines have come, art has gone, and I am far from thinking that photography would be propitious to us.'[1093] Thus he depreciates every scientific attitude in his concise and forceful way (he also denied that thanks to photography an artist would for instance be able to understand a horse better):[1094] 'As to myself, I have withdrawn very far, farther away than the horses of the Parthenon . . . to the "dada" of my childhood, the good old wooden horse.'[1095] By this Gauguin wanted to say that he had dissociated himself from every system that prevailed in the world of art before him, also mentioning the Parthenon to indicate that even Greek art could no longer be a source of inspiration to him. Egyptian art and that of the Burubudur – which is what he called the art of Cambodia – were sources of inspiration to him, for in these he found an artistic conception to which he felt akin, an art which was free of any naturalism because it most clearly manifested the iconic element in the sense in which he understood it.[1096] He considered such men as Ingres, Corot, Delacroix of the first half of the nineteenth century as his direct predecessors: 'Finally there is at present a beautiful effort which stems less from the previous epoch than from the Romantics.'[1097]

For the art of the period immediately preceding his own time too much forgot 'the mysterious centre of thought',[1098] remained too superficial, was often too much of a system, a formula, too little born of a strictly human subjectivity.

> Where does the execution of a picture begin and where does it end? At the
> moment when the extreme feelings are fusing together in the deepest part

of being, at the moment when they burst and all thought is thrown out like lava from a volcano, is not there a breaking forth of the work that is suddenly created, savage if you like, but grand and of a superhuman aspect? The cold calculations of reason have not preceded this outburst but who knows when the work was begun in the depth of being? Unconsciously perhaps?[1099]

This is a pronouncement to which both Delacroix and Baudelaire would certainly have subscribed, each in his own way.

Freedom

When at the end of his life he surveys his work, he more than ever lays the emphasis on freedom: 'I have wanted to establish the right to venture anything: my capacities have not yielded a great result, but the machine has been launched after all. The public does not owe me anything because my pictorial work is only comparatively good, but the painters who profit from this liberty nowadays owe me something.'[1100] The motif of freedom, which always played an important part but was formerly kept within bounds by the idea of synthesis in which reality also claimed its rights, now comes to the fore much more emphatically, at least in Gauguin's writings. He shows that this motif was ultimately the determining element in his aims. Freedom from any restrictive demand for naturalness in the sense of naturalism, from 'the shackles of verisimilitude',[1101] although also at this time he did not mean to take leave of recognizibility nor deliberately to seek abstraction (in the twentieth-century sense). Freedom also from the 'the academic bias' and from 'the Symbolist bias, another kind of sentimentalism'.[1102] For he also thought Symbolism too cheap. To his mind it did not dig deep enough, stuck too much to an allegorizing which could only be understood from tradition – we are referring to his rage on receiving his portrait, painted by Schuffenecker: 'A cross, flames, that is it, Symbolism.'[1103]

Gauguin no doubt had some very unpleasant characteristics. He could flare up in a very disagreeable way and he was certainly not free from a Bohemian pose. But this does not mean that we are entitled to explain his art, his work and his aims as a kind of theatrical performance intended to evoke applause and to increase the receipts (with however much talent it may have been accomplished).[1104] He himself denied this and he never sought a cheap success.[1105] A large dose of idealism not only urged him on but sustained him in all his difficulties and strengthened his willpower – the idealism of his hope that also owing to his own work, there would come a better and more beautiful art that would be more healthy and more meaningful. For it was his dream to deliver the art of painting especially from 'the mediocrities'[1106] – insufficiently aware as he was that the latter will never be lacking in any period, no matter the style, the attitude and the aims of the artists: not all men are geniuses, and a mediocre talent also has its place in the life of art, and is perhaps as important for society, for contemporary humanity, as a great reformer and leader.

In the writings of his last years rather than in his art, in which he remained a pure Synthetist, he broke with Synthetism and more and more strongly emphasized freedom. The problems evoked by it, the conflict with given reality[1107] that was bound to arise, he did not only realize intellectually; he struggled with it in the depths of his being. No doubt in this case he was influenced by Mallarmé, who also tried to realize freedom in his own way, [1108] and possibly the reading of an article like that on Harcoland in the *Mercure de France* (which was always sent to him)[1109] drove him on again in that direction.[1110] This is clear from the following passage in *Avant et Après*: 'I know, like everybody, and as everybody will ever know, that two and two makes four. It is a far cry from convention and intuition to understanding: I subject myself, and like everybody I say: Two and two makes four . . . But . . . [1111] that bores me, and deranges very much my reasoning.'[1112]

Gauguin's legacy

Indeed, the freedom preached by Gauguin in his last years especially, the heritage which he bequeathed to the next generation – as a testament – was accepted in full by the twentieth century, as well as the problems we have just indicated. In the first few years of the new century in particular, Gauguin's influence was great, and no doubt contributed a great deal to the art of the Fauves, especially in their great daring, their contempt of *raisemblance*, their relinquishing any naturalism in colour and the handling of lines. Gradually freedom is more and more stressed, reality loses more and more of its meaning until, at last, non-figurative art made its appearance – in particular that branch of it which may be called irrational.[1113] In art theory it was especially the idea of 'musicality' that was carried through to absurdity. The synthesis which determined Gauguin's work was broken up and thus Gauguin's art, in which reality continued to play an important part, became an out-dated standpoint. Nevertheless its humanity always makes his art so fascinating, and constitutes its great and permanent significance, precisely also on account of his adherence to reality, although he rejected naturalism.

The re-discovery of the iconic element was to prove very fruitful – not only for Art with a capital letter, but also for posters and illustrations and so on. Looked at in a historical perspective this is perhaps the greatest importance to be attached to this oeuvre – viewed not merely as a collection of paintings left by the artist but also as a demonstration of the principles inherent to these works. At the same time we should not underrate the importance and the influence of his writings. After all, the decorative principle of Gauguin's art, according to which a far greater emphasis was laid on aesthetic arrangement, the rhythmic and harmonious play of lines and colours, than had been done in the art of the preceding period, and which was connected with his appreciation of the iconic aspect and founded in the idea of musicality, has been of primary importance for the genesis and the development of modern French art. We are referring to Matisse and the revival of tapestry art. This was made possible because Gauguin's art emphasizes the composition on the surface, whereas the spatial effect (the ordering in depth) – also because of the influence of Japanese art and later on especially of the art of the Burubudur – becomes of secondary importance.

So Gauguin left us with the legacy of three things: the artist's freedom to find new forms apart from any tradition; an undoubtedly very fertile apprehension of the iconic character of the pictorial arts; and a new appreciation of the decorative. But it was freedom he prized above all. In a powerful way he formulated it in 1902 as the task of the new generation – and it is still the most concise formula of twentieth-century artistic striving:

> So it was essential taking account of all the efforts made and all the research (even scientific research), to dream of total liberation, to smash the windows – even though it meant cutting our fingers – and leave it to the next generation, which from now on is on its own, free of any ties, to find a solution to the problem. I don't mean it to be final for we are talking about an art which never comes to an end, with a wealth of techniques at its disposal, capable of translating all the moods of man and nature, fitted to every personality in very generation, be it in joy or sorrow.
>
> To do that we had to throw ourselves body and soul into the battle, to fight against all the schools, the whole lot, not only depreciating them, but in another way, attacking not just the dignitaries but also the Impressionists, the Neo-Impressionists, the public old and new. There is no need anymore to have wife and children who will disown you. What do insults matter? What does unhappiness matter? This as far as the way of life is concerned.
>
> And what about the work? A method of contradiction, if you like. Attempt the greatest abstractions, do everything which isn't allowed and then reconstruct and don't worry about the results. Don't be afraid to exaggerate, even do exaggerate. Learn afresh, and then, once you know, learn over again. Overcome all your fears, no matter how ridiculous the results.
>
> In front of the easel, a painter is not a slave of the past nor of the present, not of nature nor of his fellow-man. He is himself, I repeat, himself, always himself.[1114]

Bibliography

We have arranged the titles systematically. Completeness has not been pursued. For an almost all-comprehensive list see the Bibliography in Rewald's *Post-Impressionism*.

H. Dooyeweerd, *A New Critique of Theoretical Thought* (Amsterdam 1955).

H. Dooyeweerd, *Wijsbegeerte der Wetsidee* I, II, III (Amsterdam 1935).

H. Dooyeweerd, *Transcendental Problems of Philosophical Thought* (Grand Rapids. Mich., 1948)

W. Windelband, *Lehrbuch der Geschichte der Philosophie*, ed. H. Heimsoeth (Tübingen, 1948 14).

Susanna K. Langer, *Philosophy in a New Key: a study in the symbolism of reason, rite and art* (New York, 1949 2).

H. v. Oyen, *Philosophie, beknopt handboek tot de geschiedenis van bet wijsgerig denken*, I, II, ed. (Utrecht, 1947).

E. Panofsky, *Meaning in the Visual Arts* (Garden City, N.Y., 1955).

E. Schöne, *Über das Licht in der Malerei* (Berlin, 1954).

E. Bevan, *Holy Images, an inquiry into idolatry and image-worship in ancient paganism and christianity* (London, 1940).

E. Cassirer, *Der Begriff der symbolische Form im Aufbau der Geisteswissenschaften* (Vorträge Bibl. Warburg, 1921/2; Berlin, 1922).

J. Maritain, 'Sign and symbol', *Journal of the Warburg and Courtauld Institutes* I (1937)p.1.

W. Embler, 'Symbols in literature and art', *College Art Journal* XVI, 1, (1956) p.47.

Ch. Saulnier, 'Esthétique et connaissance, caractère spécial de l'attitude esthétique du point de vue cognitif', *Revue d'Esthétique* V, 4 (1952) p.411.

Th. Munro, 'Suggestion and symbolism in the arts', *Journal of Aesthetics and Art Criticism* XV, 2 (1956) p.152.

A.N. Whitehead, *Symbolism, its meaning and effect* (New York, 1927).

C. Morris, *Signs, Language and Behavior* (New York, 1946).

On art, art theory and aesthetics before the nineteenth century

E. Panofsky, 'Idea', in *Ein Beitrag zur Begriffsgeschichte der älteren Kunsttheorie* (Berlin, 1924).

J. Lemeere ,'Les concepts du Beau et de l'Art dans la doctrine platonicienne', *Revue d'Histoire de la Philosophie et d'Histoire générale de la civilisation* VI (1938) p.1 f.f.

Plotinus, *Enneads*. Transl. S. MacKenna (London, 1956).

Plotin, *Enneade* I, VI, *Du Beau*. Transl. M. Meunier (Paris, 1926).

E. Bréhier, *La Philosophie de Plotin* (Paris, 1928).

J. Daniélou, *Platonisme et théologie mystique. Essai sur la doctrine spirituelle de St. Grégoire de Nyssa* (Paris, 1944).

H.J. Hak, 'Marsilio Ficino' (Amsterdam, 1934., Diss.).

A. Chastel, *Marsile Ficin et l'art* (Genève, Lille, 1954).

A. Blunt, *Artistic Theory in Italy* 1450-1600 (Oxford, 1940).

E. Gombrich, 'Icones symbolicae. The visual image in Neoplatonic Thought', *Journal of the Warburg and Courtauld Institute* XI (1948) p.163.

E. Wind, 'The revolution of history painting', *Journal of the Warburg and Courtauld Institute* II (1938) p.116.

J.J. Rousseau, *Dialogues, Rêveries d'un promeneur solitaire*. Annot. P. Richard (Paris, 1952 54).

I. Kant, *Werke in 8 Bücher*. ed. H. Renner (Band I, II, Berlin o.J.).

F. v. Schiller, *Über die aesthetische Erziehung des Menschen* (Herford, 1948).

M. Lamm, Swedenborg *Eine Studie über seine Entwicklung zum Mystiker und Geistesseher* (Leipzig, 1922).

E. Swedenborg Clavis, *Hieroglyphica arcanorum naturalium et spiritualium per viam repraesentationum et correspondentiarum* (London, 1784).

M. Matter, *Emmanuel de Swedenborg, sa vie, ses écrits et sa doctrine* (Paris, 1863).

E.A. Sutton, *The living Thought of Swedenborg* (London, 1944).

L. Venturi, *Histoire de la critique d'art* (Bruxelles, 1938).

Philosophy and aesthetics in the nineteenth century

A. Schopenhauer, *Die Welt als Wille und Vorstellung* (Leipzig, 1844 2).

A. Schopenhauer, *Pensées, Maximes et Fragments*. Ed. J. Bourdeau, (Paris, 1880).

T. Carlyle, *Sartor Resartus* (London, 1898).

T. Carlyle, *On heroes, hero-worship and the heroic in history* (London, 1352).

H. Taine, *L'idéalisme anglais, étude sur Carlyle* (Paris, 1864).

E. Neff, *Carlyle* (London, 1932).

A.C. Taylor, *Carlyle, sa première fortune littéraire en France* (1825-1868), (Paris 1929).

Humbert de Superville, *Essai sur les signes inconditionnels dans l'art* (Leiden, 1827).

E. v. Hartmann, *Philosophie des Unbewussten* (Berlin, 1871 3) p.244

H. Taine, *Philosophie de l'art* I, II (Paris, 1924).

H. Taine, *Notes sur Paris. Vie et Opinions de M. Frédéric-Thomas Graindorge, recueilli par H.Taine* (Paris, 1867).

C. Picard, *H. Taine* (Paris, 1909).

J. Zeitler, *Die Kunstphilosophie von Hippolite Taine* (Leipzig, 1901).

J. Gibelin, *'L'esthétique de Schelling d'après la Philosophie de l'Art'* (Paris, 1933, Diss).

R. Schneider, *L'esthétique classique chez Quatremère de Quincy* (Paris, 1910).

D. Lenz, *L'esthétique de Beuron*. trad. 3. Sérusier. Introduction M. Denis (Paris, 1905).

L. Venturi, *Histoire de la critique d'art* (Bruxelles, 1938).

V. Cherbuliez, *L'art et la nature* (Paris, 1892).

Ph. Gauckler, *Le Beau et son histoire* (Paris, 1873).

J.D. Bierens de Haan, *De strijd tussen idealisme en naturalisme in de 19e eeuw* (Haarlem, 1929).

M.H. Abrams, *The mirror and the lamp Romantic Theory and the Critical Tradition* (New York, 1953).

A. Fouillée, *Le mouvement positiviste et la conception sociologique du monde* (Paris, 1896).

J. Wilcox, 'La genèse de la théorie de l'art pour l'art en France', *Revue d'esthétique* VI, 1 (1953) p.1.

A. Kuyper, 'Calvinism and Art.' *Calvinism, Six Stone Lectures* (Amsterdam-Pretoria, 1899).

A. Kuyper, 'The antithesis between Symbolism and Revelation' (Lecture delivered before the Historical Presbyterian Society in Philadelphia, Pa. Amsterdam-Pretoria-Edinburg, 1899).

A. Kuyper, 'Het Calvinisme en de kunst' (Lecture, Amsterdam, 1888).

A. Kuyper, 'Calvinism and Art', *Christian Thought, lectures and papers on philosophy, christian evidence, biblical elucidation* IX, New York, 1891/2, pp.259-282, 447-459, Transl. Rev. J. H. de Vries.

A. Kuyper, 'De verflauwing der grenzen' (Lecture, Amsterdam, 1892).

Literature and culture in the nineteenth century (up to 1885)

E.A. Poe, *The poems of* . . . (incl. 'Essay on the Poetic Principle', 'Essay on the Philosophy of Composition') Introd. H. N. Williams (London, New York 1900).

E.A. Poe, 'Lettres 1848–1849', *La Revue Blanche* (Feb. 1895).

C.P. Cambiaire, *The influence of E. A. Poe in France* (Fontenay-sous-Bois, Seine, 1927).

M. Atterton, 'Origins of Poe's Critical Theory' (University of Iowa Humanistic Studies II, 3, nd.).

C. Baudelaire, *Histoires extraordinaires par Edgar Poe*. annot. J. Crépet (Paris 1932).

C. Baudelaire, *Curiosités Esthétiques* (Paris, 1921).

C. Baudelaire, *L'Art romantique* (Paris s.d. circa 1910).

C. Baudelaire, *Les Fleurs du Mal*, ed. J. Crépet et G. Blin (Paris, 1942).

M. Gilman, *Baudelaire the Critic* (New York, 1943).

J.P. Sartre, *Baudelaire* (Paris, 1947 28).

J. Prévost, *Baudelaire* (Paris, 1953).

L. Horner, *Baudelaire critique de Delacroix* (Genève, 1956).

A. Ferran, *L'Esthétique de Baudelaire* (Paris, 1933).

W. Drost, 'L'Inspiration plastique chez Baudelaire', *Gazette des Beaux Arts* (May/June 1957) p.321.

R. Huyghe, *L'Esthétique de l'individualisme à travers Delacroix et Baudelaire* (Oxford, 1955).

Maatstaf: Maandblad voor letteren, V, 3/4, p.145 – special Baudelaire issue.

R. Michaud, 'Baudelaire, Balzac et les correspondances', *Romanic Review* XXIX, 3 (1938) p.253 ff.

G. Batault, 'A propos de Baudelaire et de Balzac', *Mercure de France* (April, 1931) p.216.

H. Balzac, *Oeuvres Complètes* XV: *Etudes philosophiques* I (Paris, 1869).

H. Balzac, *Oeuvres Complètes* XVII: *Etudes philosophiques* III (Paris, 1870).

H. Evans, *Louis Lambert et la philosophie de Balzac* (Paris, 1951).

J.d. Elst, 'Autour du 'livre mystique'; 'Balzac et Swedenborg', *Revue de la littérature comparée* X (1930) p.88.

E. Zola, *L'Oeuvre* (Paris, 1893).

E. Zola, *Les romanciers naturalistes* (Paris, 1881 2)

E. Zola, 'Les réalistes au salon' *Mes Haines* (Paris, 1866).

G. Flaubert, *La tentation de St. Antoine* (Paris, 1874).

J. Sezoec, 'Flaubert and the graphic arts', *Journal of the Warburg and Courtauld Institute* VIII (1945) p.175.

M. Raymond, *From Baudelaire to Surrealism* (New York, 1950). Transl. from French.

A. Poizat, *Le symbolisme de Baudelaire à Claudel* (Paris, 1919).

A. Tabarant, *La vie artistique au temps de Baudelaire* (Paris, 1942).

Holbrook Jackson, *Dreamers of dreams. Rise and fall of nineteenth century idealism* (London 1948).

H.A. Hatzfeld, *Literature through art. A new approach to French literature* (New York, 1952).

Kenneth Clark, *The Gothic Revival: An Essay in the History of Taste* (London, 1928).

U. Christoffel, *Malerei und Poesie. Die symbolistische Kunst des 19. Jahrhunderts* (Zurich, 1948).

P. van Tieghem, *Le Romantisme dans la litterature européenne* (Paris, 1948).

F. Strich, Die *Romantik als europäische Bewegung, Festschrift H.Wöllfflin* (1924).

M. Jean & A. Mezei, *Genèse de la pensée moderne dans la littérature* (Paris, 1950).

A. Viatte, *Les sources occultes du romantisme* I, II (Paris, 1928).

General works on nineteenth-century art

H. Focillon, *La peinture an XIXième siècle* I, II (Paris, 1927/28).

A. Springer, *Die Kunst von 1800 bis zur Gegenwart* (Leipzig, 1920).

P. Colin, *La Peinture aux XIX siècle. Le Romantisme* (Paris-Bruxelles, 1935).

J. Rothenstein, *Nineteenth-Century painting, a study in conflict* (London, 1932).

H. Sedlmayr, *Verlust der Mitte. Die bildende Kunst des 19. und 20. Jahrhunderts als Symptom und Symbol der Zeit* (Salzburg, 1951 5).

H. Beenken, 'Die Krise der Malerei', *Deutsche Vierteljahrschrift für Litt. Wissenschaft und Geistesgeschichte* XI (1933) p.421.

M. Raynal, *Histoire de la peinture moderne de Baudelaire à Bonnard* (Genève, 1949).

F.D. Klingender, *Art and the industrial revolution* (London, 1947).

Ph. Burty, *Maîtres et Petits-Maîtres* (Paris, 1877).

K. Berger, 'Poussin's style and the XIX century', *Gazette des Beaux Arts* (1955) p.161.

J. Alazard, 'L'Exotisme dans la peinture française au XIXième siècle', *Gazette des Beaux Arts* II (1931) p.241.

E.H. Gombrich, 'Imagery and Art in the romantic period', *Burlington Magazine* XCI (1949) p.153.

F. Jourdain, 'L'Art officiel de Jules Grévy à Albert Lebrun', *Le Point* (Souillac, 1949).

W. Friedlaender, *David to Delacroix* (Cambridge, Mass, 1952).

J. Piper, *British Romantic Artists* (London, 1946).

J. Alford, 'Art and Reality 1850-1950', *College Art Journal* XVII, 3 (1958) p.228.

The two sides of the medal. French Painting from Gerôme to Gauguin (Exhib. Detroit Museum of Art, 1954).

Verkannte Kunst (Cat. Exh. Kunsthalle Recklinghausen, 1957).

Catalogue illustré officiel de l'Exposition centennale de L'Art français 1800-1889 (Paris, 1900).

B. Newhall, 'Photography and the development of kinetic visualisation', *Journal of the Warburg and Courtauld Institute* VII (1944) p.42.

J. Thirion, 'L'influence de l'Estampe japonaise sur la peinture française', *Musée de France* (Oct. 1948) p.229.

C. Blanc, *Le Trésor de la curiosité* (Paris, 1958).

E.J. Délécluze, *Les beaux Arts dans les deux mondes en 1855* (Paris, 1856).

Th. Gautier, *L'Art moderne* (Paris, 1856).

H. Heine, *Der Salon I* (Rotterdam, 1860).

N. Lübke, *Die moderne französische Kunst* (1872).

Precursors of the Synthetists

L. Lopez-Rey, 'Goya and the world around him', *Gazette des Beaux Arts* II (1945) p.129.

G. Levitine, 'Literary sources of Goya's Capricho 43', *Art Bulletin* XXXVII (1955) p.56.

Xavier de Salas, 'Miscelanea Goyesca'. *Archivo Español de Arte* 92 (1950), p.335.

Bosch, *Goya et le Phantastique* (Cat. Exp. Bordeaux, 1957).

T. Hetzer, 'F. Goya und die Krise der Kunst um 1800', *Wiener Jahrbuch für Kunstgeschichte* XIV (1950) p.7.

L. Lopez-Rey, *Francisco de Goya* (Amsterdam-Antwerp, 1950).

E. Delacroix, *sa vie et ses oeuvres* (Paris, 1865).

B. Delacroix, *Oeuvres littéraires* I, II ed. E. Faure (Paris, 1923).

Journal d'Eugène Delacroix, ed. A. Joubin (Paris, 1950 2).

Lettres de Delacroix (7815-1863), (Paris: publ. p. Burty, 1878).

G. Dargenty, *E. Delacroix par lui-même* (Paris, 1885).

Tourneux, *E. Delacroix devant ses contemporains* (Paris, 1886).

A. Robaut, *L'oeuvre complète d'Eugène Delacroix, commenté par E. Chesneau* (Paris, 1885).

P. Signac, *De Delacroix au Néo-Impressionnisme* (Paris, 1899).

E. Moreau-Nélaton, *Delacroix* (Paris, 1916).

J. Meier-Graefe, *E. Delacroix. Beiträge zu einer Analyse* (München o.J.).

J. Lassaigne, *Eugène Delacroix* (Amsterdam-Antwerp, 1949).

G.H. Hamilton, 'Delacroix, Byron and the English Illustrators', *Gazette des Beaux Arts* XCI (1949), p.261.

K. Badt, *Eugene Delacroix, drawings* (Oxford, 1946 2).

P. Burty, *Maîtres et Petits-Maîtres* (Paris, 1877).

S.J. Key, *John Constable, His Life and Work* (London, 1948).

Art and art theory in the naturalistic-realistic tradition

J.C. Sloane, *French painting between the past and the present. Artists, critics and traditions from 1848 to 1870* (Princeton, 1951).

C. Mauclair, *Les états de la peinture française 1850-1920* (Paris, 1920).

F.B. Blanshard, *Retreat from likeness in the theory of painting* (New York, 1949 2).

C.E. Gauss, *The aesthetic Theories of French artists 1855 to the present* (Baltimore, 1949).

L. Venturi, 'Prémisses théoriques de l'art moderne', *Preuves* II (1952) p.37.

J. de Gruyter, *Wezen en Ontwikkeling der schilderkunst no 1850* (Den Haag, 1935).

J. Rewald, *The history of impressionism* (New York, 1946).

J.E. Blanche, *Les arts plastiques de 1870 à nos jours* (Paris, 1931).

J. Meier-Graefe, *Der moderne Impressionismus* (Berlin, 1903).

E. Klossowski, *Die Maler von Montmartre* (Berlin, 1903).

Sheldon Cheney, *The story of Modern Art* (New York, 1945).

T. Craven, *Modern Art: The Men, the Movement, the Meaning* (New York 1940).

Th. Duret, *Critique d'avant-garde* (Paris, 1885).

J.K. Huysmans, *L'Art moderne* (Paris, 1883 nouvelle ed. 1902).

E. Zola, 'Les réalistes au salon', *Mes Haines* (Paris, 1866).

W.A. van Konijnenburg, *De waarde der impressionistische schilderkunst, Ethiek en aesthetiek* (Den Haag, 1908).

Duranty, *La nouvelle peinture* (1876). Nouvelle ed. M. Guérin (Paris, 1946).

G. Moore, *Confessions of a Young Man* (Penguin Books, 1939).

M. Zahar, *Gustave Courbet* (Amsterdam-Antwerp, 1950).

M. Shapiro, 'Courbet and Popular Imagery, an Essay on Realism and Naïvete', *Journal of the Warburg and Courtauld Institute* IV (1940) p.164.

Constantin Guys (Cat. exp. Vlissingen, 1954).

F. Blei, *Felicien Rops* (Berlin o.J.).

M. Kunel, *F. Rops* (Bruxelles, 1943).

G.A. Aurier, 'C. Monet', *Mercure de France* IV (1892) p.302.

W. Seitz, 'Monet and Abstract Painting', *College Art Journal* XVI, 1 (1956) p.34.

Art and literature outside the circle of the Synthetists

Kerrison Preston, *Blake and Rossetti* (London, 1944).

J. Bronowski, *William Blake* (Penguin, 1950 6).

R. Schmutzler, 'Blake and Art Nouveau', *Architectural Review* CXVIII 704 (Aug. 1955) p.91.

D. Erdman, *Blake: Prophet against Empire* (Princeton Univ. Press, 1954).

R. Garnett, 'William Blake', *The Portfolio* (London, Oct. 1895).

J.C.E. Bassalik-de Vries, *William Blake in his Relation to Dante Gabriel Rossetti* (Diss. Zürich, 1911, Basle).

A. Blunt, 'Blake's Pictorial Imagination', *Journal of the Warburg and Courtauld Institute* VI (1943) p.190.

J. Ruskin, *Modern Painters I-V* (London, 1909).

J. Ruskin, 'The arts and pleasures of England'. *Lectures 1883/4* (London, 1907).

Holman Hunt, *Pre-Raphaelitism and the Pre-Raphaelite Brotherhood I, II* (London, 1905).

W. Morris, *Hopes and Fears for Art* (London, 1896 4).

W.M. Rossetti, *Pre-Raphaelite Diaries and Letters* (London, 1900).

J.L. Topper, 'The Subject in Art', *The Germ* (1850) p.11.

R. Ironside & J. Gere, *Pre-Rafaelite Painters* (London, 1948).

W. Gaunt, *The Pre-Raphaelite Tragedy* (London, 1943 3).

Jean Proix, *Un mysticisme esthétique* (Paris, 1928).

A. Neumeyer, 'Die präraphaelitische Malerei im Rahmen der Kunstgeschichte des 19.Jahrh.', *Deutsche Vierteljahrschrift für Litt. Wissenschaft und Geistesgeschichte* XI (1933) p.67.

Holbrook Jackson, *Dreamers of Dreams. Rise and Fall of Nineteenth-Century Idealism* (London, 1948).

H.C. Marillier, *Dante Gabriel Rossetti* (London, 1901).

Dante Gabriel Rossetti, 'Hand and Soul', *The Germ* (1850).

Dante Gabriel Rossetti, *Poems* (Leipzig, 1873).

W.M. Rossetti, 'Dante Rossetti and Elisabeth Siddall', *Burlington Magazine* I (1903) p.273.

J. Cartwright & Aymer Vallence, *Burne-Jones* (London, 1900).

H. Pater, *The Renaissance: Studies in Art and Poetry* (London, 1928).

Holbrook Jackson, *The Eighteen Nineties* (Pelican Book, 1950).

Bettina Polak, *Het fin-de-siècle in de Nederlandse schilderkunst: De symbolistische beweging, 1890-1900* (Den Haag, 1955).

A. Alexander, 'Les Arts français à l'âge critique: Les Salons de 1889 à 1890', *Gazette des Beaux Arts* I (1934) p.306.

G. Geffroy, *La vie artistique* I, II, III (Paris, 1892/3/4).

E. Bricon, *Psychologie d'Art. Les Maîtres de la fin du XIX siècle* (Paris, 1900).

T. de Wyzéwa, *Peintres de jadis et d'aujourd'hui* (Paris, 1903).

G. Ramberg, *Die moderne Kunstbewegung. Zweck und Wesen der Sezession* (Wien, 1899).

G-A. Aurier, 'Rationations familières et d'ailleurs vaines à propos des trois Salons de 1891', *Mercure de France* III (1891) p.30.

A. Fontainas, *Mes souvenirs du symbolisme* (Paris, 1928).

T. Natanson, 'L'Art des Salons', *La Revue Blanche* (1 et 15 mai 1895).

C. Chassé, *Le mouvement symboliste dans l'Art du XIXième siècle* (Paris, 1947).

H. Fierens-Gevaert, *Essais sur l'art contemporain* (Paris, 1897).

T. Natanson, 'Expositions (Utamaro, Hiroshige, Tosslouse-Lautrec)', *La Revue Blanche* (Feb. 1893).

T. Natanson, 'Expositions (des Nabis)', *La Revue Blanche* V (25, Nov. 1893) p.236.

'Fragments de Nietsche', *La Revue Blanche* (Nov. 1892).

G. Coquiot, *Les gloires déboulonnées* (Paris, 1924).

0. Uzanne, 'Victor Hugo, par la plume et le crayon', *L'Art et l'Idée* II (1892) p.1.

La Revue Fantaisiste (Paris, 1861).

J. Destrée, *L'Oeuvre lithografique de Odilon Redon* (Brussel, 1891).

J. Veth, 'Odilon Redons lithografische Serien', *Kunst und Künstler* III (1903) p.104.

O. Redon, 'A soi-même', *Journal 1867-1915* (Paris, 1922)

J. Rewald, 'Odilon Redon and Emile Bernard. Quelques notes et documents sur Odilon Redon', *Gazette des Beaux Arts* (Nov. 1956) p.81.

Musée Gustave Moreau (Catalogue sommaire) (Paris, 1926).

Charles R. Sturt (pseud. for C. Ricketts), 'A Note on Gustave Moreau', *The Dial* III (1893) London.

Gleeson White, 'The pictures of Gustave Moreau', *The Pageant* (London, 1897), p.3.

G. leRoy, *James Ensor* (Bruxelles, Paris, 1922).

L. Lebeer, *James Ensor, Etser* (Antwerp, 1952).

M. Vachon, *Puvis de Chavannes* (Paris, s.d.).

C-A. Aurier, 'E. Carrière', *Mercure de France* II (1891) p.332.

D. Sutton, 'Carrière et les Symbolistes at the Orangerie', *Burlington Magazine* XCII (1950), p.81.

O. Uzanne, 'A. Robida', *L'Art et l'Idée* II (1892) p.128.

A. Germain, 'Un peintre idéaliste-idéiste, Alexandre Séon', *L'Art et l'Idée* I (1892) p.107.

A. Rannit & K.M. Ciurlionis, 'Der erste abstrakte Maler der modernen Welt', *Das goldene Tor* (Zweimonatschrift für Litteratur und Kunst, Baden Baden, 1951).

S.M. Péladan, *Comment on devient fée* (Paris, 1893).

S.M. Péladan, *Amphithéatre des sciences mortes: Traité des antinomies, métaphysique* (Paris, 1901).

Salon de la Rose†Croix , Règle et Monitoire (Paris, 1891).

T. Natanson, 'Exposition: Le 4ième salon de la Rose†Croix ', *La Revue Blanche* (April, 1895).

A. Germain, 'L'idéal et l'idéalisme, Salon de la Rose†Croix ', *L'Art et l'Idée* I (1892) p.176.

E. Michalski, 'Die Entwicklungsgeschichtliche Bedeutung des Jugendstils', *Re pertorium für Kunstwissenschaft* 46 (1926) p.148.

E. Bayard, *Le style moderne* (Paris, a.d.).

S.T. Madsen, *Sources of Art Nouveau* (Oslo, 1956).

J.E. Blanche, 'Les objets d'art', *La Revue Blanche* (15 Mar 1895) p.163.

S. Bing, *Le Japon Artistique* I, II, III (Paris, 1888).

C. Lancaster, 'Oriental Contribution to Art Nouveau', *Art Bulletin* XXXIV (1952) p.297.

'Um 1900 – Art Nouveau und Jugendstil.' Cat. Exp. (Zürich, 1952 2).

O. Uzanne, 'Eugène Grasset', *L'Art et l'Idée* II (1892) p.193.

R. Wagner, *Quatre poèmes d'Opéra précédé d'une lettre sur la musique* (Paris, 1861).

P. Valin, 'Ceux de demain. Les jeunes et leurs revues', *L'Art et l'Idée* I (1892) p.62.

P. Valin, 'La jeune littérature', *L'Art et l'Idée* I (1892) p.136.

M.v. Wedderkop, 'Paul Verlaine und die Lyrik der Décadence in Frankreich', *Pan* (1896) p.69.

Rémy de Gourmont, 'Le symbolisme. Définition de ce nouveau mouvement littéraire', *L'Art et l'Idée* II (1892) p.47.

P. Valin, 'Les lettres prochaines: Essai sur les tendences des écrivains de demain', *L'Art et l'Idée* II (1892) p.81.

T. de Wyzéwa, *Nos Maitres* (Paris, 1895).

J. Huret, *Enquête sur l'évolution littéraire* (Paris, 1891).

A. Kuyper, *The Antithesis between Symbolism and Revelation* (Amsterdam-Pretoria, Edinburgh, 1899).

C. Moore, *Confessions of a Young Man* (Penguin Books, 1939).

J.K. Huysmans, *A Rebours* (Paris, 1903).

C. Récolin, *L'anarchie littéraire* (Paris, 1898).

P. Radiot, 'Notre Byzantinisme', *La Revue Blanche* (Feb. 1894) p.110.

M. Raymond, *From Baudelaire to Surrealism* (New York, 1950) Transl.

A. Micha, *Verlaine et les poètes symbolistes* (Paris, 1957 17).

A.G. Lehmann, *The Symbolist Aesthetics in France 1885–1895* (Oxford, 1950).

A. Barre, 'Le symbolisme', *Essai historique sur le mouvement symboliste en France de 1885 à 1900* (Paris, 1911).

P. Valéry, *Existence du symbolisme* (Paris, 1939).

C. Mauclair, *Servitudes et grandeurs littéraires* (Paris, 1922).

A. Fontainas, *Mes souvenirs du symbolisme* (Paris, 1928).

A. Poizat, *Le symbolisme de Baudelaire a Claudel* (Paris, 1919).

E. Raynaud, *Le mêlée symboliste* I, II, III (1918–1922).

G. Michaud, *Message poétique du symbolisme* I, II, III (Paris, 1947).

A.J. Mathews, *La Wallonie 1886–1892. The Symbolist Movement in Belgium* (New York, 1947).

Kindred spirits of the Synthetists, writers and painters

G.-A. Aurier, *Oeuvres posthumes. Notice de Rémy de Gourmont* (Paris, 1893).

J. Huret, *Enquête sur l'évolution littéraire* (Paris, 1891).

G. Dumur, 'Aurier et l'évolution idéaliste', *Mercure de France* VIII (1893).

T. de Wyzéwa, *Nos maîtres* (Paris, 1895).

A. Fontainas, *Mes souvenirs du symbolisme* (Paris, 1928).

A. Poizat, *Le symbolisme de Baudelaire à Claudel* (Paris, 1919).

G. Michaud, *Message poétique du symbolisme I, II, III* (Paris, 1947).

M. Raymond, *From Baudelaire to Surrealism* (New York, 1950), Transl.

A.G. Lehmann, *The symbolist aesthetics in France 1885–1895* (Oxford, 1950).

S. Mallarmé, *Oeuvres complètes*, notes par H. Mondor & G. Jean-Aubry (Paris, 1951).

S. Mallarmé, *Poésies complètes*, texte et notes établies par Y. G. le Dantec (Paris, 1948).

S. Mallarmé, *Divagations* (Paris, 1897).

G. Delfel, *L'Esthétique de S. Mallarmé* (Paris, 1951).

R. Michaud, *Mallarmé* (Paris, 1953).

A. Mellério, *Le mouvement idéaliste en peinture* (Paris, 1896).

Lettres à Emile Bernard de Van Gogh, Gauguin, Redon, Cézanne, Bloy, Bourget etc. (Paris, 1927).

C. Mauclair, *Les états de la peinture française de 1850 à 1920* (Paris, 1921).

R. Rey, *La renaissance du sentiment classique dans la peinture à la fin du XIXième siècle* (Paris, 1930).

J. Rewald, *Post-Impressionism: from Van Gogh to Gauguin* (New York, 1956).

F.B. Blanshard, *Retreat from Likeness in the Theory of Painting* (New York, 1949).

C.E. Gauss, *The Aesthetic Theories of French Artists 1855 to the Present* (Baltimore, 1949).

D. Sutton, 'Exhibition at Wildenstein's', *Burlington Mag.* XCV (1954), p.193.

H. Read, *Philosophy of Modern Art* (London, 1952).

W. Hess, *Problem der Farbe in den Selbstzeugnisse moderner Maler* (München, 1953).

J. Rewald, *P. Cézanne, Correspondances* (Paris, 1937).

A. Vollard, *En écoutant Cézanne, Degas, Renoir* (Paris, 1938).

Rainer Maria Rilke, *Brieven over Cézanne.* Transl. (Den Haag, 1945).

F. Burger, *Cézanne und Hodler* (Berlin, 1919 3).

E. Bernard, 'Cézanne', *Kunst und Künstler* VI (1908) p. 426.

E. Bernard, 'Souvenirs sur Paul Cézanne et lettres inédits', *Mercure de France* (1–15 Oct., 1907).

E. Bernard, *Erinnerungen an Paul Cézanne.* Transl. H. Graber, (Basle, 1917).

R. Fry, *Cézanne: a Study of his Development* (London, 1952 5).

K. v. Tolnay, 'Zur Cézanne's geschichtlicher Stellung', *Deutsche Vierteljahrschrift für Litteraturwissenschaft und Geistesgeschichte* XI (1933) p.78.

J. Rewald, *Cézanne et Zola* (Paris, 1936).

L. Venturi, *Cézanne–son art–son oeuvre* (Paris, 1936).

E. Loran, *Cézanne's Composition* (Berkeley-Los Angelos, 1950 5).

L .Guerry, *Cézanne et l'expression de l'espace* (Paris, 1950).

J.M. Carpenter, 'Cézanne and tradition', *Art Bulletin* XXXIII (1951) p.174.

G.H. Hamilton, 'Cézanne, Bergson and the image of time', *College Art Journal* XVI (1956) p. 2.

C-A Aurier, 'Les Isolés: Vincent van Gogh', *Mercure de France* I (1890) p.24.

Verzamelde Brieven van Van Gogh. Uitg. J. v. Gogh-Bonger (1953).

F. Bonger-v. d. Borch v.Verwolde, 'Vincent van Gogh als lezer', *Maandblad voor Beeldende Kunsten* (March 1950).

W. Fowlie, 'The religious experience of Van Gogh', *College Art Journal* IX, 3 (1950) p.317.

K. Jaspers, Strindberg und van Gogh. *Versuch einer pathologischen Analyse unter Vergleichender Heranziehung von Swedenborg und Hölderlin* (Berlin, 1926).

M.E. Tralbaut, *Vincent van Gogh in zijn Antwerpse periode* (Amsterdam, 1948).

W. Jos de Gruyter, 'Vincent van Gogh' (Introd. cat. v. Gogh Exposition, The Hague, 1953).

G. Laprade, *Seurat* (Paris, 1945).

J. Rewald, *Seurat* (Paris, 1948).

R.J. Goldwater, 'Some aspects of the development of Seurat's style', *Art Bulletin* XXIII, 2 (1941) p.117.

R.L. Herbert, 'Seurat in Chicago and New York', *Burlington Mag.* C (1958) p.146.

J. Rewald, 'Extraits du journal inédit de Paul Signac', *Gazette des Beaux Arts* (1949, p.97), (1952, p.265), (1953, p.27).

P. Signac, *D'Eugène Delacroix au Néo-Impressionnisme.* Ed. La Revue Blanche (1899).

J. Rewald, 'F. Fénéon, critique d'art', *Tijdschrift voor Beeldende Kunsten* (1950) p.67.

J. Rewald, 'F. Fénéon', *Gazette des Beaux Arts* (1947) p.45.

C. Henry, 'L'Esthétique des formes', *La Revue Blanche* (Aug. 1894, Oct. 1894, Feb. 1895).

Writings by or about the Synthetists (1885–1900)

Ch. Morice, *La Littérature de tout à l'heure* (Paris, 1889).

P. Gauguin et C. Morice, *Noa Noa* (Paris, 1924).

G.-A. Aurier, *Oeuvres posthumes (note de Rémy de Gourmont)* (Paris, 1893).

G.-A. Aurier, 'Le symbolisme dans la peinture: Paul Gauguin', *Mercure de France* II (1891) p.155.

G.-A. Aurier, 'Les peintres symbolistes', *Oeuvres posthumes*, p.293.

Maurice Denis, *Théories 1890-1910* (Paris, 1912 2)

P. Sérusier, *A.B.C. de la peinture, suivies d'une correspondance inédite* (Paris, 1950).

Sérusier reproductions, *Dekorative Kunst* IV (1899) p.129 ff.

Lettres à Emile Bernard (Paris, 1927).

E. Bernard, 'Les ateliers. Notes Diverses', *Mercure de France* XIII (1895) p.194.

E. Bernard, 'Ce que c'est que l'Art mystique', *Mercure de France* XIII (1895) p.28.

E. Bernard, 'Les musées', *Mercure de France* (XIII 1895) p.296.

P. Gauguin, 'Armand Séguin, Préface inédite au catalogue de l'exposition des oeuvres de Armand Séguin', *Mercure de France* XIII (1895) p.222.

A. Mellerio, *Le mouvement idéaliste en peinture* (Paris, 1896).

0. Uzanne, 'La renaissance de la gravure sur bois. Un néoxylographe: Félix Vallotton', *L'Art et l'Idée* I (1892) p.113.

La Revue Blanche (Paris, 1891 ff.).

Mercure de France (Paris, 1890, ff.).

L'Art et l'Idée Revue contemporaine illustrée, publ. p. 0. Uzanne, I, II (Paris, 1892).

Writings by Gauguin

M. Malingue, *Lettres de Gauguin à sa femme et à ses amis* (Paris, 1946).

Lettres de Gauguin à Daniel de Monfreid, ed. Mme Joly-Ségalen (Paris, 1950).

P. Gauguin, *Avant et Après* (Paris, 1923).

P. Gauguin, 'Armand Séguin: Préface inédite au catalogue de l'exposition des oeuvres de Armand Séguin', *Mercure de France* XIII (1895) p.222.

Notes synthétiques de Paul Gauguin, ed. H. Mahaut, *Vers et Prose* VI 22, (Juillet - Sept. 1910) p.51.

P. Gauguin, *Ancien Culte Mahorie. Présentation p. R. Huyghe, Le clef de Noa Noa*. Facs (Paris, 1951).

P. Gauguin et C. Morrice, *Noa Noa* (Paris, 1924).

P. Gauguin, *Racontars de Rapin* (Paris ,1951).

P. Gauguin, *Esprit Moderne et le Catholicisme* (ms. à St. Louis, Miss., 1897-98).

B. Dorival, *Carnet de Tahiti*. Facs. (Paris, 1954).

R. Huyghe, *Le carnet de Paul Gauguin*. Facs. (Paris, 1952).

Writings concerning Gauguin

G.-A. Aurier, 'Le symbolisme dans la peinture: Paul Gauguin', *Mercure de France* II (1891) p.155.

T. Natanson, 'Oeuvres *récentes* de Gauguin (Galerie Durand-Ruel)', *La Revue Blanche* V 26 (Dec. 1893) p.418.

J. de Rotonchamp, *Paul Gauguin* (Paris, 1906).

C. Morice, *Paul Gauguin* (Paris, 1919).

Gh. Chassé, *Gauguin et le groupe de Pont Aven* (Paris, 1921).

R. Rey, *Gauguin* (Paris, 1924).

J. Dorsenne, *La vie sentimentale de Paul Gauguin* (Paris, 1927).

M. Guérin, *L'oeuvre gravé de Gauguin*, I, II (Paris, 1927).

A. Alexander, *Paul Gauguin, sa vie et le sens de son oeuvre* (Paris, 1930).

C. Kunstler, *Gauguin, peintre maudit* (Paris, 1934).

J. Rewald, *Gauguin* (London, 1938).

M. Malingue, *Gauguin* (London-Paris, 1948).

R. Cogniat, *La vie ardente de Paul Gauguin* (exp. Galerie Wildenstein, 1936–37).

C. Estienne, *Gauguin, étude biographique et critique* (Genève, 1953).

Hans Graber, *Paul Gauguin nach eigenem und fremden Zeugnissen* (Basle, 1946 2).

R. Cogniat, *Gauguin* (Paris, n.d.).

R. Goldwater, *Gauguin* (New York, 1957).

D. Sutton, 'La perte du pucelage by Paul Gauguin', *Burlington Magazine* XCI (1949) p.103.

D. Sutton, 'The Gauguin Exhibition', *Burlington Magazine* XCI (1949) p.283.

D. Sutton, 'Notes on Paul Gauguin', *Burlington Magazine* XCVIII (1956), p.84.

H. Dorra, 'The first Eves in Gauguin's Eden', *Gazette des Beaux Arts* (March 1953) p.189, 225.

H. Dorra, Emile Bernard et Paul Gauguin, *Gazette des Beaux Arts* XLV (1955), p.227.

R. Huyghe, *Gauguin, Createur de la peinture moderne* (Gauguin, Exposition Centenaire, Paris, 1949).

D. Cooper, 'Gauguin the innovator' (Gauguin cat. exhibit., 1955) p.5.

Pola Gauguin, 'Paul Gauguin: Avant et Après', *Kunsten Idag* XXVII, I (Oslo, 1954) p.21

B. Dorival, 'Sources of the art of Gauguin from Java, Egypt and Ancient Greece', *Burlington Magazine* XCII (1951), p.118.

'D'où venons-nous, que sommes-nous, où allons-nous' (M. Harriman Gallery, New York, 1936).

Lee van Dowski, 'Gauguin als Glasmaler', *Neue Zürcher Zeitung* (4/1 1/'50).

R. Puig, Paul Gauguin, *G. D. de Monfreid et leurs amis* (Perpignan, 1958).

U. F. Marks-Vandenbroucke, 'Gauguin, ses origines et sa formation artistique', *Gazette des Beaux Arts* (98ième année, 1956) p.9.

H. Rostrup, 'Gauguin et le Danemark', Ibid., p.63.

J. Thirion, 'L'influence de l'estampe japonaise dans l'oeuvre de Gauguin', Ibid., p.95.

Jénot, 'Le premier séjour de Gauguin à Tahiti, 1891-1893', Ibid., p.115.

L.J. Bouge, 'Traduction et interpretation des titres en langue tahitienne inscrit sur les oeuvres océaniennes de Paul Gauguin', Ibid., p.161.

J. Loize, 'Gauguin sauvé du feu', Ibid., p.165.

G. Le Bronnec, 'Les dernières années', Ibid., p.189.

G. Wildenstein, 'L'Idéologie et l'esthétique dans deux tableaux clés de Gauguin', Ibid., p.127.

— 'Documents', Ibid., p.201.

J. Lindberg-Hansen, 'Discovering Paul Gauguin, the Wood-carver', *College Art Journal* XII, 2 (1953) p.117.

H. Read, 'Gauguin, return to symbolism', *Art News* 25: 122-58 (1956).

J. Rewald, *Gauguin Drawings* (New York, 1957).

L. Gowing, 'Letter on Paul Gauguin', *Burlington Magazine* XCI (1949) p.354.

C. Gorham, *Gouden Gestalten, een roman over Gauguin* (Amsterdam, 1956).

C. Chassé, 'Le sort de Gauguin est lié au Krach de 1882', *Connaissance des Arts* (Paris, Feb. 1959) p.40.

F. Daulte, 'L'art de 'transposer' chez Gauguin', *Connaissance des Arts* (Paris, Feb. 1959) p.44.

Memoirs and writings after 1900 of eye-witnesses

M. Denis, *Théories 1890-1910* (Paris, 1912 2).

M. Denis, 'Catalogue de l'Exposition Cross' (Paris, 1910).

M. Denis, *Nouvelles théories* (Paris, 1922).

M. Denis, 'Introduction' (cat. Französische Kunst des XIX und XX Jahrh., Zürcher Kunsthaus, Oct-Nov. 1917).

M. Denis, 'L'époque du symbolisme', *Gazette des Beaux Arts* I (1934) p.165.

M. Denis, *Sérusier* (Paris, 1942).

P. Sérusier, *A.B.C. de la peinture, suivi d'une correspondance inédite* (Paris, 1950).

W. Verkade, *Le tourment de Dieu* (Paris, 1926), Préface de M. Denis.

E. Bernard, 'Louis Anquetin', *Gazette des Beaux Arts* I (1934) p.108.

C. Morice, *Gauguin* (Paris, 1919).

T. Natanson, *Peint à leur tour* (Paris, 1948).

T. Natanson, *Le Bonnard que je propose* (Geneva, 1951).

A. Barre Le symbolisme. *Essai historique sur le mouvement symboliste en France de 1885 à 1900* (Paris, 1911).

C. Mauclair, *Les états de la peinture française de 1850 à 1920* (Paris, 1921).

C. Mauclair, *Servitude et grandeur littéraires* (Paris, 1922).

A. Fontainas, *Mes souvenirs du symbolisme* (Paris, 1928)

J.E. Blanche, *Les arts plastiques de 1870 à nos jours.* Introduction par M. Denis (Paris, 1931).

Later literature on Synthetism and the Synthetists

H.F., 'Studio-Talk–on Maurice Denis', *Studio* III (1910) p.235.

G. Coquiot, *Cubistes, Futuristes, Passéistes* (Paris, 1914).

A. Ségard, *Peintres d'aujourd'hui. Les décorateurs. H. Martin, Aman-Jean, Maurice Denis, Vuillard* (Paris, 1914).

Ch. Chassé, 'Gauguin et le groupe de Pont Aven' (Paris, 1921).

A. Vaudoyer & Maurice Denis, *Dedalo* II (1921/2) p.772.

J.E. Blanche, *De Gauguin à la Revue Nègre* (Paris, 1928).

T. Craven, *Modern Art* (New York, 1940).

S. Cheney, *The Story of Modern Art* (New York, 1945).

S. Bavazetti-Desmoulin, *Maurice Denis* (Paris, 1945).

C. Chassé, *Le mouvement symboliste dens l'art du XIXième siècle* (Paris, 1947).

C. E. Gauss, *Aesthetic Theories of French Artists 1855 to the present* (Baltimore, 1949).

H. Redeker, *De dagen der artistieke vertwijfeling* (Amsterdam, 1950).

L. Venturi, 'Prémisses théoriques de l'art moderne', *Preuves* II (1952) p.37.

F. Dauchot, 'Meyer de Haan en Bretagne', *Gazette des Beaux Arts* (1952) p.355.

D. Sutton, 'Paris in the 90th at Wildenstein', *Burlington Mag.* XCVI (1954) p.193.

H.H. Hofstätter, *Die Entstehung des neuen Stils in der französischen Malerei um 1900* (Freiburg i. B., 1945, Diss.).

Agnes Humbert, *Les Nabis et leur époque, 1888–1900* (Geneva, 1954).

J. Rewald, *Post-Impressionism* (New York, 1956).

J. Rewald, 'Odilon Redon and Emile Bernard', *Gazette des Beaux Arts* (1956) p.81.

0. Hølaas, 'J. F. Willumsen', *Kunsten Idag* XLIV, 2 (Oslo, 1958) p.5.

R. Puig, Paul Gauguin, *C. D. de Monfreid et leurs amis* (Perpignan, 1958).

Writings concerning Gauguin after 1959

G. Wildenstein, 'Gauguin I', *Les Beaux Arts* (Catalogue, Paris, 1964).

M. Bodelsen, 'Gauguin and the marquesan God', *Gaz. Des Beaux Arts* (1961) p167.

—'Dating of Gauguin's early paintings', *Burl.Mag.* (June 1965) p.306.

—'Gauguin the collector', Burl. Mag. LXII (1970) p.590.

—'The Missing Link in Gauguin's Cloisonism', *Gaz. Des Beaux Arts* (May/June 1959) p.329.

W. Anderson, 'Gauguin's Motifs from Le Pouldu', *Burl.Mag.* LXII (1970) p.615.

W. Jaworska, 'Gauguin et les peintres de l'école de Pont-Aveu' (1970).

T. Buser, 'Gauguin's Religion', *Art Journal 68* (XXVII) p.375.

R.S. Field, 'Gauguin's Noa Noa Suite', *Burl.Mag.* CX (Sept.1968) p.500.

S. Lövgren, 'The Genesis of Modernism: Seurat, Gauguin, v. Gogh and French Symbolism in the 1880th', *Figura 11* (Stockholm, 1959).

M. Roskill, *Van Gogh, Gauguin and the Impressionist Circle* (London, 1970).

R.T. Goldwater, 'The Genesis of a Picture: Theme and Form in Modern Painting', *Critique* (New York, October 1946).

W. Andersen and Barbara Klein, *Gauguin's Paradise Lost* (New York, 1971).

Theses Accompanying the Dissertation

I

Iconography and iconology should be sharply distinguished.

II

An iconological approach to a work of art, whereby one attempts to interpret the picture, has the advantage over a stylistic analysis in that it puts more emphasis on the general human aspect. Other branches of historical-cultural research may also benefit from this.

III

The making of an iconographical collection is of great importance for the development of the historical sciences.

IV

When studying the works of art that are united under the name of the Master of the Virgo inter Virgines, one has to take account of possible German contacts and/or influences. *Catalogus Exp. Middeleeuwse Kunst der Noordelijke Nederlanden* (Amsterdam: Rijksmuseum, 1958) pp.65-71 and the literature cited there.

V

When A. Kuyper, in his treatise 'Calvinism and Art' (*Stone Lectures*, 1899), attempted to make clear the foundations of seventeenth-century Dutch art, he refuted by this his own thesis that Calvinism has not produced a style of its own. Cf. A. Kuyper, 'Het Calvinisme en de kunst.' Lecture (Amsterdam, 1888).

VI

The evaluation of works of art in our time is characterized by a historical attitude that works in two directions: on the one hand, in the capacity for positive appreciation of all artistic expressions, without distinction; on the other hand, in a dogmatism that is convinced that only one contemporary style is possible.

VII

For art criticism to be meaningful, it has to take a subjective stand in the cultural struggle of today.

VIII

The teaching of art history at secondary schools and at tertiary institutions should not in the first place aim at aesthetic formation but be a practical education that teaches students to 'see'. Cf. A. v.d. Boom, *Kunstgeschiedenis op het Gymnasium* (Amsterdam, 1943).

IX

The Second Commandment in the Decalogue does not forbid the making of works of visual art, but prohibits their use for cultic purposes, i.e. to worship or adore them.

X

Jaffé's thesis that the non-figurative art of Mondrian can be explained by his Calvinist past – in connection with the Second Commandment – is a misapprehension. Rather, Mondrian contravened this Commandment. H.L.C. Jaffé, *De Stijl, 1917–1931*, (Amsterdam, 1956) p.85 passim.

XI

The influence of Froebel on non-figurative art should not be underestimated. C.F.M Logan, 'Kindergarten and Bauhaus', *College Art Journal* X, 1(1950) p.36ff.

XII

Any lack of appreciation for Rembrandt and van Gogh during their lifetimes should not be used to defend modern art.

XIII

Baudelaire's saying 'Le sujet fait pour artiste une partie du genie'('For the artist, the subject is part of his genius') is correct. C. Baudelaire, *Curiosités Esthétiques: Salon* de 1859, VIII (Paris, 1921) p.337.

XIV

The influence of the Japanese Zen-Buddhism on non-figurative modern American art is indicative of a common spiritual background. Cf. G.M. Cohen, 'The Bird Paintings of Morris Graves', *College Art Journal* XVIII, I (1958) p.3, and M. Tobey, 'Japanese Traditions and American Art', ibid., p.20.

XV

Gershwin's opera *Porgy and Bess* is representative neither of the culture nor of the music of the African-Americans.

XVI

The Puritan way of singing the Psalms in the seventeenth and eighteenth centuries has exercised a great influence on the formation and development of African-American music.

XVII

The rate of historical development is not uniform.

XVIII

The rate of cultural development in our time is not necessarily greater than in earlier times, although here also accelerations and decelerations can be noticed, as mentioned in the previous thesis.

XIX

A wrong choice of illustrations in popular histories can influence people to have an unfavourable picture of the fifteenth century. On the one hand, the significant innovations will be sought almost exclusively in Italy. On the other hand, the culture on the northern side of the Alps will be seen too exclusively as a 'waning' one.

XX

G.K. Chesterton in his *The Napoleon of Notting Hill* gives an excellent caricature of the aesthetic ideals of the Morris movement.

XXI

Epistemology cannot be placed ahead of ontology as a starting point for philosophy.

XXII

Descartes' thesis, that the biotic aspect is a special mechanism only, contains a tautology. R. Descartes, *Discours sur la méthode* V (Paris, 1948) p.109.

Part II

ROOKMAAKER AS ART CRITIC (1949–1956)

Note: There are further exhibition reviews by H.R.R. appearing in Volume 4 (miscellaneous reviews) and Volume 5 (on twentieth-century sculpture), of which some were written during the years 1949–1956 for *Trouw* but were felt to fit better with the topics in those volumes.

Middle Ages and Renaissance

- **Art treasures of the Lower Rhineland: grand culture from around AD 1000**[1115]

No one would have guessed that the bricklayer, sitting on the box of his cart loaded with building materials, was carrying in his arms, hidden under the gunny-sack, one of the most rare art objects in Western Europe. That object, created in the tenth century, was a gold-overlaid statue of Mary, the oldest free-standing statue still in existence as well as one of the first ever made in its genre. In 1945 the custodian of the treasures of the Minster of Essen tried to rescue it from the violence of the War and the destructive vandalism of Russian soldiers who showed little appreciation or respect for such cultural treasures. In this ingenious way the statue as well as the crosses commissioned by Mathilde, sister of King Otto II, were saved. At present they are still being held for safekeeping (rather unimaginatively) in a bank in Essen until, in the not-too-distant future, they can be publicly displayed again. The crosses, approximately 45 cm high, and representing some of the most splendid goldsmith work ever done, are in themselves the best refutation of the suggestion that the times around AD 1000 were barbaric and dark.

On the contrary, the surviving remnants of the culture of that period in the lower Rhineland attest to a purity of taste and a grandeur of vision that is anything but primitive. Look, for instance, at the Minster of Essen with its amazingly beautiful group of towers on the west side, bright and clear in their construction, tasteful and modest in their sober playfulness. This church was built during the 'reign' of Mathilde, who was not only the head of a Damenstift (a cloister-like boarding school for girls from the highest social classes) established in Essen but also administered justice there. The grandeur of this period and an excellent sense of proportions is evident in the huge seven-branched candelabra (a Menorah) which Mathilde commissioned for the church, and which is still there today. The decorations on this gilded bronze candelabra, more than two metres high, were modelled on the reliefs of the Titus Arch in Rome (which depicted the treasures stolen by Titus from the Temple in Jerusalem), but the artist incorporated the adornments with such amazing skill that they serve the work as a whole, animating it and avoiding inflexibility and rigidity. As a result there is nothing showy about this splendid and important work; although very tight in its form, it manages to convey a sense of inner peace. It is sober and simple without becoming shabby or bare.

Goldsmith work and the making of enamel were nothing new for this region. Already during the periods of migration monarchs had commissioned the making of jewelry, works which continue to be of interest today because of their artistic as well as technical merits. The various studios made great strides ahead during the flourishing cultural activity in the tenth century. If one studies the crosses mentioned above, taking note of the controlled, perfect forming of the body of Christ, and if one then compares them with the justifiably famous bronze crucifix from the nearby Werden, it becomes clear that 'primitive' is an entirely inappropriate description of this culture. On the contrary, it was a culture in which the arts flourished as richly as they did during the Renaissance.

Christianity, however, was relatively new to these parts. It was not until the arrival of Charlemagne that the region became christianized – and that, not always in the most gentle way. It is clear, however, that there had been some attempts at proselytizing prior to Charlemagne – for example, graves recently discovered in Xanten dating from around AD 750 appear to be the graves of Christians who may have been sacrificed to heathen gods (the location of an altar has also been established). The graves are located under the chancel of the church and can be reached via the crypt. The church itself dates from a much later time and, apart from the Romanesque tower, is a late-Gothic structure, just recently repaired after sustaining heavy damage during the War. Still, it is worth a visit, even if only for the sake of the wonderful statues to be seen there, works from the early sixteenth century, of which the most notable one was created by Arnt van Tricht.

But if you want to admire late Gothic artistry at its best you are advised to travel to Kalkar, which is closer to the Dutch border. In a beautifully spacious church hall, supported by a couple of rows of pillars, there are six carved wooden altars such as you will seldom find in one single location. The main altar is the most famous, especially because of the painted panels by Jan Joest of Kalkar, but in our opinion the side altar by Douwerman is even more stunning. This woodcarver was so gripped by reality and so absorbed in depicting people from his own time (whom he portrays as quarreling scribes or as Joseph, with his knapsack on his back, leading Mary and Jesus on the donkey to Egypt) that the actual biblical stories are literally relegated to the background. This altar gives us a fascinating glimpse into the world of that time, a time in which piety may have been a matter of tradition more than of reality but in which people had an eye for the many-faceted richness of human life.

Douwerman also created monumental statues. This is evident from the somewhat later altar with the large figures of a trio of saints; of these we are especially struck by the figure of Mary Magdalene who, in all her majestic holiness, still possesses something very human, appealing and lovely. The costumes are remarkable. Was there ever a time in history when people had such wonderfully discriminating taste and avoided every form of gaudiness, ostentation or kitsch as in the sixteenth century?

Truly, you do not need to travel far to see beautiful and impressive objects. For if it is your desire to look for such things outside our own country [the Netherlands], there is much to be found just across the border if you take the time to look carefully. You may be surprised that these villages or towns, which today are considered inconsequential, in the middle of a shabby industrial region, were at one time the centre of Western European culture.

• From the treasuries of the Middle Ages

The Netherlands, and Amsterdam in particular, has seen an exceptional wealth of big and important art exhibitions over the past few years. Having hosted the treasures of Vienna and Munich, the Rijksmuseum is now turning its attention to the area of West Germany. Although we do not wish to detract from the value of previous exhibitions and are indeed grateful to have accommodated them, we must refer to this exhibition as being more important and more splendid. The former collections were, after all, the property of a few museums. As such they belong together and they may be brought together again in future, but this present exhibition boasts works from many different places. Here we can see works of art regarded as the most important and most beautiful of the Middle Ages which we would otherwise have had to travel long distances to admire. (Anyway, few of us are in a position to do this, and even if we could, we would still not be able to compare the works directly.)

This exhibition is of great importance in acquainting the public with a beautiful, though in general unfortunately little known, body of art. It is equally important in encouraging scholars and art historians in particular to focus attention on the place as well as the influence of this art on the general development of art during the Middle Ages, an area of study so far largely neglected.

It is indeed astonishing that while German medieval art is generally 'advanced' it has made so little direct impact. Perhaps we must attribute this to the insignificant political position held by Germany. While the German emperors sometimes had a significant role to play, Germany itself was less affected. The struggles almost always took place in Italy. Where the outside world did affect the art of Germany, though we must not exaggerate this, outside influences were absorbed and incorporated in an entirely unique way.

Let's turn now to the works of art themselves. There is a great deal of silver/gold metal work on most of the (religious) objects. While the embellishments may be referred to as decorative, they still possess a very typical life and character. A distinction between free and decorative art had not yet emerged. All art was after all subordinate to a greater composite, be it an architectural composite like a church or a smaller-scale reliquary.

One of the most beautiful examples of this is the famous *Heribert's Shrine*. See how gracefully the two apostolic figures, embossed in gold, reach out to each other and note the fine, expressive enamel prophets between them. In the same tradition is the bronze lid of the baptismal font from Hildesheim which was made almost a century later. It beautifully portrays Mary anointing Jesus' feet, while the whole representation fits splendidly into its allotted frame.

The font itself was too heavy to transport for this exhibition, but two of the four supporting figures, portraying the four paradisical characters, have been included. It is important to realize that the placement of figures and subjects is not random, but that each one is designated a place on the basis of a well-considered 'symbolic-theological' plan. The eleventh-century depictions on the wooden door of a Cologne church, otherwise completely destroyed, superbly serve such an overall plan without losing their own significance as representations of the life of Christ.

Romanesque art has sometimes been compared with modern Expressionism. Expression is indeed a common feature of both art forms, but with one important difference: early art never sought expressiveness as an end in itself but always emphasized the subject, the image itself. This is clearly seen in the truly magnificent bronze crucifix from Werden – possibly one of the most beautiful pieces ever sculpted.

Then there is the strange and very beautiful crucifix from Brunswijk, carved a century or so later during the mid-twelfth century by Master Imerwald. Indeed, one aspect of the appeal of these sculptures is that they are amongst the earliest examples (still) in circulation. One of the oldest figures of the Madonna we know originates from a church in Essen. It is a wooden sculpture covered in gold leaf and dates back to the tenth century. It is important and interesting both for art historians and church historians, even though most of us will not find it particularly attractive.

We see a similar trend towards expressiveness – albeit much less restrained and possibly even extravagant – in the fourteenth-century figures that remind us of the flourishing mysticism of that era. Note the almost sinister reality and powerful expression of the Cologne crucifix.

We hope to return to the paintings at another time. A relatively large number of paintings from the fourteenth century has been preserved from this particular region, whereas little has survived from elsewhere in Western Europe. In the paintings too we must commend the power and realism of the works, often supported by strong lines and bright – but not too bright – colours. The reproduction of the drapings alone is a pleasure to behold.

• Painting in the late Middle Ages

The exhibition 'From the Treasure Chambers of the Middle Ages' will be on display in Amsterdam for a short period of time. It is a great privilege to be able to see these works of art assembled in one place, a unique opportunity that we may not get again. However, it is not a great spectacle that is being offered here; rather, one needs to view these pieces thoughtfully, directing one's attention to the finer points. Whoever takes time to do this well will be richly rewarded, with always another interesting detail to be discovered.

The works that we see here have withstood the test of time – a time during which peoples' tastes changed, as well as a time in which the materials used (gold, precious stone, bronze, and so forth) became attractive for other reasons than artistic ones. Works like these were often melted down or lost, but somehow these pieces were spared and kept safe from the hands of those who desired 'renewal'.

Although much German art was lost, it is fortunate that a good number of paintings from the later Middle Ages were saved, enough to give us a good impression of that period. From the first half of the fourteenth century there are two small panels here, completely in late-Gothic style, beautifully expressive in line and composition – one is tempted to call them charming!

Enormous changes took place in art during the following period, undoubtedly in response to the profound changes affecting the religious, scientific and social structures of the time. This new direction led artists to become more and more interested in the exact depiction of the outward appearance of a specific individual; and they wanted to depict common, everyday objects and scenes, treating all the various details with great care.

In Germany this new trend expressed itself in the depiction of various biblical scenes, set as ordinary, everyday events. Especially striking are the detailed, almost caricatured faces of the subjects. See, for instance, the panels from the magnificent passion-altar by Bertram of Minden from the end of the fourteenth century. How superb, for example, is the donkey on which Christ enters Jerusalem – five centuries earlier than Walt Disney's cartoons but as effective and more beautiful. And what a pleasure it is to discover in this same work the face of Peter, with his grey whiskers, bald head and incredibly engaging face. A friendly old fellow must have served as model for this one.

Master Francke, a great artist who may have come from Gelderland (part of the Netherlands), demonstrates more of a French influence – courtly, more geared to decorative and beautiful forms and richness in colour and detail. The two panels from his *St Barbara Altarpiece*, especially borrowed from Helsinki, are themselves worth the trip to the Rijksmuseum. Again we see the characteristic heads and faces, for example the executioner on the right panel who, with obvious sadistic pleasure, holds the torch to Barbara's body. Barbara and her father are of royal descent and differ significantly from the common people depicted by Master Bertram. This is a work of art that can stand up to the most rigorous critique!

In another painting, by Conrad van Soest, we see the friendly, though anxious Joseph, sitting so watchfully by Mary's bed, clothed in a beautiful blue cloak. That particular shade of blue is hardly found in any later periods, not even in our own time. The same colour is used in an even deeper and more intense hue by Stephan Lochner, the great Cologne contemporary of Jan van Eyck. Lochner's art expresses a more mystical disposition, especially seen in his *Madonna in the Rose Bower*. Maybe some children will find those little angels 'cute'? Yet Lochner's art is not detached from the trend towards exact representation. On the contrary, what other work of this period shows such a completely responsible, masterly painting of a child as the Christchild in Lochner's *Adoration of the Magi*, which is also, perhaps, the most impressive painting of the entire exhibition.

•From Gothic to Renaissance

This summer, in one of the most beautiful buildings in the Netherlands, the fascinating seventeenth-century town hall of Bolsward, an exhibition entitled 'From Gothic to Renaissance' is on display. It's an advantage that this time period – the fifteenth and early sixteenth centuries – is not represented here by the typical examples, but that common utensils are also part of this display. For thus we realize that outside the main art centres, and outside the work of the great masters, change occurred very gradually. With hardly a noticeable break, another style of representation emerged slowly.

Contrary to what we may gather from study guides, this change in style (by which, as it were, a new trend asserted itself, and in place of the old traditional motifs and accepted forms, others – derived from elsewhere – took their place) did not make a great ripple in the history of art and did not represent any kind of deep spiritual revolution. Some things did change, certainly, but oh so gradually, oh so timidly. The era defined here as 'from Gothic to Renaissance' seems in itself to contain a certain unity – it was a time of change, in which the old was making room for the new. At first this occurred just superficially in the artistic 'trends', and only gradually did it have an effect on the spirit of the times. Therefore this was also a time of great variety, full of vitality and movement, alternation and, though not evident from the works shown here, a time of strife and conflict.

The radical changes brought by the Reformation may have kept minds busy in the first half of the sixteenth century but in these artworks we see little of the repercussions from this; the reason may be that during this period the Reformation had very little influence in the Netherlands and certainly did not yet affect and fertilize our culture.

We just stated that it is a pleasure to view these pieces which, for the most part, do not find a place among the standard repetoire of 'great works'. For it helps us to discover the value of the more humble, 'ordinary', commonplace yet very acceptable art.

There is *Manna-rain* by an unknown master of the early sixteenth century – what an appealing piece! The statues of the late fifteenth century – the stone sculptures and woodcuts – are also extremely compelling. A true little masterpiece is *Carrying of the cross*, ascribed to Simon Marmion, while the *Destruction of Sodom* by Lucas van Leyden is worthy of our praise, and so is *The optician* by Jacob Cornelisz with its hard-to-decipher subject, consisting of much more than just the sale happening in the foreground.

The deposition, from around 1450, is a striking wooden sculpture, beautiful in its composition and with very refined expression. For fear of sounding like the exhibition guidebook, we will mention only one more work, the famous *Bible in rhyme* ('Rijmbijbel') by Jacob van Maerlant, which has a well-deserved reputation.

It is a total view of the era that is impressed on us by this exhibition, rather than its highlighting the excellence of a few specific pieces. Actually, even the town hall itself, in a certain sense, fits in for it represents the close of that period and its artistic development. In a similar sense the well-known Martinikerk in nearby Groningen, now largely restored, could be said to mark the beginning of that transition era, while its stunning choir benches date from the middle of the period.

• Alsation art in Delft I[1116]

In the Netherlands we have been spoiled in recent years with some very important art exhibitions. Among others, there have been the Viennese exposition, the exhibition from the Pinakothek in Munich, and the expositions of a number of paintings from the collections of the British royal family. The exhibition of drawings by old masters, shown in Rotterdam earlier this year, was also a very unique experience.

Now the art-loving public is going to have to board the train to visit the Alsatian art treasures which are on display in the Prinsenhof in Delft. One can hardly imagine a more suitable ambiance and setting for an exhibition like this, in which art from the Middle Ages is the central attraction.

The Alsace, an area stretching from Basle northwards along the left bank of the Rhine, borders on the great French and German cultural centres. Prior to the eighteenth century it belonged mainly to Germany but since then it has become part of France. However, although in the Middle Ages a strong French influence was felt here – as evidenced, for example, in the architecture of the cathedral – the Alsatian art of that time still belonged primarily to the culture of southern Germany.

It is amazing, really, to think that now you can travel to Delft to see statues that belonged to the Strasbourg Cathedral. Although the deservedly famous pieces entitled *Ecclesia* and *Synagogue* are not present here, there are a number of works that were created in the same studio. We clearly see the affinity with the sculptures of Chartres in the so-called *Small Ecclesia*, a work dating from around 1230. Considering this connection with the Chartresque sculptures of the early thirteenth century, one can gather that the leading master of this studio, the Master of Ecclesia and Synagogue, one of the greatest sculptors of the high Gothic period, was probably schooled in Chartres. In a somewhat later sculpture of an apostle which has been taken from the former choir screen of the cathedral, one can find influences from the art of Reims. But here again we also recognize some signs of the influence of Chartres and it is clear that this work too springs from the same tradition that was mentioned earlier.

In the right portal of the West façade, the five wise virgins and the five foolish virgins faced one another. The former were led by Christ, the latter by the Prince of Darkness. From this collection of statues, created around 1280, we can now see one wise virgin and the Devil himself. The former is a stately, elegant female figure with a lamp full of oil in her hand, while the Seducer of the foolish virgins leads the way with a falsely sweet smirk on his face and an apple in his hand, but carrying destruction on his back, loaded with toads and reptiles.

After these statues, which belong to the high point or, if you will, the classic period of high Gothic, the influence of a measure of mannerism can be noted, in which elegance was taken to its extreme. Among these often overly thin, overly refined, though frequently very beautiful statues, we find one dating back to 1300 entitled *Vice*, which is personified by a woman; it comes from the left portal of the West façade.

Shortly after 1460 a very talented sculptor surfaced in Strasbourg, namely Nicholas Gerhaert van Leyden, a master who undoubtedly had been influenced by the style of the great sculptor Claus Sluter who worked in Dijon in the early fifteenth century. Nicholas' self-portrait is wonderful – a sculpture, especially with respect to its plastic composition, of exceptionally high quality. His bust of an old grey-beard is also well worth a closer look.

The impressive sculpture of one of the Wise Men comes from the Laurens portal of the cathedral. It is a rather bizarre-looking figure with prominent buck teeth and the statue captures him at the moment he is removing his head-covering in readiness to kneel before the Child. Perhaps he represents the black man who, as medieval tradition would have it, was part of the Magi group?

The angel figure from around 1500, which apparently still has its original paint, is almost Rococo-like, an uncommonly appealing piece of work! The polychromy reminds us that all sculptures created in the

Middle Ages were painted. Unfortunately, since the Renaissance, artists have abandoned the painting of sculptures. In the draft sketches one can see how the colours of the sculptures blended with the design of the Gothic building.

With reference to the wood carvings, we want to direct your attention to the various groups of figures representing the birth of Christ, the worship of the shepherds, and so on, which date from around 1500. They display many engaging details for attentive observers to discover for themselves.

We hope to deal with the painted art in this exhibition in a subsequent article.

• Alsation art in Delft II[1117]

Once again we wish to draw your attention to the exceptionally important exhibition of art from the Alsace, consisting mainly of pieces from the Museum of Strasbourg which are being shown in the Prinsenhof in Delft. In general it is not necessary nor advisable to draw the public into art-historical issues concerning the attribution of specific pieces. After all, whether a piece of art definitely came from the hand of this or that specific artist does not affect in any way the artistic value of the piece in question.

In this case, however, we feel that something must be said. For in the catalogue a number of works have been attributed to masters like Schongauer, the great fifteenth- century graphic artist and painter, and to Grünewald. Concerning those so-called Schongauer pieces, the attribution is not only highly disputable on several grounds – though admittedly the panels being discussed are undoubtedly fifteenth-century works and definitely originated in the Alsace area – but is also extremely misleading. After all, in our country we are acquainted with hardly any of the works by this artist, so the impression we are given of his work is hardly flattering if it is based on these appealing but far from first-rate pieces.

The same could be said concerning the so-called Grünewalds. Grünewald would have had to undergo an extraordinary change in style, if besides his magnificent visionary altar pieces he had also painted these panels. You can get to know the 'real' Grünewald very well from the large drawing of Christ on the cross. This is an artwork that clearly shows his genius as an artist (except for the colours). Among those pseudo-Grünewalds, we wish to point out the wonderful portrait of a man with a cage, dating from around 1480 – a piece which, despite the difficult art-historical problems it presents, is of exceptional power and beauty.

And now, getting back to Schongauer, we have to say that he is, above all, one of the greatest copper engravers of all time. We can prove this to ourselves by carefully studying the copperplates on display here. Schongauer is spectacular and powerful in his *Christ carrying the cross*; he is ever so friendly in his *Flight to Egypt*; and the composition as well as the portrayal in the beautiful large censer are accomplished with masterly control. It deserves to be thoroughly enjoyed because of its exceptional qualities – do not pass it by even though it may not seem so spectacular. It is interesting that the curators have included a few plates from Schongauer's predecessor as well, the Master E.S. (we still do not know his full name). He, too, was a great artist, though without the masterful brilliance that we find in Schongauer's art.

Among the paintings, besides the ones already mentioned, there are a number of very significant works. These include a few early fifteenth-century panels (e.g. *The upbringing of Mary*) which can give us an idea of the northerly art prior to the van Eycks. The influence of these great innovators is clearly seen in the piece by Conrad Witz, a painter who worked primarily in Constanz and Basle during the Councils held there in the early fifteenth century. Notice his thorough command over the perspective and the naturalistic representation of his subjects, but also how he displays them with great love. His two female saints in a cloister is an exceptionally strong work and it gives a fair impression of his art.

From Baldung Grien (who, by the way, has not been conclusively shown to be the artist of several panels attributed to him here) there is a wonderful collection of drawings and woodcuts. This artist, who is frequently prone to wild fantasizing, excels in these works. How he allowed his fantasy to run wild in the pieces with witches, one of his favourite themes! But also in the biblical scenes and in his studies of horses he reveals great mastery. The works of several of his contemporaries and disciples are also well worth attention.

Finally, the last room is devoted to a seventeenth-century still-life artist from Strasbourg. For us Dutch, who are well acquainted with many top-quality works in this genre by our own native artists, these pieces may not be so captivating, though they do possess some good qualities. But why it was felt necessary to transport such a large number of his works to Delft is not really clear.

Nevertheless, let us be glad for all the beauty that we can find here, sculptures as well as drawings and a number of painted panels. You should certainly take advantage of this unique opportunity.

• Rhineland's art in Arnhem[1118]

We have been rather spoiled over the years with the art exhibitions that have been shown in this country, exhibitions which were set up to give a thorough and extensive overview of the art of a chosen period or theme. Let us hope that we have not become blasé about it all, or so spoiled that we would now disparage an exposition consisting of only around 80 works, judging it to be 'insignificant' or 'not really worth my time'.

The exhibition 'Rhineland's Art of the late Middle Ages', now showing in the Arnhem Museum, is certainly well worth your while. Especially striking about this particular show is the care with which each piece has been displayed, so that it can receive the full attention it deserves. This allows us to enter more profoundly and conscientiously into the spirit and the artistic qualities of each work, so much more than when there is an overabundance of pieces on display. It does not surprise us, then, that one tends to spend just as much time at this exhibition as at a much larger one.

One of the requirements of an exhibition like this, of course, is that each piece of art must be of sufficiently high quality to warrant the attention it is given; that the chosen specimens of art are worthy examples of the period or movement that they represent. In our opinion, this exhibition has been very successful on that front. Perhaps paintings from that period are not as well represented as they could have been, but the result is that some exceptionally beautiful wood carvings have more space to come into their own.

In the first place, the art of this era, as we learn from the statues, was characterized by a strong tendency towards realism. However, the artists never resorted to a dull imitation of the natural givens; rather, the wholesome truth that reality is richer, deeper and more profound than what meets the eye has stayed alive in their art. (This is something that the later nineteenth-century naturalists forgot, resulting in art that became meaningless and flat.) In the second place, these artists have not forgotten that a work of art must obey aesthetics laws. They have, in their attempt at a faithful rendering of reality, not forgotten to seek and find beautiful and gripping forms. Finally, these artists have also understood that it does not harm the truthfulness of a work of art to make use of symbols, and they often sought to express 'spiritual' truth more than just what is 'historically-correct'. Art is not required to reproduce external reality. But on the other hand, it does have to communicate something about the truth, and about the meaning of what is being represented. That is only possibly if it is not slavishly bound to reproducing the so-called 'historically-accurate' visible external appearance.

Therefore we can call a sculpture like the one of Peter and Paul truthful, even if Peter never really held a key, nor Paul a book in his hand, as they are portrayed here: this statue strikes home because of its truthful characterization of these figures by the way they serve as a foil to each other – not to mention the lovely parallelism of the folds in the clothing, which gives a subdued rhythm to the composition, making it such a treat for the eye. Then we have *Christ and the Samaritan woman*. One could give free rein to a shrewd eagerness to pick out all the 'historical inaccuracies', but the artistic image of the meeting at the well is nevertheless very accurately rendered; it is true in the deepest sense of that word.

In any truly successful work of art an artistic rendering and a meaningful representation of reality will always serve to strengthen and support each other – to form a single, inseparable unity. Viewing a work like the beautifully subdued statue of the grieving Mary is better proof of this point than any verbal argument can offer. Similarly, a study of the larger sculpture of John and Mary at the cross will show how splendidly the inner emotions of the figures have been rendered, while the lines and forms are of great beauty. Finally, how very human are those scribes in their debate with John the Baptist: such real faces, snatched out of real life, characters to feast one's eyes on, shown without contempt or hatred in all their weakness.

Among the paintings, which are certainly worthy of attention, we wish to make special mention of the work of Baegert. But more striking still are the crafted works: the gorgeous tapestries and the love and skill, and artistic excellence, that are found in a simple lectern. And do not forget to look at that magnificent copper engraving by Israël van Meckenem.

But we cannot go into more detail here. Viewers can see for themselves the grace expressed on a face, the artistry in the folds of cloth, the lovely contours; and it is in the act of discovering these things that they will find great satisfaction. Viewers can also judge for themselves the degree of truthfulness, or the rightness of vision, of the way reality has been presented in these works of art.

There is much good to say about this museum with its exceptionally beautiful display of ceramics and its stunning paintings (the one by Salomon van Ruysdael alone is already worth the trip). We should be very thankful for an exhibition like this, which so wonderfully allows each work to speak for itself.

• Beauty from the Middle Ages in the Rijksmuseum[1119]

'Art of the Middle Ages from the Northern Netherlands' is the title of a large and exceptionally beautiful exposition on display this summer in the Rijksmuseum. Because the museum is celebrating its sesquicentennial by means of this exhibition, extra attention has been devoted to making it one of especially high quality, with emphasis being given to fifteenth-century paintings, and appropriately so.

It is a curious fact that we Dutch know so little about our own art from the time prior to the seventeenth century, even though the works of artists like Geergen tot Sint Jans (Little Gerard of the Brethren of St John) and the Master of the Virgo inter Virgines are of extremely high calibre. It really is very important for us to come to understand the merits of this art as it will help us also to understand ourselves better. For truly, this is characteristically Dutch art. We would go so far as to say that in the latter half of the fifteenth century, and partly because of the work of these artists, the Dutch character acquired a definite shape based on a unique kind of piety, a form of practical mysticism (like that of the Brothers of the Common Life).

What exactly are the qualities of the Dutch character revealed in our art? They include an avoidance of everything theatrical; they include also intimacy, directness and modesty, embracing that which is genuine, shunning every excess and seeking the real worth and beauty of the ordinary, the commonplace. The art is subdued and never harsh, never violent, but always extremely refined, with richly nuanced colours. Harmonizing beautifully with one another are the subtle reds or rosy purples, the peaceful blues and greens, and these in turn are consistent with the gentle folds of the garments – all of these allow for a richness of tone. But even with all this depth of tone, the art never becomes wildly colourful. The composition of these paintings is treated in the same way: at first sight it seems so obvious, so ordinary, so nondescript. But on closer examination one begins to see how beautifully the whole has been put together, with a touch of an accent here and there, so that the whole piece comes to life with no dead spots where one's attention flags.

Sometimes a slightly more lively arrangement of the pleats in the clothing will be enough to draw attention to a certain part of the painting. In such ways the theme is communicated in an utterly sober and business-like way, without agitation, but with serenity and dignity, always probing deeply rather than seeking a false effect that is without real purpose.

This art speaks a completely different language from what followed it; the latter was deeply influenced by the Renaissance (which was introduced to the Netherlands around 1500), especially in terms of its forms. The art we are talking about here is more like the polyphonic music of that era in which the separate voices are not always distinguishable. In the same way in art the compositions are not easy to analyse and the main lines are difficult to make out, but in a wondrous way it all holds carefully together. And this is all done in such a way that the subject of the painting seems to unfold itself slowly before one's eyes. Anyone who seeks to be immediately gripped, instantly captured, has come to the wrong place: rather, this art requires concentrated and careful attention.

When that careful attention is given, one will discover that one's first impression – i.e. that the figures are quite removed and do not really participate in the action – is utterly mistaken. How delicately the emotions are rendered, with great variety, as the characters react very differently to the events occurring around them. But they do not make any grandiose gestures; rather they experience these things very privately, and their bearing and facial expressions just barely betray their feelings. They are always real flesh-and-blood people, without grandeur or a dramatic pose. Saints, and even angels are figures with great physical beauty and with super human qualities, but here they are depicted also as sober and ordinary, dead serious, with a profound inner depth and without flamboyance.

Take a good look and you will see that these people (and even these angels) are common Dutch folk resembling people you can see on the street every day, even if the style of clothing has changed a bit over the years.

These are the qualities that characterize the work of a Geergen tot Sint Jans – the greatest of them all – and of those anonymous masters whom art historians have given names such as the Master of the Virgo inter Virgines. The latter name is derived from the title of one of his works in the Rijksmuseum. That anonimity, hiding behind the work of art, does that not also fit this way of looking at the world? Take special notice of how these well-known pieces suddenly reveal their beauty now that they are surrounded by so many other Dutch works, works which so often (all too often) have left our country.

Then we come to Hieronymus Bosch with his own unique world, but unfortunately we do not really have time to deal with him here. Nor can we discuss those beautiful statues (and the strange sensation when one starts to discover their unique Dutch character), the books, the prints, the drawings and so much more.

The exposition concludes with the works of a number of great painters from the early sixteenth century. A strong secularist tendency is evident in these works, and sometimes a rather unconvincing effort to dramatically preserve more traditional values and content. Lucas van Leyden is certainly the greatest of these, whose skill is shown best in his portraits and in his completely secular scenes. Did he not also infuse his painting of the Last Judgment with that secular spirit – a piece that is striking because of its unusual light and vast spaciousness?

In conclusion we would suggest that no one should miss this exhibition. It will remain until 28 September, but do not wait until the last day because you may want to return for a second look.

• Religious art in Tournai[1120]

It is a real miracle that the famous cathedral in Tournai (Belgium), an exceptional structure of incredible beauty, was spared during World War II. It is almost entirely surrounded by the ruined buildings as most other churches and important structures fared less well. There is, however, a drive to rebuild and (though not always as successful) to restore these buildings.

In the Lakenhal, which fortunately was also spared and has been turned into a museum, there is currently an exposition of religious art. Especially the large collection of miniatures, mostly painted by artists from Tournai, is of great significance. We are thinking particularly of the fifteenth-century pieces, which most clearly show the great influence of Rogier van der Weyden on the art of his birthplace, even though later, after he had made a name for himself, he established himself in Brussels.

The only miniature by Rogier himself is of breathtaking beauty. It depicts the presentation by its writer of the chronicle of Hainault to Philip the Good, in the presence of several important noblemen (including Philip's young son, later called Charles the Bold). The colours are brilliant and have a rich glow. The parchment used as foundation gives a rich effect, especially with a master like Rogier who knows how to use its qualities to best advantage. And then, the drawing itself! Typical is the dignified regal bearing of Philip. How carefully Rogier developed those portraits, even though many of them measure no more than 2 cm, without letting them become wooden. On the contrary, they sparkle with life! Look at the fabric of the canopy, worked out in such detail – only a great master could have accomplished such excellence.

Next to the miniatures and the paintings (which, on the whole, are not very significant) you will want to take a closer look at the wood carvings, mostly from the fifteenth or early sixteenth centuries.

Finally we prefer to direct our attention to the modern religious art, which invites us to make a comparison with the religious art of the Netherlands, especially since we have recently seen a collection of the latter in Amsterdam. On the whole it does not meet our expectations. But if we bypass all the weaker works we come to the exceptional art of Gustav van de Woestijne. His *Christ in the desert* is a gripping piece. It depicts Christ all alone in the 'yellow' desolation and one can almost feel the Devil approaching with his temptations. His second piece, *The Judas kiss*, shows a strong composition but without the appeal of the first work.

Rather expressionistic are the works of André Blanc and A. Jamar. There is also much art in the spirit of Matthieu Wiegman or Colette, but its quality is not very high. Among the sculptures, we should take note of the Madonna by Elstrom, a piece influenced by Bourdelle, and a Madonna – in this case a black woman with child – in a composition created by Dupagne that has some qualities of a totem pole.

Our final conclusion may be that our own Dutch modern religious art is, when it comes to quality, superior to that from abroad.

•Burgundian splendour by Flemish masters[1121]

It is remarkable that by far the majority of artworks, displayed in exhibition at the Rijksmuseum entitled 'Burgundian Splendour', are of Flemish origin. Even a significant percentage of the works from Burgundy itself were created by Flemish masters. The new, more modern art of the fifteenth century – which was born out of a spirit very similar to the one that motivated the Italian Renaissance but without its reference to the classics – may have started primarily in France, yet its leading artists were mostly Northerners.

In the area of sculpture it was Claus Sluter, an artist apparently born in the Netherlands, who was the great innovator. He worked from approximately 1380 to 1406 (the year of his death) and thus preceded the period in which the great Italian Renaissance masters, like Donatello, created their famous works of art. Through a peculiar turn of events the Italians attained great fame and glory, while few today will even recognize the name of Sluter. Yet he was surely one of the greatest artists who ever lived. Although we cannot see his *Moses fountain* here (one would have to compare his Moses with the one by Michelangelo to prove how well his work stands up to scrutiny), we get an impression of his skill in the fragment of the beautiful Christ torso (taken from a crucifix which used to be located above the *Moses fountain*). Another wonderful sculpture is his funerary monument for Philip the Bold.

Sluter's influence had a definitive impact on fifteenth-century Burgundian sculpture, evident in the funerary monuments created for the dukes. His Madonna in the church portal of Dijon became the standard inspiration for this kind of sculpture.

Jan van Eyck was without doubt the most famous Flemish painter, a great master who brought renewal to painting style in a way that was similar to what Sluter did for scupture some twenty or thirty years earlier. To commend van Eyck's works is like carrying coal to Newcastle. Perhaps less well known, but in practice of the same superb quality, are the works of the so-called Master of Flémalle, the predecessor of Rogier van der Weyden. This exhibition gives a unique opportunity to study his art. We would like to single out his magnificent *Birth of Christ*, in which you should note particularly the landscape, and also the *Engagement of Mary*, on loan from the Prado.

The new art of the fifteenth century was launched with works by master artists, the greatest of the great. In the areas of both portrait and landscape painting they laid the foundation for later generations to build on, who rarely managed to surpass them, and certainly not in portrait painting. From the masters who followed them, van der Goes, Bouts and Memling, there are some extremely interesting works on display here which one would not wish to miss.

Also do not bypass the magnificent tapestries, representing large-scale pictorial art, nor the miniatures, representing pictorial art at its most minute. Notice that in all areas, from tiny to huge, from applied arts (considered 'fine art' at that time) to what we today consider the fine arts of painting and sculpture, the work from this period was unrivalled in quality, both artistically and technically.

• The portrait in the Old Netherlands

It appears to have become a tradition that every other year Bruges hosts an exposition that not only reveals the beauty of Flemish art but also has scientific interest. Because of the nature of the issues that concern art historians today, exhibitions have more recently tended to be organized around a certain theme rather than around specific artists or groups of artists.

The title of this exhibition, 'The Portrait', was also the title of the great exhibition displayed in Amsterdam last year. This Bruges exhibition, with its greater emphasis on Flemish and Southern Netherlandish elements, and ending at the time of the split between the North and South, is a perfect completion of what was offered there in Amsterdam. For the distinctive character of the earlier Northern portraits is much clearer when they are seen next to their Southern counterparts and the differences between the two become much more obvious.

The making of portraits began in fourteenth-century France and, more specifically, in Burgundy, where artists were attracted to the courts of the dukes and duchesses. However, it was especially Jan van Eyck and the Master of Flémalle (who, unfortunately, is not represented here by any of his best works) who managed in a brilliant way to enrich and exploit the possibilities and potential of this art form, overshadowing all previous attempts at portraiture. Their heritage, enriched by the beautiful works of Rogier van der Weyden, was developed and expanded by the next generation of artists.

See for instance the gorgeous *Portinari altarpiece* by Hugo van der Goes, commissioned by the Italian merchant Portinari and quickly transported to Florence, where it created a big sensation. The side panels with the portraits of Portinari and his wife and child are now in Bruges. Especially the right panel, showing the woman and her small daughter against the majestic figures of the patron saints Margaret and Mary Magdalene behind them – set in a landscape of gentle, rolling hills – is an unsurpassed masterpiece.

Works by Memling and Bouts are displayed too, but unfortunately none by the Northern Netherlandish Geertgen tot Sint Jans. If he had been represented too, then perhaps the development of the portrait as it occurred in the North, quite differently from what happened in the South, would have been more clearly demonstrated.

Right at the start of the sixteenth century the different temperaments of the Flemish and the Northern Netherlandish portraitists came to the fore, undoubtedly pointing also to differences in national character. In the South, where people were more receptive to and understanding of the Italian Renaissance spirit, and where the court always made its influence known, portraits were seen to be a representative manifestation of the subject. The heads, relatively large, fill the panels almost entirely and the facial expressions are of self-conscious strength and self-confidence. See for instance the portraits by Quinten Metsys, Jan Gossaert and Joos van Cleve (who painted not only royalty, but also prominent citizens). In the portraits from the North the heads are smaller compared to the size of the panel, and the whole impression is more modest, more inward, yet certainly not less beautiful even though the figures are more angular, with less concern for an ideal form. See especially the works by Lucas van Leyden, Cornelis Engelbrachtsen and Jan Mostaert.

In the next period we see more interplay between North and South – partly as a result of the fact that Gossaert had worked in the North for so long and had taught many students there (among them Jan van Scorel), but also because of the continuing influence of Italy. Northerners, such as van Scorel and Heemskerck, travelled to Italy. The art of Moro [Anthonis Mor van Dashorst], which actually had a much more international character because this court portraitist travelled so widely, cannot be understood apart from an Italian link (Titian!). Of the Southerners, Floris and Lombard particularly display clear evidence of their contact with Italy. Yet the Netherlanders also retained an own character in their portraits; it is just possible, and maybe not by such a big leap of the imagination, that an artist like Pourbus, born in Gouda and working in Bruges, linked up with the art of Memlinck and others.

It is impossible to consider all of sixteenth-century portraiture, all the best works that the century had to offer, in all its rich variety. Every work has its own unique qualities, even a personality of its own, and we are continually presented with surprises. See for instance the wonderful portrait of a woman by Coxie, an artist who had made a few copies of van Eycks and had painted some not very exceptional ecclesiastical pieces but who, in this particular work, excelled himself. The beautiful black of her dress has been equally only in works by the seventeenth-century Thomas de Keyser, and her calm, meditative expression is unrivalled.

Without suggesting that no beautiful portraits have been made since then, we do wish to point out that as a branch of the arts, portraiture flourished in the sixteenth century with unparalleled excellence.

• Jan van Scorel: universal artist

On 15 October 1550 Jan van Scorel, originally from Schoorl [in the Netherlands], and later promoted to the position of a canon in Utrecht, received the royal patent for his invention of a method of dike-building that used anchored blocks. It was a technique he developed for the purpose of reclaiming the Zijpe. That same year, he won a silver cup for restoring the famed *Lamb of God* by Jan van Eyck of Ghent. The modern reader will think: he must have been a chemist-inventor. But no, we are dealing here with one of those widely gifted individuals of the Renaissance, who in the end – as happened so often – became famous for his works of art.

Jan van Scorel was a typical Renaissance man, and that refers to more than just his painting style. One senses it in the way he describes himself on his earliest known work - *pictoris artis amator* – a 'lover of painted art'. When he painted this *Holy Kinship altarpiece* in 1520, in a late Gothic style reminiscent of his teacher, Jacob Cornelisz, he already acted no longer like an artisan but more like a proud, liberated artist. That's also why he never joined a guild, which he considered unqualified to promote art for art's sake.

We can be very thankful for the opportunity to see this altarpiece from Obervellach in Austria at the exhibition of Jan van Scorel's work in the Centraal Museum in Utrecht – not just because it has never before been removed from its village church but also because it represents the early work of Scorel in such a splendid way.

The young Scorel had left Holland to travel to Nuremberg, where he also met Dürer, and there enjoyed the patronage of an important noble family from Kärnten (Austria); he travelled with them to their ancestral castle where he painted this first-rate masterpiece, a testimony to his great talent – especially since he was only 25 years old at the time.

Soon thereafter he went to Venice, and there it was inevitable that a man so in touch with the spirit of Italian Renaissance culture would be influenced by Italian art. In 1521 he went to Rome, where Adrian from Utrecht had just become pope. This compatriot gave him one of the most enviable positions that an artist of that day could have wished for – he became Raphael's successor and was given the studio that the previous pope had furnished for Leonardo da Vinci. Unfortunately for van Scorel this did not last long, for in 1524 Adrian died and the artist returned north, enriched by a thorough knowledge of the work of Raphael and Michelangelo. So van Scorel became the one who introduced our country [the Netherlands] to this new Renaissance art, not as a slavish follower but as a man spiritually and artistically permeated with ideas and knowledge still new to the North.

The exposition in Utrecht is a beautiful testimony to his art. Certainly, his work lacks the seasoned maturity of the greatest Renaissance artists but, on the other hand, it has a freshness and clarity of colouring, a liveliness in composition, a beautifully mature rendering of landscape backgrounds and a pervading lucidity that makes viewing his work a special experience. See for instance his *Entry into Jerusalem*, the *Baptism in the Jordan* and the valuable *Mary Magdalene* from the Rijksmuseum as well as the beautiful *Madonna* from New York.

Even more poignant is Jan van Scorel's portraiture. How accurately and individually he could depict his subjects – so beautifully positioned against the background, with finely balanced light and dark contrasts. In these wonderful, delicately-painted portraits, van Scorel's art reaches its culmination: *Agatha van Schoonhoven, The Jerusalem pilgrims, The twelve-year-old boy.*

As an agent of renewal, van Scorel strongly influenced the further development of sixteenth-century painting in the Northern Netherlands, also through his very important pupil Maerten van Heemskerck. The latter's early work, painted under the influence of van Scorel, shows us a powerful and gifted artist, maybe even greater than his master. The family portrait from Kassel is stunning, one of the most impressive pieces painted in this time. The story goes that Jan van Scorel became so jealous of this pupil that he booted him out of his studio.

The exposition shows many more works by portraitists and painters of biblical scenes who were directly influenced by Jan van Scorel. Thus this is also an exhibition of great scientific importance, addressing many hitherto unresolved art-historical problems. But it is foremost an exhibition that offers the enjoyment of works of superior quality to every lover of art – especially of portraits and biblical scenes of powerful persuasiveness.

• Leonardo da Vinci: brilliant and universal

It's not easy to summarize the contributions of Leonardo in a short space. So too, it must have been not easy for the organizers of the Leonardo exhibition (being shown in the Gemeentemuseum in The Hague until 8 June in honour of the 500th anniversary of his birth) to properly select, in a comprehensive way, the most characteristic and important elements out of his great legacy. For Leonardo was an extraordinarily diverse man: musician, fortress builder, engineer, eminent equestrian, sculptor, painter, architect, anatomist, naturalist, and art theoretician. He was a man with far too diverse interests; as a result many of his ideas remained in their concept stage and he managed to carry out or complete only a fraction of all that his inventive spirit considered or imagined.

Moreover, some of his important works – the fresco of the Battle of Anghiari in Florence and the huge statue of a horseman in Milan – were destroyed during his lifetime, so that his legacy became even more fragmented.

Nevertheless, he is and will remain a figure who can only be underrated for it is hardly possible to judge him too highly. Why? Without his influence, Italian painting, especially in Northern Italy during the sixteenth century and into the seventeenth century, would certainly have developed differently.

Yet, this is not the greatest of his contributions. His buildings and designs are not without interest; neither are his writings about art theory. But in these things he was not alone. The talents that earned him such an eminent position in the court at Milan – including horsemanship, musicianship and his work as building engineer – naturally has less significance for later generations. His engineering projects, which included a design for an aeroplane, were so far ahead of his time that their true value is only now fully appreciated, yet we cannot say for sure that without Leonardo's inventions the course of technology would have developed differently. So, what essentially does give this man such and exceptional position in history?

We believe that though Leonardo was and is such a fascinating figure, it is especially in the field of drawing and science – or rather, in connecting the two – that his greatest contribution is to be found. As a student Leonardo worked for years in the studio of Verrocchio and learnt there the art of a very exact representation of reality – a number of drapery studies in the exhibition attest to this. But Leonardo was the first person to go on and make use of his new skills in the service of science. That was his greatest contribution and his greatest service to the world. He was the first one to record his anatomical findings in precise drawings – so exact that they are still of scientific merit.

Leonardo's observations in the area of the natural sciences were preserved by his never-resting drawing pencil. And in the connection between the exact sciences (in which he also broke new territory) and the art of exact drawing lies a principle upon which modern science (amongst others) is founded: modern medical science could not function without the very precise drawings which allowed Leonardo's discoveries to be shared with others. Anyone who understands the important role of drawing in engineering will realize that Leonardo's discovery also made modern applied science and technology possible. All this does not detract from his excellence as a 'free' sketcher. It is a feast to submit oneself to Leonardo's drawings – one may be tempted to say that his lines are flawless.

• Italian drawings: breaking with the Renaissance

Italy experienced the height of Renaissance art shortly after 1500, when the fifteenth-century search for an exact reproduction of nature bore fruit in a superior command of the means to that end. These means were then placed in service to the artistic ideal that aimed for ultimate harmony through a most highly-refined beauty.

Thus art became subservient to the ambition to achieve a mature, harmonious control of all of life and activity, so that complete freedom and power to control, the two most fundamental ideals of the Renaissance, were both affirmed in an aesthetic styling of all of life.

But the equilibrium between these two opposite driving forces of the Renaissance was inherently unstable, and very soon the harmony – capturing life in a purely aesthetic way – began to feel like a straitjacket; then freedom was sought again – and indulged in – much more passionately.

Thus the style called Mannerism was born, an art style that seldom reaches the extreme forms of our day but, at root, is closely related to them. It shouldn't surprise us then that currently there is a new awakening of interest in the work of those artists who first broke with the high Renaissance ideals in favour of free creative activity. The inner tensions of this Mannerism – which for its main spokesmen encompassed a complete lifestyle – are also familiar to us. And out of this interest and this understanding arises the theme for the large exhibition of drawings now showing in the Rijksmuseum, intended as a manifestation of the Italian-Dutch cultural accord, and as a response to the exhibition of Rembrandt drawings that was presented to Italy.

This exposition contains only works from large public Italian collections, drawings created between 1500 and 1540. They are mostly sketches and studies, thus giving some insight into the first surge of ideas from these wonderful artists, while at the same time revealing to us something of their perception of reality. It is as if the aestheticism of the high Renaissance goes over the top and consumes the desire for an exact rendering of nature.

The pictures are drawn in a very rapid sketching style, in which the first concern is the completely subjective shape of the line and an immediate satisfaction of the wild urge to create. That which previously was subject to the exact replication of reality now stands on its own and is assigned its own worth, almost independent of the image. The play of lines on the surface, the interplay of light and dark produced by the unfettered creative activity of the artist, is of supreme importance.

We see this supremacy of the aesthetic expressed in the drawings of Fra Bartolommeo, of whom we have some excellent pieces. A few of his contemporaries show a similar approach, demonstrated convincingly with beautiful examples.

But it is only with the younger masters – Pontormo, Rosso and Beccafumi – that this new trend asserts itself in full force. We see this clearly in Pontormo's work. Note, for instance, how his heads are sometimes sketched with a single, fiercely-drawn round line; and how he sometimes builds his bodies in a way reminiscent of the earlier Cubism which similarly built up images out of small units and then placed the head on the torso as if it was unimportant and incidental. Rosso sometimes dissolves whole compositions in the interplay of light and dark, by which the depth is almost completely lost so that the surface of the drawing, endowed with its own meaning, is emphasized. Boccafumi builds his figures with a free play of lines which at times have only a very loose connection with reality, resulting in effects that remind us of etchings by moderns like Villon and Morandi. The tormented spirit of these Renaissance defenders of artistic freedom comes to the fore more than once in an almost expressionistic tension. Notice – to mention just one of the most striking examples – the facial expressions of Pontormo's figures with their hollow eyes.

Drawings by Michelangelo, Raphael, Bronzino, and a few others make this exhibition (of which the value is further heightened by the excellent accompanying catalogue) an experience not to be missed.

Seventeenth and Eighteenth Centuries

• Caravaggio's influence on the school of Utrecht

The seventeenth-century art of our country [the Netherlands] is adorned with names like Rembrandt, Vermeer, Hals, Ruysdael and many others. Curiously absent from that list, however, are the names of the artists to whom the wonderful exhibition now showing at the Centraal Museum in Utrecht is specifically dedicated. There are reasons for that, though. In the seventeenth century Utrecht held a very unique place in the world of art because of its position as a centre for Roman Catholic culture. Here, more than anywhere else, art remained in service to the Roman Catholic Church, and it means this art had quite a different emphasis than art from other parts of Holland.

There was another factor, too, that gave this primarily Catholic art a different 'tone'. These Catholic artists were partial to Italy, and certainly felt more at home in Italian culture than Protestants did. That was why they absorbed more of the Italian influences and their outlook was much more coloured by Italian ideas. And that is why these artists could be collectively labelled with a name borrowed from an Italian master: 'Caravaggists'.

Caravaggists! It's questionable whether, in the strict sense, this name is really appropriate; it certainly presents a problem for art historians. For while all those displayed here have undoubtedly been inluenced by Caravaggio there was often at least as much, and sometimes more, influence from other Italian contemporaries. Thus, we should think of them more in terms of representing the style of this period than in terms of showing the influence of Caravaggio only.

Seen in this way, then, it is unfair, strictly speaking, to introduce this exhibition with a number of Caravaggios and to bypass other contemporary Italian artists. Various reasons could be given to justify this, however. Besides, we should be grateful for the opportunity to view six works by this unquestionably exceptional artist. Typical of his painting is the plasticity of his figures, with taut, tightly-drawn contours. Also his colouring is very remarkable and unique, in sharp contrast with the mostly uniformly dark backgrounds, and it infuses his work with an incredible dynamic power which could not but have left a strong impression on his contemporaries, as it still does on us. His figures are real, concrete, not so much because of an inordinate attention to detail but mainly because of their strong plastic quality.

The so-called Dutch Caravaggists have a preference for large figures, in common with Caravaggio and the other Italian artists of this period. Their human figures, so tightly crowded together in relation to the framework, give these works a peculiar monumental and completely unique character, very different from other seventeenth-century Dutch art.

Another typical feature of the works of the Caravaggists are their themes. First there are many ecclesiastical themes, such as 'Jesus in the Temple', 'The Evangelists' and so on. Then there are the flute and lute players, and paintings on subjects like 'The matchmaker'. These subjects were not always so 'properly' depicted, and as other Dutch artists copied these themes we see a moderation, not just in regard to the details but also in regard to the spirit of the whole – so that their work comes across with more humour and less rudeness.

Finally, we find many humanistic themes portrayed. Subjects like 'The death of Seneca', portraits of ancient poets, and so on are common. It's not surprising then that later, as this art began to lose some of its typical Caravaggist flavour, it moved steadily towards a more academic style and began to accept typically un-Dutch assignments like wall ornaments.

It is impossible to deal individually with each of the masters represented here by such stunning works. Honthorst, Stomer, Baburen, and especially the extremely important Henrick Terbrugghen, are all master artists; and the others shown here are also very worthy of our attention. See, for example, the beautiful piece by de Gheyn entitled *St Luke*. Next to these one must not forget the important group of artists from the Southern Netherlands, particularly Rubens, to whom a separate article should really be devoted.

To conclude the exhibition, the museum wanted to present a few pieces that show the influence of these Caravaggists on the rest of Dutch art – Rembrandt's early depiction of a musical social gathering, a painting by Frans Hals and one by Leyster were chosen. Finally, as a very late example of this Caravaggist influence, we see the painting that is also the most beautiful one of the whole exposition – an early painting by Vermeer, *Christ in the house of Mary and Martha*. It is worth a visit to this exhibition, including a long journey if necessary, just to see this one painting. Don't miss the chance – it normally hangs in Edinburgh, and for most of us that is too far to travel.

•Painters of architecture

With the emergence of a distinctly Dutch style of art, categories of painting flourished or came into being that had seldom or never been seen before – we think of the flower arrangement, the still life, the genre painting, the seascape. In the establishment of this new art, the northern and southern parts of the Netherlands kept pace with each other until, at the end of the sixteenth century, they diverged and developed further along very different lines, politically as well as religiously. The task of developing the new art was left completely to those in the North;

while in Flanders a different form of art emerged, belonging to the Baroque, which was determined mainly by the Counter-Reformation.

The field of architectural painting also experienced these developments and an important, major exposition has now been devoted to this in the Centraal Museum in Utrecht. It is not a collection of unconnected, lovely and interesting works of art but rather an exposition that sets out to increase our understanding of these developments.

In the fifteenth century architecture was used in paintings only as a background for 'holy objects'; in the sixteenth century this was taken even further and architecture became decor, a sort of ornamental background. Around the middle of that century people became tired of this and there emerged an architectural painting style for art's own sake. Vredeman de Vries, who published books about architectural design, was very influential at this time – and do not forget that all late sixteenth-century architecture of the Netherlands bears his stamp. These paintings became displays of architectural forms in large imaginary constructions. We see it in the works of de Vries himself, and in those of the van Steenwijks and the Neefs (of whom the youngest continued to paint this genre in the Southern Netherlands until the late seventeenth century). Moreover, this art was dominated by perspective: the artists boasted expertise in this respect. In the Northern Netherlands, Hendrick Aerts worked in this style and is undeservedly less well known, for he had a great influence on most of the important artists of the Northern Netherlands during the first half of the seventeenth century.

The first real innovator and 'Dutch-i-fier' of architectural painting was undoubtedly Saenredam: with him the emphasis is no longer on perspectival construction (he does not show off his knowledge of it) – but a sense of depth is suggested through fine nuances of colour and through differing sizes of the architectural segments he uses. He places the viewer right in the middle of his churches, also through his skilful depiction of pillars and other features from very close up.

The next generation of painters, comprising of Houckgeest, van Vliet and Emanuel de Witte – who together discovered this new genre in Delft around 1650 – continued to work in a style reminiscent of Saenredam. In their works we are completely pulled into the church interiors. They succeeded in painting colonnades from close-up, creating a sense of space from very close proximity and taking composition as well as painting style to new heights.

The story is not yet finished: we still need to mention van der Heyden and Berkheyde. Besides, we have only touched on one facet of the rich heritage of the seventeenth century, demonstrated in this exposition. Van Goyen, Salomon van Ruysdael, Cuyp, and many others have not tested their skills in vain on architectural subjects.

But history goes on and perhaps the only later artist who achieved the same skill as these seventeenth-century artists is J. Weisenbruch.

Subsequently Bosboom revived paintings of church interiors but, despite their great appeal, his works are not to be compared with the works from the 'golden age'. We will not mention our own age in this respect – perhaps its best accomplishment has been to make an exhibition like this possible.

• Dutch still lifes

Now that Rotterdam is hosting an art exhibition which shows the development of the French still life, it has been a clever move for the museum in Dordrecht to set up a display of Dutch still lifes. After viewing the one exhibit one is tempted to hop on the train and go and have a look at the other, in order to compare and gain a clearer perception of the essence of both styles, Dutch and French.

At the outset there can be no doubt that the French learned this genre from the Dutch. Moreover, the art of seventeenth-century Holland reached unprecedented heights and this genre of the still life became one of its most important forms, while the French art of the same period seldom reached such heights of excellence. It was not until the eighteenth century, and undoubtedly as a result of a strong Dutch influence, that Chardin's art came to match the quality of our own. However, during that period the Dutch produced little of comparable quality. So while our Dutch art was gaining a following in many places outside our borders, we ourselves produced little that was new or significant.

The Dordrecht exhibition does not attempt to be a comprehensive overview. That would simply be impossible. In the exhibition catalogue we are warned that these works were selected on the basis of personal choice rather than on the basis of any particular art-historical principle.

That explains why there are relatively few works by Heda and Pieter Claeszens, and a great many by van Beyeren, although the latter have been very tastefully selected. The oldest works show a multitude of objects placed closely beside each other or on top of each other, hardly a harmonious unity. But then, particularly in the works of Heda and Claeszens, unity is achieved through the use of light, the limited number of objects and the carefully constructed compositions, so that these works no longer depict collections of unconnected objects. Van Beyeren in particular, building on their work, shows skill in conveying a richness and an abundance without letting his paintings becoming too busy or overcrowded, yet also not lapsing back into a primitive style of arrangement. Kalf, van Aelst, and many others are represented here, and their works together form a symphony of simplicity. Simplicity, yes, but with such concentration and harmony that it celebrates visual art at its best.

A remarkable fact demonstrated clearly in this exhibition is the important place occupied by the Middelburg artists. With Bosschaert, van der Ast with his very appealing works, and Coorte with his gripping style, Middelburg art forms a centre of remarkable unilaterality, though certainly not without merit.

Coorte as a painter takes simplicity to its furthest extreme: his most captivating and complete painting perhaps is that single bunch of asparagus, nothing more, nothing less.

I am not really sure how to explain this, but it is striking that the French still lifes show the greatest affinity with Middelburg art. In Sterling's introduction to the Rotterdam catalogue he attributes the great sense of restraint, which is carried to an extreme in these works, to a Latin spirit.

In the eighteenth century the still life became either a down-to-earth identification of plants and flowers or a decorative ornament. With van Huysum the rocaille of the Rococo is particularly striking.

It is not until the end of the nineteenth century that the still life regained a sense of meaning and artistic worth. There was a remarkable change then from the seventeenth-century perception: in the earlier period people praised the beauty of created things, focusing their attention on their lovely subjects and, in their attempt to approximate that beauty, achieving the epitome of artistic beauty. But in the later period the beauty of the work of art itself takes priority, while the represented object becomes a means to an end, an excuse, an inducement to create the work – see here the wonderful works by Verster or Suze Robertson, to limit ourselves to a few of the very best pieces.

Among the later pieces we wish to single out Dick Ket for our attention. Here you feel (in a negative sense) the importance for an artist to work within a living and flourishing tradition of activity. The fact that, despite being obviously gifted as well as showing a singular focus on still lifes, Ket is still not able to attain the same level of excellence as perhaps one of the less talented seventeenth-century artists is undoubtedly because of the lack of a living tradition, an environment around him of artists working in the same direction. Still, his through and through twentieth-century work is definitely worthy of praise.

• The Rembrandt House in Amsterdam

In 1906, on the 300th anniversary of his birthday, Rembrandt the world-famous Amsterdammer, was honoured in a really grand way. As a result you can still find in the library the beautiful Rembrandt biography by Jan Veth, and the thick *Rembrandt Bible* by Bredius with its splendid reproductions, of such exceptionally high quality for those days.

There was also great concern at that time about the fate of Rembrandt's home, the stately dwelling in Jodenbreestraat from which he was driven because of bankrupcy in 1656; the home, subsequently divided into two, was then in a really deplorable condition.

Especially the great Rembrandt admirer Jozef Israëls worked tirelessly to establish a Rembrandt House on the exact same location. The result was that in 1911 the fully restored home was opened to the public, proof of thankful remembrance by the Dutch people.

I don't know what you think of such historic homes of famous personalities, where you can see objects like the gloves they wore, the bed in which they slept, the pen with which they wrote. We have always found them rather distasteful – so sensational and smacking of an unhealthy veneration. In Rembrandt's case we have been spared this because good taste was exercised and there are hardly any such personal items present. The Rembrandt House has real class, without pandering to a false romanticism. Not that the house is 'empty'. The fortunate decision was made to exhibit his wonderful etchings there – works otherwise only on display where a special permit has been granted, and mostly seen by only a small number of viewers. This collection of etchings is one of the largest and most complete collections of a single artist's work in the world.

To the directors of the Rembrandt House it is a real thorn in the flesh that their visitors are almost exclusively foreigners. Very few Amsterdammers set foot in the house, leaving the awe and enjoyment of such exceptional beauties to the Americans, the British, the French, the Swiss...

To stimulate interest, a 'Circle of Friends of the Rembrandt House' has been established, with free admission to the house and a bi-monthly magazine included in the membership fee. The primary goal of this organization is to raise funds for the cost of advertising in the Netherlands and for new purchases. Guided tours, evenings by candlelight and so on supply the rest.

Once a year, in the summer, a special exhibition is organized; this year its emphasis is on Rembrandt's landcape art. You can study facsimiles of drawings, original etchings from the House collection and high-quality photographs of his paintings – sufficient materials for useful comparisons. Especially instructive are the drawings and etchings, which most directly express Rembrandt's reactions to the world around him. Through them it is possible to reconstruct in unexpected ways the Amsterdam and its surroundings of his time. There are series in which Rembrandt's drawing of a certain place or area is compared with a photograph of that same place today – and it shows how much has been lost in the beauty of the landscape. Rustic spots, farms, windmills, a small town in the distance, lanes and dikes, water and bridges – we can find them all here. In the paintings, on the other hand, fantasy wins out. Wide pastures with mountains, cities and rivers, almost always presented in a dark and heavy mood, form the substance of the painted works.

It is an unrewarding task to try to critique Rembrandt's art. May the fruit of this exposition be that Dutch people – the Amsterdammers! – will stop claiming Rembrandt as the best painter of all time on the basis of what they were taught and perhaps (though not even always!) of having seen the *Nightwatch* once; rather let them claim it because they have learned to love him by seeing for themselves, again and again, these unsurpassed etchings.

• Fame and value of a great artist: Rembrandt exposition in Amsterdam[1122]

It is partly due to tradition that now, on the occasion of the Rembrandt commemoration, a large exposition has been organized in the Rijksmuseum – an exposition which will also travel to Rotterdam. But the fact that a group of very prominent museum directors and curators have enthusiastically collaborated to make this a very special event, added to the fact that they have received much cooperation from abroad, particularly from those private individuals who are in possession of Rembrandts themselves – and that these people have, almost without exception, been willing to offer a helping hand or lend a work of art – is a clear indication that here and elsewhere Rembrandt's name still has a very distinctive place. It is unimaginable that those private art collectors or the curators of those foreign museums would have been keen to part with some of the most important pieces in their collections for practically the entire summer. No, this unusual level of cooperation indicates that people are glad to be part of this Rembrandt commemoration; and that they wish to respect his reputation, not out of tradition or as an empty gesture, but genuinely and not without sacrifice.

One may wonder why it is that Rembrandt has always been so well loved all over the world. What is it that makes his work apparently universally understood and loved? For Rembrandt's art could only have originated in the seventeenth century – it is inextricably bound to his times. In addition, although he may have been an anomaly in his Dutch environment – not just because of his talent and stature, but also because of the nature of his work – his work cannot be conceived but in the local context of Amsterdam. Still, when people view Rembrandt's art they seem to require no explanations, no extensive discussions about the traditions and practices of that time, no scholarly treatises about religion or world views or art theories. That is exactly why he is able, three centuries later still, to connect with people, to appeal to them – and it goes a long way to explaining his great popularity. For it is true that there are many who speak of Rembrandt with respect, just because that is the right thing to do, but it is impossible that such an attitude or tradition could have been maintained for such a length of time unless the actual experience of becoming acquainted with his art also confirmed the qualities that it has become famous for. For that to be the case it is essential that also the uneducated and untrained viewer must be able to connect with his work and understand it. Rembrandt is an artist who has much to teach his colleagues both then and now, but no one needs to be a scholar or connoisseur to understand him.

We have established that the art of Rembrandt has a unique place in the hearts of people around the world; still, we may wonder why. What is the cause of his universal appeal? We believe that the answer is found in one single word, his *humanity*.

Certainly, if his works had not been executed with such incredible mastery, if his art did not belong, artistically speaking, to the very best of all time, then his name would not have become a household word. But when we stand before one of his paintings it is, more than any artistic or technical consideration, the pure humanity of his work that grabs and captivates us. It appeals to us in such a personal way that we feel right at home in his art. He inspires our confidence and we are not overcome by ifs and buts; his art is not problematic.

See, for example, that portrait from Munich of Hendrikje Stoffels: who would even bother to notice that she is wearing seventeenth-century clothing, or who would talk as with the Mannerists about 'a strange tension between the painted person and reality'? No, here we have a woman depicted as she really is. Rembrandt paints her with a wisdom which elucidates and touches on the richness and the unique qualities of womanhood in its essence; this painting is deeply human, without any idealizing, without hatred, but plain and full of warm affection for this fellow human being.

Or look at that wonderful piece entitled *The Holy Family with angels* – a work that most viewers will probably see here for the first time, since it is usually housed in Leningrad! We might easily forget that this is the Holy Family, because this young family is rendered so warmly human in all their joy but also anxiety. The angels look so un-angelic, more like rascal boys jumping down. Strictly speaking we have to admit that they look incongruous, even a little ridiculous. Nevertheless, we cannot deny that because they are so beautifully painted, we cannot bring ourselves to laugh at them and certainly will not make any disparaging remarks about them. Yet, though it depicts people in this familial relationship as they have appeared in all times and places, perhaps it is good to remind ourselves that this really is 'the Holy Family' – it allows Rembrandt to teach us that the holiness of Mary and Joseph had nothing to do with a supernatural aura, the scent of incense or any other worldly beauty. Rembrandt understood, as no other, what the Scriptures mean by holiness, and he depicted it with precisely such down-to-earth soberness. This is also where we see most clearly the influence of Calvinism on Rembrandt's thought and experience.

Rembrandt's art was not one-sided or restricted; something of the powerful richness of what it means to be a human being on this earth is reflected in his work. Take a look at his *Bathsheba,* his *Paul in prison,* the mighty collection of busts of the apostles from his later years, the portraits, the campfire in the night in *The flight to Egypt,* that lovely landscape from Montreal that reminds us of painters like Roelofs or J.W.A. Bilders (whose work Rembrandt certainly surpasses). Take a look at the portrait of the cavalryman, and the one of an old woman – who can take it all in with one glance, and who can fail to appreciate the rich humanness and the wisdom of life contained in them? The depth and the magnitude of our own wisdom we will find reflected in them – for our understanding can hardly reach beyond that. We have an unconscious sense that he has captured life in a wider fullness than we possess ourselves. This is exactly why, as we view these pieces, we learn from him – learn to see, learn to understand. If you really take time to study that little portrait from Stockholm of a young girl, you will learn something, gain something to take home with you. You will gain an understanding of what it means, in essence, to be a young woman – and in doing so, you will notice that time and place become irrelevant, that also the gap between 'professional' and 'amateur', between scholar and layman, disappears. Because Rembrandt's art is so entirely commonplace yet so rich that it rises far above being common.

'Rembrandt is pretty much obsolete now, isn't he?' I recently heard someone say at this exhibition. Certainly there are aspects of his art to which we can hardly relate any longer. For example, look at Saskia dressed as Flora: Rembrandt may have been too much influenced by the southern Baroque art he had seen, and by trying to translate it into the Dutch context walked the tightrope of becoming almost absurd; such a painting can really only be appreciated in a historical context, but can hardly be enjoyed. And granted, when you walk around you do encounter other pieces of lesser quality, works that have not really been successful, but perhaps this helps us to feel a little closer to Rembrandt for, despite his genius and great wisdom, we discover, he was quite human and sometimes got things wrong.

Be that as it may, the fullness of life and the humanity in Rembrandt's work assures us that he is not obsolete. It might be true that such art could never have originated in our day and age, but that is exactly why it is so crucial, culturally speaking, that he continues to be respected – for he can serve as an antidote against all the dehumanizing trends in contemporary art and lifestyles. He reminds us of sober, warm humanity that is depicted with great love – at a time when such a view of life is threatened with extinction. It is an antidote that admittedly does not do away with the ills of our time, but it may help to soften them and, in the midst of so many problems, witness to the fullness of life that we have lost. It can serve as a warning against exaggeration and schematization. Rembrandt has been called an educator of humankind. Even if he turns out to be a preserving power only, the value of his art is far greater than of artistic merit only. Also with respect to this it is a very significant exposition.

• Rembrandt as graphic artist

In 'art shops' one often sees paintings in the window that are labelled as 'oil on canvas'. Yes, in most cases that is about the only meaningful thing one can say about these concoctions. But we must ask ourselves why that phrase is used to describe this merchandise – to suggest that it is the discernment and honesty of the vendor that induces him to advertise in this way would be an overly-generous assessment. Rather, one would suspect that a certain level of quality is thought to be implied by that description; because the phrase 'oil on canvas', certainly to the Dutch, has come to suggest something valuable, worthwhile and original.

So we find in that label a reference with some universal significance. Rembrandt has become known to all as a painter, and his paintings are regarded as the epitome of his work. His drawings and etchings seem of little value in comparison. We believe that such an assessment is not typical for our time only but finds its origin in the distant past, long before Rembrandt's time. Also for him, his paintings were what he used to 'advertise' himself; they were what he presented to the public. We could draw a comparison between 'the painting' and the carefully pondered and formulated book or speech, in which the key thoughts are stated and explained. It is the official vehicle for a person with something to say by which present his or her thoughts to the public.

But the book or speech requires preparation, and notes – scribbled-down random thoughts and facts and an outline are all part of the process of preparation. The artist also needs to prepare, which is done by way of drawings. The drawing is not intended for the public – on the contrary, it is intended for private use only.

In this way, ideas and observations are noted down which may be of use when the actual work of painting has begun. This, then, is how we should view Rembrandt's drawings. And this helps us understand why we encounter an even richer world in Rembrandt's drawings than in his paintings. For there is much that he did not deem worthy enough to stand on its own as an 'oil on canvas', but that greatly interested him as studies, and that he recorded for possible future use in planning and working out the details of a landscape or a portrait. By comparing the paintings and the drawings we can gain insight into Rembrandt's different approaches to each: landscapes that directly represent a piece of actual nature are an exception in his paintings. His painted landscapes are always grandiose, poetic, with hills and valleys, vast distances and dramatic shadows, while in his sketches he recorded more factually many of the common sights, especially around Amsterdam. Also domestic scenes – women busy with their children, a man dictating a letter, a sleeping woman or a visitor at a sickbed – all are found with abundant variety in his sketches, though he did not consider them worthy of his paintbrush. Remarkable, then, how he differs from his Dutch counterparts in this regard! And next to the jotted observations are his design sketches, in which he recorded ideas that occurred to him for pictures, ideas of which some were incorporated into existing canvases or etchings and others never used again, perhaps for lack of time or perhaps because, for one reason or another, they were rejected.

So we see in Rembrandt's drawings (of which a very comprehensive exhibit of more than 270 pieces is currently showing in the Boymans-Van Beuningen Museum in Rotterdam) a greater variety, a richer vintage than we find in his paintings. Of course, these works were not intended for public viewing and therefore we also find drawings with improvements or ones that did not work so well. But even in those his genius shines through as, with just a few lines or scratches, whole worlds are called up and pictured. It is striking to see how his skills developed over the years, how he made use of the particularities of drawing by pen, for instance, with thicker lines at the beginning and thinner endings when the pen starts to run out of ink.

Look, for example, at the lion (in a late work, a landscape with Hieronymous) – the left front leg, belly and back leg are sketched in one stroke so that lifelike depth and perspective are captured. He also perfected the skill of 'washing' – an artist's term for adding a shade to a sheet of paper, covering the complete drawing with a brush stroke. Sometimes scenes suddenly become clear through this additional darkening of parts, or rather, through leaving others parts lighter. Sometimes this technique draws out the meaning of a scene, as in the drawing where the wash technique is used to heighten the threat of a brooding storm.

Rembrandt also handles chalk like no other artist, though he uses it less often than his drawing pen. Look at his elephant: whenever before has the thick, grey looseness of an elephant's hide been rendered so lifelike? It is as if, for the first time, we are made to see how it fits the animal like an oversized coat!

This series of masterly 'jottings', capturing themes that represent the wide world, cannot be passed by without great loss to anyone who wishes to better understand Rembrandt's genius. It would be impossible to mention here all the exceptional qualities of these drawings – as if it would be possible for anyone to do that in one piece of writing, no matter how extensive. One must look and discover for oneself – for example, how even just by the placement of the subject on the paper Rembrandt manages to convey so much, as in the drawing of Saskia by the windowsill: although he actually shows us no more than just the window and Saskia, it is as if we see the whole house, its height and shade, and even the whole bustling village that is observed by Saskia's eye.

There is a third 'Rembrandt' to discover, alongside the sketcher and the painter: Rembrandt the etcher. To comprehend this work, primarily intended for the connoisseur and true art lover, treasures to be kept in folders and pulled out from time to time to be admired, one must know something of the technique of etching. The artist draws, as it were, on a wax-covered copper plate, which is then dunked in an acid bath, so that the copper is 'dissolved' by the acid in all the places where the wax was scratched away. After washing, all the wax is removed, the plate is inked and an impression is made. If the artist is not pleased with the result, or if the plate becomes worn from multipe impressions and he wishes to rework or change something, he can repeat this process, as a result making several different stages of the same plate. So there is much in the art of etching that reminds us of drawing, and it will therefore not surprise us that this outstanding drawer becomes the finest etcher. Here we have artworks that were also intended for public viewing – works that were produced for the true art connoisseurs, works in which Rembrandt gave the best of his inspiration. Again we are struck by the awe-inspiring variety of subjects: landscapes composed of different natural realities or simply reflecting an actual scene, such as the stunning etch of Amsterdam as seen from a distance; beggars and domestic scenes; portraits and biblical subjects, such as many different versions of 'The flight into Egypt'. We see the small, intimate etching of a sleeping puppy, and a majestic Crucifixion – one of the most impressive works of Rembrandt's whole career. As also seen in the paintings and drawings from the period around the 1650s, this work shows the richest, deepest, greatest control of his medium. This is Rembrandt at his best – in these etchings he shines undisputably as the greatest master of all times.

Therefore we will stop trying to find ever more superlative expressions for the variety and wealth found here – superlatives start sounding commonplace in this context. We only hope that the treasures of works selected for display in the Print Gallery of the Rijksmuseum will not be passed by without due appreciation – for those who cannot appreciate the value of these small pieces are not worthy of the large paintings. Likewise, images we may have seen many times before as reproductions are found, in real life, to be a hundred times more wonderful.

• Rembrandt and the Bible

There is not a single artist who matches the popularity of Rembrandt among Calvinists. Not just because he was skilled at depicting biblical stories in such a sublime way but also because the manner in which he did this was so closely tied to his personal faith.

Although we certainly should not idealize Rembrandt – there are plenty of things we could criticize him for – we can still assert with confidence that his art conveyed a true understanding of the Scriptures.

However we may judge the man Rembrandt, we cannot deny that very few other artists have so responsibly and so vividly brought before our eyes the biblical events, and have so richly interpreted their meaning.

That is why we are so pleased to review the newly published book by J. Kalff, *Rembrandt en de Bijbel* ('Rembrandt and the Bible') (Amsterdam/Antwerp: Kosmos).

Following the biblical chronology, Rembrandt's most significant works are reproduced, accompanied by an excellent, instructive text. We are also thrilled to discover that not only his paintings but also his (unfortunately lesser known) etchings and drawings are included, for works in these genres are much less apt to lose their original character through the process of reproduction than paintings are. Also, the etchings and drawings represent some of Rembrandt's best work.

It is a real revelation, for instance, to become acquainted with the drawing *Christ on the road to Emmaus*! The etchings surprise and amaze us every time we see them, because there are always details that we missed the first time round – they present the truth in such an unadorned and genuine way.

Not only can this newly published work help us to understand better the great value and meaning of Rembrandt's work, but it may even help us understand the Scriptures more concretely.

It is a book to read and to ponder, and to come back to again and again!

• The Gospel of Rembrandt

There are few artists who have lived so closely with their open Bibles as Rembrandt did. He read the text and, with his gifted artistic imagination, visualized the scenes with his mind's eye; then he drew and etched what he saw, directly, unencumbered by traditional representations or conventions. It is precisely because he did not choose traditional biblical themes and because he was not under obligation to any church to portray commissioned subjects that we find him depicting subjects that had been (and later would be again) deemed inappropriate.

He was such a talented artist that for him it was never difficult to come up with striking compositions, which clearly tell the story and give a keen commentary on it. Thus we have this large collection of original works that render biblical themes in a fresh and meaningful way. Rembrandt viewed biblical history with a deep respect for its story but his understanding was not coloured by liturgy, doctrine or traditional holiness (which often has an otherworldly tint). He never idealized and he recognized no hierarchy, qualities that had led others, for example, to the depiction of the humble Mary delivering her child as a Queen of Heaven, dressed (in blatant contradiction with the scriptural story) in glorious array, seated on a throne, a picture of awe-inspiring beauty.

No, Rembrandt's vision was far too Protestant for this. Whether it was also a Calvinistic vision is a mute question for now: what we want to point out is that Rembrandt is the only important Dutch artist who seldomly painted or etched the daily events around him but was always dealing with the stories from Scripture and from history. There is much in his work that connects with the past, and with the world abroad, although the way in which he worked can hardly be separated from his surroundings, his times and, particularly, from Protestantism with a Calvinistic flavour.

In their unadorned beauty, honesty and faithfulness to nature, Rembrandt's etchings and drawings are unique. It is therefore a great pleasure to welcome the book *Rembrandt's Evangelie* ('Rembrandt's Gospel') (Bussum: Moussaulte, 1955), in which F. van der Meer has chosen etchings and drawings that illustrate the gospel, with appropriate words from Scripture placed alongside them. Van der Meer wrote the introduction, which briefly and clearly emphasizes the uniqueness of Rembrandt's work and does not hide the author's own Roman Catholic bias. It is a worthwhile addition to the Rembrandt section of every bookcase – or maybe the beginning of one?

• Rembrandt's pupils

If you were first to visit the huge Rembrandt expositions currently showing in Amsterdam and Rotterdam, and then to follow that up with a visit to the Lakenhal in Leiden to see the works of Rembrandt's pupils, you would probably not be going there with great expectations. What impression could those pupils possibly make, their works surely overshadowed by those of their great teacher?

You may be quite surprised, once you actually start walking around to view these pieces for yourself. It will then become clear that there is an incredible abundance of wonderful art here, and that on the whole the quality is very high. Rembrandt brought his students, through his example and his teaching, to a level which they never might have attained on their own. It is even more surprising to discover how very individual and personal their works are. Exactly because the recent Rembrandt exhibitions have offered us the possibility to discern what is typically Rembrandt, we are better equipped to recognize the personal touches that each of his students brought to their own work. If one were to see these paintings out of this context, one here and one there in a corner of a museum or as part of a larger exhibition, it would be much harder to recognize their individuality.

Ferdinard Bol was one of Rembrandt's most brilliant students. Without doubt, his portrait of a woman is one of the loveliest of this whole exhibition. How beautiful her little face with the frail, almost transparent skin; how clearly her character is revealed, not only by the expressive and clear manner in which her facial features were painted but also in the whole bearing of her figure and the particularly original play of her hands. For years this portrait was attributed to Rembrandt because of a false signature, and that fact is yet another proof of its exceptional quality!

We will not easily make such a mistake with the seventeenth-century businesswoman Bayken van Bracht, painted by Gerbrandt van den Eeckhout, for it clearly reveals the unique style of this student and close friend of Rembrandt. In both the layout of the portrait as well as its execution it deviates strongly from Rembrandt's style, although without Rembrandt's example the artist would likely never have achieved such excellence. This is truly one of the best pieces in the exhibition, an exhibition that presents us with so many lesser known works and so much unexpected beauty.

It is striking that Rembrandt's pupils almost never attempted the very marked light-dark contrasts that are so characteristic of his own work. Even Govert Flinck, during the years that he worked entirely in the style of his master's art, painted his canvases with much brighter colours and with a more uniform lighting on his subjects. Perhaps that explains why a piece like his *Isaac and Jacob* did not become a poor imitation or a failed copy of a Rembrandt, but instead became a masterpiece in its own right.

Another very gifted student of Rembrandt was Carel Fabritius. In this show we can make our acquaintance with a very unusual piece from Warsaw, which shows a much closer resemblance to Rembrandt's style than Fabritius' work usually does. Unfortunately this exhibition does not do justice to the latter's true genius, mainly because so few of his works are represented.

Besides these well-known artists, there are works by dozens more whose names are hardly known at all. Rembrandt's skill was such that he could inspire even those with only limited talents to great achievements. See, for example, the still life by Christoff Paudiss, a German who studied with Rembrandt for one year only. In the section with drawings there are also many works by such lesser-known artists.

One should definitely not skip the hall with the drawings, even if it is only to see the figure-studies by Backer, and the charming, almost unsurpassed grand Dutch landscapes by Philips Koninck.

Finally, we have to mention Aart de Gelder, Rembrandt's last pupil, who remained loyal to his teacher right into the eighteenth century. Highly original, though unmistakably influenced by Rembrandt, are his late *Scenes from the Passion*, particularly the impressive depiction of the carrying of the cross.

It seemed natural for the museum in Leiden to display at the same time some of Rembrandt's own early pieces, works that were created in this city. It is hardly the Rembrandt we have come to know and love so well.

Rather colourful, in a painting style that is still unrefined, we see the master searching for an own style. Yet these are important pieces, especially the *Flight into Egypt* from 1626, one of the oldest pieces by Rembrandt that we are aware of, and one that unmistakably shows his great talent.

• 120 Famous paintings in the Rijksmuseum[1123]

Over the past years, the Amsterdam Rijksmuseum has really spoiled us with huge and rather unique exhibitions. But not one of the exhibitions could legitimately have claimed the title of the current show from the Berlin Kaiser Friedrich Museum: '120 Famous Paintings'. For these pieces are not only of great interest to the art connoisseur and the art historian but are at the same time the works most well known and loved by the general public.

We can see the marvellous male portraits by van Eyck: *The man with the carnation*, who has an exceptionally appealing face; and Arnolfini, a less pleasant chap. Then there is a wonderful character study of Robert de Masmines painted by Campin, a contemporary of van Eyck and also an artist of superb skill. The *Portrait of a young woman* by van der Weyden, who was Campin's student, is nearly as impressive, much more so than the portrait he painted nearly twenty years later of Charles the Bold. This is truly a series of portraits that you will not quickly forget. One more portrait needs to be singled out: that of a girl by Petrus Christus, who studied under van Eyck. We may rightfully call her the Flemish 'Mona Lisa' because of her mysterious expression. The style in which she was painted reminds us of the much later painting of a girl by Vermeer because of its precise, but not fussy, brushwork and the utter simplicity of the contrasting light and shadow.

There are several landscapes by Adriaan Brouwer, exceptionally appealing and quite different from his usual style, and we appreciate them all the more for that reason. Vermeer, Terborch and de Hooch are all represented by wonderful and characteristic works: especially the famous piece entitled *The mother* by de Hooch will charm every viewer.

The masters van Dyck and Rubens are not absent either. Although the latter may not be as popular here [in the Netherlands] as elsewhere, we have to admit that he was a truly great artist, and although Van Dyck also strikes us as too courtly and theatrical at times, the beautiful and important portraits he painted in Genoa will not fail to leave a deep impression.

Then there are quite a few Rembrandts, taken from various periods during his career, but all typical representations of his much beloved style; good wine needs no commendation!

There are many more works that could be singled out for closer attention, such as the life-like portrait by Goya, the two canvases by Poussin (who is not represented by his best works here) and so forth. But we will not do that. Our goal is to whet your appetite sufficiently so that you will want to go and see for yourself – a work of art does not in the first place cry out to be described; rather, it cries out to be contemplated.

This exposition of works, which fortunately survived the War without harm, will be on view until mid-September.

• The story of the portrait in the Rijksmuseum[1124]

Exhibitions of paintings can be organized in a variety of ways. For example, a specific theme or genre can be taken as the point of departure, and one will then attempt to choose works that best illustrate the development of that theme or genre. Alternatively, works may be chosen to show the various aspects of a particular time or art-period. Or works may be selected to give an overview of the development of the art of a specific geographical area – the permanent exhibition in the Rijksmuseum which gives an overview of the best of Dutch art is a prime example of such an exhibition. Finally, it may be decided to have no real organizing principle at all but simply to display a number of works because they belong together for one reason or another. In this case the works are chosen not for any historical or art-historical purposes or because they represent a specific genre but simply on the basis of their quality and beauty. Nearly all the exhibitions that have been shown in the Rijksmuseum in recent years belong to this last genre: we were shown a specific group of paintings because they were all borrowed from the same museum. In this way we have been privileged to see a good number of very famous and exceptionally beautiful works of art.

Even though the current exhibition of 120 works taken from the Berlin Museum belongs to this last genre and we are invited to direct our attention to nothing but the beauty and quality of the paintings, we nevertheless have the privilege of seeing a series of very important portraits, together, in one place.

In the fourteenth century artists began to explore and experiment with the possibilities of portrait-making; and their work, of which very little remains today, should not be underestimated. Nevertheless, it is fair to say that it was not until the van Eycks and Campin in the early fifteenth century that the portrait came into its rightful place. These artists – all of a sudden, it seemed – discovered the right form for the portrait and started to create works of the highest quality. Although there would still come many changes after this and the portrait would undergo further developments over the succeeding generations, we can say that all these changes represent variations on a theme: the very best examples of this genre, found in the portraits by van Eyck and Campin and the early Rogier van der Weyden (which are to be seen here) have been matched by other artists, sometimes in a different style or manner, but they have never been surpassed.

A very basic requirement for any portrait is the quality of the likeness. Of course we can never judge this in the case of portraits made in the past, but we may surmise something about it, and our intuition is of great help. Another requirement which, strictly speaking, is part of the one just mentioned is that not only the outward appearance but also the spirit, character and personality of the subject should shine through in the portrait.

The earliest portraits, those by van Eyck and Campin, presented their subjects in a completely unembellished, mercilessly honest way, without idealizing or artificial beautifying. The portraits from the second half of the fifteenth century were more refined and more precise: *Charles the Bold* by van der Weyden and the portraits by Memling. The sixteenth century introduced a massive change: as a result of the Italian influence portraits now, although they appear to show more of the individual personality than the older more matter-of-fact works, give the impression of exalting and idealizing their subjects – the rich and ornate clothing, painted with utmost care, is typical in this respect. This is true especially of the Flemish pieces – the most beautiful being the one by Gossaert – which closely resemble the art of Holbein. The portraits by Cranach and Baldung Grien are quite different: what a restless, tense, forceful and incredibly dynamic figure Count von Loewenstein must have been, whose character Baldung captures so completely through the composition and layout of his portrait.

The seventeenth century brings us to the state portraits and Van Dyck. We can say in all honesty that those portraits from his earlier years include some striking character sketches. What do you think of the friendly, extremely sharp, Genoese woman sitting like a queen in all her splendour? The portraits by Rembrandt takes us into the lives of ordinary citizens with a simplicity which, in the beautiful portrait of Hendrikje Stoffels, is combined with tenderness and love that could only have come from an artist with a strong personal interest in his subject.

Finally, consider the magnificent portrait of an old woman, attributed here to Goya although it is not at all certain that he painted it – a worthy conclusion to the series with its unmistakable likeness, unembellished and almost mercilessly honest!

• Three centuries of portraits in the Rijksmuseum[1125]

The portrait is a typically Dutch art form. Not that good, high-quality portraits have never been painted elsewhere but then, as a rule, the portrait served as the dignitary's official state portrait. It had another purpose and was often painted mainly to emphasize the importance or nobility of its subjects – the portrait often either idealized the person or placed him or her on a pedestal in some other way.

In our own [Dutch] portrait art the key features are truth, lack of ostentation, and soberness . For that reason the Dutch portraits, which have sometimes been dubbed 'burgher art' (a name we should consider an honour), are so full of life and so varied. They do not stereotype and are without the embellishments that lead only to emptiness.

A beautiful exposition of portraits of Dutch families is on display in the Rijksmuseum until 3 October. It is striking how often the subjects seem very familiar to us.

The exhibition has many surprises. Because there is an agreement not to borrow art from other Dutch museums, unfamiliar works are on display that have not been shown before. That makes for many delightful surprises even though one might miss a few favourites, perhaps a little grudgingly.

What a revelation is the wonderful portrait of the family Berensteyn, of which the husband and wife had already been depicted by Frans Hals some years earlier. And there is a portrait of perhaps the ugliest man who ever lived, the painter Lairesse. Could it be the epitome of artistic skill, to be accomplished only by a master like Rembrandt, to depict such a person in all his ghastliness and yet end up with a beautiful painting? It is one of the most wonderful works in the whole show.

For that matter, Rembrandt is represented here with an unparalleled collection, including a number of less familiar pieces. The portrait of a woman reading, for example, belongs among his unsurpassed creations. Then we have the friendly girl leaning on a windowsill. One feels convinced that you know her from somewhere, that you have met her before. And then you notice that it was painted in 1645.

Jan de Bray's portrait may depict the most impressive woman of all these ancestors of ours. If this is your first acquaintance with her, you will long remember it. Amazing that the artists can manage to make us feel so close to all of these people!

It is interesting to notice how the proportions of portraits began to change during the eighteenth century. Increasingly people were painted as sitting in a large room, with space to move about freely without being cramped, very different from the 'close-ups' of the past. A number of exceptionally fine pieces were painted during that period, though on the whole their quality does not compare with the seventeenth-century works. But a painter like Troost should not be overlooked. We are also particularly delighted with the exceptionally high quality of the portrait of a woman by the virtually unknown Tace Scheltema. It forms a worthy conclusion to this exhibition, flanked as it is by the extremely impressive painting by Hodges of Revd Jona Willem te Water, who first served a church in Vlissingen and later became a professor in Leiden.

• Rubens and Antwerp

Holland is known as the land of Rembrandt, but in many respects Rembrandt is a stranger in this country, with little of his work to be seen here. In contrast, to call Flanders the land of Rubens is saying something of real substance. Rubens' work can be seen in almost every church one visits there, in every museum one enters. Moreover, one sees the influence and impact of his work in nearly every piece of art produced since his time. There is no need to visit a museum to observe this, for it is evident on the streets, in the city squares, in the public decorations and in the general proportion of things – one could almost claim to smell it in the air. We can say without exaggeration that Rubens has made Flanders what it is today.

The Dutch have some difficulty in appreciating Rubens. We find him too full of pathos, too short on humility; and we do not like his grand stance. To us he is not down-to-earth enough; he oversteps the boundaries of proper human behaviour. The grandeur and the lifestyle that appears to lack intimacy, despising the commonplace and freely indulging in sensual pleasures, revelling in the superhuman interplay of gods and goddesses, supermen and superwomen in every respect – these things do not go down well with us. We do not appreciate his style which elevates the revered saints so far above ordinary humans and, at the same time, bestows on them outward appearances and gestures characteristic of Rubensian daydreams.

Yet, those who have noticed the way these things have left their stamp on the way of life in Flanders and those who have immersed themselves in Rubens' own work know that this is not just a show; it is genuine and intentional. This was the world view and the way of life of a reinvigorated Roman Catholicism that also created space for humanism to deepen and develop. The reality of the stylized life, the truth of the grandiose gesture, the familiarity of these human figures who seem at first glance to be far too hallowed, are all to be found in Rubens' drawings.

Now Antwerp, the city on the River Schelde, which in her whole appearance testifies all too clearly to a love of her greatest son, wanted to honour him even more and have done so with an exhibition of his drawings in the Rubens House. Seldom has such a comprehensive collection of his drawings, representing all the stages of his development, been assembled in one place, taking into account also the latest discoveries in the field of Rubens scholarship.

We see here a series of drawings from his earliest period that has never been exhibited before, from when at the age of twenty he immersed himself in German woodcarvings and the paintings of old Flemish masters and copied some of the figures from them. There are drawings from his time in Italy, copies of works by Michelangelo, Raphael and Leonardo [da Vinci], and particularly of classical works. It was in Italy where he learned to see people in a new way, and the studies from nature show how this style became completely part of him.

Although, in observing these drawings, there can be no doubt that they represent the models, we notice that from the outset he stylized the human body to be more muscular, more beautiful, than it really is – more classical and ideal than the real, not-so-Olympian body. The drawings by Rembrandt, viewed in the same way, record the human body in a very down-to-earth way and technically very different.

There are also the sketches that record the initial inspiration for Rubens' large compositions. But the drawings which interest us most, apart from art-historical considerations, are the studies in which he pays close attention to each individual figure, such as the live drawings made in preparation for the huge works currently hanging in the Antwerp Cathedral, works that brought fame to this young painter returning from Italy. The technique he developed for this kind of drawing is outstanding, making effective use of black, red and white chalk on tinted paper. Over the years, Rubens' command of this technique improved, and eventually reached its climax in the beautiful sketches for the painting entitled *Garden of love*. Grandiose, improbably stylish, and yet far too realistic to be called a work of fantasy, a young man in a flowing robe strides down the stairs, and men and women indulge without embarrassment in life's sensual pleasures.

Yet more extraordinary is his close fusion of reality and stylizing, of grand living alongside the ordinary workaday world, in his drawings of landscapes, animals – powerful cows that still manage to look like cows – and farmers and their wives at work. Extraordinary, especially because we have so much Dutch art available for comparison. When viewing these marvellous Rubens drawings, one must admit that this master presented ordinary people in all their boorish existence without turning them into bloodless Arcadian shepherds, something that other Baroque and classical artists have often been guilty of. But we also sense, from the whole way in which he sings the praise of these people, that he perceives them and their land with the idealistic eye of the aristocrat, and that his dream of life elevates them imperceptibly above the mundane. As Dutch folk we simply cannot identify with such a fusion of observation and stylization, of simplicity and flourish. However, it does show that Rubens was not playing a game or posturing; he simply expressed life as he knew it.

The large exposition entitled 'Scaldis' (Schelde) shows us clearly how much Rubens contributed to the character of the city of Antwerp. In attempting to present an overview of all the art and culture of this city, many widely divergent pieces were assembled together.

It is a remarkable exposition which, as a direct result of its too widely divergent limits and its impossible attempt to be comprehensive, gives a curious impression. At times it feels as if one has ended up in a junk-filled attic, until one looks more closely and sees that what has been assembled is not that bad, and that after all there is some organizing principle. At other times one seems to stumble from one surprise to the next. For example, at one moment one is confronted with a gorgeous, completely unexpected masterpiece like a lovely golden chalice, only the next moment to be looking at half-faded photographs of a cheap-looking stained-glass window. Then again, one suddenly comes across an absolutely arbitrary group of ten sixteenth-century paintings, including several masterpieces as well as a passable copy. And there are five beautiful Rubens paintings to grab one's attention, as well as a complete series of tapestries he designed, which in themselves make a trip to the exhibition worthwhile. But to see those five paintings, one had to first walk around a showcase with . . . alas, we forgot to look.

It is a grand effort to gather together 1100 pieces with the purpose of portraying an entire bygone era – and in that grand gesture too we see a little of Rubens' mind as it still inspires the Schelde city. Why would it surprise us that in their bold effort to display everything – furniture, cannons, architecture, sculpture, fine ironwork, tapestries, chests, prints, drawings, chasubles, book bindings and so on – a few mistakes crept in?

In short, this is an exposition which would be unimaginable in our own country, where our perfectionism will never honour a gesture unless it has also proved to be completely responsible. But what we see here is alive and true, sincere and authentic; and why shouldn't we allow ourselves to be carried from one marvel to the next, so that, maybe just for once, we too can experience the fullness of life evidenced in Rubens' drawings?

• The Venetian art of painting

Changes in art sometimes take place gradually, over a number of years; at other times a new trend with a completely different character suddenly rears its head. The latter will be the case when there is a spiritual revolution that has repercussions in the world of art (as is happening today); the former will be the case when the development is determined more by purely artistic considerations, by the creative force of genius and talent. This development will reflect changes in mentality and attitudes in society at large, but there is no sudden transition from one stage to another; rather, each stage seems to follow on from strains that were slumbering in the previous one.

Such a gradual but significant change seems to have taken place during the five centuries that Venetian art flourished. If you take a look at the *Madonna* by Paolo Venetiano, painted in 1347, and exhibited in the first hall of this exhibition, and then (and this can be done if you're standing in just the right spot) glance over your shoulder at the large work by Tiepolo, *The death of Hyacinthus*, painted around 1750, you will notice a powerful contrast and profound differences between the two. But if you follow the gallery trail, from hall to hall, observing the progressive developments and stages as they are shown, beginning with the Venetiano piece and ending with the Tiepolo, you will hardly notice any break in the continuity.

We start with the art of Paolo Venetiano, Guariento and others, which continues to build on the Byzantine tradition. Then for a short period a Northern influence is seen, in the much more brightly coloured artworks by Jacobello del Fiore. Next comes the grand works by the Vivarinis and, especially, Crivelli. A single thread leads from those early beginnings to Crivelli, regardless of the various outside influences which served as stimulants or catalysts.

Crivelli's period, in turn, overlapped with that of Giovanni Bellini, the great master, who started off in a style very similar to Crivelli's but gradually changed to a completely different artistic style, the same style in which Titian started off his artistic career. Bellini is a typical representative of Venetian art: he absorbed many different influences but always incorporated them completely into his own style, so that his art did not lose its own distinctive character. An exception to this pattern might be Giorgione, that remarkable genius who died at such a young age and unfortunately is not represented here at all so that we cannot appreciate his innovative work. But we discern his influence in the works of Titian, especially in the beautiful portrait and in the piece called *Noah's drunkenness*, which is here attributed to Bellini.

Elsewhere in sixteenth-century Italy, Mannerism reigned; but in Venice the artistic community was unaffected and continued untroubled by the tensions that caused Mannerism to flourish. Art from elsewhere – the Florentine art of Raphael and Michelangelo, and the Flemish landscapes – added influences to the work of the great painters Titian and Tintoretto, and joyful, appealing works were created by Veronese and Bassano, who was more attracted to genre and landscape painting. Venetian art continued in its own direction; in the works of someone like Tintoretto this led to art which can be classified only as Baroque. By becoming acquainted with this art one gets a better understanding of the renewal that took place elsewhere at the beginning of the seventeenth century. The art of the Bolognese pioneers of Baroque could certainly find an immediate connection here.

However, when it actually came to that stage, Venice no longer produced artists of great talent. Instead, the German Liss and the Florence-educated Roman Reti now determined Venetian style – both (and particularly the former) being artists of great historical significance. Maffei, the Riccis and the Genoese Strozzi gave Venetian art in the remainder of the seventeenth century its own distinctive style, one tone in the wonderful symphony of Baroque art. However, during the eighteenth century Venice once again entered a period of greatness, through the works of widely diverse artists such as Tiepolo, Piazetta, Canaletto and Guardi. Tiepolo surely must be the greatest painter of all times of internal decoration. His influence reached far beyond Venice, to France, Germany and even Spain.

Piazetta's art, his sensitive handling of light and the beautiful peacefulness, appeals to us Dutch – he has even been called an Italian 'Vermeer'. Canaletto's cityscapes are strongly reminiscent of works by our own van der Heyden and in their genre are matched in excellence only by his works and that of Berckheyde. Guardi, with his streak of Rococo and his peculiar romanticism, is an unparalleled artist of distinction.

With this last blossoming, Venice's role is played out: sic transit gloria mundi. Today Venice has become a tourist attraction because of its wealthy heritage of art, with the 'Biennale' – its biennial international modern art exhibition – as a major attraction.

• The French landscape

Every year since the War has ended we have been spoiled with magnificently large art exhibitions in the Rijksmuseum. This year again, we are pleasantly surprised with an exposition entitled 'The French Landscape'. The display has been set up in a particularly enjoyable way, with a brilliant construction of the exhibition area to give the visitor the best possible opportunity to view and enjoy the paintings. And what an incredible variety we find here! Limiting the show to just one genre certainly has not resulted in monotony nor in a dull uniformity.

Most interesting to the Dutch public will undoubtedly be the canvases by Poussin. This seventeenth-century classicist may not have had a smooth touch, but his work is certainly not cold or lifeless. The strength of his work lies in the stunning construction of his compositions. We seldom see paintings with such a vast sense of space and depth, and with such a balanced sense of calm. Perhaps the loveliest is the landscape with Phocion, a canvas one never tires of looking at. The differences between Poussin and his contemporary Le Lorrain, who is often perceived to be Poussin's opposite, do not seem to be that great in the works exhibited here, although Le Lorrain's works are poetic in a completely different way.

Among the drawings especially those by Fragonard stand out. One can describe them only in a sort of lyrical way, if one is to capture something of their unique atmosphere. Fragonard was not an innovator or pioneer but an artist who knew how to use the best of the contemporary style to the greatest advantage.

In the special hall devoted to Watteau and his followers, this master gives evidence of the superior quality of his works, though the pieces shown here are not even among his best. Of the other eighteenth-century artists represented (besides Fragonard, whom we have already mentioned), we are especially drawn to the magnificent art of Hubert Robert and the landscapes by Moreau, who is exceptionally well represented in this exhibition.

From the works in the subsequent halls, we realize that the older French landscape art had quite a different style from Dutch landscape art. No rendering of reality for reality's sake, no effort to capture typical characteristics of the landscape and its atmosphere here, as we find in the Dutch works. Rather, there is here a kind of rhetoric in the best sense of the word – dreams of a classical, ideal world (as in Poussin's works), or of landscapes perfectly suited to the playful picnics that Watteau painted so lyrically, or of romantic strolls between lovely ancient buildings, as in the works by Robert.

In the works from the nineteenth century the influence of our own seventeenth-century landscape art becomes apparent again. A fresh wind starts to blow, and grass once more becomes real grass. No longer does it look like a lush carpet for tender feet but more like fodder for cows. No longer are we carried away to landscapes of poetic imagination, but we are taken outdoors to enjoy the beauty of the real world around us. Some of the art retains a certain lyricism, however, like those panoramas by Corot.

Then come the Impressionists, who wanted to capture the essence of sunlight on their canvases, and who introduced a much brighter palette. (Take a moment to compare the colour-values of the paintings in the first hall with those in the last!) Finally we have the reaction to that Impressionism, an anti-realism that gradually led to the modern art movement. We see Cézanne come close to this; his last works from the early twentieth century are starting to resemble the painting techniques of Cubists like Picasso.

This exhibition invites one to look, study, reflect and, above all, to enjoy.

• Swiss graphic art in the Print Gallery of the Rijksmuseum[1126]

To most people mention of Switzerland evokes images of mountains, valleys and cozy chalets – in short, the ideal vacation spot. The unique place that Switzerland holds in the history of art is much less familiar. If we leave aside the not insignificant contributions from the Middle Ages, we see that in the early sixteenth century Swiss art flourished. As far as form was concerned, this fantastic, almost wild sort of art, fierce and impassioned, built on the innovations of masters like Dürer.

The graphic art of men such as Urs Graf or Niklaus Manuel Deutsch which is now on display in the Print Gallery of the Rijksmuseum gives us a good impression of this. Their ingenious woodcuts display not classical calm but, instead, a tempestuousness that we really cannot call anything but expressionistic.

Particularly characteristic is the woodcut by Urs Graf which presents us with a snapshot image of these extremely turbulent times, when the Swiss mercenary foot-soldiers often played the deciding role in wars. We see two of these fashion-conscious fighters in full array, with a woman on the left and Death, as always, lurking in the trees above. More than ever, death held a fascination for the writers and painters of this era – see the famous *Dance of Death* by Hans Holbein the Younger, who as a Basle artist still counted as being Swiss. The small prints on display here, almost miniatures, have value far beyond that indicated by their mere size; they are also superior to the countless pieces created in similar vein. Perhaps it is not such pleasant art because of the subject matter; yet, it is true to life. There is an almost exalted humour as the artist appears to spy on Death, carrying away prelates and pompous dignitaries.

From the seventeenth-century pieces we are drawn to the topographic works by, amongst others, the master of this genre, Mattheus Merian the Elder. His cityscapes depict reality very accurately but without becoming boring or failing to capture the beauty of the landscape. This tradition was subsequently continued in drawings that focused more and more strictly on nature scenes, showing very specific mountains, streams and such, and finally leading to a rather dry, lifeless art with little depth of meaning.

Holbein celebrated his greatest triumphs in England, as did the famous son of Merian the Elder, mentioned above. Also the eighteenth-century Fussli, who worked in the spirit of those expressionists of the sixteenth century, created the major part of his strange, tormented repertoire of art in London. These fiery, impassioned works are the complete opposite of the remarkably idyllic pieces created by Salomon Gessner that were so characteristic of pre-Romanticism.

The nineteenth century, as we already pointed out, offered little but decline. After that, with the start of our own [twentieth] century, we find once again a worthy Swiss artist in Hodler, whose impressive *Student putting on his coat* (the title does not sound nearly as memorable as the painting is) is important enough to earn him a lasting name.

All these works, and much more, is currently on display in the exposition room of the Print Gallery in the Rijksmuseum.

•Drawings from two centuries in the Rijksmuseum[1127]

The Rijksmuseum in Amsterdam currently has two different collections of drawings on display: in the Print Gallery there is the collection belonging to A. Staring; and in the halls of the Archaeological Society you can see the collection owned by C. P. van Eeghen. The latter contains drawings of Amsterdam; the former concentrates on eighteenth-century Dutch art.

The art of the seventeenth century was indeed in every respect realistic, but it is striking that in their very penetrating depictions of seventeenth-century life in all its facets, these artists seldom tried to capture reality in a photographically accurate way. The artist remained an artist, always composing his art in a very personal way, building reality into his painting in a way that was certainly related to the actual subject but never just a copy of it. In seventeenth-century art, artistry and Realism forged an unbreakable bond. This unity between art and reality, which was largely responsible for the excellence of our [Dutch] seventeenth-century art, started to fall apart towards the end of the century. The two elements began, as it were, to drift apart.

With utmost precision artists subsequently attempted to represent their own reality, the world around them, which in van Eeghen's collection happens to be Amsterdam, and in Staring's collection, Dordrecht (see particularly the painting by Schouman of the house just outside Dordrecht!) as well as some other places. We find that during this period events were depicted in a narrow, realistic way, for example in the painting by Schouman of the unloading of a whaling ship at the Groothoofdkade in Dordrecht, or in the reception of William IV in Maassluis, painted by Paul van Liender. When these artists painted animals or plants the precise biological and scientific details became of prime importance. One might say that these artists, sensing somehow that the wonderful unity between artistry and reality had been lost, tried to win back something of it by attributing artistic value to the subject itself and glorifying it.

It is ironic that precisely because of this search to preserve a beautiful reality through idealizing the subject, adding lustre to the stones through colouring, the close resemblance to real life that was the great strength of seventeenth-century art, the richness of reality was lost. It became a superfluous reality, losing touch with reality because of its precision, being too lovely, too picturesque. You can see this touch of idealized unreality in the drawing by Schouman of a woman playing the mandolin.

Around 1800 artists began to recognize this; and in reaction to all the dolled-up prettification and affectation they began to cast back to seventeenth-century art. It can be clearly seen in the works of van Strij, van Hulswit and van Schotel (whose *Arrival of the British on the Merwede* has an entirely different character from other eighteenth-century drawings of similar subjects), not to bypass Barbiers, whose rich landscapes are permeated with an ambience of truth.

Romanticism followed soon thereafter, bringing with it its own unique way of transmitting dreams into reality. The Staring collection shows us a few examples of this as well.

We hope that our comments have not served to discourage you from going to see this exhibition, because the drawings of de Beyer, Jacob Cats, both artists van Liender, van Drielst and others are really very beautiful, and certainly warrant a trip to the museum.

• Gainsborough in Bath

One could say that portraiture is the true national art of the British. It's remarkable, however, that prior to the eighteenth century it was mostly foreigners who set the tone. Hans Holbein worked at the Tudor court in the sixteenth century and established a tradition which continued until the seventeenth century, when van Dyck started a completely new, highly refined style of portraiture. Artists continued working in this style, maybe because its refinement, and perhaps also its tendency to idealize, satisfied the demands of the formal lifestyle of the socialites of high society. Anglicized Dutchmen like Lely and Hanneman took on many commissions in that vein.

Not until the eighteenth century, and continuing to show influences from the tradition established by Van Dyck, a style of portraiture developed that sprang from England's own soil. Reynolds and Gainsborough, in particular, set the tone for a tradition that still continues today.

We had the privilege, during a recent visit to Bath, of seeing a large series of family portraits in several English country homes. We wish to mention Wilton House, where a whole series of Van Dyck portraits is to be seen; a beautiful hall was especially furnished and decorated for this purpose around the year 1650.

Gainsborough worked for many years (from 1758 to 1774) in Bath. This explains why it was decided to include an exhibition of his works during the Festival of Britain. Although the exhibition is by no means comprehensive, it well illustrates both the strengths and weaknesses of his art.

Negatively, one notices the inconsistent quality of his work that resulted from accepting too many commissions. Positively, one is struck by his wonderful painting technique, wherein with just a few strokes of his brush he can give shape to his figure; the fine nuances of colour, sometimes silvery in tone, but always transparent and warm, with a bit of red introduced skilfully at times to give depth and radiance to the whole; the refined shaping of the faces, paintings seemingly composed with great ease.

The *William Poyntz* of 1762 shows Gainsborough's typical style, painted a few years after he took up residence in Bath. We see how this sportsman leans against a tree, a characteristic pose for him. The man appears somewhat bored and arrogant, not because of the way he is painted but because that is how he is. The painter has portrayed him keenly, be it perhaps somewhat unsympathetically.

Another canvas of exceptional quality is the portrait of Gorrick, the great eighteenth-century Shakespearean scholar and also a friend of Gainsborough. What an accurate portrayal!

The portrait of Gainsborough's wife is more friendly, a lovely painting and one of the high points in this genre. There is the large canvas entitled *Lady Molyneux*, which simultaneously connects with the great Van Dyck tradition in its posture and attitude but, without the idealizing tendency, penetratingly characterizes its subject – one of the finest works in this exposition.

But let's leave the portraits for now and pay some attention to Gainsborough's skill as a landscape painter. In this domain England never really established its own style, so he connects with the Dutch school – though it could also be said that after its decline in the Netherlands, this art form was further developed in England. That Gainsborough was inspired by Ruysdael, Hobbema, Wijnants and others, can be clearly seen in his earlier works. But he became increasingly romantic, until he arrived at works that have become so typical of the British landscape genre, seen in this exhibition, for example *A market cart crossing a brook*. Like water-colours, very lightly brushed, romantic and maybe even sentimental in style, these paintings focus on the 'picturesque' (a word that originates from this period) – still, these are stunning pieces.

Landscapes, explored and copied by many artists of varying skill, was circulated around the world as one of the most typically British art products. Half a century later, Berrington and Constable developed a new kind of landscape art; Constable, especially, became a significant inspiration for the Barbizon school of painters and also for the school in the Hague. However, they never fully succeeded in pushing aside the older, more sentimentally-romantic genre.

• Goya's accusations

Fransisco de Goya was a celebrated artist in the circles of the nobility and the royal court in Spain during the late eighteenth century; and deservedly so, for his portraits are masterpieces in the history of art. Also his tapestries, religious paintings for churches and so on, should not simply be by-passed. On the contrary, all of these demonstrate his great genius. Events at the end of the eighteenth century, however, had such a profound effect on Goya that his art took on a completely different tone. For Goya was in close contact with people who, to an extent, supported the principles of the Revolution; at the same time he developed a serious illness which left him deaf.

As a result, Goya developed the distinct style for which he has become even more famous than for his skill as an accomplished painter of nobility. He created a series of etchings, *Caprichos*, and painted several smaller works in which he allowed his imagination free rein. Then, shortly after the turn of the century, new terrors seized Spain – wars which involved Spain, England and Napoleon. The waves of misery, the unruled passions – all these made a deep impression on Goya. Previously accepted principles and ideals crumbled; Goya observed a humanity after the Fall, stripped of pretence and idealistic slogans. Undoubtedly Goya saw and experienced these things so intensely because it was also a time of personal crisis for him, a time which brought into question all the values he had held dear. In this spirit he created his famous series of etchings *Desastros de la Guerra* ('The disasters of war'). He painted powerful works that expressed the misery, futility, capriciousness and brute force of the unrestrained passions that ruled the day.

But perhaps most clearly Goya's spirit and clear vision shine through in the etchings and in the dozens of drawings, some of which were actually preparatory sketches, which remained unused and unpublished. One seldom has opportunity to view these pieces and therefore the exhibition now on show at the Boymans-Van Beuningen Museum in Rotterdam is a very special event. The person who thinks art has a right to exist only when it is pretty and sweet, that art is only something to 'enjoy', should stay away. This art is powerful, disturbing and gruesome – though not in the sensational way of a horror story – and viewing this art is not an 'enjoyment' but an experience.

It is remarkable that in these drawings Goya does not use the easy, flowing drawing style that he used in his earlier years – a style he had in common with many of his contemporaries. One hardly dares to declare that these works are 'skilfully drawn', much less that they are 'beautiful'. On the contrary, although one could certainly criticize their technique or aesthetic value, one senses immediately that such a critique would be out of place here, for this art clearly derives from the artist's struggle to realize his vision, to give shape to that which has never been expressed before.

It is a world full of terror and cruelty, an unapologetic acting out of the basest passions; a world full of bizarre events in which every imagined horror can become reality and everything which is precious can be assaulted, where reality is more frightening than a nightmare. This is Goya's art; these are his visions, his inner experiences. These are not childish or meaningless fantasies, one has to admit, but deeply human realities confronting the viewer. However unbridled these fantasies might appear to the superficial observer, and some may appear to be nothing more than pictured hallucinations, still one senses constantly how closely they represent real life. That makes this art so gruesome for some, and so compelling and meaningful for others. This is no 'playful fantasy'; it is real, true, and deeply human.

Is it true? Maybe too true – for it shows human beings as they are now, after the Fall. It shows people's most intimate emotions; it shows us the secret depths of our own hearts. It may be only half true, for the way to deliverance from all this suffering is neither shown nor suggested. In Goya's art we read the naked truth about our world, unembellished and without easy solutions. And the inescapable accuracy of his vision gives these works a timeless quality, free from any specific historical references – a lasting message to us all for, in the words of Goya (as found in the title of one of his drawings), *Siempre sucede*, 'This happens all the time.'

Nineteenth Century

• Romantic painting: entitled to more recognition and a little fame

Without becoming embroiled in the origins and definition of the word 'romantic', we must note that the painted art of the early nineteenth century is indeed Romantic in its sensitivity and sometimes slight sentimentality, in its hankering after and obsession with the past and its willingness to transport us back into it. But when it offers us a glimpse back into the seventeenth century it is not the heroic and magnificent, as displayed in the conflicts of that time, that it depicts but rather a gentle, homely friendliness. Yes, whatever else you might say about it, this is friendly art.

It is not so long ago that the Romantic school was viewed with nothing but scornful disdain, characterized as 'those artists with their flat, lifeless pictures'. Without being so ungracious as to put to the test the 'richness of life' of such detractors (Yes, certainly their own art was different, but did it really communicate so much more depth?) one thing is certain: their judgment was too harsh and not entirely fair. Our critique should be based on a thorough consideration, after honest confrontation with the actual works, so that these works may be allowed to take their own, perhaps modest yet honourable place amongst the art of all the ages.

We have a good opportunity to do this at the exposition by the art dealer P.A. Scheen (in Zeestraat, The Hague). What a rich ambience we find in A. Eversen's *Winter in Enkhuizen*! How he manages to let us feel the piercing cold as well as the lovely winter sunshine. How beautifully it is painted, what a carefully controlled technique! Leickert is another master whose name must not be forgotten; his watercolour has much depth. How lovely is the still life of the farmyard interior by R. Vis, the exquisite rendering of the torn fabric of the jacket!

The much-reviled Ary Scheffer has pleasant surprises for those who take the time to look for them, as seen in the watercolour represented here. Fresh and pleasing is A.J. van Wijngaerdt's forest path with figures. It is impossible and pointless to ennumerate them all. Most of these artists were lost from memory after the sharp change in public art taste some seventy-five years ago. But alongside Schelfhout and Koekkoek there were others, like Leickert, who have the right to more recognition and a little fame.

• The Romantic painting

Many writers have pointed out that Romanticism is an indefinable concept, a cultural-historical notion that cannot be captured in words. One of the reasons for this is that there are different kinds of Romanticism, or rather that this name is used to describe various trends that share few similarities. Many who have read something about Romanticism will be amazed to see something quite different from what they expected when they view Dutch Romantic painting for the first time.

For in these paintings they will find none of the baroqueness, the fanaticism, the heroism, the overly sentimental approach that are sometimes perceived as the hallmarks of Romanticism. Remarkably, they may find more of that sentimental adoration of nature (which certainly can be called truly 'romantic') in the works of the eighteenth-century Dutch artists who are not even labelled as Romantics. We think, for example, of Janson and van Os whose works from the collection of the well-known art dealer Scheen are now being shown in the Old Wevershuys in Amersfoort.

What then was our nineteenth-century Romantic art? One could call it a late blooming of our seventeenth-century art. One could also call it Biedermeyer, a trend towards peaceful conventionality with no heroical or revolutionary élan, a simple, cosy, sober busying of self with ordinary matters of the day. It could be called 'smug', and certainly sometimes was, but it doesn't have to be perceived like that.

See, for example, that beautiful landscape by Schelfhout – a rare work that acquaints us with this master from the very unusual and special perspective of a quiet path through the woods, a view of the river on the left, a few people conversing – an idyllic picture of what many of us would hope to find when we go on vacation. Rest, pleasant warmth, a rural atmosphere, the scent of woods – these things can hardly be called 'romantic'; rather, they represent common, everyday, unheroic longings. We think too of the panorama painted by the young Roelofs during the same period, reminiscent on the one hand of the great Philips de Koninck and on the other hand, reminding us of the calm, pleasant utopia we long for during times of extreme stress and busyness.

We could also point to Verveer, a rare master who stands head and shoulders above his contemporaries with his beautiful and rigorously constructed compositions. What a little masterpiece of his is exhibited here! It is remarkable and intriguing that his composition is more reminiscent of Poussin than of our great seventeenth-century artists, not to mention his own contemporaries. The work by B.C. Koekkoek shown here was painted a year later and is worthy of our full attention. Too often he is undervalued because the many counterfeits attributed to him exceed the number of genuine works he painted. In this painting, more than in works by any of his already mentioned contemporaries, we find a tendency to idealize, a preference for what is exotic, ancient and mysterious. His works again and again contain capricious old oak trees. However, his paintings do not show groups of old Germans cutting each other up or swearing allegiance to one another; just a traveller on horseback, some cows, a few shepherdesses – so simple. We still have to mention the Waldorp painting, more expressive than the works already mentioned, but still emphasizing peacefulness and the beauty of the ordinary. The fact that he did not choose 'beauty spots' but rather his own regular surroundings suggests that he may be called more modern, ahead of his time.

Appreciation is growing for the works by these nineteenth-century artists. It is inevitable, for quality and clear vision will not for ever be silenced or pushed into a corner; high quality art will, even if only in the long run, always be appreciated and loved. The Hague art dealer Scheen has played an active role in raising interest in this art by carefully researching and sorting the works, and (do not underestimate this!) by continually discovering new works to surprise viewers like ourselves again and again with hitherto unknown masterpieces of lesser known works. There are many pieces here that have never before been exhibited. Amersfoort and its surrounding towns should respond with thanks to the initiative of the Old Wevershuys.

• Romantic works from the nineteenth century[1128]

There is ultimately only one conclusive argument that justifies the existence, and the significance and meaning, of a work of art: the artwork itself. Our opinions and theories may be helpful, but in the long run the work itself must be able to bear the scrutiny of a quiet, unbiased consideration. Unfortunately it is essential that we include the phrase 'unbiased consideration', because how often does it not happen that we already know ahead of time how we are going to judge a particular piece of art . . . in a spirit of 'This is the opinion that I am supposed to have if I am anybody at all.'

It is an all too common cliché that our Romantic (nineteenth-century) art, with the exception of the school of The Hague, is rather mediocre, a bit tame, rather uninspired and without any real meaning. Well, it is certainly true that a great deal of second-rate art was produced during that era, but has there ever been an era when that was not the case? On the other hand, it is equally true that the high-quality pieces produced during that period are superb, and that exactly the characteristics often quoted to justify our contempt for this art are also the characteristics that give it its greatest charm – namely, its sense of peacefulness and balance.

The fact that peace and rest can turn into lethargy and dullness is no basis for judging these works. As a matter of fact, such a critique will quickly vanish when these works are viewed. For the truth is that this art deserves the highest praise for the carefully controlled craftsmanship and expert touch of the artists.

The current exposition in the Van Looy Museum displays a large number of really excellent pieces from that period. It gives a representative impression and hopefully inspires viewers to reconsider how they evaluate the works from that time.

It is curious that this period has, on the whole, been so poorly researched. That may be one reason why we have so little appreciation for the unique and innovative touches that characterize its art (while at the same time, we should not deny the strong influences of our seventeenth century). But the innovations of that time often originated as a result of foreign influences, particularly that of the English painters Lawrence, Bonington (in the works of Nuyen) and Constable, and the influence of genre painting. These influences should not be ignored and cannot easily be overestimated.

It is nearly impossible for us to comment on every piece. Instead we will restrict ourselves to a selection of the most important ones. Nuyen's cityscape of 1837 is outstanding because of its strong atmosphere and the powerful brushwork. Schelfhout is best known for his icy winter scenes, of which there are lovely examples here. His ability to move beyond that genre is evident from the exceptionally skilful painting of sand dunes with a lighthouse, unadorned in its simplicity and truth, with the colour harmonies well balanced in the overall composition. Pieneman's superb self-portrait clearly shows British influences – painted during this period but outside the Netherlands. The trend-setting French Romantics were also largely influenced by British trends. Bilders, who actually already belongs to the following generation, shows that he was clearly influenced by both Constable and Nuyen as well as the Fountainebleau painters, especially Rousseau. Similar French influences are seen in Roelofs' work; he was one of the first to acquaint the Netherlands with this French school of painting, even though the fresh, lovely landscape with animals that we see here cannot be imagined apart from Constable's example. For a long time Leckert worked in the 'Romantic' style and his art reminds us strongly of that of his teacher, Nuyen, especially the style of his cityscapes.

We could mention many more paintings but prefer to turn our attention now to the beautiful series of drawings. Such a large number is seldom seen in one single exhibition. Springer's cityscapes are magnificent. Koekkoek excels with his lively winter scenes (how curious that there was such a preoccupation with snow and ice scenes during this period).

Of Schelfhout's work there are both some quick sketches as well as more elaborately worked-out drawings, which give clear evidence of his great talents. Although Schotel's paintings are often boring, he shows great accomplishment in his drawings. There is much more to see, of course, but this series of drawings alone already makes the trip to the Kleine Houtweg worth the trouble.

What a pleasure it is to see such a large number of nineteenth-century works together, even though it is far from a comprehensive sampling and even though some of the greatest masters of that period are minimally or only moderately well represented. We think here of J. Weissenbruch, for example, or Koekkoek (not only the famous B.C. Koekkoek but also J.H.). At the same time, we are sad that the Fodor Museum in Amsterdam has not been restored to its original state and that the Stedelijk Museum of Modern Art shows its treasures so sparingly ... in short, that as a result of the museum policies in Amsterdam this truly Dutch art has been either ignored or hardly given any exposure. We would venture to express our doubt that the modern works are really so much more worthwhile. However, the Gemeentemuseum in The Hague and the Boymans-Van Beuningen Museum in Rotterdam do give adequate attention to this period.

Do try and take time out to visit this exhibition!

• Nuyen: a gifted Romantic

What we in the Netherlands are in the habit of calling Romantic painting is not that in the true sense of the word. Rather it is a weak extension of our seventeenth-century art. That art was born out of a Calvinistic world view – which accepted the full reality in which we have been placed, as it is, with its beauty and its faults, because God created it. In the early nineteenth century, with Calvinism at a low ebb, this art had degenerated into a flat depiction of reality.

True Romantic art originated elsewhere, borne from a deep, well-grounded pursuit of the unfolding freedom of humankind – thus, the appearance of the art had to reveal this freedom. In this aspiration humankind came into conflict with reality itself.

Outside of Holland, in England (Bonington and others) and in France (Delacroix, Isabey and others), this art was further shaped and developed. And to this art the Roman Catholic Nuyen, one of our greatest nineteenth-century artists, looked for inspiration. By submitting to its influence he developed himself into a true Romantic even though, as a good Catholic, he retained his enjoyment and acceptance of the normal parameters of life.

So Nuyen became one of the few, perhaps even the only, true Romantic in our country, although his work was tempered by the tradition of our [Dutch] seventeenth-century artists as it resonated in the works of Nuyen's teacher Schelfhout and in the works of P.G. van Os and others. In his early work, between 1832 and 1833, Nuyen aligned himself with them. Works from this period are well represented in the Nuyen exhibition presently showing in the Panorama Mesdag in The Hague, organized and collected by Mr Scheen, art collector and critic of nineteenth-century Dutch art.

In 1833 Nuyen travelled to France and Germany. His small painting of a heron is truly marvellous and strongly reflects the influence of Delacroix. Nuyen was a colourist. The remarkable gift of the colourist is that, by applying just a small spot of colour, he knows how to create a truly astonishing space and ambiance around objects with a sense of real depth. Compare, for example, the incomplete painting shown in the exhibition – flat and without depth since colour has not yet been applied – with the masterpiece *The Duinkerken coast* – where, through the application of a tiny bit of green and red, the group in the left foreground jumps out at us. What a truly convincing suggestion of depth! Nuyen painted his most important works between 1835 and 1838. After that, perhaps pressurized by those around him, possibly painters like Schelfhout and Moerenhout, he lost his passion.

In 1839 this multi-gifted colourist died at age of only 26, having created such masterful works over a period of just a few years, works which singled him out as one of our greatest nineteenth-century artists.

Truly, it was no excessive luxury to bring Nuyen's works into the limelight for a closer look – we should thank Mr Scheen for his tireless efforts in gathering these pieces, which so clearly reaveal this artist's talent. And we are not thinking only of the paintings but also of the wonderful series of drawings. Unfortunately there is no space to discuss them here.

• Beautiful Nuyen discovered[1129]

Amongst the Dutch Romantics – whose art in general can be characterized as a celebration of the peaceful moods of nature, thus deviating from the melodramatic style of Romanticism which is so full of drama, movement and colour – Nuyen has a special place. His art is much closer to that of French artists like Delacroix.

Because his works are so scarce, the discovery of a new work by Nuyen is an important event. Especially so when it turns out to as beautiful a painting as the one recently discovered by the famous art dealer Scheen. The painting, which in the meantime has been purchased by the Gemeentemuseum in The Hague, is from the same period as Nuyen's *The windmill*, which this museum had previously acquired, but it surpasses the latter in integrity and splendour of vision.

At the wharf of a harbour along the French coast a paddle steamer is moored, tossing and slamming about on the waves of the stormy water, tugging at its cables; meanwhile the sailors are trying to embark. In the foreground the sails of a fishing boat are being taken down; here we find that the red of a coat and the green of a piece of cloth give colour and movement in a masterful way to the otherwise fairly monochrome composition. The seagulls in the right foreground finish off the composition brilliantly, exactly because of the simplicity and control exercised by the artist in the subdued way he introduces this motif. It is a wonderful acquisition for the Gemeentemuseum in The Hague, but it also helps us to appreciate Nuyen even better as one of our most talented artists of the [nineteenth] century. A painting such as this may deservedly be ranked among the best works of art in the world.

• The Hague school of art[1130]

It is an odd fact that when it comes to art we often fail to practise a healthy chauvinism: we study and research foreign art with great interest but neglect to examine our own indigenous art more closely. For example, it is remarkable that no one has ever been inspired to produce a thorough study of our 'Hague school of art', which is certainly not just a provincial branch of Barbizon or the Impressionists, and in its ranks include artists like Weissenbruch, whose talent matches that of the great French landscape artists like Monet, Pisarro and others, and may even surpass them.

About those French artists we know a great deal, but about Weissenbruch many people know hardly anything! So it is good that at last a book has been published entitled *De Haagse School: De vernieuwing van onze schilderkunst sinds het midden der 19e eeuw* ('The Hague School: The renewal of our painted arts since the mid-nineteenth century'), written by G. Colmjon, with 80 illustrations collected by P.A. Scheen.[1131] An excellent selection of works of art have been reproduced and the high quality of the reproductions (four of which appear in full colour) and their lavish layout make it a superbly illustrated book, for which it deserves the highest praise.

The accompanying text, although instructive and informative, is unfortunately not of the same high standard. It is somewhat lacking in focus and, because of a conscious effort to appeal to the general public, it sometimes remains too superficial, holding back information which we would have loved to have had included. At times the clarity of the explanations suffers as a result.

But despite these disappointments, we are thankful for what this book offers. It is certainly worth reading and, as an introduction to the art of this great Dutch school, it meets a real need. This is partly because it clearly shows their connection with the French artists while at the same time emphasizing the characteristic and uniquely Dutch aspects of their work. It is a book which, despite its shortcomings, we do not hesitate to recommend.

- **Verster in Lakenhal**[1132]

Peaceful, colourful, intimate, quietly compelling – these are some of the characteristics that typify the art of Floris Verster, one of the great Dutch artists from the period around 1900. Finding beauty in the ordinary, and prompting us to discover it, by opening our eyes to the loveliness that surrounds us each day if only we would take a moment to really look – that is the message of his art.

We are thinking, for example, of the three leaden Chinese tea tins: what an exceptionally picturesque beauty the artist finds in them. And have a look at the colours in a work like *Spring flowers in a glass vase*: a simple harmony of colours and yet so thoroughly refined. Well, maybe 'refined' is the wrong word, because such intimate simplicity and natural beauty are very different from an outward form of refinement. This work has a simple colour harmony that may be compared with the depth and splendour of a single chord from a Mozart symphony. But I am contradicting myself again, because the comparison with Mozart's music is perhaps even less appropriate. His music is too graceful, too playful to be compared with this sober and entirely unembellished, thoroughly Dutch art – and we mean 'Dutch' in the best sense of the word.

For a while, in his younger years, Verster was influenced somewhat by the broad and monumental expression of Breitner, but he soon left that behind. Then, in the 1890s, for a short time, he followed the decorative trend of the Style Moderne, an international art movement that originated mainly in Britain. His *Snow* in this style is a magnificent work nonetheless, as is his *Eucalyptus*. But then, rather than trying to experiment with the van Gogh style, he moved towards an art that expresses gentle, peaceful, profound beauty with a depth that does not overwhelm the looker but has to be discovered through patient observation. Utter simplicity, a refined taste and an exceptional sense of colour are the qualities that define his art.

We made mention earlier of Verster's flower paintings by pointing out one of the most successful examples, and we wish to close by directing you to that unsurpassed work entitled *Town hall in Borger*: note the balance, the careful concern with the tiniest details (there are no 'dead spaces' in Verster's works), and the obvious love of the artist for his subject!

- **Pier Pander – an overdue classicist**

What a remarkable phenomenon that we people of the mid twentieth century can value and enjoy such diverse streams of art. Walking around the city of Leeuwarden, for example, modern-day art lovers can behold the Gothic Oldenhove, apprecing its imposing grandeur; then move on to the Renaissance art of the Waag; and then they can enjoy, without any effort, some Chinese vases, Indian statues, primitive art from

New Guinea, Japanese sculptures and Indian woodcuts in the Prinsessehof. Next they can look with interest at some golden leather wallpaper and several eighteenth-century pieces of furniture, admiring each for its own unique qualities.

The same art lovers can visit the Friesian Museum to examine and enjoy imported ancient goldsmith's art, seventeenth-century paintings and who knows what else. Of course there is always the need to distinguish between high quality, lesser quality, and inferior art; between the masterpiece, the appealling work, and the junk. It is a good thing too for otherwise the world of art lovers would soon become a very drab world of sameness.

Now if the same art lovers should visit the recently established Pier Pander Museum in the Prinsentuin they may run into difficulties. Must they like this as well? Or rather, can it be called enjoyable? How about its quality? Is it high quality art, or just clever? How come that there is a classical artist around at the beginning of the twentieth century? It will become clear then that our art lovers, these connoisseurs of so many different styles, have prejudices after all.

In the first place, they judge that every piece of art must fit into the progression of the art of that particular time: it's the art-historical prejudice which deems a work to have aesthetic value only if it contributes to the orderly development of art – or at least does not belong to an outdated era.

Secondly, and this is really in conflict with their personal principles: they have a hard time liking classical art. Ingres? Well, of course he is all right. But Flaxman? And the late nineteenth-century German classicist Hildebrandt? Yes, we are naming here the ones Pier Pander undoubtedly had the closest relationship with, apart from the occasionally strong influence of the fifteenth-century Florentines – not, of course, the fierce and tempestuous art of Donatello but certainly the gracious 'Greek' art of Luca della Robbia.

Pier Pander worked in Rome nearly his whole life (1864-1919), especially after he became disabled at the age of 27. Art historians in Italy today could probably still find some of his work if they searched diligently, especially in a villa in Como. But who wants to look for the work of an overdue classicist? In his days things were viewed differently, however, and he was highly esteemed. This is apparent, for instance, from the commission to design the portrait of Queen Wilhelmina to appear on the guilder coin after her coronation.

But most art lovers today will not know what to do with his art – or for that matter with the whole revival of classicism in the late nineteenth century which has not been described in textbooks as important.

How should one view Pier Pander's small temple, opened after his death in 1923, a sort of art theory summarized in five sculptures, more suited to the 1800s in its conception and execution. Strange, isn't it, to think that this piece of art was made at the same time as Picasso's radical creations, the time of Surrealism and Expressionism?

Still, it is a worthy exercise to see if you can do it, if you can free yourself from your prejudice against classicism, against this art that refuses to take its proper place in the historical scheme of things. Perhaps it will turn out that there is a deficiency and a shortcoming in that scheme; maybe, after all, there is something beautiful to be discovered in these statues by Pier Pander, which, unfortunately, are largely made of plaster. See for instance the beautiful relief with street singers, lovely and gentle, not at all naturalistic and undoubtedly inspired by the work of Luca della Robbia.

This classicism is pure, genuine art, without any unnecessary frills: no colour, no movement, no expression, nothing but sheer beauty of form. In essence, it is art that lends itself to abstraction just as much as the apparently very different art of the modern movement. The goal is pure, spiritualized beauty – a noble goal, but impossibly hard to achieve. If Pier Pander manages it, even just in one relief or one single figure, he deserves our praise.

Noble simplicity, serene excellence – that is how the classicists defined their artistic vision, and Pier Pander has managed to bring that to concrete expression more than once. That's enough reason to set all our prejudices aside and take time to look attentively, and not through the coloured spectacles of art-historical machinations.

There are many circumstantial reasons why the money Pander left behind for the purpose of building this museum has not been used until now, and why only now his last will has finally been carried out. Maybe it is best this way, because it teaches us something; it helps weaken our preconceived prejudices – if we are willing to look with honesty.

• Constantin Guys

The French don't have a monopoly on how to see beauty in the everyday things of life. But their unique gift lies in presenting those everyday objects with a particular vivaciousness, an élan and subtlety that invests ordinary things with a special charm and unsuspected loveliness. Yes, perhaps it could be stated like this: whereas the Dutch see and paint the beauty of ordinary things, the French try to realize that beauty by experiencing it intensely and then painting it in a passionate, vehement but not necessarily less effective, way. It makes their art characteristically French – *esprit* – a word that is impossibly hard to translate.

As so often when one makes an absolute statement like this, it may be an over-generalization; perhaps this does not describe every French person. It is certainly true, though, that in eighteenth-century France – perhaps not untouched by Dutch influences – an art 'of daily life' emerged which since then has continued to boast an array of brilliant representatives. This tradition of excellent artists who sketched their world with an unbridled and extremely subtle use of line, and a free and daring use of colour, started with St Aubin and Fragonard; it was continued by Debucourt, Gavarni and Daumier; and amongst its last followers, in the late nineteenth century, were Forain, Steinlen and even Toulouse-Lautrec.

Also Constantin Guys belongs to this tradition. He was not mentioned above but fits in alongside Daumier and Gavarni. He was a typical Frenchman, born in Vlissingen, where his father was part of a detachment of soldiers stationed there during the French occupation of our country in 1802. Shortly thereafter his father left, and so did he, only a baby. But Vlissingen is no place to nurse a grudge against a French occupation and it is honouring this Frenchman, creator of such an ultra-French style of art, by hosting this truly excellent exposition.

It was no easy task to select around 125 pieces to give a representative overview of his work out of the thousands of drawings Guys has made since 1840 – some for reproduction in newspapers like the *Illustrated London News*. The organizers of the exhibition may rest assured that their effort has been successful.

The French character of the works by Guys is apparent not only in the particular genre which he preferred but also in the subjects that caught his eye and which he chose to draw. Guys – and all the other French artists we mentioned – painted everyday, ordinary life, but not the small world of the home which so attracted our own [Dutch] artists. What appealed to Guys was the world of ceremony and special occasions, the world of socializing, fun, cafés and ballrooms, processions, parades and uniforms. We have to say that the passionate, unbridled drawing style and the application of colours with much *esprit* are exceptionally suited to depict that world on paper.

The best drawings may have been created in the Crimean War, where Guys followed the troops as a sort of reporter with a drawing pencil. He also depicted the Eastern world, with special attention to the women.

We will not attempt to describe the exceedingly clever and exquisite way in which he drew carriages speeding by, filled with ladies in their crinolines; or the bustling streets, shown in a truly unequalled way just by a few lines and a bit of colour here and there; or . . . the whole sparkling world of his day. One cannot capture his images in words. Guys, though undoubtedly not as great an artist as Fragonard or Daumier, nevertheless is a master worthy of our attention and a great ambassador for French art.

• A hundred years of Norwegian painting[1133]

An especially interesting and at the same time very educational exhibition is currently being shown in the Gemeentemuseum in The Hague. Not only is it fascinating to make an acquaintance with this nineteenth-

and twentieth-century Norwegian art, until now quite unknown to us – and what a very pleasant acquaintance to make! – but we also notice how clearly the development of Norwegian art paralleled the development of European art in general. Perhaps exactly because we are not so familiar with these artists we can more clearly identify the trends that are hidden in their work.

During the first half of the nineteenth century Norwegian art was very much dependent on German art though, especially in the depiction of its own country and people, it managed to strike a distinctive note. After 1850 France became the more significant trendsetter. It is remarkable to notice a great similarity to the developments in our own country. When one looks at these pieces one is almost tempted to identify them as 'from the school of The Hague' or 'resembling such and such' (a Dutchman), though it is equally true that we can find also many personal, unique traits in them. This art is no replica of Dutch art, despite the similarities in development and in the way French influences have been incorporated; seeing it inspires us to look again at our own art and contemplate its development in a new way.

We will draw your attention to just a few of the pieces, rather than trying to cover everything. The lovely painting by Dahl, a student of Friedrich and one of the earliest Romantic painters, is entitled *Dresden by Moonlight*. It could have been described as a Romantic version of a van der Neer. Another peaceful work with a sensitive but not sentimental atmosphere is *Moonlight over Sorento* by Fearnley.

We should not bypass Munch who is, after all, one of the most influential early Expressionist painters! When you look at his *Jealousy* of 1890, that is immediately evident. The group painting with a man and a woman under the tree looks almost as if it could have been painted by a German Expressionist after 1910. The parallels in development between Munch and our own Jan Toorop are striking. There are works by Toorop displayed, from around 1890, which breathe a new spirit, similar to that of Munch. However, Toorop later abandoned Expressionism to explore new directions, while Munch stayed in the Expressionist movement.

Of the somewhat more modern works, we wish to point out the one by Sohlberg, from 1904, which reminds us of an Anton Pieck avant la lettre. The unsettling *Night work in the garden* by Astrup is also very impressive.

The separate area with drawings and graphics holds many wonderful surprises. We have space only to point out a few pieces: the gorgeous animal drawings by Borchgrevik and Munthé are important vignettes, particularly from an art-historical perspective. We were impressed by Munch's woodcut entitled *The kiss,* while his etched portrait of a woman is abundant evidence of his great talents.

• The British school of the hunting scene[1134]

'This art is the natural child of the great Dutch school of painting' – so Guy Paget typifies the British school of the hunting scene in his clear and enjoyable introduction to the catalogue of the art exhibition currently showing in the Prinsenhof in Delft. Indeed, this charming genre of art was built on the Dutch example, even as we at the same time were trading in our tradition for a French model!

This becomes clear when viewing the exposition and focusing on a few pieces represented here: the large work by van Asch and the amateur artist Verschuiring, or the painting entitled *The horse market in Delft* by Pieter Wouwermans, who is the follower and student of his much more famous brother Philips. If we then cast our glance towards the portrait of a horse by L. Palmer (from 1906), we realize how long-lived this tradition was. Even today it has not completely died out.

We would also like to single out a few works by Henry Thomas Alken for closer attention. He was a prolific artist, especially famous for his etchings of horses and other subjects. Unfortunately we do not have the opportunity to see that aspect of his work on display here, but we can view quite a few of his paintings. Although painting was not his strongest skill we may still look at his canvases with respect, for they are charming works. Also extremely appealing are his watercolours, painted in a typically early nineteenth- century style. Alken painted a number of stage-coaches, but in those he was bettered by Charles Cooper Henderson. Four of Henderson's pieces show his fresh, appealing style and the painting of the stage-coaches passing each other in the night deserves admiration.

A piece of exceptional quality is *The long driveway in the park of Windsor Castle* by Gilpin; Sandby took care of the landscape in that painting. This piece is catches the eye because of its atmosphere and its bright tone. In all these paintings the landscape is often incidental, with the main focus on the horse and the hunt. This is especially true of the works by the Wolstenholmes, in which the horses are carefully crafted with great character while the landscapes are extraneous. However charming and appealing these works might be, they certainly do not approach the high quality of our own seventeenth-century art. Few of these artists are real masters, and the truly great British artists like Gainsborough, Reynolds and so on, concentrated mainly on portraiture. We should make an exception for the art of George Morland, a truly first-rate painter. He started off as a portrait painter and made a name for himself as such, but through a number of unusual circumstances turned his attention to the genre of the hunt. His works reached their climax during the time he was residing at the country estate of C.L. Smith, surrounded by many other artists of this genre. Morland did not really belong to that group in the strict sense of the word, because he did not really paint portraits of horses and seldom depicted the actual hunt. His paintings are usually rather genre-like glimpses into a thickly forested area, with a few human figures and often several animals, but he hardly ever painted one of those noble pure-bred horses. His *Turnpike gate* is a marvellous work that excels in its composition and especially fine harmony of colours. Just note how he handled the light! His other paintings are also worthwhile in every respect, while even the prints which were made from his paintings cannot obscure or dull the freshness of the original.

Alongside Morland we would like to single out the superb works of Charles Towne, with their bright tone. There are also a number of pieces by Stubbs, whose book *Anatomy of the Horse* which appeared in 1766 established a solid foundation for artists seeking to portray horses. The pieces shown here are somewhat disappointing, though, and certainly do not represent his best works. It would be quite unfair to judge him on the basis of what is displayed here.

Naturally there is much more to see than what we described here, but you would be better off taking a look for yourself.

•Early works by van Gogh

Gallery Wisselingh on the Rokin in Amsterdam is exhibiting the early works of van Gogh. The latest work shown here comes from his early period in Paris.

It is a remarkable experience to be confronted with these pieces which are, for the most part, still quite immature. More than one of the pieces would never have survived had it not been for the fact that they bear the name Vincent, and sometimes they come frighteningly close to modern kitsch.

What is especially striking is the diversity of styles in which van Gogh worked while searching for his own unique style. The most beautiful are certainly his still lifes, which in their jagged roughness and their brown earth-tones betray a power that hints at the later van Gogh.

Also a few drawings (like the one of the farmer's wife with a wheelbarrow) are worthwhile in every respect; others call up a host of questions. Nevertheless, it is all extremely interesting, and amazing to think that the man who produced these works between 1880 and 1885 created during the subsequent five-year period a series of masterpieces which are not only unique but which also never relapsed to the awkward amateurishness that is still evident here. We do find an ungainliness in some of his later works, but then it is sublimated and meaningful – the expressions of an artist who has something important to say and who is in complete control of his medium.

We can confidently assert that if van Gogh had died in 1885 he would have remained an obscure figure. At most a single work (perhaps the still life with potatoes, because of its interesting subject and its powerful brushwork) may have been noted as indicating an artist of talent. But to be honest, some of the other pieces would not even have interested a second-hand art dealer. And that makes this exhibition so interesting: it demonstrates the successes and failures of a genius in the process of finding his way.

• Van Gogh: visual phenomenon

This is the year in which we commemorate the birth one hundred years ago of van Gogh, the great Vincent. All manner of writings have been dedicated to his honour – in women's magazines, in weekly and daily newspapers, and in scholarly journals. There cannot be a soul left who has not read about van Gogh, and some have read a great deal.

We find it hard to understand what was so special about his birth date, other than that it gives a wonderful excuse to put his art in the spotlight in a comprehensive way. And it is appropriate to focus our attention there. For van Gogh may have written many letters, and beautiful ones too, but he remains primarily a painter – and a painter must be known through his paintings.

His career may have been very interesting, but the important thing is that all his struggles and work led to amazing results, results which we are now free to view at our leisure in art museums. That's why we want to draw your attention to exactly that: the exhibition of van Gogh's art currently on display in the Stedelijk Museum of Modern Art.

Van Gogh's desire was to paint for the masses, and his dream was that his paintings would be hung in schools, in playrooms, in the homes of farmers and fishermen. It is partly because of the excellent reproducibility of his work that his wish has, to a large extent, been fulfilled.

Some of the work van Gogh produced in his later years may seem a bit strange, but in general his art is so completely wholesome that the schoolchild as well as the academic, the baker as well as the doctor, young and old, can enjoy the beauty of his work. He has something to say to each of them, to each of us – that is what makes his art great.

• James Ensor: a great graphic artist

James Ensor is one of the greatest Belgian artists since about 1880. He certainly had a very unique place in the Belgian art world, and in the rest of Europe as well, considering the international appeal of his work. He was already the odd one out during his time as member of the artists group Les Vingt, instituted in 1884. After all, this group as a whole was inclined to Impressionism. And although, particularly in the technical aspects of his work, he cannot be contemplated apart from this movement, yet his emphasis was very different from theirs: the subject always was of great significance to him. He may therefore be better viewed as a forerunner of Expressionism and Surrealism.

If our understanding of art is saturated with ideas based on Impressionism and on Hildebrand, which often unfairly render the subject unimportant and give attention only to the elements of colour, form and composition, it will be inadequate when applied to Ensor's work. Not that those elements are not present. To the contrary, we find jewels of composition among his etchings. But, and this is how it should be, his composition is always employed to impregnate his subject with meaning, to define it more sharply. See, for example, his *La mort poursuivant le troupeau des humains* ('Death persecuting the flock of mortals').

We mentioned above that Ensor was a forerunner of Surrealism, but we must keep in mind that he himself cannot yet be called a Surrealist. In common with the Surrealist movement he created a stange atmosphere at times, had a love for depicting decline and ruin, while often making use of symbols, like Redon. But in Ensor's works the subject is always understandable. As with the works of Hieronymus Bosch and Bruegel, his fantasies can be followed in thought and emotion; in Surrealism, to the contrary, the figures are often very personal dream images – which is different from fantasy – that relies too much on Freudian interpretations. The fantastic figures of Ensor are often horribly realistic. Look at his magicians riding on broomsticks through the sky – we sense that in that piece alone he already surpasses Baldung Grien. His satirical humour, a typically Flemish quality found in almost every period of Flemish art, is often very cutting, sometimes justifiably so, and sharply sardonic in lashing out at human error. Once in a while (and this must be said) he goes too far, so that his work becomes unpalatable.

There are also a number of landscapes by Ensor on display, which belong to the best of this genre. Stunning is his *Grand view of the Maria Church*; also *View of the Port of Ostende* represents his finest work. But we will not ennumerate more – the exhibition in the Gemeentemuseum in The Hague is open until 12 June.

• Bresdin: etcher and lithographer

It is a platitude to say that the nineteenth century, with regard to art, was a time of decline, a time of poverty and poor taste, although such a nineteenth century certainly did also exist. But one must not forget that the same period produced a wealth of artists of immeasureable significance, even to this day.

Among these we must include Rodolphe Bresdin, an etcher and lithographer of exceptional talent, whose work offers so much that one is hard-pressed to summarize it in a few sentences. Phrases like 'daydream', 'fantasy', 'a life lived in strained relationship with reality itself', with works that appear as 'hallucinatory', 'strangely appealing and disgusting at the same time', with a sense of being 'surrounded by unknown and unpredictable powers', frightening and yet 'natural' – all these phrases help to make this all-but-naturalistic art accessible to anyone willing to take the time and trouble to view it thoughtfully.

There is an even weaker link between Redon, who in a certain sense has continued Bresdin's style, and 'ordinary' reality. Of Bresdin it is said:

> What he wanted and sought after is nothing other than to initiate us into the impressions of his private dreamworld. The dream, mystical and strange – yes, a restless and hazy daydream. What we find everywhere in his work, from start to finish, is humanity gripped by loneliness, a world-escaping, meaningless flight without a Heaven, without a homeland, full of fear of exile, hopeless and without end.

Undoubtedly for us this describes an important aspect of Bresdin's work, but it is questionable whether it captures everything. His wildly Romantic art is more varied and more human than the modern reader, acquainted with Surrealism, might gather from Redon's quote. Nevertheless, Bresdin's work remains a compelling part of the many-faceted nineteenth-century world of art, a facet we still know too little about. Therefore we should be grateful for the beautiful exhibition of his work in the Print Gallery of the Rijksmuseum.

• Van Gogh's contemporaries

It is a very appealing exhibition that is now being shown in the Stedelijk Museum of Modern Art, containing works by well-known and famous French contemporaries of van Gogh. They are artists with whom he had a great deal of personal contact, and whose work he certainly knew well. There are just a few paintings by each of them, arranged in a tranquil and well-organized way.

Manet, the earliest artist to be displayed here, joined the Impressionist movement for a short time only in terms of the technical aspects of his art. He really belonged more appropriately with the preceding era of Delacroix and Courbet, but without their Romanticism. He rounded off the development that Courbet had set in motion. We see some very characteristic works by Manet here, but not his real masterpieces. It is clear that the museum has tried to find works produced by these masters during the time that Vincent was in France, and Manet reached the peak of his artistry before then.

Exactly during the years on which this exhibition focuses, Impressionism underwent a transition: the exact replication of the visual impression had been thoroughly explored and achieved, and these masters were now each in his own way searching for something more essential and lasting.

Monet remains the most Impressionist of these artists, typified best perhaps by the two seascapes taken from the collection of the Stedelijk Museum of Modern Art. It could be that his method of applying primary colours has to be attributed to influences by Seurat, for in his slightly older works we do not notice that (for example, in his masterly painting of a basket with apples).

Renoir aimed rather for the recovery of plasticity, though there is scarcely any evidence of that in the works on display here. The pieces seen here date mostly from the years prior to the change in his painting style and, unfortunately, they are mostly not Renoir's best works. Toulouse-Lautrec's greatest work was not produced until the subsequent decade. In these pieces from the 1880s and 1890s we can see how this master progressed, little by little taking more command of his materials. His *Woman at the piano* of 1890 is magnificent; we can actually see her reading the musical notes.

Seurat attempted the paradox of combining a super-Impressionistic technique, based on a theory of colour, with an almost classicist understanding of composition. You can see the remarkable result in works like *Le Chahut* ('The spectacle') of 1890. Seurat belonged to a younger generation – and died at a young age, in the same year as van Gogh (1891) – yet he exercised an influence on some of his elders, especially on Pissarro. This pioneer is revealed in the exposition as a very sensitive master. With modesty, and with a strong feeling for reality and a love for the French countryfolk, he made some very fine pieces, such as the one of two girls in the woods, or the one of girls talking at a hedge. When we follow Seurat's pointillist style in the later canvasses from this decade, we find that his work actually suffers by losing some of its original power.

In the last hall, we see works by Gauguin and Cézanne. Especially with the former, van Gogh had intensive contact – until their rooming together in Arles ended tragically. For both of them, this must have been a great disappointment. We are hard pressed to find van Gogh's influences in his work. Together with van Gogh and Cézanne – and perhaps also Seurat – he laid the foundations on which modern art was built. Cézanne later became extremely influential, taking over the position of Gauguin – but we cannot discuss that here. His works shown here reveal him as a mature artist, especially in his *Mont St Victoire*.

In many ways this is a very instructive exhibition; and although it includes some lesser pieces, it is one that can be viewed with much pleasure.

• Monet: a mirror of Impressionism

The name of Monet has become synonymous with Impressionism. The Monet exhibition in the Gemeentemuseum, The Hague, can therefore really be called a large exhibition of Impressionism. And we should appreciate the chance to see so many works by this pioneer artist together in one place. As an artist, his significance cannot easily be overestimated: along with a few other masters around him, he created a style which is still reflected in almost every form of art that is not part of the hyper-modern école de Paris.

We are given an excellent overview of the development of Impressionism since paintings from all the stages of Monet's development are here represented. Monet began as an artist working in the style of the older landscape school of Barbizon. His earlier works, from 1864, show his ability to handle his medium while the *Street in Normandy* (painted a year later) shows a less precise but still very strong style of painting. In Paris he was not untouched by influences from Courbet and Manet, but we cannot really call his large *Déjeuner sur l'herbe* ('Lunch on the grass') from 1866 a masterpiece. His view of Paris, painted in the same year, akin to the art of Corot is a much more succesful work – yes, a true masterpiece. But until that point there is nothing really exceptional about his work as compared to that of the older landscape school, though some of his paintings are excellent. The only unusual thing about his art during that period is that he often painted outside, something he learned from his teacher, Boudin.

As the years passed, we find a new freshness and directness in his work, precisely because of his continued effort to capture on the canvas the freshness and the colours of nature. This is evident in his *Grenouillère* ('Frogpond') of 1869.

In 1870, in reaction to the French-German war, Monet traveled to England and the Netherlands. Struck by the unique atmosphere of the latter country, with its constant light haziness that binds the colours and frees them of some of their intensity, he made great gains as a colourist, as a painter who excels at balancing the colour tones. In that respect it is instructive to compare his two paintings entitled *Canal at Zaandam*: one is harsh and lacks the typical Dutch atmosphere; the other is permeated with the silvery grey tones we know so well.

During the following years (especially from 1873 to 1874) we see a very important change in his painting style. Until that time Monet had painted the subject, the material, the substance, like all painters before him had done. But now he began to paint just the light, the impression that the colour makes on the eye, so that the object itself, which reflects the light, receded into the background. This marked the beginning of Impressionism. It can be clearly seen in comparing *Rouen Harbour* (1873) with *Seine at Argentueil* (1875). Monet continued to progress in this direction during the subsequent years, perfecting his technique and becoming more and more detached from every link to older painting style.

His colours were clear and bright, certainly when compared to those of the official academic painters of the day, but they were still quite muted. Monet had experimented a few times with strong primary colours, but not until the 1880s, influenced perhaps by Seurat's theories about light, do we see works in which the primary colours – bright blue, green, red and so on – are placed side by side in small patches. Occasionally this work became harsh and the colours almost dissonant, although we see here before us consistent Impressionism. Fairly soon, however, Monet returned to his softer, more muted colouring – as in his *Field with spring flowers* of 1887. However, his works continued to give not a true reflection of the substance of things but a subjective rendering of the individual impression that light and colour makes on the eye.

In the years after 1890 Monet's art became more lyrical and more faded, and we note that it was possible to take this line of approach much further yet. Monet's paintings of the 1880s, compared with pieces like *The Cathedral of Rouen,* his *Waterlilies* or his works from London or Venice, are still of solid and concrete substance. After 1890 everything became hazy, bathed in a sea of light that absorbed all. (See, for example, *Charing Cross Bridge,* of which we can hardly say that a real, material bridge or even the impression of one is depicted.)

So we saw how Monet's art had undergone an evolutionary process based on a very definite principle. There were many stages in between, each of which had inspired and influenced many other artists; but from the concreteness of earlier works to his 'light only' period after 1890, his development followed a steady and clear course.

Apart from all other things, Impressionism's lasting contribution to the art of painting has been the brightening of colours. The lightness and brightness that we find in true modern art has come as a direct influence from Monet. We even dare say that the brightness and the lightness of our own living interiors, of the paintings on our walls and the entire modern cityscape, are fruits of his art; though we need to add that Monet's art must be seen as the expression of a new and generally accepted way of looking at life.

Twentieth Century

• E. Munch: forerunner of modern art

We are used to hearing that modern art is built on the work of three great forerunners: van Gogh, Cézanne and Gauguin. Although there is much truth in such a statement, it is also an oversimplification. The artists who, during the first ten years of this [twentieth] century, started the new artistic movement, were much better aware of their own predecessors. That was clear from the large exhibition held in 1912 in Cologne, where a place of great honour was reserved for the Neo-Impressionists and Munch.

Munch was born in 1863. In his younger years he moved in circles that admired the writings of Dostoyevsky, Zola and Strindberg, circles where artists painted in a realistic style influenced by French Realism and Impressionism. It is Munch, then, who, in the 1880s, sought to give a different quality to his art: he tried to express the feelings and thoughts of the people he was painting. That is clear, for example, in his *Puberty*, of which a later version is at the moment hanging in the Gemeentemuseum in The Hague. Around 1890, this inclination in his art became even more distinct.

The works that Munch produced during these years are most important in the history of art. His new emphasis was most clearly revealed in the gripping and vivid painting *The scream*. In this painting we are not seeing an objective picture of what a screaming person looks like; rather, we experience what it feels like to be screaming.

During these years Munch reached perhaps his greatest expressive power in the wood carvings which, together with those by Gauguin, and even more than his paintings, were to be an inspiration to the Expressionists. The paintings, however, with their strongly subjective, unnatural colours, chosen for their particular expressive value, should not be underestimated. The colours, which have also symbolic values, certainly played a large role in the remarkable expressiveness and meaning of these works.

After 1900 Munch's art became more subdued. The landscapes he painted then are beautiful – for instance the one painted in 1901, with a train rushing past in the foreground, against the panoramic setting of the water in a bay or lake: like a poem, this painting completely captures the mood the artist was experiencing at the time. Increasingly Munch returned to the representation of objective reality, although his style always captured more than mere externals.

The exhibition in The Hague gives a good idea of this man's skill and a representative overview of the many dimensions of his work.

• Europe 1907, an important year for art[1135]

Anyone who wanders through the great summer exhibition of works exclusively from 1907 in the new wing of the Stedelijk Museum of Modern Art in Amsterdam will be struck by a certain unity and a great diversity. The latter may of course be taken for granted. After all, intellectual and spiritual movements and conflicts are oblivious to dates and so-called generations, and in any era we find great differences in attitudes and viewpoints between contemporaries. It may be questioned whether the modicum of unity that is undoubtedly discernible here is not a consequence of the selection; for these works were gathered from the perspective of 1957.

One must not make the mistake of thinking that what is presented here is a complete picture of 1907: we do not see the more or less commercial art of the Salon painters (rightly so) or the various works that people thought important at the time but which have not withstood the further testing and sifting of the last half century. It appears that perhaps too much emphasis has been placed on Expressionism, although 1907 certainly meant a high point for that movement, which evinced a strongly international character. For the most part the Expressionists were still rather young painters who had only recently appeared on the scene with their first masterpieces and who, of course, had still only barely gained recognition for their art. They were building on what had been presented by van Gogh and Seurat, and especially by Gauguin and artists influenced by him even earlier than 1900, such as Bonnard, Vuillard and others. Their art was marked by a harsh form of expression with very bright colours used in an unnatural way: an attempt to express in a violent and fiercely poetic manner the human reaction to concrete things – a landscape, a person – by means of colour and line.

These were really still just experiments, and from that point some of the results were strikingly successful. At other times the artists failed to escape a certain affectation and bizarreness, as in the case of Delaunay's portrait of Uhde, for example. While by no means desiring to lump all the French works indiscriminately together, one nevertheless gains the impression that German Expressionist work was better, more consistent, more unified in form and content, and accordingly also less contrived. This style apparently suited them better, although they built on French models. The best of the French Expressionists, known as the Fauves, was Vlaminck. His work is hardly distinguishable from that of the Germans while, not surprisingly, he is not from central France but from the north.

Happily, the important Impressionist painters who worked in this period have not been overlooked. In 1907 they were far more important than the emerging Expressionists. Monet is represented by several lovely pieces, reminiscent of the music of Debussy in their lyrical and subdued tone. Isaac Israëls fits perfectly at this international level, while even a late work by Jozef Israëls shows that an old man not inclined to adopt the innovations of the younger painters can still contribute important work – something often forgotten today. Whether Jan Sluyters is correctly hung in this company rather than with the Expressionists is a question we shall not contest; this exhibition shows clearly that the distinction between the two groups are less sharp than books sometimes imply.

Just how varied the work can be within a single period may clearly be seen in the contribution of Klimt, who worked in an entirely different context. And notice, furthermore, the two Picassos: one, fully Expressionist, already hinting at what he would go on to do much later; the other, one of the earliest Cubist works. In this same year Braque too exchanged his Expressionism for a Cubist analysis of form. Together they attest to the profound impression left by the Cézanne commemorative exhibition held in 1907.

And what work did we find the most beautiful of the whole exhibition? Perhaps the paintings of Munch. He too follows the French models and was especially strongly influenced by Gauguin. Yet he had already assimilated all that into his own distinctive style before 1900 and so became a forerunner of German Expressionism. By 1907 Munch was past his experimental stage, with riper work, more solemn and rich.

Whatever the angle from which one chooses to see this exhibition, it is unquestionably fascinating and compelling. The average standard of the works displayed, not excluding those by younger artists, is high and one gains a very clear idea of what was happening in the world of European painting at this important time. It also confirms that one must never judge works of art by the movement from which they come, nor even by their historical importance, but rather by their proper, intrinsic worth, their beauty and content. It can help to raise the awareness that modern art is often much less problematical than it is perceived to be: it is not so much the modern means of painting that causes difficulty but the content that offends. For instance, the Expressionist work by Picasso in this exhibition is such a 'weird' modern work that most people, including ourselves, are put off by it; while a Munch or a Braque or a Kirchener, by contrast, seem quite acceptable. Yet at this level too one cannot operate by seeing things in black and white only – one has to form a fresh opinion every time by taking also all the nuances into account.

• What is Expressionism?

Those who have not studied art, often ask me the question: 'What is actually the difference between Impressionism and Expressionism?' This problem is solved at once when one observes the difference. For example, compare the work of Willem Maris in the 'Five Generations' exhibition at the Amsterdam Stedelijk Museum of Modern Art with the works in the extensive exhibition of Expressionist art also being shown there. Better than any verbal explanation, the works themselves answer the question.

Impressionism and Expressionism are rooted in entirely different views of reality. But in an attempt to explain the differences as they are manifested in external form, we could say that Impressionism is naturalism-ad-absurdum: the artist attempts to capture on the canvas the transient impression that the outside world – and specifically nature – makes on him or her, one little corner of nature as it appeared in a particular light, at a particular time of day, under particular weather conditions. The focus is on the momentary impression made on the viewer – and the inner condition of the artist is considered absolutely irrelevant.

Expressionists works very differently. Thus, Expressionism can be described as a reaction to Impressionism. External reality becomes, at most, the inducement to paint the picture. Having discovered the unique aesthetic qualities of line and colour, these artists use line and colour to produce an aesthetically responsible work of art with the emphasis not on being true to life but on expressiveness. For the Expressionist, art is not a reproduction of external reality; it is therefore not naturalistic but rather a means to create a beautiful reality using the artistic medium.

Expressionism gives voice to a revolutionary mindset that no longer accepts reality, or culture, as it is; the artist wishes to build a new world. Expressionists reject the nineteenth-century faith in knowledge and technology as the means to a better world. They reject the 'materialistic' vision of that century and search instead for the universal, the absolute. These artists are called to create only out of an inner necessity and must allow themselves to be led by their very personal emotions and imaginative powers.

The statements made by Expressionists are sometimes filled with inner contradictions and are often difficult to comprehend. But what always emerges clearly is that they strive to bring forth the purely spiritual and the purely aesthetic, to free themselves from the fetters of nature, the old forms and, above all, to build with form and colour a dynamic, new expressive aesthetic reality. This is indeed related to the rising revolutionary socialistic trends of the time. Especially in Germany, where groups of artists formed collective communes.

Expressionism had its forerunners in the nineteenth century with artists who generally stood alone, rejecting the prevailing trends, and worked in a style which was not primarily concerned with the purely 'passive' reproduction of external stimuli. The most important and influential among these forerunners of Expressionism included van Gogh, Gauguin, Cézanne and Munch. What they started was continued by the Expressionists. Further, Expressionists were strongly influenced by the 'primitive' African plastic arts, as can be seen in this exhibition in the works by Heckel and by Nolde.

Expressionism sprang up simultaneously in Germany and in France around 1905, and spread into other countries a few years later – though, curiously, not into England. It is noteworthy that, although the movements in the mentioned centres were initially completely independent from each other, there was a remarkable similarity between them. One can compare the work of the German Schmidt-Rottloff with that of the French masters Dérain and Vlaminck who subsequently developed in very different directions. Also Braque, who later ended up in the more Cubist territory, hardly deviated from his fellow German artists in his views or his use of colour. Indeed Picasso himself, in his work produced during the period before he switched over to Cubism – which is closely allied with Expressionism – shows a similar tendency (though unfortunately there are no examples of his work in the exhibition).

There is no point in dealing with each of these masters in detail. We wish to point out just a few examples. Nolde, in his *Maria Egyptica*, offers us a triptych that could almost function as a symbol of the Expressionist movement. With what fierce desperation she prays before the Madonna – one could call it a piercing cry. How vividly her sinful life in Alexandria is depicted in the left panel, with all its grim reality – and how convincing. All these artists with great skill managed to communicate their perception of reality very clearly.

Also in terms of composition these works often succeed. How beautifully Marc (one of the most sympathetic) used colour and line to create a balanced whole – see, for example, his little deer. Yes, regardless of whether one agrees with the views of this movement, one has to agree that it was great gain to have the emphasis placed once again on aesthetic elements like composition and to have a break from the extreme naturalism of Impressionism (which was, after all, also very one-sided and certainly not Christian). Beckmann's *The night* communicates a nightmarish scene. If you take the time to let this work speak to you, you will find it impossible to observe it neutrally. The artist's uses of compositional lines compels the viewer to be drawn in and captured by his vision.

Finally, we wish to point out the surprising (to those who have not seen it before) early work of Sluyters. He, too, has taken up an important place in the Expressionist movement. How real are his Staphorsters, inhabitants of rural Staphorst! And that is how they are, I was assured by someone who knows that area well. Sluyters later followed more moderate streams and returned to a position closer to that of Breitner. Similary, several more of these artists after 1925 became more moderate in their expression – as seen, for example, in the works of Vlaminck, Dérain and others.

This phase in the history of modern art is exceptionally important. Viewing this exhibition helps us understand much about the background to modern art and its foundations which we may not have previously grasped. And after viewing this exhibition – which is so instructive for understanding not only modern art but also the modern world in general – just look around and observe how many elements which first appeared in Expressionist art can now be found on billboards and such.

•Beckmann: violent Expressionism

Those who like to look at pretty pictures and who demand nothing more from art than that it pleases the eye, who are averse to every sign of violence and anything problematic, should stay away from the exposition of the art of Max Beckmann, the great German Expressionist who died in 1950. For refined colour variations, lovely tones or beautiful lines are not to be found here.

But if you are willing to give this art more than a cursory look, allow it to have an impact on you, you will be gripped by images from which you can hardly tear yourself away, images that truly communicate a message. Beckmann's art is fierce and he communicates his message clearly – no explanations will be needed to interpret his powerful portrayals and compositions.

Beckmann is an Expressionist and looking at his work helps the viewer understand more about Expressionism. He does not paint nature and the world around us but the feelings, the emotions, the turmoil that humans suffer; his art is a reflection of his inner perception and not of nature as we can objectively observe it. We see this clearly, for example, in *The night* of 1918, a painting that perhaps would be better named 'The nightmare'. It takes us into a torture chamber and we as viewers, like the tortured themselves, do not see a coherent scene in front of us – our eyes (and that is precisely the skill of this composition) is drawn first to one thing, then to another; yet we experience it as one unified whole.

Undoubtedly this is not nice art to look at, but it grips one and succeeds in making its point in an almost appalling way. Also the *The trapeze*, painted in 1923, depicts the emotions of the observer, whose eyes are drawn to follow the movement.

His family portrait is almost too real, even though the whole as well as the individual parts of it rebel against a photographically realistic art style. Next there is *Monte Carlo*, in which he makes rich use of symbols – time bombs in the hands of strange and unreal creatures; sticks which, in the hands of the croupiers, appear like murderously threatening swords – to create the impression of a gambler playing a game with life and death under the suffocating threat of 'if all is lost, what then?' Finally, there is a strange triptych *Blind man*, on a theme reminiscent of the writings of Kafka and equally strange and inexplicable, hopeless and oppressive.

This great artist has succeeded in giving shape to his vision of reality in a way that has a breath-taking, choking effect on the viewer.

• Macke: pure talent

It is a delightful experience to view the 'August Macke Exhibition' currently showing in the Stedelijk Museum of Modern Art in Amsterdam. Macke is a painter who moved in the circles of the pre-World War I German Expressionists, and who has been deeply influenced by French artists like Cézanne and Matisse. He is a highly productive artist who, though he only painted for about seven years, left behind a large collection of work. In short, on the basis of this description one might not expect too much from him – is he not just another more or less immature follower of the great artists of his day, an artist whose work shows a variety of unassimilated influences?

To the contrary. Macke's art has a remarkably unique character, less strident and extreme than that of his fellow artists, and less problematic as well. His work appears to be completed, well-rounded and, with a few exceptions, the influences are incorporated in a consistently individual manner. Macke's artistic development was rapid and his artistic direction, though never shocking, was radical. Of course there are weaker pieces among his works, but the average quality is high and, although it is precisely because of his moderation that he does not hold a place among the leading artists of the day, yet his work is certainly not second-rate.

Macke's art rarely portrays the purely human. In that, he remains true to the tradition of Impressionism, with works that focus on purely artistic qualities like colour, movement, sparkling life and carefully measured, though spontaneously acquired, composition. Occasionally the movement towards abstraction, so characteristic of his time, breaks through in his work but, on the whole, he stays free of this. We enjoyed Macke best in his works of the later years, such as *The green jacket* and *Strolling three-some*, an utterly charming little piece. His art is not ambitious or monumental but intimate and modest. Therein lies its appeal, especially when we compare Macke's work with that of his often harshly outspoken contemporaries.

• Paula Modersohn-Becker

For the first time the Dutch now have the opportunity to become better acquainted with the work of Paula Modersohn-Becker – a painter who died in 1907 at the age of 30 – and it is impossible to view her work without being deeply moved by this extraordinarily talented artist.

Her work, which developed over a few years and underwent a comparatively rapid evolution, played an important role in the genesis of those modern schools of art which have sprung up in Germany subsequent to her death. We said 'a comparatively quick evolution' because it is striking how quietly and naturally her development took place, so that there is no real break between the earlier and later works – instead of displaying a revolutionary, innovative streak that wished to rid itself of the old as quickly as possible, she demonstrates a calm and carefully considered endeavor and a gradual growth. Her earliest art, from around 1900, stands completely under the spell of the late nineteenth-century French-inspired tradition or shows a certain cohesion (for example, in her *Self-portrait* of 1898) with the symbolism of a Munch. But her *Elsbeth* of 1902 strikes a different chord, though the change is subtle. It is a poetic, dreamy work of a little girl standing quietly in the countryside and it reminds one of the British art of illustration.

In the following years she painted still more children's portraits, each work a treasure in its own right. We are thinking of the sitting girl, and especially of the girl on a chair who looks so intently back at the viewer, that it is nearly impossible to turn one's attention to the rest of the canvas to view the composition as a whole: peaceful, with no harshness, mature and subdued, a moving and expressive piece.

From the period of 1903-1905 there are a number of still lifes which appear to be completely unremarkable: plain in style and conception, without a trace of Impressionism. But when viewing the *Still life with fruit* of 1905 it is not plain at all! The work is unbelievably eloquent and one can hardly find words to describe its expressive power.

During the subsequent year in Paris, she became acquainted with the work of Gauguin and other painters like Denis Vuillard and so on. It is worth noting that, though their influence is unmistakeable, she did not follow blindly but managed to incorporate the new influences into her own idiom.

Particularly the reclining nursing mother has something primitive, an almost animal quality, about it, strongly reminiscent of Gauguin, also in its composition.

Deeply expressive simplicity and immense peace characterize Modersohn-Becker's work. It is striking that her *Woman of the poorhouse* is reminscent of van Gogh's *Berceuse*, one of the works in which he most clearly incorporated and assimilated Gauguin's influence. Although a similarity to the work of van Gogh has been pointed out several times, a direct influence is out of the question.

One of her final works is the monumental *Mother and child* in which a kneeling woman breast-feeds a child. Through a simplified construction and muted colours she achieves a stern simplicity, while the mother and child have the qualities of an African sculpture that hints at an idol; a symbol of motherhood. The exposition is showing in the Gemeentemuseum, The Hague.

• Female compassion in painting: Käthe Kollwitz, Charley Toorop, and the Joffers

In the Gemeentemuseum in Arnhem there is currently an exhibition entirely devoted to the work of female artists. Do not think, however, that you will find there sweet, tender, motherly images.

On the contrary, at first glance these contemporary pieces would seem anything but 'feminine'. For example, someone previously unacquainted with the powerful art of Charley Toorop would never guess from her works represented here that the artist is a woman. We consider it unnecessary here to say much about Charley Toorop's work as most of the examples in this exhibition represent her older work; and the latest ones – which truly is new in various respects – are not really represented at all.

Then there is the impressive art of Käthe Kollwitz. Her graphic work is deeply human and illuminates especially the dark side of life – death, poverty, anxiety and conflict – but no one can deny how true and genuine her vision is. Her work was produced with a determined political agenda, but now that we stand at a distance from the events and political conflicts that inspired her, we hardly notice that. There is no hatred here, no absorption in daily politics but rather a reflection on human suffering in all ages, across social ranks, in all walks of life.

Notable is the farmer in the series *Farmers' war* - especially the almost gruesomely realistic etching of the sharpening of the scythe. Then there are the images of war – not of the front lines but of the widow, the grieving parents.

The works by Suzanne Valadon are completely different. They have a certain awkwardness, a clumsiness in the handling of the materials, yet she is no mere 'weekend painter' and at times, for example in her portrait of her husband Utter, she succeeded in creating a work of enduring value. How beautifully also she portrays adolescence in the piece *The forgotten doll* – utterly human and down-to-earth.

Finally we see the work of the Joffers of Amsterdam, a group of female artists – now all older – who around the turn of the century created their own style, a variation on late-Impressionist art. They present us with the pure art of painting, and in speaking about their work one must discuss things like colour variation and the touch of the artist. Yes, craftmanship is everything to them, and this has resulted in the creation of works for pure artistic enjoyment. What harmony of colour we see in Marie van Regteren Altena's blue bowl with the lemon and the dark shawl; as well as in the white roses painted by Coba Ritsema, or the little dead bird by Coba Surie, or the widely-spaced still life with chemist's jars by Betsy Westendorp-Osieck. There is no affectation, no pseudo-profundity, in these first-rate works of art.

• Modern Italians in the Stedelijk Museum of Modern Art in Amsterdam

It is always a fascinating but extremely complex problem to figure out what the enduring character is of the art of a particular country. One could phrase the question in this way: to what extent does such a tradition exist, and do we sometimes unintentionally just imagine it to be there, because we are not able to look at a work of art apart from the knowledge we have of that country's art tradition? For example, would we be able to look at works by modern Italians without taking into account our knowledge of the Italian people?

These and similar questions are raised by the exhibition in the Stedelijk Museum of Modern Art in Amsterdam, which is showing works by a number of renowned Italian artists from the period since 1910. One cannot find the Futurism here which was the Italian equivalent of the revolution that took place in the art world just before 1910, and which elsewhere was labelled 'Cubism' and 'Expressionism'. The museum intends to host this type of art in a forthcoming exhibition.

Quite soon after these revolutionary years, a time of reflection set in: the figure, the plasticity and the 'readability' of the paintings are recaptured, without a lapse into an imitation of the old Masters. On the contrary, the modern character of this work is undeniable.

However, to what extent one thereby connects with the old Italian tradition of art, if not in form then at least in spirit, is a question we have already touched on. Formulating an answer is extremely difficult.

One should also not ignore the fact that several of these artists found their own characteristic painting style while living abroad in Paris – Severini, Modigliani and Chirico. One also cannot separate the typical, partly-abstract canvasses by Severini (in which painted letters play a role) from the Cubism of Juan Gris and others.

On the other hand, one must admit that there are some typical characteristics common to all these painters: compositions are made up of just a few elements which maintain their own plastic value and reality – even though the combination is sometimes very modern (as with Carra and Chirico). The colour is mostly flat and quite light, and is clearly distinct from the gamut of colours used by the Cubists or the Expressionists.

Modigliani is one of the best-known artists of this group. He worked in Paris and died as early as 1920. His sculptures, mostly from his early period, clearly reflects the influence of negro sculpture. In observing this work, of which there is one example in the exhibition, we come to understand how he arrived at the characteristic shapes in his paintings. They are usually faces of women; one of the most beautiful represented here is the fine, appealing little face of the woman 'with the swan neck', which is a very typical example of his style.

Of Severini's art, we have already mentioned his earlier work. Later he developed a more 'normal' conception, of which *The harlequin* is an exceptionally successful example. Campigli's work clearly shows the influence of several archaic artists. Morandi paints primarily still lifes and constructs his canvasses with a very small number of elements. These paintings are of particular interest from a compositional point of view. By about 1912, Chirico emerged with his remarkable pieces which evoked an early surrealistic spirit. He typically built those hallucinations with the help of realistic elements: mannequins, crates and such, which have a three-dimensional quality. Carra's earlier work was certainly influenced by him, using similar motifs. Later, in the twenties Carra went on to compose very simple, peaceful beach scenes.

Finally there are some sculptures by Marino Marini, sometimes misshapen female figures, and a few horsemen, one of which is particularly appealing because it has a certain naïveté. With the exception of the latter artists, this is mostly art that, although certainly modern in its composition, does not belong to that body of art so strongly criticized by the public (and rightly so) because of its strange, incomprehensible and sometimes repulsive, character.

• The Picasso of Eindhoven

The much discussed recent purchase of a Picasso by the Van Abbe Museum is a complicated issue to sort out. In the dispute around the issue, the 'Picasso problem' – typifying the whole problem of contemporary art – has played an important role, and has, to a certain extent, muddied the waters. Let's consider the various factors that contributed to this acquisition.

In the first place, we have Picasso himself. Picasso, without doubt the most influential and powerful painter of the first half of this [twentieth] century, underwent a fascinating and remarkable development. Though he started out at the turn of the century in the style of Toulouse-Lautrec, he quickly developed his own unique style during his so-called blue and pink periods. Especially in blue tones he created masterpieces, usually of a rather melancholy nature, which, even if his career had ended there, would have earned him a place among the greatest artists of this century.

After 1905, however, he became involved in radical events in the art world that resulted in the emergence of a whole new style of art, a style that is now still called 'modern art' and has remained problematic for many people. Influenced by traditional African sculpture and by Cézanne, a typical use of forms developed that moved towards a completely new kind of art, a classic form of art, if you will; art that really could be called art. It is understandable that art moved in this direction, for the nineteenth century ended with paintings of anecdotes and stories, representations strictly of what the eye can see, in a way devoid of any depth or 'vision'. Human creative activity was choked by a slavish subjection to 'nature' and art, as a cultural activity, was dead.

As a result, there grew a longing for a more enduring art, art which would try to capture not just the external but the essence of reality, art that would record not just the all-too-fleeting present but the more enduring inner values. Perhaps it was an idle search, but certainly understandable considering the truly deplorable state of art that had followed the road of norm-less and vision-less naturalism to its bitter end. Picasso took the lead, presenting figures which were stripped of all their individuality and of all that is casual and temporal, using a cubistic style which, through analysis, sought to capture only that which is enduring. In the series of paintings he created between 1906 and 1914 the woman's head of 1909, now showing in the Van Abbe Museum, is a crucial work. It marks a milestone in the development of the immensely influential Cubist style which would have such far-reaching consequences for the twentieth century, also in the non-art world. Not just that, but it is one of the most beautiful, most successful works in the whole series. It is no surprise, then, that already in the years prior to the First World War this canvas was worth 12,000 francs (Fl 6000)!

It is possible to survey the art history of that period and to assess the place a work such as this holds in it. It is no wonder then that many museums that understand their calling, to record and preserve that which is key from the past, are searching for important works from that period, works that will help to clarify what we are seeing around us now, including some of the forms we see in the world of design. So, when the Van Abbe Museum saw an opportunity to get hold of this first-rate canvas, a painting which had been lost track of and for which many museum directors were 'on the prowl', it was obvious that they would try to acquire it if at all possible. In this, as in many other spheres of life, price is determined by supply and demand. Occasionally, if one is fortunate, one can find a good deal – as happened with the important Chagall of 1911 (almost as important as this Picasso) – but such luck is a rare occurrence. In this case it was necessary to pay the full price, and that price was determined by the fact that it is a stunning and important painting of great historical value, and one that is in great demand.

Is this price, 126,000 guilders, justifiable? The price is not exorbitant, it is not fixed with a view to the snobbish buyer's market, as has been the case more than once with the later Picasso's. These really problematic Picassos did not emerge till after 1920, when it seemed that something inside the artist snapped and his development no longer showed a logical progression. Instead, in constantly new ways, he exhibited destructive images that were a denial of all values and reality.

The question of whether or not to purchase such a work is in the first place a question of museum management. Should a museum attempt to build up a collection that shows the highlights of modern art? Is this how the museum should understand its task – to show the public the very best from the beginnings of modern art? And should a small museum also see this as its task? Or should that be left to the larger museums, and especially to the large American collections? This question was answered in Eindhoven in the affirmative.

The second question is even more fundamental. Is it permissible to spend so much money on a museum? Should art not be more 'alive', and is it not so that museums are more of a public burial place for art?

When asking such questions it is important not to forget that museums are also a part of the cultural world. They radiate a stabilizing kind of power; they stimulate; they prevent a sense of uprootedness by pointing to our link with the past. By showing the best, they offer us a standard by which to measure new forms and new creations.

Is it responsible to buy such a painting? Are there not many social needs that should first be taken care of? Certainly, but those needs will always be with us, and if one goes by that, then all cultural activity should come to a standstill (thereby unintentionally doing a disservice to the 'social' side of life).

One must not forget that, apart from the investment value, it has a tourist value, as well as value related to the the task of a museum as such. Though we must not let social needs out of our sight, we also should not allow culture to become paralysed.

There must be a prioritizing of values. Was it responsible for the Van Abbe Museum to buy this canvas – and with public money? Perhaps they did try to acquire a piece 'out of their league'. Possibly they became too caught up in the competition-fever between the various bidding museums. Possibly. But the fact remains that a small gallery with just six paintings, which include a Chagall, a Kandinski, a Braque, and now this Picasso, makes Eindhoven famous across the world, and not just because of Philips.

• Picasso's Guernica in Amsterdam

The small Basque village of Guernica was the first place in the world to be demolished from the sky. It happened on 28 April 1937 during the Spanish Civil War and was done by German pilots who were sympathetic to the Franco cause. Though many people were alarmed by this dreadful event, few today remember it and the word 'Guernica' is more likely to bring to mind Picasso's masterpiece.

A masterpiece by Picasso? Yes, there are many who would question such a statement, and ask 'How can you call it such? Are you trying to be highbrow? Is it an intellectual conclusion you reached? Or is this just repeating what a small group of self-proclaimed elitists are dictating that everyone should believe? Are you joining the tyranny of that clique that threatens to call everyone else ignorant, stupid, behind-the-times or simply dull?'

If one should persist in asking whether this painting can really be called 'beautiful' – this *Guernica*, a 8x3.5-metre canvas painted in greyish shades that express the artist's own reaction to the news of the bombing – we are inclined to answer, 'No, not at all!' On the contrary, it is a horrible work, anything but sweet or lovely, and certainly not 'aesthetically pleasing' or harmonious. But this does not say anything about its quality.

How would it be if this painting was exhibited anonymously, without the aura that has come to surround it? We would probably glance at it, be surprised or annoyed and walk past. Ten minutes later we may start to wonder what it actually meant and consult our guide to find the name *Guernica*, shrug our shoulders and walk away, maybe to return a little later for another look.

That evening we may be surprised to find that certain of its details have embedded themselves in our memory with irresistable power and we may find that we have to deal with the piece emotionally whether we wanted to or not. And that is the typical impact of an impressive masterpiece: we cannot escape its message.

At first the design may appear strange and bizarre, so that we cannot possibly understand it at all, and certainly cannot figure out why it calls up such strong emotions in us. Yet it appears that the inner logic of the scene, the convincing power of its symbolic language, takes hold of us and irresistably works itself into our soul. No, *Guernica* is not beautiful, and yet.

It is amazing that, the longer one immerses oneself in this painting, and the more one ponders it, the less strange the figures appear, and the more clear and human they become. The figures may be completely different from the reliably recognizable shapes in the older paintings we have become used to and yet, we see here, very convincingly portrayed, the sorrow, anxiety, hopelessness and desperation that grip a suffering people in the depths of their soul. And it begins to occur to us that it is particularly through the way these figures were drawn that they express these emotions so profoundly. No, do not come and look here for a pretty painting, a lovely design; but the work is filled with power that betrays incredible artistic talent.

Picasso did not try to picture the bombarded town; rather, he symbolically expressed the emotions of the people during the bombing and thereby elevated this work to become an enduring 'writing on the wall'.

Chunks of a man, his sword still clutched in his hand, lie scattered on the ground. A woman whose child has been killed becomes a monument of sorrow and hopelessness. A terrified, dismayed figure drags itself along, and another raises his hands to heaven in his utter distress. These figures are not individual people but symbolic figures who collectively express the misery of all. The figure on the right, for example, with arms raised to the sky, reminds us of the Zadkine statue in Rotterdam, which has the well-deserved title *Demolished city* even though it shows 'only' one single human figure.

Then we have the woman jerking her head out of a window and holding out an oil lamp. This figure, relentlessly powerful, could have been imagined only by a truly great artist. Are these the masses, trying to find out in panicked terror what is actually happening, since the bombardment was completely unexpected and unforeseen? To the left there is a bull, the symbol of the Spanish people, conscious of its own might, unmoved, for Spain will not capitulate! The horse also appears as a symbol of Spain, but this time in fear and agony.

Words can hardly do justice to this work. So purely artistic is the arrangement of the whole, with its underlying unity that allows no unnecessary line or speck of colour. The whole surface expresses the artist's coming to grips with one single theme: *Guernica*, a complexity of human emotions ranging from rebellion to desperation, from despair to confidence in the future.

There is nothing coincidental about the fact that one of the most impressive masterpieces in all of modern art is a piece such as this. The theme of terror, which one finds again and again with many varying nuances in Picasso's work, is most appropriate. For although modern art may sometimes be perceived as a new visual language, it must be remembered that it started out as a way of voicing those emotions that are normally experienced only in a nightmare or a terrifying daydream.

This painting by Picasso, just like Zadkine's best sculpture, the one in Rotterdam, expresses horror with a wealth of emotion that could never have been achieved as convincingly had the subject been omething idyllic or cheerful.

All Picasso's work from that period carried the potential for a piece like *Guernica* to be conceived. Special circumstances, as it were in a single blow, turned the possibility into reality. In January 1937 he was commissioned to create a painting for the Spanish Pavilion at the World Fair in Paris, but by late April nothing had come of it. Not even one idea had borne fruit. Then, on 28 April, the bombing took place. By 1 May the preparatory sketches were ready – these are on display as part of the exposition dedicated to *Guernica* in the Stedelijk Museum of Modern Art. In these early studies we find various elements that have been incorporated as dominant parts into the finished work. By 11 May the main lines had been sketched on the canvas and a month later, only slightly deviating from the earliest sketches, the work was completed. It is clear from this that Picasso was ready for a theme such as this, while the substantial events that finally led to its creation ensured that it did not result in a meaningless play of forms or in idle metaphysics but in a work pregnant with deep human significance.

When considered together, all this helps us to understand why *Guernica* could, or rather, why it had to become the signature masterpiece of modern art.

• De Stijl in the Stedelijk Museum of Modern Art[1136]

'Definition, clarity is demanded in life and art,' wrote Mondrian in 1919, and the ideal that he had in mind was, again in his own words, 'to attain to a balance between nature and not-nature in and around us.' When that is achieved, then 'building, sculpture and painting merge into architecture, that is into our environment.' This is what De Stijl (the 'Style Group') that was established in 1917 by van Doesberg, together with Oud, van der Leck, Mondrian, Huszar and a few others, always tried to achieve.

And so it was accurate to write in the jubilee edition of their paper *De Stijl* in 1927: 'The stylistic discipline, now cherished for years, has had its hygienic influence in every respect.' For this movement, whether one concurs with its theories and slogans or not, provided healthy ideas in the realm of style and art, particularly where people applied these to architecture, furniture and the applied arts. And indeed, with the work of architects like Oud and Rietveld proceeding in close contact with the work of the painters of this movement, a new art and style arose that had a profound and wholesome influence on our architecture and interiors in general. Here too they envisioned a unity in style between all the elements that form an environment. They did not hesitate to use modern materials and to take advantage of the possibilities these offered. It was also a movement that did not despise or disregard machine products and techniques but aimed, instead, at aesthetically responsible designs attuned to modern requirements.

In this they connected with Berlage and other forerunners, yet it was the painter Mondrian in particular who most strongly defined their style of design. After all, when De Stijl began there was little or no architecture that met their requirements, while the painters, continuing in the somewhat older Cubism, had by then already given solid shape to their vision. That is how it came about that strictly functionalist notions created an entirely new style that did indeed give rise to aesthetically responsible buildings, furniture, typography, and so on. No wonder that such a wholesome principle, allied with a new and strong feeling for style, could exercise tremendous influence not only in the Netherlands but throughout the world. Our country thereby made a very positive contribution indeed to this [twentieth] century.

The Congress for Art Critics discussed De Stijl extensively. It is impossible to recount all they concluded but Jaffé's thesis, that this movement was closely connected with Calvinism, perhaps deserves our attention. And then we must not think of any direct influence but rather of the deep impression that Calvinism left on the Dutch national character, so that people in this country more deeply resist any over-exaggerated individualism and detest specious displays and an empty outward show. In all of this, we see the continuing fruit of the good and wholesome effect of the Reformation in this country [the Netherlands].

• Bart van der Leck

Why, in the first quarter of this [twentieth] century, were so many artists all over Europe drawn to abstraction, to the freedom from representation, to the search for a pure, unadulterated and absolute art form?

Undoubtedly this tendency was revolutionary, but it will not do to attribute it simply to charlatanism and snobbery. These ideals were more deeply rooted than one might have suspected and gave expression to an intellectual movement (and certainly not an insignificant one) that is peculiar to our time. The result – abstract, non-figurative art, at least when it comes to the visual arts – is open to debate. Yet it has had a positive influence too and one that should not be underestimated; it has contributed much to the aesthetic improvement of the applied arts and as such shaped the tastes of today.

In connection with the latter, the group called De Stijl, which was started in 1917 by van der Leck, amongst others, is of great interest. Although van der Leck soon withdrew from the group, his influence was deeply felt – especially by van Doesburg, the greatest propagandist of the philosophy of De Stijl, as well as by Mondrian. It's interesting to follow his development in the comprehensive exhibition of his work now showing in the Stedelijk Museum of Modern Art in Amsterdam.

Around 1900 he started out in a rather ordinary (for that time) painting style; two beautiful portraits from that period can be seen. Then between 1900 and 1910 he became a little more vehement in his expression. After 1910 he started placing the heads and bodies in rank and simplifying them in a cubistic ordering of reality, which was achieved with planes of simple and always strictly primary colours – especially the colours red, blue and yellow which came to play such a key role in the tradition of De Stijl.

In 1917, by holding on to these principles but abandoning representation, van der Leck moved towards composition in abstract blocks. In time, this work became calmer, more refined. He never abandoned his typical white backgrounds. Around 1925, in the abstract interplay between blocks and lines, recognizable figures appear again through an extreme simplification and abstraction of reality, as seen in the drawings that are also exhibited here. A single book design is enough to demonstrate his contribution to a more beautiful style of typography.

This is an important and interesting exhibition, and it gives a good understanding of the origin of the modern style in general; and of a modern perception of beauty, for example, in the design of many utensils we use daily.

• Guggenheim collection in the Gemeentemuseum[1137]

In the Gemeentemuseum in The Hague one can now see a part, the most important part, of the art collection owned by the Guggenheim Museum, a private foundation in New York. The goal of this unique institution is to purchase what is qualitatively the best that the twentieth century has to offer, in order to create a standard of value. On the basis of this standard they then endeavor to assess recent works and add to the collection, with a view to encouraging the development of contemporary art. Completeness in a historical or any other sense is not their intention.

We intentionally made a small error in what we just said. We namely wrote that the goal was to find works from the 'twentieth century', but what we should have used is the word 'modern'. If anything, this exhibition makes it clear that the two terms are not synonymous. For although it is certainly true that we see here a series of extremely important works from the modern movement, we believe at the same time that these can by no means be said to be representative of the twentieth century. They reflect just one facet, namely works that can be called 'modern'. For a great deal of work has been, and is being, produced in this century that is of no less quality and in no sense merely mimicking the past. Why should a recent Kandinsky be better, more important, beautiful, real and contemporary than a recent landscape by Gestel? Why should a Desnoyer be inferior to a Manessier?

Certainly there is a deep divide between contemporary art that continues to manifest an interest in reality and humanity and the works of this modernistic movement that proceeds from entirely different premises than all the art of earlier centuries. It is not in the first place the way of working that is different, the artists' manner of expressing themselves. No, the great difference lies in the first place in the content, in what is depicted. It is what this art has to say that is so different. And that lies so far outside the normal perspective that even now, some fifty years after the first real modern works were created, most people remain puzzled when confronted by it – even though many of the modern methods and principles of visualization are by now also widely applied in advertising and in paintings and sculptures that lack any modernist intent or empathy at all.

When, in spite of this, an institution continues to make propaganda for modern art in every way it can, there is more at work than just familiarizing the general public with new art. They are preaching a new view of reality: an existentialist one, to characterize it briefly. Reality is experienced as an alien power, irrational, strange, imprisoning humankind with its laws. But maximum freedom is desired for humankind and anything that impedes this is experienced as an illegitimate restriction. Within this world view, people are often deeply averse to the created world and attempt to escape from it with a free interplay of line and colour or by giving vent to their hatred and estrangement. They experience their own lives as meaningless accidents and feel they have been thrown into a sick reality. They are strangers within the created world because they no longer want to acknowledge the Creator and because they have fundamentally repudiated the God of Holy Scripture.

It is remarkable to see at this exhibition how the departure from every element of humanism and every remnant of a Christian world view led, within less than half a century, to terminal nothingness. Marc's *Landscape in Tyrol*, an Expressionist work from 1913, provides an exuberant release of emotion which, however, retains a connection with what is given, while Kandinsky's work from the same period – *Painting with white surface* – does practically the same but without any residual connection with reality; it portrays absolute subjectivity, total freedom. Yet this latter work is much poorer. And as the development continues we witness how these principles eventually result in an empty, insolent throwing down of colours in dollops of paint on a surface. Such works may at times be beautiful in colour and even betray some vestigial control of form, but they are empty and say nothing. These artists are absolutely free from reality, yes, but they have also become detached from everything that is valuable and meaningful; they have lost connection with all of positive value. Such freedom is slavery and it has taken art ever deeper into a dismal, more uniform nothingness, into tedious boredom. A Mondrian is still harmoniously and beautifully balanced. Kline achieves no more than the insolent rendering of a few heavy stripes. An uncontrolled emotional release it may perhaps be, but it lacks the power to convey anything more. This is death.

We do not say these things in order to blast this kind of art. These artists are certainly serious, unquestionably talented, and their works definitely worth viewing, if for no other reason than to become aware of what their art means: a world, a humanity without God. But we do criticize this: that people want to assert that only such art is meaningful and valuable today, and that everything else is without value and out of touch with our times. At the same time we want to point out the poverty and emptiness of the dogma of these academicians of the twentieth century, just as boring, even more boring, than that of the academicians and Salon painters of the preceding century who, for want of a vision knew nothing better than to copy reality like a photographic machine. We find ourselves wishing that people would now finally break through the dogma of modernity and open their eyes to other facets of our century which, qualitatively speaking, may not be inferior at all. Perhaps it would encourage the public to take a greater interest in art again if something is exhibited that they may recognize as meaningful and/or true. For the rest the Cézanne and two small Seurats on display here are by themselves worth the trip to the museum.

• Unbelief as emptiness

In the catalogue of the huge Miró exposition that is currently being shown at the Stedelijk Museum of Modern Art in Amsterdam we are advised to put aside any preconceived bias and allow these works to affect us without questioning them, simply giving them room to speak their own language. If we heed this advice we will see canvases on which the paint has been placed with great precision and a refined sense of colour; where, with pure intuition, a red, green or yellow blotch of colour has been painted in just the right spot. These are inexplicably wonderful compositions which are perplexing and sure in their construction, never jolting.

And in this we see how Miró, like all great artists who forge new ground, who discover new shapes, new colour combinations, and new principles of composition, created something that could fruitfully be referred to in advertising, typography and so on, and which certainly exerts a strong influence.

But viewers of this work also realize that they cannot leave it as such. This is not just a decorative playing around with colours and random shapes. There is a poetry here, a symbolic quality that never describes, never posits, but continually evokes and hints at more. It is exactly because we know these are symbols of a poetic language, elusive, indescribable, not to be captured in words or in a single concept, that many people feel uncomfortable and incapable of handling this art; they feel irritated by the insoluble problem that it apparently presents.

What on earth is this *Head of a Catalan farmer*, a huge painting in which, on a blue background, a few irrational shapes and a few small patches of colour are placed. Is that title an *épater le bourgeois* (to bewilder the small-minded middle class), a matter of free play, 'silliness' (in the everyday sense of that word), or is it a description of an element of the unconscious that evokes an existential and irrational experience? Is this meaningless child's play, a hoax, or a deeply profound immersion into the cosmic whole, a mysticism that evaporates into irrational nothingness, an experience that may be freeing, obsessive or frightening? Or, perhaps all three at the same time?

One should not approach this art with an attitude of 'I can do that!' Because, apart from the artistic talent betrayed here by colour and design, these weighty fantasies are based on real experience, fed by a mystical, existential, irrational perception of reality.

We are dealing here with feelings of *Geworfen-sein*, which Heidegger spoke about, a profound experience of the irrationality and arbitrariness of all being, 'swaying' on the edge of the abyss of universal 'nothingness'. Based on the fundamental experience of creation as an unfathomable, arbitrary, irrational, cosmic happening without structure or plan, which views the cosmos as simultaneously wonderful and terrifying – based on the view that 'we are drifting in a meaningless void', without structure, without coherence, 'just because' – based on such beliefs one can comprehend a work like *The grasshopper*. And one can then also understand the countless number of interpretations evoked by Miró's titles. Titles like *The eagle flies to the mountains, which have been hollowed out by comets, to proclaim the word of the poet* are nonsense, but meaningful nonsense. The painting interprets this given meaninglessness in an abstract as well as poetic way, irrationally, mystically, so that modern viewers are pushed to the very edges of reality, where they encounter the huge, irrational, frightening mystery of meaningless emptiness. Somehow, this is accepted as a positive thing.

An artist teaches us how to see. Undoubtedly Miró is capable – through his strange combination of cogwheels, patches of tar and a child's broken drum, for instance – of elevating these objects above their worthless existence to give them a poetic, cosmic interpretation. He integrates them emotionally into our human experience by making them symbols of the 'cosmic whole' that we referred to earlier.

So this art is poetic and prophetic, and we can certainly understand how it could be said of Miró that he hands us the key to a wonderful way of living, a way that is genuine, authentically genuine, and that exposes the asininity of a world mired in false problems. However, in order to say this one must agree with Miró that there are neither Creator nor norms. For those who live out of the conviction that they have been placed here by their Lord to live in a creation that he maintains, and that this God is faithful, for such persons this art is at best understandable and revealing, for it helps them to better understand what it is that drives today's world. But to respond to this art with a positive 'Yes', to be positively gripped by it, is not possible. But, yes, we should be alarmed by this straightforward expression of godlessness (literally), this surrender to the most fundamental aspects of a radical nihilism. And yes, as such this art can strengthen our faith and help us to see more clearly what it means to know God.

• Collection Urvater in Museum Kröller-Müller[1138]

It is not easy to write a review of the exhibition of the Belgian private collection Urvater that one can view until 2 September in the Kröller-Müller Museum. For the collector evinces a pronounced preference and love for Surrealist work, and the body of works we can see here has accordingly become a statement, as it were, of Surrealism. Naturally some weaker works are included, but one can be assured that most of what is on display belongs to the best of this genre.

What must we say then? Is it enough to assert that all these artists undeniably have talent and that they have succeeded in giving precise and pure form to their vision? Is it enough to say that on average the quality is very high? Or, in saying that, do we really fail to touch upon what is essential? Is it not inevitable in connection with precisely this art that we should also delve into the content of the works, into their message, into what they have to say? I believe it is not only inevitable but also mandatory that we do so. If art is to have meaning, if it is to have anything to say to us as human beings, then there must be more to it than a beautiful arrangement of colours and forms. A painting is not an ornament or a utilitarian artifact. Surely we expect more from a book than from a signpost?

To say these paintings have recognizable quality is to assert at the same time that we can have a meaningful discussion about them, even argue about them. One cannot have a serious discussion about junk – that would pay it too much respect and border on the ridiculous. The strangeness that leads many a 'lay' person wandering through this exhibition to say 'I do not understand much of it', arises not from a new form but from the content. And then I do not believe such 'lay' persons are correct in saying they do not understand it. The only thing they do not understand is that there are people who have such a view of reality. They believe that a work of art must be beautiful and that it must reflect the human world as it is given and experienced by them.

Yet what do we see here? The work of artists who hate such 'ordinary' reality, who experience reality instead as a strange, irrational, capricious, illicit jumble of coincidences without meaning or purpose, without norms or law, and at times even as a hostile power. These artists present what they regard to be true and correct, and they state their concern about a reality with which they have lost touch. They are no longer genuinely able to love the things around them but believe they can discover the demonic in them; at times they even experience this demonic as something positive.

Every artist imbues his or her work with an own vision and chooses themes and a way of handling them so that he or she says, consciously or unconsciously: 'Yes, this is how it is.' Thus we see here what, with a play on words, we might call 'daymares' – awful, terrifying series of works that bespeaks the artists' experience of meaninglessness and the demonic.

It often seems as if they search for a new myth whereby to interpret the given cosmos. But they remain vague, for every well-defined picture would evoke immediate criticism – who, after all, really believes in a myth today, since biblical Christianity has unmasked all myths as human fabrications. At times here it is as if we are gazing into hell – and is this not hell, life without God, without human contact with the given creation, existing as strangers in a world for which love or interest can no longer be generated, a world of which the meaning and structure is no longer understood, desired or accepted?

Is this all beautiful? We do not believe so. For we cannot apprehend the 'daymare' as a beautiful dream and cannot underwrite its terrible oppression as something true and beautiful. The fact that it may at times have been painted with great talent and skill or that it may have expressed these feelings with great purity does not detract from that; on the contrary, it reinforces it. Nevertheless, one might object, there are also non-Surrealist works, abstract works of various kinds. Certainly there are: yet one of the discoveries one makes in this exhibition is just how close an affinity there is between the abstract works and Surrealism. In the abstract works one observes a similar freakishness of form with a lack, in a certain sense, of structure; a similar estrangement from reality.

Happily one can still see other art in the museum as well, including some magnificent works from the sixteenth and seventeenth centuries and a great many van Goghs and works by his contemporaries. Yet we should not be disappointed that the museum decided to exhibit these Surrealists. It is one of the tasks of a museum to show us what has been produced in our time, in order to edify us, however that may be. Yet we hope that on another occasion the museum will show us that our times have also produced different art, more wholesome and fresh, warmer and more human.

• Willink, envisioner of existential angst

A large exposition that gives an overview of the interesting work of the famous painter A.C. Willink is being shown in the Townhall-Palace in Tilburg until 19 September. Interesting, because whatever one may think of Willink's art, the exhibition is worth seeing, and his art is worthy of our contemplation and consideration. Willink began work as a young painter around 1920 in the style of the abstractionists. He was subsequently influenced by another contemporary modern movement, led primarily by Léger and Le Fauconnier. An interim period followed, with a very unique and interesting contribution to what could be called a controlled Surrealism, in a work like *The sémaphore*. Something from each of these periods is to be seen in the exhibition. Finally, around 1930, he found himself in an art style that people have attempted to call by various names; we wish to add to the list the label of 'Romanticism'.

Willink's art speaks first of all of the unique way in which he experiences nature, especially the mountainous terrain of France which he loved so much. Although he fully experienced the beauty of this scenery, he never presents the pure charm, the quiet, the picturesque side of it. Instead, there is always something of a suppressed tension, a sense of threat, a grandeur. In short, there is something overwhelming about these mountain landscapes which are shown in panoramic view. There is a very peculiar aura about them, which is further accentuated by the dark clouds, so somber and heavy. This view of nature as a mighty power, against which humans are small and insignificant creatures, a vastness to be viewed with anxiety and fear, is a typically Romantic notion, although Willink does not try to imitate Romanticism.

Very occasionally he painted landscapes only; usually his paintings include a castle, or a terrace with statues, to draw our attention. The observant viewer will note the remarkable absence of people in these paintings; the terraces are empty, the palaces are uninhabited, the statues are neglected and damaged, and everything appears empty and deserted. It is a melancholic view of a past world. Unlike earlier artists, he does not fill his terraces and palaces with people from eras when these buildings were still new, for he realizes that this would be immediately identified as a masquerade. For him it is all about barrenness and desolation – in our times we are no longer able to achieve the grandiose lifestyle of an earlier era. It is past, gone, beyond recollection.

And nature does not smile benignly, but hovers threateningly around these doomed cultural creations, witnesses to a past time of glory. When he does include people in his paintings they are always tourists, accentuating the loneliness and abandonment, the transience of everything – tourists who are too ignorant to realize how out of place they are on these terraces alongside the crumbling beauty of past times.

Is such melancholy, such a barely suppressed longing for a grander past, such a not-to-be-silenced yearning, such a silent lamentation, not typical of Romanticism? Understand me well, it is not the Romanticism of the past, for Willink's starting point is completely contemporary. His portrayal of France is very different from that of his colleagues, who return year after year with portfolios full of colourful and more or less cheerful valleys and fields. His work is different but, we believe, not less true. Because what Willink portrays will impress anyone familiar with the past glories of the French palaces and esplanades.

Indeed, the Modernists may shrug their shoulders about Willink and say that he is out of touch with his own times. Thus they demonstrate their small-minded narrowness, for if they are interpreting modern ideas and experiences, he is doing the same. They are often impressed by the nauseating, the boring or are gripped by the angst of existence. Perhaps Willink is too, but besides this he has a sense of the values that have been lost; and it is his calling to express that.

There are also his portraits – beautifully painted and, I was informed, excellent likenesses. Yet they are, in one way or another, very disturbing. There is no distortion, nothing odd in the portrayal as such, but as soon as one attempts to describe the impression of these hard faces, one feels powerless. Something of the restlessness, the tension, the estrangement from one's own society that his other work attests to in a different way is also evident in these paintings. They cannot really be compared to anything else in our time or from the past. These beautiful portraits are further evidence that Willink is an artist who experiences the times he is living in very intensely and expresses it an artistic form.

• W. Schumacher: magical and Romantic[1139]

There is currently an exposition of the work of the 60-year-old artist W. Schumacher in the Stedelijk Museum of Modern Art in Amsterdam. He is a remarkable artist, from whom we have heard little in recent years. He is one of the artists who, after initially following Expressionism already in the 1920s turned back to paint more 'normally'.

This turn did not mean a return to nineteenth-century naturalism. On the contrary, a type of art came into being which one can perhaps best refer to as 'Romantic'. Reality is depicted very precisely here; yes, so precisely that sometimes because of the advanced detail a remarkably unnatural tension is evoked, while in the manner of composition a twentieth-century imaging is evident, which could not have come about without the preceding influence of Expressionism. These paintings, with their strange lighting, reveal a peculiar tension and dynamism – we are, as it were, lead into an unreal reality which, externally looks quite ordinary but has something ethereal and dreamlike to it, and at the same time something very tense. The landscapes painted in this way, with not a single human figure, appear to be rigid and in all their pale lightness they are cold and tenuous. Exactly because the precisely drawn reality is represented in such a slight and dreamlike manner, in very tense compositions, it appears scary and threatening, as if they are about to burst apart. When he paints figures they too have a peculiar real-unreal character.

This element is less prevalent in the portraits and the different figures of sitting women, although never totally absent. Various still lifes complete our picture of this Romanticist, whose art can be understood by everybody. Sometimes, through using skulls, his Romantic disposition is especially striking as in the *Portraits of dead birds*, which render the downfall motif of Romanticism in a very penetrating way. This is very interesting art with regard to the problems it poses; much enjoyment can be found in its highly developed technical qualities.

• German art after 1945

In the early part of the twentieth century Germany played an important role in the development of modern art; the movement called Expressionism put its deepest roots down there, carving out for itself a place of permanence, very different from France where, under the direction of Picasso, artists quickly dispersed in different directions. However, after 1933 a *Dritte Reichs Kunst* ('Third Reich art') was established – a sort of officially sanctioned kitsch; while real German art (which certainly was ultra-German) was declared to be 'degenerate'.

In 1945 the German artists suddenly received back their freedom, and then, yes, then the problem for the young could be summed up in the words, 'Now, what?' Their response was two-fold. In the first place they checked the pulse of the older German art to see what vitality it might still hold; the result was a series of expositions of early twentieth-century German art, through which the young were given the opportunity to become acquainted with their own past and to align themselves with their national tradition. At the same time there was an increased contact with other countries in an attempt to bring Germans 'up-to-date with the times'.

In all of this, of course, the artists who survived the Nazi era and had not escaped to America or elsewhere, played an important role – Hofer, Baumeister and Mataré. And so German art was modernized. A remarkable result of this revival was that people looked at modern art in a new way, without the burdens which elsewhere have not only dominated the discussions surrounding modern artists but have determined the artworks themselves. The German modern artists seem to be free of this; for them, what is modern speaks for itself and modern art is created in a straightforward way, without metaphysical theorizing or seemingly-profound artistic problematics. As a result there is a direct and unaffected quality about their work.

Perhaps the reflection will come later and perhaps the recent works by German artists that we can now view in the Amsterdam Stedelijk Museum of Modern Art are still products expressing the pure joy of their recovered freedom to create, to paint and do art again.

Of the older generation – those who had achieved some success prior to the Nazi era – the works of Nolde, Schmidt-Rottluf, Hofer and Heckel are represented. These artists could delve back into their own past work, free at last to make public that which for years had to be done in secret. We were impressed by the marvellous aquarelles by Nolde, and by the still, powerful, pure Expressionism of Schmidt-Rottluf. Hofer's work, despite the Kafka-like quality of his 'black rooms', was very disappointing.

And the younger artists? We were struck that few human values are present in their work; in their art the human element is almost completely absent. Apart from a few very striking sculpted portraits, people play no role in this art, except occasionally to serve as a point of departure for a composition that has meaning only and purely as a composition. Truly, the purely aesthetic gets all the emphasis and nearly all of these works are playing with hints of abstraction. Still, we seldom find here (as so often happens these days in France) that a painting comes down to nothing more than a few pleasing colours. Rather, most of the works are marked by a poetic expression which gives them content and meaning, and which elevates them above the ornamental. See, for example, Meisterman's huge composition, awesome in a strange and indefinable way and reminiscent of Chagall in its use of colours. Also note the works of Winter, Ritschl, Luckner and Werner.

The poetic expression of these works is seldom light and cheery; more often they speak of modern tensions and a sense of *Unheimlichkeit* ('lugubriousness') that will not surprise anyone; still, playfulness and joyful movement are not totally absent from these works.

It is surprising then that there is a certain unity to be found here, though it is hard to pinpoint exactly what constitutes it. The connection with earlier German art is certainly present, though it plays a subordinate role. This art shows a strong international character – not surprising, considering its affiliation with the latest modern foreign art. Yet it is an exhibition with its own unique character and therefore most worthy of a visit.

• Joseph Zaritsky: chaotic work without clear substance

It seldom or never happens that, because of a freak of fashion, the work of an artist is greatly overestimated and then later generations determine that this high estimation was a sorry mistake; that the work was like an empty wrapper whose shiny exterior had blinded the viewer. On the contrary, art history shows that much more frequently artists who were honoured in their day are found to have been worthy of this honour, and that their work does have substance and significance – although the relative level of appreciation, with all that influences it, may vary.

Thus, when we read that since 1923 Joseph Zaritsky has held a prominent position in the art world of Israel; when we hear that he is perceived as a man of importance, a teacher and a leader for the younger generation; when we read that the director of an art museum, after seeing a few of Zaritsky's works for the first time, immediately wanted to purchase some of his work; and when we read the praises that introduce his work in the guidebook to the current exhibition, we had to conclude that this is an artist of importance whose work has substance, has something to say of artistic significance.

We do not dare to simply say, therefore, that we found Joseph Zaritsky's work (currently showing at the Stedelijk Museum of Modern Art) to be worthless. We do dare to say plainly that we saw nothing in it, that his work did nothing for us, and that more than once we were unsympathetically struck by the chaotic resolution of work that appears to consist of lines of paint randomly thrown about. It occured to us that perhaps this art is not really so rich in ideas or beauty.

But at the same time we must add that we were not able to connect with the spirit behind this work; we could not even work up a desire to contemplate it for any length of time. So our conclusion can only be that there must be something here, but we were not able to find it. We will not pretend to be profound, then, but will just leave it at this.

• Belgian art

The Belgian artists currently being displayed in the Stedelijk Museum of Modern Art in Amsterdam could be divided into three groups: the abstractionists, the Surrealists, and the rest – any other connection between them is hard to find, and we will not speculate about that.

First, the abstractionists: that is to say, artists who produce art that does not seek to represent anything. In this genre, art has ultimately no other purpose than the purely aesthetic – it does not actually have a subject, for it would be a betrayal of abstractionist principles to have one.

The qualities of abstractionist art must thus be defined purely by the interplay of lines, planes and colours – in varying degrees of beauty. Viewed in this way, the work of van Lint and Mendelsohn satisfies these high demands; especifically the former makes a strong statement with his compositions in graded shades of blue-grey tints – full of movement, balanced and appealingly beautiful. Mendelsohn's work varies in quality but, since the last time his work was shown in Amsterdam, he has matured considerably. His successful works are some of the best ones in this exhibition.

Contrary to what one may think, in this type of art – in which decoration gains, as it were, an independent quality – one can distinguish a number of very refined qualities. When artists approach this genre thinking that it will be easy, they are terribly mistaken. Some of the works of the other abstractionists are definitely of inferior quality, underworked, often untidy and full of 'empty spaces'. We think of Collaert, for example – with the exception of his *Boats*, which have a great strength of design – and Bonet. Also in Bertrand's work we find little that satisfies. Ongenae is a close follower of Mondrian and not without talent, but his work does help us to better appreciate the refinement and strength of the works of the great master.

Second, the Surrealists: Delvaux and Magritte are not unknown here. Magritte paints jokes, quasi-profound sayings and word-plays. Delvaux is very different; he is a Surrealist who, with real power and sometimes very convincingly presents us with his view that the world and our lives are meaningless, that 'the smell of death clings to them', that everything beautiful is past. He has not always scorned subjects that are popular and easy. The crucifixion with skeletons, for example, will appeal to certain snobbish viewers but is nevertheless, in every respect, of inferior quality. Other works, for example *Cyrialide*, are very effective. His characteristic work, *Penelope*, demonstrates how ridiculous and meaningless every beauty, every classic pose, is in these days of electric lights, with everything flat and without sparkle, robbed of all zest for life. Even the little flag hangs listlessly in the wind, not to mention the 'frozen flesh' of the female figure.

The rest: these are hardly worth any further attention. Brusselmans may have played a role in the development of art in Belgium, but his work has little to offer, even though it is hundred times better than the boring quasi-accidental art of Guiette. Mortier and van Roy are not without merit and do say something, but their works failed to awake any enthusiasm in us.

The final verdict? A number of works are not without merit; a few are exceptional; but on the whole, rather mediocre.

• Three friends who gave expressions to a Flemish view of life

In the minds of the general public, modern art is still something new, strange and almost indigestible. However, for those who, because of some special connection or interest, or because of their occupation, have come into more frequent contact with this art, it is a movement that is already half a century old. This art manifested itself with great energy in the early part of the twentieth century, but then continued its progression in a calmer way – as most artistic styles throughout the ages have done. Yet, that gradual evolution did occasionally experience some sudden explosions.

We notice this when we view the exhibition of three Flemish Expressionists in the Van Abbe Museum in Eindhoven. Apart from forerunners like Ensor, Expressionism emerged simultaneously around 1905 in France and Germany; since then it has steadily evolved and developed, and continues to do so. Between 1920 and 1930 it manifested itself in an especially unique and very recognizable way, with heavy shapes and angular, monumental forms of people and things with a lumpish, earthy, animal feel. The clear, vivid colours of the original Expressionism became heavier and darker, but still remained very strained. In the Netherlands we think of Gestel and Chabot; in Germany, especially of Feininger; and in Belgium we must certainly include the three masters whose work, now being displayed in Eindhoven, shaped the 'countenance' of this time.

It is remarkable that many recent critiques of the art of this era (and such critiques are abundant, due to the exhibitions of Schlemmer and Feininger in Amsterdam, and this one in Eindhoven) comment: 'It's passé, it was just a passing movement that did not last.' We cannot see such comments as having much integrity. After all, art historians are able to narrow down the date of an ancient work of art to within ten years. Is it then problematic that this is true of modern art too? There has never been an art style that has endured; they have all come and gone!

Permeke is certainly the most impressive of these three artists. His large works, imposing in their presentation and, in a strange way, fierce in their expressions, have mostly farm folk as their themes. The subjects are larger than life, created as symbols so that they become expressions of primeval powers, of earthy life. We will not find any tenderness or gentleness here – nor, in a sense, anything spiritual. Even a theme like motherhood lacks anything tender or loving. Rather, we have a symbolizing here of the purely animal, primeval power of nature, of the constant regeneration and maturing of new life.

In his later works he softens his almost inhuman, symbolic and weighty style, and a more sensitive, human side emerges. Even then the form and colour remain imposing. We are reminded of Rubens' landscapes – not that there is any influence of Rubens in his style but because here, in modern form, we experience a similar perception of nature – grand and gripping and cosmically-directed.

Van den Berghe is more philosophical, and one might call some of his works more vitalistic. Here we find heavy, simplified forms with a touch of Cubist influences, symbolism and a tendency to generalize. He is less earthy than Permeke though, similarly, his figures too have no individuality. After 1930 van den Berghe's style changed. His presentation became freer, more poetic. A profound influence by Ensor is apparent here, with a reality that is just as sinister. We can see this in the impressive portrait of Eduard Anseele if we look carefully at the listening crowd.

Gustave de Smet is the most appealing, the most refined of the three. Yes, he has a similar earthiness and uses a similarly ponderous simplification of forms. But his art retains something warmer, more human. Especially in his portraits (which for his contemporaries was an unthinkable genre) we can almost characterize him as a modern-day

Rik Wouters. De Smet's art is more direct, less fierce and also less monumental and less symbolic. Especially in his later works, a sensitive human spirit is expressed – see his portrait of the girl with flowers.

It is unfortunate that none of the works prior to 1920 are represented here of these three friends, who so often worked closely together. For that would perhaps have helped shed more light on the development of modern art, and perhaps would have helped us, in a historical sense, to better understand the artistic origins of the work of the 1920s. Instead, we are here presented with their mature styles, without an introduction as to how they arrived there. This is especially unfortunate because it is so difficult in our country to get to see anything of that earlier, perhaps more passionate work, even though de Smet and van den Berghe worked in the Netherlands for many years, both during and after the First World War.

• G. Rouault: modern Christian art

Rouault is a remarkable artist. His work is being shown in the Stedelik Museum of Modern Art in Amsterdam. He is one of the undisputed masters of modern art and, at the same time, one of the most human. His work does present us with questions, but they are of a very different nature than the questions raised by the average modern painting: after all, his work, though in its composition undoubtedly product of our times, yet, like the work of his equals in the past, can be understood without deeply theoretical contemplations.

Rouault is a Roman Catholic; knowing this is fundamental to understanding his work. It also helps to explain the two-sided nature of his art: on the one hand it is revolutionary and rebellious, narrowly allied with ultra-modern directions; on the other hand it is thoroughly devout, with the intention of depicting what is sacred.

In his training with Gustave Moreau he painted works that were certainly not without merit, but which did not give evidence of his formidable expressive power. At the beginning of this [twentieth] century, his work started to express rebellion. During this time he maintained a close contact with a movement led by Leon Bloy that aspired to spiritual renewal. Rouault painted evil and sin as perhaps it had never been done before. His works from this period are not pretty; sin is also not pretty. Prostitutes, judges, so-called 'chique ladies' (as in *In the Salon*) are presented as they really are: ugly and proud, without human dignity.

This is not caricature; it is biting irony, mocking and scornful. Conventions are unmasked as the artist shows himself to be a rebel, who will not accept the world as it is, acutely aware of sin and without pity or tenderness. Sin is clearly depicted, and every belief in the goodness and purity of human life is denied, but there is nothing upbuilding here, and no sense of co-participation in the guilt. Veneration, respect for established values, a forgiving spirit – these are all foreign to his work, and this makes it through and through revolutionary.

Gradually, however, with the passing of the years, we see alongside this type of art the appearance of a completely different angle. The clown, the Pierrot, becomes the primary theme: a person who has to act cheerful and comical, though inside he is lonely and full of tragic melancholy. It describes the human condition of the modern person, who has unmasked everything as glitter and emptiness, yet has to carry on with the daily drudgery of superficial joys and pleasures. The *Miserere* becomes his main theme: he created a large series of etchings with this title which shows people continually weighed down by sorrow and suffering. This work is deeper, and more human, than his previous art.

During the same period he also made many paintings of the Christ figure: pious works that have a typically Roman Catholic flavour but are completely free of all sentimentality and the one-dimesional Christ that we see, for example, in devotional pictures.

In addition he created a series of marvellous landscapes during this time. It is remarkble that the work of his later years, when he was in his eighties, was painted more and more thickly, becoming like relief paintings. This is mature art that testifies to wisdom: on the one hand, wisdom gained from life experience and, on the other hand, a highly artistic control and excellence. Thus his work gained an almost timeless quality of humanness and meaningful clarity in the midst of a continuing revolution, showing up the artistic talk of many of his contempories as foolishness.

• Healthy French art

Art dealer De Boer (Keizersgracht 542, Amsterdam) has taken the initiative to exhibit the work of a contemporary French artist. Of course, now and then in art museums we do come across French artists, but then it is usually the 'big names', the ultra-modern painters, whose bold outlandishness causes the viewer to respond with either surprise or despair. No, Carrega is not a man dear to the hearts of today's avant-garde, who appreciate only what is extreme. We will not try to determine how much snobbishness is involved here, but it is certain that Carrega's work is not inferior to that of the Modernists who do not belong to the great masters.

That is to say, he is an excellent painter. But, alas, these days that is not enough, for above the heads of artists a storm is brewing about artistic direction, with the result that people can only appreciate works that correspond with their own opinions. And yet, we believe that artists like Carrega may be more avant-garde than those who are celebrated as such. For he is an artist who wants to bring the human element back into art. One must begin with the human, he says. And then that human quality, which consists of more than purely aesthetic values, must be crafted in an artistic way. For certainly, the human element alone does not make for a good painting.

Well, Carrega has certainly succeeded in creating some very acceptable work, both with regard to composition as well as to the actual painting. He presents us with works that one is able to enjoy, even to like – in short, art that one can connect with and can discuss in ordinary language, without quasi-philosophical profundity. He often chooses his subjects on the coast, in harbour towns like Le Havre, among the fishermen of Bretagne – themes that the nineteenth century laboured to a point of death. Modern art started in reaction to that tendency to show us the same thing over and over again. But here the subject is worked out in a new way, with a new vision and painting style and a comletely contemporary interpretation, and without short-changing the subject.

We do not suggest that Carrega is a genius. If only he was, the future of painting might have looked brighter; then perhaps even the so-called avant-garde would be convinced. But, however it may be, perhaps he is one of the first birds to announce the arrival of a new spring. Let us welcome him as such.

• Works by André Petroff

It is easy for an art critic to write about a follower or imitator. All the critic has to do is to place the artist under consideration into the proper box; then to make a judgment about the quality of his work; and everything has been said. It is a very different matter to consider the work of an original artist – one who really cannot be compared with anyone else. Then one discovers that words are not enough to capture the language of painting. Petroff is such an artist.

Petroff has his own views. He says that in every time period there are 'primitives', by which he means artists who paint out of the richness of their personality – having grown up in a specific country with its own climate and landscape, rooted in an own tradition – with all their talents, their emotions and intelligence, without allowing themselves to be pushed into a certain mold, and without adhering to specific standard methods. He admires such 'primitives' of other eras and other lands (and since he has travelled to nearly every corner of the globe, he has seen their art for himself); among them he includes van Gogh, Rembrandt, and especially our fifteenth-century [Dutch] artists.

Despite this he is well aware – and has experienced it himself – that it is impossible (at least if one wants to be oneself) to stop being, for instance, a Russian. People cannot renounce or strip themselves of their heritage, their land of birth with its unique characteristics and peculiar artistic traditions (and here he is thinking of the so-called Russian 'primitives' like Rublev.

Judged by his own criteria, Petroff is indeed such a 'primitive'. He looks at things in new ways, as if with different eyes, without falling back into old formulas – drawing on his own personal emotions. Staking all his knowledge and abilities, he realizes his vision. It is mature work, drawn from his own experience, that does not do away with common sense (as so often happens today) that dictates that one has to work and study hard in order to be able to express oneself in a convincing and satisfying way.

It is very hard to characterize Petroff's work. It is thoroughly twentieth-century art, not disconnected from Expressionism and Impressionism, but also not to be captured by those style terms. His favourite theme is the sailing vessel of southern France, depicted in every possible light and position – now in a dynamically active composition, bathed in light and full of movement; then again lying in a corner of the harbour in quiet water beside some old houses, rustic and romantic, in utter peace, though never without a measure of tension, for the ship will sail again and this peace will not last. He continually shows us at other aspects of this recurring pattern (for that is how he sees it) in works that fascinate us especially because of their compositional qualities. Sometimes it is the harmony of colour that gives the work meaning, at other times it is the unique rhythm of the lines, sometimes the perception of depth. Especially the rhythmic play of lines is characteristic of his art with their underlying criss-crosses, diverging into many different directions – these are used to build the compositions and give them their typical dynamic tension.

Very special (and we won't mention any other pieces) is his painting of the windmill, which he uses as a symbol to express what is typically Dutch: the sturdy strength, embodying the struggle against the sea by using the readily available power of the wind; with a proud bearing in peaceful simplicity. And truly – what we have here is not a windmill in a landscape, but a windmill at the centre of everything, with the landscape and the depth dependent on it. All this is accomplished by a subtle but very unique choice of viewpoint that strongly underscores the majesty of the scene.

• Humour in drawing: mirror of modern life

An exceptionally entertaining exposition entitled 'Masters of Caricature' is at present being shown in the Amsterdam Gemeentemuseum. The show begins with Daumier, whose biting caricatures mocked the values that were held by the people of his time (or that they pretended to hold) – from the most highly-respected classics to the battle for freedom on the barricades, from monarch to blue-stocking to the person in the street.

Much more human and tender, and less revolutionary, is the humour of *Punch*, the British magazine that became well known around the middle of the nineteenth century. It commented on the current events of those days with a single drawing and caption that depicted a specific situation in a certain light. Initially the captions were very long and made the main point. In contrast with Daumier (and later political cartoons, such as the keenly artistic and beautiful drawings found in the German *Simplissimus* of around 1900) who drew figures that represented specific groups or powers, *Punch* portrayed ordinary people experiencing those accidental and amusing things that happen to us all from time to time. This style has endured and can be found also in the works of Frenchmen like Willette and Steinlen, when they finally dropped their preoccupation with the political and social situation.

A third type of caricature is found in the works of Lear, who published *A Book of Nonsense* for children in which he drew pictures to accompany rhymes that, in the manner of English nursery rhymes, play on words and sounds, without any deeper meanings. We wish to emphasize that Lear was strictly concerned with the play on words and thoughts, a certain kind of childlike, unbridled fantasy, which breathes a completely different spirit than that of the modern caricature (or 'cartoon' as it is called in in America these days). In the latter one can hardly speak anymore of political satire or caricature; rather, a grim sort of humour is all that remains. There is some madness in the work of Steinberg, the most influential illustrator of our time; and an ominous absurdity in the work of Addams, who creates a sinister atmosphere by placing ordinary objects in very out-of-the-ordinary contexts. The drawing itself becomes completely autonomous in these often very nihilistic caricatures, which satirize everything and never offer solutions, thereby making everything appear meaningless, picturing all as being rotten and every ideal as a whimsical fantasy without logic or reason. The modern world finds in this art a most exact and clear reflection of its own likeness.

This is an educational and sometimes also amusing exhibition. It is a pity that the British artists prior to Daumier, specifically Fillray and Rowlandson, are not represented. We also missed Gavarni.

• Saul Steinberg's mockery: nihilistic games

One could invent a new proverb – 'By his humour, a man is known' – to be applied to the work of Saul Steinberg, a Romanian presently working in America, who has received many accolades for his work in the field of burlesque art.

With his humourous drawings (so-called 'cartoons') he has established himself as a celebrity, but in this exhibition we see something more than just humour emerging. Or rather, it is hard to tell where the humour ends and something else begins – art? Or just a game? We can gather from the reactions of the viewers that this sort of art appeals to twentieth-century people, that it reflects their spirit and that they can connect with it – another reason why our opening proverb is so applicable.

In our assessment this art holds no more than bitter sarcasm (at which our fellow viewers were heard snickering); we felt it expressed a hatred that our fellow viewers could not help laughing about and calling 'fantastic'. We must conclude that those who do not understand the truly modern spirit and own it will be hard pressed to determine what is, and what is not, so funny.

There is a strong twentieth-century world view in this work, a perception of reality which finds an expression in toppling structures, in train stations with their jumbled tangle of tracks and gloomy steel constructions, in cityscapes with their caricature of flashy American automobiles and movie theatres that flaunt glittery, Rococo-like facades. To sum up Steinberg's work in a few words, 'He has no respect.' Anything that was once considered sacred, that was loved or adored, everything that gave joy or caused awe, is depicted with biting sarcasm in all its meaninglessness, emptiness and its pretence.

But along with the ugliness of our present time and the pretenses of the past, anything of true worth, every tradition, everything historically achieved, every perception of rank or standing, is jeered at. Thus, these pseudo-historical documents manage to connect with a generation which has no sense of history, which views important documents as ugly things with fancy signatures. The pleasures that youth have always enjoyed (yes, even the people of our own time) are 'unmasked' as futile, empty, idle games – just hollow fun.

Diplomas? How ridiculous! Yes, that's how this man with his sharp drawing pen perceives them, for to him values are meaningless, nothing is sacred; everything is an ugly sham. Is there then nothing that matters anymore?

These drawings speak of hatred, not only towards that which realy is false and hypocritical (that would be laudable), but towards anything cultural and traditional, every accomplishment and every product of responsible and historical development. Thus the humour fails to be liberating; it lacks that which makes true humour healthy and refreshing, namely a love for and empathy with the people it humours. Instead, we find a revolutionary hatred expressed here that feeds a biting and destructive spirit of sarcasm.

• Modern American graphic art[1140]

It is difficult to judge the importance of the exhibition of modern American graphics at the Gemeentemuseum in The Hague. Whether this is great and important art or just empty showmanship may be a matter for discussion. What is clear is that we are presented here with wealth and multiplicity of technical possibilities, which at times render even an otherwise insignificant work fascinating. Here one can see the most diverse processes and the most complex printing techniques applied.

It is more difficult, as we have said, to define the artistic value of the work. By far the greater part of what we see is 'abstract' art, but, putting aside for the moment every possible objection, it is seldom a boring or uninspired rehashing of what has been done excellently before. It has to be said that this art is alive, with no sign of becoming bogged down in theories and slogans like so much of the modernistic art we encounter.

On the other hand, it strikes me as an acute danger for the further development of this art that what is interesting and fascinating and alive about it is often, far too often, traceable exclusively to the technical experimentation. Undoubtedly, that is always an important aspect of graphic art that one would neglect at one's peril, yet ultimately technique must be harnessed in the service and articulation of a vision, a view of reality that the artist musters and needs to communicate.

Yet in abstract art we often discern nothing more than the flight from reality or, if there is any expression of emotion at all, it is a negative emotion of hatred and revulsion for the creation. Practically speaking, this means that abstract art seldom gets any further than super-ornamentation, being beautiful without any further content. In itself that certainly does not have to be worthless. Mondrian is proof enough of that! But ultimately it is only enjoyable if it arises from exceptional purity and intensity. The moment the spell of supreme beauty is broken, one is left with an empty vessel. Less superb abstract art is ultimately intensely boring, empty, hollow, and unutterably indigent. The danger confronting graphic art at the moment is this: as soon as the spell of the captivating experiment is broken a tenuous nothing remains and, in the end, nothing of lasting value has been gained.

It would serve no purpose to name the exhibitors who, to the best of my knowledge, are all displayed in Europe for the first time. It would be futile too to discuss the few works that are not abstract separately, for in a technical sense what they have to say is not much different from the purely abstract ones. There is one exception. I cannot neglect to mention the piece I enjoyed most: Frasconi's *Good catch* – a rhythmic play of little boats on the waves, strongly reminiscent of Japanese art, a special effect attained by printing the grains of a plank. Well then, until 6 December.

• Comparative exposition of modern art[1141]

Over the summer months a very interesting exhibition is showing in the new wing of the Stedelijjk Museum of Modern Art in Amsterdam. It shows modern art in various different contexts. On the lower level modern art is confronted with primitive art, primarily from New Guinea and the surrounding islands as well as from Africa. The intention, of course, is to point out the similarities between this art and modern art. There are some truly striking specimens among these – for example, the statue of a corpse from Tojo that is compared with a statue by Schmidt-Rottluf.

There is certainly a strong resemblance between these two works, but that is not surprising: Schmidt-Rottluf had consciously incorporated influences from the kind of art that has been included here for purposes of comparison. The same could be said of Picasso. Anyone with some knowledge of the history of modern art knows that in his early cubistic period he was strongly influenced by the African masks that we see placed next to his art here.

Yet, it is a remarkable fact that modern artists have so frequently drawn inspiration from primitive art. Modern art can be understood as a reaction against the naturalism of the nineteenth century; instead of just imitating reality it sought to express something of reality in a symbolically artistic way. To this end, artists began to study many types of old art based on a similar inspiration. Modern art is also an expression of a broken relationship with reality; there are tensions because reality is perceived as a strange, incomprehensible, irrational power. Herein too the moderns found a deep affinity with the primitives, even though their perceptions had different causes and were experienced differently. With the moderns it is all very self-consciously done and very carefully considered. That is why the comparison with a child's drawing is less compelling, even though there are some similarities: both make use of imagery that is not naturalistic, and colours are used for the sheer enjoyment of colour itself, for the joy of 'self-expression', as it is called today.

However, there is one big difference between modern and primitive art, namely the tendency towards abstraction. Of course, the art of all times, including that of the primitives, have been acquainted with adornment, with decoration that uses the interplay of lines and colours and shapes without any special meaning. But today abstractions in form and colour are perceived to have value in themselves, to possess their own meaning as independent works of art.

On the upper exhibition level one can see how the forms discovered by the modern art movement have had their effect on modern life. Yes, in many different ways they directly express the emotions and sensations that are offered by our times. We often know the world abstractly, in a mathematically formulated way and, by playing around with these mathematical forms and formulas we think we can control reality.

We did not always find the chosen examples convincing, however indisputable the insight may be that is at the heart of this exposition. Nevertheless, some real discoveries await the viewers – for example, the comparison of Mondrian's *Victory boogie woogie* with a photograph of New York in the evening that clearly shows the contemporary realities Mondrian was attempting to express.

• The Experimental in (or out of) the Stedelijk Museum of Modern Art

As soon as we enter the international exhibition of the Experimentals currently showing at the Amsterdam Stedelijk Museum of Modern Art, we notice the slogan on the wall: 'We abolish this lyricism.' Under it, a number of books have been stuck to the wall, and a thick red line has been crossed through them all. Then it becomes apparent that it is the lyricism of people like Werumeus Buning and Kees van Doorne that has been damned. We might have our own objections to some of those renounced poets too, but what are we given in their place? Well, we don't have to wait long for the answer. On the same wall also the 'Experimental' poem by Elburg is inscribed. It starts as follows:

> They would do boats
> through the water, the dry sand
> through the stones cut into mirrors
> of foot and by bicycle paths
> they would do boats, comrades.

This small fragment, better than a profusion of words, perfectly conveys the spirit of this exhibition in which a number of Amsterdam painters (Appel, Constant and others) are also represented.

One might ask whether such work really belongs in a museum. Is the government required to display everything that calls itself art? Must the enlightened state go so far that every 'newness', no matter how crazy or foolish or artistically weak and irresponsible, must be displayed to the public? Certainly there should not be a one-sided instruction, as the Stedelijk Museum of Modern Art seems to be doing in its promotion of this 'new' trend.

Yes, we have put the word 'new' in quotation marks, because what we find here is nothing more than the prolonging of a revolution that has happened long ago and was then just as radical as it is still perceived to be. It is a movement that repeats what has been stated, if only more emphatically, more wildly, more brashly and, in our opinion, certainly with less talent and with much more charlatanry. For the ideas expressed here are already found in the Futurist movement of 1909 and in the Dadaism of 1919 and are closely allied with people like Klee and the great artist Kandinski.

What are those ideas? Well, let's listen to what the Experimentals themselves have to say. We come across slogans like: 'It's our longing that brings about the revolution.' 'Culture permits beauty to excuse the ugly.' 'No civility in art – art is just brute desire.' 'The best painting is the one that excludes reason.' Such cries are to be found throughout their writings.

Experimentalism is the most consistent kind of nihilism: people don't believe in anything any more, not even in the world created by the revolution itself. The result is a constantly prolonged and renewed revolution. Civilization, conventions, norms, morality, beauty, these are obsolete concepts to be rid of. They cause all the misery, because they stifle the true essence of being human and prevent it from being expressed. The only honesty is to let oneself go, unbounded by any external norms or laws. The (psycho-somatic) life, which houses the true inner self, must express itself directly, unrestrained and unfettered by the detestable mind. Well, when we hear talk like that, we know well where it will end. Is it not written, 'For from within, out of men's hearts, come evil thoughts . . . slander, arrogance, and folly' (Mark 7:21)?

But, these artists say, in a time such as this people can't expect sweet, wholesome art. Decadent times produce, by necessity, decadent art. We will provide it, we will accept this task.

But how did a time 'such as this' come about? Do not people themselves create their art (as well as other things), through their own desires and efforts? Yes, that's true – they answer – but we know no way out. The only salvation would be a complete detachment from the basics of our culture . . . so we just keep trying things. Instructed by the experience of experimenting in an environment of unrestrained freedom, we will discover new laws for a new creativity.

As if those who in the past have refused to bow the knee to anything will suddenly be willing to subject themselves to new laws! Sin gives birth to sin, and revolution to revolution. And in the end they both result in death.

Truly we have here a most extreme expression of the spirit of our times. Therefore let us not mock all this or call it charlatanry. For charlatans look for a public; they look for a willing ear and therefore they direct themselves to current ideas. Charlatans must be willing to identify themselves eagerly with their public. No, this is much more serious and the world ought to be shocked by these extremes.

Let us take note of them. Here we have those followers of false teachers who take lessons from evil spirits and who 'have delighted in wickedness' (2 Thessalonians 2:12), those who 'call evil good' (Isaiah 5:20); here we have persons filled with terror and dread (Isaiah 2:21) who 'still did not repent of the work of their hands' (Revelation 9:20–21). And it is only in repentance that a solution can be found. Therefore, let us not mock all this, or call it charlantry; let us not cry 'woe and alas' but let us take note of this sign of the times. For it is here, right here in these extreme expressions in painting and poetry, that the spirits make themselves manifest.

•Domela Nieuwenhuis

C. Domela Nieuwenhuis is exhibiting work at Huinck and Scherjon in the Herengracht in Amsterdam. In an attempt to define this work, one could ask whether it should be called painting or embossment. In either case, it is abstract, non-figurative art.

The public (and not only they) often wonder what abstract artists are actually trying to say, what their work is supposed to mean. Although one could explain how the concept of abstract art started at the beginning of this century, prompted by a specific world and life view, that would still not help us answer the question of what a specific work really means. Perhaps it is more fruitful not to pose the question at all, but to view this type of art only as decoration, work that does not really mean to portray anything and should rather be regarded as a sort of ornament.

When viewed in this way, Domela's work certainly has some very special qualities. With various kinds of wood inlays, a few painted pieces of wood, copper wire and copper tape he constructs decorative panels that often breathe a sense of peace and harmony and could very appropriately be used to break up the emptiness of a large wall.

If one disregards the question we began with and asks altogether fewer questions (which perhaps should be answered by the artist anyway – and even then his answer may not be satisfying), one ought not have any problem with this kind of art, which certainly has strengths. One can appreciate it for its own worth and can enjoy its craftmanship in the beautiful interplay of lines and colours.

• Modern art as national property

As one wanders through the hallways of the Prinsenhof in Delft, where presently a huge variety of high-calibre works by contemporary Dutch artists have been assembled, one is struck by the fact that the phrase 'the Netherlands, mid-twentieth century' – a term that will undoubtedly be used in the future by art historians – definitely describes a very clearly defined body of works. There is a distinct unity of style; not more so than in previous eras – it is no boring uniformity – but also no less so than in past periods.

It may have been true in the early years of this [twentieth] century that chaos reigned in the world of art. At present, though, now that the new principles conceived during that time have had a chance to be worked out, the relative unity that the art of any era usually displays – almost impossible to define and yet definitely there – can unquestionably be found here too. Certainly much art is still being done in the older styles, also in this country, but that too is not unique to our time and an unmistakeable epigonism is almost always present in such work.

It is remarkable too that the progressive works classified as 'ultra-modern' – Experimental, and so on – which can be found here as well, still fall within the general framework of this exhibition; hanging in between high-quality modern art pieces that are more understandable and less strange, they nevertheless do not appear out of place or incongruent in the context of the artistic whole.

If one wants to attempt to define what it is that constitutes this unity, one must begin by recognizing clarity of colour, a vivid palette, determined by the primary colours. In addition to unity of colouring one finds unity also in the brush technique – the style of painting. Broad lines, a lack of attention to detail, and fluid and clear strokes are common to almost all of these works, as well as the shapes that are used. Then, too, one finds hardly any of these works have real content in the sense of having a specific meaning, something to say or to tell. The reaction to the 'story art' of the previous century was so vehement and strong that now almost every human reference, everything generally thought of as meaningful, has disappeared from art. These paintings make sense only in a strict artistic way: purity of line and colour, and their combination, lively brush technique and, in short, all that relates strictly to the pictorial and to the technique of painting, determine the value of these works, whether we are dealing with a still life or a landscape, an interior or even a human figure – all of these are no more than an inducement to the artist to create something.

Whereas painters in the past would have made a poem about a still life, today they would make a poem with the still life: colour, shape and volume are used as building blocks in constructing the work of art. There is little that differentiates between art that is completely subject-less – for even when something recognizable remains, the art plays havoc with actual reality – and works in which we can still find some hint of Impressionism; what difference there is, relates more to the method of painting and colouring than to a fundamentally different view of reality.

No, the modern art of today does not speak in a pictorial-poetic way about reality; it plays around with the givens taken from reality, intent on composing a work with pure artistic merit. Beauty can be found here, but rarely anything with value in terms of its human reference – except in an artistic sense. With this in mind, one should not be surprised that the Coronation painting was a failure: for such an assignment our modern artists can hardly be expected to come up with an appropriate style.

Of course, the world view of today is also clearly apparent in these works. To a greater or lesser degree, we find in their composition and their expressive power a reflection of the stresses of modern life – anxiety, the notion of insignificance, an alienation from created reality. Form and content may be in agreement, but it is the manner of its representation rather than the theme of the work that explores these notions. Composition, form, and colour, in their mutual relationship, become symbols. Occasionally we find symbols in the usual, narrower sense of the word, but there is never an appeal to a commonly understood language of imagery. Such a language hardly exists anymore as it did in past centuries, when a lily beside Mary indicated her purity, and a dove denoted the Holy Spirit. It is possible that these paintings are so inaccessible to the viewing public precisely because of the absence of such figurative language – and the fact that these works (even when they are recognizable) give us nothing more than pictorial beauty or, at best, a fundamental awareness of reality (again, only in a purely artistic sense). After all, the public seeks clearly represented human content, a story, a poem about the beauty of things, and understands little or nothing of this art that plays around with given realities as if they are elements with which one can more or less freely do as one wishes.

After all the experiments and all the 'painting exercises' we believe it is now time for artists to go back to content. Holding on to their newly acquired skills, the human aspect must be given its place again, and art must become 'meaningful' again. We know this is possible when we observe the different tapestries of the series *The prodigal son*. Perhaps it is also indicated in some of the works by, for example, the artists from The Hague: Berserik, Drayer, Andrea, van Eysden and Huib Hierck. But besides the grammar that these artists know so well, they will have to find a pictorial language again – and that will not be easy. Shall we make this the assignment for the near future, and will the second half of the twentieth century see the completion of the task? Unfortunately, we are not very confident of this.

This large and very important exposition has given an account of our art – just as our Government has wanted to give an account of its acquisitions and commissions, and just as former governments (monarchies, dynasties, and republics) also did in their own time, in their own way. Nevertheless, the acquisitions are of a high quality and certainly not one-sided; it has become a truly representative collection. It invites us to an overall picture that turns out to be much better than we ever expected – our ears still ringing with the buzzing, screaming and bleating of the many isms of a good twenty to thirty years ago.

• Meritorious work of Paul Citroen[1142]

Paul Citroen is being honoured with an exhibition in the Gemeentemuseum in The Hague. And we believe the praise is justified. For Citroen is an important figure in the artistic life of The Hague. Not only because of his own work, yes, perhaps least of all because of that personal oeuvre. For Paul Citroen has an open-minded spirit and is prepared to do things for others; he is a man who encourages young artists in the right way, alert to what is interesting and good in their work, who does not hide the light he finds under a bushel, a man with many ideas who can turn every dialogue into a significant encounter. Citroen is, in short, a man who never lets himself be carried away by any fad or movement and who, precisely for that reason, has been able to fulfil a mediating role, showing those from one movement what those from another, were achieving.

Yet in spite of all that, yes, perhaps as a condition for all that, Paul Citroen has never occupied a place in the foreground. He prefers to remain in the background. He does not talk much about his own work but more about art, about this piece or that movement. Therefore it is good to have the spotlight turned on him for a change. This exhibition of his work reveals an artist of considerable talent who has a vision and something to say. He himself seems bemused that, while he has such a love for the diverse currents in modern art and has done so much to promote it, seeing great importance in this movement – for example, he was the first person in the Netherlands to publish anything about modern artists! – yet he has been unable to work in a modern idiom himself. We believe we know the reason why. He is far too open-minded a spirit, far too interested in the people around him, far too full of life. He could not have been satisfied by producing the designs in which much of modern art has become stranded. He could never have pursued the general, the abstract or stylized in art when it is precisely the distinctive and the characteristic that so engages and fascinates him.

His magnificent portrait drawings, a generous 'bouquet' of which we see displayed here, attest to his knowledge of people and his understanding of real life. They show us that Paul Citroen knows what a work of art is: a meaningful spiritual reality that says something about what it depicts, that expresses a vision, a statement of thoughts and ideas. But not only that. Art is also a playful interaction with materials, constructing the whole in such a way that it stresses what the artist desires to say, that it communicates clearly through lines and composition. The portrait drawings must be called exceptional. Piece for piece they demonstrate that one does not have to be modernistic in the way one works – abstract, surrealistic or expressionistic – in order to belong to our times. Citroen's portraits certainly belong to our day and age. They present a view that is totally 'now'. Indeed, one will consult the past in vain to find an art that is of the same sort or style. No, Citroen's art is alive, arising directly from intense empathetic contact with the people around him.

There are also landscapes, which we will not discuss extensively here, even if that were possible. Somewhat romantic in mood, they manifest a pure beauty that cannot be captured in words. Citroen's drawings, impressions of Florence, are very beautiful as well, though executed more broadly and directly. Almost all of them depict the fountain on the great square in Florence, yet observed with such freshness and intelligence and with so much taste that many will realize after having seen these drawings just how much this fountain – inspired by the great bronze horses – has for the artistically trained eye to discover, though it is easily overlooked because there is so much else of 'importance' to see in Florence.

In short, this is an exhibition where people will see a great deal that they can talk about in a warm and human way without stumbling into all kinds of issues concerning alienation. For this reason too it is an important exhibition by an important artist.

• Charley Toorop: mature talent in full bloom

The Huinck and Scherjon Art Dealers (Herengracht 469, Amsterdam) are currently showing the works of Charley Toorop that were painted in the years following the War.

Actually this announcement should be sufficient, for Charley Toorop has fully deserved her reputation and anyone unacquainted with her work is lacking some basic knowledge about twentieth-century Dutch art; they should hurry and catch up quickly. On the other hand, anyone who has seen her remarkable work once, or more, will need no description.

However, we can imagine there might be some who are curious about her most recent developments. It is remarkable that we see neither the slightest sign of any slackening in her pace, nor do we find Toorop repeating herself at all – remarkable, especially when we consider her state of health. On the contrary, her most recent work radiates with vitality and daring, with utmost control and tension.

Her work, which now consists of many still lifes, betrays a concern for the 'ordinary' things of daily living. She paints with a richness of colour that is perhaps at times less balanced than before, which we may regard as the price she had to pay for the freshening, the brightening and clarifying of her palette. *In Tree in the living room* she reaches a vividness of colour that we have not seen in her work before, while the general quality of her work has remained the same. A number of self-portraits and a beautifully drawn portrait of Roland Holst complete this exhibit.

It is not without sadness that one leaves this exhibition. It denotes the end of an era as the exhibiting art dealer is closing down soon, and, while its owner deserves and needs a rest after a very busy life, it nevertheless is an ominous sign for our present culture that no one could be found to take it over. The end of this show signifies the end of a period characterized by names like Mendez da Costa, Redeker, Bremmer, Charley Toorop and others. Little activity in the realm of contemporary art remains, and another piece of Amsterdam culture and tradition will disappear. Let us raise a final salute to one of our greatest female artists, and to this art dealer who has done so much for our culture.

• Berserik: one of the best

H. Berserik, one of the most gifted among the younger artists of The Hague, has, in the years after the War, left a deep impression with his expressionistically tinted works. Especially boats were a well loved theme and, through some deformation, he managed to breathe into them an almost demonic dynamism. This art had a fairly important influence on the artists' circles in The Hague.

Last year, however, in an exhibition by the group De Verve (to which he belongs), we noted that he had broken with that style and was now searching for a more direct, more conventional mode of expression. However, the resulting work has not been very satisfying, and we pointed out that Berserik still had to find his own style in this new, less exalted, less forced artistic direction.

With much pleasure we can state that, at the exposition of drawings and graphic art by Liernus in the Zeestraat, his most recent works witness that he has found such a style. And how! No deformities, no unbearable and unnatural tensions anymore; instead, a wholesome, normal kind of art. This art recognizes that it has not been called upon to copy reality but that it is permitted to represent nature in its own way; it knows how to present honest human emotion without exaggerated stress. See, for instance, the beautiful drawing of a man, standing on a bridge and looking out over the grandeur of the surrounding landscape – how real, true, natural; and yet, artistic, and far removed from a dull realism.

How human, the etching of a pregnant woman, drawn and characterized with so much love, with such a deep understanding of her private emotional state, and far removed from every crudeness or forced realism that can make such themes disgusting in modern art. And then too with what a truly artistic *économie des forces* he controls his medium.

Among the woodcuts, perhaps not always sufficiently free from Roozendaal's influence, we could mention some beautiful examples.

Finally we should point out the coloured chalk drawing of a harbour. In this work the contrast with his former style is most striking, as formerly he displayed a special affinity for themes like this. There are no extraordinary tensions in this drawing; only a revelation of the beauty of colour, of contrasts and movement that elevate this work to a masterpiece.

In conclusion, notice how in the drawing of the house between the trees, light and sun and colour are present even though there are only a few black lines. It is a simple contrast of black and white that – without striving for effect – achieves this.

Truly, in this exposition Berserik reclaims the position that he deserves. Here we have thoroughly wholesome, truly level-headed Dutch art in the best sense of the word; it is art that places Berserik in the top ranks of the younger Dutch artists.

• Escher's graphic art: puzzling cleverness

How narrow is that view which states that art must only give us beauty; that it can and may be nothing other than 'art for art's sake'! For such a view does not do justice to art's full range of possibilities. Certainly art must embrace beauty too, but the tangible work of art can offer us so much more than that. Art can reveal depths; it can serve as a symbol; it can convey humour or become a game – yes, art is deeper and wider than beauty alone. Think too of the technical aspect: are there not works that amaze us purely because of their technical excellence, the artist's incredible control of materials and media?

We speak of these issues with a view to the work of Escher, the well-known Dutch graphic artist whose work is being displayed in the Stedelijk Museum of Modern Art in Amsterdam. For his art is not only great from the standpoint of its technical rendering of the design onto the block that the print is made from, but the mathematical construction of these works is also a technical achievement – puzzling cleverness. We say 'puzzling', although this time, by allowing us to see his study materials, Escher has revealed to us something of the way in which he works. It might seem so simple to us: you cover a page with parallelograms, then take two animals, drawing them so that they border each other in a particular way inside a parallelogram, and you end up with an endlessly-repeated motif full of movement and life, rhythm and humour. But I doubt there are many who, following those directions, could duplicate such playfulness, such perfection and sophistication. No, I don't believe that anyone but Escher would know where to turn with those basic building blocks.

But Escher doesn't leave it at the endlessly-repeated motif; he circumscribes it and plays around with it in a great number of ways. It is often a romp between real and unreal: think of the little crocodile, this motif inside a basic pattern, which being invested with volume and life starts to walk around and then fades back into the flat design. Famous, too, are the little black and white men who fit precisely into each other, who, after taking leave of their flat plane, come together and shake hands. In Escher we often also find a fascinating play between the reality of what is drawn, on the one hand, and what, on the other hand, is artistically suggested by it. The playfulness is full of humour but also, on more than one occasion, plain creepy. We think of the hands that are drawing each other; or, in a very different trend, the staircase-houses with strange little monsters, where the floor of one becomes a a wall for another and a ceiling for yet another – a supreme toying around with perspective and other old naturalistic ways of representing reality.

One could perhaps lump all of this into a term like 'the irrationality of the rational'. For Escher plays with mathematical and structural reality and discovers in them a strangeness and coincidence and unreasonableness which, paradoxically, are at the same time humourous and horrible. In all of this, his art is fully twentieth-century, an expression of a world view filled with inner contradictions and tensions.

Playful and at the same time profound, full of rollicking fun and simultaneously a nightmare – this work with all its technical precision gives us much more than just beauty, which makes it all the richer. If one should ask whether beauty is to be found here at all, we would have to answer 'Yes', exactly because of all the elements we just mentioned, elements that have all-too-often been reasoned away from having a legitimate place in art.

• Graphic work of Henk Krijger

In the showroom of the Corvey Paper Wholesale Business at the Keizersgracht 289 in Amsterdam, Henk Krijger is displaying his graphic work. Throughout the ages artists have represented reality in their own way; they (and this includes the so-called naturalists) have always had a specific vision of reality. Seldom – or perhaps never – does one encounter an exact representation of reality that also has compositional beauty; the artist always changes and transforms nature so that the result is an aesthetically responsible whole – a whole which, as such, was not exactly present in reality. Also Henk Krijger, whose work bears his very unique stamp, 'deforms' reality, specifically placing the images in a way that shows their mutual connectedness, a way that is obedient to aesthetic laws. He never loses the sense that visual art must represent reality; therefore he never sacrifices the recognizability and understandability of the images he is portraying.

Very occasionally in Krijger's work one could say that what he depicts cannot be found like this in reality, but in those cases the entire work possesses such a compositional and visionary strength, and is so artistically convincing, that the question of the 'realisticness' doesn't even occur to us. In his work Krijger places great emphasis on the decorative element – and therein lies his strength. For that reason, too, his art is so well suited as book illustrations, and so on. Among the works displayed here are the pen-drawn designs for the illuminations of H. de Bruin's *Paul in Ephesus* and A. Coolen's *Fairytales for grown-ups* – but we will not describe these in more detail here. We are constantly struck by the exceptionally convincing, extremely personal stylizing of reality, from which Krijger's compositions derive their decorative and expressive effect. This work, though not untouched by contemporary artistic influences (but then, which art would claim that?), nevertheless takes its own honourable place in the ranks of contemporary art.

• Poorly organized exposition

The St Luke Painters' Association has been given the first privilege of exhibiting in the new exhibition building of the Amsterdam Stedelijk Museum of Modern Art; this is also an opportunity to view the exceptional features of that building. A fairly large number of artists is represented, as usual, which makes exhibitions like this quite unfruitful. The few works per artist cannot give a proper impression; they are too 'alone' and it is nearly impossible to really 'get into them'.

Also the atmosphere that forms the spiritual background against which a work is viewed and weighed, is not conducive, since the work hangs among others of a completely different inclination. What the viewer misses in exhibitions like this is a unity of direction. A profusion of conflicting styles are presented, making it difficult to approach and immerse oneself in any of the works shown.

As is the case with so many exhibitions of this type – and truly, St Luke is not alone in this – there is a mixture here of mature and novice, of first-rate and mediocre, of this style and that. In short, it is a chaotic mess that distracts from the enjoyable task of viewing these artworks. Our patience and goodwill were severely tried as we attempted to stop and look at each piece.

It may be difficult for an association like St Luke to organize an exhibition in a different way, but this sort of display (even more than any showing of the most extreme modern art) contributes to the fact that there is little appreciation, understanding or interest in the visual arts of our time. On the contrary, to choose, say, ten artists and show a large number of each one's work would be a meaningful and instructive display, for the excellence of an individual work would not then be lost because it was hung next to a piece that clashed with it in one way or another.

The problem is certainly not with the building or with the method used to hang the works, for that was done very well. The problem is with the guiding principle behind the choices, which prevents what is valuable from being appreciated as such and brings discredit to the whole field of painted art. The impression is created that whether one tries this, or that, none of it really matters much. Thus, many artists are treated unfairly, not because the public is at fault but because of the ridiculous standards used for organizing the show. What would you think of an anthology of poetry from many periods and countries, of varying quality and content but with no real organizing principle? Even the most sympathetic critic would be inclined to call it rubbish. Or, a musical potpourri made up of excerpts from a symphony, an opera, a waltz, a passion, and an operetta? It is unimaginable!

We have no desire to mention any artists or single out any works from this exposition, with the exception of the cheerful *Girl in the door* by the sculptor Dobbelman. Whether we would have even noticed it had it been of smaller proportions is questionable.

Thus, our assessment is that despite the many individual works of high quality this is a quite unbearable exposition.

• Christian art in Amstelveen[1143]

It is very understandable that Protestant visual artists, in a time such as ours, should associate to discuss their particular task and style. Unfortunately this is not the case in the Circle of Christian Visual Artists; we are dealing here with an association for the single purpose of exposition. Even if their activities together did extend beyond this, the results are barely noticeable, for what can be seen in The Bosrand until 18 April is no more than a mediocre following of that which has been achieved elsewhere. The only positive thing – and for this we would demand full appreciation – is that they keep themselves far from all modernism, which violates people and creation with its destructively oriented imagery.

But, we can hardly be enthusiastic about what is presented here. It is striking that these artists are apparently dependent on a Roman Catholic way of thinking when using 'religious' themes. A real low point in the whole exhibition is the way in which the *Mourning of Christ*, *The Crucifixion*, *Christ bearing the Cross* are treated – mostly in a fundamentally un-Reformed and at times somewhat 'mystical' way, though this is not even a real mysticism. Jan Ooms, strongly influenced by the modern Roman Catholic style, in his windows and his design for the new church in Amstelveen attains an acceptable level, although we should not overestimate his work.

Moreover, where the artists stick to portraits or landscapes, the quality of what is presented is usually below the average standard expected for an exposition. We have to mention as exceptions the successful watercolours of Glasener, which are worth looking at, and the portrait of the family D. by Mrs. Ameenk-Knap, which actually dates from before the War! Together with another set of four works, these are the only ones of an artistically acceptable level. We regret that we are not able to be more enthusiastic; unless stricter criteria are maintained for the selection of works to be exhibited, visitors cannot but be disappointed and feel they might have spent their time better elsewhere.

• Van Meegeren: genius forger and decadent artist

Modern art, now already half a century old, has presented modern viewers with some strange problems. This modern art looks so strange, so unapproachable. The emphasis is heavily placed on what is purely artistic; the stress is on an individual expression of personality; reality is radically and freely transformed (and sometimes malformed). No wonder that persons, who are unwilling – and perhaps even unable – to immerse themselves in this world of imagination because its sentiments are so foreign to their way of thinking, find this art quite inaccessible. It looks like madness to them, like a wilful destruction of all traditional values, truth and beauty.

The art of the past seems so much superior, so much more profound and beautiful than the art of the modern day. However, we must note that this older art, found in museums, is the result of an ages-long process of elimination to indeed select the true masterpieces, the cream of the crop. In becoming acquainted with modern art, however, we are required to choose for ourselves from what is offered and, naturally, much that is presented will be of lesser quality, less beautiful, less artistically powerful. So it is often unkind and unfair to compare modern art with older art, for one is comparing a very inclusive body of untried, untested works with works that have passed the test of time and have been selected out of a much larger pool of possibilities.

That's why the old sometimes seems so much more technically perfect, so much more wholesome, so much more human. If we add to this the possibility that it not only seems more wholesome, but that it really was healthier and more human, then one is prone to lament, 'Why can't we go back to that kind of art? Why have all those old values been lost?'

That is perhaps the background to the van Meegeren drama. Van Meegeren didn't just leave it at a lament. Instead, he tried to bring back into art those elements he felt it had lost, both technically and in terms of its subject matter: consummate beauty and a more human quality. So he tried to do the impossible by simply imitating the old painting style. He failed to understand that to make art that is more wholesome, one must begin with an equally wholesome attitude, and that one must look into one's own time for new solutions to artistic problems.

One more thing needs to be mentioned, which actually sparked off the whole 'van Meegeren debate', namely that van Meegeren was a man filled with hatred. This is not the most appropriate disposition for one who is trying to return wholesomeness to art. He hated the art critics who refused to recognize him as a master, who refused to acclaim his work as pure and excellent, not his seventeenth-century imitations but his own genuine and spontaneous works of art. I doubt one could find a single art critic today willing to defend these works, for they truly betray a decadent spirit. The best drawings, still often seen in shop windows, of a deer and of a type of crane, are actually of quite acceptable quality, although the former does merit some criticism, but the rest . . . However it may be, van Meegeren wanted revenge on the art critics who were not so agreeable towards his work.

He did this in a very odd way. Instead of getting back at the critics themselves, he wreaked his vengeance on the art scholars and those who were are experts of the art of the past. His earlier attempts at works in the old seventeenth-century style, combined with his awful interpretations of modern themes, were not accepted; well then, he would fool the experts with an original painting worked in perfect seventeenth-century technique and form. Thus it happened that the experts in those older art styles were completely deceived and the art critics, who indeed often have little expertise in that difficult field, accepted the judgment of the professionals.

These experts presumed *The men on the road to Emmaus* to be an authentic work. For the reasons mentioned at the beginning of this article, they often had little knowledge of the art of their own day. It didn't interest them, for they could find no beauty in it. And that's how it could happen that these scholars, with a few exceptions, did not recognize those characteristic van Meegeren faces. Besides, most of these experts held to the value judgments set by one of our greatest art scholars, at that time an old man, who had done some pioneering work and to whom the Dutch people were still quite beholden – he had enriched our art holdings with a very commanding series of masterpieces, including a number of Rembrandts. In deference to this leader, because of the confidence they placed in his knowledge, and in a scientifically-critical stance toward their own methods which perhaps did see some van Meegeren-like characteristics but left open the possibility that, by coincidence, a true Vermeer could display those same traits, these experts kept quiet. They also relied on the assumption that the museum purchasing the piece would have researched the situation critically and thoroughly – though in fact this had not been done adequately at all.

Certainly a critical error was made by the art scholars, but where do such errors never occur? If a doctor makes a critical error, the patient dies. Here the mistake was costly in financial terms, but it does not give the public the right to say: 'You see, they don't know anything!' The public, who in our culture and our artistic development has often been quite ignorant concerning the appraisal of art, vented its feelings of inferiority: 'Ha, the art world has been put in its place! It's just as we suspected: they don't know any more than we do!'

The van Meegeren issue is now past and he will forever appear in the chronicles of history as one of the most clever forgers of all time. In technical terms, his imitation of Vermeer was the work of a genius. Not in the history of art. His misdirected attempt at revenge failed miserably. But the issue that so consumed the public has not disappeared and we now have Jan Basjou coming out with the book *Han van Meegeren: De alchemist van Roquebrune* ('Han van Meegeren: The alchemist of Roquebrune') (Antwerp-Tilburg: P. Vink). It resurrects the not-so-healthy fascination with the issue in a kind of fictionalized biography, in which all the other participants in this drama appear under fictitious names but are presented with near-complete accuracy. This somewhat exaggerated melodramatic account, especially of the court case – somewhat 'wood-be', to use the 'strange' spelling of Basjou – is, in our opinion, inappropriately sentimental.

Although not entirely successful, the situation, as seen from van Meegeren's own point of view and in the light of his own humanness, is clearly depicted. It is a human drama, full of misunderstandings, tensions and often misdirected hatred, as well as an overblown self-estimation. The problem and conflict generated by the nature of modern art, does become clearer to us, though we find that Basjou tends to present the issues rather superficially, focusing too much on the opinion of he person in the street, while against that the rather romanticized emotional perception of artistry that he attributes to van Meegeren's defense lawyer is unconvincing because of its lack of common sense.

It is too bad that through research the real course of events and a correct description of the situation did not come to the fore. This book, instead of being helpful, is unconvincing and can give rise to all manner of further misconceptions. Fortunately van Meegeren is not portrayed as a hero, though his endeavours are romanticized in an unfortunately superficial way.

• Contact between art and the public

It is an undeniable fact that art and the public have grown apart, especially after around 1850. Artists no longer know how to serve the public, and the public no longer knows the art that is being made because, rightly or wrongly, it is considered impossible to understand.

It is not so easy to grasp the reasons for this alienation and even more formidable a task to come up with a solution that will put an end to this unsatisfactory situation for both the public and the artists. A renewed contact between artists and the public is needed that will acquaint the public with modern art, where artists may be available to respond to questions, critical observations and comments from the public. If artists prefer to live in an ivory tower, they should not be surprised when the public simply passes by with, at the most, a shrug.

In this connection we have to appreciate the initiative taken by the Dutch Art Institute (*Nederlands Kunstichting*), formerly named *Kunst en Gezin* ('Art and Family'), under the conviction that this lost connection must be gradually re-established, and that this is possible only in a casual, unforced way.

To this end they have organized art exhibitions in places where people normally congregate and where there is no special 'museum atmosphere', which gives many people the feeling of having been forced into a forbidden ivory tower. So the Institute places paintings in the cafeterias of factories, where people can get to know them in a casual way, without any fuss. It organizes these exhibits in such a way that one can view the art without first having to work up the courage to visit a 'real' exhibition – it also sets up exhibits in, for example, town parks (in Groningen, Assen, Leiden and, with great success, in the Keukenhof).

We had the privilege of visiting a number of these expositions in the cafeterias of the Philips-Roxane Factory in Weesp, in the University

House in Utrecht, and at the Polak & Schwartz Essence Factory in Hilversum. Again and again we were struck by how natural and relaxed these exhibits worked. No one was compelled to look and no high-brow atmosphere existed. Some of the factories offered a completely voluntary tour of the exhibition. Of course, the exhibits were changed regularly.

Naturally, it is difficult to gauge the results of this effort. But more than once we were told that it did heighten interest and created also (and not less importantly) a more critical attitude in making subsequent purchases of 'arts and crafts' items.

However that may be, we believe that this process will certainly help foster a kind of growing mutual understanding and appreciation that will be very beneficial for all sides.

The Dutch Art Institute is a non-profit organization. However, the one who stands to lose the most in our society is the artist. That is one reason why we appreciate this rental arrangement, whereby the artist is paid a certain remuneration for the privilege of displaying his or her art. The Institute does not draw much attention to itself; that is why we decided to draw attention to this initiative here. We hope that more and more establishments will make use of their services. The address of the Institute is Keizersgracht 743, Amsterdam.

•Monumental arts

The role of the visual arts in society is to express the feelings and emotions peculiar to a specific period of time by portraying and summarizing in visual terms its understanding of, and attitude towards, reality. To do this, artists must find a form that will allow those thoughts and feelings to be expressed in the spirit of the period, and in such a way that the external is in harmony with the internal. It is inconsequential whether an artist is looking for this consciously or subconsciously.

Unfortunately, for a long time now there has been a deep gulf between artists and the public. The industrial revolution, Romanticism, the individualism of the nineteenth century – all of these contributed to the fact that the artist was pushed out of the common environment and into an ivory tower. And the public figured it did not need to show any interest in the curiosities that would occasionally come from that tower.

But the rift is beginning to heal. Almost imperceptibly, the public is becoming comfortable with the artistic language of our times, since it has increasingly pervaded advertising, book illustrations, magazine layout and so on. Industry has also become more artistically aware in the design of products. So it hardly strikes us as strange when the prints on fabrics for clothing or drapes display modern designs, possibly created by Miró, Picasso or Appel. And so the ivory tower is crumbling into a ruin from the past.

We are not so far yet, but we do see a gradual lessening of the disharmony in Western culture, where the outer appearance was not in touch with the internal reality. It is not surprising, either, that architecture and visual art are beginning to find more agreement. Naturally, architecture must meet the demands of our day with its own peculiar qualifications, but it does this (at least, in its best products) wonderfully by playing around with the possibilities offered by new materials and new techniques. The shapes used – square, angular, pointed, sometimes streamlined – truly belong to the 'spirit of our times', and are not at all in contradiction with the expressive style of modern art. Rather, the latter finds a logical place in it, a place that does not jolt at all.

The possibilities are shown in the marvellous exposition 'Opdracht' (Commission) currently on view in the Amsterdam Stedelijk Museum of Modern Art. Anyone eager to learn and understand what the coming years will bring should not miss this. We see new and amazing possibilities devised and developed. For example, we see glass in concrete, a distant relation of leaded glass but one better suited to address the spirit of our times than leaded glass. See for example the gorgeously decorative window by Wildschut. It is completely modern in its use of colour and line and could work wonderfully in a modern building as a decoration that is much more than just ornamental. Perhaps every viewer will remark with surprise, 'Really, it doesn't seem so crazy or strange after all!'

But glass has many more possibilities. What does the viewer think of the beautifully austere but simple window designed by Kurpershoek for a chapel or a church? It shows the Christ-symbol in bright white against a tinted background, a circle . . . Well, it is beyond description, one has to see it for oneself. Also the decorative panels with stained glass offer new perspectives, even though we consider the end result as we find it here, for example in the work by Lalaster, too sloppy and superficial. The works by van Soest or Alma are better examples of how it should be done.

Modern art always uses a free interplay of line and colour on a surface to depict things. Just see what that can mean on a linoleum floor, as designed by Haanstra, or an inlaid floor by Kurpershoek: *Jonah and the whale*, which truly has a powerful effect.

In all this we see that the experiments of modern art, already half a century old, suddenly bear fruit that is accessible and completely acceptable. Or does anyone still have problems with something like the metal 'relief' by Timmer, designed for the entrance hall of a zoo? With its bright colours and playful designs, this modern art can be an invigorating and meaningful decoration of modern architecture, which would otherwise be rather bare. See the creations by Hendriks for the outer walls of a few otherwise quite simple Reformed church buildings. But perhaps you have already been acquainted with the work of this artist, for he designed the concrete wall with glass for the Koningskerk here in Amsterdam.

In closing, as proof that contemporary painting is more than capable of fulfilling a difficult commision, even one that is not more or less decorative or ornamental, we wish to draw attention to the beautiful large painting by Schrofer, in which he portrays the professors of the Theological Faculty of the University of Amsterdam. It's a wonderfully lucid solution to the problem that we Dutch know so well from our old 'marksmen' paintings. The problem is solved brilliantly, without becoming bizarre, a true milestone in the evolution of the group portrait.

• Emergence of a style

The place of the visual arts is not easy to define, but is certainly much greater and more far-reaching than many people realize. Although visual artists themselves are often hardly aware of this, one of the most important facets of their work is the creation of forms which then penetrate society and give shape to almost every object in daily use, from architecture to irons, from fashion to furniture, from typography to cars and trains. All of these things are given an individual character, which then collectively is called the style of that period. Directly connected with the spiritual heart of a certain period is the development of the look of the entire cultural surroundings of that era.

Modern art is now nearly 50 years old. Abstract art, especially as practised by Mondrian and his followers, has exercised an influence on architecture and typography that should not be underestimated. In the early years after the last World War, creativity was often squeezed out by the urgency to rebuild. But after some time for contemplation and, shall we say, a return to normal, there is now a growing interest in the artistic aspect of everything related to building and shaping, as well as a growing recognition that this has value for society.

So what are the principles behind the latest style of design, as we see it displayed in an exposition like the 'E55', and in two extremely interesting exhibitions being held in the Stedelijk Museum of Modern Art – one by the 'Society for Renewal in the Visual Arts' (*Vereniging Nieuw Beelden*), which chose this particular problem as its field of study; and one devoted to the submissions for a contest held by the 'Architectural Society' (*Vereniging Architectura et Amicitia*) for a community centre in Amsterdam North?

In relation to architecture we find free and playful yet controlled constructions, with rectangular shapes and cubes that penetrate one another, creating a remarkable openness and spaciousness. Insofar as one can define architecture as the creation of living space, we believe that our era, with these new principles, has found a style that can compete with the very best from the past. At the same time this new style is completely adjusted to modern materials, needs, and possibilities, and it therefore does not aesthetically bypass reality (something we encountered often in the styles of the era just past).

In relation to interior decoration and design we find a whimsical interplay of form, sometimes mathematical, yet functional and in accordance with the characteristics of the specific materials and always strongly influenced by the shapes of abstract art. It may be true that abstract art is poor in human content, and that it falls far short of the mark when it comes to the visual arts; yet in terms of its contribution to form for decorative purposes, or for the creation of furniture and other useful objects, it has produced a wealth. On the basis of what we see in these exhibits, we predict this will be increasingly so.

We must frankly admit that we found many of the experimental paintings in the exposition of the Society for Renewal in the Visual Arts to be boring and meaningless. But in a frieze such as the one by Will Leeuwens, in the work of van Kruiningen, in the free play with rounded forms by Frieda Hunziker, in the decorative work by Volten and Ongenae, we found much that is gripping and meaningful and entirely functional as regards its decorative purposes. Nieuwenhuis, who moved from the experimental arts to a kind of constructivism, presents abstract constructions without architectonic purpose, limping along behind architecture. Yet his monument to honour the determination and achievement of the Dutch, made for the E55, is an impressive, emotionally moving experience for every viewer, and truly contemporary. Also the furniture, so comfortable and yet with such whimsical playfulness, fits perfectly here. In such an interior, one can feel in complete harmony with the motion of an abstract sculpture such as the one by Breetveld.

The similarity in style revealed by the submissions for the Community Centre Contest is remarkable. If such a construction should indeed be realized, Holland would thereby (and also with a building like the Provincial House in Arnhem) take first place in the development of modern architecture. We are glad that decoration, so long neglected as being superfluous and therefore purposely overlooked, is being given its rightful and completely appropriate place again. The bareness of modern constructions, as if it has passed through an obligatory period of cleansing, thus will make way for a warmer and also – in terms of the details – more striking whole.

It is good to recognize that we live in a period that is well on the way to develop a truly great style – which has been a *fata morgana* for the past century and a half. Therefore it is a good idea to make acquaintance with the new, which will likely constitute our future and which, in truth, has already arrived. We hope, then, that many will take the time to view these interesting exhibits; they will only remain until 18 July though we are hoping that perhaps the time will be extended.

•Poster art, a living art[1144]

In the Stedelijk Museum of Modern Art in Amsterdam an exhibition is under way that will attract a tremendous amount of interest: an exhibition of posters and advertising broadsheets from the last fifty or sixty years, exclusively from abroad. Alas it was thought that the Dutch poster is generally familiar: that is undoubtedly so with respect to the present-day, but not for the beginning of the century. I have in mind the works of Roland Holst, for example!

Yet we may still be most grateful for what is on offer: modern art has lost touch with the people, with the masses, many despair as they cast about sometimes here and sometimes there in an effort to assign the blame for that. Yet the poster is a true art form of our time. This is art alive, which not only satisfies the demands people often make of art, namely that it should expresses the present age, but also enjoys everyone's interest. Never before has 'popular' graphic art, the everyday pictorial 'folk' art, attained such a high level of artistic quality. One is inclined to say that art is not dead but that it lives 'underground' in the poster!

For the origins of modern poster art we must turn to England and France. In the latter, one of the first to produce coloured, artistically responsible advertising broadsheets was Chéret, an artist of formidable stature who was able to achieve outstanding results within the restrictions of a few colours: red, blue and yellow. In England the group called the Pre-Raphaelites took a great deal of interest in graphics, particularly in relation to the publications prepared by William Morris, and attained an exceptional level of skill. Beardsley's posters are from this tradition; and the influence of Morris's 'school' on artists such as Steinlen, Toulouse-Lautrec and others, should not be underestimated. A textbook example of a poster from this tradition is the one from 1907, extremely simple, suggestive and decorative, and above all, elegant. Alas, there are not many of these English posters from the 1890s on display here. This sort of art undoubtedly also influenced the develoment of modern art during its earliest period, though it will be no simple matter to define that influence precisely.

Excellent poster examples are on display representing all the artists already mentioned – Chéret, Lautrec, Steinlen, Beardsley and others. These are head and shoulders above the 'standard' turn-of-the-century posters: very naturalistic, yes sometimes even semi-classical genre pieces of low artistic quality and, in our eyes often amusing. See, for instance, the early advertisements for bicycles: a rider on a bicycle leaves his old-fashioned fox-hunting colleagues on horseback far behind, or an explorer with a smug look on his face leaves a wild aboriginal tribe in the dust as he speeds out of the jungle on his bicycle, and so on.

It is an exhibition that requires little further explanation: this is art that everyone can understand and appreciate. The contrasts too are marked enough to be observed and correctly assessed by any so-called 'layman', so that we can do nothing better here than whet your appetite to go and see it for yourself. A large series of posters from the Nazi period adds significant importance to the exhibition – these genuine historical documents are perhaps the best sources for examining the history of that period! One should not be irritated by the eccentric catalogue, which for the sake of being different has this time been made from fine sandpaper – not a great choice, to put it mildly!

Notes to Volume I

Part I: Gauguin and Nineteenth-Century Art Theory

The publishers have moved the foreign-language quotes, which originally appeared in the main text, and replaced these with their English translations. Foreign quotes now appear in these notes. Some abbreviations used in these notes are as follows:

Windleband-Heimsoeth: W. Windelband, *Lehrbuch der Geschichte der Philosophie*, ed. H. Heimsoeth (Tubingen, 1948 14)

Cur. Esth.: C. Baudelaire, *Curiosités Esthétiques* (Paris, 1921)

Ferran, *Esth.*: A. Ferran, *L'Esthétique de Baudelaire* (Paris, 1933)

Malingue: M. Malingue, *Lettres de Gauguin à sa femme et à ses amis* (Paris, 1946)

Denis, *Théories*: Denis, *Théories 1890-1920* (Paris, 1912 2)

ABC de la peinture: P. Sérusier, *ABC de la peinture suivi d'une correspondance inedited* (Paris, 1950)

[1] Previously published as *Synthetist Art Theories* (1959) and as *Gauguin and 19th Century Art Theory* (1972), both by Swets and Zeitlinger, Amsterdam.

[2] 'Le XIXième siècle, après avoir, pendant quatre-vings ans, proclamé, dans son enthousiasme enfantin, l'omnipotence de l'observation et de la déduction scientifiques, après avoir affirmé qu'aucun mystère ne subsistait devant ses lentilles et ses scalpels, semble enfin s'apercevoir de la vanité de ses efforts, de la puérilité de ses vantardises. L'homme marche toujours au milieu des mêmes énigmes, dans ce même formidable inconnu, devenu plus obscur encore et plus troublant depuis qu'on s'est déshabitué de le considérer. Bien des savants, aujourd'hui, s'arrêtent avec découragement, comprenant enfin que cette érudition expérimentale, dont ils tiraient vanité, a mille fois moins de certitude que la plus bizarre théogonie, que la plus folle rêverie métaphysique, que le moins acceptable rêve de poète, et pressentent que cette hautaine science, qu'ils appelaient en leur fierté, positive, n'est peut-être que la science des relativités, des apparences, des 'ombres' comme disait Platon, et qu'ils n'ont, eux, rien à mettre dans les vieux Olympes dont ils ont arraché les divinités et décroché les astres.' G.-A. Aurier, *Les peintres symbolistes*, pp.293 ff.

[3] 'La copie myope des anecdotes sociales, l'imitation imbécile des verrues de la nature, la plate observation, le trompe-l'œil, la gloire d'être aussi fidèlement, aussi banalement exact que le daguerréotype. G.-A. Aurier, *Les peintres symbolistes*, p.294.

[4] See Rewald, *Impressionism*, p.23.

[5] Cf. W. Friedlander, *David to Delacroix*, transl. R. Goldwater (Cambridge, Mass, 1952) p.7 ff.

[6] Cf. Delacroix, *Oeuvres Littéraires* (1923) I, pp.24/25; C. Mauclair, *Les stats de la*

peinture française 1850-1920 (1921) p.30 passim; John Rothenstein, *Nineteenth Century Painting* (London, 1932) pp.25 ff.

7 'Au début du XIXième siècle, l'art n'est plus une langue comme autrefois, dans chaque pays, avec le souvenir des belles traditions. C'est en quelque sorte un volapuk formé avec des recettes. Un langage unique, enseigné par des professeurs brevetés, donnant l'assurance du parfait et d'une immense médiocrité. Ce volapuk se parle encore.' P. Gauguin, *Racontars d'un rapin*, p.61/62; here as quoted, a bit shortened, by Kunstler, p.177.

8 Quatremère de Quincy, *Essai sur l'idéal dans ses applications pratiques aux oeuvres de l'imitation propre des arts de dessin* (Paris, 1837) pp.314 ff.

9 They were even able to appeal to Ingres himself. Ingres, *Roconte par luimême et ses amis*, (Paris, 1947), pp.48/49, 64/65. See also in this connection the pictures of painters of the 'Salons' collected by F. Jourdain in 'L'art official de Jules Grévy à Albert Lebrun', *le Point* (XXXVII, 7, April, 1949, Souillac). They prove – and this is even more marked in the black-and-white reproductions, of course – that the nudes at the Salons differ from the photos obtainable at present in 'photobooks' of studies from the model or 'Nudes', only in as far as the material – in the literal sence of the word – and the proportions are concerned. Here this 'art' has sought a 'refuge' now that the walls of the museums have been denied to it. These photos are made for the same kind of public who must, however, do without the sanction that this kind of work, which they desire, is 'great art'.

10 A. Springer, *Die Kunst von 1800 bis zur Gegenwart*, 7th edition (Leipzig, 1920) fig. 197.

11 'un Lupanar obligatoire'. Gauguin, *Racontars d'un rapin*, p.70.

12 *Catalogue officiel illustré de l'exposition centenale de l'art français, 1800-1809* (Paris, 1900). Cf. also *The two sides of the Medal: French Painting from Gerôme to Gauguin* (Detroit Museum of Art Exhib., 1954).

13 Ibid.

14 Castagnary, 'Le Salon de 1866', in *Salons 1857-'70* (Paris, 1872) I, p.224, quoted by Rewald, I*mpressionism*, p.126.

15 George Besson, *La peinture française au XIXième siècle* (Paris, n.d.) fig. 56.

16 There has been a recent attempt made by Sloane to promote Henri Regnault, who died in 1870, to a real master of the 'Salon'-world. The question whether or not Regnault's work justifies such an attempt can only be settled after more work of his can be seen together. Cf. J. C. Sloane, *French Art between the Past and the Present, Artists, Critics and Traditions from 1848 to 1870* (Princeton, New Jersey, 1951) pp.176 ff. There are no reproductions of the work of this artist, nor of that of Bastien-Lepage or Lhermitte, in the fiercely critical publication of Jourdain mentioned in our previous note (see note 8). They are not prime examples of tastelessness and artistic emptiness.

17 Van Gogh, *Brieven* III, Sept. 1885, Letter 423.

18 'Sans le savoir is die academie une maîtresse die verhindert dat er eene meer serieuze meer warme meer vruchtbare liefde in U wakker wordt. Laat die maîtresse loopen en wordt tot over de ooren verliefd op uwe eigentlijke beminde dame nature of réalité ... Elle renouvelle elle retrempe elle donne la vie! Cette dame Nature cette dame Réalité.' Van Gogh, *Brieven* IV, R. 4.

19 'les flots d'articles de pur commerce ... il n'y serait point question d'art, point

d'artistes, mais simplement d'une industrie de luxe ...' *Mercure de France*, (III,1891) p.30.
20 'la médiocrité ... règne plus que jamais ... ' *Cur. Esth.: Salon 1859*, I, p.248.
21 *Cur. Esth.: Salon 1846*, V, p.122.
22 E. Wind, 'The Revolution of History Painting', *Journal of the Warburg and Courtauld Institute* (II, 1938, '39) p.116.
23 Cf. *Burlington Magazine* (XCVI, 1954) the Géricault number, pp.233 ff.
24 Cf. W. G. Constable, 'A Note on the Birth of Modern Painting, as Examplified in Landscape', *Actes du XVIIième Congrès International de l'Histoire de l'Art* (La Haye, 1955) p.480. Cf. Kenneth Clark, *Landscape into Art* (London, 1949) pp.74 ff.
25 Humanism as a view of life and the world arose in the fifteenth century and has dominated Western culture since that time. It is always essentially driven on by a dynamic motif of a religious character. Its basic motif is found in the human freedom to selfconstitution. However, there is no absolute freedom realizable, as in the striving after such freedom the structure of reality operates as a counter instance to which also man is bound. This is especially true with respect to the natural aspects of reality with their unavoidable laws. The attempt is then to make this nature subservient to man by submitting to its laws in order thus to realize the humanistic ideal. This, however, entails the risk that human freedom has to suffer. In this way there arises a dialectic of a fundamentally religious nature not necessarily explicit, as the issue is the basic attitude of a person in the heart of his or her existence towards God, his creation and his law (or his norms). Compare with this, e.g. Delacroix's pronouncements referred to in note 69); and also *Oeuvres Littéraires* I, p.115 'L'homme domine la nature et en est dominé. Il est le seul être de la création qui, non seulement lui résiste, mais la dompte ou en élude les lois et qui étende son empire par sa volonté et son activité. Mais que la création ait été faite pour lui, c'est une proposition qui est loin d'être évidente.' ('Man dominates nature and is dominated by it. He is the only being of the creation who does not only resist it, but subjects it or eludes its laws and who extends his empire by his will and his activity. But that the creation was made for him is a proposition which is far from evident.') Compare a more detailed account of these things in H. Dooyeweerd, *A New Critique of Theoretical Thought* (Amsterdam 1955), pp.169 ff.; *Transcendental Problems of Philosophic Thought* (Grand Rapids, Mich. 1948) p.73 ff. and 'De transcendentale critiek van het wijsgerig denken en de grondslagen van de wijsgerige denkgemeenschap van het avondland', *Philosophia Reformata* (VI, 1941) pp.1ff., and his 'De vier religieuze grondthema's in de ontwikkelingsgarig van het wijsgerig denken van het avondland', *Philosophia Reformata* (VI, 1941) pp.161 ff.
26 'un coin de la nature vu par un tempérament' On Zola, cf. L. Venturi, *Histoire de la critique d'art*, p.300, with a.o. quotations from his *Salon* of 1866. Ditto, Rewald, *Impressionism*, pp.123 ff.
27 Cf. Ellis Waterhouse on this subject in the introduction to the *Catalogue of the English Landscape Art* (Boymans' Museum 1955), and also J. Piper, *British Romantic Artists* (London, 1946 2) p.19.
28 Cf. also Rewald, *Impressionism*, p.213, with a telling pronouncement by Monet.
29 J. Ruskin, *Modern Painters* (Part VII, Chapter IV, 18) V (London, 1904) p.162.
30 Goya, *Caprichos* No. 43, F. J. Sanchez Canton, *Los Caprichos de Goya y sus debujos preparatorios* (Barcelona, 1949).

31 G. Levitine, 'Literary Sources of Goya's Capricho 43', *Art Bulletin* (XXXVII, 1955) pp.56 ff.

32 E. H. Gombrich, 'Imagery and Art in the Romantic Period', *Burl. Mag.* (XCI, 1949) pp.158 ff.

33 Very telling is the text that Goya wrote on the drawing for his etching No. 43: 'Ydioma universal. El autor soñando. Su yntento solo es desterrar bulgaridades perjuciales y perpetuar con esta obra de caprichos el testimonio sólido de la verdad' ('Universal idiom. The author dreaming. His only purpose is to make an end to senseless prejudices and to perpetuate with this work of caprichos the testimony only of truth.') F. J. Sanchez Canton, *Las Caprichas de Goya y sus debujos preparatorias* (Barcelona, 1949) p.87.

34 To prevent confusion we shall have to make a sharp distinction between the terms naturalism and realism. Naturalism refers to the way of representing things. It is the attempt to call up an image, analogous to what the eye sees, by means of lines and colours, and as accurately as possible. Realism is concerned with the subjects, the facts represented. In Realism the artist only wants to depict what can he observed in the reality around him. Thus, e.g., an angel (a nonrealistic subject) may be rendered in a naturalistic way – recall van Eyck – while it is also possible to represent a realistic theme in a non-naturalistic way – e.g., by means of colour symbols, expressive lines elucidating the meaning of what is depicted, as is often done by the Expressionists. As a matter of fact every caricature is realistic – non-naturalistic.

35 Cf. E. H. Gombrich, 'Tobias and the Angel', 'Harvest I', 'Travel' (London, 1948) p.63.

36 A. de Vesme, *Le peintre graveur italien* (Milan, 1906) p.382, 'Vari Capricci' (3-12), 'Scherzi di Fantasia' (13-35).

37 'ces contorsions, ces faces bestiales, ces grimaces diaboliques sont pénétrées d'humanité' *Cur. Esth. Caricaturistes Etrangers* II, p.430.

38 'tous les vices que l'esprit humain peut concevoir,' *Cur. Esth.* p.428.

39 No. 76 of the series E. Lafuente Ferrari, *Goya, Desastros de la Guerra y sus debujos preparatorios* (Barcelona, 1952).

40 The first edition of articles etc. by Delacroix appeared in 1865, the editor being Piron, but this impression consisted of a very small number of copies. His *Journal* was published in 1893, compiled by Paul Flat and René Picot, whereas some time before a number of his letters had been published by Burty, in two volumes, one of 1878 and one of 1880. Baudelaire's work was easily accessible in the publication of the *Curiosités Esthétiques*, Collected 'Salons', supplemented by a few other articles, in 1884, and there was also a great deal to be found of his works, e.g., in the prefaces to the translations of Poe's works.

41 Van Gogh, *Brieven* III, 'Letter 401'.

42 P. Signac, *D'Eugène Delacroix au néo-impressionisme* (ed. La Revue Blanche, 1899).

43 'Il Faudrait faire ... des tableaux esquisses qui auraient la liberté et la franchise des croquis.' Delacroix, *Journal*, 5 Oct. 1847.

44 'Le hasard a l'air d'avoir assemblé les tons et agencé les lignes de la composition. L'idée poétique ou expressive ne vous frappe pas au premier coup d'oeil.' Delacroix, *Journal*, 19 Sept. 1847.

45 E.g. Gauguin in 'Diverses Choses' (1902), quoted by Kunstler, p.182.

46 'Il y a une impression qui résulte de tel arrangement de couleurs, de lumières et d'ombres etc ... C'est ce qu'on appellerait la musique du tableau...' Delacroix, *Oeuvres littéraires*, I. pp.63, 64, also quoted by Ferran, *Esth.* p.147.

47 'L'imagination chez l'artiste ne se représente pas seulement tels ou tels objets, elle les combine pour la fin qu'il veut obtenir; elle fait des tableaux, des images qu'il compose à son gré.' Delacroix, *Oeuvres littéraires*, III, p.45, quoted by M. Gilman, *Baudelaire the Critic* (New York '43) p.226.

48 'Mais si, à une composition déjà intéressante par le choix du sujet, vous ajoutez une disposition de lignes qui augmente l'impression, un clair-obscur saisissant pour l'imagination, une couleur adaptée aux caractères, vous avez résolu un problème plus difficile, et, encore une fois, vous êtes supérieur: c'est l'harmonie et ses combinaisons adaptées à un chant unique.' Delacroix, *Journal* 1853, 20 May, quoted in English J. C. Sloane, *French Art 1850–1870* (1951) p.115.

49 'Ne peignent plus seulement les sentiments; ils décrivent l'extérieur, ils analysent tout.' Delacroix, *Journal* 9 April, 1856.

50 'Mes intentions sont plus prononcées et les choses inutiles éloignées.' Delacroix, *Journal*, 12 October 1853.

51 'L'exécution la plus soignée dans les détails ne donnera pas cette unité qui résulte de je ne sais quelle puissance créatrice dont la source est indéfinissable,' Delacroix in notes for 'Le réalisme et l'idéalisme' quoted by R. Rey, *La Renaissance du sentiment classique*, p.25.

52 Delacroix, *Journal*, 12 Oct. 1853.

53 Of course, we need not think of a particular philosopher, but more generally of the way in which the epistemological problem regarding the relation of man to reality was posited and the direction in which the answer was sought.

54 Cf. Windelband-Heimsoeth, § 34. *Die Erkenntnis der Aussenwelt*, pp.391 ff.

55 'Le fait est comme rien, puisqu'il passe. Il n'en reste que l'idée réellement même-il n'existe que dans l'idée puisqu'elle lui donne une couleur ... (C'est) ce qui s'y passe quand la faculté créatrice s'empare d'elle (l'idée) pour animer le monde réel (which is given in the 'faits passagers') et en tirer des tableaux d'imagination. Elle compose, c'est-à-dire qu'elle idéalise et choisit.' Delacroix, *Oeuvres Littéraires* I, p.114, quoted by M. Gilman, *Baudelaire the Critic* (New York, '43) p.226.

56 'Ces figures, ces objets, qui semblent être la chose même à une certaine partie de votre être intelligent, semblent comme un pont solide sur lequel l'imagination s'appuie pour pénétrer jusqu'à la sensation mystérieuse et profonde dont les formes sont en quelque sorte l'hiéroglyphe ...' Delacroix, *Journal*, 17 Oct. 1853. Cf. *Journal*, 14 May 1824.

57 This old method was certainly not primitive or naïve because science had not yet advanced sufficiently and so there was no possibility of exactness. On the contrary, here we are confronted with a quite different conception of the past and its significance for the present, which was, therefore, reflected in the work of art. Cf. H. v. d. Waal, *Drie Eeuwen Vaderlandse Geschiedenis-Uitbeelding* (Den Haag, 1952).

58 Cf., e.g. H. Heine, *Der Salon* I (Rotterdam, 1860) p.18.

59 Delacroix, *Journal*, 27 Dec. 1853.

60 'Sans cette philosophie que j'entends, nulle durée pour le livre ou le tableau, ou plutôt nulle existence.' Delacroix, *Journal*, 17 Oct. 1853.

61 'Je désire être ramené vers les dioramas dont la magie brutale et énorme sait m'imposer une utile illusion ... Ces choses, parce qu'elles sont fausses, sont infiniment plus près du vrai; tandis que la plupart de nos paysagistes sont des menteurs, justement parce qu'ils ont négligé de mentir.' *Cur. Esth.: Salon 1859* VIII, p.338.

62 'magnifique imagination' *Cur. Esth.: Salon 1859* VIII, p.338.

63 *Cur. Esth.: Quelques caricaturistes français* II, pp.411/412.

64 'désordre et étalages sans pudeur', Ferran, *Esth.*, p.500.

65 'Plaignez-moi, ou plutôt plaignez-nous, car j'ai beaucoup de frères comme moi; c'est la haine de tous et de nous même qui nous a conduits vers ces mensonges. C'est par désespoir de ne pouvoir être nobles et beaux suivant les moyens naturels que nous nous sommes si bizarrement fardé le visage. Nous nous sommes tellement appliqués à sophistiquer notre coeur, nous avons tant abusé du microscope pour étudier les hideuses excroissances et les honteuses verrues dont il est couvert et que nous grossissons à plaisir, qu'il est impossible que nous parlions le langage des autres hommes... Nous avons altéré l'accent de la nature, nous avons extirpé une à une les pudeurs virginales dont était herissé notre intérieur d'honnête homme. Nous avons psychologisé comme des fous qui augmentent leur folie en s'efforçant de la comprendre ... Malheur, trois fois malheur aux pères infirmes qui nous ont fait rachitiques et mal venus. Ferran, *Esth.* p.98.

66 We are referring here to Humanism as a view of life and the world. Cf. 25

67 P. v. Tieghem, *Le romantisme dans la littérature euroéenne* (Paris, 1948) p.179 passim.

68 Margaret Gilman, *Baudelaire the Critic* (New York, 1943) pp.65 ff.

69 Cf. also what Delacroix says about reality, inclusive of his own body, in his *Journal* of 4 June, 1824; 5 May, 1847; and 5 Sept. 1847; 'Est-il dans la création un être plus esclave que n'est l'homme? La faiblesse, les besoins, le font dépendre des éléments et de ses semblables ... Il ne veut pas non plus de la hiérarchie en quoi que ce soit; c'est en cela il trouve surtout le christianisme odieux ... soumission à la loi de la nature, résignation aux douleurs humaines, c'est le dernier mot de toute raison (et partant soumission à la loi écrite, divine ou humaine)' ('Is there in the creation a being that is more of a slave than man? His weakness, his needs make him dependent on the elements and on his equals ... He does not want any hierarchy either, in whatever it may consist; that is what he especially hates in Christianity ... submission to the law of nature, resignation to human sorrows, this is the last word of every reason (and consequently submission to the written law either divine or human)'. The same thing also elsewhere in Baudelaire, 'La nature qui pose devant nous, de quelque côté que nous nous tournions, et qui nous enveloppe comme un mystère' ('Nature, which confronts us wherever we may turn, and envelops us like a mystery'), *Art Romantique*, p.311.

70 'l'hostilité de l'atmosphère', Baudelaire, *Art Romantique*, p.100.

71 'die Klage einer früh in den Stürmen des Lebens verdorrten Seele über die Leere und Nichtigkeit des Daseins.' M. v. Wedderkop, *Paul Verlaine und die Lyrik der Decadence in Frankreich* (Pan., 1896) pp.69 ff.

72 'tout cette oeuvre ... ressemble à un hymne terrible composé en l'honneur de la fatalité et de l'irrémédiable douleur.' Baudelaire, *Art Romantique*, p.30.

73 '0, Mort! / Verse nous ton poison pour qu'il nous réconforte!/ Nous voulons, tant ce feu nous brûle le cerveau, /Plonger au fond du gouffre, enfer, ou

ciel qu'importe! / Au fond de l'inconnu pour trouver du nouveau.' Also quoted by Barre, *Le Symbolisme*, p.54.

74 'au fond de l'inconnu' Cf. also what he writes in connection with Hugo, *Art Romantique*, p.318.

75 This is why he wrote about the *fleurs du mal* ('the flowers of evil'), in which he wanted *d'extraire la beauté du m*al ('to extract beauty from evil'). (*Les Fleurs du Mal*, ed. critique Jacques Crépet et Georges Blin (Paris; 1942) p.211: 'Projet de Préface pour une édition nouvelle'.)

76 'Qu'est-ce que l'art pur suivant la conception moderne? C'est créer une magie suggestive contenant à la fois l'objet et le sujet, le monde extérieur à l'artiste et l'artiste luimême.' Margaret Gilman, *Baudelaire the Critic*, p.166.

77 Romanticism here refers to Baudelaire's own ideals, not to the older movement.

'Le romantisme n'est précisément ni dans le choix des sujets, ni dans la vérité exacte, mais dans la manière de sentir' 'Il faut donc, avant tout, connaître les aspects de la nature et les situations de l'homme, que les artistes du passé ont dédaignés ou n'ont pas connus.' *Cur. Esth.*, pp.85/86.

78 *Ia reine des facultés* ('the queen of the faculties') comprises analysis and synthesis. Here the word 'synthesis' is intended to denote the opposite of analysis, and is not used in the sense indicated above – as later on the term is generally used, which we hope to prove.

79 'C'est l'imagination qui a enseigné à l'homme le sens moral de la couleur, du contour, du son et du parfum. Elle a créé, au commencement du monde, l'analogie et la métaphore. Elle décompose toute la création, et, avec les matériaux amassés et disposes suivant les règles dont on ne peut trouver l'origine que dans le plus profond de l'âme, elle crée un monde nouveau, elle produit la sensation du neuf. Comme elle a créé le monde on peut bien dire cela, je crois, même dans un sens religieux – il est juste qu'elle le gouverne.' *Cur. Esth.* pp.264, 265.

80 W. Windelhand-Heimsoeth, pp.537,538.

81 As a matter of fact, throughout the century French contemporary philosophy had hardly any influence on the literati (and the painters), not even in those cases that clearly show spiritual affinity. Recall Ravaisson and Lachelier.

82 'L'imagination est la reine du vrai, et le possible est une des provinces du vrai.' *Cur. Esth.* p.263.

83 'Ia formule principale ... de la véritable esthétique', will be: 'Tout l'univers visible n'est qu'un magasin d'images et de signes auxquels l'imagination donnera une place et une valeur relative; c'est une espèce de pâture que l'imagination doit digérer et transformuler.' *Cur. Esth.*, p.274. Cf. Baudelaire, *Art Romantique*, p.13.

84 Delacroix, *Journal* I, May 14, 1824, e.g.

85 Baudelaire, *Art Romantique*, pp.9, 10.

86 'tout doit servir à illuminer l'idée génératrice et porter encore sa couleur originelle, sa livrée, pour ainsi dire.' *Cur. Esth.*, p.272.

87 'une vision produite par une intense méditation.' *Cur. Esth.*, p.289.

88 'un tableau doit avant tout reproduire la pensée intime de l'artiste, qui domine le modèle, comme le créateur la création.' *Cur. Esth.*, p.104.

89 This appears from his introduction to *Les Fleurs du Mal*: 'In this atrocious book I have put all my heart, all my tenderness, all my religion (travestied), all my hate.' Marcel Raymond, *From Baudelaire to Surréalism* (New York, 1950), p.13. 'L'art pour l'art' really meant the absolute liberty of the artist to treat anything he liked without heeding ethical or other norms. Cf. Recolin, *L'Anarchie littéraire* (Paris, 1898) p178, and J. Wilcox, 'La genèse de la théorie de l'art pour l'art en France.' *Revue d'esthétique* VI (1, 1953) p.1 ff.

90 'tout ce qu'il faudra inventer, si tout cela n'existait pas.' *Cur. Esth.*, p.337.

91 *Cur. Esth.*, pp.196/198.

92 Ferran, *Esth.*, p.500.

93 'l'absence nette du juste et du vrai dans l'art équivaut à l'absence de l'art', because 'l'homme entier s'évanouit.' Baudelaire, *Art Romantique*, p.301.

94 Baudelaire, *Art Romantique*, p.301.

95 Dr. A. Kuyper, *The Antithesis between Symbolism and Revelation* (1899) p.15.

96 'l'imagination est la plus scientifique des facultés, parce que seule elle comprend l'analogie universelle, ou ce qu'une religion mystique appelle la correspondance.' *Correspondances* I, 130, publ. Gautier et le Dantec, commented on by M. Gilman, *Baudelaire the Critic* (New York, 1943) p.121.

97 A. Viatti, *Les sources occultes du romantisme* 1770-1820 (1928, Paris) and R. Michaud, 'Baudelaire, Balzac et les correspondances.' *Romanic Review* (Oct. 1938 XXIX, 3) p.254 note.

98 Literature on Swedenborg: M. Matter, *Swedenborg* (Paris, 1863); M. Lamm, *Swedenborg: Eine Studie über seine Entwicklung zum Mystiker und Geisterseher* (transl. Leipzig,1922); A. Viatti, *Les sources occultes du romantisme* (Paris, 1928) I, pp.72 ff.; H. de Geymuller, *Swedenborg et les pénomènes psychiques* (Paris, sd.); E.A. Sutton, *The Living thoughts of Swedenborg* (London, 1944).

99 M. Lamm, op.cit., p.20.

100 Ditto, pp.30 ff.

101 Ditto, pp.62,63,111,112.

102 Ditto, pp.256 ff., Sutton, op.cit., pp.71ff.

103 Ditto, pp.51, 73, 74.

104 Ditto, p.89; on Plotinus, cf. E. Bréhier, *La philosophie de Plotin* (Paris, 1928) pp.47ff.

105 'Omnia enim Divina sunt exemplaria, intellectualia, moralia et civilia sunt typi et imagines naturalia vero et physica sunt simulacra', M. Lamm, *Swedenborg. Eine Studie über seine Entwicklung zum Mystiker und Geisterseher* (transl. Leipzig, 1922) p.108, a quotation from Swedenborg's 'Clavis Hieroplyphica arcanorum naturalium et spiritualium per viam Repraesentationum et Correspondentiarum' (1784, London).

106 Bréhier, op.cit., pp.36, 42.

107 'L'âme ajoute aux quatre éléments la forme du monde dont elle leur fait don; 'mais c'est l'intelligence qui lui fournit des raisons séminales.' E. Bréhier', *La philosophie de Plotin* (Paris, 1928) p.87, quoted from the *Enneads* V, 9, 3.

108 Bréhier, op.cit., p.55; Lamm, op.cit., p.109.

109 Swedenborg's 'Clavis Hieroglyphica arcanorum naturalium et spiritualium per viam Repraesentationum et Correspondentiarum' (London, 1784) pp.19 ff., also quoted by Lamm, op.cit., p.110, cf. Bréhier, p.124 (*Enneads* V, 8, 6).

110 E. H. Gombrich, 'Icones Symbolae, The Visual Image in Neoplatonic Thought', *Journal of the Warburg & Courtauld Institute* (XI, 1948) pp.167 ff., cf. also I. L. Zupnick, 'The Aesthetics of the Early Mannerists', *Art Bulletin* (XXXV, 1953) p.305.

111 H. Evans, *Louis Lambert et la philosophie de Balzac* (Paris, 1951) p.248.

112 Margaret Gilman, *Baudelaire the Critic* (New York, 1943) p.16.

113 Humanistic taken in the sence of classical philology (here not in the sense of the life and world view of modern times).

114 The freedom motive was concretized in the life and world view (cf. note 25) as the ideal of human being as an autonomous rational-moral personality, whereas the motive of nature found expression in the science ideal, namely that a person can (only) gain an insight into reality by means of the (natural) sciences. Cf. also the writings quoted by Prof. Dr. H. Dooyeweerd in note 25.

115 'L'éternel dialogue de l'idée et du fait, qui l'a toujours tourmenté, Balzac le résout finalement en faveur de l'idée, mais le fait subsiste, dans son oeuvre comme image de l'idée', H. Evans, *Louis Lambert et la philosophie de Balzac* (Paris, 1951) p.250; Compare Balzac, *Louis Lambert* (ed. Conrad) p.104, quoted by J. v. d. Elst, 'Autour du "Livre Mystique": Balzac et Swedenborg', *Revue de la littérature comparée* X (1930) p.92.

116 J. v. d. Elst, 'Autour du "Livre Mystique": Balzac et Swedenborg', *Revue de la littérature comparée* X (1930) pp.88 ff.

117 E.g., Gauguin, cf. Charles Morice, *Paul Gauguin* (Paris, 1919) p.37.

118 Quoted and analysed by M. Raymond, *From Baudelaire to Surréalism* (New York, 1950) pp.17ff.

119 R. Michaud, 'Baudelaire, Balzac et les correspondances', *Romanic Review* (Oct. 1938, XXIX) p.257.

120 'que le son ne pût pas suggérer la couleur, que les couleurs ne pûssent pas donner l'idée d'une mélodie, et que le son et la couleur fussent impropres à traduire des idées; les choses n'étant toujours exprimées par une analogie réciproque (another word for 'correspondance'), depuis le jour où Dieu a proféré le monde comme une complexe et indivisible totalité.' Baudelaire, *Art Romantique*, art. on Wagner, pp.207 ff., quoted by Lehmann, *Symbolist Aesth.*, p.264.

121 'Cette vérité que tout est hiéroglyphique, et nous savons que les symboles ne sont obscurs que d'une manière relative, c'est-à-dire selon la pureté, la bonne volonté ou la clairvoyance native des âmes. Or, qu'est-ce qu'un poète – je prends le mot dans son acception la plus large – si ce n'est un traducteur, un déchiffreur? Chez les excellents poètes il n'y a pas de métaphore, de comparaison ou d'épithète qui ne soit d'une adaptation mathématiquement exacte dans la circonstance actuelle, parce que ces comparaisons, ces métaphores et ces épithètes sont puisées dans l'inépuisable fonds de l'universelle analogie, et qu'elles ne peuvent être puisées ail'eurs.' Baudelaire, *Art Romantique*, p.317.

122 Cf. article quoted in note 110.

123 'C'est cet admirable, cet immortel instinct du Beau qui nous fait considérer la Terre et ses spectacles comme un aperçu, comme une correspondance du Ciel.' Baudelaire, *Art Romantique*, pp.166-173; and *The Poems of Edgar Allen Poe* (London, New York, 1900) pp.191/192.

124 'Le soit insatiable de tout ce qui est au delà, et que révèle la vie, est la preuve la plus vivante de notre immortalité.' Ditto.

125 'C'est à la fois par la poésie et à travers la poésie, par et à travers la musique, que l'âme entrevoit les splendeurs situées derrière le tombeau.' Ditto.

126 'Le témoignage d'une mélancolie irritée ... d'une nature exilée dans l'imparfait et qui voudrait s'emparer immédiatement, sur cette terre même, d'un paradis révélé.' Ditto.

127 It might be possible to posit that Poe starts more directly from Plato, whereas Baudelaire's thought rather goes in the direction of Plotinus. For the latter has converted the Platonic Eros which strives after the highest into the knowledge of the intelligible. In the third chapter we shall revert to the relation between Plato and Plotinus.

128 'Je veux illuminer les choses avec mon esprit et en projeter le reflet sur les autres esprits.' *Cur. Esth.*, p.275.

129 This was also Delacroix's thought. 'Il est donc beaucoup plus important pour l'artiste de se rapprocher de l'ideal qu'il porte en lui, et qui lui est particulier, que de laisser, même avec force, l'idéal passagère que peut presenter la nature' (Journal 12 Oct. 1853, II, p.87). Cf. M. Gilman, *Baudelaire the Critic* (New York, 1943) p.39. (It is, therefore, much more important for the artist to approach the ideal that he carries within himself and which is peculiar to him, than to give – even if it is done with vigour – the fleeting ideal presented by nature . . .)

130 'L'idéal, c'est l'individu redressé par l'individu.' *Cur. Esth.*, p.140.

131 Cf. *Cur. Esth.*, p.104.

132 *The Poems of Edgar Allen Poe* (London, New York, 1900) pp.211 ff.

133 This thought is also found in Delacroix, who, most probably, influenced him directly in this matter. *Cur. Esth.*, p.105. Cf., e.g., *Journal* II, 17 Oct., 1853.

134 *Cur. Esth.*, p.325.

135 H. de Balzac, *Seraphita, Oeuvres Complètes.* XVII *Etudes Philosophiques* III. *Etudes Analytiques* (Paris, 1870) pp.429/430.

136 'La fantasia abandonada de la razón produce monstruos impossibles: unida con ella, es madre de las artes y origen de sus marabillas.' Translation by Levitine F. J. Sanchez Canton, *Los Caprichas de Goya y sus debujos preparatorios* (Barcelona, 1949) p.87.

137 *The Opal* (Virginia ed. XIV, 1845) p.187.

138 *Cur. Esth.*, p.92, passim.

139 'intimité', 'spiritualitè', 'aspiration vers l'univers', *Cur. Esth.*, p.86.

140 'Je me suis contenté de sentir; ... je préfère parler au nom du sentiment, de la morale et du plaisir.' *Cur. Esth.*, pp.215,217.

141 It is true Baudelaire here speaks of Delacroix's biblical, or his traditionally ecclesiastical pictures. But Delacroix does nothing different from what so many before him had done (since the Renaissance): he makes use of such subjects to render his own vision from his own standpoint. The term 'religion' at the beginning of our quotation can only relate to the traditional Roman-Christian subjects, but when he uses this term the second time it is clear that to Baudelaire the issue is the real all-embracing attitude and commitment of man's life and not some Roman-ecclesiastical viewpoint. Especially when he speaks of the 'catholicité' of this basic sence of life (which might be the best translation of his word 'religion' in this case) his real meaning may be clear also in connection with 'liberté à l'individu' (the freedom of the individual person). When Baudelaire states that Delacroix is the best artist among his contemporaries as regards the paint-

ing of 'religious' subjects, he does not at all mean to describe Delacroix as a believing Roman Catholic.

142 'Mais pour expliquer ... que Delacroix seul sait faire de Ia religion, je ferai remarquer à l'observateur que, si ses tableaux les plus intéressants sont presque toujours ceux dont il choisit les sujets, c'est-à-dire ceux de fantaisie – néanmoins la tristesse sérieuse de son talent convient parfaitement à notre religion, religion profondément triste, religion de la douleur universelle, et qui, à cause de sa catholicité même, laisse une pleine liberté à l'individu et ne demande pas mieux que d'être célébrée dans le langage de chacun – s'il connaît la douleur et s'il est peintre.' *Cur. Esth.*, p.109.

143 On Poe, cf. C. D. Cambiaire, *The Influence of E. A. Poe in France* (Fontenay-sous-Bois, 1927). M. Alterton, *Origins of Poe's Critical Theory* (University of Iowa Humanistic Studies, II, 3, w.d.)

144 Cambiaire *op.cit.*, p.44, quotes from the introduction of *Histoires Extraordinaires* (Paris, 1922) p.29; ditto edition Paris 1932, p.XXVIII.

145 Thus Gautier in the preface to Baudelaire's *Les Fleurs du Mal* (1868), quoted in Cambiaire, op.cit., p.37.

146 M. Alterton, op.cit., p.68.

147 Cf. note 145.

148 'Poe, une littérature nouvelle, la littérature du XXième siècle, le miraculeux scientifique, la fabulation par A + B ... De l'imagination à coup d'analyse, Zadig juge d'instruction, Cyrano de Bergerac élève d'Arago ... enfin le roman de l'avenir appelé à faire plus l'histoire des choses qui se passent dans la cervelle de l'humanité que des choses qui se passent dans son coeur.' *Journal des Concourts*, under the 16th of July, 1856, C. D. Cambiaire, *The Influence of E. A. Poe in France* (Fontenay-sous-Bois, 1927) p.44.

149 C. Mauclair, in the *Fortnightly Review* (Sept. 1923), 'E. A. Poe as an Inspirer of Ideas', translation, quoted in Cambiaire, op.cit., p.64.

150 'le sens profond qu'il a de cet aspect non encore observé de la nature et de l'humanité ... le grotesque et l'horrible ... le sens de l'Exception, le sens Spirituel de la Beauté dans l'intensité, et enfin le sens lyrique de la Science – voilà les trois plus glorieux titres de Poe à l'admiration éternelle' Ch. Morice, *La littérature de tout à l'heure* (Paris, 1889) pp.200,203.

151 'C'est la matière qui est l'esclave de l'artiste, elle lui appartient.' Ch. Morice, *Paul Gauguin* (1919, Paris) p.37 – we have been unable to find out the origin of this quotation, if it is not a free summary on the part of Gauguin himself.

152 Gauguin was fond of these books, thus C. Morice in his biography of Gauguin, (Paris, 1919) p.37. And Sérusier writes in a letter: 'sur la table, *Louis Lambert*, dont je lis une page avant de travailler.' ('on the table *Louis Lambert*, a page of which I read before starting to work.') *A.B.C. de la peinture*, p.66, in a letter to Verkade.

153 Schopenhauer, *Pensées, Maximes et Fragments* (Paris: par J. Bourdeau, 1880 2).

154 Thus Morhardt in *Nouvelle Revue* (LXXXV, Febr. 1892) quoted in Lehmann, *Symbolist Aesth.*, p.66.

155 Justi, *Winckelmann und seine Zeitgenossen*, especially I, p.148.

156 'Die Welt ist meine Vorstellung' (publ. Leipzig, 1844 2) p.1.

157 Schopenhauer, *Die Welt als Wille und Vorstellung* (publ. Leipzig, 1844 2) par. 30, pp.191 ff.

158 'Der, wie gesagt, mögliche, aber nur als Ausnahme zu betrachtende Uebergang von der gemeinen Erkenntnisz einzelner Dinge zur Erkenntnisz der Idee, geschieht plötzlich, indem die Erkenntnisz sich vom Dienste des Willes losreiszt, eben dadurch das Subjekt aufhort ein blosz individuelles zu sein und jetzt reines, willenloses Subjekt der Erkenntnisz ist, welches nicht mehr, dem Satze vom Grunde gemäsz, den Relationen nachgeht, sondern in fester Kontemplation des dargebotenen Objekts, auszer seinem Zusammenhange mit irgend andern, ruht und darin aufgeht... In solcher Kontemplation nun wird mit einem Schlage das einzelne Ding zur Idee seiner Gattung und das anschauende Individuum zum reinen Subjekt des Erkennens. Ditto, par. 34, pp.201-202.

159 Ditto, par. 36, p.208.

160 'Ihr einziger Ursprung ist die Erkenntnisz der Ideen, ihr einziges Ziel Mittheilung dieser Erkenntnisz', to which we should add that ... Wesen des Genius besteht eben in der überwiegenden Fähigkeit solcher Kontemplation.' *Ditto*, par. 36, pp.208,209.

161 'Le monde, c'est l'enfer, et les hommes se partagent en âmes tourmentées et en diables tourmenteurs.' Schopenhauer, *Pensées, Maximes et Fragments* (Paris: par J. Bourdeau, 1880 2) p.41.

162 'Un roman est d'un ordre d'autant plus noble et élevé qu'il pénètre dans la vie intérieure et qu'il a moins d'aventures... La tâche du romancier n'est pas de nous raconter de grands événements, mais de rendre les petites choses intéressantes,' Ditto, p.139. 'Le style est la physionomie de l'esprit.'

163 *Pensées*, etc. quoted in note 61, p.140, 141.

164 'spekulative Resultate nach induktiv-naturwissenschaftlicher Methode' E. v. Hartmann, *Philosophie des Unbewussten* (Berlin, 1871 3) p.11 – in 1877 a French translation appeared in two volumes: *La Philosophie de l'Inconscient*, trad. p. M.D. Nolen.

165 Rewald, *Post-Impressionism*, p.298.

166 Ditto, p.295, illustr., Cull. Q. A. Shaw Mc. Kean, Boston.

167 'Les faits saisis par cette imagination véhémente s'y fondent comme dans une flamme... Les idées, changées en hallucination, perdent leur solidité; les êtres semblent des rêves... Le mysticisme entre comme une fumée dans les parois surchauffées de l'intelligence qui craque.' G. Michaud, *Messages Poétiques du Symbolisme* (Paris, 1947) p.203 quote.

168 Th. Carlyle, *Sartor Resartus* (London, 1898) p.193.

169 Ditto, p.196.

170 Ditto, p.198.

171 Ditto, p.227.

172 Ditto, p.252.

173 Ditto, p.254.

174 Ditto, p.257.

175 Ditto, p.258.

176 Margaret Miller, 'Géricault's Paintings of the Insane', *Journal of the War-burg and Courtauld Institute* (IV, 1940) p.151.

177 'défiler devant vos yeux, dans sa réalité fantastique et saisissante, tout ce qu'une grande ville contient de vivantes monstruosités.' *Cur. Esth.*, p.405.

178 R. Rey, *La renaissance du sentiment classique dans la peinture française a la fin du XIX siècle* (Paris, 1931).

179 Baudelaire, *Art Romantique*, p.54 ff.

180 See chapter 1: The art of the Salons.

181 We here concentrate on the important years in which he struck out new paths and so caused a great deal of discussion. In his work after 1860 his strict realism was broken through or mitigated – recall his nudes and his landscapes.

182 'J'ai été étonné de la vigueur et la saillie de son principal tableau; mais quel tableau! quel sujet! La vulgarité des formes ne ferait rien; c'est la vulgarité et l'inutilité de Ia pensée qui sont abominables; et même, si cette idée, telle quelle, était claire.' Delacroix, *Journal*, 15 April 1852.

183 'La peinture est un art essentiellement concret et ne peut consister que dans la représentation des choses réelles et existantes. Un objet abstrait, non visible, n'est pas du domaine de Ia peinture. L'imagination dans l'art consiste à savoir trouver l'expression le plus complète d'une chose existante.' Co*urrier du Dimanche*, 25th December, 1861, quoted by L. Venturi, *Histoire de la critique d'art*, p.291.

184 'Le beau, comme la vérité, est une chose relative au temps où l'on vit et à l'individu apte à le concevoir.' Ditto.

185 Cf. Rewald, *Impressionism*, p.107 *passim*.

186 Rewald, *Impressionism*, p.126-131.

187 Ibid.

188 See eg. R. W. Lee, 'Ut pictura poesis, the humanistic theory of painting', *Art Bulletin* XXII (1940) p.228.

189 W. G. Constable, 'A note on the birth of modern painting, as exemplified in landscape', *Actes du Congres International d'Histoire de l'art* (La Haye, 1955) p.476–481.

190 'Revue Critique de productions de peinture, sculpture, gravure exposées au Salon de 1824', Par M., quoted in Gustave Geffroy, J.B.C. Corot, *Winternumber Studio* 1902/3, pag. C. VI.

191 This term is used in a very broad sense here, comprising eighteenth-century French scientialism and nineteenth-century positivism proper, not restricting ourselves to Comte.

192 'Et puis il tombe dans le fameux défaut moderne, qui naît d'un amour aveugle de la nature, de rien que la nature; il prend une simple étude pour une composition.' *Cur. Esth.*, p.329.

193 'Je comprends qu'un esprit appliqué à prendre des notes ne puisse pas s'abandonner aux prodigieuses rêveries contenues dans les spectacles de la nature présente.' *Cur. Esth.*, p.333.

194 Geffroy, *Corot* op.cit., p.C. VII.

195 Ch. Blanc, *Les artistes de mon temps* (1876), quoted Ferran, *Esth.*, p.425.

196 For instance Castagnary and de Goncourts, see J. C. Sloane, *French Art 1850-1870* (1951) pp.100ff.

197 The *Orpheus*: Ill. C. 15 in *Studio* no. quoted in note 190 (New York and London: Coll. Cottier & Co.).

The *woman*, ill. J. Basehet, *Pour une Renaissance de la peinture française* (Paris, 1946) p.45, Coll. M. G. Wildenstein.

198 Compare Rewald, *Impressionism*, p.295/297.

199 'Et ce que veut le dessin, dans ces modernes ambitions, c'est justement de reconnaître si étroitement la nature, de l'accoler si fortement, quil soit irréprochable dans tous les rapports des formes, qu'il sache l'inépuisable diversité des caractères. Adieu le corps humain, traité comme un vase, au point de vue du galbe décoratif; adieu l'uniforme monotone de Ia charpente, de l'écorché saillant sous le nu; ce qu'il nous faut, c'est la note spéciale de l'individu moderne dans son vêtement, au milieu de ses habitudes sociales, chez lui ou sur la rue. La donnée devient singulièrement aiguë, c'est l'emmanchement d'un flambleau avec le crayon, c'est l'étude des reflets moraux sur les physionomies et sur l'habit, l'observation de l'intimité de l'homme avec son appartement, du trait spécial que lui imprime sa profession, des gestes qu'elle entraîne à faire, des coupes d'aspect sous lesquelles il se développe et s'accentue le mieux.' Duranty, *La nouvelle peinture, à propos du Groupe d'Artistes qui expose dans les Galeries Durand-Ruel 1876*, Nouvelle édition, ed. M. Guérin (Paris, 1946) p.42.

200 Duranty, *La nouvelle peinture, à propos du Groupe d'artistes qui expose dans les Galeries Durand-Ruel 1876*, Nouvelle édition, ed. M. Guérin (Paris, 1946) p.41.

201 Rewald, *Impr.*, p.176; Rewald, *Post-Impressionism*, p.157; Mme Thirion, 'L'influence de l'estampe japonaise sur la peinture française.' *Musée de France* (Oct. 1948) p.229.

202 Ibid.

203 'Une nouvelle esthétique, une esthétique plus libre, un dessin de premier jet, une exubérante fantaisie en même temps qu'une servilité de bon aloi à suivre la nature dans ses transformations les plus rapides.' A. Renan, 'La Mangua de Hokusai.' *Le Japan Artistique*, Documents d'Art et d'Industrie réunies par S. Bing (Paris, 1888) I, p.93.

204 We do not enter into a discussion of the question whether or not Renan and his contemporaries interpreted Japanese art correctly, and whether they did not too much overlook its strong stylization according to a fixed traditional pattern. Perhaps painters like Gauguin and his fellows had a better understanding of these things.

205 'IL est évident qu'il y a deux hommes dans l'auteur de Ia Mangua: le naturaliste et l'idéaliste. Il ne faut pas s'étonner de ce dernier terme. Hokusai n'est pas seulement un amant de la nature visible; il est aussi rêveur, un peintre imaginatif.' A. Renan, 'La Mangua de Hokusai', *Le Japon Artistique*, Documents d'Art et d'Industrie réunies par S. Bing (Paris, 1888) p.109.

206 'N'est-ce pas une chose remarquable que de trouver chez un artiste de l'Extrême-Orient la réalisation plastique de ces rêves d'au-delà', de ces songes nostalgiques que l'école la plus avancée de la littérature anglaise et française a cru être seule à entrevoir?' A. Renan, *op.cit.*, p.110/111.

207 W. Blake, 'A vision of the last judgment', in Kerrison Preston, *Blake and Rossetti* (London, 1944) p.84.

208 A. Blunt, 'Blake's Pictorial Imagination', *Journal of the Warburg and Courtauld Institute* (VI, 1953) pp.190 ff.

209 Cf. note 207.

210 J.C.E. Bassalik-de Vries, *William Blake in his relation to D. G. Rossetti* (1911, Basle) p.11. Here also more discursive on the *correspondances*. Compare Blake, *op.cit.*, p.76.

211 Bassalik-de Vries, *op.cit.*, p.11.

212 Blake, *op.cit.*, p.82.
213 Cited from the Rossetti manuscript in Kerrison Preston, *op.cit.*, p.63.
214 Blake, *op.cit.*, p.75.
215 Bassalik-de Vries, *op.cit.*, p.8.
216 We agree with this view on Blake's profetic books. See J. Bronowski, *William Blake* (London, 1954 2) pp.24 ff.
217 Contradictory thought proceeds from a view of the cosmos as a co-incidentia oppositorum. This view was introduced into Western thought by Heracleitos (cf. Dr. D. H. Th. Vollenhoven, *Geschiedenis der Wijsbegeerte I*, (Franeker, 1950) pp.74 ff.) and it is more than once found again with the mystics – e.g. in Eckhardt (cf. Windelband-Heimsoeth, p.282) and in Sebastian Franck (ditto, p.306,308 and J. W. Tunderman, *Marnix van St. Aldegonde en de subjectivistische stromingen in de 16e eeuw* (Goes, n.d.) p.123 ff.). Blake's Heracleitism is very clear in Kerrison Preston's Summary (*Blake and Rossetti*, p.62) 'Blake's way of Twofold vision, of seeing the soul through the body, the universal through the particular, the eternal through the temporal, can be acquired by anybody with Imagination, which is the Divine Vision, but Blake wanted everyone to go further and "be an Artist", or Prophet, completing the process of vision by reversing it, taking in and also giving out, like continuing the circumference of a semi-circle to the starting point and making the perfect round. This means translating the universal back into the particular, giving the soul a visible body, manifesting eternity in time and space, as an artist does with paint and paper.' This also shows the background of his method of working, which will be discussed in more detail in what follows. Bronowski, *William Blake*, (London 1954 2) p.63. Kerrison Preston, *Blake and Rossetti* (London, 1944) p.62.
218 Bronowski, *op.cit.*, p.127, cited from Blake's *Jerusalem*.
219 F. D. Klingender, *Art and the Industrial Revolution* (London, 1947) p.105, cited from Blake's *Milton*.
220 Kerrison Preston, *op.cit.*, p.65.
221 For reproductions of his biblical illustrations see e.g. *Catalogue of Christie's Sale of Robertson Collection*, 22 July 1949
222 Naturalism refers to the way of representing things, in a plastic manner, in three dimensional reality, e.g., by means of perspective, etc., so it refers to the way of depiction and not to the subjects.
223 John Ruskin, *Modern Painters* (London, 1909) III, p.30.
224 Ditto, p.158 *passim*.
225 Ditto, p.264 ff.
226 Ditto, p.327 ff.
227 Ditto, p.326.
228 *Modern Painters* I, p.13.
229 In our opinion there is here some misconception on the part of Ruskin. Also the great Dutch landscapists such as van Goyen and Ruysdael are rather concerned with a total view, a summary of the structure of, e.g., a Dutch riverscape or of a Guelder wood than with a meticulous representation of a particular subject. The latter is found with the (later) topographically-minded painters. The distance in this respect between van Goyen and Turner is certainly not so very great. The difference is the consequence of

a different kind of vision. As a matter of fact we often get the impression that this Dutch art suits Ruskin's theories better than the often rather too romantically vague achievement of Turner – who gives his 'imagination' (in Ruskin's sense) rather too much rein (cf. what follows in this paragraph). In addition, it is remarkable that Ruskin has so little to say about Constable, who had certainly also studied nature in its forms of appearance and its structures in a way similar to Ruskin's – e.g. by his study of clouds. Ruskin's criticism of Constable in a note to the preface of the second edition of *Modern Painters* (ed. 1909, p.XLIV) is, however, far from clear.

230 Ditto, p.XXXIII and XXXIV.

231 Ditto, p.450.

232 Ditto, p.451/2.

233 Ditto II, p.166. Cf. p.176.

234 'L'homme a dans son âme des sentiments innés que les objets réels ne satisferont jamais, et c'est à ces sentiments que l'imagination du peintre et du poète sait donner une forme et une vie... L'exécution la plus soignée dans les détails ne donnera pas cette unité qui résulte de ce je ne sais quelle puissance créatrice dont la source est indéfinissable.' Delacroix, cited R. Rey, *Le Renaissance du sentiment classique*, p.25.

235 Compare F. Hoffet, *L'Impérialisme protestante, Considérations sur le destin inégal des peuples protestants et catholiques dans le monde actuel* (Paris, 1948). See the author's 'De constituerende factoren ener historisehe daad.' Philosophia Reformata (XIX 1954) p.129 ff. See also Ruskin, *Modern Painters* V, p.376 ff. on unbelief and its consequences.

236 W. Holman Hunt, *Pre-Raphaelitism and the Pre-Raphaelite Brotherhood* (London, 1905) I, p.73.

237 Ditto, p.91.

238 Repr. R. Ironside and J. Gere, *Pre-Raphaelite Painters* (London, 1918) No. 25, Manchester Art Gallery.

239 Ditto Repr. 7, Manchester City Art Gallery.

240 Holman Hunt, op.cit. I, p.XV.

241 Repr. Ironside & Gere, op.cit., p.28 and 29, Coll. C. Anderson esq.

242 *Déjeuner sur l'Herbe*, Louvre, Paris. Cf. P.Fehl, 'The hidden genre: a study of the Concert Champêtre in the Louvre', *Journal of Aesthetics and Art Criticism* (XVI, 2, 1957) p.153.

243 Holman Hunt II, p.436. Repr. Ironside and Gere, *op.cit.* repr. 33 (Wilmington, Delaware: Bancroft Foundation).

244 'Hand and Soul', reprinted in Kerrison Preston, *Blake and Rossetti* (London, 1944) p.88.

245 Ditto, p.92.

246 J. C. E. Bassalik-de Vries, *William Blake in his relation to Dante Gabriel Rossetti* (Basle, 1911) p.49.

247 Ditto, p.17.

248 Ditto, p.24.

249 Kerrison Preston, op.cit., p.95 ff.

250 A pencil-drawing of 1855, Ironside & Gere, op.cit. repr. 32, Coll. Miss Munro.

251 Ironside and Gere, op.cit. Repr. 44, Tate Gallery.

252 Kerrison Preston, op.cit., p.93.

253 Holbrook Jackson, *The Eighteen Nineties* (Pelican 1950 6) p.286 ff.; Miss Dr. Bettina Polak, *Het fin-de-siècle in de Nederlandse schilderkunst* (The Hague, 1955) p.255.

254 A. Muthesius-Trippenbach, 'Das moderne englische Bilderbuch.' *Die Kunst* (München, 1902) p.300 ff.

255 Gauguin visited England. This follows from some comments in a letter to Mette, in which he compares Sidney and Melbourne to London (Malingue, *Letters* CXXIV 1891). Cf. D. Sutton, 'Notes on Paul Gauguin', *Burl. Mag.* (XCVIII 1956) p.84 ff. Gauguin was still with his children in the early eighties, and he may have looked into these books with them. He certainly has known them, see D. Sutton, 'The P.Gauguin Exhibition', *Burl. Mag.* (XCI 1949) p.285, note 26.

256 Ironside and Gere, op.cit., p.18.

257 Kenneth Clark, *The gothic revival, an essay in the history of taste* (London, 1928) p.265.

258 W. Gaunt, *The Pre-Raphaelite Tragedy* (London, 1948 3) p.68.

259 Cf. a letter of Ruskin of 1862, cited by Holbrook Jackson, *Dreamer of Dreams* (1948) p.95 ff.

260 Gaunt, op.cit., p.135; G. Bell, *The art of William Morris* (1897); Holman Hunt, op.cit. II, p.218.

261 Holbrook Jackson, op.cit., p.247 ff.

262 James Grady, 'Nature and the Art Nouveau', *Art Bulletin* (XXXVII, 3,1955) p.187; *Le Japon Artistique* I, p.112,113.

263 R. Schmutzler, Blake and Art Nouveau, *Architectural Review* (CXVIII 704, Aug. 1955) p.91.

264 Holbrook Jackson, *op.cit.*, p.23 passim and p.31ff.

265 Ditto p.56.

266 Ditto p.272 ff.

267 Ditto p.60. Baudelaire is mentioned more than ten times in this book, although French influences as such, are not discussed.

268 These works are reproduced: Ricketts' *Oedipus* and Sturge Moore's scenes from Coleridge, in *The Pageant* (London, 1896); *Pan-Island* by Sturge Moore, Savage's *Behemoth* and a woodcut by Lucien Pissarro in *The Pageant* (1897); W. Heath Robinson's Poe illustrations in *The Poems of Edgar Allen Poe* (London, New York, 1900); Beardsley's work in R. A. Walker, *The Best of Beardsley* (London, 1948); *Pan-Island* by Sturge Moore and work by Lucien Pissarro in *The Dial*, ed. C. S. Ricketts and Ch. Shannon (London, 1897); Savage's *Centaurs* in *The Dial*, No. 3 (1893); Savage's *Behemoth* in *The Dial* No. 2 (1892); Ricketts' *Daphnis and Chloe*, in P. James, *English Book Illustration 1800-1900* (London, New York, 1947) p.59; Burne-Jones' works in J. Cartwright, *Life and Work of Edward Burne-Jones* (London w.d.).

269 Ibid.

270 Ibid.

271 Holbrook Jackson, op.cit., p.104 ff.

272 Whistler's art was intermediate between Impressionism and the Pre-Raphaelites discussed here, and also underwent Japanese influences. He is a typical exponent of this period, although characteristically his own

in his poetry. He stood apart from the tendencies and schools of his time. Yet this generation of 1890 could welcome him as a congenial spirit.

273 Yeats' *Collected Works* (Stratford on Avon, 1908) VI, p.132.

274 Cited by Holman Hunt, *op.cit.*, p.365.

275 It is not so easy to classify Watts. He no doubt shows affinity with the Pre-Raphaelites, both with those who worked in the same direction as Holman Hunt, and with those who were rather of Rosetti's mind. Yet his work is more akin to the style of the Salon art. He did not play an important part in either of the groups, however, and he had no influence of any importance, This is why it was unnecessary to discuss him more elaborately. Cf. M.S. Watts, *George Frederic Watts* (London, 1912).

276 'qui ont, jusqu'à une certain point, accompli en France une oeuvre analogue à celle des préraphaelites anglais, ou du moins de certains de ceux-ci, notamment Rossetti, Watts et Burne-Jones. Ce mouvement a été une protestation à la fois contre l'École et le réalisme, et c'est en cela il est curieux à étudier.' C. Mauclair, *Les états de la peinture française* (1921) p.83.

277 'images mort-nées'.

278 G. Geffroy, *La vie artistique III* (Paris, 1894) p.371.

279 'Il nous serait donné d'assister, simplement, à la concentration des forces idéalistes, au renouveau de Ia mysticité définitivement victorieuse de la science, du matérialisme, de la Révolution, des temps modernes.' G. Geffroy, *La vie artistique II*, Le symbolisme – article of March, 11, 1892 discussing the Salon de la Rose†Croix.

280 'L'art, c'est ni un torse, ni un tête, ni une corps, c'est l'âme, la foi, la passion, la douleur ... Tout art est idéographique.' A. Germain, 'Un peintre idéaliste-idéiste, Alexandre Séon (symbolisme des teintes)', *L'Art et l'Idée* (I, 1892) p.107.

281 Cf. Kahn's writings cited Rewald, *Post Impressionism*, p.148/149, also in our chapter 3, p.62. A. Germain, 'L'idéal at l'idéalisme, Salon de la Rose†Croix', in *L'Art et l'Idée* (I, 1892) p.176.

282 A. Springer, *Die Kunst von 1800 bis zur Gegenwart* (Leipzig 1920 7) p.286.

283 *Mercure de France* (II April 1891) p.236 ff. about the exposition of the XX in that year.

284 We refer to the elaborate study by Miss Dr. Bettine Polak, *Het fin-de siècle in de Nederlandse schilderkunst* (Den Haag, 1955) (title shortened here: B. Polak).

285 B. Polak, p.25,89,102,293.

286 This even applies to a Toorop: influences of Schwabe, see B. Polak, p.127/128 (repr. 27, 28) concerning contacts with Péladan, ditto, p.115.

287 B. Polak, p.28 ff.

288 'de schijn der dingen, maar de mooie herinnering, die er van is bij gebleven', ... bijjvoorbeeld als een sterk omtekend stuk witte kleur ... met sterretjes eromheen, lijntjes die stil bewegen en zeggen hoe mooi zij was, hoe teer haar hele bestaan, dat zij zóó volmaakt was,' B. Polak, p.173.

289 'Travers symbolistes, autre genre de sentimentalisme.' *Lettres de Gauguin à Daniel de Monfreid*, ed. Mme Joly-Segalen (Paris 1950, letter of June 1901) p.177 ff.

290 For example B. Polak, repr. 47.

291 'Donc, MESURER figure et forme, enchâsser sa composition dans une ossature d'arabesques décoratives, élire luminosité et teintes en rapport avec le

sujet à traiter ... enclore sa fiction dans la vraisemblance.' A. Germain, 'Un peintre idéaliste-idéiste, Alexandre Séon', *L'Art et l'Idée* (I, 1892) p.107 ff.

292 Cf. G. Michaud, *Message poétique* III, p.468.

293 Reproduced in the *Illustration*, special number devoted to the Salon of that year.

294 'misérables déformations des Symbolistes?' B. Polak, p.19.

295 'peintres de l'âme' M. Denis *Théories 1890-1910, Du symbolisme de Gauguin vers un nouvel ordre classique* (1912 2, Paris) p.33.

296 'Á confondre les tendances mystiques et allégoriques, c'est-à-dire la recherche de l'expression par le sujet, et les tendances symbolistes, c'est-à-dire la recherche de l'expression par l'oeuvre d'art.' Denis, *Théories*, p.17.

297 B. Polak, p.292, repr. 41.

298 'Motifs' is here intended in the sense of subject matter, thought, themes, and not in that of visual objects – in which sense e.g. Cézanne uses the term.

299 'Nu kan ik in de symbolieke schilderkunst niets anders zien dan het meest geoutreerde individualisme, dat in de waan bevangen is van algemeen metaphysische dingen uit te drukken dus het tegenovergestelde van individuele dingen, en tot deze waan is gekomen door het element der reflexie, en door het werken met anti-naturalistische motieven. Maar wat anti-naturalistisch is, is nog niet supra-naturalistisch, nog minder metaphysisch en naderend tot het absolute.' B. Polak, p.205, citation.

300 See scheme, p.644 of Michaud, *Message Poétique III*.

301 Cf. Michaud, *Message Poétique I*, p.34, 35.

302 Michaud, *Message Poétique II*, p.204.

303 'les tristes vers', 'l'égoïste rêverie' 'la poésie décadente' Michaud, *Message Poétique II*, pp.314 ff., p.328.

304 The terminology is not simple. For in this period there was often a sharp opposition between the various tendencies that we have distinguished here, but it was rarely attempted to give one's own group a name which was clearly different from the other groups. As a matter of fact such distinctive names are not found before the first decades of the twentieth century. Yet we have tried to keep as closely as possible to the linguistic usage of that time and to abstain from introducing new names and new characterizations. It is, therefore, always indispensable to realize what a particular name means. We shall stick to the following terms: by Symbolists we refer to the poets mentioned above who were of the same mind as the Synthetist painters – Gauguin, etc – whereas 'decadents' is the name for the men of letters who are akin to symbolist painters such as Toorop, etc. Thus we get the same name for two different groups, but this is unavoidable if we do not want to introduce artificial terms.

305 'Tel est le contenu de la poésie décadente: le monde intérieur, mais réduit à ses couches les plus basses, aux émotions indéfinissables, aux sensations exacerbées, aux rêves que commandent les désirs refoulés et les exigences de la chair.., expression neuve... correspondances subjectives entre la musique des mots et la musique de l'âme, saisi en son courant mobile et fuyant.' Michaud, *Message Poétique II*, p.404.

306 Rewald, *Post-Impressionism*, p.148/149.

307 In one term we see here the great difference from the attitude of life founded in Holy Scripture: a believer is at home in this world (in the sense of this cosmos, the creation of his heavenly Father), and a stranger in the

midst of the world (by which the unbelievers are meant, human society following the lead of conceptions which are often contrary to the Scriptures). The unbeliever, however, the worldling, is at home among his or her fellows who constitute the majority, but feels himself or herself as a stranger in the cosmos (called 'nature' here) from which he or she has got estranged by refusing to recognize the Creator as such. The latter attitude justifies our term 'a negative sense of reality'.

308 'Ainsi, voyant dans les choses des rapports qui n'y sont guère et cherchant ce que je n'obtiendrai jamais, étranger dans la nature réelle, ridicule au milieu des hommes, je n'aurai que des affectations vaines: et soit que je vive selon moi-même, soit que je vive selon les hommes, je n'aurai dans l'oppression extérieure ou dans ma propre contrainte que l'éternel tourment d'une vie toujours reprimée et toujours misérable. Cited by Morice, *La Littérature*, p.184, note.

309 Cited by Morice, *La Littérature*, p.185.

310 'Je cherche ailleurs, un bien inconnu dont l'instinct me poursuit. Est-ce ma faute si je trouve partout des bornes, si tout ce qui est fini n'a pour moi aucune valeur' Thus the main person in Chateaubriand's 'René', cited Barre, *Le symbolisme*, p.35.

311 By 'religious' we do not mean the cult in the service of God, nor a Christian attitude of life. By 'religious' we mean to say that it is a matter of the heart. The issue is the fundamental and most central commitment of people with respect to God – and hence also with respect to his creation and to their fellow persons, their fellow creatures. The religious commitment of the heart is decisive for people's attitude with regard to things, it directs all their efforts and determines their aim, and is manifested in their view of life and the world. See note 25 and the literature mentioned there, and also the writer's 'De constituerende factoren ener historische daad', Chapter IV, *Philosophia Reformata* (XIX, 1954), pp.169 ff., with an English summary on p.191.

312 Cf. the literature quoted in note 25.

313 'Pour trouver et combiner les développements et les péripéties de son poème et de son drame, il n'a eu qu'à pousser à leurs extrêmes conséquences ses sentiments imaginaires, mais sincères, les sentiments qui lui ont bouleversé l'âme alors qu'il se demandait, exalté par la propre fumée de son génie et par l'électricité de l'air orageux 'Si j'avais la toute-puissance, que ferais-je de mes ennemis, que ferais-je du monde?' Morice, *La Littérature*, p.124.

314 *Sartor Resartus*, p.222.

315 'son roi, son prêtre et son Dieu'.

316 Cf. H. Dooyeweerd, *Dictaat Inleiding tot de Encyclopedie der Rechtswetenschap* (Amsterdam) p.22, the same, *Wijsbegeerte der Wetsidee* I, p.30 ff. and II, p.252 ff.; *A New Critique of Theoretical Thought* I, p.65 ff. and II, p.299 and the literature quoted in note 25.

317 As such it is the concrete form of the humanistic freedom motif. Dooyeweerd, *Wijsbegeerte der Wetsidee* I, p.154 ff.

318 'Si, délicatement l'humanité en proportion des jouissances nouvelles qu'il – i.e. sciencialism – lui apporte, le progrès indéfini ne serait pas sa plus ingénieuse et sa plus cruelle torture; si, procédant par une opiniâtre négation de lui-même, il ne serait pas un mode de suicide incessamment renouvelé, et si, enfermé dans le cercle de feu de la logique divine, il ne ressem-

blerait pas au scorpion qui se perce lui-même avec sa terrible queue, cet éternel desideratum qui fait son éternel désespoir?' *Cur. Esth.*, p.220.

319 'Il a vu, dans le masque uniforme que la science jette sur la nature partout où elle est en relation directe avec l'homme, l'humanité s'en aller des choses, les choses reprendre, dans un silence menaçant leur vie personnelle, étrangère à l'humanité ainsi vaincu par sa victoire et impuissante à reconquérir ses ruines qui retournent à la nature.' Morice, *La Littérature*, p.221.

320 'Une robe de Nessos dont rien ne peut nous délivrer.' Lehmann, *Symbolist Aesthetics*, p.238, cited from *Nouvelle Gauche* XI, 1882

321 'Seulement celui qui nous rêve ferait bien de hâter le couvage de son opium.' Lehmann, *Symbolist Aesthetics*, p.49, cited from Laforgue, *Mélanges posthumes* (1882) p.280.

322 'Notre vie étant cette chose affreuse, tant que l'art n'a pas eu les moyens d'une réalisation parfaite de nos rêves de bonheur, il devait en effet se maintenir dans le deuil des joies que la vie nous refuse et qu'il pouvait encore réaliser en rêve.' Morice, *La Littérature*, p.203.

323 'Impuissance dont souffrent surtout les artistes, incapables de réaliser pleinement leur rêve, c'est-à-dire de revêtir une pensée éternelle d'une forme véritablement réelle.' Pierre Valin, 'Les lettres prochaines', *L'Art et l'Idée* (II, 1892) p.83.

324 'Les conseils de la perversité qui veut toutes choses détournées de leurs limites et de leur équilibre naturels.' Pierre Valin, 'Les lettres prochaines', *L'Art et l'Idée* (II, 1892) p.84.

325 Cf. Windelband-Heimsoeth, p.550,551.

326 'L'esprit est devenu incapable de hiérarchie.' P.Radiot, 'Notre Byzantinisme.' *La Revue Blanche* (Feb. 1894) p.111.

327 'Ce n'est plus le général en chef âme qui a la parole, mais chacun de ses soldats mutinés, les nommés Sens.' P.Radiot, 'Notre Byzantinisme.' *La Revue Blanche* (Feb. 1894) p.111.

328 'Le présent n'est blessant et laid que par sa matérialité.' 'Ne faisons-nous autre chose, en croyant inventer les plus fabuleuses chimères, que d'évoquer les visions, inconsciemment ressouvenues, des temps où nos âmes se prélassaient dans le merveilleux Eden des Idées pures?' G.-A. Aurier, *Oeuvres*, p.31.

329 'Losqu'elle se prélasse dans les douceurs ephémères de la contingence; immortelle, lorsqu'elle sait s'élever jusqu'au paradis des absolus., G.-A. Aurier, *Oeuvres*, p.31.

330 Cf. Jean Lemeere, 'Les concepts du Beau et de l'art dans la doctrine platonicienne.' *Revue d'Histoire de la Philosophie et d'histoire générale de la civilisation* (VI, 1938) p.1ff., especially, p.10 ff.

331 M.H. Abrams, *The mirror and the lamp, Romantic theory and the critical tradition* (New York, 1953) p.42. ff; B. Panofsky, *Idea, ein Beitrag zur Begriffsgeschichte der älteren Kunsttheorze* (Berlin, 1924) p.11.

332 B. Panofsky, *op.cit.*, p.39 ff.; I. L. Zupnick, 'The "aesthetics" of the early Mannerists,' *Art Bulletin* (XXXV 1953) p.302 ff.; A. Blunt, *Artistic Theory in Italy 1450-1 600* (Oxford, 1940).

333 85. Abrams, *Mirror and the lamp*, p.43, p.126 ff. See also P. v. Tieghem, *Le romantisme dans la litterature européenne* (Paris, 1948) p.271 ff.

334 Abrams, ditto, p.44.

335 R. F. Beerling, Sjestow (Baarn, w.d.) p.74 ff.; see E. Panofsky on Suger: *Meaning in the visual arts*, p.132.

336 'Le point de départ de la spéculation de Plotin ... est un sentiment de malaise, le sentiment que la vie humaine, sous la forme actuelle, est une vie arrêtée ou diminuée par des obstacles dus aux corps et aux passions.' E. Bréhier, *La Philosophie de Plotin* (Paris 1928) pp.24 ff.

In this connection it is interesting to find the following distinction made by Gregorius of Nyssa there are three stages of knowledge Chaldaean philosophy related to appearances, symbolic philosophy related to abstract truths, and apophatic philosophy, *apophainoo*, is no doubt used here in the sense of 'to reveal' – directed to spiritual reality. Each of these ways of knowledge corresponds to special organs: *aisthesis* for the forms of appearances, *phantasia katalèptikè* for abstractions, *pistis* for reality (Jean Daniélou, *Platonisme et théologie mystique. Essai sur la doctrine spirituelle de St. Grégoire de Nyssa* (Paris, 1944) p.155). It is typical of the strong bond with old traditions that these distinctions could be so readily used by the Symbolists – in the wide sense of the word. The first way was the science of nature characterized by them in a similar manner; the second was concerned with themselves (in this even the 'imagination' was applied in an identical way), while the third method was rejected by them as an impossibility, as all of them, with a few exceptions only, refused to recognize the divine revelation – so that they often assigned to art the role of revealing reality, thus remaining within the limits of Gregorius' second way of knowledge.

337 M. Denis, *Théories*, p.160.

338 'Son besoin d'échapper à l'horrible réalité de l'existence, à franchir les confins de la pensée, à tâtonner sans jamais arriver à une certitude, dans les brumes du de l'au delà de l'art. J. K. Huysmans, *A Rebours* (Paris 1903) p.143.

339 'L'ordre naturel' so that 'si tout ce qui vit vit esclave, rien n'est selon les lois de la nature.' There is no freedom, as 'toute vie est enchaînée par une autre vie, ou par un vice, ou par de factices obligations que résume la Société telle qu'elle est.' Morice, *La Littérature*, p.367.

340 H. Redeker, *De dagen der artistieke vertwijfeling* (Amsterdam, 1950) p.31.

341 Ditto, p.154,155,143.

342 Cf. above, p.44.

343 See Rewald, *Post-Impressionism*, p.154 passim.

344 'Anywhere out of the world' is a quotation form Thomas Hood's 'Bridge of Sighs', a poem that Morice perhaps knew from Poe's *The Poetic Principle* in which it occurs in full (Poe, *The Poetic Principle*, pp.202 ff.).

345 'Cette plainte est de ce temps et c'est bien plus qu'une plainte: c'est la loi suprême de l'Art suprême.' Morice, *La'Littérature*, p.282.

346 'il s'éloignait, de plus en plus, de la réalité et surtout du monde contemporain qu'il tenait en une croissante horreur; cette haine avait forcément agi sur ses goûts littéraires et artistiques, et il se détournait le plus possible des tableaux et des livres dont les sujets délimités se réléguaient dans la vie moderne.' Huysmans, *A Rebours*, p.238, compare p.136.

347 'La nature est laide, et je préfère les montres de ma fantaisie à la trivialité positive.' *Cur. Esth.*, p.263.

348 'J'ai trouvé la définition du Beau, de mon Beau. Cest quelque chose d'ardent et de triste, quelque chose d'un peu vague ... je ne conçois guère (mon cerveau serait-il un miroir ensorcelé) un type de Beauté où il n'y ait du

Malheur. Appuyé sur d'autres disent obsédé parces idées, on conçoit qu'il me serait difficile de ne pas conclure que le plus parfait type de Beauté virile est Satanà la manière de Milton'. From the *Journaux Intimes, Oeuvres complètes*, ed. le Dantec 1938 II, p.633, cited by Denys Sutton. 'The Paul Gauguin Exhibition', *Burlington Magazine* (XCI 1949) p.284; Cf. 'Projets de Préface pour une édition nouvelle', *Les Fleurs du Mal*, in the edition of Jacques Crépet et Georges Blin, (Paris 1942) p.211; see also Marcel Raymond, *From Baudelaire to Surrealism*, (New York 1950) p.13, both notes.

349 Dr. B. Polak, *Het fin-de-siècle in de Nederlandse schilderkunst* (The Hague, 1955) p.20 ff.

350 Cf. Barre, *Le Symbolisme*, p.133.

351 See Holbrook Jackson, *The Eighteen Nineties*, p.26, 60.

352 He wrote articles on the Salons, collected in *L'Art.moderne* (Paris, 1902 2/first impression, 1883).

353 'Et peintre fier de mon génie / Je savourais dans mon tableau / L'énivrante monotonie / Du métal, du marbre et de l'eau ... / Et des cataractes pesantes / Comme des rideaux de cristal, / Se suspendent éblouissantes / À des murailles de cristal.'

Cited by Ch. Chassé, *Le mouvement symboliste* (1947) p.24.

354 'Il y avait dans ses oeuvres désespérées et érudites un enchantement singulier, une incantation vous remuant jusqu'au fond des entrailles, comme celle de certains poèmes de Baudelaire.' Huysmans, *A Rebours*, (1903) pp.71ff.

355 'Décameron satanique. Cette île des rêves fantastiques renferme toutes les formes de Ia passion, de la fantaisie, du caprice chez la femme, la femme dans son essence première, l'être inconscient, folle de l'inconnu, du mystère, éprise de mal sous forme de séduction perverse et diabolique. Rêves d'enfants, rêves des sens, rêves monstrueux, rêves mélancoliques, rêves transportant l'esprit et l'âme dans le vague des espaces, dans le mystère de l'ombre, tout doit ressentir l'influence des sept péchés capitaux, tout se trouve dans cette enceinte satanique, dans ce cercle des vices et des ardeurs coupables, depuis le germe encore innocente, jusqu'aux fleurs monstrueuses et fatales des abîmes ... Au loin, la ville morte, aux passions sommeillantes. Et cette ville, c'est Ia vie réelle, la vie vraie, ce qui est caché, renfermé dans des murailles sombres, sous des toits surbaissés. Mais les routes montueuses ... se dressent et des figures ... montent toujours s'accrochant aux aspérités de cette roche aride et dure ... Peut-être arriveront-elles jusqu'it cette croix redemptrice qui se dresse humblement dans l'Ether, dernière étape de la Vie, dernière épreuve génératrice et bienfaisante, dernier refuge de l'Etre qui a pu éviter ou vaincre après les épreuves cruelles le rêve chimérique, le rêve terrible de ruine, de douleur et de mort.' *Catalogue Musée Moreau*, 1926, No. 39, p.11/12, ill. p.42.

356 'courbe son front attristé, dans un regret d'esclavage et d'exil, tandis qu'à ses pieds s'entasse la sombre phalange des monstres de l'Erèbe et la Nuit' ... while there is also question of an 'ascension vers les sphères supérieures vers le Divin', by which 'Le grand Mystère s'accomplit.' *Catalogue Musée Moreau*, p.2, no cat, no., with reprod. Cf. text concerning cat, no. 13, p.4, *Oedipus and the Sphinx*.

357 See e.g. *Les licornes*, cat, no. 213, repr. on p.66.

358 'Le Salomé de Gustave Moreau nous hantait' A. Fontainas, *Mes souvenirs du Symbolisme* (Paris 1928) p.96.

359 A. Fontainas, *Mes souvenirs du Symbolisme* (Paris, 1928) p.326.

360 *The Dial* (1893, No. 3) p.10 ff., article signed Charles R. Sturt, pseudonym of Ricketts, see U. Bridge, *W. B. Yeats and T. Sturge Moore, their correspondence 1901-1937* (London, 1953) letter of 7 November 1921.

361 Gleeson White, 'The pictures of Gustave Moreau.' *The Pageant* (1897) p.3 ff.

362 Ditto, p.11.

363 G. Michaud, *Message Poétique* II, p.221.

364 'Le concret sans loi tout ce qui reste à l'homme après le départ des dieux– la surnature civilisée, irrationnelle et psychique, engendre des fantômes qui peuplent le roman noir. Le fantôme n'exprime pas les mythes de la nature ou l'infini du réel, comme le dieu grec ou la fée. C'est un événement particulier qui se transforme en psychisme, une partie du réel transposée à l'intérieur de l'homme, et qui se réincarne – dans l'irréalité. Ces créations immatérielles expriment l'angoisse des hommes menacés par le mal extérieur devenu psychisme.' Marcel Jean & Arpad Mezei, *Genèse de la pensée moderne* (Paris, 1950) p.44.

365 Catalogue of etchings and lithographs by Rodolphe Bresdin, Print Room Amsterdam, 1955, cat. no. 45.

366 'Ce qu'on retrouve partout, presque d'un bout à l'autre de son oeuvre, c'est l'homme épris de solitude, fuyant le monde, fuyant éperdument sous un ciel sans patrie, dans les angoisses d'un exil sans espoir et sans fin.' Odilon Redon, 'A soi-même', *Journal 1867–1915* (Paris, 1922) p.161.

367 Ensor might have been mentioned here, but he was of no importance to France–at least we have not found any reference to his work. The question might be asked whether Ensor's prints of the eighteen-eighties had been created under the influence of Redon's lithographs.

368 Rewald, *Post-Impressionism*, p.166 ff.

369 'par ce simulacre du vrai', Odilon Redon, 'A soi-même', *Journal 1867–1915* (Paris, 1922 p.93.

370 'autant que possible, la logique du visible au service de l'invisible.' Odilon Redon, 'A soi-même', *Journal 1867-1915* (Paris, 1922) p.29.

371 'mal de vie', Cf. Redon, *op.cit.*, p.84.

372 'frisson de peur dans l'infini de la nuit', G.-A. Aurier, *Oeuvres*, p.306.

373 Cf. e.g. Jan Veth, Odilon Redon's lithografische Serien, *Kunst und Künstler* (III, 1903) p.104.

374 E.g. Odilon Redon, 'A soi-même.' *Journal 1867–1915* (Paris, 1922) p.71.

375 In L'art moderne 1883, cited by Jules Destrée, *L'oeuvre lithografique de Odilon Redon* (Brussels, 1891) p.8.

376 Michaud, *Message Poétique* III, p.644.

377 'La nature est laide et je préfère les monstres de ma fantaisie à la trivialité positive.' *Cur. Esth.*, p.263.

378 'Mais j'ai mille et mille fois horreur de ces mélancolies à la Meryon.' Van Gogh, *Brieven*, letter 546.

379 Here we again give a brief summary of the terminology used by us. Decadents are the men of letters that came to the fore about 1885 in the footsteps of Verlaine and Huysmans. To these the Symbolist painters of the Rose†Croix were akin. A different milieu was formed by the symbolistic writers round Mallarmé, with whom we class Aurier and Morice. They are nearest akin to the Synthetist painters. This terminology has been chosen because it is nearest to the non-systematic and often confusing

terminology used by their contemporaries. We have been unable to avoid using the same term for two different movements. But we prefer this to the introduction of names of our own devising.

380 'Méfie-toi des préraphas.' J. Rewald, 'Lucien Pissarro: Letters from London 1883-1891.' *Burl. Mag.* (XCI, 1949) p.192. Cf. Van Gogh, *Brieven III*, letter 615.

381 Here the 'Synthetists' are meant.

382 'les tendances mystiques et allégoriques, c'est-à-dire la recherche de l'expression par le sujet, et les tendances symbolistes, c'est-à-dire la recherche de l'expression par l'oeuvre d'art.' Denis, *Théories*, p.17.

383 This term may be read in English as well as in French. Cf. Windelband, p.377 ff.

384 *'Traité de sensations'* Windelband-Heimsoeth, p.383.

385 Rewald, *Impressionism*, p.234, cf. p.271 ff.

386 Cf. Windelband-Heimsoeth, p.381, about Hume.

387 Gauss, *Aesthetic Theories*, p.21, 22; cf. Duranty, *La nouvelle peinture*, p.39.

388 Rewald, *Impressionism*, p.131.

389 Rewald, *Impressionism*, p.431.

390 'L'oeil et la main, ah! superbes, et ce fut assez mais rien d'autre.' Mauclair, *Servitude et grandeur littéraires* (Paris, 1922) p.192.

391 'Au fond, ils n'avaient rien à voir ensemble, c'était la communauté de réaction contre les méchancetés de la presse qui les reliait' Mauclair, *Servitude et grandeur littéraires* (Paris, 1922) p.194.

392 Cf. L. Venturi, *Cézanne* (Paris, 1936) p.29.

393 See e.g. P.A. Scholes, *The Oxford Companion to Music* (Oxford, 1947 7) 'Impressionism'.

394 Fontainas, *Souvenirs*, p.91 ff.

395 Rewald, *Impressionism*, p.119.

396 They also tried to stimulate this 'dream' (*rêverie*) in the parks laid out in the second half of the eighteenth century. Cf. H. Sedlmayer, *Verlust der Mitte* (Salzburg 1951 5) p.19 ff. This is very clear in the theories of C.C.L. Hirschfeld, *Théories de l'art des Jardins* (*traduit de l'allemand*) (Leipzig 1780, 5 volumes), from which we quote, II, p.76: 'Lorsque nous entrons sous des voûtes ténébreuses de feuillage, le repos se répand sur tous nos sens notre âme se trouve soudain dans une situation qui lui fait retirer son activité en elle-même; bientôt elle ne s'occupe plus que de soi, elle commence à se livrer entiérement à l'imagination.' ('When we enter underneath the dark arches of the foliage, the feeling of repose spreads over all our senses our soul is suddenly in a situation which makes it withdraw its activity into itself; soon it is only occupied with its own self, it commences to deliver itself entirely to the imagination.') Monet's 'Nymphéas' represents a similar attitude towards nature, although very probably Monet never occupied himself with Rousseau, and even less with such a kind of literature as we have just quoted. After all Rousseau's ideas had penetrated all French thought. Cf. Lehmann, p.81 ff.; J. J. Rousseau, *Dialogues, Rêveries, Correspondance*, ed. P.Richard (Larousse, 1938) p.17ff.

397 Cf. Lehmann, p.102/3.

398 'Il est permis ... de blâmer ce constant sacrifice des formes significatrices et ce parti-pris de plonger les êtres dans ces atmosphères si splendidement embrassées qu'ils semblent s'y vaporiser; sans doute, aussi est-il légitime de

souhaiter un art moins immédiat, moins directement sensationnel, un art de rêve plus lointain et d'idée.' Aurier, 'C. Monet.' *Mercure de France* (IV, 1892) p.302.

399 'd'instinct et d'instantanéité', P.Signac, *D'Eugène Delacroix au Néo-Impressionnisme* (Ed. La Revue Blanche 1899) p.58.

400 Also Baudelaire had advanced thoughts on colour that were found again in Seurat and his fellows. Thus, e.g., in the section 'De la couleur' in the *Salon* of 1846, *Cur. Esth.*, p.87. The *Curiosités Esthétiques* had appeared in 1884, and it is hardly conceivable that such a man as Seurat should have remained ignorant of it. This is a clear instance of the confluence of Baudelaire's and Delacroix's influence on this generation of painters. P.Signac, *D'Eugène Delacroix aux Néo-Impressionnisme* (Ed. La Revue Blanche 1899) p.62.

401 P.Signac, *D'Eugène Delacroix an Néo-Impressionnisme* (Ed. La Revue Blanche, 1899) p.21.

402 'conférer à la nature, que laissait à la fin sa réalité précaire, une authentique réalité; P.Signac, *D'Eugène Delacroix an Néo-Impressionnisme* (Ed. La Revue Blanche 1899) p.76. Cf. Rewald, *Post-Impressionism*, p.84.

403 'Synthétiser le paysage dans un aspect définitif qui en perpétue la sensation.' J. Rewald, *Seurat* (Paris 1948) p.81. From an article of F. Fénéon in *L'Art Moderne* (1887).

404 Laprade *Seurat* (1945) cited from a letter of Seurat to Beaubourg of 1890 'Le moyen d'expression est le mélange optique des tons, des teintes', etc. ('The means of expression are found in the optical mixing of tones and hues.')

405 'L'art, c'est l'harmonie. L'harmonie, c'est l'analogie des contraires, l'analogie des semblables de ton, de teinte, de ligne, considérés par la dominante et sous l'influence d'un éclairage en combinaisons gaies, calmes ou tristes.' Quotation from beginning of a letter of Seurat to Beaubourg of 1890. Laprade, *Seurat* (1945).

406 Typical of this is the announcement of the 'Bibliothèque scientifique internationale', including also Brucke and Helmholz, *Principes scientifiques des beaux-arts, suivis de l'optique et la peinture* (trad. 1878); a.o. it says 'La Bibliothèque scientifique internationale ne comprend pas seulement ouvrages consacrés aux sciences physiques et naturelles, elle aborde aussi les sciences morales, comme la philosophie, l'histoire, la politique et l'économie sociale, la haute législation, etc. mais les livres traitant des sujets de ce genre se rattacheront encore aux sciences naturelles, en leur empruntant les méthodes d'observation et d'experience qui les not rendues si fécondes depuis deux siècles.' ('The *Bibl. scientifique internationale* not only comprises works devoted to physical and natural sciences, it also deals with moral sciences, such as philosophy, history, politics, social economics, legislation, etc.; but the books dealing with such subjects will be connected with the natural sciences by borrowing from them the methods of observation and experience which have rendered these so fruitful for two centuries already.') This announcement is found at the back of Schopenhauer, *Pensées, maximes, et fragments*, ed. J. Bourdeau (Paris, 1880 2).

407 Later on (in chapter 8) we shall enter in more detail into the iconic aspect. For the present only briefly this by 'iconic' we mean that in the picture something is told about reality in a manner analogous to language. Also outside art proper we find iconic representations (just like language,

which also exists apart from literature or poetry) – a pure, non-artistic, use of iconic means is found, e.g., in maps, visual-statistics, etc.

408 Rewald, *Post-Impressionism*, p.100 passim.

409 'soumettant la couleur et la ligne à l'émotion qu'il a ressentie et qu'il veut traduire, le peintre fera oeuvre de poète, de créateur.' P.Signac, *D'Eugène Delacroix au Néo-Impressionnisme* (Ed. La Revue Blanche 1899) p.59.

410 'Les règles ne gênent pas la spontanéité de l'invention ni de l'exécution malgré leur caractère absolu ... La science délivre de toutes les incertitudes, permet de se mouvoir en toute liberté et dans un cercle très étendu ... Toutes les règles étant puisées dans les lois mêmes de la nature, rien n'est plus facile à connaître par principe, ni plus indispensable. Dans les arts, tout doit être voulu.' Rewald, *Seurat*, p.119, cited out of D. Sutter, 'Les phénomènes de la vision', *L'Art* (1880). Cf. Rewald, *Post-Impressionism*, p.86.

411 'Il faut voir la nature avec les yeux de l'esprit et non uniquement avec les yeux du corps, comme un être dépourvu de raison.' Ditto quotation from Sutter.

412 'Une esthétique scientifique' *Revue contemporaine* (II, 4 August 1885). Also cited by Morice, *La littérature*, p.275, note.

413 'L'esthétique des formes' *La Revue Blanche* (August and October 1894) illustrated by Signac.

414 'Cercle chromatique et sensation de couleur.' *Revue Indépendante* (VII, 19 May 1888).

415 Cf. Rewald, *Seurat*, concerning his apprenticeship, when he made copies of Raphael, Holbein, Ingres, etc.

416 Article in *L'Art Moderne* (1 May 1887) cited by Rewald, *Post-Impressionism*, p.99.

417 Verhaeren, 'Le salon des Vingt Bruxelles.' *La Vie Moderne* (Feb. 26, 1887) cited by Rewald, *Post-Impressionism*, p.104.

418 R.J. Goldwater, 'Some aspects of the development of Seurat's style.' *Art Bulletin* (XXIII 1941) p.124.

419 'Il eut le mérite de tenter la réglementation de l'impressionisme – ce premier effort contre la liberté', M. Denis, *Théories*, p.257.

420 Gauguin had in his cabin at Atuana among others a photograph of Puvis' Hope–of which he had made a lithography at an earlier date. Cf. Rewald, *Post-Impressionism*, p.162, 459. And in a letter to Fontainas of 1899 (Malingue CLXX) Gauguin wrote: 'Puvis de Chavannes (en) est le haut example.' (Puvis de Chavannes is the best example).

421 Cf. Aurier, 'Les symbolistes.' *Revue encyclopédique* (April, 1892), cited by Rewald, *Post-Impressionism*, p.165.

422 'Ils ne sont point par un vain caprice désincarnés mais strictement figurés selon les nécessités essentielles de la matière.' Fontainas, *Souvenirs*, p.99.

423 'Pour toutes les idées claires il existe une pensée plastique qui les traduit.' Quoted Denis, *Théories*, p.50, by Chassé, *Le Mouvement Symboliste*, p.52 also by Rewald, *Post-Impressionism*, p.162.

424 'Je cherche un spectacle qui la (idée) traduise avec exactitude.' Cited by Denis, *Théories*, p.50.

425 E. Bernard, *Erinnerungen an Paul Cézanne* (Basle, 1917) transl. H. Graber, p.34, 35; G. Geffroy, *La vie artistique* III, 1894, p.249.

426 Rewald, *Impressionism*, p.356, 358.

427 Cézanne, *Correspondances*, p.98/99, letter of 1866.

428 'moyen d'expression de sensation', Cézanne, *Correspondances*, p.153, letter of 1878.

429 'sur nature', Cézanne, *Correspondance*, p.264, letter of July 1904.

430 Cited in L. Venturi, *Cézanne, son art, son oeuvre* (Paris, 1936) letter to Mans of 1889 on p.42.

431 'Toutes les théories sur le génie pictural de Cézanne, tous les boniments sur son art de synthèse, ont été faits après coup, je les ai vu naître.' Mauclair, *Servitude et grandeur littéraires* (1922) p.189.

432 Those of Gasquet and of Vollard.

433 This is a clear refutation of the view that art will be all the better, greater, and more profound as the artist is poorer and more lonely. On the contrary, it is only very human that exactly by being recognized, and stimulated also by purchases, etc. the artist will be encouraged to go on in a particular direction and to give the best he can – unless he has such a weak character that he will soon fall a victim to the urge of winning an easy and immediate fame, and is thus forced to pander to the taste of his patrons. It is very doubtful whether in such a case the artist would have achieved anything of importance if he had been obliged to strive against the stream of indifferent neglect.

434 Rewald, *Impressionism*, p.324.

435 'faire de l'impressionnisme quelque chose de solide et de durable comme l'art des musées.' Denis *Théories*, p.242. This as well was written down later, and it is not possible to know whether Cézanne would have said this in the eighties.

436 Rewald, *Impressionism*, p.358.

437 'Voyez Cézanne, l'incompris, la nature essentiellement mystique de l'Orient ... il affectionne dans la forme un mystère et une tranquillité lourde de l'homme couché pour rêver, sa couleur est grave comme le caractère des orientaux', and he continues saying 'plus je vais plus j'aborde dans ce sens de traductions de la pensée par tout autre chose qu'une littérature.' Malingue, *Lettres* XI, Letter of January 14, 1885. See also chapter VI.

438 Rewald, *Cézanne et Zola*, p.286.

439 Rewald, *Post-Impressionism*, p.308.

440 'ce qu'il faut, c'est refaire le Poussin sur nature.' Vollard, *En écoutant Cézanne*, p.50. Cf. the statement as given by Bernard: 'Wir müssen durch die Natur, d.h. durch die Sinneseindruck wieder klassisch werden' ('We have to become classic again through nature, that is through sensation'), in *Erinnerung an P.C.*, p.27.

441 'Dans le peintre, il y a deux choses l'oeil et le cerveau, tous deux doivent s'entr'aider; il faut travailler à leur développement mutuel, mais en peintre à l'oeil par la vision sur nature, au cerveau par la logique des sensations organisées qui donnent les moyens d'expression.' Rewald, *Cézanne et Zola*, p.274.

442 'On n'est ni trop scrupuleux, ni trop sincère, ni trop soumis à la nature; mais on est plus ou moins maître de son modèle, et surtout de ses moyens d'expression. Pénétrer ce qu'on a devant soi, et persévérer à s'exprimer le plus logiquement possible.' Cézanne, *Correspondances*, p.262, letter of 1904.

443 'la nature est toujours la même, mais rien demeure d'elle de ce qui nous apparaît. Notre art doit, lui, donner le frisson de sa durée avec les éléments, les apparences, de tous ces changements.' L. Guerry, *Cézanne et l'expression de l'espace* (1950) p.187, note 28, cited from Gasquet.

444 'le peintre concrétise, au moyen du dessin et de la couleur, ses sensations, ses perceptions' Cézanne, *Correspondances*, p.262, letter of 1904. Cf. p.257, in which he speaks of his 'sensation forte de la nature' ('strong sensation of nature').

445 'La connaissance des moyens d'exprimer notre émotion.' Cézanne, *Correspondances*, p.257, letter of 1904.

446 'J'ai voulu copier la nature – je n'y arrivais pas. J'ai été content de moi lorsque j'ai découvert que le soleil par exemple (les objets ensoleillés) ne se pouvait pas reproduire mais qu'il fallait le représenter par autre chose que ce que je voyais – par la couleur.' Denis, *Théories*, p.259, note 2.

447 'La reconstruction d'art que Cézanne avait commencée avec les matériaux de l'impressionnisme, Gauguin l'a continué avec moins de sensibilité et d'ampleur, mais avec plus de rigueur théorique. Il a rendu plus explicite la pensée de Cézanne.' Denis, *Théories* p.262.

448 Cf. F. Bonger-v. d. Borch van Verwolde, 'Vincent van Gogh als lezer.' *Maandblad voor Beeldende kunsten* (Maart, 1950) and M. E. Tralbaut, *Vincent van Gogh in zijn Antwerpse periode* (Amsterdam, 1948).

449 Cf. *Brieven* No 423 from his early period.

450 'Ah, il est sans doute sage, juste, d'être ému par la Bible; mais la réalité moderne a tellement pris sur nous que même en cherchant abstraitement à reconstruire les jours anciens dans notre pensée, les petits événements de notre vie nous arrachent à ce même moment à ces méditations et nos aventures propres nous rejettent en force dans les sensations personnelles – joie, ennui, souffrance, colère, ou sourire.' *Brieven* IV B 21, cited by Rewald, *Post-Impressionism*, p.307/8.

451 Rewald, *Post-Impressionism*, p.338, *Brieven* IV T 10.

452 *Brieven* No. 615.

453 *Brieven* No. 566 – he says to do so under Delacroix's influence. Cf. IV B 19.

454 Malingue, LXXVIII, letter of Dec. 1888.

455 *Brieven*, 626 a, and 595.

456 See note 454.

457 The word 'instinctive' is properly speaking incorrect. For this 'instinct' is the result of the formation of ideas under the influence of a particular view of life and the world for centuries at a stretch, a formation which will continue its influence even a long time after this view of life has lost its hold on people. Cf. again F. Hoffet, L'*Impérialisme protestante. Considérations sur le destin inégal des peuples protestants et catholiques dans le monde actuel.* (Paris, 1948) This 'instinct', therefore, is not something natural implied in the structure of man as such, but a complex of standards of judgment that has been formed in the cultural process.

458 *Brieven* IV B, 21.

459 'mélancolie à la Meryon,' Van Gogh, *Brieven*, letter No 546.

460 See note 458.

461 Karl Jaspers, *Strindberg und van Gogh. Versuch einer pathografischen Analyse under vergleichender Heranziehung von Swedenborg und Hölderlin* (1926, Berlin) p.124 ff.

462 'Sans le savoir is die academie eene maîtresse, die verhindert dat er een meer serieuze meer warme meer vruchtbare liefde in u wakker wordt – Laat die maîtresse loopen en word tot over de ooren verliefd op uwe eigentlijke beminde dame nature of réalite.' *Brieven* IV, R 4.

463 'Welnu, dat algemeene mooi doen tegen elkaar van de tonen in de natuur, men verliest het door pijnlijk letterlijke nabootsing, men behoudt het door herschepping in een kleurengamma evenwijdig, maar desnoods niet precies of lang niet eender aan 't gegevene.' Van Gogh, *Brieven* No. 429.

464 Rewald, *Post-Impressionism*, p.371.

465 'Sans doute comme tous les peintres de sa race, il est très conscient de la matière, de son importance et de sa beauté, mais aussi, le plus souvent, cette enchanteresse matière, il ne la considère que comme une sorte de merveilleux langage destiné à traduire l'Idée. Il est presque toujours un symboliste ... sentant la continuelle nécessité de revêtir ses idées de formes précises, pondérables, tangibles, d'enveloppes intensément charnelles et matérielles.' Aurier Les Isolés Vincent van Gogh, *Mercure de France* (Jan. 1890), cited by Rewald, *Post-Impressionism*, p.368.

466 'J'ai toujours l'espoir de trouver quelque chose là dedans. Exprimer l'amour de deux amoureux par un mariage de deux complémentaires, leurs mélange et leur oppositions, les vibrations mystérieuses de tons rapprochés. Exprimer la pensée d'un front par le rayonnement d'un ton clair sur un fond sombre.' Van Gogh, *Brieven* IV B 8, cited by Rewald, *Post-Impressionism*, p.235.

467 *Brieven* No. 554, cited by Rewald, *Post-Impressionism*, p.235.

468 'et ce n'est pas le moyen de synthétiser.' Van Gogh, *Brieven* No. 614.

469 *Brieven* No. 520.

470 'Je ne peux pas travailler sans modèle. Je ne dis pas que je ne tourne pascarrément le dos à la nature pour transformer une étude en tableau, en arrangeant la couleur, en agrandissant, en simplifiant.' Van Gogh, *Brieven* IV B, 19.

471 The latter also applies to the classicists who depict an ideal world, as they conceive of it, in a naturalistic way, while correcting the real object by purifying it from its (supposed) faults. In this case we need not at all speak of the Salon artists, for they were in actual fact the adherents of the most rigorous kind of naturalism (cf. our chapter 1).

472 'Ce n'est pas un retour au romantique ou à des idées religieuses, non. Cependant en passant par le Delacroix cela apparaît davantage, par la couleur et un dessin plus volontaire que l'exactitude trompe-l'oeil, on exprimerait une nature de campagne.' Van Gogh, *Brieven* No. 595, cited by Rewald, *Post-Impressionism* p.337.

473 'Pour te rappeler que pour donner une impression d'angoisse, on peut chercher à la faire sans viser droit au jardin de Gethsémané historique; que pour donner un motif consolant et doux il n'est pas nécessaire de représenter les personnages du sermon sur la montagne.' Van Gogh, *Brieven* IV B 21.

474 'Je reviens plutôt à ce que je cherchais avant de venir à Paris, et je ne sais si quelqu'un avant moi a parlé de couleur suggestive, mais Delacroix et Monticelli tout en n'en ayant pas parlé, l'ont faite.' Van Gogh, *Brieven* No. 539.

475 *Brieven* IV R. 30.

476 Cf. R. Huyghe, *Le carnet de Paul Gauguin* (Paris, 1952) p.78.

477 B. Klossowski, *Die Maler von Montmartre* (Berlin, 1903) p.5 passim. A. Barre, *Le symbolisme*, p.67ff.

478 'Rops n'a rien du mystique ni du névrosé. C'est un esprit sain dans un corps sain, dédaigneux de toutes les faiblettes pudeurs, heureux d'exalter sa virilité...' Maurice Kunel, F*élicien Rops (*Bruxelles 1943) p.30.

479 'Je tâche tout bêtement et tout simplement de rendre ce que je sens avec mes nerfs et ce que je vois avec mes yeux: c'est là toute ma théorie artistique.' Maurice Kunel, *Félicien Rops* (Bruxelles 1943) p.30.

480 'Personne jusqu'alors n'a touché aussi profondement la notion catholique de la luxure, le plaisir démoniaque de la perversité, l'au-delà du mal.' Kunel, op.cit., p.32.

481 Maurice Kunel, *Félicien Rops* (Bruxelles, 1943) p.30 ff.

482 'Conter la vie de tous les jours, montrer le ridicule de certaines douleurs, la tristesse de bien des joies, et constater rudement quelquefois par quelle hypocrite façon le Vice tend à se manifester en nous c'est mon projet. Chercheur fantaisiste, j'irai partout, m'efforçant de rendre d'un trait net et immédiat, aussi sincèrement que possible, les impressions et les émotions ressenties ...' G. Geffroy, *La Vie Artistique* (III, Paris 1894) p.227 ff.

483 'Les symbolistes dédaignaient le Chat Noir et les artistes de Montmartre ils étaient rive-gauchers, hermétiques, assez pontifiant, et s'ils admettaient l'humour ils eussent trouvé indigne d'eux le rire de la blague.' C. Mauclair, *Servitude et grandeur littéraires* (Paris 1922) p.47.

484 Realism in this case is what we have called naturalism.

485 'Ce n'est pas là du trompe-l'oeil réaliste mais n'est-ce pas une chose réellement existante?' Van Gogh, *Brieven* No. 531.

486 'Nous allions à ceux-là qui faisaient table rase non seulement de l'enseignement académique mais encore et surtout du naturalisme, romantique ou photographique, alors universellement admis comme la seule théorie digne d'une époque de science et de démocratie.' Denis, *Théories*, p.254.

487 Denis, *Théories*, p.160.

488 'Les sciences naturelles, ou sciences inexactes, par opposition aux sciences rationnelles ou exactes, étant, par définition, insusceptibles de solutions absolues, conduisent fatalement au scepticisme et à la peur de la pensée. Il faut donc les accuser, elles, de nous avoir fait cette société sans foi, terre à terre, incapable de ces mille manifestations intellectuelles ou sentimentales qu'on pourrait classer sous le nom de dévouement. Elles sont donc responsables... de la pauvreté de notre art, auquel elles ont fixé pour unique domaine l'imitation, seul but constatable par les procédés expérimentaux.' Thus we have arrived at 'l'animalité pure et simple' and that is why a reaction is needed. 'Il faut recultiver les qualités supérieures de l'âme.' Aurier, *Oeuvres*, pp.175,176,202.

489 It is remarkable and striking that here Baudelaire simply speaks of 'vrai' (true), thus implicitly accepting positivism. Only as a guide for artistic creation it is depreciated. It appears that positivism was by no means overcome and subjected to an intrinsic criticism – its 'truth' was recognized as such.

490 'Chez nous le peintre naturel ... est presque un monstre. Le goût exclusif du Vrai c... opprime ici et étouffe le goût du Beau ... Il (l'artiste) sent ou plutôt il juge successivement, analytique.' *Cur. Esth.*, p.257.

491 Delacroix, *Journal* 9 April, 1856.

492 'Nous (this refers to Western civilization) sommes tombés dans l'abominable erreur du naturalisme' Morice, *Gauguin*, p.27 as cited by Morice from memory.

493 'Ils cherchèrent autour de l'oeil et non au centre mystérieux de la pensée, et de là tombèrent dans les raisons scientifiques.' *Lettres de Gauguin a Daniel de Monfreid* (Paris, 1950) p.121, letter of March 1898.

494 'la force de créer' Malingue CLXXXI, April 1903 to Morice, p.319.

495 'la copie myope des anecdotes sociales, l'imitation imbécile des verrues de la nature, la plate observation, le trompe-l'oeil, la gloire d'être aussi fidèlement, aussi banalement exact que le daguerréotype, ne contente plus aucun peintre ... digne de ce nom.' Aurier, *Oeuvres*, p.294.

496 'Ils ont propagé la haine du naturalisme.' Denis, *Théories*, p.26.

497 'Où commence l'exécution d'un tableau, où finit-elle? Au moment où des sentiments extrêmes sont en fusion au plus profond de l'être, au moment où ils éclatent et que toute la pensée sort comme la lave d'un volcan, n'y a-t-il pas une éclosion de l'oeuvre soudainement créée? Les froids calculs de la raison n'ont pas présidé à cette éclosion.' *Lettres & Daniel de Monfreid*, March 1898, p.206. Cf. Delacroix's pronouncement 'unité qui résulte de je ne sais quelle puissance créatrice dont la source est indéfinissable' ('the unity that is the result of I do not know what creative power whose source is indefinable') (From his notes for 'Le réalisme et l'idéalisme') quoted in R. Rey, *La renaissance du sentiment classique*, p.25). There is also a striking agreement with the thought expressed in a stanza by Poe:

These were the days when my heart was volcanic / As the scoriac rivers that roll – / As the leaves that restlessly roll / Their sulphurous currents ...

(from the second stanza of 'Ulalume', in *The Poems of Edgar Allan Poe* (London, 1900) p.23). It is possible that Gauguin knew this, maybe as a result of his contact with Mallarmé. The image however can be traced much further back in history. 'The familiar Neoplatonic figure of the soul as a fountain, or an outflowing stream, is also frequent in romantic poetry, although this, too, is usually reformed to imply a bilateral transaction, a give-and-take, between mind and external object.' (M.H. Abrams *The Mirror and the Lamp; Romantic Theory and Critical Tradition* (New York, 1953) p.61. This book deals mainly with English writers like Shelley and Coleridge. In a later context we shall revert to this very old Neoplatonic tradition which has penetrated very deep into Western thought (especially in artistic circles). This general state of affairs is not in the least affected by the possibility that Gauguin may have been indebted to Poe for his image – Poe, himself was of course much more directly influenced by the English authors, such as Coleridge, and/or by German Romantic thought.

498 'Au lieu de travailler autour de l'oeil nous cherchions au centre mystérieux de la pensée, comme disait Gauguin. L'imagination redevient ainsi, selon le voeu de Baudelaire, la reine des facultés. Ainsi nous libérions notre sensibilité et l'art, au lieu d'être la copie devenait la déformation subjective de la nature.' Denis, *Théories*, p.260.

499 'vu à travers d'un tempérament.' 'signe visible de ce tempérament' ...'le Symbole de l'ensemble idéique et sensitif de l'ouvrier.' Aurier, *Oeuvres*, p.298.

500 'Nous aspirions à la joie de s'exprimer soi-même' que réclamaient les jeunes écrivains d'alors,' Denis, *Théories*, p.164.

501 Aurier, *Oeuvres*, p.301.

502 'Qu'est-ce-que le Poème? Une synthèse de toutes les idées générales perçues par un moi donné.' Aurier *Oeuvres*, p.XIV.

503 'l'art pur suivant la conception moderne', viz., 'créer une magie suggestive contenant à la fois l'objet et le sujet, le monde extérieur à l'artiste et l'artiste lui-même' M. Gilman *Baudelaire the Critic* (New York 1943) p.166, cited from a not finished article 'L'art philosophique' in *Qeuvres* (II Le Dantee) p.367.

504 'L'artiste ne revèle que lui-même ... Il a été son roi, son prêtre et son dieu.' *Cur. Esth.*, p.221.

505 Cf. note 25.

506 Motif has really been derived from *movere*.

507 'L'art primitif procède de l'esprit et emploie la nature. L'art soi-disant raffiné procéde de la sensualité et sert la nature. La nature est la servante du premier et la maîtresse du second. Mais la servante ne peut oublier son origine, elle avilit l'esprit en se laissant adorer par lui. C'est ainsi que nous sommes tombés dans l'abominable erreur du naturalisme.' Morice, *Gauguin*, p.26, 27 (cf. note 494). It is not impossible for Gauguin to have borrowed this thought from van Gogh. He already expresses it in a similar way in a letter to van Rappart, *Brieven* IV R 4.

508 This refers to Cross.

509 'A Paris, chaque année, aux Indépendants ... il voit quel travail s'opère, en apparence vers plus de liberté, en réalité vers plus de raison et d'ordre, un ordre nouveau, paradoxal, un ordre issu de la tourmente symboliste et dont le succès marque le triomphe de l'esprit de synthèse sur l'esprit de l'analyse, de l'imagination sur la sensation, de l'homme sur la nature.' Denis, Introduction to *Catalogue Exposition Cross* (Paris, 1910).

510 Morice, *Gauguin*, p.243.

511 Abstraction here has nothing to do with the use of this term in the first decades of the twentieth century by modern painters. Here it refers to the forming of images, of iconic representation. The term is used in opposition to the direct 'imitation' of the naturalists. Compare also van Gogh's use of the term in his letter to Bernard, B 21, in which he characterizes his work after the manner of Gauguin, e.g. *La Berceuse*, in this way.

512 'Il était donc nécessaire, tout en tenant compte des efforts faits et de toutes les recherches, même scientifiques, de songer à une libération complète, briser les vitres, au risque de se couper les doigts, quitte à la génération suivante, désormais indépendante, dégagée de toute entrave, à résoudre généralement le problème. Je ne dis pas définitivement, car c'est justement un art sans fin dont il est question, riche en techniques de toutes sortes, apte à traduire toutes les émotions de la nature et de l'homme. Il fallait pour cela se livrer corps et âme à la lutte contre toutes les Écoles, toutes sans distinction, non point en les dénigrant, mais par autre chose, affronter non seulement les officiels mais encore les Impressionnistes, les Néo-Impressionnistes, l'ancien et le nouveau public ... En tant que travail, une méthode de contradiction, si l'on veut, s'attaquer aux plus fortes abstractions faire tout ce qui était défendu, et reconstruire plus ou moins heureusement, sans crainte d'exagération, avec exagération même. Apprendre à nouveau, puis, une fois su, apprendre encore. Vaincre toutes les timidités, quelque soit le ridicule qui en réjaillit. Devant son chevalet, le peintre n'est esclave, ni du présent, ni de la nature, ni de son voisin. Lui, encore lui, toujours lui. Cet effort, dont je parle, fut fait, il y a une vingtaine d'années, sourdement, en état d'ignorance, puis il alla s'affermissant.' Gauguin, *Racontars de rapin* (Paris, 1951) p.75 ff.

513 'Leur idéal, sans doute, n'est pas le même que le romantique, ils ne se plaisent pas à la fougueuse expression des passions ni des sentiments du coeur ... ils couvrent une vérité abstraite d'un vêtement d'éblouissantes réalités.' P.Valin, 'Ceux de demain, Les jeunes et leurs revues', in *L'Art et l'Idée* (I, 1892) p.62 ff.

514 'Ce n'est pas le fond des passions, c'est leur gesticulation extérieure, leur manifestation active' Morice, *La littérature*, p.110.

515 As is said with emphasis by Denis, *Théories*, p.33.

516 'peintres de l'âme,' Denis, *Théories*, p.33.

517 Cf. Michaud, *Message Poétique*, p.416: 'La poésie ne saurait plus s'opposer à la science ... pas de cette science qui faisait abstraction du monde psychique et intellectuel ... mais de la science véritable, celle qui se propose pour objet de connaître la réalité tout entière.' ('Poetry could no longer be opposed to science, not that science which abstracts from the psychic and intellectual world ... but to true science, that which aims at knowing the whole of reality.') And also A. Fouillé, *Le mouvement positiviste et la conception sociologique du monde* (Paris, 1896) p.1: 'Montrer comment, dans leurs conclusions ultimes, peuvent se concilier la philosophie positive et la philosophie idéaliste, tel est le but de cet ouvrage', which will bring about 'une représentation plus large de l'humanité et du monde.' ('To show in their ultimate conclusions how positive philosophy and idealistic philosophy can be reconciled, this is the purpose of the present work.' which will bring about 'a much more ample representation of humanity and the worldly'.)

518 'C'étaient des esprits passionnés de vérité, vivant en communion avec la nature ... S'ils furent amenés à 'déformer', à composer ... c' est aussi pour apporter plus de sincérité dans le rendu de leurs sensations.' Denis, *Théories*, p.33.

519 'Cet intense et contemporain désir de l'esprit humain de faire confluer en un seul large et vivant fleuve de Beauté réuni à la Vérité dans la Joie le courant mystique et le courant scientifique.' Morice, *La Littérature*, p.175.

520 'L'art intégral.' Morice, *La Littérature*, p.60.

521 'Je prétends que celui qui se jette dans l'allégorie, s'impose la nécessité de trouver des idées si fortes, si neuves, si sublimes, que sans cette ressource, avec Pallas, Minerve, les Gràces, l'Amour, la Discorde, etc. rétournés de cent façons diverses, on est froid, obscur, plat, commun.' Delacroix, *Journal* II, p.343.

522 Morice, *Gauguin*, p.37.

523 On the co-operation of Morice and Gauguin, cf. R. Huyghe, *Présentation de l'Ancien culte Mahorie* (Paris, 1951) Introduction.

524 Actually Gauguin never let go of reality, 'nature', and the following pronouncement of Morice is quite correct: 'Gauguin a une constante préoccupation de la réalité. Dans les contrées lointaines et primitives ou il est retiré ... il observe sans cesse, directement, il se renseigne, accumulant les documents, croquis ... notes écrites.' Morice, *Gauguin*, p.190. ('Gauguin is constantly concerned with reality. In the remote and primitive parts where he has withdrawn from the world ... he unceasingly observes, directly, he makes inquiries, accumulates documents, sketches ... written notes.')

525 '(L'artiste) est le maître de la vérité, de la vie. Il t'apporte la nature vivante. L'invention que tu lui reprochais, dont tu te défiais, c'est précisément l'âme de son oeuvre, le souffle qui la vivifie, c'est la chaleur et c'est l'eau qui manqueraient aux fleurs coupées, tôt desséchées' – it his is a reference to the science ideal and its shortcomings – 'C'est l'invention qui fait la vie de l'esprit comme elle fait la vie des oeuvres, l'invention qui circule comme un sang dans les éléments empruntés par l'imitation à la Nature ... un grand artiste a couronné de son génie quelqu'une des innombrables figures belles de la NATURE, quand l'artiste, enfant

lui-même de la NATURE, nourri par elle, vivant d'elle, se lève pour dire la beauté de sa mère quand la Nature laisse un des aspects changeants de son mystérieux visage éterniser le mot de son énigme dans l'oeuvre d'art.' Gauguin and Morice, *Noa Noa* (Paris, 1924) p.10.

526 Here creation is synonymous with nature, the created world.

527 'Peut-être un jour arriveront-ils à la Nature: c'est-à-dire que leur conception des choses pourra devenir assez complète, assez profonde, pour que l'oeuvre d'art réalisée par eux conserve tous les rapports logiques qui sont le caractère essentiel de la Nature vivante, et qu'ainsi il y ait plus d'analogie entre l'objet et le sujet, entre la création et l'image qu'ils en auront reconstituée.' Denis, *Théories*, p.28.

528 'De la toile elle-même, surface plane enduite de couleurs, jaillit l'émotion amère ou consolante, 'littéraire' comme disent les peintres, sans qu'il soit besoin d'interposer le souvenir d'une autre sensation ancienne (comme celle du motif de nature utilisée).' 'Dans l'un c'est la forme qui est expressive, dans l'autre c'est la nature qui veut l'être.' Denis, *Théories*, p.10. Of course the controversy is carried on here against naturalism, but perhaps much more directly against (pictorial) Symbolism, for the latter sought the new art in the first place in the choice of subjects, which were strongly allegorical.

529 'Observez dans l'immense création de la nature et vous verrez s'il n'y pas des lois pour créer avec des aspects tout différents et cependant semblables dans leur effet, tous les sentiments humains.' Malingue, XI, 14/1/1885, p.44.

530 'Au lieu d'évoquer nos états d'âme au moyen du sujet réprésenté c'est l'oeuvre elle-même qui devait transmettre la sensation initiale, en perpétuer l'émotion.' Denis, *Théories*, p.245.

531 'Se rappeler qu'un tableau – avant d'être un cheval de bataille, une femme nue, ou une quelconque anecdote – est essentiellement une surface plane recouverte de couleurs en un certain ordre assemblées. Denis, *Théories*, p.1. Cf. the elaborate discussion on page 164 ff.

532 Cf. for example letter from Arles to Bernard, Malingue no. LXXVIII, p.154.

533 Cf. chapter 4: Van Gogh.

534 A name for synthetism.

535 'Il faillait justifier (l'art idéiste) par d'abstraites et compliquées argumentations, tant il semble paradoxal à nos civilisations décadentes et oublieuses de toute révélation initiale.' Aurier, *Oeuvres*, p.163.

536 'En outre, Sérusier nous prouvait par Hegel, et les lourds articles d'Albert Aurier insistaient sur ce fait que logiquement, philosophiquement, c'était Gauguin qui avait raison.' Denis, *Théories*, p.164.

537 Gauguin was certainly a reader of books. This is clear from the letter to Morice, Tahiti November 1897, Malingue, CLXVI.

538 It is impossible to prove this from the direct source material.

539 In 1885 the following books were published: A. Robaut, *L'Oeuvre Complète de Eugène Delacroix* 'commenté par E. Chesneau', with an introduction by the latter; and also P.Dargenty, *Eugène Delacroix par lui-même*. But Gauguin will not yet have been able to read either of them in January when he wrote his letters from Copenhagen. But some older publications, like the *Lettres de Delacroix*, published by P. Phil. Burty, Paris 1878 – although this contains little that is important in an art-theoretical respect – and the important *Oeuvres littéraires de Delacroix*, published in 1865 – although much rarer – he may have known. Some of Delacroix's thoughts were also spread by means

of articles. Van Gogh, e.g., at Nuenen already knew about Delacroix's theories (cf. *Brieven* 401).

540 'C'est un bonheur de rêver, et c'était une gloire d'exprimer ce qu'on rêvait.' *Cur. Esth.*, p.262.

541 'Il y a des tons gais et folâtres, folâtres et tristes, riches et gais, riches et tristes, communs et originaux.' *Cur. Esth.*, p.92.

542 'L'oeuvre de Eugène Delacroix contient la sensation, l'émotion constante, l'emotion aiguë qui conduit en un instant le spectateur par toutes les phases de l'activité intellectuelle surexcitée. L'idée fixe du maître, si je ne me trompe pas, a été de rendre pour ainsi dire palpables, visibles au moyen des couleurs et des formes, les combats qui s'agitent au secret des âmes.' Robaut, *L'oeuvre complète de Eugène Delacroix* (commenté par E. Chesneau, Paris, 1885) p.XXXIX (cited from an article of Chesneau of about 1863).

543 In *Lettres à Daniel de Monfreid* on page 178 a watercolour is reproduced that bears strong resemblance to the painting of Delacroix referred to. Is it a copy by Gauguin, or had he made it from memory?

544 'De même chez Delacroix les bras et les épaules se retournent toujours d'une façon insensée et impossible au raisonnement, mais cependant expriment le réel dans la passion.' 'Rien que la peinture, pas de trompe-l'oeil.' And 'le trait chez lui (est) un moyen d'accentuer une idée.' Malingue, *Lettres* XXII, p.62, 63.

545 This formulation looks paradoxical. It is not meant as such, however, but Gauguin had not yet the correct words for the new thoughts he tried to formulate. He means to say that we must seek for pictorial means to express the human view of things iconically – which may result in an image that deviates strongly from that of the naturalists – in which, however, the structure of the given object should be retained.

546 'Pour moi le grand artiste est la formule de la plus grande intelligence, à lui arrivent les sentiments, les traductions les plus délicates et par suite les plus invisibles du cerveau. Observez dans l'immense création de la nature et vous verrez s'il n'y a pas de lois pour créer avec des aspects tout différents et cependant semblables dans leur effet, tous les sentiments humains ... j'en conclus qu'il y a des lignes nobles, menteuses, etc.' Malingue XI.

547 Humbert de Superville mentioned it in his *Essai sur les signes inconditionnels dans l'art* (1827). It is very doubtful if Gauguin had known this work. Perhaps Seurat had read it and told him about it. (Seurat himself wrote about the meaning of the direction of the lines only later on). Aurier turned out to have read it later on (in his article 'Les peintres symbolistes', *Oeuvres posthumes*, p.302).

548 'Les couleurs sont encore plus explicatives quoique moins multiples que les lignes par suite de leur puissance sur l'oeil. Il y a des tons nobles, d'autres communs, des harmonies tranquilles, consolantes, d'autres qui vous excitent par leur hardiesse.' Malingue, *Lettres* XI, p.45-47.

549 'Les lignes et les couleurs ne nous donneraient-t-ils pas aussi le caractère plus on moins grandiose de l'artiste.' Malingue, *Lettres* XI, p.45-47.

550 Malingue here has *abonde*, which does not make sense, in our opinion. The emendation is ours – *abonde* may very well be a clerical error. The same thing applies to the word *pour*, which we changed into *par*.

551 'Plus je vais, plus j'aborde dans ce sens de traductions de la pensée par tout autre chose qu'une littérature.' Malingue, *Lettres* XI, p.45-47.

552 'travaillez librement et follement . . . un grand sentiment peut être traduit immédiatement, rêvez dessus et cherchez-en la forme la plus simple.' Malingue, *Lettres* XI, p.45-47.

553 Rewald, Gauguin, p.16 note 73; cf. also H. H. Hofstätter, *Die Entstehung des 'Neuen Stils' in der französischen Malerei um 1890* (Freiburg im Breisgau, 1954) (mimeographed) p.22. Even though Devallée, who tells us about it, is perhaps not entirely reliable (Rewald, *Post-Impressionism*, p.185 and note 2, page 239), we need not suppose with Hofstätter that at this time Gauguin meant something different by synthesis than later on, or that he had not yet thought of synthesis at all. The term is characteristic enough of Gauguin's thought and aims, also in the time immediately after 1885.

554 It is true, Gauguin's ceramic work is quite different from what was made by others in this period. It shows strong Peruvian elements. We may no doubt refer in this case to Gauguin's reminiscences of his youth, when he must have seen Inca pots in his childhood in Peru. Cf., for example, the pot in the portrait of Laval (reproduced in Rewald, *Post-Impressionism*, p.187) and very especially the pot with the portrait head of Gauguin himself (Rewald, op.cit., p.442), which also occurs in the still-life represented on page 443 there).

555 Rewald, *Post-Impressionism*, pp.74,75,186.

556 Rewald, *Impressionism*, pp.378/9.

557 Rewald, *Impressionism*, pp.323,351.

558 Chapter 6: The events of the summer of 1888.

559 Rewald, *Post-Impressionism*, p.187.

560 Rewald, ditto, p.190.

561 Rewald, *Post-Impressionism*, p.289. So we do not agree with Hofstätter who discovers all kinds of new elements in this work, p.25 of his *Entstehung des neuen Stils*.

562 'Je n'ai jamais eu une peinture aussi claire, aussi lucide (par exemple beaucoup de fantaisie).' Malingue, LVII, p.117.

563 Rewald, ditto, p.56.

564 A few times, as for example in the landscape of St Briac reproduced in Rewald, P*ost-Impressionism*, *p.*192.

565 Rewald, ditto, p.195 repr.

566 Here we use the term in the same way that he uses it. This indicates that in the work the emphasis is laid on the play of lines over the surface, and on the mutual relations between the colours.

567 E.g., the oval shape on Bernard's work in 1887, reproduced in Rewald, *Post-Impressionism*, p.195.

568 Cf. list of Bernard's works by H. H. Hofstätter, *Die Entstehung des 'Neuen Stils' in der französischen Malerei um 1890* (Freihurg im Breisgau, 1954, mimeographed) p.258.

569 Van Gogh, *Brieven* B 21, cited by Rewald, *Post Impressionism*, pp.363/4.

570 Cf. e.g. his statements in connection with his *Potato-eaters*, collected by Dr. J.G. van Gelder, *De aardappeleters van Van Gogh* (Amsterdam, Antwerp, 1949) pp.10,11.

571 See Rewald, *Post-Impressionism*, pp.22, 56/9; Hofstätter, pp.27/29.

572 Cf. e.g. Van Gogh, *Brieven* B 9 (end of June 1888) in which van Gogh discusses one of his poems.

573 We express ourselves so cautiously on purpose, for it does not seem quite certain that Bernard pronounced or wrote down these opinions in 1888 literally like this. The quotation is from E. Bernard, *Souvenirs inédits sur l'artiste peintre Paul Gauguin et ses compagnons*, (1939) p.11 – quoted by H. Dorra, Emile Bernard and Paul Gauguin, *Gazette des Beaux Art*, (April, 1955) p.227 ff. The remarkable elliptic form of this sentence we leave as it is without any attempt at correction. The meaning will no doubt be clear. This quotation is a very good illustration of Puig's pronouncement on Bernard's style of writing: 'Et ce style était souvent un peu compliqué, et même prétentieux.' ('And this style was often a little involved and even pretentious.') R. Puig, *P.Gauguin, C. D. de Monfreid, et leurs amis* (Perpignan, 1958) p.73.

574 'Puisque l'idée est la forme des choses recueillies par l'imagination, il fallait peindre non plus devant la chose, mais en la reprenant dans l'imagination, qui l'avait recueillie, qui en conservait l'idée, ainsi l'idée de la chose apportait la forme convenable au sujet du tableau on plutôt à son idéal (somme des idées) la simplification que l'essentiel des choses perçues et par conséquent en rejette le détail.' E. Bernard, *Souvenirs inédits sur l'artiste peintre Paul Gauguin et ses compagnons* (1939) p.11, cited in translation by H. Dorra: E. Bernard and Paul Gauguin, *Gazette des Beaux Arts* (1955) p.238.

575 'poésie fantastique' (of Rimbaud cs.). Cf. p.61.

576 Michaud, *Message Poétique*, p.327 ff.

577 Rewald, *Post-Impressionism*, p.148.

578 Quoted by us in chapter 2: Delacroix.

579 Dargenty, *Delacroix*, p.125.

580 'La signification symbolique que peut contenir le dessin abstrait et mystique ... tes recherches relatives aux propriétés des lignes à mouvements opposes.' Van Gogh, *Brieven* B 14–in B 15 van Gogh says he is happy that B. is with Gauguin at that moment, which implies that the letter to which van Gogh refers in B. 14 was at any rate written before this contact.

581 Rewald, *Post-Impressionism*, p.193.

582 'un contingent d'idées psychologiques et quasi-littéraires'; 'cette prédominance absolue du principe décoratif dans toutes les branches de l'art'; 'le goût naturel de la synthèse.''un instinct merveilleux des ressources de la couleur.''une connaissance approfondie des lois de leur harmonie.''une délicatesse infinie à varier leur emploi.' *Le Japan Artistique*, (documents d'art et d'industrie réunis par S. Bing, publication mensuelle, le fasc. March 1888) pp.13,14. The head at the right hand side of the bottom of Bernard's *Bretonnes dans la prairie*, reproduced in Rewald, *Post-Impressionism*, p.251, shows a striking resemblance to a head in Hokusai's composition representing a row of men, depicted with the article quoted here. It might very well be a borrowing, but this is not so evident on the other hand, that we should he warranted in drawing the conclusion that Bernard had read this article.

583 Denys Sutton, 'The Paul Gauguin Exhibition.' *Burl. Mag.* (XCI 1949) p.285, note 26.

584 Hofstätter also mentions this influence in his *Entstehung des neuen Stils*, and then refers to Mackmurdo.

585 Rewald, *Post-Impressionism*, p.197 repr.

586 Ibid.

587 In this part of our study we do not intend to repeat the excellent articles on this period and these artists written by Huyghe, Dorra, Rewald and a few others. We are exclusively concerned with the art theories of these painters, but in the discussion about them it is unavoidable for us to enter into their art as such.

588 On the origin of this term, cf. Rewald, *Post-Impressionism*, p.194. It will have been used by Dujardin to denote some analogy with Limoges enamel.

589 See Rewald, *Post-Impressionism*, p.191 reproduction in connection with the letter to Schuffenecker. Malingue LXVI, p.133.

590 'Ce n'est pas du tout des Degas.'

591 Van Gogh, *Brieven* 539, cited by Rewald, *Post-Impressionism*, p.201.

592 'vit en vérité dans mon travail et éprouva par l'exposé de mes idées tout ce que l'on pouvait tirer de Cézanne.' Chassé, Le *mouvement symboliste*, p.100 cites a letter of Bernard to the writer.

593 See Hofstätter, p.66.

594 This is confirmed by a later letter of Gauguin's, published in Rewald, *Post-Impressionism*, p.283, Nov. 1889 of Gauguin to Theo van Gogh (cf. Rewald, *op.cit.*, p.311, note 21).

595 Malingue LXXV.

596 In a letter to Schuffenecker, Malingue LXVII.

597 Rewald, *Post-Impressionism*, p.192 repr.

598 Rewald, *Post-Impressionism*, p.61 repr.

599 In this connection Denis' remark is remarkable as well as elucidating 'La reconstruction d'art que Cézanne avait commencée avec les matériaux de l'impressionnisme, Gauguin l'a continué avec moins de sensibilité et d'ampleur, mais avec plus de rigueur théorique Il a rendu plus explicite la pensée de *Cézanne*.' (Denis, *Théories*, p.262). ('The reconstruction of art begun by Cézanne with the materials of impressionism has been continued by Gauguin with less sensibility and fullness, but with more theoretical rigour he has made Cézanne's thought more explicit.')

600 Chassé, *Le mouvement symboliste*, p.99.

601 Delacroix had already developed similar ideas. Cf. his *Journal*, 12 October 1853.

602 Rewald, *Post-Impressionism*, p.193 cites articles of Bernard of 1934 on Anquetin and another of 1940 concerning the history of symbolism.

603 We express some reserve because we are not at all certain that Morice's note to the story we are quoting is correct: 'Ces lignes datent de son second séjour à Pont Aven (1888).' These lines date from his second stay at Pont Aven. Morice, *Gauguin*, p.230 ff. Rotonchamp in his book on Gauguin gives the same 'legend' of Mani-Vehli-Zumbul-Zadi (p.215), adding 'Gauguin a lui-même exposé, en une fantaisiste parable, les éléments de sa technique propre.' Gauguin himself has shown the elements of his own technique in a fantastic parable. Its source is not given here either. Finally we find this story in *Avant et Après* (p.55) – if we should have to look upon this passage as the original source, Morice would have been mistaken, and ought to have said: 1898, during the second stay in Tahiti. The ideal to give quiet, stately figures in the art of painting, which is also expressed in this story, admirably suits the work of this period, better than it would do the earlier one.

R. L. Herbert, 'Seurat in Chicago and New York,' *Burlington Magazine* (C 1958) p.151, note 21, tells us that before 1886 Gauguin had lent a manuscript to Seurat containing the copy of a Turkish painter's guide, that of the Turkish poet Vehli-Mohamed-Zumbul-Zadi (t 1809). If the source from which Herbert draws in this case should have to be considered as reliable, it would be very interesting, because then this manuscript might have influenced Seurat in the direction of a classical ideal of style. But then the question remains where Gauguin had copied the fragment from. *The Encyclopaedie des Islam IV* (Leiden-Leipzig 1934) and J. v. Hammer-Purgstall, *Geschichte des osmanischen Dichtkunst* (Pesth, 1838) IV, pp.554-573 and E. J. W. Gibb, *A History of Ottoman Poetry*, ed. E. G. Browne (London, 1905) IV, pp.242-265, give all of them elaborate views of Sumbulzade Wehli, and the only work relevant to this question seems to be the *Lutfiyya*. However, there is nowhere any mention made – in spite of the extremely detailed bibliographies – of a translation of this work into French or into any other West-European language. The only possibility would be for a Turcologist of the middle of the nineteenth century, such as, e.g. C.A.C. Barbier de Meynard, to have given a translation of some passage in a non-scientific publication. In the bibliographies bearing on this there is however not even the merest indication of such an article to be found. But the character of the Turkish poet's work, and in particular that of the *Lutfiyya*, in no way suggests that such a passage resembling Gauguin's story really occurs in it. And in addition it is questionable whether a Turk would speak of the art of painting in such a way, while on the other hand it is certainly possible for Gauguin to have formulated similar views on the nature of the art of painting, also around 1885.

We think we are warranted to suppose that this story was written by Gauguin himself – in which case it is difficult to fix the date with any degree of certainty. Gauguin would then have introduced the figure of Mani-Vehli-Zumbul-Zadi, because he somewhere found this name and thought it poetical, strange and remote enough to function as the principal character in this legend. There is a certain analogy in it with Nietzsche's *Also sprach Zarathustra*, which was published in 1884. So Gauguin may have heard or read about the latter. The addition of 'Mani' to the Turkish poet's name, which was not very accurate either, points in this direction. It is not a falsification, but may be a legend invented by Gauguin in order to express some of his ideas in a literary form.

604 'Mieux est de peindre de mémoire, ainsi votre oeuvre sera vôtre; votre sensation, votre intelligence et votre âme survivront alors à l'oeil de l'amateur... Cherchez l'harmonie.' Morice, *Gauguin*, p.213.

605 Abstraction in this case has little or nothing in common with the abstraction intended or practised after 1900 (synonymous with nonfigurative). Cf. Note 513. We again refer to this in connection with the note given by Malingue with Letter LXVII of August 1888 to Schuffenecker. 'Abstraction' is here perhaps best translated by 'stylization' although the former term implies a little more than the rather technical ring of the word 'stylization'.

606 'Un conseil, ne peignez pas trop d'après nature. L'art est une abstraction, tirez-la de nature en rêvant devant et pensez plus à la création qui en résultera.' Malingue, LXVII.

607 'Ne se servant de la couleur que comme une combinaison de tons, harmonies diverses, donn(e)nt l'impression de la chaleur etc.' Malingue, LXXV.

608 'C'est en quelque sorte elle (the shadow) qui est à votre service.' Malingue, LXXV.

609 'synthèse d'une forme et d'une couleur en ne considérant la dominante.' Malingue LXVII (cited by Rewald, *Post-Impressionism*, p.196).

610 'Que me parlez vous de mon mysticisme terrible. Soyez impressionniste jusqu'au bout et ne vous effrayez de rien.' Malingue, LXXIII.

611 It is quite possible that Schuffenecker here reacted to a letter in which Gauguin explained his thoughts. We must certainly not exclude the possibility of some letters having got lost. Another possibility might be found in letter LXXI, in Malingue. There is also the chance of oral communication via men like Sérusier of the ideas of Gauguin, while finally, apart from all this, (or in collaboration with it) it is quite possible that Schuffenecker wrote in response to some pictures he had seen but had not quite understood (e.g. *Vision après le sermon*).

612 Van Gogh, *Brieven* No. 539.

613 In a letter by Gauguin to van Gogh, Rewald, *Post-Impressionism*, p.202, not published before.

614 In the manner of working of the *Vision après le sermon* it is very plausible that Gauguin was influenced by Bernard – in the *cloisonné*. But, quite different from what Bernard pretented, this was not the essential thing (to Gauguin). For a short time after he again made various other works in which he experimented with different techniques. We are referring to the works reproduced in Rewald, *Post-Impressionism*, p.248, 259, 258. With Gauguin the strict *cloisonnéism* is only a very transitory phase.

615 'Je vois du Puvis à faire mélangé de japon.' Malingue, LXXV.

616 Van Gogh, *Brieven* No. 531.

617 Rewald, *Post-Impressionism*, p.209, where again a not published letter of Gauguin is cited.

618 Ibid.

619 'une source de beau style moderne,' Malingue LXXV.

620 Cf. reproduction Rewald, *Post-Impressionism*, p.254.

621 Van Gogh, *Brieven* No. 562.

622 'un souvenir de notre jardin à Etten,' Van Gogh, *Brieven*, No. 562.

623 Rewald, *Post-Impressionism*, p.255 repr.

624 'Heb ik met de kleur al een wiegeliedje gezongen laat ik aan de critici over.' Van Gogh, *Brieven*, No. 571a.

625 'Peut-être dans la *Berceuse* il y a un essai de petite musique de couleur d'ici.' Van Gogh, *Brieven*, No. 567.

626 Van Gogh, *Brieven* B 21.

627 Ditto 533 and 555.

628 'littérature décadente', Denis, *Théories*, p.160 ff.

629 For this purpose he could consult the elaborately annotated French translation made by M.N. Bouillet and published in 1875.

630 Rewald, *Post-Impressionism*, p.206.

631 'Un paysage informe, à force d'être synthétiquement formulé, en violet, vermillon, vert veronèse et autres couleurs pures, telles qu'elles sortent du tube, presque sans mélange de blanc.' 'Comment voyez-vous cet arbre, avait dit Gauguin devant un coin du Bois d' Amour il est vert? Mettez donc du vert, le plus beau vert de votre palette; et cette ombre, plutôt bleu? Ne craignez pas de la peindre aussi bleue que possible.' Denis, *Théories*, p.160.

632 'Ainsi nous fût présenté pour la première fois, sous une forme paradoxale, inoubliable, le fertile concept de la 'surface plane recouverte de couleurs en un certain ordre assemblées.' Ditto.

633 'Tout oeuvre d'art était une transportation, une caricature, l'équivalent passionné d'une sensation reçue.' Ditto.

634 Denis, *Théories*, p.160.

635 'Gauguin n'était pas professeur ... C'était au contraire un intuitif. Dans sa conversation comme dans ses récits, il y avait des aphorismes heureux, des aperçues profondes, enfin des affirmations d'une logique pour nous stupéfiante.' Denis, *Théories*, p.162.

636 Rewald, *Post-Impressionism*, p.272.

637 Also later on Sérusier repeatedly came back to Le Pouldu.

638 In this case we follow Rewald's on the whole convincing chronology. Rewald, *Post-Impressionism*, p.310, note 4 and p.283.

639 Rewald, *Post-Impressionism*, p.282 ff.

640 Cf. Malingue, LXXXV, XCII, XCIV; Rewald, *Post-Impressionism*, p.289.

641 It is not clear why Rewald dates this work in 1890 (p.441). From Letter XCIII in Malingue, dated (not by way of conjecture) November 1889, it appears clearly that the work was finished then.

642 'Le renard symbole indien de la perversité.' Malingue, LXXXVII.

643 Repr. Rewald, *Post-Impressionism*, p.295.

644 Repr. Rewald, *Post-Impressionism*, p.299; Cf. Denys Sutton, 'The Paul Gauguin Exhibition.' *Burl. Mag.* (XCI, 1949) p.284.

645 Repr. Rewald, *Post-Impressionism*, p.299.

646 Rewald, *Post-Impressionism*, p.298.

647 'il y a à faire dans les deux Sens.' Malingue LXXXVII.

648 'le manque de l'au-delà.' Ditto.

649 It will not be easy to discover the exact meaning of this indication of the day. Probably this is an instance of the esoteric jargon the 'Nabis' used among themselves.

650 'Ce qui m'a surtout embarrassé, le voilà: quelle part la nature doit-elle avoir dans l'oeuvre? Où s'arrêter? Enfin, au point de vue matériel de l'exécution, faut il travailler d'après nature, ou seulement regarder et se souvenir?' Sérusier, *A.B.C. de la peinture*, p.39.

651 'Je me repens de ce que je t'ai dit sur Gauguin, il n'a rien d'un fumiste, du moins à l'égard de ceux qu'il sait pouvoir le comprendre.' Ditto, p.42.

652 We may suppose that by this he means those theories that he had mentioned to Denis in his letter from Le Pouldu 1889 under a) 'Principes immuables' (*ABC de la peinture*, p.42).

653 'De toutes mes théories cherchées cet hiver, cette loi simple me reste éviter de rapprocher deux tons trop écartés comme valeur, à moins qu'ils n'aient entre eux une parenté de couleur.' Ditto, p.45.

654 Morice, *Gauguin*, p.25/29; cf. Rewald *Post-Impressionism*, p.489, note 25 and p.452.

655 'L'art primitif procède de l'esprit et emploie la nature. L'art soi-disant raffiné procède de la sensualité et sert la nature. La nature est la servante du premier et la maîtresse du second. Mais la servante ne peut oublier son origine; elle avilit l'esprit en se laissant adorer par lui. C'est ainsi que nous sommes

tombés dans l'abominable erreur du naturalisme...' Morice, *Gauguin*, p.25/29; cf. Rewald, *Post-Impressionism*, p.489, note 25 and p.452. It is at most the formulation which is new. For similar thoughts had already clearly occurred in his earlier letters, as we have already seen more than once.

656 C. Chassé, *Le mouvement symboliste*, p.69.

657 'Gauguin va revenir, j'ai reçu de ses nouvelles. Il a, me dit-il, étudié sans chercher du symbolisme. OH! tant mieux. Il a surgi des gens qui me font détester même ce mot.' Sérusier, p.63

658 'entraves du symbolisme.' *Gauguin à Daniel de Monfreid*, Nov. 1901, p.333. Symbolism is here clearly intended in the sense of the art of Moreau, the people of the Rose†Croix, etc. As has been explained before, it is very difficult to find a terminology which is clear and does not deviate too much from the terminology used in the nineteen-nineties. As a matter of fact we have been content to adopt the inconsistent terminology of the period, and preferred it to a series of neologisms, although we are thus compelled every time to describe in more detail what was meant in our opinion.

659 Rewald, *Post-Impressionism*, cites a letter published by J. Loize, 'Un inédit de P.G.', *Nouvelles Littéraires*, 7 May 1953.

660 Concerning these *poètes maudits* and the meaning to be attached to this term, cf. P. Rodenko 'Baudelaire en de *poètes maudits*.' *Maatstaf* (V 3/4 Juni, Juli, 1957) p.198 ff.

661 Repr. Rewald, *Post-Impressionism*, p.451.

662 Rewald, *Post-Impressionism*, p.455.

663 Rotonchamp, *Gauguin*, p.21.

664 Malingue, CLXVI.

665 Morice, *Gauguin*, p.37.

666 *Avant et Après*, p.1.

667 Rewald, *Post-Impressionism*, p.466/7 and Denys Sutton, 'La perte du Pucelage by Paul Gauguin.' *Burl. Meg.* (XCI 1949) p.103.

668 'Il 'philosophe' quand il manifeste sa manière de comprendre les idées générales ... (saying) 'La philosophie est lourde, si d'instinct elle n'est pas en moi. Douce au sommeil avec le rêve qui lui donne parure – ce n'est pas science ... elle est une conséquence comme de graves personnages voudraient nous l'enseigner, mais bien une arme qu'en sauvages nous seuls fabriquons par nous-mêmes. Elle ne se manifeste pas comme une réalité, mais comme une image tel un tableau, admirable si le tableau est un chef-d'oeuvre.' Morice, *Gauguin*, p.82/83.

669 Cf. A. Fontainas, *Mes souvenirs du symbolisme* (Paris, 1928) p.31 ff.

670 'Érigent en dogmes qui n'auront plus d'hérétiques parmi les vrais poètes.' Morice, *La littérature*, p.267.

671 'la vulgarisation des sciences,' Ditto, p.2.

672 'Médiocrité. Produit fatal de la 'diffusion de lumières' – cette énorme plaisanterie, cette monstrueuse extase moderne.' Ditto, p.2.

673 'Ils ne veulent plus que des formules, 2 et 2 font 4, il n'y a que cela au fond de tout.' Ditto, p.7.

674 Morice's mysticism is characteristically intellectualistic, like that of Plotinus. Cf., e.g., his pronouncement 'Poète ... n'oublie pas ... que ta joie doit être cérébrale.' ('Poet, do not forget that your joy is cerebral.') *Littérature de tout à l'heure*, p.360.

675 'Émanations de Dieu, étincelles échappées du Foyer de la Toute-Lumière, ils -the poets-y retournent.' Ditto, p.14, cf. Dr. D. Loenen, 'De wijsbegeerte van den hellenistisch-romeinschen tijd,' in *Philosophia* I, ed. H. van Oyen (1947) p.134/5 (where Plotinus is discussed).

676 'l'universelle loi de la vie', 'des âmes'. These souls 'sont les manifestations extérieures de Dieu qui les émet avec la mission de coopérer, toutes diversement, à la lumineuse harmonie mondiale.' Morice, *La littérature*, p.14.

677 'Le livre, l'objet d'art, la phrase musicale, la pure pensée elle-même ... sont des éternisations du Moi. C'est que nous en faisons autant de moyens de dégager notre Moi des contingences et c'est qu'aussi, par la-même et dès qu'il échappe aux contingences, le Moi humain recourt ... au foyer de l'absolu, au lieu metaphysique des Idées, à Dieu.' Ditto, p.30.

678 'La forme, dans l'oeuvre ainsi parfaite et idéale, n'est que l'appât offert à la séduction sensuelle pour qu'ils soient apaisés, endormis dans une ivresse délicieuse et laissent l'esprit libre, les sens enchantés de reconnaître les lignes et les sons primitifs, les formes non trahies par l'artifice et que trouve le génie dans sa communion avec la Nature.' Ditto, p.33.

679 'l'apparition vague et charmante d'une entité divine de l'infini.' Ditto, p.33.

680 'Ainsi entendu, l'Art n'est que le révélateur de l'infini il est le moyen même d'y pénétrer. Il y va plus profond qu'aucune Philosophie, il y prolongue et répercute la révélation d'un Évangile.' Morice, *La littérature*, p.33.

Here Dr Abraham Kuyper's criticism started, which we will examine more closely in the following chapter.

681 'C'est là le grand, le principal et premier signe de la Littérature nouvelle, c'est là, dans cette ardeur d'unir la Vérité et la Beauté, dans cette unité désirée de la Foi et de la Joie, de la Science et de l'Art' - 'l'Art Intégral' ('Integral Art'). Ditto, p.59.

682 'Nous cherchons la Vérité dans les lois harmonieuses de la Beauté, déduisant de celle-ci toute métaphysique -car l'harmonie des nuances et des sons symbolise l'harmonie des âmes et des mondes -et toute morale.' Ditto, p.65.

683 Morice, *La littérature*, p.175.

684 'De faire confluer en un seul large et vivant fleuve de Beauté réuni à la Vérité dans la Joie le courant mystique et le courant scientifique.' Ditto, p.177.

685 Cf. Windelband-Heimsoeth, p.221 ff., Dr R. J. Dam, 'Karakter en functie van het lelijke.' *Philosophia Reformata* VI (1941) p.105 ff., especially, p.126/7; H. Dooyeweerd, 'Grondthema's van het wijsgerig denken van bet avondland.' *Philosophia Reformata* (VI, 1941) p.169, 170.

686 Morrice, *La littérature*, p.267.

687 'En attendant que la Science ait décidément conclu au Mysticisme, les intuitions du rêve y devancent la Science, y célébrent cette encore future et déjà définitive alliance du Sens religieux et du Sens scientifique dans une fête esthétique où s'exalte le désir très humain d'une réunion de toutes les puissances humaines par un retour à l'originelle simplicité.' Morice, *La littérature*, p.355.

688 Rewald, *Post-Impressionism*, p.454/5.

689 Morice also uses the word *simplicité* with respect to painting. Cf. *La littérature de tout d l'heure*, p.283.

690 'De suggérer tout l'homme par tout l'art.' Ditto, p.358.

691 'La synthèse ne peut se localiser ni dans la pure psychologie passionnelle, ni dans la pure dramatisation sentimentale, ni dans la pure observation du monde tel que nous le voyons dans l'immédiat, puisqu'elle risquerait de cesser d'être la Synthèse et de redevenir l'Analyse' Morice, *La littérature*, p.358, 359.

692 'L'oeuvre d'art est une transaction entre le tempérament de l'artiste et la nature.' Morice, *La littérature*, p.362.

693 We have the word 'christian' printed in small type on purpose, not in capital letters the search for a synthesis between Christian – i.e. biblical – Truth and ancient pagan philosophy was certainly understandable in the earliest Christian thinkers who themselves had been educated and formed in the ancient pagan spirit – the conversion of an entire manner of thought and of a mental attitude is not such a simple and immediately realizable process. And sometimes this synthesis will have been unconsciously due to the fact that long-established terms were used which, somehow, carried along something of their own original 'burden'. But this synthesis as such is not typically Christian, and more than once it actually caused the Christian thinkers, against their will, to get into conflict with Holy Scripture itself. Especially in mystical circles this 'christianized' Neoplatonic thought had a prolonged influence, and a little more than half-a-century ago its influence was still strong.

694 Cf. note 25.

695 'L'art est une reprise par l'âme de ses propres profondeurs, que ('in order that') l'âme s'y libère de toutes entraves pour la joie et l'intelligence du monde et d'elle-même.' Morice, *La littérature*, p.367.

696 Cf. page 66.

697 'Toute vie est enchaînée par une autre vie.' 'Le désordre du monde.' Morice, *La littérature*, p.367.

698 'cette reprise de soi dans la liberté', ditto, p.170.

699 'un sentiment de puissance illimitée', ditto, p.170.

700 Cf. page 63.

701 'La gloire de l'homme dans le monde est de se reduire à n'être, au lieu de l'élu contestable d'un chimérique titre royal que le réel ministre de la Nature [with a capital letter!] et son confident. Ici, la Science naturelle intervient pour conclure avec la Métaphysique le pacte d'une alliance féconde.' Ditto, p.170.

702 'L'instant contemporain.' For, 'le Rêve s'échappant de lui-même peut atteindre aux apparences des réalités quotidiens.' Ditto, p.373.

703 'La suggestion peut ce que ne pourrait l'expression (i.e. 'the explicit description'). La suggestion est le langage des correspondances et des affinités de l'âme et de la nature.' 'La suggestion seule peut rendre par quelques lignes l'entre-croisement perpétuel et la mêlée des détails auquels l'expression consacrerait des pages.' 'Elle est remontée aux sources même de tout langage aux lois de l'appropriation des sons et des couleurs des mots aux idées.' Ditto, p.378.

704 'Le poète est l'intermédiaire nécessaire entre l'humanité et, non pas seulement la nature, mais aussi la pensée. Les arts se hiécharchisent plus ou moins selon les moyens qu'ils fournissent au poète pour accomplir sa fonction intermédiaire.' H. Mahaut, 'Notes synthétiques de Paul Gauguin.' *Vers et Prose* (VI, 1910) p.51ff.

705 'La peinture est le plus beau de tous les arts; en lui se résument toutes les sensations, à son aspect chacun peut, au gré de son imagination, créer le roman, d'un seul coup avoir l'âme envahie par les plus profonds souvenirs; point d'efforts de mémoire, tout résume en un seul instant. Art complet qui resume tous les autres et les complète.' Ditto.

706 'La science du coloriste.' 'Pour entrer en relation intime avec nature.' Ditto.

707 'Vous pouvez rêver librement en entendant la musique comme en regardant un tableau.' Ditto.

708 Literature dealing with Mallarmé: G. Delfel *L'esthétique de SM.* (Paris, 1951) (review by C. Lalo, *Revue d'Esthétique* (VI, 1, 1953) p.108); A. Barry, *Le symbolisme* (Paris, 1911) p.198 ff.; M. Raymond, *From Baudelaire to Surrealism* (New York, 1950) p.23 ff; G. Michaud, *Le message poétique du symbolisme* (I, Paris, 1948) p.159 ff.; J. Huret, *Enquête sur l'évolution littéraire* (Paris, 1891) p.60 passim; A. Poizat, *Le symbolisme de Baudelaire à Claudel* (Paris, 1919) p.70 ff.; A. G. Lehmann, *The symbolist aesthetics in France 1885–1895* (Oxford, 1950) p.50 ff. and passim, *Poésies complètes de Stéphane Mallarmé* (textes et notes p.Yves-Gérard le Dantec, Paris 1948).

709 Cf. N. Westendorp Boerma, 'Engelse Verlichting van Francis Bacon to David Hume', in *Philosophia* II (ed. H. v. Oyen, Utrecht, 1949) p.87, on Berkeley.

710 Lehmann, *Symbolist Aesthetics*, p.162.

711 'Ia divine transposition, pour l'accomplissemenr de laquelle existe l'homme, va du fait à l'idéal.' Mallarmé, *Divagations* (Paris 1897) p.121; cf. A. Micha *Verlaine et les poètes symbolistes* (Paris 1943 17) p.53.

712 This quotation is very difficult to translate; it is certainly incapable of anything like a literal rendering, as Mallarmé's style is strongly suggestive and even relies for its meaning and effect on the sound of his language. This attempt was, therefore, only an approximation. 'Abolie, la prétention, esthétiquement une erreur, quoiqu'elle régit les chefs-d'oeuvre, d'inclure au papier subtil du volume autre chose que par exemple l'horreur de la forêt, ou le tonnerre muet épars au feuillage non le bois intrinsèque et dense des arbres ... Les monuments, la mer, la face humaine, dans leur plénitude, natifs, conservant une vertu autrement. attrayante que ne voilera une description, évocation dites, *allusion* je sais, *suggestion*: cette terminologie quelque peu de hasard atteste la tendance, très décisive, peut-être, qu'ait subit l'art littéraire, elle le borne en exemple. Son sortilège, à lui, si ce n'est libérer, hors d'une poignée de poussière ou réalité sans l'enclore, en livre, même comme texte, la dispersion volatile soit l'esprit, qui n'a que faire de rien outre la musicalité de tout.' Mallarmé, *Divagations*, pp.245/6.

713 'Rien ne nous révélerait le sens de l'allégorie.' Malingue, CLXX.

714 'Mon rêve ne se laisse pas saisir, ne comporte aucune allégorie; poème musical, il se passe de libretto.' Citation Mallarmé:'Par conséquent immatériel et supérieur, l'essentiel dans une oeuvre consiste précisément dans 'ce qui n'est pas exprimé il en résulte implicitement des lignes, sans couleurs ou paroles, il n'en est pas matériellement constitué.' Malingue, CLXX, Tahiti, March 1899, p.288.

715 It is not quite clear whether this remark refers to what precedes it or to what follows. In either case the influence is clear. But we have not been able to locate the literal wording of the quotation – Gauguin may be quoting something from memory that he had heard from Mallarmé on one of the occasions of his meeting him. For it is clear that Mallarmé's thought turned in this direction. We refer, e.g., to his pronouncement: 'Nomminer un objet, c'est supprimer les trois-quarts de la jouissance d'un pokme qui

est faite du bonheur de deviner, peu à peu.'('Giving a thing a name is suppressing three quarters of the enjoyment of a poem which is constituted of the happiness of devining little by little.') J. Huret, *Enquête sur l'évolution littéraire*, p.57.

716 See note 715.

717 Cf. G. Mauclair, *Servitude et grandeur littéraires* (Paris, 1922) p.29 ff.

718 Here and elsewhere we have presupposed a general knowledge of Gauguin's life. Therefore we do not feel compelled to refer to existing literature when facts like these are concerned.

719 'Fuir! Là-bas, fuir! Je sens que des oiseaux sont ivres / D'être parmi l'écume inconnue et les cieux / [. . .] / Je partirai! Steamer balançant ta mature, / Lève l'ancre pour une exotique nature!'

Ch. Chassé, *Le mouvement symboliste* (Paris 1947) p.86, from 'Brise Marine' of 1865, published 1886, 1887, 1893 (and 1899). *Oeuvres Complètes* (1951) p.38, pp.1432/3.

720 Cf. Rewald, *Post-Impressionism*, p.400.

721 Cf. Malingue, CII, CIII, CV, etc.

722 'Libre enfin, sans souci d'argent et pourra aimer, chanter et mourir.' Malingue, C.

723 'L'Occident est pourri en ce moment et tout ce qui est Hercule peut comme Antée prendre des forces nouvelles en touchant le sol là-bas.' Malingue, CVI.

724 'Mon centre artistique est dans mon cerveau et pas ailleurs et je suis fort parce que je ne suis jamais dérouté par les autres et que je fais ce qui est en moi.' Malingue, CXXVII.

725 Malingue, CXXVII.

726 'Si ... je prends ... un (homme) intelligent et je le transporte dans une contrée lointaine, je suis sûr que ... elle créera en lui un monde nouveau d'idées ... toute cette vitalité inconnue sera ajoutée à sa vitalité propre; quelques milliers d'idées et de sensations enrichiront son dictionnaire de mortel.' *Cur. Esth.*, pp.213/214.

727 'En outre Madagascar offre plus de ressources comme types, religion, mysticisme, symbolisme.' Malingue CIX. It is also possible to think of a distant influence of Plotinus about whom one of those who were acquainted with the subject in this respect may have talked to him, such as Morice, Meyer de Haan, Bernard, or Sérusier. Bréhier summarizes Plotinus' view as follows: 'Plotin allait demander aux Barbares ... la réalité, l'intuition vivante que risquaient de faire perdre les constructions savantes et compliquées de la philosophie grecque.' ('Plotinus would demand from the barbarians . . . reality, the living intuition, the loss of which was risked by the learned and complicated constructions of Greek philosophy.') p.124.

728 Rewald, *Post-Impressionism*, pp.191,192,366.

729 Ditto, p.366.

730 Cf. Rewald, *Post-Impressionism*, p.559. This knowledge is implied in his statements on quite a number of painters.

731 He calls them Symbolists himself.

732 'Ce formidable inconnu.' G.-A. Aurier, 'Les peintres symbolistes', in *Oeuvres Posthumes* (1893) p.293. We will refer to this article as Aurier 2.

733 'Dépositaires de l'éternel savoir.' Aurier 2, p.294.

734 'Antinomie de tout art la vérité concrète, l'illusionnisme, le trompe-l'oeil,' Aurier, 'Le symbolisme en peinture, Paul Gauguin.' *Mercure de France* (II 1891) p.162. We will cite this article as Aurier 1.

735 'Copie myope des anecdotes sociales, l'imitation imbécile des verrues de la nature la plate observation.' Aurier 2, p.294.

736 'Pauvre stupide prisonnier de l'allégorique caverne (de Platon).' Aurier 1, p.159.

737 This 'azure' is found in a poem entitled 'L'Azur' by Mallarmé. 'L'azur symbolizes the poet's artistic ideal', says A. Micha, note 4, to page 54 in *Verlaine et les poètes symboliste*. It has been printed here. Originally it was published in L'Artiste, later on in *Le Parnasse contemporain*.

738 'De toutes parts on revendique le droit au rêve, le droit au pâturage de l'azur, le droit de l'envolement vers les étoiles niées de l'absolue vérité.' Aurier 2, p.294.

739 Aurier 2, pp.296,304. (Cf. note 734.)

740 'Ils se sont efforcé de comprendre la mystérieuse signification des lignes, des lumières et des ombres, afin d'employer ces éléments, pour ainsi dire, alphabétiques, à écrire le beau poème de leurs rêves et de leurs idées.' Aurier 2, p.296.

741 'Ces caractères directement significateurs (formes, lignes, couleurs, etc.).' Aurier 1, p.164.

742 Aurier 2 p.294.

743 'L'art, mode suprême d'expression, ne puisse exprimer l'universalité des psychés.' Aurier 2, p.299.

744 Bréhier translates *Nous* by 'Intelligence' (cf. Bréhier, *La Philosophie de Plotin*, p.81), compare also note 748.

745 'La forme ... le corps tout ... objet est ... la tangible modalité de son être, c'est-à-dire la signification visible d'une pensée.' Aurier 2, p.299/301.

746 'À travers tout ce rébarbatif jargon et toute cette hirsute scolastique.' Aurier 2, p.299/301.

747 Dans la nature, tout objet n'est, en somme, qu'une Idée signifiée.' Aurier 2, p.299/301.

748 This is also found in Plotinus. About this Bréhier says, 'The Intelligence corrresponds with the platonic ideas.' (*op.cit.*, p.81).

749 Aurier 2, p.301.

750 'Les intelligences supérieures de notre pauvre aveugle humanité.' Aurier 2, p.301.

751 'l'exprimeur des êtres absolus / homme supérieur / dompteur du monstre illusion / sait se promener en maître dans ce temple fantastique où de vivants piliers laissent parfois sortir de confuses paroles ... alors que l'imbécile troupeau humain, dupé par les apparences qui lui feront nier les idées essentielles, passera éternellement aveugle à travers les forêts de symboles qui l'observent avec des regards familiers.' Aurier 1, p.161/2, quoted from Baudelaire's poem 'Correspondances'.

752 'Les diverses combinaisons de lignes, de plans, d'ombres, de couleurs, constituent le vocabulaire d'une langue mystérieuse, mais miraculeusement expressive.' Aurier 1, p.161/2.

753 'Cette langue, comme toutes les langues, a son écriture, son orthographe, sa grammaire, sa syntaxe, sa rhétorique même, qui est le style.' Aurier 2, p.302.

754 'Beaucoup de personnages disent que je ne sais pas dessiner parce que je fais des formes spéciales. Quand donc comprendra-t-on que l'exécution, le dessin et la couleur (leStyle) doivent s'accorder avec le poème?' Morice, Gauguin, p.122, a letter to Morice from Tahiti concerning Gauguin's *D'où venons-nous* ...

755 'J'agis un peu comme la Bible dont la doctrine ... s'énonce sous une forme symbolique présentant un double aspect; une forme qui d'abord matérialise l'Idée pure pour la rendre plus sensible ... c'est le sens littéral, superficiel, figuratif, mystérieux d'une parabole; et puis le second aspect donnant l'Esprit de celle-ci. C'est le sens non plus figuratif; mais figuré, explicite de cette parabole.' Malingue, *Lettres* CLXXII.

This view of the Bible shows close agreement with Swedenborg's, which Gauguin may have known via Balzac, whose *Séraphita* was one of the painter's favourite books and in which similar ideas were expounded (p.154).

756 'comme minimum un fragment de la spiritualité de l'artiste, comme maximum cette entière spiritualité de l'artiste plus la spiritualité essentielle des divers êtres objectifs', Aurier 2, p.303.

757 'Qui est la synthèse de deux âmes, l'âme de l'artiste et l'âme de la nature.' Ditto.

758 'C'est cet influx, ce rayonnement sympatique ressent à la vue d'un chef-d'oeuvre, que l'on nomme le sentiment du beau, l'émotion esthétique.' Ditto.

759 'L'esthétique de Plotin est en effet imprégnée de cette idée que la beauté ne s'ajoute pas aux choses comme un accident extérieur, mais en constitue véritablement l'essence (*Ennéades* I, 2) ... il faut donc que la beauté ... soit le reflet d'une Idée, qui fait de cet être ce qu'il est. Valeur esthétique et valeur intellectuelle coincident.' B. Bréhier, *La Philosophie de Plotin* (Paris 1928) p.85.

760 'quelque boueuse sexualité' 'l'animalité pure et simple', 'il faut réapprendre l'amour, source de toute compréhension'; Aurier *Oeuvres*, p.202 (from a not previously published 'Essay sur une nouvelle méthode de critique').

761 It is characteristic of Aurier to accept the results of positivism, notwithstanding, however much he may have depreciated it. He does not suggest a new view which is really directed against the fundamental tenets of positivism and is therefore able to regret its results.

762 'Un seul amour nous est encore loisible, celui des oeuvres d'art. Jetons-nous donc sur cette ultime planche de salut.' Aurier, *Oeuvres*, p.202.

763 Baudelaire, *Art Romantique*, p.311ff.

764 In the next chapter we will revert to this thought and examine Dr. A. Kuyper's criticism of it (especially in connection with the conceptions of the meaning of a symbol). 'Ainsi entendu l'art n'est que le révélateur de l'Infini ... De nature donc, d'essence, l'art est réligieux.' Morice, Littérature, p.34, 35, cited by Lehmann, Symbolist aesthetics, p.116.

765 'Se trouve, de plus, au fond, identique à l'art primitif, à l'art tel qu'il fut deviné par les génies instinctifs des premiers temps de l'humanité.' Aurier 1, p.163, cf. 2, p.304.

766 Cf. p.119 above.

767 'C'est, on pourrait presque dire, du Platon plastiquement interprêté par un sauvage de génie.' Aurier 2, p.305.

768 Aurier 1, p.164. (Cf. our note 734).

769 Aurier I, p.162.

770 'Idéiste, puisque son idéal unique sera l'expression de l'Idée.' Aurier 1, p.162.

771 'Symboliste, puisqu'elle exprimera cette Idée par des formes.' Ditto.

772 'Synthétique, puisqu'elle écrira ces formes, ces signes, selon un mode de compréhension générale.' Ditto.

773 Cf. p.161.

774 'Subjective, puisque l'objet n'y sera jamais considéré en tant qu' objet, mais en tant que signe d'idée perçue par le sujet.' Ditto.

775 Aurier 1, p.460.

776 '(C'est en conséquence) decorative – car la peinture décorative proprement dite, telle que l'ont comprise les Egyptiens, très probablement les Grecs et les Primitifs, n'est autre chose qu'une manifestation d'art à la fois subjective, synthétique, symboliste et idéiste.' Ditto.

777 *Lettres à Daniel de Monfreid*, Oct. 1897, p.113.

778 Denis, *Théories*, p.162.

779 'Sérusier nous prouvait par Hégel, et les lourds articles d'Albert Aurier insistaient sur ce fait, que logiquement, philosophiquement, c'était Gauguin qui avait raison.' Denis, *Théories*, p.162.

780 Above, p.115 ff.

781 'Se rappeler qu'un tableau – avant d'être un cheval de bataille, une femme nue, ou quelconque anecdote – est essentiellement une surface plane recouverte de couleurs en un certain ordre assemblées.' Denis, *Théories*, p.1.

782 Rewald, *Post-Impressionism*, p.498, note 10, p.536.

783 'Ainsi nous fut présenté, pour la première fois, sous une forme paradoxale, inoubliable, le futur concept de la 'surface plane recouverte de couleurs en un certain ordre assemblées.' Denis, *Théories*, p.161.

784 'Ainsi nous connûmes que tout oeuvre d'art était une transposition, une caricature, l'équivalent passionné d'une sensation reçue.' Ditto.

785 'L'art, c'est quand ça tourne.' Ditto, p.10.

786 'De la toile elle-même, surface plane enduite de couleurs, jaillit l'émotion amère ou consolante, 'littéraire' comme disent les peintres, sans qu'il soit besoin d'interposer le souvenir d'une autre sensation ancienne (comme celle du motif de nature utilisé).' Ditto.

787 'Un Christ byzantin est symbole; le Jésus des peintres modernes, fût-il coiffé du plus exact kiffyed, n'est que littéraire. Dans l'un c'est la forme qui est expressive, dans l'autre c'est la nature imitée qui veut l'être.' Denis, *Théories*, p.10.

788 By 'in its proper sense' we mean in the sense in which this term was generally used by the painters. Properly speaking, the term is wrong, as 'literary' is not at all identical with naturalistically descriptive.

789 Here 'symbolistic' means 'synthetistical'. By that mystical tendency he refers to those we have called Symbolists, the painters who were related to the decadent poets.

790 'Nous nous étonnons que des critiques renseignés ... se soient plu à confondre les tendances mystiques et allégoriques, c'est-à-dire la

791 'Ceux qui I ont inauguré étaient des paysagistes, des nature-mortistes, pas du tout des 'peintres de l'âme.' Denis, *Théories*, p.33.

792 Deformation is not used here in the sense of twentieth-century art, which interferes with the structure of the natural object. Here we use it in a way such that we can say Raphael deforms.

793 By 'content' we mean that which Panofsky renders by the word 'meaning', as in his introduction to his *Meaning in the visual arts* (Garden City, N. York, 1955) p. 40 passim.

794. 'hermétique', meaning 'elevated above reality'.

795 'L'art est la sanctification de la nature, de cette nature de tout le monde, qui se contente de vivre. Le grand art qu'on appelle décoratif, des Hindous, des Assyriens, des Egyptiens, des Grecs, l'art du Moyen-Age et de la Renaissance (that is to say all art that was really important) et les oeuvres décidément supérieures de l'art moderne (referring to Gauguin and Cézanne), qu'est-ce? sinon le travestissement des sensations vulgaires – des objets naturels – en icones sacrées, hermétiques, imposantes.' Denis, *Théories*, p.12.

796 We use the term 'realistic' here in a sense which is not identical with 'naturalistic'. By 'realistic' we mean that the subject has been derived from everyday reality, whereas 'naturalistic' refers rather to the manner in which the subjectmatter (which is perhaps, not at all realistic, e.g., in Bouguereau) has been rendered. And, in addition, we use the term 'motifs' in the same sense as Panofsky does in his introduction just mentioned .

797 'Triomphe universel de l'imagination des esthètes sur les efforts de bête imitation, triomphe de l'émotion du Beau sur le mensonge naturaliste.' Denis *Théories*, p.12.

798 'Ils voulurent se soumettre aux lois d'harmonie qui régissent les rapports des couleurs, les agencements des lignes (recherches de Seurat, Bernard, C. Pissarro); mais c'est aussi pour apporter plus de sincérité dans le rendu de leurs sensations.' 'Il y avait donc étroite correspondance entre des formes et des sensations.' Denis, *Théories*, p.33.

799 'Au point de vue objectif, la composition décorative, esthétique et rationnelle ... devenait le contrepartie, le correctif nécessaire de la théorie des équivalents. Celle-ci autorisait en vue de l'expression toutes les transpositions même caricaturales, tous les excès de caractère la déformation objective obligeait à son tour l'artiste à tout transposer en Beauté. En résumé la synthèse expressive, le symbole d'une sensation, devait en être une transcription éloquente, et en même temps un objet composé pour le plaisir des yeux.' Denis, *Théories*, p.260.

800 'Nous faisions un singulier mélange de Plotin, d'Edgar Poe, de Baudelaire et de Schopenhauer.' Quoted from *Nouvelles théories*, cited by Ch. Chassé, *Le mouvement symboliste* (1947) p.152.

801 Denis, *Théories*, Préface.

802 In a letter in the summer of 1893, to Verkade, in *A.B.C. de la peinture* (1950) p.66.

803 Cf. Agnes Humbert, *Les Nabis*, p.54 passim; W. Haftmann, *Malerei im 20. Jahrhundert* (München 1954) p.51.

804 Cf. ditto. p.28 ff.

805 *Cur. Esth.*, p.92, 272.

806 *Cur. Esth.*, p.241.

807 'Une collection de règles réclamées par l'organisation de l'être spirituel.' *Cur Esth.*, p.274.

808 Baudelaire, *Art Romantique*, p.207 ff., cited here in chapter 2, p.28.

809 'Par l'ensemble, par l'accord profond, complet, entre sa couleur, son sujet, son dessin, et par la dramatique gesticulation de ses figures.' *Cur. Esth.*, p.243.

810 *Cur. Esth.*, p.274.

811 Cf. p.16 ff.

812 Baudelaire, *Art Romantique*, p.317, cited in chapter 2, p.28.

813 Cf. p.122 ff.

814 'Il y avait donc étroite correspondance entre des formes et des sensations.' Cf. note 799.

815 'Je veux un dessin ferme et simple, fini. J'entends par là non pas que tous les détails y soient, mais que toute ligne soit voulue et ait son rôle, expressif et décoratif, dans l'ensemble; je veux que toute ligne soit nécessaire ... Mais pour arriver à ce but il faut bien connaître son sujet.' *ABC de la peinture*, p.61.

816 'Le spectacle direct de la nature, suscitant les sensations – la mémoire, qui les rappelle – l'imagination, qui les crée par combinaisons – nous mettent dans un état d'âme involontaire. Puis l'Idée se forme dans l'esprit, supérieure aux limbes génératrices par sa logique et son harmonie, elle apparaît à l'artiste. Il s'efforce de l'exprimer dans son intégrale intensité, résultat qu'il obtiendra d'autant mieux que, négligeant les détails, il ne retiendra que les seules caractéristiques. Alors l'artiste place ainsi le spectateur dans l'état d'âme où lui-même s'est trouvé – ce qui est le but d'art.' Mellerio, *Le mouvement idéaliste*, p.45.

817 'Nous avons suivi de bonnes voies, cherchant l'Idée exprimée par les formes décoratives, expliquée par les couleurs simples'. *ABC de la peinture*, p.77.

818 Denis, *Nouvelles Théories*, cited by Ch. Chassé, *Le Mouvement symboliste* (1947) p.155.

819 In our discussion of the preceding writers we have not repeatedly dealt with this question, above all in order not to lay too heavy a burden on our argument. But we purposely bring in this problem here because in Sérusier the synthesis has been realized in the purest way, and his expositions have been least mixed with all kinds of secondary motifs and ideas derived from Plotinus and others. When studying Bernard and also in the next chapter we shall enter into more detail about the problems indicated.

820 'Je crois que notre époque est plutôt moins avancée comme Art chrétien qu'aux premières époques du christianisme. Je crois donc qu'on peut appliquer à notre époque ce qu'il (P.Didier) dit de ces temps: que la recherche de la beauté empêcherait l'expression directe et naturelle des idées, exprimons-nous n'importe comment, et soyons surtout sincères avec nous-mêmes: c'est en cela que consiste l'esprit des primitifs; la correction viendra peu à peu, elle ne peut précéder les idées sans leur barrer la route. Du reste, nous ne nous entendons pas sur le sens du mot Beauté ... Je crois que tu prends ce mot dans le sens objectif, tandis que je le prends dans le sens subjectif. C'est cette différence qui sépare les Écoles de ce siècle, qui ont abouti à Cabanel et Bouguereau, de celle que j'ai embrassées.' *ABC de la peinture*, p.117.

821 'Je crois actuellement que la seule chose que puisse faire un artiste est d'établir une harmonie en formes et en couleurs. L'harmonie est le seul moyen, comme la prière, de nous mettre en communion avec Dieu. Tout le reste, dans l'Art, n'est qu'illustration, sentiment personnel, individualisme, poésie humaine. Quant à la copie d'objets naturels, surtout de modèles, qui ne sont même pas naturels, elle me fait horreur.' *ABC de la peinture*, p.122.

822 No doubt in this connection Desiderius Lenz of the Beuroner school had some influence on him. Here, however, this influence is chiefly concerned with the elaboration of details, for at bottom the Beuroners and Sérusier were of the same mind before they entered into a more intensive discussion with each other. This is why we shall not go into these matters which were certainly not unimportant to Sérusier personally. Sérusier translated Lenz's German work of 1865: D. Lenz, *L'esthétique de Beuron* (Paris: trad. Sérusier, 1905), cf. Agnes Husobert, *Les Nabis*, p.56/7.

823 *ABC de la peinture*, p.7 ff.

824 In passing we would refer to the agreement with Aurier's idea of style (cf. p160). Of course, Sérusier may have learnt and borrowed something from it.

825 'Une qualité supérieure, langage commun à toute intelligence humaine. Sans quelque trace de ce langage universel, il n'existe pas d'oeuvre d'art ... Ces éléments sont inhérents à notre constitution, donc innés.' *ABC de la peinture*, p.12.

826 There occurs a remarkable passage on page 21 of his *ABC de la peinture*:'Il est une notion sans laquelle aucun être animé, même le végétal, ne pourrait exister C'est celle de l'équilibre. La ligne droite horizontale et la verticale sont les signes de l'équilibre; la première pour la matière dite inerte, la seconde pour la matière vivante. Il est à remarquer que ces deux lignes n'existent pas dans la nature; elles sont des conceptions de notre esprit ... alors que la nature ne procède que par des courbes ... Tout manque d'équilibre est une souffrance.' ('There is a notion without which no animate being, even of the vegetable kind, could exist: it is that of equilibrium (balance). The horizontal straight line and the vertical line are signs of balance; the former for so-called inert matter, the latter for living matter. It must be observed that these two lines do not exist in nature; they are conceptions of our mind ... whereas nature does not proceed except along curved lines ... Every lack of equilibrium is distress.') The passage is remarkable on account of the close resemblance to the ideas of Mondrian and his circle. In the first place, both speak of balance. Thus Mondrian considered as his ideal purpose: 'Universal harmony; to be realized in art, but in life as well. In art and life, it means the reign of serene, unchangeable equilibrium.' H.L.C. Jaffé, *De Stijl, 1917–1931* (Amsterdam, 1956) p.129.

Further in his distinction of natural forms from artistic ones (compare Sérusier's pronouncement just quoted with those of van Doesburg (Mondrian's nearest congenially minded fellow-artist) quoted on p.55 of Jaffé, *op.cit.*, taken from the periodical *De Stijl*). It is not impossible for Sérusier to have heard this – it is even possible that Sérusier had heard van Doesburg speak at Paris in 1921 (Jaffé, *op.cit.*, p.177), as precisely in this latter year the former published his *ABC de la peinture*. Another agreement is seen in their positing the meaning of what is vertical and horizontal, although Sérusier's formulation is slightly different. Van Doesburg summarizes Mondriaan's 'equations' as follows Vertical = male = space = statics

= harmony; horizontal = female = time = dynamics = melody, etc. (Jaffé, *op.cit.*, p.58). Finally, the thought that the breaking of harmony entails pain, in this connection has its parallel in Mondrian's ideas of the tragic. (Cf. Jaffé, *op.cit.*, p.130 passim). Although we should certainly consider the possibility of Sérusier being influenced by De Stijl, we should not think of some direct dependence – for such dependence the formulations are not sufficiently identical. As a fact, Sérusier borrows nothing from the philosophical-theosophic implications, nor from Mondrian's utopian doctrines, while he does not in the least attempt to defend abstraction qua talis. On the other hand, we should also take into account the possibility that Sérusier himself may have influenced the formation of the ideas of De Stijl, perhaps in a direct way, perhaps via (the work of) Delaunay, at the time when Mondrian and van der Leek were at Paris. Cf. Jaffé, op.cit., p.48 passim, and W. Haftmann, *Malerei ins 20. Jahrhundert* (München, 1954) p.165/6.

827 Cf. Aurier's pronouncement quoted on p.132–133.

828 'Or, les pensées et les qualités morales ne peuvent être représentées que par des équivalents formels. C'est la faculté de percevoir ces correspondances qui fait l'artiste.' *ABC de la peinture*, p.23.

829 'Le monde extérieur dans ses lois et non dans ses accidents'. *ABC de la peinture*, p.33.

830 In a letter to Denis of 29 Febr. 1915, *ABC de la peinture*, p.146.

831 J. E. Blanche, *Les arts plastiques*, p.243.

832 Compare e.g., Sérusier's *Die Sage* ('The saga') reproduced in *Dekorative Kunst*, Band IV, 2nd year, p.129, with Gauguin's *Vision après le sermon*, from which it derived its inspiration. Sérusier's work is really what it has been called in this magazine, a *dekoratives Gemälde* (a 'decorative painting'), and this reduces the fascination of Gauguin's conception into something far less novel. This is further clarified when we understand that Gauguin represents his subject 'after the Japanese manner', as if he had looked down upon it from the top, whereas Sérusier's 'direction of observation' lies much nearer to the horizontal, in conformity with Western traditions. The figures, too, are much more 'academic' in style. Lastly, the remarkable kind of realism inherent in Gauguin's painting has been turned into a poetic-symbolistic vision ('real' people in the foreground see, behind trees, a procession of figures belonging to a saga), which, indeed, is much more in accordance with the poetry of the 1890s. On the other hand, this is clearly at a distance from Art Nouveau and the symbolistic painters (in the sense defined above).

833 Cf. on this H. Dooyeweerd, *Transcendental Problems of Philosophic Thought* (Grand Rapids, Mich., 1948) p.62 ff. and H. Dooyeweerd, 'Grondthema's van het wijsgerig denken van het avondland', *Philosophia Reformata* (VI 1941) p.164 ff. As a short summary we would submit the following quotation from this article 'The form-matter-scheme of Greek philosophy ... was ... deeply rooted in the Greek religious consciousness of an irreconcilable tension between the older, tellurian, chthonic and ouranic religions of nature on the one hand ... and the younger cultural religion of form, measure, and harmony on the other.' These thoughts have been elaborately treated in H. Dooyeweerd, *Reformatie en Scholastiek* (I. Franeker, 1949) and in his *A New Critique of Theoretical Thought* (Amsterdam, 1955) I, p.62 ff.

834 In the philosophical elaboration of this theme there are a great variety of conceptions possible – which give an answer to such questions as, e.g., in what is the *principium individuationis* to be found, or where does the caesura lie between the sphere of the principle of matter and that of form. Of course, we shall leave these questions for what they are. Cf. D.H.Th. Vollenhoven, *Geschiedenis der Wijsbegeerte* (I, Grieksche Philosophie, Franeker 1950) p.40 ff. Compare also the work of H. Dooyeweerd, mentioned in the previous note, in which these problems are further examined especially in connection with Plato's philosophy.

835 The basic motives mentioned here are of a religious nature. Cf. note 25 in chapter 2 and the literature quoted there.

836 Cf. on this synthesis D. H. Th. Vollenhoven, 'Christendom en humanisme van Middelecuwen tot Reformatie', *Philosophia Reformata* XI, 1946, p.102 ff.; H. Dooyeweerd, 'Grondthema's van het wijsgerig denken van het avondland', *Philosophia Reformata*, VI, 1941, pp.169 ff; Windelband-Heimsoeth, pp.210 ff. H. Dooyeweerd, *Transcendental Problems of Philosophic Thought* (Grand Rapids Mich., 1948) p.70 ff.

837 'Car, si les choses sont la figure des choses invisibles'; 'l'essence de l'homme, tenant du divin et douée d'harmonie, coordonne et transforme la nature selon sa suprématie pour lui faire exprimer son origine propre et surnaturelle.' Bernard, 'Ce que c'est que l'Art mystique?' *Mercure the France* (XIII, 1895) p.29.

838 'Il y a donc en l'homme – de par Dieu – une création latente et supérieure au monde visible.' Ditto.

839 Bernard cites *Oeuvres de Saint Denys l'Aréopagite* (Paris: trad. p. l'Abbé Dulac, 1865).

840 The passages quoted by Bernard are the very same in which a doctrine has been explained that shows a close resemblance to that of Swedenborg, so exactly those thoughts that also Gauguin advanced as more or less self-evident. Cf. p.160 (Pseudo-) Dionysius represents a phase in early Christian thought that seeks for a marked synthesis with Neoplatonic philosophy, but in which there is not yet any question of the nature-and-grace-scheme which was to dominate mediaeval philosophy later on (we might say that the division between the Christian and the Greek inheritance had not yet been realized).

841 'Le Beau qui est le résultat d'une illumination particulière et qui est le don du Saint-Esprit.' Bernard quotes *Oeuvres de Saint Denys l'Aréopagite* (Paris: trad. p.l'Abbé Dulac, 1865) p.39. This is greatly emphasized in Bernard's thesis, that only a Christian can be a Synthetist, i.e., only he who possesses the *donum super additum*. For he said: 'Le symbolisme est d'essence chrétienne. C'est l'invisible manifesté par le visible et c'est cela qu'à la faveur de la foi chrétienne je tentai de ressusciter en 1890. Pour y parvenir, il fallait être croyant et professeur des théories catholiques.' ('Symbolism is essentially Christian. It is the invisible manifested by the visible, and this is what I tried to restore to life again for the benefit of the Christian faith in 1890. To attain it one must be a believer and profess catholic theories.) Quoted after P. Normand, by R. Puig, *Paul Gauguin, C. D. de Monfreid et leurs amis* (Perpignan, 1958) p.74

842 'Les lignes ont leurs accords plus ou moins significatifs, les couleurs sont des caractères, leurs unions des phrases ... Les formules jeunes ou vieilles sont donc une manière d'écrire que nous devons toujours entendre, toujours connaître et ne point nier.' Bernard, op.cit., p.39.

843 'Dans la nature, il n'est pas une forme qui ne soit un signe pour l'esprit (viz, the Greek 'nous' or Aurier's 'pensée'), la nature toute entière est donc elle-même symbole.' *Lettres à Emile Bernard* (1927) p.62.

844 'Un travail intérieur s'est fait inconsciemment; tout ce qui est inaliénable à mon tempérament s'est effacé de moi; ce qui reste est réellement propre à lui.' Ditto.

845 'Grandes directions des lignes, simplification de la couleur, devenant plutôt significative du sujet que réprésentative de la lumière ou du ton propre.' Ditto, p.63.

846 For the sense of these terms, cf. W. Schöne, *Über das Licht in der Malerei*, (Berlin, 1954) p.112, p.188 ff., and 218/9; *Indifferenzlicht is light in a picture which is neither natürliches* ('natural'); nor *künstliches* ('artificial'); nor *sakral Leuchlicht* (the 'sacral light' of Christ or an angel); it is light that cannot somehow be explained from the scene represented, but on the other hand is not the same light found, for example, in Ottonian miniatures, which Schöne calls *Eigenlicht, op.cit.*, p.14, 12. It is exactly on these points that the great difference is seen between the new art of Synthetism and the older nineteenth-century art which would only use light that could be explained naturally when rendering the given object (cf. note 362 on p.193 in Schöne, op.cit.).

847 Cf. p.109.

848 'd'unir la vérité visible du monde et le divin de la vie intérieure', E. Bernard, 'Note relative au symbolisme pictural 1888–1891' in *Lettres à Emile Bernard* (1927) p.190.

849 Cited in F. D. Klingender, *Art and the industrial revolution* (London, 1947) p.31.

850 'L'art soi-disant raffiné procède de la sensualité et sert la nature'; 'procède de l'esprit et emploie la nature.' Morice, *Gauguin*, p.26.

851 'Ainsi se forme chez l'artiste moderne, par choix et synthèse, une certaine habitude éclectique et exclusive d'interpréter les sensations optiques.' Denis, *Théories*, p.2.

852 'C'est ... surtout l'oubli complet du style, du vrai style, qui au fond n'est que la compréhension de l'intellectualité des formes, et qui est devenu impossible, d'abord par l'oubli de toute synthèse en art ... 'G-A. Aurier, 'Rationations familières et d'ailleurs vaines à propos des trois Salons de 1891', *Mercure de France* (III, 1891) pp.37/38.

853 'ses dernières toiles, d'un symbolisme poétique, d'une belle et savante synthèse de lignes et de couleurs, font présager un artiste de premier ordre', G-A. Aurier, 'Les symbolistes, Littérature et Beaux Arts', *Revue Encyclopédique* (Avril 1892), quoted by Sérusier, *ABC de la peinture*, p.56 note.

854 'La synthèse consiste à faire rentrer toutes les formes dans le petit nombre de formes que nous sommes capables de penser, lignes droites, quelques angles, arcs de cercle et d'ellipse; sortis de là nous nous perdons dans l'océan des variétés.' Quoted by C. Chassé, *Le mouvement symboliste* (1947) p.129; cf. *ABC de la peinture*, p.161.

855 'Ce qui domine, c'est l'idée de synthèse. Pas de classique qui ne soit économe de ses moyens, qui ne subordonne toutes les grâces de détails à la beauté de l'ensemble, qui n'atteigne la grandeur par la concision.' Denis, *Théories*, p.228.

856 It is remarkable that somebody who was far away from France and from the circle of people that we are studying here wrote: 'He (the savage) had begun first by making a complete synthesis of certain points that interested him and ... had assumed to himself and others that this synthesis–which was not a copy of nature, this arrangement and coordination of certain facts of sight–would he understood by others and represent the thing seen.' John la Fargue, quoted by R. Berenson Katz, 'John la Fargue, Art Critic,' *Art Bulletin* (XXXIII 1951) p.105. In the next chapter we intend to revert to la Fargue again.

857 'Le triomphe de l'esprit de synthèse sur l'esprit d'analyse, de l'imagination sur la sensation, de l'homme sur la nature.' Denis, *Introduction to Catalogue Cross Exhibition 1910*.

858 Cf. B. Littré in Dictionnaire de la langue française (Paris, 1889), 'synthèse'. Also A. Lalande, *Vocabulaire technique et critique de la philosophie* (Paris, 1951).

859 'Il sent, ou plutôt il juge successivement, analytiquement'; 'sentent tout de suite, tout à la fois synthétiquement.' *Cur. Esth.*, p.257.

860 'langue synthétique'; 'qui exprime des rapports complexes par un seul mot, et qui groupe les idées accessoires autour de l'idée principale dans des phrases périodiques.' A. Hatzfeld and A. Darmesteter, *Dictionnaire général de la langue française* (Paris w.d., after 1871).

861 One of the writers of the dictionary which we have just quoted, viz. Darmesteter, is mentioned by Fontainas (in his *Mes souvenirs do symbolisme*, p.110): 'En linguistique on prônait Littré ... Darmesteter.' ('In linguistics they extolled Littré ... Darmesteter.')

862 See present chapter: 'Rêve'.

863 This term is used thus at a very early date by Mallarmé – in a letter on 5 August 1867 'En créant une parfaite synthèse des choses' [by creating a perfect synthesis of things] (Michaud, *Message poétique*, p.178). Possibly Mallarmé was the man who circumscribed this term in the sense intended here and under whose influence it became popular in this environment.

864 'Au fond de leur pensée il y a le désir de TOUT. La synthèse esthétique, voilà ce qu'ils cherchent.' Morice, *La littérature*, p.297.

865 'C'est là, dans cette ardeur d'unir la Vérité et la Beauté, dans cette unité désirée de la Foi et de la Joie, de la Science et de l'Art.' Ditto, p.59.

866 Very clearly and explicitly the two poles of the Humanistic view of reality are opposed to each other in what follows: 'Tout objet a deux aspects: l'aspect matériel et l'aspect idéal. Il y a donc bien authentiquement deux mondes: l'un phénomenal, frappant l'âme par les sens et s'y introduisant en notations directes, l'autre intuitif, produit de l'âme, et empruntant pour se traduire les formes du premier ... Il s'ensuit que le réalisme et l'idéalisme sont deux tournures de l'esprit, deux manières d'envisager la vie.' (Dumur, 'Aurier et l'évolution idéaliste', *Mercure de France* (VIII, 1893) p.295). ('Every object has two aspects: the material aspect and the ideal aspect. There are, therefore, really two authentic worlds the one is phenomenal and strikes the soul by means of the senses and enters into it in direct notations, the other is intuitive, a product of the soul, and borrows the forms of the first one to express itself ... from this it follows that realism and idealism are two attitudes of the mind, two ways of considering life.')

867 'Qu'est-ce que le Poème? Une synthèse de toutes les idées générales perçues par un moi donné. La synthèse des sensations constitue les sciences. La synthèse des sciences constitue les philosophies. La synthèse des philosophies constitue les dogmes. La synthèse des dogmes: le poème. Le poème est donc, par excellence, la conclusion intellectuelle, le poème est l'essentielle synthèse du moi.' Aurier, *Oeuvres*, p.XV.

868 'un être nouveau... puisqu'il a pour l'animer une âme, qui est la synthèse de deux âmes, l'âme de l'artiste et l'âme de la nature'. Aurier, *Oeuvres*, p.303.

869 'Vouloir ... faire entrer la vie contemporaine dans la littérature constituait une des tendances les plus nouvelles, les plus hardies ... du mouvement romantique; le plus difficile aussi à réaliser, si l'on tenait à maintenir et à développer les droits de l'imagination, de la sensibilité, de l'idéal, à garder la divine robe de la poésie pure de toute souillure au contact de la réalité terre à terre, à éviter le prosaïsme de la forme et la vulgarité du fond.' Van Tieghem, *Le Romantisme*, p.345.

870 Here synthesis does not mean more than artistic form-giving, style. This passage, however, was written before Morice and the synthetists had said and written such a great deal about synthesis. Here we clearly see the transition from a neutral technical use of the word to an accurately defined use for the purpose of denoting only one movement.

871 'La vie moderne ne nous demeure point interdite ... Mais il sera permis de transfigurer dans une synthèse autre que celle donnée jusqu'à ce jour par l'impressionnisme du roman. Nous ne la peindrons pas telle qu'elle se subjective dans la cervelle du palefrenier ou du peintre d'enseignes, mais telle que nous la fera notre rétine individuelle, notre vision plus largement embrassante. Nous y introduirons les fantômes du rêve, de l'hallucination, du souvenir, les évocations imaginaires, parce que cela se trouve dans la vie et le fait.' P. Adam, 'La Presse et le Symbolisme.' *Le Symboliste*, 7/14 Oct. 1886, cited by Barre, *Le Symbolisme*, p.118/119.

872 'Voici les sujets repoussés ... Toute représentation de la vie contemporaine ou privée ou publique'; 'L'interprétation de théogonies orientales, sauf celles des races jaunes'; 'l'allégorie soit expressive comme 'modestie et vanité', soit décorative comme l'oeuvre du Puvis de Chavannes.' *Salon de la Rose†Croix, Règle et Monitoire* (Paris 1891) p.8/9.

873 See note 869 of this chapter.

874 With the impressionists the artist's personality is expressed in the manner of painting. The composition thereby gets much less emphasis. With them there is really no question of 'objective deformation', and this on purpose.

875 'L'art, au lieu d'être la copie, devenait la déformation subjective de la nature. Au point de vue objectif, la composition décorative, esthétique et rationnelle à laquelle les impressionnistes n'avaient pas pensé parce qu'elle contrariait leur goût de l'improvisation, devenait la contrepartie, le correctif nécessaire de la théorie des équivalents. Celle-ci autorisait en vue de l'expression toutes les transpositions même caricaturales, tous les excès de caractère la déformation objective obligeait à son tour l'artiste à tout transporter en Beauté. En résumé la synthèse expressive, le symbole d'une sensation, devait en être une transcription éloquente, et en même temps un objet composé pour le plaisir des yeux.' Denis, *Théories*, p.260.

876 Cf. Denis, *Théories*, p.164.

877 'Entre tous autres, la peinture est l'art qui préparera les voies en résolvant l'antinomie du monde sensible et de l'intellectuel'. Quoted in Gauguin, *Avant et Après*, p.40.

878 'Reales und Ideales als gleich ursprünglich im Bewusztsein gesetzt und aufeinander bezogen sind.' Windelband-Heimsoeth, p.489/90.

879 'Im Bereiche menschlicher Vernufttätigkeit wird also die gesuchte Synthesis von Freiheit und Natur, von Zweckmäszigkeit und Notwendigkeit, von praktischer und theoretischer Funktion durch das Genie repräsentiert, das in absichtsloser Zweckmäszigkeit das Werk der schönen Kunst erzeugt.' Windelband-Heimsoeth, p.474/5, cf. Kant, *Kritik der Urteilskraft*, Einleitung IX and § 30 and § 44 ff.

880 Windelband-Heimsoeth, p.505/5 12 passim.

881 Aurier quotes Schiller (*Oeuvres*, p.176) from *Lettres sur l'éducation esthétique*. We have not been able to find a possible French edition. The quotation is taken form *Ueber die aesthetische Erziehung des Menschen* (Herford, 1948) pp.22/23.

882 A. Delaroche mentions Schelling in his article on Gauguin taken over in *Avant et Après*, p.41. In his *Histoire de la critique d'art* L. Venturi summarizes Schelling's ideas as follows 'Le génie artistique fait coïncider le fini et l'infini, le conscient et l'inconscient, alors que la science opère sans génie uniquement sur le fini et le conscient.' ('The artistic genius causes the finite to coincide with the infinite, the conscious with the unconscious, whereas science operates without genius exclusively on the finite and the conscious.') These ideas have been explained in Schelling's *Ueber das Verhältniss der bildenden Künste zu der Natur*, 1807. The French were probably informed of Schelling's work by such treatises on him as, e.g., M. Matter, *Schelling ou la Philosophie de la Nature et la Philosophie de la Révélation* (Paris, 1845). We have not been able to find a nineteenth-century French translation of Schelling's work.

883 Cf. eg. Michaud, *Message poétique*, p.200; Lehmann, *Symbolist Aesthetics*, p.37 ff.; Fontainas, *Mes Souvenirs*, p.110.

884 Nowhere does one find the dialectics of the humanistic basic motif elaborated more clearly than precisely in Kant. Cf., his *Kritik der Urteilskraft*. Einleitung II. In his attempt to do justice to both of them, the personality-ideal and the science ideal each have its own domain assigned to it, the former being treated in *Kritik der praktischen Vernunft* and the latter in *Kritik der reinen Vernuft*. In his *Kritik der Urteilskraft*, Kant makes an attempt at a synthesis. This term is found rarely as such, only in a note at the end of the *Einleitung*. It is true we come upon the term in *Kritik der reinen Vernunft* viz., as the combination of a plurality of representations brought about by the subject (§ 15). So we do not find this term 'synthesis' with respect to art used in *Kritik der Urteilskraft*. Windelband's use of the term in the quotation given in the text (on p.151) is not Kant's, although virtually the same idea is expressed in *Kritik der Urteilskraft*.

885 'Le mouvement auquel nous appartenons était antérieur aux influences allemandes. En philosophie nous parlions de Platon, d'Aristote, des Neoplatoniciens et jamais de Kant.' Sérusier in a letter to Denis, 29-2-1915, *ABC de la peinture*, p.146.

886 'In ihr erscheint der Geist als die synthetische Funktion, welche aus ihrer hoheren Einheit die Vielheit erzeugt. Von diesem allgemeinen Gesichtspunkt aus haben die Neuplatoniker die Psychologie des Erkennens unter dem Prinzip der Aktivität des Bewusstseins durchgefuhrt. Denn die "höhere Seele" kann hiernach nicht mehr als leidend, sondern ihrem Wesen nach auch in allen ihren Funktionen nur als tätig angesehen werden. All ihre Einsicht beruht auf der Zusammenfassung (sunyesis)

verschiedener Momente; selbst da, wo die Erkenntnis sich auf das sinnlich Gegebene bezieht, leidet nur der Körper, während die Seele in dem Bewusztwerden sich aktiv verhält und dasselbe gilt von den sinnlichen Gefühlen und Affekten.' Windelband-Heimsoeth, p.195. We shall not examine whether Windelband does not slightly distort Plotinus' thought owing to the fact that W. (as a neo-Kantian) considers him too much from the standpoint of W.'s own basic idea, and, therefore, too little from the ancient Greek idea. Cf. however the next paragraph.

887 Whosoever looks for a genuine art theory in Plotinus will be disappointed. Windelband's conclusion (p.208, op.cit.) is, therefore, not quite supported by the texts: 'die Schönheit, welche die Griechen geschaffen und genossen batten – sie wird nun erkannt als das sieghafte Walten des Geistes, in der Veräszerlichung seiner sinnlichen Erscheinungen. Auch dieser Begriff ist ein Triumph des Geistes, der in der Entfaltung seiner Tätigkeiten zuletzt sein eigenes Wesen erfasst und als Weltprinzip begriffen hat.' ('the beauty that the Greeks have created and enjoyed – it is only now recognized as the victorious rule of the Spirit, in the exteriorization of its sensory appearances. This concept, too, is a triumph of the Spirit which in the development of its activities has at last grasped its own essence and has recognized it as the principle of the world.') When Plotinus speaks of beauty he does not emphasize what we call 'art', but an internal kind of beauty. What arouses love of beauty? 'No shape, no colour, no grandeur of mass: all is for a soul, something whose beauty rests upon no colour, for the moral wisdom the soul enshrines and all the other hueless splendour of the virtues. It is that you find in your-self or admire in another, loftiness of spirit; righteousness of life; disciplined purity; courage of the majestic face; gravity, modesty that goes fearless and tranquil and passionless; and shining down upon all, the light of godlike Intellection. All these noble qualities are to be reverenced and loved, no doubt, but what entitles them to he called beautiful?' (*Enneads* I, 6, 5). In his aesthetics Plotinus wants to give an answer to the latter question, and while doing so he also sometimes speaks of sensory beauty in things as if in passing (e.g., *Enneads* I, 6, up to and including 3, and especially V, 8, 1 up to and including 6). Perhaps we should rather credit Ficino (cf. A. Chastel, *Marsile Ficin et l'Art* (Genève, Lille, 1954) pp.64/65) with the achievement that Windelband attributes to Plotinus.

888 Cited by H. J. Hak, *Marsilia Ficino* (Amsterdam, 1934) p.102. Cf. A. Chastel, *Marsile Ficin et l'Art* (Genève, Lille, 1954) p.64/65.

889 'Le rapport synthétique de l'Idée avec ses apparences ne peut être fixé que par un style archétype et complexe.' Barre, *Le Symbolisme*, p.221.

890 Rewald, *Post-Impressionism*, p.298.

891 Ditto, p.281.

892 'Synthèse d'une forme et d'une couleur en ne considérant que la dominante.' Malingue, *Lettres* LXVII.

893 See p.152 ff.

894 Rewald, *Post-Impressionism*, p.206 and p.239, note 28. This quotation would seem to be a very good summary. It cannot be a real source, because this document is too late and too much derived for that. But thus we avoid giving quotations that have already been used before and at the same time we can be concise.

895 Paris, 1873.

896 'La manifestation vraie de l'Unité de l'être par des phénomènes finis.' Gauckler, p.44.

897 'Modern' here very probably means the naturalism of the Salons.

898 'Bafouée par les modernes qui ne la comprenaient pas et dédaignent de la comprendre, elle a été appréciée des Anciens, qui sous le nom d'inspiration lui attribuaient une origine divine.' Gauckler, p.55.

899 'la nature n'est qu'un dictionnaire'; 'Ceux qui n'ont pas d 'imagination, copient le dictionnaire. Il en résulte un très-grand vice, le vice de la banalité.' Baudelaire, *Art Romantique*, p.10.

900 'le vrai peintre est celui chez lequel l'imagination parle avant tout. Delacroix, *Journal*, 12 Oct. 1853 II, p.85.

901 'L'imagination chez l'artiste ne se représente pas seulement par tels ou tels objects, elle les combine pour la fin qu'il veut obtenir; elle fait des tableaux, des images qu'il compose à son gré'. Delacroix, 'Notes pour un Dictionnaire des Beaux Arts,' *Imagination* III, p.242.

902 'Au lieu de travailler autour de l'oeil, nous cherchions 'au centre mystérieux de la pensée' comme disait Gauguin. L'imagination redevient ainsi, selon le voeu de Baudelaire, la reine des facultés.' Denis, *Théories*, p.259.

903 Cf. Lehmann, *Symbolist Aesthetics*, p.85 ff.

904 'Le rêve! le rêve! mes amis, embarquons-nous pour le rêve.' Cited by Michaud, *Message poétique* II, p.260. The book was by G. Vicaire & H. Beauclair.

905 'Son rêve d'art commençait à prendre corps.' Vollard, *En écoutant Cézanne* (1938) p.11.

906 'Ce qui trompe-l'oeil c'est l'identité. Ce qui réjouit l'esprit et l'élève – car un tableau est avant tout un rêve écrit, et, à un certain point de vue, pour l'esprit lui-même une sorte d'illusoire tremplin – c'est l'harmonie, le senti.' Bernard, 'Les ateliers', *Mercure de France* (XIII 1895) p.203.

907 'Rêver éveillé, c'est à peu près la même chose que rêver endormi. Le rêve endormi est souvent plus hardi, quelquefois un peu plus logique.' Gauguin, *Avant et Après*, p.112.

908 This term has been aptly translated in the *Catalogue of the Gauguin Exhibition in London*, 1955. See No. 56 – *Te Rerioa* ('Le Rêve, Day-Dreaming').

909 'Tout est rêve dans cette toile; est-ce l'enfant, est-ce la mère, est-ce le cavalier dans le sentier ou bien est-ce le rêve du peintre! Tout cela est à côté de la peinture, dira-t-on. Qui sait? Peut-être non.' *Lettres de Gauguin à Daniel de Monfreid* 12 March 1897, p.102.

910 'Mais le rêve est aussi moyen de connaissance, mode de perception du réel, ou plutôt d'une surréalité 'dont notre univers stable n'est que la simplification et, pour ainsi parler, la caricature.' Cited by Michaud, *Message poétique*, p.57 from *Paradis Artificiels* III.

911 'Il admit la réalité du monde, mais il l'admit comme une réalité de fiction. La nature, avec ses chatoyantes féeries, le spectacle rapide et coloré de nuages, et les sociétés humains effarées, ils sont rêves de l'âme; réels mais tous rêves ne sont-ils point réels?' Wyzéwa in *Vogue* 11, 5/VII/1886, quoted by Lehmann, *Symbolist Aethetics*, p.89.

912 'qui remarque les événements sous le jour propre au rêve.' 'Artifice de la réalité, bon à fixer l'intellect moyen entre les mirages d'un fait; mais elle repose par cela même sur quelque universelle entente: voyons donc s'il n'est pas, dans l'idéal, un aspect nécessaire, évident, simple, qui serve de type.' *Divagations*, p.20 and *Poésies complètes de Stéphane Mallarmé*, textes et notes par Y.G. le Dantec (Paris, 1984) p.180.

913 See D.H.Th. Vollenhoven, 'Hoofdlijnen der logica.' *Philosophia Reformata* XIII 1948, p.93, 96. For this reason it seems to us that Michaud's observation (*Le message poétique*, p.200) is quite right: 'Si, pour certains, le criticisme kantien semblait préparer les voies de la science moderne en fixant les limites de la raison, du même coup son idéalisme transcendental, affirmant la subjectivité de tout connaissance, rendait au moi et à l'esprit une prépondérance qui allait permettre toutes les audaces.' ('If, to some people, the Kantian criticism seemed to pave the way for modern science by fixing the limits of reason, his transcendental idealism, asserting the subjectivity of all knowledge, gave to the self and to the mind a preponderance that would permit all kinds of audacities.')

914 Cf. George Levitine, 'Literary Sources of Goya's Capricho 43.' *Art Bulletin* (XXXVII, 1, 1955) p.56. See also our chapter 2: Goya.

915 'Beauté ... le Rêve du Vrai. Mais qu'est-ce que cette jouissance des 'sens spirituels' sinon le rayonnement de la Vérité en des symboles qui la dépouillent des sécheresses de l'Abstraction et l'achèvent dans les joies du Rêve?' Morice, *La Littérature*, p.33.

916 We have not entered into the discussion of the use of the terminology of men like Redon, or of men of letters like Rémy de Gourmont, etc. We abstained from it on purpose as we wanted to restrict ourselves to the circle of the Synthetists. We have followed this policy throughout.

917 'L'idole ... faisant corps dans mon rêve'; Et tout cela chante douloureusement en mon âme et mon décor, en peignant et rêvant tout à la fois' ; 'mes yeux se ferment pour voir sans comprendre le rêve dans l'espace infini qui fuit devant moi'. Malingue, *Lettres* CLXX, p.288/9. This reminds us of Clovio's letter rediscovered shortly after 1920 containing the story of El Greco refusing to go out one fine day, because the daylight would disturb his inner light – he planned his projects with his eyes shut. Quoted in Panofsky, *Idea*, p.56.

918 'Il n'y a de symbolisme qu'à ce prix le symbole n'étant autre chose que l'esprit présenté sous la forme, l'idéal sous le sensible.' *Lettres à Emile Bernard*, 'Note relative au Symbolisme Pictural de 1888–1890', p.190.

919 The difference between the two movements is found firstly in their subjects and their styles. Only with respect to what we call the iconic element (which we shall examine further later on) do they differ greatly, also as far as theory is concerned; as far as we can see, the term and the idea of 'synthesis' is used less frequently by the Symbolist painters (and decadent men of letters).

920 'Les décadents s'étant ralliés au subjectivisme ... ne regardaient plus les choses qu'à travers le miroir déformateur qu'était leur âme rêveuse. Et comme, d'autre part, ils étaient en même temps très raisonneurs, ils en vinrent assez vite à ne plus voir dans les choses ainsi réfléchies et immatérialisées en eux que des emblèmes et des symboles.' Poizat, *Symbolisme*, p.145.

921 The use of the image of a bouquet here is characteristic. It is also found in Balzae's Seraphita and in Baudelaire's *Fanfarlo* – in which case the flowers have a symbolic sense as to their choice and arrangement. The connection is undeniable in this case.

922 'Töne und Worte, Farben und Formen, das Erseheinende überhaupt, sind jedoch nur Symbole der Idee, Symbole, die in dem Gemühe des Künstlers aufsteigen, wenn es der heilige Weltgeist bewegt, seine Kunstwerke sind nur Symbole, wodurch er andern Gemütern seine eigenen Ideen mittheilt

'... Ist der Künstler so ganz willensfrei bei der Wahl und Verbindung seiner geheimnissvollen Blumen? Oder wählt und verbindet er nur, was er muss? Ich bejahe diese Frage einer mystischen Unfreiheit ... In der Kunst bin ich Supernaturalist. Ich glaube, dass der Künstler nicht alle seine Typen in der Natur auffinden kann, sondern dass ihm die bedeutendsten Typen, als eingeborene Symbolik eingeborner Ideen, gleichsam in der Seele geoffenbart werden.' H. Heine, *Der Salon* (I, Rotterdam, 1860) p.27/28.

923 Baudelaire himself also quotes the passage from Heine just mentioned. *Cur. Esth.*, p.103.

924 'Chez les excellents poètes, il n'y a pas de métaphore, de comparaison, ou d'épithète qui ne soit d'une adaption mathématiquement exacte dans la circonstance actuelle, parce que des comparaisons, ces métaphores et ces épithètes sont puisées dans l'inépuisable fond de l'universelle analogie et quelles ne peuvent être puisées ailleurs.' Baudelaire, *Art Romantique*, p.317.

925 '(Pour le poète à composer) la vision seul est digne: le réel et suggestif Symbole d'où, palpitante, pour le rêve, en son intégrité nue se lèvera l'Idée première et dernière, ou vérité.' R. Ghil, *Traité du Verbe*, (1885) p.33, cited by Michaud, *Message poétique*, p.329.

926 Bernard, 'Ce que c'est que l'Art Mystique.' *Mercure de France* (XIII 1895) p.28.

927 'Aussi avons-nous généralement peine à croire les paroles relatives aux divins mystères que nous ne contemplons qu'à travers l'enveloppe de sensibles symboles... les diverses formes dont un symbolisme sacré revêt la divinité, car, au dehors, ne sont-elles pas remplies d'une inadmissible et imaginaire monstruosité.' Bernard, 'Ce que c'est que l'Art mystique.' *Mercure de France* (XIII 1895) p.30, cited from *Oeuvres de Saint Denys l'Aréopagite* (Paris: trad. Abbé Dulac, 1865).

928 'il doit chercher l'éternel dans la diversité momentanée des formes, la Vérité qui demeure dans le Faux qui passe, la logique pérenne dans l'Illogisme instantané', Remy de Gourmont, 'Le Symbolisme, Définition de ce nouveau mouvement littéraire.' *L'art et l'Idée* II, p.51.

929 Aurier, 'Le Symbolisme en peinture, P.Gauguin.' *Mercure de France* (II, 1891) p.155.

930 'Or ceci admis, c'est concéder la possibilité et la légitimité pour l'artiste d'être préoccupé, en son oeuvre, par ce substrat idéiste qui est partout dans l'univers et qui, selon Platon, est la seule vraie réalité.' Aurier, *Oeuvres*, p.301.

931 *Sartor Resartus*, p.254.

932 'Celle (l'oeuvre d'art) qui révèle, celle dont la perfection de la forme consiste surtout à effacer cette forme pour ne laisser persister à l'ébranlement de la Pensée que l'apparition vague et charmante, charmante et dominatrice, dominatrice et féconde d'une entité divine de l'Infini.' Morice, *La littérature*, p.33.

933 'une simple imitation des matérialités ne signifiant point une quelconque spiritualité n'est jamais de l'Art, en d'autres termes, qu'il n'y a pas, qu'il n'y a jamais d'Art sans symbolisme', Aurier, *Oeuvres*, p.298.

934 See Thesis IV to Hak's dissertation on Ficino 'The theology of Ficino distinguishes itself in this from Scholasticism and Neoplatonism, that it declares the human spirit to be independent of God and of matter and makes it the centre of the Universe.'

935 Cf. Hak, *Ficino*, p.102. Also A. Chastel, *Marsile Ficin*, p.65.

936 'Qu'est-ce que le Poète? C'est une des incarnations sous lesquelles se manifeste le Révélateur, le Héros, l'homme que Carlyle appelle "un

messager envoyé de l'impénétrable Infini avec des nouvelles pour nous."
Cette conception du Héros, exprimé par un visionnaire de génie, est la
directe conséquence d'une autre conception universellement admise par
les occultistes et les mystiques, et formulé ainsi par Novalis: "Tout être créé
est une revelation." ' V.E. Michelet. *De l'Esotérisme dans l'art* (1891) p.9,
cited by Michaud, *Message poétique* III, p.468.

937 'Quelque part hors du monde, dans le ciel de la joie et de la beauté, c'est
jour de suprême épiphanie quand un grand artiste a couronné de son
génie quelqu'une des innombrables figures belles de la NATURE; quand
l'artiste, enfant lui-même de la NATURE, nourri par elle, vivant d'elle, se
lève pour dire la beauté de sa mère quand la Nature laisse un des aspects
changeants de son mystérieux visage éterniser le mot de son énigme dans
l'oeuvre d'Art.' *Noa Noa* (ed. 1924) p.11.

938 L'art n'est que le révélateur de l'Infini il est au Poète un moyen même d'y
pénétrer. Il y va plus profond qu'aucune Philosophie, il y prolonge et
répercute la Révélation d'un Evangile, il est une lumière qui appelle la
lumière.' Morice, *La littérature*, p.33.

939 'Nous cherchions la Vérité dans les lois harmonieuses de la Beauté,
déduisant de celle-ci toute métaphysique – car l'harmonie des nuances et
des sons symbolise l'harmonie des âmes et des mondes–et toute morale'.
Morice, *La littérature*, p.65.

940 The examination of Kuyper's correspondence preserved in the Kuyperhuis
at the Hague did not yield a single indication of the reason why he delivered his speech on 'The Antithesis between Symbolism and Revelation' for
the Historical Presbyterian Society in Philadelphia in 1898/9. He was in
the USA. for the Stone Lectures, but alongside those gave many other
addresses. Nowhere does Kuyper appear to possess special knowledge of
art, but he has no doubt occupied himself with it. A number of publications are evidence of his interest. In addition to the lecture discussed here
we may mention: 'Calvinism on Art' in *'Christian Thought', Lectures and
Papers in Philosophy, Christian Evidence, Biblical Elucidation* (IX, New York,
1891–1892) pp.259–282, 447–459, translated by Rev. J. H. de Vries, *Het
Calvinisme en de Kunst* (rectorial address, Amsterdam, 1888) 'Calvinism on
art' (The Stone Lectures, Amsterdam/Pretoria, 1899).

941 There is no doubt some connection between the Liturgical Movement in
Protestant Churches then and now – it may be a movement which asserts
itself at different times with varying emphasis. Cf. also the book cited in the
next note, pp.63, 158.

942 We may think of the ecumenic movement which arose with increasing force
in those years and of which the World Council of Churches, constituted
after the Second World War, is an important result. Cf. C. van der Waal,
Antithese of Synthese? De oecumenische beweging beschreven en getoetst.
(Enschede, 1951) pp.29 ff.

943 He means the orthodox Calvinistic churches.

944 A. Kuyper, 'The antithesis between Symbolism and Revelation.' p.9.

945 Ditto, p.10.

946 Ditto, p.10.

947 'Pauvre enfant! Ne te désole point ... Il existe une redemption – Où la
trouverais-je? – En toi ... Descends en ton âme! ... Ai-je donc en moi, sans
le savoir, pareille puissance? Porté-je donc en ma chair tout un univers? –
Un univers, enfant, plus grand et plus beau que l'univers! Un univers dont
tu es le Dieu ... Ne faisons-nous autre chose, en croyant inventer les plus

fabuleuses chimères, que d'évoquer les visions, inconsciemment ressouvenues, des temps où nos âmes se prélassaient dans le merveilleux Eden des Idées Pures?' Aurier, *Oeuvres*, p.11.

948 R. Kroner, 'The year 1800 in the development of German Idealism.' *Review of Metaphysics* (I, 4, June, 1948) p.22.

949 *Ongeloof en Revolutie* (Kampen, 1904) p.347 ff.

950 Cf., the article cited in note 948: 'No longer do the practical issues, the ideals of moral man, the principles of volition and action dominate thought, but instead intuition and imagination, contemplation and speculation assume supremacy' (p.7).

951 The text says 'beautiful'. We thought we were entitled to correct this – the English of this lecture is sometimes far from beautiful, and obviously the work of a translator who had great difficulty with the text.

952 Kuyper, *op.cit.*, p.13.

953 Ibid.

954 Ditto, p.14.

955 The thought briefly formulated here had already been Kuyper's in 1892, and was elaborately developed in his rectorial address, 'De Verflauwing der Grenzen' (Amsterdam, 1892) pp.12 ff.

956 Ditto, pp.15,16.

957 Baudelaire, too, had discovered that this revelation via art was in reality nothing but the positing of the artist's view from the standpoint of the latter's view of life and the world. Cf. p.24.

958 Ditto, p.16.

959 Morice, who had originated from a Roman-Catholic environment, probably refers to saints' legends, to the belief in relics, etc.

960 'La critique moderne ne permet plus qu'on croie à des choses incroyables, et pourtant l'esprit moderne comme l'esprit ancien, reste avide de beaux mystères: comment n'a-t-il pas compris, Wagner, que, puisque la religion ne peut vivre pour l'art qu'autant qu'elle voile son élément de vérité sous un entassement toujours croissant de choses incroyables, et puisque, cependant, les hommes ne veulent plus que ces belles chimères soient proposées à leur raison, c'est à leur imagination SEULEMENT qu'il faut les offrir!' Morice, *La litterature*, p.199.

961 Lehmann, *Symbolist Aesthetics*, p.306.

962 W. B. Yeats, *Collected Works* (Stratford-on-Avon, 1908); especially VI, 'Ideas on Good and Evil'; concerning magic, p.23 ff., on symbolism in painting, p.176,224. Cf. Holbrook Jackson, *The Eighteen Nineties*, p.69, 147 ff; Lehmann, *Symbolist Aesthetics*, p.281 ff.

963 Lehmann, op.cit., p.308.

964 Ditto, p.313.

965 Ditto, p.306.

966 Even the most naturalistic way of representation only seemingly copies reality – and does so merely because of the age-long custom of using a particular kind of pictorial means (such as perspective, etc.). Thus the idea got fixed in the minds of both adherents and opponents that art was really an 'imitation'.

967 In literature it will no doubt always be realized that we are dealing with language, even though the peculiar nature of language may I have been

lost to sight because of the view that a word is identical with an idea or a concept. However this may be, also naturalism in literature had caused a great deal of the peculiar character of art to be lost, for art is more than 'copying' the life of every day. Thus Lehmann's thesis quoted above, which bears on literature, can be understood.

968 The term 'iconique' even occurs a few times. For instance, '(les) milles nuances (de la couleur) sont aptes à complémentariser la symbolisation iconique d'un état d'âme' ('the thousands of shades (of colour) are suitable to complement the iconic symbolization of a state of mind') A. Germain, 'Un peintre idéaliste-idéiste, Alexandre Séon (Symbolisme des Teintes).' *L'Art et l'Idée* (I, Paris, 1892) p.109.

969 By modalities we mean the different aspects of reality, which are facets that (in principle) can be discovered in everything, or spheres of experience in which every human being functions as a subject. They are not modes of thought – whoever should assert this would thereby reduce all the aspects of reality to subordinate parts of the logical modality. On the theory of the modalities, cf. H. Dooyeweerd, Wijsbegeerte der Wetsidee II, pp.1 ff., or his *A New Critique of Theoretical Thought,* II, pp.3 ff., or his *Transcendental Problems of Philosophic Thought* (Grand Rapids, Mich., 1948) p.42 ff.

970 We might mention as an example the Japanese way of representing depth in works of art, using entirely different means from that of perspective. In this example we point out differences in pictorial representation in different cultural spheres.

971 'Il n'y a plus de contours qu'il n'y a de touches dans la nature. Il faut toujours en revenir à des moyens convenus dans chaque art, qui sont le langage de cet art.' *Journal,* 13 January 1857.

972 See notes 550 and 551. 'Plus je vais plus j'aborde dans ce sens de traduction de la pensée par tout autre chose qu'une littérature'.

973 'Vous discutez avec Laval sur les ombres et me demandez, si je m'en fous quant à l'explication de la lumière, oui. Examinez les Japonais qui dessinent pourtant admirablement et vous verrez la vie en plein air et au soleil sans ombres. Ne se servant de la couleur que comme une combinaison de tons, harmonies diverses, donnant l'impression de la chaleur, etc.' Malingue, LXXV.

974 'toutes ces couleurs fabuleuses, cet air embrasé mais tamisé, silencieux. Mais tout cela n'existe pas!' ('this is the critic's objection,' Gauguin replies) 'Oui, cela existe comme équivalent de cette grandeur, profondeur de ce mystère de Tahiti, quand il faut l'exprimer dans une toile d'un mètre carré.' Cited Rotonchamp, *Gauguin,* p.122, spoken in connection with the exposition of 1893. Cf. Malingue, CLXX.

975 'Le strict devoir du peintre idéiste est, par conséquent, d'effectuer une sélection raisonnée parmi les multiples éléments combinés en l'objectivité, de n'utiliser en son oeuvre que les lignes, les formes, les couleurs générales et distinctives servant à écrire nettement la signification idéique de l'objet'. Aurier, 'Le symbolisme en peinture.' *Mercure de France* II, 1891, p.162.

976 'Cela revient à constater que les objets, c'est-à-dire, abstraitement, les diverses combinaisons de lignes, de plans, d'ombres, de couleurs, constituent le vocabulaire d'une langue mystérieuse, mais miraculeusement expressive, qu'il faut savoir pour être artiste. Cette langue, comme toutes les langues, a son écriture, son orthographe, sa grammaire, sa syntaxe, sa rhétorique même, qui est le style', Aurier, *Oeuvres,* p.302.

977 We are referring to those who may call themselves Iconologists, and to S. K. Langer in the field of art theory, in her *Philosophy in a New Key* (New York, 1949, 2).

978 The new insight was expressed most clearly by an artist who was strongly influenced by Gauguin in the years 1890-1892, viz. J. F. Willumsen, a Danish painter. On an etching entitled 'Fertility', of 1891, he wrote 'L'art ancien a son ancienne langue que le monde peu à peu a appris à comprendre. Un art nouveau a une langue nouvellement formée que le monde doit apprendre avant de la comprendre.' ('Ancient art has its ancient language which the world has gradually learnt to understand. A new art has a newly formed language which the world must learn before understanding it.') Reproduced in *Kunsten Idag* (XLIV, Oslo, 1958, 2) p.13.

979 'Méditons ce mot de Cézanne 'J'ai voulu copier la nature ... je n'arrivais pas. J'ai été content de moi lorsque j'ai découvert que le soleil par exemple (les objets ensoleillés) ne se pouvait pas reproduire mais qu'il fallait le représenter par autre chose que ce que je voyais – par la couleur'. Denis, *Théories*, p.259, note 2.

980 M. Denis, Introduction to the *Catalogue of the exhibition 'Französische Kunst des XIX. Jahrhunderts'*, Züricher Kunsthaus, Oct-Nov. 1917, p.10.

981 Morice, *Gauguin*, p.225 e.g.

982 'Nous avons substitué à l'idée de la 'Nature vue à travers un tempérament' la théorie de l'équivalence ou du symbole nous affirmions que les émotions ou états d'âme provoqués par un spectacle quelconque, comportaient dans l'imagination de l'artiste des signes ou équivalents plastiques capables de reproduire ces émotions ou états d'âme sans qu'il soit besoin de fournir la copie du spectacle initial; qu'à chaque état de notre sensibilité devait correspondre une harmonie objective capable de le traduire.' Denis, *Théories*, p.267.

983 'Or, les pensées et qualités morales ne peuvent être représentées que par des équivalents formels.' 'C'est la faculté de percevoir ces correspondances qui fait l'artiste. Tout homme, en naissant, a cette faculté en puissance; son travail personnel la développe; une mauvaise éducation peut l'annihiler'. Sérusier, *ABC de la peinture*, p.23.

984 'enfin je compris encore que dans l'icône... tout doit être empreint d'un caractère simple, explicatif, exact et symbolique, que chaque acteur doit avoir une dimension proportionnée à l'importance de son rôle'. Bernard, 'Ce que c'est que l'Art mystique.' *Mercure de France* (XIII 1895) p.37.

985 It shows a keen insight to speak of 'Jesus' here – for we are only concerned here with the human being who was on earth at one time in history. On this human being all our attention is concentrated in this kind of work, whereas his divine office as the Messiah is ignored as well as His divinity. In contradistinction to this attitude Byzantine Art chiefly and pretty well exclusively paid attention to Jesus Christ's divine nature.

986 'Un Christ byzantin est symbole. Le Jésus des peintres modernes, fût-il coiffé du plus exact kiffyed, n'est que littéraire. Dans l'un c'est la forme qui est expressive, dans l'autre c'est la nature imitée qui veut l'être.' Denis, *Théories*, p.10.

987 He speaks about a photo of a Giotto in *Avant et Après*, p.97, of a 'Mary Magdalene disembarking at Marseilles'. This probably refers to a fresco of the series of scenes from the life of Mary Magdalene in the Magdalene Chapel of the Lower Church of Assisi, represented in G.H. Weigelt, *Klassiker der Kunst : Giotto* (1925) p.181.

988 Cf. B. Dorival, 'Sources of the art of Gauguin from Java, Egypt and Ancient Greece.' Burlington Magazine (XCIII, April 1951) p.118. That he took photos of the Burubudur for works from Cambodia clearly appears from his letter to Bernard in 1889 in which he wrote (on the occasion of the World Exhibition at Paris) on the works exhibited in the Dutch-East-Indian Pavillion: 'Tout l'Art de l'Inde se trouve là et les photographies que j'ai du Cambodia se retrouvent là textuellement.' *Lettres à Emile Bernard*, p.66. ('The whole art of India is found there and the photos I possess of Cambodia are found back again there literally.') For in our opinion his term textuellement means 'literally', exactly agreeing with, not merely as to style generally.

989 Ditto, p.44.

990 On the term 'modality' cf. note 969. Briefly we would describe the structure of a work of pictorial art as follows: first, a structure of an objective psychical qualification – oil-paint on canvas, applied in such a way that particular colours and lines are noticed in our sensory perception – in this bottom structure another one is founded, viz, one of an iconic qualification – for, the configurations of colours and lines given in sensory perception have been aranged in such a way that to the observer, to the human subject, they have an iconically signifying sense, in short, that they render something, depict some thing – while, finally the iconic structure is the foundation of the aesthetically qualified one – and in the latter qualification we are confronted with the meaning and the peculiar nature of the work of art as such. However this may be, the iconic and the aesthetic aspects of a work of art are together the key functions, which are closely interrelated, as we try to show in more detail in this part of our study. In connection with this, cf. Dooyeweerd, *Wijsbegeerte der Wetsidee* III, pp.71 ff.; or ditto, *A New Critique of Theoretical Thought*, III, pp.104 ff.

991 Here we have to deal with an anticipatory element within the iconic modality opening and expanding the latter and deepening its meaning. Cf. Dooyeweerd, op.cit. II, pp.112 ff., and *A New Critique*, II, pp.181 ff.

992 This is a retrocipatory moment within the structure of the aesthetic modality. Cf. Dooyeweerd II, op.cit., p.106; *A New Critique* II, pp.181 ff.

993 We are, e.g., referring to Weelkes' 'As Vesta was from Latmos hill descending' in the of the anthology *Triumphs of Oriana*(1601), published in honour of Queen Elizabeth I. In it descent is musically characterized when the choir sings 'running down amain', while in the next line 'two by two' is sung by two voices, 'three by three' by three voices, and 'together' by the whole choir, etc.

994 Cf. my article 'Ontwerp ener aesthetica.' *Philosophia Reformata* XI, 1946, p.144, where some more examples are given.

995 'Symbolism' is, properly speaking, an unfortunate term, as it is also used by the authors and artists we are discussing, with a very particular meaning. By this term 'aesthetical symbolism' we want to express that we are concerned with an element which is exclusively qualified by the aesthetic modality, although it is connected with the linguistie-iconic aspect of reality. A neologism like 'aesthetical iconism' seems awkward to us, for which reason we have resorted, after all, to the term 'symbolism'.

996 'Au lieu d'évoquer nos états d'âme au moyen du sujet représenté, c'est l'oeuvre elle-même qui devait transmettre la sensation initiale, en perpétuer l'émotion.' Denis, *Théories*, p.245.

997 'Qu'il me suffise d'avertir le visiteur que Gauguin est un cérébral – je ne dis pas, certes, 'un littéraire' – qu'il exprime non ce qu'il voit mais ce qu'il pense par une originale harmonie de lignes, par un dessin curieusement compris dans l'arabesque.' Gauguin, 'Préface inédite au catalogue de l'exposition des oeuvres d'Armand Seguin', in *Mercure de France* (XIII, 1895) p.222.

998 'Il était naturel que la synthèse conduisit l'artiste au symbole. Des sacrifices et un ordre dans la composition qui avaient pour but de rendre intelligible la pensée de l'auteur, un affranchissement des sujétions immédiates de l'observation directe, devaient inspirer à l'artiste le désir de retenir de la nature les aspects seulement où il lisait une allusion significative à cette pensée et de réunir ces aspects en quelque grande image, à la fois libérée de toute vraisemblance (scl. naturalistic mimesis instead of iconic representation) et profondément, c'est-à-dire vitalement et artistiquement, vraie.' Morice, *Gauguin*, p.166.

999 See pp.170–171.

1000 From the way in which D. expresses himself it might appear that the term was by no means unusual. It was a current metaphor, which D. defines more closely, however, giving it a sharply outlined meaning.

1001 'Il y a un genre d'émotion qui est tout particuliere à la peinture ... Il y a une impression qui résulte de tel arrangement de couleurs, de lumières et d'ombres etc ... C'est ce qu'on appelle la musique du tableau. Avant même de savoir ce que le tableau représente, vous entrez dans une cathédrale et vous vous trouvez placé à une distance trop grande du tableau pour savoir ce qu'il représente, et souvent vous êtes pris, par cet accord magique: les lignes seules ont quelquefois ce pouvoir ... C'est ici qu'est la vraie supériorité de la peinture sur l'autre art, car cette émotion s'adresse à la partie la plus intime de l'âme ... Elle ajoute à ce que serait le spectacle de la nature cet élément qui vérifie et choisit, l'âme du peintre, son style particulier.' Delacroix, Oeuvres littéraires I, p.63.

1002 'Un tableau de Delacroix, place à une trop grande distance pour que vous puissiez juger l'agrément des contours ou la qualité plus ou moins dramatique du sujet, vous pénètre déjà d'une volupté surnaturelle ... Et l'analyse du sujet, quand vous vous approchez, n'enlèvera rien et n'ajoutera rien à ce plaisir primitif, dont la source est ailleurs et loin de toute pensée secrète. Je puis inverser l'exemple. Une figure bien dessinée vous pénètre d'un plaisir tout à fait étranger au sujet. Voluptueuse ou terrible, cette figure ne doit son charme qu'à l'arabesque qu'elle découpe dans l'espace.' *L'Art Romantique*, p.18/19.

1003 'La bonne manière de savoir si un tableau est mélodieux est de le regarder d'assez loin pour n'en comprendre ni le sujet ni les lignes. S'il est mélodieux, il a déjà un sens, et il a déjà pris sa place dans le répertoire des souvenirs.' *Cur. Esth.*, p.92.

1004 'Il y a des tons gais et fôlatres, fôlatres et tristes, riches et gais, riches et tristes' Ditto.

1005 'Die Musik ... (malt) menschliche Gefühle auf eine übermenschliche Art, weil sie uns alle Bewegungen unsers Gemüts unkörperlich, in goldne Wolken lustiger Harmonien eingekleidet, über unserm Haupte zeigt.' W.H. Wackenroder, 'Die Wunder der Tonkunst', in Tieck und Wackenroder, *Phantasien über die Kunst* (Stuttgart o.J: Deutsche National-Litteratur 145, 1799) p.58, quoted by Abrams, *Mirror and the Lamp*, p.50 (in English).

1006 'Und ebenso ist es mit dem geheimnisvollen Strome in den Tiefen des menschlichen Gemütes beschaffen, die Sprache zählt und nennt und beschreibt seine Verwandlungen, in fremden Stoff; – die Tonkunst strömt ihn uns selber vor ... In dem Spiegel der Töne lernt das menschliche Herz sich selber kennen; sie sind es, wodurch wir das Gefühl fühlen lernen.' Ditto, p.71, quoted by Abrams op.cit., p.93. Abrams deals elaborately with the question we are talking about here.

1007 *Poetica I*, 2 and 4. A. Gudeman, *Aristoteles über die Dichtkunst* (Leipzig, 1921) p.1.

1008 Cited by Abrams, *Mirror and the Lamp*, p.92.

1009 Edition of 1852, pp.129/130.

1010 See note 913.

1011 This metaphor in connection with art had occurred at a much earlier date already. Cf. M. H. Abrams, *The Mirror and the Lamp*, pp.32 ff. –where this term is even used in the title of the book. The metaphor goes back to a very old Neoplatonic tradition.

1012 'Une oeuvre d'art n'est réellement oeuvre d'art qu'à condition de refléter, ainsi qu'un miroir, l'émotion psychologique éprouvée par l'artiste devant la nature ou devant son Rêve. Cette émotion peut, à la dernière limite, n'être qu'une sensation pure: sensation d'un accord particulier de lignes, d'une symphonie déterminée de couleurs.' Aurier, article on the Salons of 1891, *Mercure de France* (III, 1891) p.37.

1013 For we admit the existence of 'musicality' in this sense of aesthetic symbolism, but we deny the supposed correctness of the subjectivistie application of this phenomenon.

1014 *Diverses Choses*, cited by Rotonchamp, Gauguin, p.214. Cf. note dp.

1015 'Pensez aussi à la part musicale que prendra désormais la couleur dans la peinture moderne. La couleur qui est vibration de même que la musique est à même d'atteindre ce qu'il y a de plus général et partant de plus vague dans la nature sa force intérieure', Malingue, CLXX. In this letter Gauguin quotes from Delaroche's article, consequently he makes the latter's words fully his own. That article, 'D'un point de vue esthétique à propos du peintre Paul Gauguin', was also copied by him in his *Avant et Après*, p.33, with this passage on page 40.

1016 'Les sons, les couleurs, les mots ont une valeur miraculeusement expressive, en dehors de toute représentation, en dehors même du sens littéral des mots.' M. Denis, *Sérusier*, Paris 1942, cited by Agnes Humbert, *Les Nabis*, p.15. The pronouncement is Sérusier's.

1017 Ruskin, *Works* XX, Aratra Pentelici 207. Cited by C. Dougherty, 'Ruskin's views on non-representational art.' *College Art Journal* (XV, 2, 1955) p.114.

1018 Dougherty, op.cit.

1019 Ditto, p.117.

1020 M. Raymond, *From Baudelaire to Surrealism* (New York, 1950) p.46/47.

1021 See note 712. 'Les monuments, la mer, la face humaine, dans leur plénitude, natifs, conservant une vertu autrement attrayante que ne voilera ni description, ni évocation dites, allusion je sais, suggestion: cette terminologie quelque peu de hasard atteste la , très décisive, peut-être, qu'ait sub l'art littéraire, elle le borne et l'exempte. Son sortilège, à lui, si ce n'est libérer, hors d'une poignée de poussière ou réalité sans l'enclore, au livre, même comme texte, la dispersion volatile soit l'esprit, qui n'a que rien àfaire outre la musicalité de tout.'

1022 'Oui, je le sais, nous ne sommes que de vaines formes de la matière – mais bien sublimes pour avoir inventé Dieu et notre âme. Si sublimes, mon ami! que je veux me donner ce spectacle de la matière, ayant conscience d'être, et, cependant, s'élançant forcément dans ce Rêve qu'elle sait ne pas être, chantant l'âme et toutes les divines impressions pareilles qui se sont amassées en nous depuis les premiers âges, et proclamant devant le Rien qui est la vérité, ces glorieux mensonges! Tel est le plan de mon volume, lyrique et tel sera peut-être son titre, la Gloire du Mensonge ou le Glorieux Mensonge. Je chanterai en désespéré.' Letter to Cazalis, March 1866, cited by Michaud, *Message poétique*, p.172.

1023 This existentialistic terminology admirably fits in with Mallarmé's views, whom we may call a precursor of this twentieth-century movement in many respects.

1024 J. Huret, *Enquête sur l'évolution littéraire* (Paris, 1891) p.60.

1025 Cf. Michaud, *Message poétique*, p.190.

1026 Ditto, p.172.

1027 'La poésie est l'expression, par le langage humain ramené à son rythme essentiel, du sens mystérieux des aspects de l'existence elle voue ainsi d'authenticité notre séjour et constitue la seule tâche spirituelle.' Michaud, Message poétique, p.197.

1028 'C'est le mysticisme qu'il faut aujourd'hui, et c'est le mysticisme qui seul peut sauver notre société de l'abrutissement, du sensualisme et de l'utilitarisme. Les facultés les plus nobles de notre âme sont en train de s'atrophier ... nous serons revenus, par la science positive, à l'animalité pure et simple. Il faut réagir. Il faut recultiver les qualités supérieures de l'âme. Il faut redevenir mystiques. Il faut rapprendre l'amour, source de toute compréhension.' Aurier, *Oeuvres*, p.201.

1029 'Leurs définitions reposent sur la théorie de l'inspiration directe. Dégager, par l'initiation, ce 'moi intérieur', cette 'étincelle divine' existant dans la personnalité humaine, jouir de cette 'intuition', de cette 'Intelligence' profonde des choses qui repose sur 'une illumination spirituelle', de 'ces relations d'un genre exceptionnel avec les habitants du monde invisible', posséder la 'vision intime du principe de la réalité du monde', telles sont bien les espérances des adeptes.' A. Viatte, *Les sources occultes du romantisme 1770-1820: I de Préromantisme* (Paris, 1928) p.18.

1030 'Bien des âmes, dédaigneuses des chemins battus, s'enquièrent de voies nouvelles ou ignorées. Nées sous l'ombre tutélaire d'une Église, ou dans l'absence de toute croyance, le doute se combine chez elles avec l'anxiété réligieuse.' A. Viatte, *Les sources occultes du romantisme 1770-1820: I de Préromantisme* (Paris, 1928) p.19.

1031 Cf. W.H. Beuken, *Ruusbroec en de Middeleeuwse Mystiek* (Utrecht, Brussel, 1946); J. W. Tunderman, *Marnix van St. Aldegonde en de subjectivistische stromingen in de 16e eeuw*, hoofdstuk II: 'Subjectivistische Themata in de eeuwen voor de Reformatie' (Goes, z.j.) p.26.

1032 'Le livre, l'objet d'art, la phrase musicale, la pure pensée elle-même ... sont des éternisations du Moi. C'est que nous en faisons autant de moyens de dégager notre Moi des contingences et c'est qu'aussi, par là même et dès qu'il échappe aux contingences, le Moi recourt ... au foyer de l'absolu, au lieu métaphysique des Idées, à Dieu.' Morice, *La littérature*, p.30.

1033 Aurier, 'Le symbolisme en peinture, P. Gauguin.' *Mercure de France* (II, 1891) p.159.

1034 To a Greek of the Platonic school only the world of the ideas was the true reality, all other things were merely their adumbrations – recall Plato's myth of the cave in which man looks at the shadows of true events and takes them to be 'authentic'. What is relative and transitory thus only has a derived kind of reality, at best.

1035 'Puisqu'il s'agit d' atteindre l'absolu, le langage poétique ne doit-il pas rechercher des symboles nécessaires, qui échappent à toute relativé?' Michaud, *Message poétique*, p.327.

1036 'Et en effet, de ces trois vertus fondamentales, Liberté, Ordre, Solitude, résulte aussitôt un sentiment de puissance illiminitée, qui est le conseil-même de l'Infini; aussitôt, l'âme acquiert la certitude de sa propre éternité dans cette solitude d'exception, et qu'il n'y a pas de mort comme il n'y a pas de naissance, et que la vie véritable est d'être un des centres conscients de la vibration infinie.' Morice, *La littérature*, p.367.

1037 'Car, si les choses visibles sont la figure des choses invisibles, l'essence de l'homme, tenant du divin et douée d'harmonie, coordonne et transforme la nature selon sa suprématie pour lui faire exprimer son origine propre et surnaturelle.' Bernard, 'Ce que c'est que l'art mystique.' *Mercure de France* (XIII, 1895) p.29.

1038 W. Haftmann, *Malerei im 20. Jahrhundert* (München, 1954) p.77; 'Dekorative Kunst, Ill.' *Zeitschrift für angewandte Kunst* (I, München, 1898) p75/76, an article by A. Endell

1039 Cf. B. Smith, 'European Vision and the South Pacific.' *Journal of the Warburg and Courtauld Institute*(XIII, 1950) p.65.

1040 H. la Fargue, 'John la Fargue and the South Sea Idyll.' *Journal of the Warburg and Courtauld Institute*(VII, 1944) p.34; F. Fairchild Sherman, 'Some early oil paintings by John la Fargue.' Art in America (Feb. 1920) p.85.

1041 Charles Kunstler, *Gauguin, peintre maudit* (Paris, 1934) p.8.

1042 'Et on les appelle des sauvages? Ils chantent, ne volent jamais ... n'assassinent pas. Deux mots tahitiens les désignent Iorama (bonjour, adieu, merci, etc.) ... et Onatu (je m'en fiche, qu'importe, etc) et on les appelle sauvages?' Malingue CXVI (1891). It is remarkable that Gauguin never alludes to classical antiquity in this connection – a proof that he had got estranged from any kind of classicism which idealized Greek-Roman antiquity. The only author who refers to the anything other than idyllic and ideal conditions existing among the Tahitian population, is Th. Craven, *Modern Art: The Men, the Movements and the Meaning* (New York, 1940) p.133 passim.

1043 See note 1041

1044 P. Gauguin, *Ancien Culte Mahorie*: Présentation par R. Huyghe, Le Clef de Noa Noa (Paris, 1951).

1045 Malingue, CXXVII.

1046 'J ai bien des tracas et si ce n'était nécessaire à mon art (j'en suis sûr), je repartirais de suite.' Malingue, CXXVII.

1047 'son imagination a dans le réel son point de départ et ses références'. Morice, *Gauguin*, p.190.

1048 'Paul Gauguin, en vérité, fut plutôt un peintre décorateur qu'un peintre symboliste; car jamais dans aucun de ses tableaux une idée quelconque n'apparaît.' *Lettres à Emile Bernard*, p.62.

1049 'Son imagination, prisonnière jusqu'alors dans le réel, s'était éveillée, désireuse de s'exprimer par les images dont se sont servis les grands maîtres. Il reconnut tout à coup combien il etait vain de s'attacher aux aspects passagers de son temps ... au savoir sommaire de la palette et des pratiques courantes, il opposait la grande science de l'art; aux faux styles, la forme; à l'anémie des méthodes, la force; aux sujets immédiats, les grands lieux communs de l'humanité ... ne plus une belle Parisienne à la toilette, mais une nymphe guetté par un satyre.' E. Bernard, 'Louis Anquetin.' *Gazette des Beaux Arts* (1934, I) p.117.

1050 Morice, *Gauguin*, p.190.

1051 'le plus raide et celui que je tiens à garder ou vendre cher', Malingue, CXXXIV. Now in the A. Conger Goodyear Collection, reproduced in almost every book on Gauguin.

1052 *Noa Noa*, p.29, cited by Morice, *Gauguin*, p.199.

1053 'Une jeune fille canaque est couchée sur le ventre, montrant une partie de son visage effrayé. Elle repose sur un lit garni d'un paréo bleu et d'un drap jeune de chrome clair. Un fond violet pourpre, semé de fleurs semblables à des étincelles électriques: une figure un peu étrange se tient à côté du lit. Séduit par une forme, un mouvement, je les peins sans aucune autre pré-occupation que de faire un morceau de nu. Tel quel, c'est une étude de nu un peu indécente, et cependant je veux en faire un tableau chaste en donnant l'esprit canaque, son caractère, sa tradition. Le paréo lié intimement à l'existence d'un canaque, je m'en sers comme dessus de lit. Le drap d'une étoffe d'écorce d'arbre doit être jaune, parce que de cette couleur il suscite pour le spectateur quelque chose d'inattendu; parce qu'il suggère l'éclairage d'une lampe, ce qui m'évite de faire un effet de lampe. Il me faut un fond un peu terrible. Le violet est tout indiqué. Voilà la partie musicale du tableau tout échafaudée.

'Dans cette position un peu hardie, que peut faire une jeune fille canaque toute nue sur un lit? Se préparer à l'amour? Cela est bien dans son caractère, mais c'est indécent, et je ne veux pas. Dormir? L'action amoureuse serait terminée, ce qui est encore indécent. Je ne vois que la peur. Quel genre de peur? Certainement pas la peur d'une Suzanne surprise par des vieillards. Cela n'existe pas en Océanie.

'Le Tupapaou (Esprit des Morts) est tout indiqué pour les canaques, c'est la peur constante. La nuit, une lampe est toujours allumée. Personne ne circule sur les routes, à moins d'avoir un fanal, et encore ils vont plusieurs ensemble. Une fois, mon Tupapaou trouvé, je m'y attache complètement et j'en fais le motif de mon tableau. Le nu passe au deuxième plan.

'Que peut bien être, pour une canaque, un revenant? Elle ne connaît pas le théâtre, la lecture des romans, et, lorsqu'elle pense à un mort, elle pense nécessairement à quelqu'un déjà vu. Mon revenant ne peut être qu'une petite bonne femme quelconque. Le sens décoratif m' amène à parsemer le fond de fleurs. Ces fleurs sont des fleurs de Tupapaou, des phosphorescences, signe que le revenant s'occupe de vous. Croyances Tahitiennes.

'Le titre, Manao Tupapaou, a deux sens ou elle pense au revenant, ou le revenant pense à elle.

'Récapitulons. Partie musicale lignes horizontales ondulantes, accords d'orange et de bleu, reliés par des jaunes et des violets, leurs dérivés, éclairés par étincelles verdâtres; partie littéraire l'Esprit d'une vivante lié à l'Esprit des morts. La nuit et le Jour.

'Cette genèse est écrite pour ceux qui veulent toujours savoir les pourquoi, les parce que. Sinon, c'est simplement une étude de nu océanien.' From *Notes Eparses*, cited by Robert Rey, *Gauguin*, p.38.

1054 'Tout cela est à côté de la peinture, dira-t-on. Qui sait. Peut-être non.' *Lettres à de Monfreid*, p.102, March 12, 1897.

1055 Of course the traditional manner of naturalism was equally iconic, but those means had become so familiar that they were no longer experienced as such – this is why we can formulate the issue as we did.

1056 Toorop, *Klanklijnen* ('Lines representing sounds'), e.g., in his *Drie bruiden* ('Three brides') reproduced in B. Polak, *Fin de Siècle*, ill. 24 and 26).

1057 Cf. e.g. H. Kauffmann, 'Jan van Eyck's Arnolfini's Hochzeit.' *Geistige Welt* (1950, 2) p.45; J. G. van Gelder, *De Schilderkunst van Jan Vermeer* (Utrecht, 1958).

1058 We are referring to the poetic language that multiplies motifs derived from antiquity and which has continued since the fifteenth century till the present day – e.g. Giorgione (cf. P. Fehl, 'The Hidden Genre, a Study of the Concert Champêtre in the Louvre.' *Journal of Aesthetics and Art Criticism* (XVI, 1957)) p.153 – and in our time, e.g. Anquetin and others.

1059 In view of this state of things we do not think it correct that in America Gauguin's work now bears the title 'Where do we come from? What are we? Where are we going?' (In reproductions and in the texts relating to it produced by the M. Harriman Gallery, New York, 1936). The title had better be rendered as 'Whence? What? Whereto?' or 'Whence? What? Whither?'

1060 *Modern Painters* I, p.12.

1061 The whole of this study, inclusive of this chapter, had been written before the publication of the special Gauguin issue of the *Gazette des Beaux Arts*, in March 1958, marked the 98th year, dated January-July, 1956. The article by G. Wildenstein, 'L'idéologie et l'esthétique dans deux tableaux – clés de Paul Gauguin', discusses the same work especially from the viewpoint of the motifs used, which have heen borrowed from older paintings by Gauguin himself; this article is only an additional support for our thesis. Wildenstein leaves the problems with which we are occupied entirely undiscussed.

1062 P. Rodenko, 'Baudelaire en de 'Poètes maudits', *Maatstaf* (V, 2/3, 1957) p.220.

1063 'J'ai terminé un ouvrage philosophique sur ce thème comparé à l'Évangile ... je crois que c'est bien.' *Lettres à de Monfreid*, p.119 ff., Feb. 1898.

1064 Bettina Polak, *Fin de siècle*, p.37, 67.

1065 'Que mes paroles revêtent les brillantes formes de rêves, qu'elles se parent d' images, flamboient et descendent sur toi ... Comprends-tu par cette pensée visible la destinée de l'humanité? d'où elle vient, où va-t-elle? ... Comprends-tu ... de tels spectacles emporteraient et déchireraient ton intelligence ... comprends-tu?' Balzac, *Séraphita*, p.429.

1066 'Une figure ... lève les bras en l'air et regarde, étonnée, ces deux personnages qui osent penser à leur destinée.' *Lettres à de Monfreid*, p.119 ff., Feb. 1898.

1067 The influence of Carlyle's work on Gauguin becomes all the more probable when we notice how clear the direct relation to Carlyle is in the case of an artist who temporarily worked under the strong impression of Gauguin's art and ideas. Thus the Danish painter Willumsen left France in 1892 for Norway, where he made a few more or less symbolic paintings inspired by the mountains near Jotunheimen and the North Cape, entirely viewed in the manner of Carlyle, and in the frame, some figures to render the latter's thoughts of humanity – cf. *Sartor Resartus*, p.242 ff, where Teufelsdrockh asks himself if this most important idea could ever be painted. Cf. also, in the same work, pp.180 ff. See also O. Hølaas, J. F. Willumsen, *Kunsten Idag* (XLIV, Oslo 1958, 2) pp.13 ff.

1068 Carlyle derives his image from the sign of the Lord's presence during Israel's journey through the desert, Exodus 13:21.

1069 *Sartor Resartus*, p.193.

1070 *Sartor Resartus*, p.68. Carlyle had had a Christian education and no doubt knew Bunyan's Pilgrim's Progress thoroughly. There is perhaps in this utterance a reminiscence of Bunyan's introduction, in which occurs:

This book it chalketh out before thine eyes / The man that seeks the everlasting prize: / It shows you whence he comes, whither he goes.

1071 Ditto, pp.254/5.

1072 Both works were written almost simultaneously, without influencing each other, hut only agreeing in that they derived from the same sources. Carlyle's work dates from 1831, Balzac' s was written between 1833 and 1835.

1073 Ditto, p.306.

1074 Repr. Rewald, *Post-Impressionism*, p.295. Cf. D. Sutton, 'The Paul Gauguin Exhibition.' *Burlington Magazine* (XCI, 1949) p.284.

1075 From his comparison in a letter to Mette of Melbourne and Sydney with London, we must conclude that Gauguin had once been in England with her. He also knew English children's books from around 1880 (cf. D. Sutton, 'The Gauguin Exhibition.' *Burlington Magazine* (XCI, 1949) p.285 and note 26). He must have had some knowledge of English, but there is no proof for more than 'some'.

1076 In spite of his criticism, Taine appears not to have escaped from the inspiring influence of Carlyle's Sartor Resartus. He wrote a French imitation of this work, *Opinions de M. Frédéric-Thomas Graindorge ... publiées par H. Taine, son exécuteur testamentaire* (1867). It is a characteristically French trait that in this book Mr. Graindorge was not, like Teufelsdröckh an incomprehensible philosopher, but an amiable epicurean, remarking about the girls, the mistresses and the balls of Paris.

1077 H. Taine, *L'idéalisme anglais, étude sur Carlyle* (1864) p.108.

1078 See note 1059.

1079 'Puvis explique son idée, oui, mais il ne la peint pas. Il est grec'; 'tandis que moi je suis un sauvage', i.e., its opposite. 'Puvis intitulera un tableau Pureté et pour l'expliquer peindra une jeune vierge avec un lys à la main – Symbole connu, donc on le comprend. Gauguin au titre Pureté peindra un paysage aux eaux limpides; aucune souillure de l'homme civilisé, peut-être un personnage. Sans rentrer dans des détails il y a tout un monde entre Puvis et moi. Puvis comme peintre est un lettré tandis que moi je ne suis pas un lettré mais peut-être un homme de lettres.' Malingue, CLXXIV.

1080 'Ici, près de ma case, en plein silence, je rêve à des harmonies violentes dans les parfums naturels qui me grisent. Délice relevé de je ne sais quelle horreur sacrée que je devine vers l'immémorial. Autrefois, odeur de joie que je respire dans le présent. Figures animales, d'une rigidité statuaire je ne sais quoi d' ancien, d'auguste, religieux dans le rythme de leur geste, dans leur immobilité rare. Dans des yeux qui rêvent, la surface trouble d'une énigme insondable. Et voilà la nuit – tout repose. Mes yeux se ferment pour voir sans comprendre le rêve dans l'espace infini qui fuit devant moi, et j'ai la sensation de la marche dolente de mes espérances.' Malingue, CLXX.

1081 'ce qui n'est pas exprimé'; 'il en résulte implicitement des lignes, sans couleurs ou paroles, il n'en est pas matériellement constitué', Malingue, CLXX.

1082 'Dans ce grand tableau:

Où allons-nous? / Près de la mort d'une vieille femme, / Un oiseau étrange stupide conclut. / Que sommes-nous? / Existence journalière. / L'homme d'instinct se demande ce que tout cela veut dire. / D'où venons-nous? / Source. / Enfant. / La vie commune.

'L'oiseau conclut le poème en comparaison de l'être inférieur vis-à-vis de l'être intelligent dans ce grand tout qui est le problème annoncé par le titre.

'Derrière un arbre deux figures sinistres, enveloppées de vêtements de couleur triste, mettent près de l'arbre de la science leur note de douleur causée par cette science même en comparaison avec des êtres simples dans une nature vierge qui pourrait être un paradis de conception humaine, se laissant aller au bonheur de vivre' Malingue, CLXXIV.

1083 In Morice's Gauguin, p.113, the text is printed in three parallel columns in the part of this letter that contains the indication of the contents of the three parts of the title. This is how Gauguin had it in his letter, logical, clearly arranged, and explanatory. Cf. the reproduction of this part of the letter in G. Wildenstein, 'L'idéologie et l'esthétique dans deux tableaux clès de Gauguin.' *Gazette des Beaux Arts* (98th year, Jan-July 1956) p.132.

1084 We are confronted in it with a very old tradition, concerning the direction of handwriting and the way in which the illustrations, done in miniature in the scrolls, were unrolled, in the literal sense of the word. Cf. A. C. Soper, 'The Illustrative Method of the Tokugawa "Genji" pictures.' *Art Bulletin* (XXXVII, 1955) p.1.

1085 B. Dorival, 'Sources of the art of Paul Gauguin from Java, Egypt and Ancient Greece.' *Burlington Magazine* (XCIII, 1951) p.118.

1086 'cherchez l'harmonie ... que tout chez vous respire le calme ... Évitez la pose en mouvement. Chacun de vos personnages doit être à l'état statique ... Appliquez-vous à la silhouette de chaque objet.' Gauguin, *Avant et Après*, p.55.

1087 See note 603.

1088 'se remettre entre les mains de son Créateur, c'est s'annuler et mourir'. *Avant et Après*, p.224.

1089 'L'idole (in this painting) est là ... faisant corps dans mon rêve devant ma case avec la nature entière, régnant en notre âme primitive, consolation imaginaire de nos souffrances (mind this word 'imaginaire') en ce qu'elles comportent de vague et d'incompris devant le mystère de notre origine et notre avenir.' Malingue, CLXX. Also in his writing which was begun in these same years and was entitled 'Esprit moderne et le catholicisme' (in the Museum at St. Louis, Mo., USA, at the exhibition of French drawings from American collections in Boymans-Van Beuningen Museum, 1958, cat. no. 172) he occupied himself with this subject. Thus on the first page he wrote in the dedication to Morice: 'D'où venons-nous, que sommes-nous, où allons-nous? L'éternel problème qui nous punit de l'orgueil – ô Douleur tu es mon maître – Fatalité que tu es cruelle et toujours vaincu je me révolte – La raison reste: folle sans doute mais vivante – Et c'est alors que la frondaison commence.' ('Whence? What? Whither?

The eternal problem that punishes our pride – Oh, Sorrow, thou art my master – fate, how cruel thou art, and always vanquished I revolt – Reason remains: foolish, no doubt, but alive – And then the foliage begins to come out.')

1090 'Puis vous savez que si les autres m'ont gratifié d'un système, moi je n'en ai pas et je ne veux pas être condamné à cela. Peindre à ma guise, clair aujourd'hui, foncé demain, etc ... du reste l'artiste doit être libre ou il n'est pas artiste.' *Lettres à de Monfreid*, p.109, 14 July 1897.

1091 'si l'oeuvre d'art était de hasard, toutes ces notes seraient inutiles'. *Avant et Après*, p.24.

1092 'tout de rayons jusqu'au centre vital de mon art.' *Avant et Après*, p.24. Cf. Baudelaire, *Cur. Esth.*, p.102: 'Rien n'est plus impertinent ni plus bête que de parler à un grand artiste, érudit et penseur comme Delacroix, des obligations qu'il peut avoir au dieu du hasard. Cela fait tout simplement hausser les épaules de pitié. Il n'y a pas de hasard dans l'art, non plus qu'en mécanique.' ('Nothing is more impertinent or stupid than talking concerning a great artist, a scholar and thinker, such as Delacroix, of the obligations he may be under to the god of chance. This simply evokes only a shrug of the shoulders out of pity. There is no chance in art, no more than in mechanics.')

1093 'Les machines sont venues, l'art s'en est allé, et je suis loin de penser que la photographie nous soit propice.' *Diverses Choses*, quoted by Morice, *Gauguin*, p.224.

1094 Delacroix still thought he could use photography (e.g. of nudes) as 'inots d'un dietionnaire' Cf. *Journal* 21 May, 1853.

1095 'Quant à moi, je me suis reculé bien loin, plus loin que les chevaux du Parthénon ... jusqu'au dada de mon enfance, le bon cheval de bois.' *Diverses Choses*, quoted by Morice, *Gauguin*, p.224.

1096 *Lettres à de Monfreid*, p.113, Oct. '97.

1097 'En somme aujourd'hui il y a un bel effort et venant bien moins directement de l'époque précédente que des romantiques.' *Lettres à de Monfreid*, p.134, Dec. 1898.

1098 'le centre mystérieux de la pensée' cited by Morice, *Gauguin*, p.153.

1099 'Où commence l'exécution d'un tableau, où finit-elle? Au moment où des sentiments extrêmes sont en fusion au plus profond de l'être, au moment où ils éclatent, et que toute pensée sort comme la lave d'un volcan, n'y a-t-il pas une éclosion de l'oeuvre soudainement créée, brutale si l'on veut, mais grande et d'apparence surhumaine? Les froids calculs de la raison n'ont pas procédé à cette éclosion, mais qui sait quand au fond de l'être l'oeuvre est commencée? Inconscient peut-être?' *Lettres à de Monfreid*, p.121, March 1898.

1100 'J'ai voulu établir le droit de tout oser: mes capacités n'ont pas donné un grand résultat, mais cependant la machine est lancée. Le public ne me doit rien puisque mon oeuvre picturale n'est que relativement bonne, mais les peintres qui aujourd'hui profitent de cette liberté, me doivent quelque chose.' Quoted in Morice, *Gauguin*, p.243.

1101 'les entraves de la vraisemblance'. *Lettres à de Monfreid*, p.183, 17 November 1901.

1102 'travers académiques'; 'travers symbolistes, autre genre de sentimentalisme'. Ditto.

1103 'Une croix, des flammes, v'lan! ça y est, le symbolisme.' Ditto, p104, April 1897.

1104 As e.g. Th. Craven, *Modern Art: the Men, the Movements, the Meaning* (New York, 1940) p.118 ff.

1105 Cf. Malingue, CLXVIII.

1106 Ditto.

1107 Carlyle's Teufelsdröckh went through all this already in his youth: 'Thus already Freewill often came in painful collision with necessity.' *Sartor Resartus*, p.122.

1108 Michaud, *Message Poétique*, p.174; C. Delfel, *L'esthétique de Stéphane Mallarmé*, p.34 ff.

1109 Malingue, CLXXVI.

1110 In the article on the American dramatist Harcoland, by C. Tigell in *Mercure de France* (XIII, 1895) p.290, we find the following quotation from one of the dramatist's works: 'Les lois sont la honte de l'humanité. Le premier législateur qui osa endiguer les torrents de l'âme attenta sinistrement à la liberté morale, le premier juge fut le coupable. Voici la ligne à suivre! pourquoi tenir cet hypocrite langage au nouveau-né et l'arracher dés l'aurore à sa spontanéité ou le plonger dans le canal des généralités asservies? ... L'homme libre aide à l'harmonie; l'homme esclave la contrarie.' ('Laws are the shame of humanity. The first legislator who dared to fence in the torrents of the soul committed a sinister assault on moral liberty, the first judge was the culprit. This is the policy we should follow! why should we talk in such a hypocritical way to the newly born and from the first moment of their day tear them loose from their spontaneity, in order to plunge them into the canal of servile generalities? ... Free man is a support to harmony; enslaved man is the opposite.')

1111 The dots are Gauguin's.

1112 'J'ai su, tout le monde aussi, tout le monde le saura, que deux et deux font quatre. Il y a loin de la convention, de l'intuition à la compréhension je me soumets, et comme tout le monde je dis 'Deux et deux font quatre ... Mais ... cela m'embête, et cela me dérange beaucoup dans mes raisonnements.' Avant et Après, p.5.

1113 We are not concerned here with the tendency that was probably indirectly influenced by Sérusier and of which the greatest master was Mondrian; but we are dealing with the other non-figurative movement, leading to Manessier, etc.

1114 Il était donc nécessaire, tout en tenant compte des efforts faits et toutes les recherches, même scientifiques, de songer à une libération complète, briser les vitres, au risque de se couper les doigts, quitte à la génération suivante, désormais indépendante, dégagée de toute entrave, à résoudre généralement le problème. Je ne dis pas définitivement, car c'est justement un art sans fin dont il est question, riche en techniques de toutes sortes, apte à traduire toutes les émotions de la nature et de l'homme, s'appropriant à chaque individualité, à chaque époque, en joies et en souffrances.

'Il fallait pour cela se livrer corps et âme à la lutte, lutte contre toutes les Écoles, toutes sans distinction, non point en les dénigrant, mais par autre chose, affronter non seulement les officiels, mais encore les Impressionnistes, les Néo-Impressionnistes, l'ancien et le nouveau public. Ne plus avoir de femme, d'enfants, qui vous renient. Qu'importe l'injure? Qu'importe la misère? Tout cela en tant que conduite d'homme.

'En tant que travail, une méthode de contradiction, si I'on veut, s'attaquer aux plus fortes abstractions, faire tout ce qui était défendu, et reconstruire, plus ou moins heureusement, sans crainte d'exagération, avec exagération même. Apprendre à nouveau, puis, une fois su, apprendre encore. Vaincre toutes les timidités, quelque soit le ridicule qui en rejaillit.

'Devant son chevalet, le peintre n'est esclave, ni du passé, ni du présent, ni de la nature, ni de son voisin. Lui, encore lui, toujours lui.'

Part II: Rookmaaker as Art Critic (1949–1956)

1115 *Trouw*, 30 July 1957.
1116 *Trouw*, 11 April 1949.
1117 *Trouw*, 28 May 1949.
1118 *Trouw*, 30 December 1952.
1119 *Trouw*, 28 July 1958.
1120 *Trouw*, 22 September 1949
1121 *Trouw*, 7 August 1951.
1122 *Trouw*, 26 May 1956.
1123 *Trouw*, 12 June 1950.
1124 *Trouw*, 1950.
1125 *Trouw*, 1953.
1126 *Trouw*, 6 November 1954.
1127 *Trouw*, 26 April 1955.
1128 *Trouw*, 19 August 1950.
1129 *Trouw*, 18 December 1951.
1130 *Trouw*, 10 March 1951.
1131 Rijswijk, the Netherlands: Leidse Uitgeversrij, 1950.
1132 *Trouw*, 26 April 1952.
1133 *Trouw*, 24 January 1950.
1134 *Trouw*, 10 January 1950.
1135 *Trouw*, n.d.
1136 *Trouw*, September 1951.
1137 *Trouw*, n.d.
1138 *Trouw*, n.d.
1139 *Trouw*, 5 July 1954.
1140 *Trouw*, n.d
1141 *Trouw*, November, 1954.
1142 *Trouw*, n.d.
1143 *Trouw*, 7 April 1952.
1144 *Trouw*, n.d.

www.ingramcontent.com/pod-product-compliance
Lightning Source LLC
Chambersburg PA
CBHW031603210526
45464CB00004B/1402